LSAT®
DECODED
For PrepTests 72–81

The Staff of The Princeton Review

PrincetonReview.com

Penguin
Random
House

The Princeton Review
110 East 42nd St, 7th Floor
New York, NY 10017
E-mail: editorialsupport@review.com

ISBN: 978-1-5247-5779-3
eBook ISBN: 978-1-5247-5780-9
ISSN: 2575-5188

Editor: Meave Shelton
Production Editors: Liz Rutzel and Kathy G. Carter
Production Artist: Deborah A. Silvestrini

Printed in the United States of America on partially recycled paper.

10 9 8 7 6 5 4 3 2 1

Editorial
Rob Franek, Editor-in-Chief
Casey Cornelius, VP Content Development
Mary Beth Garrick, Director of Production
Selena Coppock, Managing Editor
Meave Shelton, Senior Editor
Colleen Day, Editor
Sarah Litt, Editor
Aaron Riccio, Editor
Orion McBean, Associate Editor

Random House Publishing Team
Tom Russell, VP, Publisher
Alison Stoltzfus, Publishing Director
Jake Eldred, Associate Managing Editor
Ellen Reed, Production Manager
Suzanne Lee, Designer

Acknowledgments

Many thanks to Chad Chasteen, Karen Hoover, Bobby Hood, Spencer LeDoux, Fiona Muirhead, Shaina Walter Bowie, and Craig Patches for their invaluable work in the creation of this title.

Special thanks to Adam Robinson, who conceived of and perfected the Joe Bloggs approach to standardized tests, and many of the other successful techniques used by The Princeton Review.

We are also, as always, very appreciative of the time and attention given to each page by Liz Rutzel, Kathy Carter, and Debbie Silvestrini.

Contents

Get More (Free) Content

1 Go to **PrincetonReview.com/cracking.**

2 Enter the following ISBN for your book: 9781524757793.

3 Answer a few simple questions to set up an exclusive Princeton Review account. (If you already have one, you can just log in.)

4 Click the "Student Tools" button, also found under "My Account" from the top toolbar. You're all set to access your bonus content!

Need to report a potential **content** issue?

Contact **EditorialSupport@review.com**.
Include:

- full title of the book
- ISBN number
- page number

Need to report a **technical** issue?

Contact **TPRStudentTech@review.com** and provide:

- your full name
- email address used to register the book
- full book title and ISBN
- computer OS (Mac/PC) and browser (Firefox, Safari, etc.)

The **Princeton** Review®

Once you've registered, you can...

- Access a handy spreadsheet of the LSAT scores accepted by top law schools
- See rankings of the best law schools in the country
- Check to see if there have been any corrections or updates to this edition
- Get our take on any recent or pending updates to the LSAT

Chapter 1
General Information

DECODING THE LAW SCHOOL ADMISSION TEST

This book is designed to help you figure out questions on LSAT PrepTests 72–81 as part of your LSAT preparation. Each chapter tackles a different PrepTest and provides complete explanations for each question of these real Law School Admission Council (LSAC) tests. These explanations also include strategies and tips about how to eliminate certain answers.

Work through each PrepTest on your own, and then review your performance using our explanations. This will help you identify your strengths and weaknesses and better understand the logic of the LSAT. We've also categorized the various questions and labeled their corresponding explanations with tabs, to help you exploit any shortcuts or patterns you find within them.

In the following introduction, we'll look at how to identify those categories from the question stem and provide one key point about each. We'll also look at some efficient and standardized ways to approach each of the three main sections of the test: Analytical Reasoning (Games), Logical Reasoning (Arguments), and Reading Comprehension.

STRUCTURE OF THE LSAT

The LSAT is a tightly timed, multiple-choice test that almost always consists of 99 to 102 questions. By tightly timed, we mean that the test is designed so that the "average" test taker (someone scoring around the fiftieth percentile) should not be able to comfortably complete all the questions in the time allotted.

This experimental section can be Arguments, Games, or Reading Comprehension.

To be more specific, the LSAT is made up of five 35-minute multiple-choice sections and one 35-minute essay. Two of the five multiple-choice sections will be Logical Reasoning (Arguments), one will be Analytical Reasoning (Games), and one will be Reading Comprehension. The remaining section (which is usually one of the first three to be administered) will be an experimental section that will not count toward your score.

Because the essay is unscored, this book does not include samples. However, a scan of your essay is sent to each school that you apply to, so if you're feeling uncomfortable with this section, we recommend checking out some of the successful submissions found in *Law School Essays That Made a Difference.*

As you may have already noticed, the order of these sections changes with each administered PrepTest. This is because the only consistent thing about the format of the LSAT is the 15-minute break given between sections 3 and 4, and that the essay will be at the end of the test. Also, bear in mind that the experimental section is not included in LSAC's official PrepTest book. If you're trying to prepare for the pacing of this test, you might consider using one or two sample tests to supplement the others. (For instance, insert the Reading Comprehension section from PrepTest 76 after the first Arguments section in PrepTest 72. Just make sure you keep track of which tests you've already taken.)

WHEN IS THE LSAT GIVEN?

The LSAT is administered four times a year—February, June, September/October, and December. Typically, students applying for regular fall admission to a law program take the test during June or September/October of the previous calendar year. You can take a test in December or February, but many schools will have filled at least a portion of their seats by the time your scores hit the admissions office.

Note that as of June 2018, the test will be offered six times a year, with tests in June, September, November, January, March, and again in June.

HOW IS THE LSAT SCORED?

The LSAT is scored on a scale of 120 to 180, with the median score being approximately 152. You need to answer about 60 questions correctly (out of 99–102) to get that median score of 152, which means you need to bat about 60 percent. Very few people earn a perfect score, mainly because the test is designed so that very few people can correctly answer all the questions, let alone do so in the time allotted. Along with your LSAT score, you will receive a percentile ranking. This ranking compares your performance with that of everyone else who has taken the LSAT for the previous three years. Because a 152 is the median LSAT score, it would give you a percentile ranking of approximately 50. A score of 156 moves you up to a ranking of about 70. A 164 pulls you up to a ranking of 90. And any score over 167 puts you above 95 percent of all the LSAT takers.

As you can see, small numerical jumps (five points or so) can lead to a huge difference in percentile points. That means you're jumping over 20 percent of all test takers if, on your first practice test, you score a 150, but on the real test, you score a 155. Small gains can net big results. The following table summarizes the number of questions you can skip or miss and still reach your LSAT goal. Notice that 93 percent of those taking the test make more than 15 errors. Take this into consideration as you develop your strategy of exactly how many questions you intend to answer or skip.

Approximate Number of Errors (out of 102)	LSAT Score	Percentile Rank (approximately)
1	180	99++
5	175	99+
8	170	98+
15	165	91+
22	160	80+
32	155	66+
43	150	45+
52	145	27+
62	140	14+
69	135	5+

Because you're working with official PrepTests that have already been administered and graded, be sure to review the "Computing Your Score" pages in the *10 Actual, Official LSAT PrepTests Volume VI* book. That will give you the most precise assessment of your grade.

What Is a Good Score?

A good score on the LSAT is one that gets you into the law school you want to attend. Many people feel that they have to score at least a 160 to get into a "good" law school. That's pure myth. Remember, any ABA-approved law school has to meet very strict standards in terms of its teaching staff, library, and facilities. Most schools use the Socratic method to teach students basic law. Therefore, a student's fundamental law school experience can be very similar no matter where he or she goes to school—be it NYU or Quinnipiac Law School.

GENERAL STRATEGIES

Before we get into specifics, there are several key things you should do when taking any multiple-choice test, especially the LSAT. We recommend that you at least give all of these mantras a shot as you work to develop a test-taking method that works for you—they are the sum of more than 20 years' worth of our experience in researching and preparing hundreds of thousands of test takers to take the LSAT.

Technique #1: Don't Rush

As we showed on the scoring table, you can get into the 98th percentile even with several wrong answers in each section. Most test takers do their best when they don't try to answer every question.

Most test takers believe that the key to success on the LSAT is to go faster. Realize, though, that your accuracy is also a key factor in how well you perform. Generally speaking, the faster you work, the higher the chance of making an error. What this means is that there's a pacing "sweet spot" somewhere between working as fast as you can and working as carefully as you can. That's where official PrepTests come in handy, as they'll help you to find the proper balance for yourself in each of the three sections.

Your mantra: *I will fight the urge to rush and will work more deliberately, making choices about where to concentrate so I can answer questions more accurately and end up with a higher score.*

Technique #2: Fill in Every Bubble

Unlike some tests, the LSAT has no penalty for guessing, meaning that no points are subtracted for wrong answers. Therefore, even if you don't get to work on every question in a section, make sure to fill in the rest of the bubbles before time is called. Even if you do only 75 percent of the test, you'll get an average of five more questions correct by picking a "letter of the day" and bubbling it in on the remaining 25 questions.

Don't wait to start implementing this strategy; you should work through the PrepTests as you plan to work through the actual test. By the time you've gone through a couple of tests, this should be a habit that you employ without even thinking about it. If you're concerned that this won't show your "real" score, remember that your "real" score will come from a bubble sheet that you've (hopefully) completely filled out, so don't hold back. Use this book of explanations to ensure that you know how to solve the questions you might have guessed correctly.

Your mantra: *I will always remember to bubble in answers for any questions I don't get to, giving me better odds of getting a higher score.*

Technique #3: Use Process of Elimination

One solace (perhaps) on multiple-choice tests is the fact that all of the correct answers will be in front of you. Naturally, each will be camouflaged by four incorrect answers, some of which will look just as good as, and often better than, the credited response. But the fact remains that if you can clear away some of that distraction, the right choice is right in front of you. Don't expect that the correct answers will just leap off the page at you. They won't. In fact, choices that immediately catch your eye are often just tricky distractors.

Process of Elimination (POE) may be a very different test-taking strategy from what you are used to. If you look first at the answer choices critically, with an eye toward trying to see what's wrong with them, you'll do better on almost any standardized test than by always trying to find the right answer. This is because, given enough time and creativity, you can justify the correctness of any answer choice that you find appealing. That skill may be useful in certain situations, but on the LSAT, creativity of that sort is dangerous.

Your mantra: *I will always try to eliminate answer choices using Process of Elimination, thereby increasing my chances to get each question right and, therefore, a higher score.*

ANALYTICAL REASONING

In this section, we'll look at the broad structure of the Analytical Reasoning, or Games, section and lay out key strategies for each question type.

Games: A Step-by-Step Approach

Analytical Reasoning is deeply rooted in logic, even if no formal training in that subject is required. To that end, we've devised a series of steps to help methodically work through even the trickiest of games.

Step 1: Diagram and inventory

Your first step will be to determine the appropriate diagram for the game by evaluating both the setup and the clues. You will be given enough information to understand the basic structure of the game. Your diagram is described by the setup and will become the fixed game board onto which you will place the elements—your game pieces. You should make an inventory of the elements next to the diagram, so that you'll have everything in one place and will be able to keep track of it easily. Don't rush through this step, because this is the heart of your process. People often want to start scribbling a diagram as soon as something pops out at them from the setup. Take the time to evaluate the setup thoroughly, and you'll be well equipped for the rest of the process.

Step 2: Symbolize the clues and double-check

After you've drawn your diagram, transform the clues into visual symbols. Your symbols should be consistent with the diagram and with each other. The goal is to change the clues into visual references that will fit into your diagram. Here are the three Cs of symbolization: Keep your symbols clear, consistent, and concise. Never forget that correctly symbolizing every clue is the key to improving accuracy and efficiency.

The most valuable 30 seconds you can spend on any game is double-checking your symbols to make sure that they perfectly match all the information in the clue. Do not merely reread each clue and glance at your symbol again. If you misread the clue once, you might do it again. Instead, work against the grain when you double-check. Number each of your symbols. Then articulate in your own words what each symbol means and carry that back up to the clues you were given. When you find a match, check off that clue. Finally, be sure to go back over the information presented in the setup as well, because some games may include restrictions or extra rules that should be treated like clues. Once you're sure everything is all accounted for, you're ready to move on.

Step 3: Make deductions and size up the game

Now that you're sure you have everything properly symbolized, it's time to make any deductions that you can from the information that was given by the clues.

Look for overlap between the clues and the diagram and among the clues that share the same elements. See if there is anything else that you know for sure. Making deductions is not merely suspecting that something may be true; a deduction is something that you know for a fact. It is something that must always be true or must always be false. Add your deductions to the information you already have.

You'll notice that many deductions give you concrete limitations about where elements are restricted—where they can't go—rather than where they must go. Consider each clue individually to see what it says about the placement of an elements. Then look for overlap between different clues.

Step 4: Assess the questions

Not all games questions are on the same level of difficulty. As a result, you should move through the questions from easiest to most challenging.

First, look for what we call Grab-a-Rule questions. Grab-a-Rule questions do not appear on every game, but they are common. They have historically been the first question of a game. These are questions that give you full arrangements of the elements in every answer and ask you which one doesn't break any rules. Remember, if the question does not deal with every element and every space on your diagram, it is not a true Grab-a-Rule.

Next, look for Specific questions. These questions will further limit the initial conditions of the game and provide you with more information. They will usually start with the word "if." Specific questions tend to be fairly quick since the question itself constrains some of the vagueness of the game. Once you've done all the Specific questions, you'll have a diagram with several valid permutations—or "plays"—of the game.

The third style of question you should work is the General questions. These questions are typically open-ended and ask what could happen without placing specific restrictions. These questions usually begin with the word "which." By saving these for later, you can often use your prior work from the Specific questions to eliminate bad answer choices.

The final question type that you may see is Complex questions. Complex questions can change the original game by adding, changing, or deleting a rule. They can also ask which answer choice could be substituted for a rule without changing the game. No matter what form they take, Complex questions should be saved for last since they function differently from the rest of the questions. These questions can also be very time-consuming for little gain. Never forget that the Complex question is worth the same number of points as the Grab-a-Rule. It is always worth considering how much you need to get that one question correct. For most test takers, the best strategy on these questions is to bubble in your letter of the day and move on to the next game. Remember that you can always come back and work a Complex question if you have time.

There is one last thing to know about the questions. No matter what the question type, the question stem will affect how the credited response is reached. The

You may note that we sometimes refer to questions out of chronological order. This is because we've found that there are efficient ways to use the information from one question to rule out choices in another. You'll definitely want to use our explanations to practice this and refine your notes and diagrams so that the specific premises of a Complex question are not accidentally used in another, independent problem.

four question stems are must be true, could be true, could be false, and must be false. The LSAT has a wide variety of phrasing, but every question will ultimately use one of these four stems. Make a habit now of underlining each question stem. This will help you to determine the best approach to the question and the type of answer you'll need.

Step 5: Act
Each question task requires its own strategy. Using the proper strategy leads to saving time on a given question without sacrificing accuracy. Plus, by approaching the questions in an efficient order, you'll find that the work you've done on earlier questions will often help you to find the right answer on a later question.

Step 6: Answer using Process of Elimination
Different question stems require POE to different degrees. Sometimes you'll be able to go straight to the right answer from your deductions, but often you'll need to work questions by finding the four wrong answers. As a last resort, you may need to test answer choices one at a time to find the right one.

The Structure of a Games Section
You will be given four "logic games" in a 35-minute section. Each game will have a setup and a set of conditions or clues that are attached to it. Then five to seven questions will ask you about various possible arrangements of the elements in the game. The four games are not arranged in order of difficulty.

The Four Types of Games Questions
A large part of the six-step method involves being able to quickly identify the four different question types so that they can be worked through in the most efficient way possible. As you compare your test results to our explanations, feel free to use the identifying tabs beside each question to check your process. Additionally, here's a core takeaway for each of the four question types you'll find in the Games section.

Grab-a-Rule
- Compare each of the given rules to the answer choices, looking to eliminate the choices that violate the rules.

Specific
- Work the given information into your notes/diagram and only then compare the answer choices.

General

- Use some of the valid solutions that you have already created for other question types to help narrow down choices.

Complex

- Because these questions mix up the rules, be careful to properly modify the assumptions made in your diagrams, or better still, start them from scratch (if you have the time).

THE LOGICAL REASONING SECTION

Here, we'll break down the process for working through the Logical Reasoning, or Arguments, section and present key strategies for each question type.

Working Arguments: A Step-by-Step Process

In the context of the LSAT, Logical Reasoning revolves around careful analysis, without using outside knowledge that may complicate things. For that reason, it helps to have a specific, formal process for working through even the most complex arguments.

Step 1: Assess the question

Reading the question first will tip you off about what you need to look for in the argument. Don't waste time reading the argument before you know how you will need to evaluate it for that particular question. If you don't know what your task is, you are unlikely to perform it effectively.

Step 2: Analyze the argument

You've got to read the argument critically, looking for the author's conclusion and the evidence used to support it. When the author's conclusion is explicitly stated, mark it with a symbol that you use only for conclusions. If necessary, jot down short, simple paraphrases of the premises and any flaws you found in the argument.

To find flaws, you should keep your eyes open for any shifts in the author's language or gaps in the argument. Look for common purpose and reasoning patterns. The author's conclusion is reached using only the information on the page in front of you, so any gaps in the language or in the evidence indicate problems with the argument. You should always be sure that you're reading critically and articulating the parts of the argument (both stated and unstated) in your own words.

Our explanations clearly identify each question task (Step 1) as well as the conclusion, premise, and common flaws (Step 2). If you're attempting to get a routine down, we suggest comparing your train of thought against ours, even on questions that you got right.

Step 3: Act

Each question task will have different criteria for what constitutes an acceptable answer. Think about that before going to the choices.

The test writers rely on the fact that the people who are taking the LSAT feel pressured to get through all the questions quickly. Many answer choices will seem appealing if you don't have a clear idea of what you're looking for before you start reading through them. The best way to keep yourself from falling into this trap is to predict what the right answer will say or do before you even look at the choices, and write that prediction down on your test!

Step 4: Answer using Process of Elimination (POE)

Most people look for the best answer and, in the process, end up falling for answer choices that are designed to look appealing but actually contain artfully concealed flaws. The part that looks good looks really good, and the little bit that's wrong blends right into the background if you're not reading carefully and critically. The "best" answer on a tricky question won't necessarily sound very good at all. That's why the question is difficult. But if you're keenly attuned to crossing out those choices with identifiable flaws, you'll be left with one that wasn't appealing, but didn't have anything wrong with it. And that's the winner because it's the "best" one of a group of flawed answers. If you can find a reason to cross off a choice, you've just improved your chances of getting the question right. So be aggressive about finding the flaws in answer choices that will allow you to eliminate them. At the same time, don't eliminate choices that you don't understand or that don't have a distinct problem.

The Structure of an Arguments Section

There will be two scored Arguments sections, each lasting 35 minutes, on your LSAT. Each section has between 24 and 26 questions. Tests in the past frequently attached two questions to one argument, but LSAC has more or less phased out this style of question; you will almost certainly see one question per argument. Typically, the argument passages are no more than three or four sentences in length, but they can still be very dense and every word is potentially important, making critical reading the key skill on this section. The arguments are not arranged in strict order of difficulty, although the questions near the beginning of a section are generally easier than those at the end.

The Fourteen Types of Arguments Questions

Our explanations have been tagged with different identifiers for each question type, so as to help you more readily associate the strategies you're practicing with the various questions you'll encounter. Here's a breakdown of the main takeaways for each of the fourteen question types you'll find in the Arguments section.

Main Point

Key Words in Question Stem: "main point," "main conclusion," "argument is structured to lead to which conclusion."

Strategy: Keywords and opinion language can often lead you to the main point. You can confirm you found the main point by asking why the author believes a certain statement is true. The other sentences in an argument are all premises that answer that question. We sometimes refer to this as the Why Test.

Reasoning

Key Words in Question Stem: "X responds to Y by," "claim that…plays what role," "technique/method/strategy of argumentation/reasoning."

Strategy: Try to describe the overall structure and logic to these arguments before matching an answer choice to the argument.

Necessary Assumption

Key Words in Question Stem: "assumption on which the argument depends/relies," "assumption required."

Strategy: Help these arguments by providing an important assumption. Confirm the credited response to these questions by negating the answer choices. A negated necessary assumption will make the conclusion invalid. We sometimes refer to this as the Negation Test.

Sufficient Assumption

Key Words in Question Stem: "if assumed, allows the conclusion to follow logically," "allows the conclusion to be properly drawn."

Strategy: Help these arguments by finding a credited response that will prove the conclusion is true.

Strengthen

Key Words in Question Stem: "most supports/justifies the argument above," "most strengthens."

Strategy: The best way to strengthen an argument is to fill in any gaps in logic. Identify the argument's weakness and find the answer choice that fixes it the best.

Principle-Strengthen

Key Words in Question Stem: "principle that, if valid, justifies the argument."

Strategy: Help these arguments by providing a guiding principle, or rule, that will prove the conclusion is true based on the set of facts in the argument.

Weaken

Key Words in Question Stem: "most undermines," "calls into question," "casts doubt on."

Strategy: The best way to weaken an argument is to attack it where it is weakest. Find the argument's weakness and then find the answer choice that exploits that logical mistake.

Flaw

Key Words in Question Stem: "flaw/error in reasoning," "vulnerable to criticism."

Strategy: Describe the logical error made in each of these arguments before looking at the answer choices.

Inference

Key Words in Question Stem: "statements above, if true, support," "must/could be true/false."

Strategy: The credited answer to these questions must be strongly supported by the facts in the passage. Avoid making any assumptions as you find the answer choice that is true.

Point at Issue

Key Words in Question Stem: "committed to disagreeing about."

Strategy: Compare each answer choice to each person's argument individually. The credited response will be one in which the two people take an opposing stance.

Resolve/Explain

Key Words in Question Stem: "puzzling statement," "apparent contradiction," "paradox," "resolution," "explanation."

Strategy: Identify the two sides of the issue before looking at the answer choices. The credited response will be a new piece of information that allows both statements to be true.

Parallel

Key Words in Question Stem: "most analogous," "similar pattern of reasoning."

Strategy: Diagram the main argument and each answer choice, and then choose the answer with the most similar diagram.

Principle-Match

Key Words in Question Stem: "conforms/illustrates...principle/proposition."

Strategy: Match these arguments by applying the principle rule to the argument. The best answer will work with the rule to come to the same conclusion.

Evaluate

Key Words in Question Stem: "helps to evaluate" or "most useful in evaluating."

Strategy: Treat these like any other help or hurt question by identifying the conclusion, premises, and assumptions. The credited response will ask a question for which the answer will confirm or deny the assumption.

READING COMPREHENSION

The rest of this chapter will clarify the components of the Reading Comprehension section and provide key strategies for each question type.

Reading Comprehension: A Step-by-Step Process

Whenever you're reading dense, complicated material, it helps to be methodical and to know what you're looking for. The following method helps to break things down.

Step 1: Prepare the Passage

A. Preview the questions, looking for lead words and/or line references that tell you what parts of the passage will be especially relevant.

B. Work the passage efficiently, focusing on the main claims made by the author.

C. Annotate the passage, circling key words that relate to the question topics or that provide clues to the structure and tone of the author's argument, and making brief marginal notes.

D. Define the Bottom Line of the passage as a whole: the main point, purpose, and tone of the text.

Step 2: Assess the Question
Translate exactly what each question is asking you to do with or to the passage.

Step 3: Act
Just as some Games questions require you to make new deductions before you attack the answers, or some Arguments questions are best answered by first identifying or analyzing certain aspects of the paragraph, most Reading Comprehension questions are most accurately and efficiently attacked by doing some work with the passage text before looking at a single answer choice.

Step 4: Answer
Use a combination of your understanding of the question and of the relevant part or parts of the passage to use Process of Elimination on the answer choices. Look for what is wrong with each choice, keeping in mind that one small part of the choice that doesn't match the passage and/or the question task means the choice is bad.

The Structure of a Reading Comprehension Section
In this 35-minute section, you will be given four Reading Comprehension passages of about 60 to 80 lines each. Three of the passages will be written by one author; the fourth will be a combination of two shorter passages from two different sources discussing the same general subject. In each case, between five and eight questions will be attached to each passage. This is probably something you're familiar with from the SAT, the ACT, or any of the other myriad standardized tests you might have taken over the years. These passages are not arranged in any order of difficulty.

The Five Types of Reading Comprehension Questions
Being able to quickly pinpoint strategies for each type of question should help you to more efficiently work through the Reading Comprehension section. These are the main identifiers and strategies to recognize and know:

Big Picture
- Develop your own version of the Bottom Line of a passage by putting the overall point, tone, and purpose of the passage in your own words, and then look for the answer choice that comes closest to it.

Extract-Fact
- The credited response will match something directly stated by the author in the passage, so look to the exact language of the text.

Extract-Infer

- The best answer will always be supported by the text; avoid using outside information or making assumptions.

Structure

- These questions ask about the organization of the passage or paragraph, which means you should compare each choice to the relevant section of the text.

Reasoning

- Identify the argument being made in the passage, and describe it in your own words before looking at the answer choices.

SUMMARY

For all these tips, strategies, and explanations of what to expect on the LSAT, at the end of the day, it all comes down to you and the test. The practice found in those official LSAT PrepTests should help to iron out timing issues and point out any immediate problem spots that need additional focus, and the explanations in this book should help to solidify your test-taking process and raise both your comfort level and familiarity with the test's tricks. But if a mantra or a specific technique isn't working for you, don't feel beholden to it. With five tests to work through, you have the space to try different things and the time to turn a successful strategy into a muscle memory. Once you know the test and understand the explanations, it's just a matter of doing what you've done here on one more official test. You've got this!

Chapter 2
PrepTest 72:
Answers and
Explanations

ANSWER KEY: PREPTEST 72

Section 1: Reading Comprehension	Section 2: Arguments 1	Section 3: Arguments 2	Section 4: Games
1. D	1. D	1. C	1. B
2. E	2. C	2. B	2. E
3. C	3. B	3. D	3. B
4. A	4. A	4. E	4. D
5. B	5. E	5. C	5. A
6. D	6. C	6. C	6. E
7. B	7. E	7. A	7. E
8. B	8. D	8. A	8. C
9. C	9. D	9. E	9. D
10. A	10. C	10. D	10. A
11. C	11. C	11. A	11. E
12. D	12. E	12. C	12. B
13. B	13. C	13. C	13. B
14. B	14. C	14. B	14. A
15. D	15. D	15. B	15. E
16. C	16. D	16. D	16. A
17. D	17. B	17. D	17. C
18. D	18. E	18. C	18. C
19. A	19. C	19. D	19. A
20. C	20. B	20. B	20. E
21. A	21. B	21. E	21. C
22. C	22. C	22. E	22. E
23. E	23. A	23. C	23. E
24. D	24. A	24. A	
25. D	25. B	25. D	
26. B	26. D		
27. B			

EXPLANATIONS

Section 1: Reading Comprehension

Questions 1–6

The main point of the first paragraph is that the success in fighting wildfires in North America may actually be worse for forests, because many of them depend on periodic fires for long-term stability. The second paragraph goes on to argue that land management policies should recognize the essential role of fires in maintaining stability. The third paragraph concludes that the best method for controlling wildfires is the use of selective harvesting and prescribed fires to control the supply of fuel. The Bottom Line of the passage is that land managers should shift to a new system of wildfire management focused on using prescribed fires to control fuel supply in order to protect forests over the long term. The overall tone of the passage is persuasive: The passage criticizes the current system of wildfire management and advocates for a change to a new system.

1. **D**   **Big Picture**

    Use the Bottom Line to choose an answer. Watch out for answers that are too narrow (a purpose that's not primary) and answers that don't match the Bottom Line of the passage.

    A. No. This answer does not match the overall tone of the passage. The passage does not discuss ideological dogma impeding the adoption of a new system, but rather suggests that new information is leading foresters and ecologists to consider this new system necessary.

    B. No. This answer does not match the purpose of the passage. The passage does not merely compare the effects of two policies; it advocates for a change to a new policy.

    C. No. This answer does not match the passage. The passage does not discuss funding or any need for a substantial increase in funding.

    D. Yes. The first and second paragraphs discuss the current policy and evidence of its potential devastating effects, and the third paragraph advocates for a new system of wildfire management.

    E. No. This answer does not match the passage. The passage discusses the current system for fighting wildfires and advocates for a proposed new system; the passage does not discuss two seemingly contradictory goals of one policy.

2. **E**   **Extract Fact**

    The question asks what the phrase "maintenance burns" in line 55 refers to. The correct answer should match the meaning of that phrase in context, likely located within five lines of line 55. In lines 51–52, the passage provides the definition: "intentional lighting of controlled burns" and "allowing fires set by lightning to burn."

    A. No. This answer does not match the passage. Maintenance burns are controlled burns that the passage recommends as part of a new fire-management system. While they are similar to fires that regularly occurred in ancient forests, they are different in that they are managed and controlled.

    B. No. This answer contradicts the passage. According to the third paragraph, the goal of maintenance burns is to protect mature (larger, fire-tolerant) trees from destruction.

C. No. This answer contradicts the passage. According to the second paragraph, the fires that are likely to occur today would result in total devastation.

D. No. This answer contradicts the passage. According to the first paragraph, this type of fire typically occurred at intervals between 5 and 25 years.

E. Yes. The passage describes maintenance burns in lines 51–52 as the intentional lighting of controlled burns as well as allowing fires set by lightning to burn under certain conditions.

3. **C**   Complex

The question asks which sentence would most logically complete the last paragraph. Eliminate answers that contradict the passage, bring up new topics, or do not match the Bottom Line or the overall tone of the passage.

A. No. This answer brings up a new topic. The passage does not address damage to developed property.

B. No. This answer contradicts the passage. The second paragraph states that foresters are becoming increasingly aware of the danger of too much firefighting. Nothing in the passage indicates that foresters would resist this new proposal.

C. Yes. The fourth paragraph indicates that the proposal will reduce the damage of inevitable wildfires once fuels are reduced by maintenance burns, which implies that in the meantime the risk of devastating fires will continue.

D. No. This answer brings up a new topic. The passage does not address the economic impact of the new proposal.

E. No. This answer brings up a new topic. The passage does not indicate that large financial resources will be needed for the new proposal.

4. **A**   Structure

The question asks for the function of the factors of topography, weather, and fuel in the passage. Look for the claim that these factors are used to support, likely located within 5 lines of the factors. The third paragraph mentions that topography, weather, and fuel are the factors that affect fire behavior, and concludes that, since fuel is the only factor land managers can control, they should focus on reducing fuel to control wildfires.

A. Yes. The function of topography, weather, and fuel in the passage is to support the claim of the third paragraph: that land managers should focus on reducing fuel to combat wildfires.

B. No. This answer goes too far and contradicts the passage. The passage does not state that land managers' efforts will always be somewhat ineffective.

C. No. This answer is from the wrong part of the passage. The second paragraph discusses the reason forest fires may be unnaturally devastating, but the third paragraph discusses topography, weather, and fuel.

D. No. This answer does not match the passage. The passage does not discuss the relationship of fuel types and forest densities to topography or weather.

E.   No. This answer is from the wrong part of the passage. The third paragraph discusses forest fires started by lightning as part of the proposed new wildfire management system. Like the factors of topography, weather, and fuel, this answer contains additional evidence supporting the claim of the paragraph: that land managers must conserve fuel.

5.   **B**   Extract Infer

The question asks which answer is true of ancient ponderosa forests. Ancient ponderosa forests are mentioned in line 9 of the passage. Look for an answer choice that is proved by statements in the passage about the ancient ponderosa forests, likely located within five lines up or down from line 9. Avoid answers that contradict the Bottom Line or include strongly worded language or comparisons that are not supported by statements in the passage.

A.   No. This answer makes an unsupported comparison. The passage does not discuss genetic differences between ancient and modern ponderosas.

B.   Yes. This answer makes a comparison that is supported by the passage. The first paragraph states that ancient ponderosa forests were stable in part because fires maintained open forests and cleared brush and young trees, while the second paragraph states that fuel builds up in modern forests.

C.   No. This answer makes an unsupported comparison. The passage does not discuss differences in weather patterns in ponderosa forests.

D.   No. This answer makes an unsupported comparison. The passage does not discuss differences in diversity of plant species in ponderosa forests.

E.   No. This answer contradicts the passage. The second paragraph states that wildlife might escape low-intensity fires, and the passage does not state that fires helped control wildlife populations.

6.   **D**   Extract Infer

The question asks how the author would regard a policy in which all forest fires started by lightning were allowed to burn until they died out naturally. The passage states in line 51 that fires started by lightning could be allowed to burn when the weather is damp enough to reduce the risk of extensive damage. This implies that the author believes extensive damage might occur if the weather were not damp.

A.   No. This answer contradicts the passage. According to line 53 of the passage, allowing all fires to burn even when the weather is not damp would risk extensive damage to the forest, and so it would not be a viable means of restoring the forest.

B.   No. This answer contradicts the passage. According to line 53 of the passage, allowing all fires to burn even when the weather is not damp would risk extensive damage to the forest, and so it would not be an essential component of a new wildfire management plan.

C.   No. This answer contradicts the passage. According to line 53 of the passage, allowing all fires to burn even when the weather is not damp would risk extensive damage to the forest, and so it would not be beneficial to forests with older trees.

D.   Yes. This answer matches the statement in line 53 of the passage that fires may cause extensive damage if the weather is not damp.

E.   No. This answer is not supported by the passage. The passage does not discuss public perception of the consequences of fires, and it does not suggest that a solution is politically infeasible.

Questions 7–13

The main point of the first paragraph is that Mali's restrictions on exporting of cultural artifacts actually resulted in looting of artifacts, and thus the loss of important knowledge about them. The second paragraph notes that many societies condemn such looting and have adopted policies that such artifacts belong to the country where they are found. The third paragraph argues that Mali's regulations ironically resulted in lootings that led to loss of information about cultural artifacts. The fourth paragraph suggests that if Mali had actually allowed and licensed excavations rather than prohibiting them, the excavations of artifacts might be less well conducted than careful archaeological excavations, but the information gained about the artifacts might be worth it. The Bottom Line of the passage is that a system that allows and licenses the excavations of cultural antiquities, although flawed, might be preferable to the alternative, where restrictions lead to looting and loss of valuable information. The overall tone of the passage is persuasive: The passage criticizes the current system and describes an alternative solution.

7.   B   **Big Picture**

Use the Bottom Line to choose an answer. Watch out for answers that contradict the Bottom Line, are too narrow (a point that is not the main point), or go beyond the statements in the passage.

A.   No. This answer is too narrow; it matches the main point of the second paragraph only.

B.   Yes. This answer matches the Bottom Line. The passage suggests in the fourth paragraph that a more flexible solution may be preferable to the damage caused by the restrictive policies described in the second and third paragraphs.

C.   No. This answer does not match the tone of the passage, and it goes beyond the passage. The passage does not suggest that Mali should resist the dictates of international bodies or that Mali must find a unique solution.

D.   No. This answer contradicts the passage. The passage does not suggest that only accredited archaeologists should be licensed for excavations.

E.   No. This answer does not match the passage. The passage does state that Mali's restrictive policies seem to have done more harm than good, but the passage does not suggest that the idea that cultural artifacts are the property of the state does more harm than good.

8.   B   **Extract Fact**

The question asks which answer represents a way some countries have made use of the UNESCO doctrine. Since the UNESCO doctrine is mentioned in line 17, the answer should be located somewhere in the second paragraph. Look for an answer choice that is proved by a statement in the passage about the use of the UNESCO doctrine. Avoid answers that contradict the Bottom Line or include strongly worded language or comparisons that are not supported by statements in the passage.

A.   No. This answer does not match the passage. The passage does not state that UNESCO regulations require the origins of all antiquities sold to collectors to be fully documented.

B.   Yes. In lines 23–25, the second paragraph states that a number of countries have declared that all antiquities originating within their borders are state property and cannot be freely exported.

C.   No. This answer is from the wrong part of the passage. In the third paragraph, the author suggests that Mali could have adopted a plan that involves educating people about the proper excavation of antiquities, but this plan does not relate to the UNESCO doctrine, which concerns the sovereign power of a country over antiquities originating within its borders.

D.   No. This answer does not match the passage. The passage does not discuss countries with borders containing an ancient culture's territory.

E.   No. This answer does not match the passage. The passage does not discuss the restoration of antiquities or the commitment of substantial resources to such a plan.

9.   **C**   **Structure**

The question asks for the author's purpose in asking the reader to suppose that Mali had imposed a tax on exported objects. Look for the claim that this request supports, likely located within five lines of the statement. In this case, the request is made in support of the main point of the fourth paragraph: A flexible plan of licensing would be preferable to a strict prohibition on excavation and export of antiquities.

A.   No. This answer does not match the purpose of the request. While the new tax would help fund the acquisition of pieces by the national museum, the purpose of the discussion of the new task is to support the main idea of the fourth paragraph: A more flexible policy would be preferable to the more restrictive policies currently in place.

B.   No. This answer contradicts the tone of the passage. The passage is critical of the Malian government's past policies concerning cultural antiquities.

C.   Yes. This answer matches the purpose of the request. The purpose of the discussion of the new task is to support the main idea of the fourth paragraph: A more flexible, pragmatic approach may be preferable to past restrictive policies.

D.   No. This answer does not match the purpose of the request. While the passage does suggest requiring that records be kept, the purpose of the discussion of the new tax is to support the main idea of the fourth paragraph: A more flexible policy would be preferable to the more restrictive policies currently in place.

E.   No. This answer is from the wrong part of the passage. The UNESCO doctrine is discussed in the second paragraph, while the purpose of the discussion of the new tax is to support the main idea of the fourth paragraph: A more flexible policy would be preferable to the more restrictive policies currently in place.

10.   **A**   **Extract Infer**

The question asks which answer the author would be most likely to agree with regarding UNESCO. Since UNESCO is mentioned in various locations in the passage, look for an answer choice that is proved by a statement in the passage about UNESCO. Avoid answers that contradict the Bottom Line or include strongly worded language or comparisons that are not supported by statements in the passage.

A.   Yes. This answer is supported by the passage. The first sentence of the fourth paragraph asks to reader to suppose that UNESCO helped Mali to exercise its rights by licensing excavations and educating people. This statement suggests that the author believes that UNESCO can play an important role in stemming abuses relating to cultural artifacts.

B.   No. This answer goes beyond the passage. The passage does not suggest that UNESCO's policies came about in response to Mali's situation.

C.   No. This answer makes an unsupported comparison. The passage does not compare UNESCO's success in single-state versus multi-state initiatives.

D.   No. This answer goes beyond the passage. The passage does not discuss whether UNESCO pays enough attention to countries like Mali.

E.   No. This answer goes beyond the passage. The passage does not discuss the level of funding received by UNESCO.

11.   **C**   Extract
                Infer

The question asks which answer the author would be most likely to agree with regarding regulations governing trade in antiquities in countries like Mali. Since these regulations are discussed throughout the passage, look for an answer choice that is proved by a statement in the passage about the regulations. Avoid answers that contradict the Bottom Line or include strongly worded language or comparisons that are not supported by statements in the passage.

A.   No. This answer contradicts the tone of the passage. The passage argues for flexible regulations, not regulations that must be approved by archaeologists.

B.   No. This answer contradicts the Bottom Line of the passage. The fourth paragraph suggests that it may be preferable to allow cultural antiquities to be exported, so long as information about the artifacts is recorded and registered.

C.   Yes. This answer is supported by a statement in the passage. In the fourth paragraph, lines 54–55 state that some people would still have been able to avoid the proposed regulations, and yet this may still be preferable to the actual results with the current regulations.

D.   No. This answer contradicts the tone of the passage. The passage argues for flexible regulations, not for strict punishment of violators.

E.   No. This answer makes an unsupported comparison. The passage does not discuss the idea that the regulations would be most effective when they are easy to understand.

12.   **D**   Extract
                Infer

The question asks which statement about cultural antiquities the author would be most likely to agree with. Since cultural antiquities are discussed throughout the passage, look for an answer choice that is proved by a statement in the passage about the antiquities.

Avoid answers that contradict the Bottom Line or include strongly worded language or comparisons that are not supported by statements in the passage.

A.   No. This answer goes beyond the passage. The passage suggests a policy that would provide funding for the country's national museum to acquire important pieces, but the passage does not suggest that artifacts must be owned and protected by the national museum.

B.   No. This answer contradicts the Bottom Line of the passage. The passage suggests that a flexible policy allowing the export of artifacts would be preferable to restrictive policies prohibiting export of cultural artifacts.

C.   No. This answer contradicts the passage. The fourth paragraph suggests that the country's national museum should acquire important artifacts.

D.   Yes. This answer is supported by a statement in the passage. In the fourth paragraph, lines 51–54 state that excavations not conducted by accredited archaeologists may be inferior and less informative, which implies that excavations conducted by accredited archaeologists would be preferred.

E.   No. This answer contradicts the passage. The fourth paragraph suggests that only licensed excavations of artifacts should be permitted; the passage does not state that artifacts belong to anyone who finds and registers them.

13.   **B**   **Big Picture**

The question asks about the author's attitude toward foreign collectors of terra-cotta sculptures from Djenne-jeno. Look for a statement about the foreign collectors that includes words indicating the author's attitude: In line 8, the passage states that terra-cotta sculptures were sold to foreign collectors who rightly admired them, which indicates that the author believes the foreign collectors correctly thought the sculptures were admirable.

A.   No. This answer does not match the author's attitude. The author is critical of such collecting, calling it "pillaging" that is "natural to condemn" in line 13.

B.   Yes. This answer matches the author's attitude. The author states that the foreign collectors rightly admired the sculptures, which indicates that the author approved of their artistic judgment.

C.   No. This answer does not match the author's attitude. The author does not discuss the idea of foreign collectors taking action against illegal exportation.

D.   No. This answer does not match the author's attitude. The author does not discuss whether the foreign collectors are concerned for the people of Mali.

E.   No. This answer does not match the author's attitude. The author states that the foreign collectors rightly admired the sculptures, which indicates that the author approved of their artistic judgment, but this does not mean the author had sympathy with their motives.

Questions 14–21

The main idea of the first paragraph is that in a clinical trial comparing a new treatment to a currently accepted treatment, experts traditionally believed that the physicians participating in the trial should be unbiased toward each treatment option. The second paragraph suggests that this requirement of neutrality ("theoretical equipoise") may be too strict, because it is effectively an impossible standard for clinical trials to meet. The third paragraph suggests that a new standard be developed ("clinical equipoise") that eliminates unreasonable restrictions while maintaining strict ethical standards. The fourth paragraph suggests that this new standard would be possible because absence of consensus among clinical experts is enough to ensure that the process meets ethical standards. The Bottom Line of the passage is that traditional standards for clinical trials are overly restrictive, and they should be replaced with a new standard that would allow a physician to prefer one method of treatment and yet remain in the study, so long as the physician recognizes the lack of consensus among clinical experts. The overall tone of the passage is persuasive: The passage advocates for the replacement of traditional, restrictive requirements for clinical trials with new, more flexible requirements.

14.   **B**   **Big Picture**

Use the Bottom Line to choose an answer. Watch out for answers that are too narrow (a purpose that's not primary) and answers that don't match the Bottom Line of the passage.

A.   No. This answer does not match the purpose of the passage. The passage does not merely explain the difference between two conceptions; rather, it advocates for a change to a new conception.

B. Yes. This answer matches the purpose of the passage. The passage advocates for a change from theoretical equipoise, a more restrictive requirement, to a new standard of clinical equipoise, which is less restrictive.

C. No. This answer contradicts the Bottom Line of the passage. The passage argues that a change in the standards would improve the standards of clinical trials, not endanger them.

D. No. This answer does not match the purpose of the passage. The passage does not advocate that researchers more closely examine the conceptions; rather, it advocates for a change to a new conception.

E. No. This answer does not match the purpose of the passage. The passage does not argue for a change in the scientific methods used in clinical trials; rather, it argues for a change in the ethical standards governing the state of mind of physicians participating in clinical trials.

15. **D**   **Structure**

The question asks for the primary purpose of the second paragraph. The second paragraph suggests that the requirement of theoretical equipoise may be too strict, because it is effectively an impossible standard for clinical trials to meet. Eliminate answers that contradict the Bottom Line or that are too narrow (i.e., that describe a purpose that is not the primary purpose of the second paragraph).

A. No. This answer does not match the purpose of the second paragraph. The second paragraph does not provide a view that contrasts with the arguments in favor of clinical equipoise; instead, it provides reasons why theoretical equipoise may be too strict, thereby supporting the idea that clinical equipoise may be preferable.

B. No. This answer does not match the purpose of the second paragraph. While the second paragraph does discuss the factors underlying physicians' preferences regarding treatments, this is just a topic discussed in the second paragraph. The purpose of the second paragraph is to argue that the traditional conception of equipoise is too strict.

C. No. This answer contradicts the Bottom Line. The passage does not disagree with the moral principle that underlies theoretical equipoise; rather, it suggests a new, less restrictive standard that would still achieve the same moral principle.

D. Yes. This answer matches the purpose of the second paragraph. The second paragraph suggests that the requirement of theoretical equipoise may be too strict, because it is effectively an impossible standard for clinical trials to meet.

E. No. This answer does not match the purpose of the second paragraph. The second paragraph does not criticize the general notion of equipoise; rather, it argues that the requirement of theoretical equipoise imposes standards that are virtually impossible for clinical trials to satisfy.

16. **C**   **Extract Fact**

The question asks which answer is true according to statements in the passage. Since the answer could be supported from a statement located anywhere in the passage, look for a statement in the passage that would prove an answer choice true. Eliminate answers that contradict the Bottom Line or include strongly worded language or comparisons that are not supported by statements in the passage.

A. No. This answer contradicts the Bottom Line of the passage. The passage argues that the requirements of theoretical equipoise are effectively impossible for clinical trials to satisfy.

B. No. This answer goes beyond the passage. The passage does not discuss how often clinical researchers are forced to suspend trials in this manner.

C. Yes. This answer is supported by a statement in the passage. In lines 50–53, the passage states that even if one or more researchers has a decided clinical preference as to treatment, this situation would be no ethical bar to participation in a trial, which implies that a physician holding such a preference would not render the clinical trial unethical.

D. No. This answer contradicts the Bottom Line of the passage. The passage suggests that the standard of theoretical equipoise is too restrictive, and it proposes clinical equipoise as a less restrictive alternative; therefore, a clinical trial that meets the standard of clinical equipoise would not necessarily meet the standard of theoretical equipoise.

E. No. This answer contradicts the Bottom Line of the passage. The passage suggests that theoretical equipoise is the traditional standard applied to clinical trials, and it argues that a new standard of clinical equipoise should be adopted. However, the passage does not state that researchers already do try to conduct trials in accordance with the clinical equipoise standard.

17. **D**   Complex

The question asks which answer would be significantly more likely to jeopardize theoretical equipoise than clinical equipoise. Look for an answer that describes a violation of the standard of theoretical equipoise but that would comply with the standard of clinical equipoise. According to the second paragraph, theoretical equipoise requires that the researcher consider the evidence for the treatment regimens being compared to be exactly balanced. According to the third paragraph, clinical equipoise provides that a researcher may prefer one treatment over another based on evidence, so long as clinical experts disagree as to which treatment is superior and the researcher recognizes this lack of consensus.

A. No. This answer would not achieve the goal stated by the question. If, during a clinical trial, most clinical specialists came to favor one treatment over another, there would be no lack of consensus among medical experts, and therefore this scenario would violate the standard of clinical equipoise.

B. No. This answer would not achieve the goal stated by the question. If preliminary results indicate that the two treatments are equally effective, then researchers participating in the study would have no reason to prefer one treatment over another, and this scenario would not jeopardize theoretical equipoise.

C. No. This answer would not achieve the goal stated by the question. If physicians participating in the study prefer one treatment to another, then this scenario would jeopardize theoretical equipoise, but if there is no lack of consensus among clinical experts, then this scenario would also jeopardize clinical equipoise.

D. Yes. This answer achieves the goal stated by the question. If physicians participating in the study prefer one treatment to another, then this scenario would jeopardize theoretical equipoise, but if there is a lack of consensus among clinical experts and the physicians in question recognize this, then this scenario would not jeopardize clinical equipoise.

E. No. This answer would not achieve the goal stated by the question. If physicians participating in the study believe both treatments are equally effective, then this scenario would not jeopardize theoretical equipoise.

18. **D** | Big Picture

Use the Bottom Line to choose an answer. Watch out for answers that are too narrow, go too far, or contradict the Bottom Line of the passage.

A. No. This answer is too narrow. This is the main idea of the second paragraph only. It does not address the main ideas of the third and fourth paragraphs: that a new standard of clinical equipoise should be adopted instead.

B. No. This answer does not match the Bottom Line. While the passage does say in the second paragraph that the conception of theoretical equipoise is almost impossible to satisfy, the passage goes on in the third and fourth paragraphs to propose a new standard that should be adopted.

C. No. This answer is too narrow. This is the main idea of the fourth paragraph only. This answer does not address the main point, which is that the restrictive conception of theoretical equipoise should be replaced with the less restrictive conception of clinical equipoise.

D. Yes. This answer matches the Bottom Line. The second paragraph argues that theoretical equipoise is too restrictive, and the third and fourth paragraphs argue that clinical equipoise is less restrictive and therefore should be adopted.

E. No. This answer is too narrow. The passage argues that a clinical trial that does not meet the standard of theoretical equipoise but does meet the standard of clinical equipoise should not be considered unethical.

19. **A** | Extract Fact

The question asks which answer represents a group of people referred to by the term "community," as used in line 41 of the passage. Look for a statement located likely within five lines of line 41 that would support the answer choice. In this case, eliminate answers that contradict the Bottom Line or include strongly worded language or comparisons that are not supported by statements in the passage.

A. Yes. This answer is supported by a statement in the passage. In lines 40–42, the passage refers to the expert clinical community and its opinions over which treatment is better for patients with a given illness. This implies that the community is a group of people who focus on a common set of problems (patients with a given illness) using a shared body of knowledge (expertise in clinical treatment of a given illness).

B. No. This answer is not supported by the passage. The passage does not discuss the geographical area where clinical experts work or live.

C. No. This answer makes an unsupported comparison. The passage does not discuss the differences of opinion of clinical experts with other groups.

D. No. This answer is from the wrong part of the passage. This answer is a paraphrase of the last sentence of the first paragraph, but the physicians and ethicists referred to by this sentence are not the community of clinical experts referred to in lines 40–41.

E. No. This answer is not supported by the passage. The passage does not indicate that the community of clinical experts are employed in unrelated disciplines.

20. **C**   **Extract Fact**

The question asks which answer is true according to statements in the passage. Since the answer could be supported from a statement located anywhere in the passage, look for a statement in the passage that would prove an answer choice true. Eliminate answers that contradict the Bottom Line or include strongly worded language or comparisons that are not supported by statements in the passage.

A. No. This answer contradicts the passage. The last sentence of the second paragraph of the passage states that few trials could comply with the standard of theoretical equipoise.

B. No. This answer makes an unsupported comparison. The passage does not suggest that clinical trials would be conducted more often if a more reasonable standard were in place; rather, the passage suggests that more clinical trials would be able to satisfy that new standard than the current standard.

C. Yes. This answer is supported by a statement in the passage. The last sentence of the second paragraph of the passage states that few trials could comply with the standard of theoretical equipoise.

D. No. This answer goes too far. While the last sentence of the first paragraph does state that most physicians and ethicists have traditionally agreed that traditional equipoise is appropriate for physicians in clinical trials, the passage does go so far as to state that most of them believe the currently accepted ethical requirements are adequate.

E. No. This answer goes beyond the passage. While the third paragraph does discuss conflicts of opinion in the expert clinical community, the passage does not suggest that most comparative trials are undertaken to help resolve such conflicts of opinion.

21. **A**   **Complex**

The question asks which answer, if true, would most weaken the author's argument in the third and fourth paragraphs. Treat this question the same as a Weaken question in the Arguments section. The author's conclusion in the third and fourth paragraphs is that a new standard called "clinical equipoise" should be developed. The author supports this conclusion with the premise that a physician participating in a clinical study who develops a preference for one treatment over another should be allowed to continue to participate so long as a lack of consensus exists among clinical experts, and the physician acknowledges this lack of consensus. Look for an answer that suggests a problem with this plan to develop a new standard of clinical equipoise.

A. Yes. This answer weakens the argument in the third and fourth paragraphs. If most comparative clinical trials are undertaken to prove that a treatment considered best by a consensus of relevant experts is superior, then the standard of clinical equipoise would be jeopardized, because the standard of clinical equipoise requires that a lack of consensus exist among clinical experts as to which treatment is superior.

B. No. This answer strengthens the argument. If physicians rarely ask to leave trials when they believe early data favors one treatment over another, then the study does not satisfy the requirement of theoretical equipoise. This supports the plan to develop a new standard of clinical equipoise that would allow those physicians to remain in the study so long as they acknowledge a lack of consensus among medical experts.

C. No. This answer is irrelevant. The number of clinical trials being conducted annually does not affect the decision whether to develop a new standard of clinical equipoise.

D. No. This answer is irrelevant. The opinion of medical ethicists compared with the opinion of clinical researchers is not relevant to whether a new standard clinical equipoise should be developed.

E. No. This answer is not strong enough to weaken the argument. Even if it is rare that researchers begin a trial with no preference, then later develop a strong preference, the standard of clinical equipoise would still be needed to deal with such situations; furthermore, the standard of clinical equipoise would also still be needed to deal with other situations, such as allowing researchers to participate in a trial even if they begin the trial with a preference for one treatment over another.

Questions 22–27

The main point of the first paragraph of passage A is that the flat tax seems to work fine in the real world, despite past objections that it works only in theory. The second paragraph notes that the first objection to the flat tax is generally that it is unfair because it is not progressive. The third paragraph argues that this is untrue, because the flat tax can be made progressive by exempting a certain amount of income from the tax, and then notes that high-income earners pay about the same rate under both systems, because typical progressive tax systems include numerous legal loopholes that reduce the taxes for the high-income earners. The Bottom Line of passage A is that the flat tax can be instituted fairly, despite objections to the contrary.

The first paragraph of passage B argues that a graduated tax rate is fairer than a flat tax, because people are treated equally, but dollars are not. The second paragraph argues that dollars should be treated unequally, because the first dollars earned are needed for survival expenses, while excess dollars earned are not as important. The third paragraph argues that, even if a flat tax exempts some low income levels from taxes, the higher-income taxpayers will pay less, and therefore the middle class will end up paying more. The Bottom Line of passage B is that a flat tax is unfair to the middle class.

22. C   **Big Picture**

The question asks which one of the answers is addressed by both passages. Use the Bottom Line of each passage to choose an answer. Eliminate answers that are addressed by only one of the two passages or that are not addressed by either passage.

A. No. This question is addressed only by passage A. The first paragraph of passage A discusses whether a flat tax is practical in the real world, but passage B does not address whether a flat tax can be implemented.

B. No. This question is addressed only by passage B. The first paragraph of passage B states that graduated tax rates treat all taxpayers equally, but passage A does not address this issue.

C. Yes. This question is addressed by both passages. Passage A argues that a flat tax can be fair to all taxpayers, while passage B argues that a flat tax is unfair to middle-class taxpayers.

D. No. This question is addressed only by passage B. The first paragraph of passage B discusses objections to progressive taxes, but passage A discusses objections only to flat taxes.

E. No. This question is addressed only by passage A. The third paragraph of passage A discusses incentives to avoid taxes legally and illegally, and it suggests that flat tax regimes would reduce such avoidance, but passage B does not address illegal tax avoidance.

23. E Structure

This question asks which technique is used by both passages to advance their arguments. Look for supporting evidence in each passage that matches an answer choice.

A. No. This technique is used only by passage A. The second paragraph of passage A suggests that those who initially said flat taxes were impractical in the real world then offer a further instant objection that they are unfair when they see that they have been successfully implemented. This is an example of shifting one's ground (changing a position once the first position has been proved wrong). Passage B, on the other hand, does not make any similar suggestion.

B. No. This technique is used only by passage A. The first paragraph of passage A discusses historical developments in Estonia as evidence, but passage B does not discuss any specific historical developments.

C. No. This technique is used only by passage B. Passage B uses an analogy to compare the dollars earned by the working poor to the dollars earned by middle-wage earners. However, passage A does not use any comparisons to advance its argument.

D. No. This technique is used only by passage B. In lines 51–53, passage B asks this question: "…[W]hy go suddenly from one extreme…to the other..?," which is a rhetorical question. However, passage A does not use any rhetorical questions.

E. Yes. This technique is used by both passages to advance their arguments. In lines 17–19, passage A corrects the misunderstanding described in the previous paragraph (that a flat tax is unfair to lower-income taxpayers). Similarly, in lines 33–36, passage B corrects the misunderstanding described in the previous sentence (that progressive tax rates seem unfair).

24. D Complex

Treat this question like a Strengthen question in an Arguments section. The question asks which answer, if true of a country that switched from a progressive tax system to a flat tax, would support the position of passage B over passage A. The position of passage B is that switching to a flat tax will shift more of the tax burden from the high-income earners to the middle class, while the position of passage A is that the flat tax is fair and will result in high-income earners paying approximately the same amount. Look for an answer that supports the idea that middle-class taxpayers will pay a greater share of taxes under a flat tax than under a progressive tax system.

A. No. This answer is irrelevant. Whether total revenues collected will remain the same does not address the issue of whether middle-class taxpayers will pay a greater share.

B. No. This answer is irrelevant. Whether the tax codes have been simplified does not address the issue of whether middle-class taxpayers will pay a greater share.

C. No. This answer is irrelevant. Whether high-income taxpayers believe they are overtaxed does not address the issue of whether middle-class taxpayers will pay a greater share.

D. Yes. This answer supports the position of passage B over that of passage A. If middle-income taxpayers tend to pay higher taxes, this supports the position of passage B over passage A, which indicates that high-income taxpayers would pay about the same (and therefore implies that middle-income taxpayers would pay about the same as well).

E. No. This answer is irrelevant. Whether some legislators favor a return to the former system does not address the issue of whether middle-class taxpayers will pay a greater share.

25. **D** Extract Fact

The question asks which answer is a conclusion for which passage A argues but that is not addressed by passage B. Look for an answer that is supported by the argument in passage A but that is not addressed in passage B. Eliminate answers that reverse the relationship or that are addressed in both passages.

A. No. This answer is addressed by both passages. The last paragraph of passage B addresses whether exempting a threshold amount enables a flat tax to avoid unfairness, so this answer does not match the requirement that the answer is not addressed by passage B.

B. No. Passage A argues against this conclusion. The main idea of the first paragraph of passage A is that the flat tax is actually practical in the real world, so this answer does not match the requirement that the answer is a conclusion argued for by passage A.

C. No. This answer is an outside knowledge trap. Neither passage addresses how taxes may inhibit investment or economic growth.

D. Yes. This answer is a conclusion argued for by passage A, and it is not addressed in passage B. The third paragraph of passage A argues for the idea that a flat tax would eliminate opportunities for high-income earners to avoid tax, but passage B does not address this issue.

E. No. This answer is not supported by either passage. Passage A argues that the flat tax is not unfair, but passage A does not argue that a progressive tax system is unfair. Passage B, on the other hand, argues that the flax tax is unfair, but it does not argue that a progressive tax system is unfair.

26. **B** Extract Fact

Treat this question like a Point-at-Issue question in an Arguments section. Look for an answer that is supported by the a statement in one passage but contradicted by a statement in the other. Eliminate answers that are supported by both passages or not supported by either passage.

A. No. This answer is supported by both passages. Both passage A and passage B state that a flat tax can be modified to exempt a threshold amount, which would technically make the flat tax system progressive.

B. Yes. The authors of the two passages would likely disagree over this statement. The last sentence of passage A argues that high-income earners usually pay about the same amount under a flat tax as under a progressive tax system. On the other hand, the last sentence of passage B argues that high-income earners would pay less under a flat tax than under a progressive tax system.

C. No. The authors of both passages would disagree with this statement. The last sentence of the first paragraph of passage A contradicts this statement by saying that a flat tax seems to work as well in practice as it does in theory. Passage B argues that the flat tax is unfair, and therefore the author of passage B would disagree with the idea that the flat tax is fine in theory.

D. No. The authors of both passages would agree with this statement. The second paragraph of passage A supports this statement, as does the first paragraph of passage B.

E. No. Neither passage supports this statement. The third paragraph of passage A argues that a certain portion of every individual's income should be exempt from taxation, as does the third paragraph of passage B.

27.   B   Complex

Treat this answer like a Weaken question in an Arguments section. The question asks which answer, if true, would be a reasonable response for the author of passage B to make to the final argument of passage A. The final argument of passage A is that progressive tax systems include numerous incentives for avoidance of taxes by high-income taxpayers, and these incentives would be removed by the flat tax. Look for an answer that is consistent with the Bottom Line of passage B and that suggests that the flat tax would not actually remove the incentives and opportunities to avoid taxes.

A.   No. This answer does not weaken the final argument of passage A. Even if some high-income taxpayers could avoid taxes under a flat-tax system by under-reporting their income, the flat tax may still have eliminated various other incentives and methods for avoiding taxes.

B.   Yes. This answer weakens the final argument of passage A. If tax avoidance is the result of tax loopholes and special deductions, and not the nature of the progressive tax system itself, then similar loopholes and tax deductions might eventually be added to the flat tax as well, which means the flat tax might not actually remove those opportunities.

C.   No. This answer does not match the Bottom Line of passage B. Passage B argues that the flat tax is unfair to middle-income taxpayers, not high-income taxpayers; furthermore, the fact that people at all income levels have been known to avoid taxes is irrelevant to the comparison between the progressive tax and the flat tax.

D.   No. This answer is irrelevant. Which system is preferred by more taxpayers is not relevant to the question of whether the flat tax eliminates the incentives and opportunities for high-income earners to avoid taxes.

E.   No. This answer is irrelevant, and it does not match the Bottom Line of passage B. Passage B does not address the idea of taxes on consumption of goods and services; rather, passage B argues that the flat tax is unfair and that a progressive tax system is fair.

Section 2: Arguments 1

1.   D   Principle
Strengthen

This argument makes the claim that you should use praise and verbal correction to train your dog rather than using edible treats. This claim is based upon the fact that even though dogs learn quickly when trained with treats, most dogs will not obey commands without seeing a treat. The argument continues that it is not possible to always have treats. The argument assumes that praise and verbal correction are both an effective alternative to training and that it is better to use a stimulus that is always available. The credited response will provide a strong general rule that forces one of these assumptions to be true.

A.   No. The speed at which a dog learns and the likelihood the owner will use a certain stimulus is irrelevant to the conclusion that verbal praise and correction should be used instead.

B.   No. This answer choice directly contradicts the premise that treat commands are less effective since dogs will not obey without the stimulus.

C. No. This answer choice does not fully support the claim that verbal training should be used instead of treats since treat stimulus is a somewhat effective method according to the premises. Therefore, "some circumstances" could include either the treat training or verbal training methods.

D. Yes. This rule, if true, would suggest that verbal training would be better than treat training since verbal commands can be supplied in all circumstances.

E. No. The focus of this answer choice is reversed from the conclusion. The claim is about what owners should do, not what they should not do.

2. **C**   **Weaken**

The archaeologist's argument makes the claim that a similar fate of high salinity soil is likely to occur to modern civilizations that rely heavily on irrigation for agriculture. This is based upon a comparison with the ancient Sumerians who depended upon irrigation. The irrigation used by the ancient Sumerians led to a toxic buildup of salts, which in turn led to a collapse of the civilization when agriculture failed. The argument assumes that ancient Sumerians and modern practices of agriculture are similar enough to warrant comparison. The credited response will exploit this comparison flaw by suggesting some reason that agricultural practices in modern times are different from those used by the ancient Sumerians.

A. No. This answer is irrelevant since the issue in the conclusion is the likely collapse of modern civilizations that rely on irrigation, not whether they could feed themselves. If anything, this answer choice would strengthen the archaeologist's claim.

B. No. This answer is irrelevant since the question task is to weaken the claim that modern civilizations will likely collapse.

C. Yes. This answer choice provides a reason to doubt the validity of the comparison between ancient Sumerian irrigation practices and modern ones.

D. No. This is irrelevant to the conclusion since the claim stipulates "civilizations that rely heavily on irrigation." Just because many do not rely heavily on irrigation does not weaken a claim about those that do.

E. No. This answer is irrelevant to the conclusion since the premises state explicitly that the practice of irrigation led to the buildup of toxicity in the soil. The presence of toxic compounds in the soil before irrigation does not weaken the comparison.

3. **B**   **Strengthen**

This argument makes the claim that mineralized dinosaur bones and dinosaur tracks in dried mud flats are rarely found together. The only evidence supplied for this claim is that scavengers most likely went to mud flats to find carcasses. The researcher assumes that the cause of the lack of tracks and bones together was scavengers and ignores other possible causes for the observed phenomenon. The credited response will strengthen the causal assumption by providing some proof that scavengers could in fact cause a lack of fossilized bones in mudflats or will rule out an alternative cause for the tracks and bones being found separately.

A. No. This is irrelevant since the claim is focused on what occurs in the mud flats.

B. Yes. This answer choice provides additional information on scavenger habits that would strengthen the claim that they are a reason for the lack of bones where dinosaur tracks are found.

C. No. This is irrelevant since the claim is focused on the fact that fossilized tracks and bones are rarely found together. The relative frequency of tracks to bones does not strengthen this claim.

D. No. This answer is irrelevant since it discusses items that are neither tracks nor bones.

E. No. While this answer choice provides a difference between tracks and bones, it does not strengthen the claim that it is scavenger activity that led to the two items rarely occurring together. If anything, this answer choice would weaken that claim.

4. **A**   Main Point

This argument concludes that stovetop burners would cause fewer fires if the burners were limited to a temperature of 350 degrees C. This claim is based upon the premise that this would provide enough heat for cooking while remaining below the ignition temperatures of cooking oil and common fibers. The author assumes that at least some fires are caused by stovetops igniting cooking oil or fibers. The credited response will identify the conclusion and will match it in both tone and scope.

A. Yes. It matches the argument's conclusion in both tone and scope.

B. No. This is a premise in support of the claim that limiting burners to 350 degrees would cause fewer fires.

C. No. This is a premise in support of the claim that limiting burners to 350 degrees would cause fewer fires.

D. No. This is a premise in support of the claim that limiting burners to 350 degrees would cause fewer fires.

E. No. This claim is not found within the argument.

5. **E**   Flaw

This argument opens by summarizing a statement made by Jenkins that his movie was not intended to provoke antisocial behavior and that a director's best interest is to prevent that behavior. The author concludes that this claim by Jenkins must be rejected. As evidence, the author claims that the movie produced antisocial behavior. The speaker assumes that the new evidence is sufficient to cast doubt on Jenkins's claim. There is a language shift from an intended action to a result. Specifically, the speaker assumes that since the movie had a certain effect (antisocial behavior) that this effect must have been intended. The credited response will identify some weakness in the new evidence.

A. No. This choice describes an ad hominem flaw, which is not found in the argument.

B. No. This describes a correlation as causation flaw, which is not found in the argument.

C. No. This describes a part to whole comparison flaw, which is not found in the argument.

D. No. This answer has the wrong focus of people acting in a way contrary to the intentions that they themselves stated. The argument confuses intentions with effects upon others.

E. Yes. It describes the confusion between the actual effects of the film with the intended effects of the film's director.

6. C `Principle Strengthen`

This argument claims that the word "loophole" should not be used in news stories unless there is evidence of wrongdoing. This conclusion is based upon the premise that "loophole" is a partisan word and that its use causes news stories to read like editorials. Since the conclusion is a conditional statement, it can be diagrammed as "If use loophole → evidence." The contrapositive is "if ~evidence → ~ use loophole." There is also a language shift in this argument between the perceptions of the word "loophole" and evidence mentioned in the conclusion. The credited response should provide a strong general rule that forces evidence to be required before the word "loophole" is used in a news story.

A. No. This answer wrongly focuses on wrong doing or scandal. It is irrelevant to the conclusion that evidence is necessary for the use of the word.

B. No. This answer choice compares editorials and news stories. This principle cannot be applied to the conclusion that the use of "loophole" requires evidence.

C. Yes. This answer choice states a general rule that new stories must provide evidence for suggestions of wrong doing. Since the premises stated that the word loophole suggests wrongdoing, this principle is applicable.

D. No. This principle would actually contradict the conclusion that reporters should provide evidence in this situation.

E. No. Public interest is not an issue in the argument, so this principle cannot be applied to the conclusion.

7. E `Strengthen`

This argument concludes that widespread food shortages are inevitable. This argument opens by stating a claim by some people that there is no reason for concern over food supplies since food production currently increases faster than population. The expert then suggests that the current resources can increase only a little more than their current levels after which no increase is possible. The expert makes a time comparison flaw by assuming that since a trend has occurred in the past, it will continue to occur in the future. To support this comparison, the credited response should provide some reason that this time comparison is valid by ruling out alternatives or by providing additional evidence for its validity.

A. No. Whether or not food sources are renewable is irrelevant to the claim that shortages are inevitable.

B. No. Whether ocean resources will be fully utilized does not support the claim that shortages are inevitable. This can be viewed as a premise restatement since the expert has already claimed that food can be produced only a few times higher than the current amount.

C. No. This answer choice would weaken the argument by providing a reason that the time comparison is invalid.

D. No. The occurrence of regional shortages in the past is irrelevant to the claim that widespread food shortages in the future are inevitable.

E. Yes. This answer choice shows that the current trends in both food production and population growth will continue to a point at which population growth outpaces food production.

8. **D** **Sufficient Assumption**

The argument concludes that in respect to technical sophistication, newer video games are less compelling to players. This is based upon a brief comparison between the earliest video games and newer ones in which newer video games have more detailed characters. The argument states that players cannot identify as well with newer game characters since they can clearly see that these characters represent other people. There is a language shift from "identify" to "compelling" games. The credited response should help the conclusion by building a bridge between one's ability to identify with a character and how compelling that makes a video game. The credited response should move from the premises to the conclusion.

A. No. This response focuses on one of the premises rather than on the conclusion. It is irrelevant.

B. No. This response discusses compelling aspects of video games other than technological sophistication. This answer choice is irrelevant.

C. No. This answer choice is necessary for the conclusion to be true, but it is not sufficient to force the conclusion that technological sophistication makes games less compelling.

D. Yes. This answer choice links the premises about a player's ability to identify with a character and how compelling that makes the game.

E. No. This answer choice moves in the wrong direction, moving from the conclusion to the premises. Thus, it does not support the conclusion.

9. **D** **Resolve/ Explain**

This states that many regions in North America would be suitable for pumpkin crops where pumpkins would be able to grow without danger of destruction by frost. The argument then poses a paradox by stating that instead, pumpkin production is located in regions of North America where there are long winters and a high degree that the crops will be destroyed by frost. The credited response will provide a viable explanation for why pumpkins are grown in regions with long winters rather than in more temperate regions.

A. No. This would not explain why pumpkins are grown predominately in colder regions.

B. No. This would not explain why pumpkins are grown predominately in colder regions. If anything, this answer would make the discrepancy worse.

C. No. This would not explain why pumpkins are grown predominately in colder regions. If anything, this answer would make the discrepancy worse.

D. Yes. This answer choice provides a reason why colder climates would be preferable for pumpkin crops despite the danger of early frost.

E. No. This would not explain why pumpkins are grown predominately in colder regions. If anything, this answer would make the discrepancy worse.

10. C   **Weaken**

The argument concludes that it is necessary to adopt an alternative code of procedure. This claim is based upon the fact that the current code has many obscure and unnecessary rules that cause fighting and a loss of public confidence. The speaker acknowledges that the code is entrenched but counters by stating the public confidence is necessary for their endeavors. The speaker assumes that the proposed solution is complete and effective. The speaker also assumes that the solution is the sole possible manner in which the problem can be addressed. Specifically, the council chair assumes that the only viable option for fixing the problem of fighting and loss of confidence is the alternative code. To weaken this claim, the credited response will provide either a problem with the alternative code or suggest a different possible solution to the issue at hand.

A. No. This answer choice suggests that the problems might not be common. However, it does not weaken the claim that the alternative code should be adopted.

B. No. While this answer suggests that the alternative code has been used for personal ends, it does not clearly show that the reason for this is inherent to the alternative code. As a result, this answer choice is not strong enough to cast doubt on the claim that the alternative code should be adopted.

C. Yes. This answer choice suggests that an alternative solution to the problem is under consideration casting doubt on the necessity of adopting the alternative code.

D. No. This answer choice is irrelevant to the conclusion. Just because it is not always necessary to adopt an alternative does not preclude the necessity to do so in this specific situation. This answer choice is too softly worded to cast doubt on the conclusion.

E. No. This answer choice moves in the wrong direction. It would strengthen the claim that the alternative code should be adopted.

11. C   **Resolve/ Explain**

This argument says that among similar businesses, those that used customer surveys to improve profits saw a decline in profits when they used the surveys. Businesses that did not employ the surveys did not see a corresponding drop in profits. Since the businesses are of the same type, the credited response will state some reason that helps explain why the use of surveys seemed to lead to the opposite of the desired effect.

A. No. This answer choice is irrelevant since it does not mention surveys.

B. No. This is stated in the argument. The general use of surveys does not explain why profits dropped among those who did use them.

C. Yes. This answer choice resolves the dilemma by showing that the use of surveys is motivated by complaints, which could lead to a decline in sales and profits. If a business has no complaints, it would have no reason to use a survey.

D. No. Whether the surveys are accurately completed does not explain why businesses who use them see a drop in profits.

E. No. This answer choice addresses only one side of the issue. It might explain why those who used the surveys saw a drop in profits but does not explain why businesses who do not use surveys saw no drop in profits.

12. E Necessary Assumption

This argument claims that humans are unable to choose more wisely. The premises state that human emotional tendencies are essentially unchanged from the earliest members of our species. The argument allows that technology broadens our range of social and individual choices. The language shift in this argument is the notion of choosing wisely. The author assumes there is a link between emotional tendencies and wise choices and that this assumed link is not affected by technological advances. The credited response will provide a link between the premises and the conclusion or will rule out an alternative interpretation of the premises.

A. No. This is irrelevant to the conclusion about wise choices. This is also a broader version of the first premise.

B. No. While this statement mentions both wise choices and emotions, it is not necessary to the argument since there is no information about being in control of those emotions.

C. No. This answer choice has the wrong scope and is thus irrelevant. This answer choice discusses becoming wiser and the emotional predisposition to be so. However, the conclusion discusses making wise choices, which is not the same as becoming wiser.

D. No. This is too strongly worded to be necessary to the argument. This answer choice states that humans choose on the basis of emotions alone. This is not necessary to the conclusion that humans are generally unable to choose more wisely.

E. Yes. This answer choice says that a change in humans' emotional disposition is necessary for wise choices. This answer choice builds a bridge between the conclusion and premises. Negated, this answer choice would read "A change in human emotional disposition is NOT necessary for wise choices," which would destroy the conclusion.

13. C Reasoning

This argument concludes that songbirds are threatened by deforestation and that, despite reforestation, the situation continues to get worse. This claim is based upon the premises that open spaces caused by deforestation reduce the distance between songbird nests and their predators. The role that reforestation plays in the argument is as a premise in support of the second conclusion that the situation is getting worse. The credited response should match this claim in tone and scope.

A. No. This does not match the argument since extinction is not mentioned.

B. No. This answer choice contradicts the argument that songbirds are threatened.

C. Yes. Reforestation is something that occurs but is still compatible with the conclusion that songbirds continue to be threatened.

D. No. This is not the conclusion of the argument, so this does not match.

E. No. The claim is about songbirds, not their predators.

14. C Flaw

This argument concludes that by reducing excessive chocolate consumption, adults can almost certainly improve their mood. The premises state that a diverse sample of 1,000 adults was studied and that those who ate the most chocolate were the most likely to be depressed. There are several possible flaws here. The first is a causal flaw the argument assumes because the two things (chocolate consumption and depression) occurred together that one must cause the other. This could be either reverse causation, in which depression could cause chocolate consumption, or correlation equals causation, in which the two things share no direct causal relationship. Another possible flaw is survey sample. The premises state that the group is diverse, but that doesn't preclude all pertinent information being gathered. The credited response will point out either the causal flaw or a problem with the methodology of the survey.

A. No. This answer seems close on first read. However, it does not correctly match the conclusion. The conclusion states "improve their mood," while this answer choice states "eliminate that condition."

B. No. While there is a sample group under study, the premises state that it is a diverse group so it is likely to be representative.

C. Yes. This answer choice correctly identifies the correlation equals causation flaw.

D. No. This answer choice describes a necessary as sufficient flaw, which is not what this argument does.

E. No. This is not the flaw in the argument.

15. **D** Necessary Assumption

This argument concludes that scientific fraud is a widespread problem among authors who submit to a particular journal. This is based upon the premise that after careful examination by computer software, dozens of digital images had been manipulated in ways that violated the journal's submission guidelines. The major flaw in this argument is the language shift from manipulation of images to "scientific fraud." The author assumes that manipulation occurs, at least in part, to defraud the scientific findings. The credited response will build a bridge between the conclusion and the premises.

A. No. This answer choice is not necessary to the conclusion that scientific fraud is widespread.

B. No. The presence of digital images in all articles is not necessary to the conclusion. This answer choice is too strongly worded.

C. No. The argument does not assume that digital imagery is necessary for fraud to be possible. This is too strongly worded.

D. Yes. This answer correctly builds the bridge between premises and conclusion. When negated, it would state, "NONE of the scientists who…." This would destroy the conclusion.

E. No. This answer choice is not necessary to the conclusion that scientific fraud is widespread in this journal. It is too strongly worded.

16. **D** Flaw

This argument concludes that contemporary artists, who believe their works enable others to feel aesthetically fulfilled, are mistaken. This is based upon the premise that there are more works in the world than anyone could appreciate and that those works are capable of satisfying any taste imaginable. The author assumes that the existence of artworks is alone sufficient to lead to aesthetic fulfillment instead of being necessary to that fulfillment. The credited response will either identify this flaw in abstract language or will identify some situation in which this factor alone is not sufficient for aesthetic fulfillment.

A. No. This directly contradicts the conclusion and thus is not the flaw.

B. No. This does not match the conclusion, which states that art "enables" people. The author does not assume that all people will actually become aesthetically fulfilled.

C. No. The value of an artwork is not mentioned. This is irrelevant.

D. Yes. This answer choice demonstrates that access to all non-contemporary art is also a necessary precondition for aesthetic fulfillment by showing that contemporary art might be one of only a few types of art accessible.

E. No. This does not match the argument. The author does not assume that contemporary art is less fulfilling due to the volume of other art.

17. **B** | Inference

This argument states that the government will not pay for the anti-flu medication until the drug company provides information on cost-effectiveness. The drug company responds by arguing that that information will require massive clinical trials, which in turn require widespread circulation which itself requires government funding for the drug. These statements can be diagrammed as follows:

Govt: ~pay → ~ info on cost effectiveness;
Drug Co: info → trials → widespread circulation → govt. funding.

These two conditional chains are mutually exclusive meaning that both situations can never occur simultaneously. The credited response will identify this.

A. No. This is a bad contrapositive of the first statement. It is too strongly worded.

B. Yes. This correctly describes the conflicting conditional statements.

C. No. Whether patients will pay is new/unsupported information.

D. No. What the government should do is unsupported.

E. No. The cost-effectiveness of the drug is an unsupported evaluation.

18. **E** | Flaw

This argument concludes that dislike of vegetables is genetically determined. This is based upon a study taken from a large, diverse group of participants. All of the participants in one group enjoyed eating vegetables, but all of those in the other group disliked them. After analyzing blood samples from the group that disliked vegetables, all of the volunteers in that group had a gene in common. The flaw in the argument is a survey/sample flaw. The premises state that the sample is representative; however, pertinent information is missing that would allow for a more accurate evaluation of the study. The credited response will identify some relevant information that is missing.

A. No. This does not match the conclusion.

B. No. This contradicts the first sentence of the argument.

C. No. Translate the abstract language if necessary to read "ignores the possibility that even when dislike of vegetables is genetically predetermined, dislike of vegetables can occur for other reasons." This is granted by the conclusion, which states "at least in some cases."

D. No. This does not match the conclusion since the conclusion does not assume monocausality.

E. Yes. From the premises it is unknown whether the vegetable liking group had this gene. This is missing pertinent information.

19. **C** **Point at Issue**

Ana concludes that she opposes the ban on smoking since it is not the government's place to prevent people from harming only themselves. Pankaj points out that the ban is limited only to public spaces and that people could smoke at home. Ana and Pankaj disagree about whether the ban prevents smokers from harming themselves or not.

A. No. Ana would agree with this statement, but there is not enough information to determine Pankaj's position.

B. No. It is not known whether either person would agree with this.

C. Yes. Ana would agree with this statement based on her premise; Pankaj would disagree since smokers can still smoke at home.

D. No. Pankaj would definitely agree with this. There is not enough information to make a clear statement about Ana.

E. No. It is not known whether either person would agree with this.

20. **B** **Flaw**

The agricultural scientist concludes that apples were probably not cultivated 5,000 years ago on the grounds that wild apples are much smaller than cultivated apples. The apples found from a time close to the beginning of cultivation are no larger than those that grow wild. The assumption in this argument is a time comparison. The agricultural scientist assumes that there are no changes to cultivated apples that occurred after these apples but before modern supermarket ones. The credited response will identify some reason to doubt this comparison.

A. No. This does not match the conclusion that specifically states "this region."

B. Yes. This is a reason that the time comparison is not valid. If size changes took place gradually, then cultivated and wild apples would not immediately appear different.

C. No. This does not match the argument, which compares apples from only a specific region.

D. No. This is not found in the argument.

E. No. This common flaw (circular reasoning) is not found in this argument.

21. **B** **Necessary Assumption**

This argument concludes that the happy life tends to be the good life. The premises define the good life as a morally virtuous life and that genuine happiness derives from a sense of approval of one's character and projects. The hole in the argument is the jump between approval of one's character and morally virtuous life. The credited response will link these premises together.

A. No. This is too strongly worded to be required by the argument.

B. Yes. This correctly bridges the two premises. The negation of this answer destroys the conclusion.

C.   No. This is not relevant to the argument's conclusion.

D.   No. This is not relevant to the argument's conclusion.

E.   No. This is not relevant to the argument's conclusion.

22.   **C**   Parallel Flaw

This argument concludes that returning organic wastes to soil is a good solution for waste disposal problems small-scale organic farms face. This is based upon the premise that this good solution requires that wastes be non-toxic and have low transport energy requirements. The premises then state that these conditions are met by small-scale organic farms. These premises can be diagrammed as follows:

P1: Good solution → non toxic AND not too much energy;
P2: non toxic AND not too much energy → Conclusion: good solution.

The diagrams make it clear that this is a necessary as sufficient flaw in which the statement was flipped but not negated. The credited response must have the same flaw. If two answer choices share this flaw, then the argument will also match structure and scope.

A.   No. This argument claims that greenhouse plants are healthy because they have moisture, light, and nutrients. The premise states that if they have these three things they will thrive. This is a valid argument.

B.   No. This argument concludes that the desired results will be seen in 20 years, based on the premise that every country will be globalized in 20 years, so every country will have a way to optimize its resources. This is a language shift, which is a different type of flaw.

C.   Yes. This argument claims your idea has three conditions, so it is viable. In this conclusion, the three conditions are treated as sufficient. The premise states those three conditions are necessary factors for a viable idea.

D.   No. This argument claims your idea has three conditions, so it is viable. In this conclusion, the three conditions are treated as sufficient. The premise states those three conditions are necessary factors for a viable idea.

E.   No. This argument concludes that what I ate was not nutritious. The premises state that carbohydrates and protein are requirements for nutritious meals and that 80 percent of the calories in the lunch were from fat. This argument shifts from needing carbohydrates and protein to fat content, so it does not match the original flaw.

23.   **A**   Strengthen

This argument concludes that phenazines serve as molecular pipelines that give interior bacteria essential nutrients from the area around the colony. The premise states that some bacteria produce antibiotic molecules known as phenazines. The flaw in the argument is that there is no support at all for phenazines to serve as nutrient pipelines. The credited response will strengthen this claim by either providing evidence that phenazines do in fact involve nutrient transfers or that a lack of phenazines can lead to a lack of nutrients.

A.   Yes. This answer choice indirectly supports the conclusion by suggesting that bacteria without phenazines have an alternative method of providing nutrients to interior bacteria.

B. No. The rate of production is not relevant to the claim that they are nutrient pipelines.

C. No. This answer choice would weaken the claim by suggesting that phenazines are not necessary for nutrients.

D. No. A bacteria's ability to fend off other bacteria is not relevant to the conclusion.

E. No. This answer choice would weaken the claim by suggesting that phenazines do not transport nutrients to interior bacteria.

24. **A** Inference

This argument deals with how quantity statements interact. The argument states that most of the culturally significant documents will be restored, some questionable authenticity documents will be restored, only manuscripts whose safety will be restored, and no infrequently consulted manuscript will be restored.

A. Yes. Since at least one suspect document will be restored and since frequently consulted documents will be restored, this must be true.

B. No. This is too strongly worded to be supported.

C. No. The argument does not state that all safe to restore manuscripts are also frequently consulted. This is too strongly worded to be supported.

D. No. Information about manuscripts susceptible to deterioration is unsupported.

E. No. Which manuscripts are rarely consulted is unsupported information.

25. **B** Strengthen

This argument concludes that the perception of direct mail being bad for the environment is misguided. This is based on the premise that most of the products advertised are for the home and that because of direct mail, millions of people buy products over the phone or online rather than driving to the store. The premises establish a causal link between home purchases and direct mail; however, the argument assumes that there are no other factors that need to be considered. The credited response will either limit other possible interpretations of the premises or will establish that direct mail has only the one effect.

A. No. This answer would weaken the claim by suggesting that more people might drive rather than less.

B. Yes. This answer strengthens the argument by limiting the scope of direct-mail purchases to needed goods, thus making the advertising for them necessary rather than superfluous.

C. No. Magazine advertisements are irrelevant to the conclusion that direct mail is not bad for the environment.

D. No. Why the advertisements are sent is not relevant to the claim that they are not bad for the environment.

E. No. Just because more products are being purchased from home than were before does not strengthen the claim that direct mail is not bad for the environment. This is irrelevant.

26. **D** Parallel

This argument concludes that if a country is new, it is probably not ruled by a monarch. This is based upon the premise that most countries are not ruled by monarchs and that the older a country is, the more likely it is to be ruled by a monarch. This can be abstracted to read as follows: more A then more likely B. B is rare. Conclusion: if ~A then likely ~B. The credited response will match this structure but not necessarily the order of this argument.

A. No. The structure of this argument reads "B is rare. More A then more likely B. Conclusion: ~A so likely ~C." The conclusion introduces a new piece, so this is not parallel.

B. No. The structure of this argument reads "B is rare. More A then more likely B. Conclusion: More A then more likely B." The conclusion in this argument does not align with the original conclusion.

C. No. The structure of this argument reads "B is rare. If less A then less likely B. Conclusion: If more A then more likely B." Neither the second premise nor the conclusion aligns with the original argument.

D. Yes. The structure matches exactly: "B is rare. If more A then more likely B. If ~A then likely ~B."

E. No. The structure reads "B is rare. More A then likely more B. Conclusion: ~A so likely B." The conclusion does not align with the original conclusion.

Section 3: Arguments 2

1. **C** Resolve/ Explain

In this question, the credited response will explain how two seemingly disparate statements can both be true. The dentist states that brushing after a meal will remove sugars that cause tooth decay but if brushing is not an option, the dentist suggests chewing gum to prevent tooth decay, even if the gum contains sugar. The credited response will show why gum with sugar is better than the alternative when brushing is not an option.

A. No. The fact that gum contains any sugar makes gum a confusing recommendation since sugar causes tooth decay.

B. No. This choice does not explain the recommendation to chew gum despite the fact that gum contains sugar, which causes tooth decay.

C. Yes. This choice explains the recommendation to chew gum since by showing that it provides a benefit that reduces tooth decay.

D. No. This choice does not explain the recommendation to chew gum despite the fact that gum contains sugar, which causes tooth decay.

E. No. While this choice references beneficial effects of chewing gum, it does not explain the recommendation to chew gum despite the fact that gum contains sugar, which causes tooth decay.

2. B | Weaken

In this question, the credited response will hurt the conclusion by attacking the flaw in the argument. The author disagrees with the theory that New Zealand's bird population exists due to a lack of competition from mammals, based on evidence that states that fossils have been found that prove the existence of indigenous mammals in New Zealand. The author assumes that the existence of indigenous mammals proves that those mammals competed with birds, but the evidence is not strong enough to prove that claim.

A. No. This choice would strengthen the claim that mammals competed with birds.

B. Yes. This choice would hurt the argument by showing that the mammals did not compete with birds in New Zealand.

C. No. Other types of animal fossils discovered at the site are not directly relevant to the question of whether mammal species competed with birds in New Zealand.

D. No. This would strengthen the claim that mammal species compete with birds.

E. No. What is true of other islands is not relevant to what is true of New Zealand.

3. D | Main Point

In this question, the credited response will match the conclusion of the argument. The restaurant owner claims that the newspaper reporter who panned the restaurant is not a true restaurant critic. The premises state that the reporter has no special expertise in food and that one cannot be called a drama critic if one does not have special training in theater. Use the Why Test to confirm that the conclusion is supported by the other facts in the argument.

A. No. This is a premise.

B. No. This is a premise.

C. No. This is a premise.

D. Yes. This matches the conclusion of the argument.

E. No. This is a premise.

4. E | Necessary Assumption

In this question, the credited response will help the argument by filling in the gap. The argument concludes that the hypothesis that our solar system was formed from a cloud of dust and gas produced by a supernova is false. This is based on the premise that if the hypothesis is correct, there would be iron-60 present in the early history of the solar system but that scientists have not found iron-60 in early meteorites. The argument assumes that if iron-60 were present in the early history of the solar system that it would be found in early meteorites so the credited response will address this assumption.

A. No. The argument does not assume that early meteorites did not contain elements from the supernova. It actually assumes the opposite.

B. No. The material used to form other solar systems is not relevant to whether the meteorites indicate that our solar system was formed from dust and gas from a supernova.

o. The argument states that a majority of users of the trail will share a certain characteristic.

o. There is no attack on the members of the citizen group.

question, the credited response will help the conclusion, which states that those people who pre-
catastrophic shortage of scientists and engineers are wrong based on premises that state that there
e upward pressure on salaries for these positions and unemployment is as high in these fields as
s. The argument assumes that a lack of upward pressure on salaries and "normal" unemployment
dications of a field that is not in danger of imminent shortage.

No. The proportion of research done by corporations is not relevant to the question of whether
upward salary pressure or unemployment are indications of an imminent shortage of researchers.

No. Financial success is not directly relevant to the question of whether upward salary pressure
and unemployment are indications of an imminent shortage of researchers since there is no information about the financial success of researchers.

Yes. This would provide an additional reason to support the claim that there is no imminent
shortage because the number of people in the field has increased.

No. Specializations within the field of science are not directly relevant to the question of whether
upward salary pressure and unemployment are indications of an imminent shortage of researchers
since the argument talks about the field of science generally.

No. Professional development is not relevant to the question of whether upward salary pressure
and unemployment are indications of an imminent shortage of researchers.

Principle
Strengthen

n this question, the credited response will help both arguments. Rhonda argues that you should use
our time, energy, and money to help others as long as the cost isn't too great. She bases this on the
premise that charitable people live richer lives than miserly hermits. Brad argues that you should focus
generosity on friends and relatives because they will remember sacrifices and return kindness.

A. No. This would not help Brad's argument since his argument says to ignore complete strangers.

B. No. The golden rule does not help Brad's argument since his argument says to ignore complete
strangers.

C. Yes. This would help Rhonda's argument because she says that charitable people live richer lives so
helping oneself in that situation would be to act charitably in order to live richer. This would help
Brad's argument by showing that helping friends and relatives would lead to returned kindnesses
for oneself in the future.

D. No. This would not help Rhonda's argument because she does not indicate whether charitable
people lead richer lives due to their returning kindness.

E. No. Neither Rhonda nor Brad discuss pride.

C. No. Other types of iron than iron-60 are not relevant to whether the lack of iron-60 in meteorites
indicates that our solar system was formed from dust and gas from a supernova.

D. No. Late forming meteorites are not relevant to whether the early meteorites indicate that our
solar system was formed from dust and gas from a supernova.

E. Yes. This helps the argument. Use the Negation Test. If this were not true, then the failure to find
iron-60 in meteorites would not itself disprove the original hypothesis.

5. C   **Resolve/**
        Explain

In this question, the credited response will explain how two seemingly disparate statements can both
be true. The argument states that tuna is sometimes treated with carbon monoxide to prevent it from
turning brown as it ages. On one hand, the argument states that carbon monoxide in this usage is not
harmful to humans. On the other hand, people are more likely to get sick from eating tuna that has
been treated with carbon monoxide.

A. No. This does not explain why people are more likely to get sick from eating tuna that has been
treated with carbon monoxide.

B. No. This does not explain why people are more likely to get sick from eating tuna that has been
treated with carbon monoxide.

C. Yes. This explains how eating tuna that has been treated with carbon monoxide could cause people to get sick even though carbon monoxide used in this way is not itself dangerous.

D. No. Other ways to prevent tuna from turning brown would not explain why people are more
likely to get sick from eating tuna that has been treated with carbon monoxide.

E. No This does not explain why people are more likely to get sick from eating tuna that has been
treated with carbon monoxide.

6. C   **Sufficient**
        Assumption

In this question, the credited response will help the conclusion by providing strong evidence that the
assumption is valid. The astrophysicist claims that the descriptive labels "long" and "short" used to
describe Gamma ray bursts are not useful. This is based on the premise that a "long" GRB has many
characteristics of "short" GRBs. The argument assumes characteristics of GRBs other than duration
are important.

A. No. This choice does not link the possibility of unique characteristics with the "short" or "long"
descriptions in the argument.

B. No. This would hurt the argument by showing that duration alone is important in some situations.

C. Yes. This choice states the assumption in the argument. If true, the argument's conclusion must
also be true.

D. No. This choice states another factor that is not important, which provides more evidence for the
claim that duration alone is important.

E. No. The argument is not concerned with the ability to label with non-descriptive labels.

ecoded PrepTests 72–81   PrepTest 72: Answers and Explanations | 47

7. A | Flaw

In this question, the credited response will hurt the argument by describing the flaw. The conclusion states that hospital patients with a greater tendency to laugh are helped more when they laugh a little than other patients who laugh more. The premises refer to a study that indicated that immune systems grew stronger when patients watched comic videos indicating that laughter can aid recovery. The study also noted that immune system gains were stronger in people who had a greater tendency to laugh. The argument is flawed in that it assumes that the patients who had a greater tendency to laugh did not in fact laugh more at the comic videos in the study than did others.

A. Yes. This describes the flaw in the argument.

B. No. The conclusion argues that the comic movie helped aid the recovery process regardless of the level of immune system that a patient started with.

C. No. The conclusion is not about the general population since it is specifically about hospital patients.

D. No. There is no concern about the direction of causality since the gains in the immune system came after the comic movie was shown.

E. No. The argument states that these patients were aided more, but there is no evidence that those patients recovered more quickly.

8. A | Strengthen

In this question, the credited response will help the conclusion of the argument by providing additional evidence. The conclusion states that a male guppy will change its courting patterns based on feedback from a female. The premises state that females preferred male guppies with more orange showing and that males tended to show females their more orange side when courting. The argument assumes a causal relationship between male and female preferences by establishing a correlation.

A. Yes. This would strengthen the claim by showing that the female feedback was responsible for the behavior of male guppies since it shows that a lack of female feedback results in no shift in behavior by the male guppies.

B. No. The preferences of females of other species of guppies are not relevant to the behavior of males of this species.

C. No. The lack of research into this question is not relevant to the argument's study.

D. No. The coloration of female guppies is not directly relevant to the behavior of males of this species.

E. No. This would weaken the argument by showing that the behavior may have been caused by an inability to interact.

9. E | Main Point

In this question, the credited response will match the conclusion of the argument. The politician concludes that acting on the basis of an argument that proposes to unilaterally reduce nuclear arms is dangerous. This is based on premises that state that the argument for unilateral nuclear arms reductions

does not consider countries that are on the verge of ci... upon to conform to an international policy.

A. No. There is no direct evidence that these countr... the premises state that these countries cannot be tr...

B. No. This is contradictory to the claims of the argum...

C. No. There is no mention of disclosure of nuclear ca... the main point.

D. No. There is no direct evidence that countries woul... premises state that some countries cannot be trusted t...

E. Yes. This choice matches the conclusion of the argumen...

10. D | Weaken

In this question, the credited response will address the flaw... should take the full LIC treatment after any accident that inv... on premises that state that many types of accidents can produ... lash. The advertisement assumes that the types of motion that... involve a fall or a head bump.

A. No. The conclusion does not state that people shoved from... ment for whiplash.

B. No. This would help the argument by linking auto acciden... whiplash.

C. No. Other causes of whiplash wouldn't hurt the argument th... ment for accidents involving the most common types of motio...

D. Yes. This would weaken the argument by showing that accident... are unlikely to cause whiplash and would not need treatment fo...

E. No. The methods of treatment are not relevant to the question... ences certain accidents should go through the treatment for whip...

11. A | Flaw

In this question, the credited response will describe the flaw in the argu... that a development proposal should move forward since the objections o... a hiking trail are groundless and that most trail users would be hikers wh... The argument assumes that the only reason the proposal may not move fo... group's argument is valid when there may be other reasons to avoid the de...

A. Yes. This describes the flaw. An argument is not necessarily correct ju... argument are wrong.

B. No. This argument does not have a part-to-whole comparison flaw.

C. No. This argument is not circular because the premises are different fro...

D. N...

E. N...

12. C | Str...

In thi... dict a... is litt... other... are i...

A.

B.

C.

D.

E...

13. C

14. **B** `Flaw`

In this question, the credited response will hurt the argument by describing the flaw. The columnist disagrees with the position of wildlife activists who claim that cable TV lines should not be strung along with electric wires above ground. As a premise, the columnist cites the fact that animals are electrocuted by power lines even when cable TV lines are above ground. The argument assumes that because the wildlife activists' argument would not completely address the issue of electrocuted animals that the proposal is invalid.

A. No. The argument does not confuse necessary and sufficient conditions.

B. Yes. This describes the flaw in the argument.

C. No. Advantages to the proposal are not directly relevant to the logic of the argument.

D. No. The author does not criticize the wildlife activists.

E. No. The author does not discuss other proposals that would be effective.

15. **B** `Reasoning`

In this question, the credited response will describe the role of the sentence in question. The argument concludes that *Thrinaxodon* was probably warm-blooded. This conclusion is based on premises that state that *Thrinaxodon* had skull features that suggest it had whiskers, and that if it had whiskers, it probably also had hair on other parts of its body that would serve as insulation to regulate body temperature and insulation would not be useful to a cold-blooded animal. The credited response will state that the sentence in question is a premise that supports the conclusion.

A. No. The conclusion does not state that insulation would not be useful to a cold-blooded animal.

B. Yes. This describes the role of the sentence in the argument.

C. No. The sentence is not the conclusion.

D. No. The author agrees with the sentence.

E. No. The sentence is used as a premise to support the conclusion.

16. **D** `Inference`

To determine the answer to this question, fill in the blank with an answer choice that is supported by the remaining text. The economist states that countries use taxation to fund expenditures but an income tax does not promote savings and investment whereas taxing consumption encourages savings. The economist also states that the only way to improve economies for most countries is to increase savings rates.

A. No. The author does not discuss taxing savings or investments.

B. No. There is no evidence that the rate of economic improvement would be rapid.

C. No. There is no evidence that taxing consumption alone would be enough to fund government.

D. Yes. This conclusion is supported by the text since one way to accomplish the important goal of improving economies is to encourage savings by taxing consumption instead of income.

E. No. The author says taxing income does not help a country's economy, but the passage does not state that taxing income would be harmful.

17. **D**   **Weaken**

In this question, the credited response will hurt the argument by attacking its flaw. Meade argues that governments are justified in outlawing behavior that puts one's own health at risk because people who are injured due to risky behavior inevitably impose emotional and financial costs on others. The argument is flawed in that it assumes that the government is justified in passing laws that prevent certain behaviors to protect others.

A. No. The ability to harm oneself is not in question.

B. No. Personal obligations are not relevant to the question of whether the government can pass laws that prevent certain behaviors in order to protect others.

C. No. This would strengthen the argument by connecting the government actions to the premises.

D. Yes. This choice would hurt the argument by showing that the law is not justified only because it protects harm to others.

E. No. This would strengthen the argument by showing that harm to others is more important than personal freedom.

18. **C**   **Necessary Assumption**

In this question, the credited response will help the argument by providing an important assumption. The conclusion states that Sanderson's omission was morally wrong. This is based on premises that lying is morally wrong, an intentionally misleading statement is a lie, and that there is no moral difference between a statement and an omission done with the same intent. The argument assumes that Sanderson's omission was intentionally misleading.

A. No. What Sanderson's cousin wanted is not relevant to the argument.

B. No. What other people did or did not say is not relevant to whether Sanderson was morally wrong.

C. Yes. Use the Negation Test. If Sanderson did not believe that the overheard statement was correct, then his omission was not intentionally misleading.

D. No. Hypothetical situations are not required assumptions.

E. No. Use the Negation Test. If Sanderson did not have something to gain, the act of omission could still have been intentionally misleading.

19. **D**   **Principle Match**

In this question, the credited response will match the principle in the argument, which states that a judge must follow precedent that is not contrary to basic moral values and that in the absence of precedent judges may use their own legal views to decide a case as long as those views are not contradictory to widespread public opinion.

A. No. By deciding the case on his own legal views that contradict public opinion, Judge Swoboda did not use the principle as stated.

B. No. By deciding the case on his own legal views that contradict public opinion, Judge Valenzuela did not use the principle as stated.

C. No. By deciding the case without applying the precedent that doesn't violate basic moral values, Judge Wilson did not use the principle as stated.

D. Yes. Judge Watanabe used her own legal view in a situation where there was no precedent and her own legal view did not contradict any widespread public opinion.

E. No. By deciding the case without applying the precedent that doesn't violate basic moral values, Judge Balila did not use the principle as stated.

20. **B**   Inference

In this question, the credited response will be supported by the text of the passage. The passage states that in a study of people with amusia, volunteers were unable to tell the difference between tones when there was a shift in pitch. The volunteers were able to perceive changes in timing.

A. No. There is no evidence that there is a compensatory relationship between perceiving shifts in tone and changes in timing.

B. Yes. This must be true because volunteers with amusia were unable to perceive shifts in tone but were able to perceive changes in timing.

C. No. There is no evidence that there is a compensatory relationship between perceiving shifts in tone and changes in timing.

D. No. There is no evidence that the perception of a melody has no relationship with discerning timing.

E. No. There is no evidence for the reasons behind people's ability to perceive timing or shifts in pitch.

21. **E**   Principle Strengthen

In this question, the credited response will help the conclusion by providing a rule that would make the conclusion true. The literary critic argues that there is little of social significance in contemporary novels. This is based on the premise that readers can't get into a literary world unless they can experience that world through the moral understanding of its characters and contemporary novels have sensationalistic spectacles that serve only to make readers wonder what will happen next. There is a gap between the conclusion about social significance and the premises based on experiencing a world.

A. No. This would hurt the argument by showing that what is true of classic literature may not be true of contemporary literature.

B. No. This goes in the wrong direction and discusses the wants of a novelist rather than the existential question of whether novels have social significance.

C. No. There is no indication that a novel is to be considered a work of art.

D. No. While attractive, this conditional is the opposite of what is needed. To strengthen the argument, this choice would have to say "If a novel does NOT allow a reader to understand injustice, it will not be socially significant."

E. Yes. This links the premises with the conclusion.

22. **E** Flaw

In this question, the credited response will hurt the conclusion by describing its flaw. The argument concludes that the recommendations for avoiding infection is counter-productive because people who follow the recommendations are more likely to contract diseases from those pathogens than those who deviate considerably from the recommendations. The argument assumes that there is no other causal factor that would make a person who follows the recommendations to become infected.

A. No. Foods that are not meat-based are not relevant to this argument.

B. No. The argument states that is true so it cannot assume this fact.

C. No. The recognizability of the symptoms is not directly relevant to the argument without also assuming that people that do not follow the recommendations are sick without knowing it.

D. No. The argument says that following the recommendations causes a greater number of infections, so it does not assume that people who follow the recommendation will not be infected.

E. Yes. This choice says that the people who are most likely to follow the recommendations are the same people who are most likely to become infected due to a susceptibility to infection.

23. **C** Parallel

In this question, the credited response will match the structure of the original argument. The argument states that no nonfiction book published by Carriage Books has been profitable and that they made a profit on every book published last year and concludes from these premises that Carriage Books must not have published a nonfiction book last year. This is a logically appropriate argument that uses elimination of alternatives to draw a conclusion. The credited response will match this structure.

A. No. This argument is invalid because the premises are contradictory. There are no circumstances in which it is possible that no actor has ever played an important role and that every actor last year played an important role.

B. No. This argument does not match because it is linear and does not eliminate alternatives to draw a conclusion.

C. Yes. This argument matches. It states that Pranwich Corporation has never given a bonus to its marketing division but that it did give bonuses to every analyst last year. Therefore, it is not possible that an analyst worked in its marketing division.

D. No. This argument does not match because it is linear and does not eliminate alternatives to draw a conclusion.

E. No. This argument does not match because it does not eliminate alternatives to draw a conclusion. Also, this argument is flawed because it assumes that if it has never done something in one area that it has never done that thing anywhere.

24. **A** Inference

In this question, the credited response will be supported by the text of the passage, which states that all unemployed artists are sympathetic to social justice and that no employed artist is interested in great personal fame.

A. Yes. If there are artists that are interested in great personal fame, they are unemployed and therefore must be sympathetic to social justice.

B. No. There is no evidence that artists uninterested in personal fame (those that are employed) are sympathetic to social justice.

C. No. There is no information about how unemployed artists feel about great personal fame.

D. No. It is possible that employed artists are also sympathetic to social justice.

E. No. It is possible that some employed artists are neither interested in personal fame nor sympathetic to social justice.

25. **D** Parallel Flaw

In this question, the credited response will have a flaw that matches the flaw in the original argument. The argument claims that there are two suspects for a burglary and that since one of them has an alibi that the other must be the burglar. The argument assumes that the burglar must be one of the suspects and not some other person. The credited response will have an argument where there are two likely possibilities, but one is found to be not possible so the other must be chosen without considering a third alternative.

A. No. This argument is the opposite of the original argument because it assumes that since one option will be chosen, the other option will not also be chosen.

B. No. This argument confuses necessary and sufficient conditions to draw its conclusion.

C. No. This is a valid argument so it does not contain a flaw that matches the flaw in the original argument.

D. Yes. This matches the original argument. Baxim Corporation has two choices that are likely, but since one option has been ruled out, the other option must be true. Like the original argument, this choice assumes that no other option is possible.

E. No. This argument states that there are only two possible situations, so this is a valid argument and does not have a flaw that matches the original argument.

Section 4: Games

Questions 1–6

This is a grouping game with two groups and a twist. The groups are segment 1 and segment 2—put these on top of the diagram. Segment 1 has three spaces and segment 2 has two spaces. The inventory consists of 5 reports—I and N are general and S, T, and W are local. Since there are two groups and more than one category in the inventory, this sets up just like a 2D In/Out game. The twist is that order matters in each group. Programs proceed from longest to shortest in each group, so label the first space in each group "longest" and the last spot in each group "shortest." The first two clues contain information about how to set up the diagram, and the remaining clues are fixed and range. There is one wildcard.

Clue 1. Use this information to set up your diagram.

Clue 2. Mark the first spaces in each group as "longest" and the last space in each group as "shortest."

Clue 3. Local in both segments; this can be noted as ~TWS in segment 1.

Clue 4. NG longest

Clue 5. SL shortest

Clue 6. IG—WL

Deductions: Since NG is the longest program, it will have to go first in whatever segment it is in. You can note this on top of your diagram. Since SL is the shortest, it will have to be in the last space in whatever segment it is in. You can also note this on top of your diagram. It is important to note that clue 6 comes into play only if both IG and WL are in the same segment. Also note that NG and IG cannot be together in segment 2 since there are only two spaces in segment 2 and both segments must contain a local report (clue 3). So one, or both, of them must be in segment 1. TL is the least restricted element.

Your diagram should look like this:

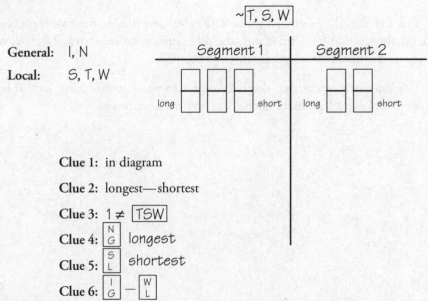

1. **B**   `Grab-a-Rule`

Use rules to eliminate answer choices; then choose the remaining answer.

A.   No. This violates clues 2 and 4 because N is longer than I.

B.   Yes. This choice does not violate any of the clues.

C.   No. This violates rules 2 and 5 by putting S before T.

D.   No. This violates rules 2 and 6 by putting W before I.

E.   No. This violates rule 3 since there is no room for a local report in segment 2.

2. **E**   `Specific`

Make a new line in your diagram and add the new information. If T is the last report in the first segment, then according to the deductions, S must be in the last spot in the second segment, making (E) the credited response.

3. **B**   `Specific`

Make a new line in your diagram and add the new information. If N is the first report in the second segment, then I is forced into the first segment and one of S, T, or W is the second report in the second segment. Eliminate (E) because there are only five reports and N is in the second segment. Eliminate (D) because S must be in the last spot in a segment (clues 5 and 2). Now, since I is in the first segment, if W is in the same segment, it cannot be first because of clue 6. Eliminate (C). So, the first spot in the first segment cannot be N, S, or W. That leaves I and T. If I is first, then W can be second and S can be third, pushing T into the second segment. This is just one possibility, but since it works, try putting T in the first spot in segment 1. If T is first, I would be second and S or W would be third. This works as well, so eliminate (A) and select (B), the credited response.

4. **D**   `General`

Use the deductions, prior work, and trying the answers to determine which answer choice must be false.

A.   No. I was one possibility for the first report in the first section in question 3.

B.   No. N was in the first spot in the first segment in the credited answer to question 1.

C.   No. N was in the first spot in the second segment in the question stem of question 3.

D.   Yes. Since N must be the first report in one of the segments, if W is the first report in segment 1, then N is the first report in the second segment. Since the second report must be local (clue 3), this forces I into the first segment, and according to clue 6, I is longer than W, so putting W in the first spot violates clue 2.

E.   No. W is in the last spot in segment 2 in the credited response to question 6.

5. **A**   General

Use the deductions, prior work, and trying the answers to determine which answer choice provides enough information to lock each report into exactly one position.

A. Yes. If I is the last report in the first segment, then S must be the last report in the second segment (clues 5 and 2) and W must be in the second segment as well because of clue 6. This forces N into the first spot of the first segment, leaving T in the second spot in the first segment.

B. No. N was in the first spot of the first segment in question 2 and there were multiple possible arrangements of the other elements.

C. No. N was in the first spot of the second segment in questions 3 and 6 and there were multiple possible arrangements of the other elements.

D. No. S was in the last spot of the second segment in question 2 and there were multiple possible arrangements of the other elements.

E. No. W could have been in the last spot in the first segment in questions 4 and 6 with multiple possible arrangements of the other elements.

6. **E**   Specific

Make a new line in your diagram and add the new information. If T is the first report in the first segment, then N has to be the first report in the second segment (clues 2 and 4). This will force I into segment 1 since clue 3 dictates that there must be a local report in each segment. You are looking for what could be true, so cross off anything that must be false.

A. No. I must be in the first segment.

B. No. N could never be the second report. This would violate clue 4.

C. No. Since I must also be in the first segment, W cannot be the second report in the first segment.

D. No. N must be the first report of the second segment (clues 2 and 6).

E. Yes. S, T, and W can all be the last report of the second segment, so this could be true.

Questions 7–12

This is a 1D order game with 1-1 correspondence. There are five houses—Q, R, S, T, and V—shown one at a time, so put 1–5 across the top of the diagram. There are no wildcards.

Clue 1. R = 1 or 2

Clue 2. T = 1 or 5

Clue 3. 3 = Q or V

Clue 4. ~QS ~SQ

There is not much to work with here, but make sure to put the information from the clues into the diagram. The elements are very restricted by the clues, so once you start filling in information from the questions they should fall into place with only a few possibilities.

Your diagram should look like this:

Q, R, S, T, U

Clue 1: R = $\frac{1}{2}$
Clue 2: T = $\frac{1}{5}$
Clue 3: 3 = $\frac{Q}{V}$
Clue 4: QS or SQ

7. E   Specific

Make a new line in your diagram and add the new information. If Q is in spot 4, then according to clue 3, V must be in spot 3, making (E) the credited response.

8. C   General

Use the deductions, prior work, and trying the answers to determine which answer choice forces each inventory element into only one space.

A. No. If Q is in spot 3, then S cannot be in spots 2 or 4 (clue 4), but it can be in either spot 1 or spot 5, interchangeable with T, without violating any other clues.

B. No. If R is in the first spot, then T is in spot 5. Q cannot be in the third spot as this would leave only spots 2 and 4 open, which would force S next to Q (rule 4), so Q must be in either spot 2 or 4, interchangeable with S.

C. Yes. If S is second, then R must be first (clue 1), T must be fifth (clue 2), V must be third (clues 3 and 4), and Q must be fourth.

D. No. If Q is in spot 3, then S cannot be in spots 2 or 4 (clue 4), but it can be in either spot 1 or spot 5, interchangeable with T, without violating any other clues.

E. No. This scenario was demonstrated as having multiple options in question 9.

9. D   Specific

Make a new line in your diagram and add the new information. If S must be shown before Q, and S and Q cannot be consecutive (clue 4), then the new clue should look like S _ –Q. This means that Q cannot be first or second, and S cannot be fourth or fifth. Try putting Q in 3. This would force R and S into the first two spots, which in turn would force T into spot 5 and V into spot 4. Now try Q in spot 4. This would force V into spot 3, R and S into the first two spots, and T into spot 5. If you try to

72: Answers and Explanations | 59

put Q in spot 5, then the first three spots would still have to be R, S, and V since S cannot be immediately next to Q (rule 4), and that would force T into spot 4, which violates clue 2. So, T must be in
spot 5, making (D) the credited answer.

10.   **A**   General

Use the deductions, prior work, and trying the answers to determine which answer choice could be
true. Eliminate any answer choice that must be false.

A.   Yes. This scenario was demonstrated in question 11.

B.   No. If Q is fifth, then T is first (clue 2), R is second (clue 1), and V is third (clue 3). The only spot
     left for S is fourth, right next to Q, which doesn't work (clue 4).

C.   No. If V is first, then R is second (clue 1), Q is third (clue 3), and T is fifth (clue 2). The only spot
     left for S is fourth, right next to Q, which doesn't work (clue 4).

D.   No. If V second, then R is first (clue 1), Q is third (clue 3), and T is fifth (clue 2). The only spot
     left for S is fourth, right next to Q, which doesn't work (clue 4).

E.   No. If V is fifth, then T is first (clue 2), R is second, (clue 1), and Q is third (clue 3). The only spot
     left for S is fourth, right next to Q, which doesn't work (clue 4).

11.   **E**   Specific

Make a new line in your diagram and add the new information. If V is third and R is first or second
(clue 1), then either Q or S must be before T because if T is first, then Q and S will be forced together
in violation of clue 4. So, no matter what, T must be in spot 5 (clue 2), making (E) the credited
response.

12.   **B**   Complex

This question is asking for a replacement clue for R, which must be first or second. The credited
response will force R to be first or second.

A.   No. Just because R can't be fourth doesn't mean it can't be fifth. Try it. If R is in 5, then V could
     be third, T could be first, and Q and S can be in either spots 2 or 4.

B.   Yes. If R must be earlier than V, then if V is third, this forces R into spots 1 or 2, and if V is
     fourth, then Q is third (clue 3) and R must still be in spots 1 or 2.

C.   No. Without any other constraints on R, just limiting V to spot 3 or 4 does not limit R to spots 1
     or 2.

D.   No. With this new clue, if Q is third, then R must be second, which is too limiting since R cannot
     also be first.

E.   No. This would be a good replacement for clue 2, but you need a replacement for clue 1. As it is, if
     the first clue is not in effect, then this new information does nothing to limit R.

Questions 13–18

This is a grouping game with three groups—Iceland, Norway, and Sweden—which should go across the top of the diagram. The inventory consists of five artifacts—V, W, X, Y, and Z—which are each used exactly once. While this game seems very straightforward, there is a twist that if missed, can make this game quite difficult. It is possible for Norway, and even Sweden, to be empty and all the artifacts to be in just two groups. There are no wildcards.

Clue 1. WY

Clue 2. X = N or S

Clue 3. I > N

Clue 4. VI → ZS ; ~ZS → ~VI

Deductions: The trick here is to note that there is nothing that prevents N or S from being an empty group. I cannot be empty because of the third clue. If there are always more artifacts from I than from N, then I cannot be empty. Since X must be in N or S, I cannot have all 5 artifacts. Note that X cannot be in I on your diagram. According to clue 4, if V is in I, then Z is in S. This means that I can have at most three artifacts—W, Y, and V or Z. According to clue 3, since I > N, that means N can have 0, 1, or 2 artifacts. There are not any restrictions on what can go in S, but the maximum number of artifacts that S can have is 4 since I must have at least 1.

Your diagram should look like this:

V, W, X, Y, Z

Clue 1: [WY]
Clue 2: X = N/S
Clue 3: I > N
Clue 4: V = I → Z = S
      ~Z = S → ~V = I

	I	N	X	S

13. **B** **Grab-a-Rule**

Use the rules to eliminate wrong answers and be left with the credited response.

A. No. This violates clue 1 since W and Y are not from the same country.

B. Yes. This does not violate any clues.

C. No. This violates clue 3 because I and N have the same number of artifacts.

D. No. This violates clue 4. V is in I, but Z is in N, not S.

E. No. This violates clue 2 since X must be in N or S, not I.

14. **A**

Make a new line in your diagram and add the new information. If both Y and Z are in I, then W is also in I (clue 1). V cannot be in I since that would force Z into S (clue 4), but V could be in N, as could X (clue 2). So, all of the artifacts could be from I and N, which means that there is no minimum number that must be in S. Choice (A) is the credited response.

15. **E**

Use the deductions, prior work, and trying the answers to determine which answer choice must be false. Eliminate any answer that could be true.

A.   No. If V and X are in N, then W, Y, and Z would have to be in I (rule 3). This does not violate any other rules and so could be true.

B.   No. V and Y (with W) can be in I as per the discussion above in the deductions.

C.   No. Question 14 demonstrates that both W and Z can be in I.

D.   No. If W and Z are in S, Y is also in S, then V would have to be in I (clue 3) and X would have to be in S (clue 3). This could be true.

E.   Yes. If W and Y are in N, then according to clue 3, the remaining artifacts would have to be in I. However, if V is in I, then Z is in S (clue 4), which means that W and Y cannot ever be in N.

16. **A**

Add a new line to the diagram and fill in the new information. If W and X are in S, then Y is in S (clue 1), which leaves only V and Z to go elsewhere. Since I must have more artifacts than N (clue 3), one of V or Z must go in I and the other must go in S. N cannot have any artifacts, making (A) the credited response.

17. **C**

Use deductions, prior work, and trying to put the elements into N to determine how many artifacts could be in N. X can be in N according to clue 2 and demonstrated in questions 14 and 15. V can also be in N as shown in the same questions. Z can be in N as long as V is not in I (clue 4). If W and Y are in N, then according to clue 3, the remaining artifacts would have to be in I. However, if V is in I, then Z is in S (clue 4), which means that W and Y cannot ever be in N. So, the maximum number of artifacts that could be in N is three, making (C) the credited response.

18. **C**

Use deductions, prior work, and trying the answers to determine what must be false. Eliminate any answers that could be true.

A.   No. This choice is demonstrated to be possible in question 16.

B.   No. This could be true. If V and Z are in S, then X is in N (clue 2) and W and Y are in I (clues 1 and 3).

C.   Yes. This must be false. If W and Y are in S, then X must be in N (clue 2) and V and Z in I (clue 3). But if V is in I, then Z is in S (clue 4), so this does not work.

D. No. This could be true. If X and Z are in S, then W, Y, and V could all be in I together. There are other possible combinations, but you need only one to prove that this could be true.

E. No. This could be true. If V, W, Y, and X are in S, then Z is in I (clue 3).

Questions 19–23

This is a mapping game that requires you to keep track of whom each of 4 employees—J, K, L, and M—can pass a project to from day to day. While order seems to be a factor (Monday through Thursday), it isn't really since every employee must have a project and pass a project every day.

Clue 1. ~JM

Clue 2. ~KJ

Clue 3. ~LJ

Since the clues all indicate who cannot pass to whom, it is important to determine who can pass to whom. There are only 4 employees, so just go through them systematically.

J—can pass to K and L

K—can pass to L and M

L—can pass to K and M

M—the only one who can pass to J, so ALWAYS passes to J since every employee must receive a project every day.

Indicate these connections on your test. It may be useful to use a standard diagram with M—F across the top to keep track of multiple exchanges.

Your diagram should look like this:

Clue 1: ~ JM
Clue 2: ~ KJ
Clue 3: ~ LJ

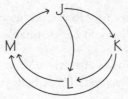

19.   **A**   Grab-a-Rule

A. Yes. This does not violate any clues.

B. No. This violates the rule given in the setup that an employee can work on only one project on any given day.

C. No. This violates the third clue by passing a project from L to J.

D. No. This violates the second clue by passing a project from K to J.

E. No. This violates the first clue by passing a project from J to M.

20. **E**   `General`

Don't let the wording confuse you. No projects are passed on the beginning of Monday—that is, the first day each employee works on his own project before passing it to someone else on Tuesday, and so on. From the deductions, you know that M is the only one who can pass to J and so must pass to J every day, making (E) the credited response.

21. **C**   `Specific`

Use your map to interpret the new information given. If one project gets passed back and forth between only two people, the only two who can pass to each other are K and L, making (C) the credited response.

22. **E**   `Specific`

Use your map to interpret the new information given. If L works the same piece on Tuesday and Thursday, then it must have received it from K or L on Tuesday and then passed it to K on Wednesday. Since L can pass only to K or M, if L passed the piece to M, then M would pass it to J, since M cannot pass to anyone else (deductions). So, in order to get the piece back on Thursday, it must pass the piece to someone who can pass the piece back—K. This makes (E) the credited response.

23. **E**   `General`

Use your map, deductions, and prior questions to help eliminate answers that must be false since you are looking for what could be true about Tuesday.

A. No. If J passes to K, K passes to M, and M can pass only to J (deductions), so L is left out of the loop.

B. No. If J passes to L, L passes to M, and M can pass only to J (deductions), so K is left out of the loop.

C. No. J cannot pass to M—this violates the first clue.

D. No. If K and L transfer to each other on the same day, then M would pass to J, but J cannot pass to M (clue 1) so J would be left unable to pass on his piece.

E. Yes. If K passes to L, L passes to M, and M passes to J (deductions), then J can pass to K. NO one is left out of the loop or left not being able to pass.

Chapter 3
PrepTest 73:
Answers and
Explanations

ANSWER KEY: PREPTEST 73

Section 1: Reading Comprehension	Section 2: Arguments 1	Section 3: Games	Section 4: Arguments 2
1. A	1. C	1. B	1. D
2. B	2. E	2. C	2. D
3. D	3. A	3. B	3. E
4. B	4. D	4. E	4. C
5. A	5. D	5. E	5. A
6. E	6. D	6. D	6. E
7. C	7. C	7. A	7. E
8. B	8. B	8. A	8. D
9. A	9. C	9. B	9. D
10. D	10. A	10. A	10. E
11. C	11. B	11. C	11. B
12. E	12. A	12. C	12. A
13. E	13. B	13. E	13. B
14. B	14. E	14. A	14. C
15. B	15. B	15. D	15. A
16. C	16. A	16. D	16. E
17. B	17. B	17. B	17. C
18. E	18. E	18. E	18. C
19. A	19. B	19. A	19. B
20. E	20. E	20. B	20. D
21. A	21. E	21. E	21. E
22. B	22. A	22. A	22. D
23. A	23. C	23. C	23. E
24. D	24. D		24. E
25. E	25. C		25. E
26. D			26. A
27. A			

EXPLANATIONS

Section 1: Reading Comprehension

Questions 1–7

The main point of the first paragraph is that, despite Charles Darwin's objection, strict construction Darwinians believe that natural selection explains all biological phenomena. The second paragraph explains what natural selection is and what the consequences of a strict constructionist view would be, and it introduces that there are many counterexamples. The main point of the third paragraph is that population genetics shows that most mutations are nonadaptive and not explainable by natural selection. The main point of the fourth paragraph is that paleontological studies of mass extinctions also undermine the strict constructionist view. The Bottom Line of the passage as a whole is that the strict constructionist view that natural selection is responsible for all biological phenomena is false. The overall tone of the passage is negative toward the strict constructionist claim.

1. **A**   **Big Picture**

Use your Bottom Line of the passage to help you to evaluate the choices. The correct answer will describe the main point of the passage.

A. Yes. The author uses evidence from population genetics and paleontology to dispute the strict constructionist point of view.

B   No. While strict constructionist Darwinians do claim that natural selection is responsible for the success or failure of the species, the main point of the passage is to disagree with such claims.

C   No. The passage states at the end of the third paragraph that natural selection does not explain neutral, nonadaptive mutations.

D. No. While this answer choice accurately captures what strict constructionists believe, the main point of the passage is to disagree with strict constructionists.

E. No. The author does not dispute that natural selection exists, only that the strict constructionist view that it is responsible for all evolution.

2. **B**   **Extract Fact**

The question is asking what the author said about why mammals were able to survive catastrophic environmental changes. This is discussed in the last paragraph of the passage. The correct answer will be explicitly mentioned in the passage.

A. No. This is contradicted by the passage in line 55.

B. Yes. In lines 43–44, the passage states that "smaller animal species are generally better able to survive."

C. No. Intelligence of mammals is not mentioned in the passage.

D. No. The environments of mammals were not mentioned in the passage.

E. No. Mammal reproduction was not mentioned in the passage.

3. **D** Extract
        Fact

The passage is asking for something that the author states about mutations of genetic material. The correct answer will be explicitly supported by the passage.

A. No. This is not supported by the passage. Persistence from one generation to the next is mentioned at the end of the third paragraph, but the other does not claim that a majority of mutations are not passed on.

B. No. The passage does not discuss when mutations occur.

C. No. The passage does not discuss whether mutations affect behavior or appearance, only whether they enhance reproductive success.

D. Yes. This is explicitly stated in lines 31–33.

E. No. The passage does not discuss the relative occurrence of mutations in larger and smaller species.

4. **B** Extract
        Infer

The correct answer will be the statement that is best supported by evidence within the passage text.

A. No. While the author refutes the strict constructionist view by providing evidence of exceptions, he or she does not claim that those exceptions account for the majority of traits in existing species.

B. Yes. In the fourth paragraph, the author discusses that the success of small mammals in the Cretaceous period was a result of "dumb luck" rather than adaptation to environment.

C. No. The author discusses in the third paragraph many neutral, nonadaptive mutations persist from one generation to the next but are not explainable by natural selection.

D. No. Watch out for deceptive language. The author claims that smaller species are generally better able to survive catastrophic climate changes, but catastrophic changes are not the same thing as harsh environmental conditions.

E. No. The author defines natural selection as generally held to shape both form and behavior.

5. **A** Extract
        Infer

The correct answer will be the statement that is best supported by evidence within the passage text and will agree with the Bottom Line and the overall tone of the passage.

A. Yes. At the end of the second paragraph, the author introduces that there are numerous examples that refute the strict constructionist Darwinian view and the third and fourth paragraphs detail two of those examples.

B. No. The author spends the bulk of the passage refuting the strict constructionists. This answer choice is not strong enough.

C. No. The author takes a position against the strict constructionists.

D. No. The author takes a position against the strict constructionists.

E. No. The author takes a position against the strict constructionists.

6. **E** Structure

The question is asking for the role that the second paragraph plays. The correct answer will discuss the strict constructionists' claims and the introduction of the evidence against those claims.

A. No. This paragraph introduces objections to the strict constructionists, not their objections.

B. No. The evidence against the strict constructionists' claims is laid out in the third and fourth paragraphs.

C. No. While the paragraph does describe the strict constructionists' view, there is no discussion of whether the evidence in the subsequent paragraphs has received any attention.

D. No. The passage does not discuss any arguments for the strict constructionist view, only the evidence against that view.

E. Yes. This accurately captures the discussion of the strict constructionists' claims and the introduction of the evidence against those claims.

7. **C** Big Picture

Use your Bottom Line of the passage to help you to evaluate the choices. The correct answer will describe the primary purpose of the passage to refute the strict constructionists' claims.

A. No. The passage is disputing the strict constructionists' claims.

B. No. This answer choice is too neutral. The author disagrees with the strict constructionist point of view.

C. Yes. This accurately captures that the author is refuting the strict constructionists' claims.

D. No. While the author is criticizing a theory, the strict constructionists' view is not a traditional theory.

E. No. The author mentions that the strict constructionist view is rising to prominence, but does not discuss why.

Questions 8–15

The main point of the first paragraph is that Julia Margaret Cameron's "fancy-subject" pictures derive their peculiar charm from their less-than-seamless elements. The main point of the second paragraph is that the realism of photography lends a depth to the pictures and captures the "doubleness" of imaginary and real personas that is not possible in theater or narrative painting. The main point of the third paragraph is that Cameron's pictures succeed because of their combination of amateurism and artistry, with *The Passing of Arthur* as an example. The Bottom Line of the passage as a whole is that the combination of reality and fantasy in Cameron's fancy-subject pictures results in peculiar treasures of photography. The overall tone of the passage is positive toward Cameron's work.

8.   **B**   Big Picture

Use your Bottom Line of the passage to help you to evaluate the choices. The correct answer will describe the main point of the passage.

A.   No. While this answer is partly true, the passage does not discuss Cameron's intentions and this answer does not capture the author's appreciation of Cameron's work.

B.   Yes. This is an accurate paraphrase of the Bottom Line.

C.   No. The author's attitude toward the fancy-subject pictures is positive.

D.   No. The passage discusses that the charm of Cameron's pictures is derived in part from the obviousness that the sitters are actors along with the imaginary scenes.

E.   No. The passage discusses that the charm of Cameron's pictures is derived from both the sitters and the imaginary scenes.

9.   **A**   Structure

The question is asking why the author brought up the props in the picture. The passage states that they are obviously broomsticks and muslin, but that those details are insignificant, supporting the paragraph's claim that the combination of amateurism and artistry is what makes the pictures special.

A.   Yes. The author introduces *The Passing of Arthur* with "for example," and the broomsticks and muslin support the claim of amateurism.

B.   No. The transformative power of theater is discussed in the second paragraph.

C.   No. The author never discusses Cameron's ingenuity.

D.   No. The passage never claims that Cameron's work is intended to be ironic.

E.   No. The author has a positive appraisal of the work, calling it magical and mysterious.

10.   **D**   RC Reasoning

The question is asking for an additional piece of information that will support the claim that we can suspend our disbelief when we look at a narrative painting but we cannot when we look at a photograph.

A.   No. The length of sitting time does not impact the viewer's willingness to suspend disbelief.

B.   No. This would make the viewer less likely to suspend disbelief when viewing paintings.

C.   No. This has no impact on the viewer's reaction to a painting.

D.   Yes. This is in line with the author's discussion of the difference between paintings and pictures: In pictures there is always the doubleness of reality and fantasy, but that is not the case in paintings. The suppression of conflicting details would allow a viewer to more easily suspend disbelief.

E.   No. This has no impact on whether the viewer would be likely to suspend disbelief.

11. **C**   `RC Reasoning`

The question is asking for an analogous relationship to that between Cameron and her fancy-subject pictures. Cameron uses ordinary people in costume to portray scenes from literature.

A.   No. The author does not claim that Cameron tried to preserve an aesthetic distance between her characters and the audience.

B.   No. The author does not claim that Cameron designed her pictures to subvert the meaning of the works she portrays.

C.   Yes. Cameron's works use ordinary people in costumes to portray grand scenes from literature.

D.   No. The author does not claim that Cameron's work was designed to be functional.

E.   No. The author does not claim that Cameron's goal was to give the appearance of authenticity.

12. **E**   `Extract Infer`

Four of the answer choices will be supported by the passage text, and the correct answer will disagree with the passage.

A.   No. In the second paragraph, the author states that we can more easily suspend our disbelief when we look at a narrative painting than we can with a photograph.

B.   No. In the third paragraph, the author claims that amateurism is part of what gives Cameron's pictures their special quality.

C.   No. In the first paragraph, the author states that the comical conditions under which the pictures were taken are what give the pictures their charm.

D.   No. In the second paragraph, the author states that theater transcends its doubleness only some of the time.

E.   Yes. At the end of the first paragraph, the author discusses that the charm of Cameron's work is due in part to the fact that she did not succeed in making seamless works of illustrative art.

13. **E**   `Extract Infer`

The correct answer will be the statement about the Victorian era that is best supported by evidence within the passage text.

A.   No. The passage does not discuss what people were interested in during Cameron's time.

B.   No. The passage does not discuss photographers other than Cameron and gives no indication of her socioeconomic standing.

C.   No. The passage never mentions publicity stills, nor does it discuss what was popular in the Victorian era.

D.   No. The fact that Cameron used ordinary people does not necessarily mean that there were no professional models available.

E.   Yes. In the second paragraph, the author mentions that the subjects of Cameron's pictures were "trying desperately hard to sit still," which implies that taking a picture took some time.

14. **B**   Structure

The question is asking why the author brings up the suspension of disbelief in the second paragraph. The suspension of disbelief is brought up to contrast how people view narrative paintings and narrative photographs.

A. No. The main conclusion of the passage is that Cameron's work succeeds because of its peculiar combination of reality and fantasy.

B. Yes. The author discusses the suspension of disbelief to contrast how people view narrative paintings and narrative photographs and how that contrast adds to our appreciation of the photographs.

C. No. The author views Cameron's work positively.

D. No. There is no criticism of Cameron's work in the passage.

E. No. The contrast is between narrative paintings and narrative photographs.

15. **B**   Big Picture

Use your Bottom Line of the passage to help you to evaluate the choices. The correct answer will describe the primary purpose of the passage to praise Cameron.

A. No. The passage discusses attributes of Cameron's pictures and *The Passing of Arthur* in particular, but it does not discuss her development.

B. Yes. This accurately paraphrases the Bottom Line of the passage.

C. No. The passage does not argue that Cameron's vision is essentially theatrical.

D. No. This answer choice is too extreme. There is no indication that Cameron's goals were doomed, only that they did not, in fact, succeed.

E. No. The passage does not mention distractors of *The Passing of Arthur* and the discussion of that picture is only one part of the passage.

Questions 16–21

The first paragraph introduces Herbert Marcuse's critique of advertising: that it creates false needs and leads people to succumb to oppression. The main point of the second paragraph is that Marcuse claims that advertising links real needs to products, resulting in people never really being satisfied. The main point of the third paragraph is that Marcuse's distinction between real and false needs, and therefore his critique, is extremely problematic. The fourth paragraph argues that people are savvier than Marcuse gives them credit for and that advertising does not subvert free will. The Bottom Line of the passage as a whole is that Marcuse's critique of advertising is problematic because it does not account for the fact that adults are not passive victims; rather, they makes choices about how to obtain fulfillment and can find a kind of fulfillment in products. The overall tone of the passage is critical of Marcuse.

16. **C** Big Picture

Use your Bottom Line of the passage to help you to evaluate the choices. The correct answer will describe the main point of the passage.

A. No. While the passage does mention that consumers sometimes get enjoyment from advertisements, this is not the main point of the passage.

B. No. The passage argues that consumers understand and recognize forces of persuasion and do not passively react to them.

C. Yes. This accurately paraphrases the Bottom Line.

D. No. While this answer choice is tempting, the author discusses only Marcuse's critique of advertising and does not generalize to what other critics typically do.

E. No. The author's criticism of Marcuse does not focus on the distinction between real and false needs; rather, it targets the assumption that people are unwittingly manipulated by advertising.

17. **B** Extract Fact

The correct answer will be directly supported by evidence in the passage. The author discusses what Marcuse believed in the first and second paragraphs.

A. No. The passage never mentions psychological research findings.

B. Yes. The author attributes this to Marcuse in lines 17–21.

C. No. This is something the author believes, not something that Marcuse believed.

D. No. The passage does not discuss what Marcuse believed about independent decision making.

E. No. The passage says that Marcuse accused advertisers of creating false needs, but there is no mention of whether advertisers accept or deny that accusation.

18. **E** Structure

The question is asking how the first paragraph fits into the passage as a whole. The correct answer should reflect that the first paragraph introduces Marcuse's theory.

A. No. The first paragraph does not discuss political or economic context.

B. No. This is discussed in the second paragraph.

C. No. This is not discussed in the passage.

D. No. The first paragraph discusses only one view.

E. Yes. This accurately captures the main point and purpose of the first paragraph.

19. A   **Extract**
         Fact

The correct answer will be directly supported by evidence in the passage. The author discusses what Marcuse believed in the first and second paragraphs.

A.   Yes. The author attributes this to Marcuse in lines 6–9.

B.   No. The passage does not discuss earlier societies.

C.   No. This is more in line with what the author believes than with what Marcuse believes.

D.   No. While Marcuse does think that advertising can be a tool of oppression, there is no discussion of totalitarian political regimes.

E.   No. Marcuse criticizes false needs, not real needs.

20. E   **Extract**
         Infer

The question is asking what "forces of persuasion" refers to. The correct answer will be best supported by evidence in the third paragraph, which discusses separating real needs from those false needs created by the manipulation of advertisers.

A.   No. The passage does not claim that advertisers' claims are intentionally dishonest.

B.   No. The passage discusses that these forces might inform our instinctive judgments, not that they are them.

C.   No. The passage says that these forces are prevalent in society, but that does not mean they are exerted by society.

D.   No. There is no claim that the state is involved in indoctrination.

E.   Yes. This accurately captures the author's discussion of Marcusian theory in the second and third paragraphs.

21. A   **Big Picture**

Use your Bottom Line of the passage to help you to evaluate the choices. The correct answer will summarize the author's argument.

A.   Yes. This accurately captures that the author disagrees with Marcuse but does not take a position on whether advertising is actually harmful.

B.   No. The author does not agree that Marcusian claims are justified.

C.   No. This is outside the scope of the passage. The author does not discuss the perception of human nature held by corporate leaders.

D.   No. The author does not claim that advertising has numerous social benefits. There is only a minor mention that some advertising can be entertaining.

E.   No. The author does not argue that advertisers exert economic power.

Questions 22–27

Passage A

The first paragraph introduces the principles of justice in acquisition and justice in transfer with respect to property. The second paragraph explains these principles. The third paragraph discusses the principle of rectification that should apply when situations don't conform to the previous two principles. The Bottom Line of passage A is that these three principles are fundamental to a theory of justice regarding property. The overall tone of the passage is neutral.

Passage B

The first paragraph introduces the Indian Nonintercourse Act as a way for Native Americans to hold onto their lands. The second paragraph discusses how an argument could be made that land that was wrongfully taken from Native Americans should be returned. The Bottom Line of passage B is that one might argue that land should be returned to Native Americans to the degree feasible in order to right the original wrong. The overall tone of the passage is neutral. Here's the relationship between the passages: Passage A outlines general principles, while passage B discusses a specific case involving those principles.

22. **B** **Big Picture**

The correct answer will reflect the Bottom Line of each passage.

A. No. While the principle of rectification in passage A arguably offers a solution to a moral problem, passage B does not criticize a solution.

B. Yes. This accurately describes the general nature of passage A and the specific application in passage B.

C. No. The description of passage A is too narrow—it does not reflect the principle of rectification—and passage B does not claim that the Native American case is ideal.

D. No. Passage A describes principles but does not argue for them, and passage B does not discuss any assumptions.

E. No. Passage A describes principles but does not argue for them, and passage B does not discuss a counterexample.

23. **A** **Extract Fact**

The correct answer will be directly supported by evidence in the passage.

A. Yes. Transfer of property is mentioned in lines 6–8 in passage A and in lines 37–39 of passage B.

B. No. This is discussed in passage B, but not in passage A. Passage A discusses only principles.

C. No. This is discussed in passage A, but not in passage B.

D. No. This is discussed at the end of passage B, but not in passage A.

E. No. This is discussed in passage B, but not in passage A.

24. **D**   **Big Picture**

The question asks for the relationship between the two passages. The correct answer will reflect that passage A outlines general principles and the second paragraph of passage B discusses remedying previous illicit taking of land.

    A.   No. Passage B involves specific details, and passage A involves general principles.

    B.   No. Passage A does not make an argument; it merely outlines a principle.

    C.   No. Both passages share the same subject matter—justice with respect to land ownership.

    D.   Yes. This accurately describes the relationship between the passages. The principle of rectification in passage A supports passage B's claim about what should happen with the land.

    E.   No. Passage B is consistent with passage A.

25. **E**   **RC Reasoning**

The question is asking for an analogous relationship to that of passage A and passage B, specifically that passage A outlines general principles and passage B discusses a specific case involving those principles.

    A.   No. These two documents disagree with one another.

    B.   No. These two documents disagree with one another, and the first document is too specific.

    C.   No. These two documents are on different topics.

    D.   No. These two documents disagree with one another, and the first document is too specific.

    E.   Yes. The first document outlines general ideas, and the second document applies those ideas to a specific project.

26. **D**   **Extract Infer**

The question is asking for the point of view of passage A with respect to the Indian Nonintercourse Act. Since the Act is in line with the principle of justice in transfer outlined in passage A, passage A would characterize the act positively.

    A.   No. The purpose of the Act is to protect Native American land.

    B.   No. The purpose of the Act is to remedy the results of past laws.

    C.   No. The Act is in line with the principle of justice in transfer, not acquisition.

    D.   Yes. This accurately captures the function of the Act.

    E.   No. The Act is in line with the principle of justice in transfer, not rectification.

27. **A**   **Big Picture**

The question is asking about the relationship between the two passages. The correct answer will reflect that passage A outlines general principles and the second paragraph of passage B discusses remedying previous illicit taking of land. Both passages are neutral in tone.

A. Yes. This answer accurately describes the purpose of each passage.

B. No. Passage A does not discuss competing views.

C. No. Passage A does not make a policy recommendation.

D. No. Passage A does not make an argument.

E. No. Passage A does not make an argument.

Section 2: Arguments 1

1. **C**   **Necessary Assumption**

This argument makes the claim that the city hired a contractor with 60 percent unqualified technicians. This is based upon the fact that only 40 percent of the technicians employed have a certification from the Heating Technicians Association. There is a language shift between having a certification and being unqualified. The credited response will link the premise to the conclusion explicitly.

A. No. The amount technicians are paid is irrelevant to the claim that some are unqualified.

B. No. Other contractors are not at issue in this argument, so this is irrelevant.

C. Yes. This answer choice correctly links a lack of certification to being unqualified.

D. No. The original installers of the heating systems are not at issue here. This is irrelevant.

E. No. The contractor having ties to the city is not required for the employees to be unqualified. This is irrelevant.

2. **E**   **Resolve/ Explain**

This argument notes a discrepancy in the way that people respond in different situations. In the argument, people tend to respond to a "Thank you" from a salesperson with another "Thank you," while they respond with "you're welcome" to thanks from a friend. The credited response will build a bridge between these two responses by establishing a situation for both responses to occur.

A. No. This is too one-sided and doesn't explain the difference.

B. No. This says only that customers are free to respond in any form, but it does not explain why people respond differently.

C. No. The focus of the argument is on what customers, not salespeople, say.

D. No. Just because their response is dictated by habit does not explain why people have different responses for two different situations.

E. Yes. This provides a reason why a person might say "Thank you" in a sales situation, but not in a favor situation.

3. **A** Flaw

This argument claims that selling movie rights to popular video games is rarely a good idea. This is based upon an example of a video game, *Nostroma*, being sold and disliked by both critics and the public. There is some additional information given that future sequels of the game sold poorly. There are two problems with this claim: causal and survey/sample. The author provides no causal connection between the movie being disliked and the future low sales. Also, the broad claim "rarely a good idea" is supported with only this single example, which may not be representative. The credited response will identify one of these flaws.

A. Yes. This answer choice describes a sampling flaw by stating that the claim is based upon only one example.

B. No. The claim is not focused on who disliked the game.

C. No. This is not circular reasoning.

D. No. This does not match the argument since the video game was popular while the movie was disliked.

E. No. This is not a necessary as sufficient factor flaw.

4. **D** Principle Match

This principle is an if…then statement that can be diagrammed. If the consultant has business interests with the company, then the executive is likely to be overcompensated. The contrapositive is as follows: If the executive is not likely to be overcompensated, then the consultant does not have business interests at the company. The credited response will describe a situation that matches this conditional statement.

A. No. The principle cannot be applied to this answer since there is no mention of a consultant.

B. No. The principle cannot be applied to this answer since there is no mention of a consultant.

C. No. The principle cannot be applied to this answer since it cannot be determined what might occur if a company does not hire a consultant.

D. Yes. This answer choice correctly matches the conditional since it claims the executive is likely overpaid since the firm used a consultant who has many other contracts with the company.

E. No. This is too strongly worded. The principle is not sufficient to guarantee the executive is not overpaid; it can suggest only that the executive is not likely to be overpaid.

5. **D** Flaw

This argument makes the claim that Lemaître's theory must be considered inadequate. The argument describes Lemaître's theory and establishes that its predictions are valid. However, it then introduces an alternative theory that makes the same prediction. The flaw in the argument is that the writer provides no evidence against Lemaître's theory other than the existence of the alternative. The credited response will point out some form of a lack of evidence for the conclusion.

A. No. This answer choice describes an appeal to authority, which is not the flaw in the argument.

B. No. This answer choice describes equivocation, which is not the flaw in the argument.

C. No. This answer choice describes a causal flaw, which is not the flaw in the argument.

D. Yes. This answer choice points out that the existence of one theory with correct predictions cannot be used as evidence against the validity of another theory with the same correct predictions.

E. No. This argument does not establish an either/or situation with the two theories since the author uses the new theory as evidence against the old one.

6. D `Principle Strengthen`

This argument claims that the criticism of a popular comedy for being unrealistic is misguided. This is based upon the premise that the stylized characters are not problematic for a comedy since the result is funny, which is what matters. The credited response will describe a general rule that forces the conclusion to be true.

A. No. This answer choice would actually weaken the argument since the premises state that the characters were too stylized.

B. No. This answer choice is not relevant to the conclusion. The issue is not the popularity of the film but whether the film was successful as a comedy.

C. No. This answer choice cannot be applied to the conclusion. The fact that film comedies find their humor in stylistic portrayals does not make the criticism misguided.

D. Yes. This answer choice makes the criticism misguided by establishing that since the stylized characters made the film funny, and since the film is a comedy, the film has been successful.

E. No. The specific genre of film is not at issue here. This answer choice is irrelevant.

7. C `Parallel Flaw`

This argument proceeds by noting that Party X has been accused of illegal actions by Party Y. The argument then concludes that these accusations are ill-founded based upon the fact that three years ago Party Y itself was involved in a scandal. The flaw here is an appeals and attacks flaw. The argument attacks the Party Y itself without addressing the specific argument against Party X. The credited response must match an attack flaw above all other considerations. The credited response should also match the other pieces and tone of the original argument.

A. No. This argument does not make an attack against the accusing party.

B. No. This argument makes an attack on the plaintiff; however, the conclusion is focused upon the plaintiff being hypocritical rather than the argument being unfounded. Therefore, this answer choice is not fully parallel with the original.

C. Yes. This argument concludes that the plaintiff's accusations are ill founded since the plaintiff recently did the same thing that the defendant had done.

D. No. The premise in support of the accusations being ill-founded does not attack the plaintiff.

E. No. This argument describes an attack flaw without actually making one.

8. **B** `Necessary Assumption`

This argument claims that eyes are adapted only to an animal's needs rather than to some abstract sense of how a good eye should be designed. This is based upon the fact that box jellyfish have eyes capable of forming sharp images with fine detail; however, their retinas are too far forward, causing their vision to be blurry and lacking fine detail. There is a language shift from the function of the box jellyfish's eyes and the notions of adaptation to need. The credited response will build a bridge from the premises to the conclusion.

A. No. Whether this is true only of the box jellyfish is irrelevant to the conclusion that adaptations are based only upon need.

B. Yes. This answer choice links the notion of need to the specific adaptations found in the box jellyfish eye. When negated, this answer would destroy the conclusion.

C. No. This answer choice would undermine the conclusion if anything by suggesting that the needs of the jellyfish are not met by its adaptations.

D. No. The origin of current box jellyfish is irrelevant to the claim about adaptations occurring based upon an animal's needs.

E. No. This answer choice does not explicitly link this method of identifying prey to a need of the jellyfish, so this answer choice is irrelevant to the conclusion.

9. **C** `Weaken`

This argument claims that there are grounds for disputing claims made by tobacco companies that advertising has no causal impact on smoking. This is based upon research that has shown that there has been a significant reduction in smoking in countries that have also imposed restrictions on advertising. This argument assumes the correlation between the advertising restrictions and the reduction of smoking is actually a causal relationship. The credited response will weaken the causal flaw in some way.

A. No. This answer choice does not weaken the claim that advertising has a significant effect on smoking since it focuses only on existing smokers. The argument specifically mentions first-time smokers.

B. No. How stringent the restrictions are in different media does not weaken the claim that advertisement restrictions cause a reduction in smoking.

C. Yes. This answer choice weakens the conclusion by introducing an alternative cause for both the reduction in smoking and for the advertising restrictions.

D. No. This answer choice is irrelevant since it does not deal with smoking advertising.

E. No. This answer choice is irrelevant. The argument is concerned about those that advertising affects.

10. **A** `Sufficient Assumption`

This argument makes the claim that Brecht's plays are not genuinely successful dramas. This is predicated upon the fact that the roles in these plays are so incongruous that audiences and actors find it difficult to discern the characters' personalities. The argument then states that for a play to be successful, audiences must care what happens to some of its characters. The gap in this argument is between the inability to discern personalities of characters and caring about those characters. The credited response will provide an answer that makes the reasoning solid and forces the conclusion to be valid.

A. Yes. This answer choice establishes a link between discerning a character's personality and caring for that character.

B. No. What determines a character's personality is not relevant to the claim that the plays are not successful.

C. No. While this answer choice does establish that a lack of caring about a character is directly related to the lack of success of a play, this answer choice does not connect these ideas to Brecht's plays specifically. Therefore, this answer choice is not sufficient to force the conclusion.

D. No. This answer choice essentially rephrases the known premises as an if...then statement. However, the premises already state that both actors and the audience find it difficult to discern the motives. Linking these two things is not sufficient to force the conclusion.

E. No. This is irrelevant since the claim is about Brecht's plays being unsuccessful.

11. **B** Main Point

This argument claims that there would be no problem in accepting the mayor's proposal to accept a gift of lights despite fears that the company wants to influence the city. This conclusion is supported by a speculation on a single ulterior motive. The argument claims that favoritism is not an issue with the gift due to a competitive-bidding procedure. The credited response will paraphrase the conclusion and match it in both tone and scope.

A. No. This answer choice is too strongly worded to match the conclusion. The argument states that there is no problem with accepting the lights, not that the fear itself is unfounded.

B. Yes. This answer choice correctly paraphrases the conclusion.

C. No. This answer choice is the opposite of what the argument is claiming.

D. No. This is a premise in support of the claim that accepting the lights is not problematic.

E. No. This is a premise in support of the claim that accepting the lights is not problematic.

12. **A** Sufficient Assumption

This argument claims that the chairperson should not have released a report to the public. This is based upon the fact that the chairperson did not consult any other commission members before releasing it. There is a language shift here between not consulting with other members and not releasing the report. The credited response will link these two ideas and make it clear that the chairperson should not have released the report.

A. Yes. This answer choice makes the consent of a majority of the commission members a prerequisite for the report's release. Since this prerequisite was not met according to the premise, then the release of the report could not have been permissible.

B. No. This answer choice moves in the wrong direction. The credited response should make it wrong for the chairperson to release the report.

C. No. The issue at hand is not whether the commissioner was justified, but whether the report should have been released at all.

D. No. The issue at hand is not whether the commissioner was justified, but whether the report should have been released at all.

E. No. This answer choice is not strong enough to force the conclusion. Just because at least one member was against the report's release does not mean that it was wrong to do so.

13. **B**   **Flaw**

This argument concludes that putting more people into prison cannot help to reduce crime. This is based upon a survey that shows that there has been no significant reduction in the crime rate in the last 20 years, despite increases both in the population and in the amount spent on prisons. There are two flaws in this argument. The first is a survey/sample flaw in which relevant information might be left out. The next flaw is a causal flaw in which the author assumes that because there has not been a decrease, then there is no link at all between the current incarceration rate and the crime rate. The credited response will identify one of these commonly occurring flaws.

A. No. This is not a flaw that occurs in the argument. There is no causal link assumed between the population and the reported statistics.

B. Yes. This answer choice points out that the author ignores the fact that the current imprisonment rate might be having some effect on crime.

C. No. This is a premise explicitly stated in the argument.

D. No. The reformer does not make any alternative suggestion. Instead, the reformer merely concludes that imprisonment cannot help reduce crime.

E. No. This flaw is not found in the argument.

14. **E**   **Reasoning**

Inez makes the claim that we cannot afford not to invest in space exploration. She bases her claim on the premise that space programs lead to many technological advancements with everyday applications, making the cost of a space program affordable. Winona rebuts this argument by arguing that technology should be funded directly, noting that it is absurd to justify an expenditure in space programs for a side effect of that program. The credited response will match a paraphrase of how Winona addresses Inez's argument.

A. No. Winona does not dispute Inez's claim that space exploration leads to technological development.

B. No. Winona does not suggest that there is direct evidence against the space program.

C. No. Winona does not point out a contradiction in Inez's premises.

D. No. Winona does not mention that technological innovations are too expensive.

E. Yes. Winona points out that the same goal Inez desires can be reached more directly than through the space program.

15. **B**   **Flaw**

The marketing consultant concludes that the marketing campaign is ill-conceived. This argument is based upon the fact that the consultant predicted that this campaign would be unpopular and ineffective. The consultant then points out that this season's sales figures are down, especially for LRG's new products. The flaw in the argument confuses the correlation of these two events with a causal relationship. The credited response will point out some form of causal flaw or will mention an alternative causal factor that has been ignored or overlooked.

A. No. The claim is that the competitor's campaign was ill-conceived, not whether sales would have been even lower. This is not the flaw in the argument.

B. Yes. This answer choice identifies that the downturn in sales could have been driven by an alternative economic cause rather than the unpopular advertisement campaign.

C. No. The author does not assume this.

D. No. The conclusion is on the ill-conceived advertising campaign, not on the sales of existing products. This answer choice is irrelevant.

E. No. The marketing consultant does not make a necessary as sufficient flaw.

16. **A** Reasoning

This argument concludes that it would be better to award the top prize in architecture to the best building rather than to the best argument. This claim is based upon an analogous comparison with the movie industry by arguing that buildings, like movies, are collaborative efforts and not like scientific discoveries. The argument also notes that the Pritzker Prize is currently analogous to the Nobel Prize. The credited response will identify the pattern of reasoning in this argument.

A. Yes. This answer choice correctly identifies the analogy that occurs in the argument between the movie industry practice and what the writer feels should occur with the architecture prize.

B. No. The distinction made in the argument between science and movies is not used to attribute value. This is not in the argument.

C. No. This answer does not match the conclusion in the argument. The argument does not try to apply the criticism of the movie industry to those of the architecture prize.

D. No. The argument does note that the science industry is disanalogous to the architecture industry, but the argument does not try to refute claims related to these two fields.

E. No. This answer does not match the argument. The argument does not focus on what is inappropriate but on what is appropriate.

17. **B** Parallel

This argument opens with a conditional statement that if Suarez is not the most qualified for sheriff, then Anderson is. The argument concludes that if the most qualified candidate is elected and if that is not Suarez, then it will be Anderson. This argument can be abstracted as Premise: ~A most → B most; Conclusion: If most chosen and ~A chosen → B chosen. The credited response will match this pattern in tone, scope, and direction.

A. No. The premise does not align because it does not set up Caldwell as only one of two lowest bidders.

B. Yes. The premise establishes either Ramsey or Dillon as the lowest bidder. Premise: ~A lowest → B lowest. The conclusion states if the conclusion goes to the lowest and it is not Dillon, it will be Ramsey. Conclusion: If lowest chosen and ~A chosen → B chosen.

C. No. This argument is not parallel in tone since it does not establish either Kapshaw or Johnson as being the lowest or highest bidders.

D. No. This argument does match the direction of the original argument. The original argument was who would receive the contract, not who would not.

E. No. This conclusion does not align with the original argument. This conclusion does not contain the sufficient condition "if awarded to the lowest."

18. **E**   Flaw

This argument opens by summarizing an art historian's position that fifteenth-century painters had a greater mastery of painting than did those of the sixteenth century since their paintings were more planimetric. The critic concludes that this is wrong and supports this claim with the premise that the degree to which a painting is planimetric is not relevant to mastery. This is a disagreement flaw in which the critic assumes that the new evidence is sufficient to disprove the old position. Specifically, this is an absence of evidence argument. The critic assumes because some of the support for the art historian's claim is not valid, then the entire argument is invalid. The credited response will describe a common flaw that is found in the argument.

A. No. This answer choice describes an ad *hominem* attack. This flaw is not in the argument.

B. No. This answer choice describes equivocation. This flaw is not in the argument.

C. No. This answer choice describes a necessary as sufficient flaw. This flaw is not in the argument.

D. No. The conclusion that the art historian is wrong is based upon a single claim.

E. Yes. This answer choice describes an absence of evidence flaw.

19. **B**   Weaken

This argument concludes that a carved flint object found in a Stone Age tomb in Ireland must be the head of a speaking staff. This is based upon the premises that it is too small to be a warrior's mace, and because the shape is that of a head with an open mouth speaking. Finally, the premises describe a speaking staff as a communal object. This argument is predicated upon several assumptions. First, the author assumes that because the object seems analogous to a talking head, it must belong to a speaking staff. Additionally, the author assumes that because it is too small to be a mace, it must be a speaking staff without providing clear justification for this. The credited response will weaken this claim by either suggesting an alternative detail or by providing another consideration that would cast doubt on the claim.

A. No. A lack of weapons in the tomb has no bearing on what this object is. This is irrelevant to the conclusion.

B. Yes. This answer choice presents an alternative consideration. If communal objects were passed from one generation to the next, it casts doubt on the claim that it is such an object since it was found in a tomb.

C. No. The level of artistry in the object is not relevant to the object's function.

D. No. If anything, this answer choice would lend support to the claim that it is a speaking staff.

E. No. The symbolism inherent in a speaking staff is not relevant to the interpretation of the object from the tomb.

20. E **Necessary Assumption**

This argument claims that farmers will need to abandon the use of chemical fertilizers in order to improve the soil structure. This conclusion is based upon the premises that due to fertilizer use, farmers have abandoned the planting of "green-manure" crops to improve soil. This in turn has hurt the soil structure in the region. There is a language shift in the conclusion that farmers must "abandon" the use of fertilizers. The credited response will either build a bridge from the premises to the conclusion or will rule out an alternative possibility.

A.   No. This answer choice goes in the wrong direction. This is sufficient, but not necessary, for the conclusion to be true.

B.   No. The effect of fertilizers on green-manure crops is not something assumed by the argument.

C.   No. This answer choice is irrelevant to the conclusion that farmers need to abandon fertilizer use.

D.   No. This answer choice is not relevant to the claim that they need to abandon fertilizer use in order to improve soil structure.

E.   Yes. The answer choice establishes that abandoning chemical fertilizers is a necessary factor of growing green-manure crops.

21. E **Inference**

This argument contains two quantity statements. First, most of the students in Spanish 101 attended every class last semester. Second, each student who received a grade lower than a B minus missed at least one class. The credited response will be the answer choice that must be true based on the statements in the argument. Specifically, the quantity statements must be supported.

A.   No. There is not enough information in the argument to support a statement about students who scored an A minus.

B.   No. This statement goes in the wrong direction. The final sentence can be diagrammed as follows: "if <B minus → miss at least one." This answer is a bad contrapositive.

C.   No. This information is unsupported because the argument does not stipulate how many students made a B minus exactly.

D.   No. This is unsupported. There is nothing in the argument that will support a statement about students who miss a class and who scored higher than a B minus.

E.   Yes. This is the valid contrapositive of the final statement: "if <B minus → miss at least one" becomes "if miss none → not lower than a B minus (B minus or higher)."

22. A **Strengthen**

This argument claims that each of the sockeye salmon populations has adapted genetically to its distinct habitat. This is based upon the fact that the populations split into two non-interbreeding groups that now differ genetically. This argument is predicated upon a causal assumption that the sole cause of the different genes is due to adaptation to the environment. The credited response either will introduce some new evidence in support of this causal link or will rule out an alternative possible cause.

A.   Yes. This answer choice rules out an alternative possibility for the different genes by stating that neither population has interbred with the native salmon population.

B. No. This answer choice is irrelevant to the conclusion, which is about how the current salmon population has different genes.

C. No. This answer choice is irrelevant to the conclusion. Where salmon spend their time does not affect the conclusion since a premise states that the two populations do not interbreed.

D. No. The similarity of one of the current groups to the originally introduced salmon does not strengthen the claim that they have adapted. This is irrelevant.

E. No. The size of the current salmon population is not relevant to the claim that the two salmon populations have genetically adapted.

23. **C** Inference

This argument states that if business people invest in modern industries that have not been pursued in a country, then that country can substantially increase its economic growth. However, the argument notes that there is high risk to the endeavor and little incentive for business people to take the risk. The credited response will be the answer choice that is most strongly supported by the facts. Unsupported information should be crossed off.

A. No. This answer choice is an unsupported prediction. There is not enough information in the argument to make a statement about what will happen after the first modern industry has been started.

B. No. This is an unsupported comparison. There is not enough information to support a statement about which industries have the most competition.

C. Yes. This answer choice is supported. The argument states that economic growth is the result of investment by businesspeople but there is little incentive for them to do so. This statement suggests that if incentives are increased, then the country will increase the chance of the first statement occurring.

D. No. This is too strongly worded to be supported. This statement makes investment in modern industries a requirement for economic growth rather than being a factor sufficient to cause growth.

E. No. This is an unsupported comparison. There is not enough information to support a statement about when industries have little risk.

24. **D** Resolve/ Explain

On the one hand, almost all of a city's concertgoers were dissatisfied with the local hall and wanted wider seats and better acoustics. However, even though they were told that it was not feasible to modify the existing hall, most were opposed to the idea of tearing it down and replacing it with a new one. The credited response will provide a reason why concertgoers do not want the hall torn down despite their dissatisfaction with it.

A. No. This answer choice does not resolve the problem because it does not explain why the concertgoers would be against the hall being torn down.

B. No. The survey deals with concertgoers, not with residents in the vicinity of the hall.

C. No. The benefits to the city do not explain why the concertgoers were against the hall being torn down. If anything, this answer choice would make the situation worse.

D. Yes. This publicized plan suggests a reason that concertgoers would not want the hall to be torn down despite their dissatisfaction with it. This plan would suggest a valid alternative use that the concertgoers might support in lieu of tearing down the building.

E. No. This answer choice does not explain why the concertgoers were against the hall being torn down. If anything, this answer choice would make the situation worse.

25. **C**   Main Point

This argument states several premises and asks for the ultimate conclusion to be identified in the answer choices. This argument states that without a book, a citation would not be accurate, which in turn is necessary for the inclusion of a quotation. However, the paper will be much better with the quotation. The credited response will properly conclude this argument and will match the tone and scope of the premises.

A. No. This violates the premise that the student will be unable to include the quotation without the accurate citation.

B. No. The final sentence states that the research paper will be completed. This violates a premise.

C. Yes. This answer choice sufficiently concludes the argument. The paper would be better with the quotation; however, without the book the quotation cannot be included.

D. No. This violates the premise that the student cannot include the quotation without an accurate citation.

A. No. This violates the premise that the student will produce a completed paper.

Section 3: Games

Questions 1–7

This is a 1D ordering game with all range clues, so it is a ranking game. The inventory consists of five songs—R, S, T, V, and W—with 1-to-1 correspondence and no wildcards.

Clue 1: S—V

Clue 2: T—R & S OR R & S—T

Clue 3: W—R & T OR R & T—W

Deductions: From clue 1 you know that S cannot be last and V cannot be first. Put this information straight into your diagram. Since clue 2 and clue 3 have two scenarios each, there will be multiple possible arrangements.

Your diagram should look like this:

R, S, T, V, W

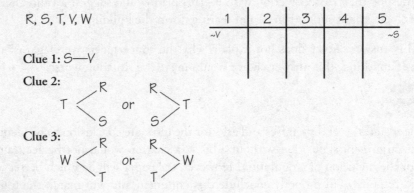

Clue 1: S—V

Clue 2:

Clue 3:

| 1 | 2 | 3 | 4 | 5 |

~V   ~S

1. **B**   Grab-a-Rule

   A.   No. This violates clue 2 because T is between R and S.

   B.   Yes. This choice does not violate any of the clues.

   C.   No. This violates clue 3 because W is between R and T.

   D.   No. This violates clue 1 because V is before S.

   E.   No. This violates clue 2 because T is between S and R.

2. **C**   Specific

   Make a new line in your diagram and add the new information. If S is fourth, then V is fifth (clue 1). S is also in clue 2. Since T cannot be after S, then T must be before S and before R. That means that (C) is the credited response.

3. **B**   Specific

   Make a new line in your diagram and add the new information. Combining clues 2 and 3: R must come before both T and W. Write deductions into the diagram. S must have T, W, and V after it, so it cannot be 3, 4, or 5. This means S must be second. T cannot be first, second, or last, so it must be either third or fourth. V cannot be first or second, so it can be third, fourth, or fifth. W cannot be first, second or third, so it must be either fourth or fifth. You are looking for what could be true, so eliminate anything that must be false.

   A.   No. T cannot be second because both R and S must come before T.

   B.   Yes. V could be third, which would make T fourth and W fifth. This does not violate any clues.

   C.   No. W cannot be third because R, S, and T must all come before W.

   D.   No. S cannot be fourth because T, W, and V must all come after S.

   E.   No. T cannot be last because W must come after T.

4.   **E**   Specific

Make deductions into the diagram. If T is second, then W must be first. R cannot be first or second, so it could be third, fourth, or fifth. S cannot be first, second, or fifth, so it must be either third or fourth. V cannot be first, second, or third, so it must be either fourth or fifth.

A.   No. S cannot be first because it must come after T.

B.   No. R cannot be first because it must come after T.

C.   No. V cannot be third because W, T, and S must all come before it.

D.   No. W cannot be fourth because it must come before T.

E.   Yes. R can be last. The line-up would be W, T, S, V, R. This does not violate any clues.

5.   **E**   General

Use the deductions, prior work, and trying the answers to determine which answer choice could be the first two pieces, in order.

A.   No. This would cause V to be before S, which violates clue 1.

B.   No. This violates clues 2 and 3 because it would force T to be between R and S and force W to be between R and T.

C.   No. This violates clue 2 by forcing T to be between S and R.

D.   No. This violates clue 3 by forcing W to be between T and R.

E.   Yes. This does not violate any rules and can be seen in the setup for question 7.

6.   **D**   Specific

Make a new line in your diagram and add the new information. If V is second, then S has to be first (clue 1). This will force R to be before T. W can be either before R and T or after R and T. This means there are only two possible orders.

A.   No. S must be first, not W (clue 1).

B.   No. S must be first (clue 1).

C.   No. If T is third, then it is between S and R, which violates clue 2.

D.   Yes. This is the first order in the diagram above.

E.   No. This would force T to be between S and R, which violates clue 2.

7.   **A**   Specific

Make deductions into the diagram; then look for something that cannot be true in either scenario. The first deduction, with T before R and S, was used in question 4, so you don't need to write it out again. The second deduction, with T after R and S, has not been used in a prior question, so you need to work it out. R cannot be first or last, so it could be second, third, or fourth. T cannot be first, second, or third, so it must be either fourth or fifth. S cannot be first, fourth, or fifth, so it must be either second or third. V cannot be first or second, but it could be third, fourth, or fifth.

A. Yes. T cannot be third in either scenario described above.

B. No. V could be third in the second scenario described above.

C. No. S could be fourth in the first scenario described above and in question 4.

D. No. V could be fourth in the first scenario described above and in question 4.

E. No. T could be fifth in the second scenario described above.

Questions 8–13

This is a 2D order game. There are five speakers—L, M, X, Y, and Z. Each speaker gives one speech at either 1 P.M. or 2 P.M. in either the Gold Room or the Rose Room. One person will give a speech at 3 P.M. Since order matters, put the times across the top of the diagram and the rooms on the side. This will give you six spaces for five inventory elements—one space at 3 o'clock is not used. There is a mix of range and conditional clues. There are no wildcards.

Clue 1: M—L same room

Clue 2: Z—X & Y; Z & X—Y; OR Z & Y—Y

Clue 3: LG → XR and ZR

XG or   ZG → LR

Since M must be before L, note that M cannot be at 3 P.M. and L cannot be at 1 P.M. Also, since Z must always be before X or Y or both, note that it, too, cannot be at 3 P.M. Since M and L must always be in the same room, that means some combination of at least two of X, Y, and Z must be in the other room (clues 1 and 3). If all three are in the same room, then Z must be at 1 P.M. (rule 2). If Z is in the room with one other, then it must still be at 1 P.M. (rule 1), and if X or Y is at 1 P.M., then Z must still be at 1 P.M.

Your diagram should look like this:

L, M, X, Y, Z, empty

Clue 1: M—L same room

Clue 2:

Clue 3: LG → XR and ZR
XG or ZG → LR

8. A `Grab-a-Rule`

    A.   Yes. This arrangement does not violate any clues.

    B.   No. This violates clue 2 since X is earlier than Z.

    C.   No. This violates clue 3 since L and X are in the same room.

    D.   No. This violates clue 1 because L is earlier than M.

    E.   No. This violates clue 1 because L and M are not in the same room.

9. B `General`

Use the deductions, prior work, and trying the answers to determine which pair of speeches cannot happen at the same time (1 P.M. or 2 P.M.).

    A.   No. Draw this one out. Both L and Y could be at 2 P.M. if M and Z are at 1 P.M. and X is at 3 P.M.

    B.   Yes. Since M must always be before L, then L can never be at 1 P.M. (clue 1), and since Z must always be at 1 P.M. (deduction), then L and Z can never be at the same time.

    C.   No. Both M and X could be at 2 P.M. as seen in question 12.

    D.   No. Both X and Y could be at 2 P.M. as seen in question 11.

    E.   No. Both Y and Z could be at 1 P.M. as seen in question 12.

10. A `Specific`

Make a new line in your diagram and fill in the information given. If X is at 3 P.M., it could be either with M and L or with Y and Z. Either way, M and Z are at 1 P.M. and Y and L are at 2 P.M. You are looking for what must be false, so eliminate anything that can be true.

    A.   Yes. L cannot be in the same room with Y since L must also be with M, which would mean X would have to be at 2 P.M. in the same room with Z.

    B.   No. This could be true. See the description above.

    C.   No. This could be true. See the description above.

    D.   No. This could be true. See the description above.

    E.   No. This could be true. See the description above.

11. C `General`

This is a partial Grab-a-Rule. The answers do not involve all the inventory in all the spaces, but you may still be able to eliminate some of the answers that directly violate a rule. Then try any remaining answers and eliminate ones that don't work.

    A.   No. This answer violates clue 1 because L is before M.

    B.   No. This rule violates clue 1 because it includes M but not L.

73

C.   Yes. This does not violate any clues. If M, Y, and L are in G in that order, then Z and X are in R at 1 P.M. and 2 P.M. respectively.

D.   No. This violates clue 2 since Y is before Z.

E.   No. This violates clue 3 since Z is listed with M and L in G.

12.   **C**   **Specific**

Make a new line in your diagram and fill in the information given. If Y is at 1 P.M. and Z must also be at 1 P.M., then Y must be with M and L, which will be at 2 P.M. and 3 P.M., respectively; therefore, Z and X must be in the other room at 1 P.M. and 2 P.M., respectively.

A.   No. L must be at 3 P.M. in both scenarios.

B.   No. L must be at 3 P.M. in both scenarios.

C.   Yes. M is at 2 P.M. regardless of which room M is in.

D.   No. X must be at 2 P.M., not 3 P.M.

E.   No. X must be at 2 P.M., not 1 P.M.

13.   **E**   **Complex**

This is a Complex question that asks for a parallel clue, and it can be very time consuming. Try the answer choices until you find one that gives you the same deductions you got at the beginning of the game, but without the second clue. First, take stock of your remaining clues and deductions: Clues 1 and 3 are still in effect, so all you are missing is something that will force X and Y to not be before Z.

A.   No. Forcing L to be at 3 P.M. does nothing to the relationship between X, Y, and Z.

B.   No. This would mean that Z could never be at 3 P.M., but it has no impact on the relationship between X, Y, and Z.

C.   No. This is on the right track but doesn't go far enough. If one of X or Y must be after Z, one of them could still be before Z.

D.   No. This does nothing to force Z ahead of X and Y. One of them could still be before Z.

E.   Yes. This is exactly what you deduced at the beginning of the game. If Z must be at 1 P.M., then there is no way for either X or Z to be before it.

Questions 14–18

This is a group game with fixed assignment. The inventory consists of five buildings—F, G, I, M and S—which are each assigned to one of three families—T, W, and Y. Every family owns at least one building and the clues are a mix of spatial, anti-blocks, and conditional clues. There is one wildcard.

Clue 1: W > Y

Clue 2: ~FI & ~FM

Clue 3: ~St → Iy

      ~Iy → St

Deductions: Since W has more buildings than Y, then W must have at least two buildings, and Y can have only one building. This now accounts for four out of the five buildings. The last building can belong either to T, meaning T = 2, W = 2, and Y = 1, or to W, meaning T = 1, W = 3, and Y = 1. Next, combine this information with clues 2 and 3 to limit the possible scenarios. Since Y can own only one building, if it's I, then F and M must be split up between T and W. S can be in W, meaning that G can be in either T or W, or S can be in T, forcing G to be in W.

If S is the only building in T, then there must be three buildings in W. Since F and M cannot be in the same group and F and I cannot be in the same group (clue 2), then M, G, and I must be in W and F must be in Y. This is the only way to keep F away from both I and M.

If S and one other building are in T, then there will be two buildings in W. There are many possible arrangements in this scenario.

If S is in T and I is in Y, then F and M still need to be split between T and W, and G will have to be in W in order for W to have more buildings than Y (clue 1).

Your diagram should look like this:

F, G, I, M, S

	T	W	Y
(1)	_ _	_ _	_
(2)	_	_ _ _	_

Clue 1: W > Y

Clue 2: F̶I̶ F̶M̶

Clue 3: S ≠ T → I ≠ Y

      I ≠ Y → S ≠ T

14. **A** Grab-a-Rule

   A. Yes this does not violate any clues.

   B. No. This violates clue 3 because S was not in T and I was not in Y.

   C. No. This violates clue 2 because F is with M.

   D. No. This violates clue 1 since there are fewer buildings in W than in Y.

   E. No. This violates clue 1 since there are the same number of buildings in W and Y.

15. **D** General

   Use the deductions, prior work, and trying the answers to determine which answer choice contains two buildings that CANNOT be together in T.

   A. No. If F and G are in T, then I must be in Y (clue 3). This leaves M and S together in W, which is consistent with the first scenario in the diagram above.

   B. No. If G and M are in T, then I must be in Y (clue 3). This leaves F and S together in W, which is consistent with the first scenario in the diagram above.

C. No. If S and G are in T, then I must be in W (if it's in Y, it would force F and M to be together in W, which violates clue 2). So, M and I must be in W and F must be in Y.

D. Yes. If I and M are in T, there is no way to fulfill the requirement of clue 3. There is no room to add S to T, and I can't be in Y if it's in T.

E. No. If I and S are in T, then I is not in Y, which means that M and F have to be split between W and Y, leaving G to be in W.

16. **D**   Specific

Make a new line in your diagram and fill in the information given. If M is in Y, then S must be in T (clue 3). You now have to find places for F, I, and G. F and I cannot be in the same group (clue 2), so one of them must be in T and the other in W. Since W must have more spaces than Y, that means G must be in W. This makes (D) the credited response.

17. **B**   Specific

Make a new line in your diagram and fill in the information given. If G and I are in the same group, then they cannot be in Y, which has only one space. This will force S into T (clue 3) and G and I into W since T cannot have three spaces. F and M are unaccounted for, but they cannot be in the same group. So one of F/M is in Y. The other of F/M could be in W (M in W and F in Y) or in T. Since everything is locked in place except for F and M, look for an answer that involves one of these buildings. This makes (B) the credited response.

18. **E**   Specific

Make a new line in your diagram and fill in the information given. If T has one space, then W has three. The question asks for a list of buildings that could each be in T alone. Clue 3 means that S must be on that list, so eliminate (A), (B), and (D). Choice (C) does not work because if I is not in Y, then S must be in T (clue 3). I cannot be the only building in T because I could not be in Y and S could not be in T. Eliminate (C). This leaves (E) as the credited response.

Questions 19–23

This is a group game with variable assignments. The groups consist of three bouquets—1, 2, and 3—and the inventory is made up of five kinds of flowers—L, P, R, S, and T. The inventory can be repeated across the groups or left out entirely. Each group has at least one space, but could potentially have up to five. While it is sometimes easier to work a variable assignment game by putting the inventory on top of the diagram to create smaller potential groups, the clues are mainly about the relationships between the bouquets rather than the flowers, meaning it will be easier to symbolize and work with the clues if you use a more traditional diagram. There are no wildcards.

Clue 1. $1 \rightarrow \sim 3$
$3 \rightarrow \sim 1$

Clue 2.   2 and 3 exactly 2 spaces in common

Clue 3.   S = 3 put into diagram

Clue 4. L → R and ~S

S or ~R → ~L

Clue 5. T → P

~P → ~T

Deductions: Since S is in group 3 (clue 3), it cannot also be in group 1 (clue 1) and L cannot be in group 3 (clue 4). Since groups 2 and 3 have two flowers in common, that means those groups have at least two spaces each. You cannot conclude that S must be in group 2, because the two flowers in common could be other than S and each group could have more than two flowers. There is not much else to conclude up front, and there are many possible combinations of flowers among the groups.

Your diagram should look like this:

L, P, R, S, T

1 ~S   2   3 ~L

__ __ | __ __ | S__ __

Clue 1: 1 → ~3

3 → ~1

Clue 2: 2 & 3 exactly

2 in common

Clue 3: S = 3

Clue 4: L → R and ~S

~R or S → ~L

Clue 5: T → P

~P → ~T

19. **A**   Grab-a-Rule

A. Yes. This arrangement does not violate any clues.

B. No. This violates clue 1 because groups 1 and 3 both have P.

C. No. This violates clue 5 since group 2 has T but no P.

D. No. This violates clue 4 because group 3 has L and S.

E. No. This violates clue 3 because group 3 does not have S.

20. **B**   Specific

Make a new line in your diagram and fill in the information given. If L is in group 1, then so is R (clue 4). This means that R cannot be in group 3 (clue 1). Since S is already in group 3, this means that the only other flower options are P and T. You need exactly two spaces in common between groups 2 and 3 (clue 2) so one of them might be S, and if there is only one other flower, then it would have to be P, since P does not guarantee T. If S is not one of the flowers in common, then groups 2 and 3 would both have to have T and P since L and R cannot be in group 3. Either way, the only thing that must be true in both scenarios is that P must be one of the common elements in the two groups, making (B) the credited response.

21. **E** Specific

Make a new line in your diagram and fill in the information given. If T is in group 1, then so is P (clue 4) and neither of them can be in group 3 (clue 1). Since group 3 cannot have L (clue 4) and now cannot have T or P, that leaves just S and R to be the two flowers that groups 2 and 3 have in common (clue 2). There is nothing restricting group 2 from having more flowers, but the list cannot include L (clue 4). You are looking for a list of one potential flower combination that could occur in group 2. Since the group must include S and R, you can eliminate (A), (B), (C), and (D), leaving (E) as the credited response.

22. **A** General

Use the deductions, prior work, and trying the answers to determine which answer choice CANNOT be the only flowers in group 2.

A. Yes. This cannot work since groups 2 and 3 must have two flowers in common (clue 2) and L cannot be in group 3 (clue 4).

B. No. If group 2 has P and T, then group 3 must also have P and T (clue 2) and group 1 cannot (clue 1). Group 1 can still have L and R, so this could work.

C. No. This combination was in group 2 in question 23. If P, R, and S are the flowers in group 2, then S must be one of the shared flowers in group 3. Group 3 cannot have more than 2 flowers though since group 1 cannot have any flowers in common with group 3 (clue 1). So, if group 3 has R, then group 1 can have T and P, and if group 3 has P, then group 1 can have L and R. This could work.

D. No. This combination was in group 2 in question 19.

E. No. If group 2 contains P, R, S, and T, then group 3 can have only two of those flowers (clue 2) and it already has S (clue 3). It cannot have T since that will require it to also have P (clue 5), but it can have P without T, as seen in question 20. This would leave L and R to be in group 1, so this could work.

23. **C** General

Use the deductions, prior work, and trying the answers to determine which answer choice must be false.

A. No. This combination could be true as seen in question 20.

B. No. This combination could be true as seen in question 21.

C. Yes. If group 2 has L, P, and R, then group 3 will have to have P and R along with S since it cannot have L (clue 4). This means that group 1 cannot have S, P, or R (clue 1). All that remains is T, which needs P to be with it (clue 5), or L, which needs R to be with it (clue 4). This combination does not work.

D. No. This combination was seen in question 22.

E. No. This combination was seen in question 20.

Section 4: Arguments 2

1. **D** **Weaken**

   The argument concludes that chocolate interferes with one's ability to taste coffee. This is based on an experiment of ten people in which a group of five people who ate chocolate with coffee were unable to taste differences, while those that did not have chocolate were able to taste differences. The argument assumes that there is no other factor that caused the chocolate group to taste no difference and that the study was valid. The credited response will hurt the conclusion.

   A. No. Random assignment despite group requests would not address the validity of the study and would not hurt the conclusion.

   B. No. This would strengthen the argument by improving the validity of the study.

   C. No. The state of matter of each item in the study is not relevant to the validity of the study.

   D. Yes. This would hurt the conclusion because it would indicate that chocolate was not the cause of the inability to taste the difference in chocolate.

   E. No. The significance of the difference is not relevant to determining whether there was a noticeable difference.

2. **D** **Principle Strengthen**

   The argument states that residents are opposed to the building of a large house because it will alter the pristine landscape and hence damage the community's artistic and historic heritage despite the fact that the house will not violate any town codes. The credited response will help the reasoning by providing a rule that indicates a house that would alter the artistic heritage of a community should not be built.

   A. No. There is no mention of historic buildings in the argument.

   B. No. Since the purchase of the land by the community is not mentioned in their argument against the building of the house, this choice would not help their argument.

   C. No. The argument is about the community opposing the building on the land, not the artist, so this rule would not support the community's argument.

   D. Yes. If this is true, then the community would be supported in their claim that the family should not build the house.

   E. No. There is no mention that the building of the house would limit access to historic sites.

3. **E** **Flaw**

   Moore argues that sunscreens, which are designed to block skin-cancer-causing ultraviolet radiation, do not do so effectively because people who use these products develop as many skin cancers as those who do not use them. The argument assumes that people who use these products would not develop more skin cancers if they did not use the sunscreen.

   A. No. The argument's conclusion is specifically about the ability of sunscreen lotions to block skin-cancer-causing UV radiation.

B. No. The severity of the cases of skin cancer are not relevant to whether the sunscreens block skin-cancer-causing UV radiation.

C. No. The argument's conclusion is specifically about the ability of sunscreen lotions that claim to block skin-cancer-causing UV radiation.

D. No. The evidence used to support the claim is not based on probability since it is based on actual numbers of people with skin cancers.

E. Yes. The argument assumes that the people who use the sunscreen lotions in question do not have more instance of skin-cancer-causing experiences.

4. C   Reasoning

The psychologist disagrees with a position held by some people that Freudian psychotherapy is most effective because it is difficult and time-consuming. The psychologist offers another situation in which the same explanation would be invalid. The credited response will describe the psychologist's argument by pointing out that it uses a comparison.

A. No. The psychologist does not offer a contradictory principle.

B. No. The psychologist does not attack the premises of the argument with which he disagrees.

C. Yes. The psychologist uses an analogy to make the argument.

D. No. The psychologist uses an analogy in his own argument but does not claim that the point with which he disagrees is based on a similar analogy.

E. No. The psychologist does not address a causal argument.

5. A   Main Point

The argument claims that biodiversity does not require the survival of every currently existing species because while biodiversity requires there to be various ecological niches that must be filled, many niches can be filled by more than one species. The credited response will match the conclusion of the argument.

A. Yes. This matches the conclusion of the argument.

B. No. This is a premise.

C. No. This is a premise.

D. No. This is a premise.

E. No. The argument does not mention any specific species that fill multiple niches.

6. E   Evaluate

The clinician argues that patients should take this new drug in addition to the drug that helps to pre-serve existing bone. This conclusion is based on premises that state that a new drug that helps grow bone cells has been developed and that patients with immune disorders take drugs that increase the risk of osteoporosis. The argument assumes that these patients need to grow bone cells in addition to preserving existing bone and that the combination of the drugs would not impede the effectiveness in curing osteoporosis.

A. No. The size of the class of drugs that increase the risk of osteoporosis is not relevant to the question of whether patients need to grow bone in addition to preserving existing bone.

B. No. The reason patients take drugs that cause osteoporosis is not relevant to the question of whether patients need to grow bone in addition to preserving existing bone.

C. No. The price of the drug is not relevant to the question of whether patients need to grow bone in addition to preserving existing bone.

D. No. The length of time of use of a drug is not relevant to the question of whether patients need to grow bone in addition to preserving existing bone.

E. Yes. The answer to this question would provide information about the assumption that would allow you to evaluate the argument.

7. **E**   **Principle Match**

The critic argues that while the city's concert hall is located on a hilltop, it does not fulfill the purpose of a civic building because it is located far from the city center. The art museum that is in a densely populated area is a more successful civic building that promotes social cohesion and makes the city more alive. The credited response will be a rule that matches the argument.

A. No. While the passage mentions the "city on a hill," it does not indicate that civic buildings should be situated on an elevated location.

B. No. The passage is about what makes a civic building successful.

C. No. The passage does not indicate that the spectacular site is connected to a building's success.

D. No. The passage is not about how a downtown should be designed.

E. Yes. This matches the passage that says that the art museum is a more successful civic building and that it promotes social cohesion.

8. **D**   **Inference**

The passage states that fluoride enters a region's groundwater when rain dissolves fluoride-bearing minerals in the soil and that fluoride concentrations in groundwater are significantly higher in areas where the groundwater also contains a high concentration of sodium.

A. No. There is no evidence that fluoride comes from other sources.

B. No. The study held rainfall constant, so there is no way to know if rainfall has an effect on fluoride concentrations in groundwater.

C. No. Since the passage does not indicate why concentrations of fluoride and sodium were higher in some places, there is no evidence that sodium-bearing minerals dissolve faster than fluoride-bearing minerals.

D. Yes. Since fluoride is elevated in locations that have high concentrations of sodium, and fluoride enters groundwater by dissolving, it must be true that sodium increases the amount of fluoride that is dissolved.

E. No. There is no mention of a pathway for sodium to enter groundwater in a region, so it cannot be known whether sodium-bearing minerals are present in a location based on the text of the passage.

9. D — Reasoning

The argument concludes that Fraenger's assertion is unlikely to be correct. Fraenger's assertion is that Bosch belonged to the Brethren of the Free Spirit. This is based on premises that state that there is evidence that Bosch was a member of a mainstream church, and no evidence that he was a member of the Brethren. The credited response will indicate that sentence in question is a premise.

A. No. The sentence is a premise, but there is no guarantee of the falsity of Fraenger's assertion.

B. No. That there is evidence Bosch was a member of a mainstream church is a premise.

C. No. The argument does not question Fraenger's credibility.

D. Yes. The argument states that there no evidence that he was a member of the Brethren as a note that the evidence to support Fraenger's assertion is insufficient.

E. No. The argument does not attempt to say that Bosch's choice of subject matter remains unexplained.

10. E — Flaw

The salesperson concludes that the Super XL vacuum is a better vacuum because it picked up dirt that was left behind by the other vacuum. The argument assumes that the Super XL vacuum would have picked up the dirt the other vacuum picked up in addition to the extra dirt that was picked up by the Super XL.

A. No. The argument does not assume that the Super XL picked up all dirt, only that it picked up dirt the other vacuum did not.

B. No. The argument does not assume that the Super XL will be a better vacuum cleaner in the future.

C. No. The argument does not state that Super XL is the best vacuum cleaner available.

D. No. The argument does not compare the relative amounts of dirt picked up by the two vacuum cleaners to determine the better cleaner.

E. Yes. In stating that the Super XL is better because it picked up dirt left behind by the other vacuum cleaner, the author assumes that the other vacuum cleaner would not have performed better had the order of cleaning been reversed.

11. B — Main Point

The manager argues that it would be irresponsible not to address today a problem that will occur in the future. The manager bases the argument on an analogy that a financial planner who made a similar argument about not worrying about a future problem would be guilty of malpractice.

A. No. This is a premise.

B. Yes. This matches the conclusion.

C. No. This is a premise.

D. No. The argument makes an analogy to financial planners that is a premise.

E. No. The manager is not making an argument about what financial planners should advise.

12. A **Inference**

The passage states that more books were sold worldwide last year than any previous year and that most of these books were cookbooks, and rather than books for beginners, more cookbooks than ever were purchased by professional cooks. Additionally, one of only a few books available on all continents is a cookbook for beginners. The credited response will be supported by the text of this passage.

A. Yes. This must be true if "For the first time ever, most of the cookbooks sold were not intended for beginners."

B. No. There is no evidence that the book available on all continents was the best-selling cookbook.

C. No. There is no evidence that sales of cookbooks for beginners was not also higher than previous years despite the claim that more cookbook sales were not for beginners. It is possible that the overall sales of cookbooks was significantly greater than in previous years and that both books for beginners and books for professionals increased (and that sales of books for professionals increased at a greater rate).

D. No. There is no mention of other types of books, but it is possible that books not purchased for beginners were predominantly purchased by experienced home cooks.

E. No. The passage does not state how many copies of *Problem-Free Cooking* were sold.

13. B **Necessary Assumption**

The argument states that any methane in the Martian atmosphere must have been released into the atmosphere relatively recently. This is based on premises that state that scientists detected methane in the atmosphere of Mars and that Methane is a fragile compound that falls apart when hit by the ultraviolet radiation in sunlight. The argument assumes that ultraviolet radiation in sunlight would destroy methane on Mars that was not released relatively recently.

A. No. The argument does not make any claims about the atmosphere on Mars prior to discovery of Methane there in 2003.

B. Yes. This is required by the argument. Use the Negation Test. If not all methane in the Martian atmosphere is exposed to sunlight, then it not necessary for Methane to have been released recently since it might not break down due to radiation.

C. No. The argument assumes that the methane on Mars had not fallen apart due to UV radiation.

D. No. The argument indicates that Methane exposed to UV radiation would fall apart, so it does not assume that the Methane on Mars had been exposed.

E. No. What happens to methane in Earth's atmosphere is not relevant to the argument about methane on Mars.

14. C **Inference**

The environmentalist states that consumers would pollute less if gasoline prices were higher because the cost of pollution from gasoline burned by cars is not included in the price of gasoline so does not affect consumer's decisions to drive. The credited response will be supported by the text of this passage.

A. No. The author does not indicate a reason why the cost of pollution should be built into the price of gasoline, only that if it were, that consumers would pollute less.

B. No. The environmentalist does not state a reason that higher taxes would cause consumers to pollute less, only that it will.

C. Yes. This must be true since higher taxes would reflect the cost of pollution and that these higher taxes would cause a reduction in pollution.

D. No. There may be other factors considered by drivers such as length of time in the car or amount of wear and tear on the vehicle. All that is known is that pollution caused by gasoline is NOT a factor since it is not included in the cost of gasoline.

E. No. The passage provides one way to accomplish a reduction in pollution but does not indicate that it is the only way to reduce pollution.

15. **A**   Resolve/ Explain

The argument states that the larvae of Hine's dragonfly survives in water where they are subject to predation by species including the red devil crayfish. At the same time, the dragonfly populations are more likely to be healthy in areas where red devil crayfish are present. The credited response will explain why populations are more likely to be healthy in areas with red devil crayfish.

A. Yes. If the crayfish dig holes that fill with water, the larvae that are not preyed on could survive when the surrounding areas dry up.

B. No. This would not explain why the total population is healthier when a species that preys upon larva is present.

C. No. This would make the problem worse by eliminating a possible reason that larva survive in areas with red devil crayfish: that the crayfish eliminate other threats to the larva.

D. No. The fact that the red devil crayfish is found in locations where Hine's dragonflies do not exist does not explain why the dragon flies are healthier in areas where both are located.

E. No. This fact alone does not explain why the dragonfly populations are more likely to be healthy in areas where red devil crayfish are present. It would need to assume the red devil crayfish prefer to prey on other species than Hine's dragonfly.

16. **E**   Inference

The passage states that stress is a common cause of high blood pressure, that some people can lower their blood pressure by calming their minds, and that most people can calm their minds by engaging in exercise. The credited response will be supported by this text.

A. No. The passage does not state that blood pressure causes or relieves stress.

B. No. The passages states that some people can do this, but there is no evidence that most people with high blood pressure could do so.

C. No. The passage indicates that exercise can help reduce stress, but it does not state that a lack of exercise causes higher stress.

D. No. The passage states that exercise can cause some people to calm their minds and thereby reduce stress, which can cause a reduction in blood pressure. The relationship between exercise and blood pressure is therefore not a direct one.

E.   Yes. This must be true since exercise can cause some people to calm their minds and thereby reduce stress, which can cause a reduction in blood pressure.

17. **C**

The argument states that soot itself probably does not cause a certain ailment since cities with large amounts of soot in the air usually have high concentrations of other pollutants. The argument assumes that other pollutants could be the cause of the ailment.

A.   No. This would strengthen the argument by proving that other pollutants are more likely the cause of the ailment.

B.   No. The argument says the opposite of this is true.

C.   Yes. This would weaken the argument by showing that other pollutants are not likely the cause of the ailment since the ailment occurs in areas that do not contain other pollutants.

D.   No. This would strengthen the argument by showing that other pollutants could be the cause of the ailment.

E.   No. This would strengthen the argument by showing that other pollutants could be the cause of the ailment.

18. **C**   Parallel Flaw

The argument claims that it will probably rain in the valley in the next week because there has been no rain in the valley this summer, there is usually a few inches of rainfall each summer, and there is only one week left in summer. The argument assumes that what is usually true of a summer will probably be true of this summer. The credited response will make a similar assumption.

A.   No. This argument says that there are *sometimes* errors and that there *may* be errors in the unchecked pages, which does not match the original argument.

B.   No. This argument claims that there are no errors in the unchecked pages despite the fact that there are generally few errors. This is the opposite of the claim the original argument makes.

C.   Yes. This argument claims that there are usually errors in the pages of the magazine and that there will probably be errors in the unchecked pages. This matches the original argument.

D.   No. This argument states that there are usually no errors and there probably won't be errors in a future issue. This argument has a comparison flaw, which does not match the original argument.

E.   No. This argument assumes that since Aisha has found no errors, that she is mistaken, not that there are likely errors in unchecked pages; this does not match.

19. **B**   Necessary Assumption

The argument claims that we must enable our children to believe that better futures are possible. This is based on premises that state that young people believe efforts to reduce pollution, poverty, and war are doomed to failure; that people lose motivation to work for goals they think are unrealizable, and we must do what we can to prevent this loss of motivation; and that pessimism is probably harmful to humanity's future. The argument assumes that enabling children to believe that better futures are possible will prevent the loss of motivation that is harmful to our future.

A. No. The author's argument does not address how he or she believes we can enable children to believe in better futures.

B. Yes. Use the Negation Test. If enabling people will not prevent the loss of motivation, then there is no valid reason to say that we must enable people to believe in better futures.

C. No. Optimism about an illusory future is not directly relevant to enabling children to believe in better futures.

D. No. The author's argument does not address the need to eliminate war, poverty, or pollution.

E. No. The author makes no assumptions about the reasons for current war or poverty.

20. **D**   Strengthen

The argument concludes that glutamate leaking from damaged or oxygen-starved nerve cells is a cause of long-term brain damage resulting from strokes. This conclusion is based on premises that state that those who showed continued deterioration of the nerve cells in the brain after the stroke also had the highest levels of glutamate in their blood and that glutamate can kill surrounding nerve cells if it leaks from damaged or oxygen-starved nerve cells. There is a language shift that shows that the argument assumes that the glutamate in the blood is leaked from damaged or oxygen-starved nerve cells.

A. No. Other types of neurotransmitters are not relevant to the argument about glutamate.

B. No. This would weaken the claim by offering other possible reasons for long-term brain damage.

C. No. Other neurotransmitters that leak from damaged or oxygen-starved nerve cells are not relevant to the argument about glutamate.

D. Yes. If the only source for the increased glutamate in the blood of patients is from leaking damaged or oxygen-starved nerve cells, then it is more likely that the glutamate in these patients is causing long-term brain damage.

E. No. The author does not make any assumptions about the cells that leak glutamate.

21. **E**   Parallel

The argument concludes that if the next song Amanda writes is not a blues song, it probably will not involve more than three chords. This is based on premises that state that the only songs Amanda has ever written are blues songs and punk rock songs and that most punk rock songs involve no more than three chords. The credited response will match this argument.

A. No. This does not match because the beginning of the conclusion that refers positively to parrots instead of saying "not a fish."

B. No. This argument does not match because it draws a conclusion about pets the Gupta family has already owned rather than a pet they will own in the future.

C. No. This does not match because it draws a conclusion about any pet the Gupta family will ever own and not just the next pet the Gupta family owns.

D. No. This does not match because the conclusion should refer to a parrot by saying "not a fish."

E. Yes. This matches the structure of the original argument.

22. **D** Resolve/ Explain

The argument states that advertising usually has a greater influence on consumer preferences on yogurt than on milk but that LargeCo's advertising has increased sales of its milk brand more than its yogurt brand. The credited response will explain the difference for LargeCo.

A. No. Since there is no information about milk, this does not explain why the advertising caused a greater increase in the sale of its milk brand than its yogurt.

B. No. Since there is no information about how the advertising impacts shoppers, this does not explain why the advertising caused a greater increase in the sale of its milk brand than its yogurt.

C. No. Since both milk and yogurt are dairy products, this does not explain why the advertising caused a greater increase in the sale of its milk brand than its yogurt.

D. Yes. A national trend away from the sale of yogurt would correspond with a similar trend at LargeCo and could explain why the advertising caused a greater increase in the sale of its milk brand than its yogurt.

E. No. Since both the milk and yogurt in question are store brand, this does not explain why the advertising caused a greater increase in the sale of its milk brand than its yogurt.

23. **E** Principle Strengthen

The problem states that Shayna will either misrepresent her feelings toward Daniel or hurt his feelings. The principle states that one should not be insincere except possibly when the recipient would prefer kindness to honesty. The credited response will show how Shayna may choose to misrepresent her feelings in order to avoid hurting Daniel's feelings as long as Daniel prefers kindness to honesty.

A. No. The principle requires that Shayna believe Daniel prefers kindness to honesty to congratulate him and this is not known based on this answer choice.

B. No. The principle requires that Shayna believe Daniel prefers kindness to honesty to congratulate him and this is not known based on this answer choice.

C. No. The principle requires that Shayna believe Daniel prefers kindness to honesty to congratulate him and this is not known based on this answer choice.

D. No. The principle requires that Shayna believe Daniel prefers kindness to honesty to congratulate him and this is not known based on this answer choice.

E. Yes. In this case, Shayna does not believe Daniel prefers kindness to honesty so it would be inappropriate for her to congratulate him and misrepresent her feelings.

24. **E** Sufficient Assumption

The argument concludes that a democracy cannot thrive without effective news media. This is based on premises that state that a democracy cannot thrive without an electorate that is knowledgeable about important political issues, and an electorate can be knowledgeable in this way only if it has access to unbiased information about the government. The argument assumes that because one way to achieve the goal of having a knowledgeable electorate is to have an effective news media, that such a news media is required in order to have a knowledgeable electorate.

A. No. This choice does not improve the argument because it does not address the necessary/ sufficient relationship between having a knowledgeable electorate and having an effective news media.

B. No. This choice does not improve the argument because it does not address the necessary/ sufficient relationship between having a knowledgeable electorate and having an effective news media.

C. No. This choice does not improve the argument because it does not address the necessary/ sufficient relationship between having a knowledgeable electorate and having an effective news media.

D. No. This choice does not improve the argument because it does not address the necessary/ sufficient relationship between having a knowledgeable electorate and having an effective news media.

E. Yes. This choice proves that an effective news media is required to have a knowledgeable electorate.

25. E   **Flaw**

The argument concludes that Roberta is almost certainly irritable because she is irritable and loses things only when she is tired and she's been yawning all day and lost her keys. The argument would correctly conclude that Roberta is tired, but in concluding that she is irritable, the argument assumes that she is always irritable when she's tired (which may or may not be true based on the facts of the argument).

A. No. The argument would correctly conclude that Roberta is tired since she lost her keys and she loses things only when she is tired.

B. No. The conclusion confuses necessary and sufficient conditions, but it is not circular.

C. No. The argument uses what is always true to make a conclusion about a specific instance.

D. No. The argument does not confuse necessary and sufficient around losing things. It would properly conclude that because Roberta lost her keys that she is tired.

E. Yes. The premises state that she is irritable only when she is tired, but the conclusion states that because she is tired, she must be irritable.

26. A   **Necessary Assumption**

The argument concludes that using genetically engineered crops more widely is likely to help wildlife populations to recover. This is based on premises that state that crops genetically engineered to produce toxins that enable them to resist insect pests do not need to be sprayed with insecticides and that excessive spraying of insecticides has harmed wildlife populations near croplands. The argument assumes that there are no downsides to the possible solution of using more genetically engineered crops.

A. Yes. This choice helps the argument by providing the assumption. Use the Negation Test. If using more genetically engineered crops would not result in less harm to wildlife, it would be inappropriate to claim that genetically engineered crops will help wildlife populations.

B.   No. The ability of wildlife populations to recover without genetically engineered crops is not relevant to the argument about genetically engineered crops helping wildlife populations to recover.

C.   No. This choice is too extreme. Use the Negation Test—the fact that crops could sometimes be sprayed with insecticides would not hurt the argument because it might reduce the overall amount of insecticides.

D.   No. The costs of pesticides are not relevant.

E.   No. Use the Negation Test. Hypothetical situations are not assumed by the argument.

73

Chapter 4
PrepTest 74:
Answers and
Explanations

ANSWER KEY: PREPTEST 74

Section 1:
Arguments 1

1. C
2. C
3. B
4. C
5. C
6. A
7. E
8. A
9. E
10. E
11. D
12. E
13. A
14. D
15. E
16. D
17. A
18. A
19. A
20. E
21. B
22. E
23. D
24. B
25. D

Section 2:
Games

1. C
2. D
3. E
4. A
5. E
6. E
7. B
8. E
9. A
10. A
11. A
12. C
13. E
14. D
15. B
16. A
17. E
18. D
19. B
20. B
21. A
22. B
23. C

Section 3:
Reading
Comprehension

1. D
2. E
3. A
4. A
5. B
6. B
7. B
8. D
9. C
10. B
11. D
12. A
13. D
14. E
15. A
16. D
17. B
18. A
19. B
20. C
21. C
22. E
23. A
24. B
25. B
26. D
27. E

Section 4:
Arguments 2

1. B
2. C
3. E
4. D
5. D
6. B
7. A
8. B
9. B
10. C
11. A
12. D
13. D
14. A
15. C
16. E
17. E
18. E
19. C
20. D
21. A
22. C
23. E
24. D
25. A
26. B

EXPLANATIONS

Section 1: Arguments 1

1. **C**   `Sufficient Assumption`

This argument makes the claim that children should be dissuaded from reading Jones's books. This claim is based upon an analogy with candy, which has short-term benefits but is not sufficiently nourishing. The argument also states that candy diminishes one's taste for superior foods. The argument assumes that Jones's books share the same characteristics as candy. Thus, the credited answer will fill in the blank by stating that Jones's books have similar characteristics, but with regard to books and reading.

A. No. This answer focuses on the premise, eating candy, rather than the conclusion. It is irrelevant.

B. No. This answer is too extreme to match the conclusion in tone and scope.

C. Yes. Impeding appreciation for more challenging literature is analogous to losing one's taste for better-quality food.

D. No. Parents are not mentioned in the argument. This answer is irrelevant.

E. No. This answer is too extreme to match the conclusion in tone and scope.

2. **C**   `Strengthen`

The author hypothesizes that, in order to carve Parthenon's columns with identical bulges in the center, stonemasons might have referred to a scale drawing. This is based on the discovery of such a drawing etched into a temple at Didyma, which depicts a column surrounded by a grid. The grid allows the correct width to be found at every height of the column. The author assumes that the Parthenon's stonemasons would have had access to a scale drawing and that the drawing would have helped them carve the columns identically. The credited answer will provide additional evidence that the stonemasons used a scale drawing or that such a drawing would be useful.

A. No. Modern attempts are irrelevant to the conclusion.

B. No. The hypothesis states that stonemasons referred to a similar drawing to the one at Didyma, not necessarily the same drawing. This answer is irrelevant.

C. Yes. If scale drawings were commonly used, that increases the likelihood that the Parthenon's stonemasons would have used one. This is the credited answer.

D. No. The actual columns at Didyma are not relevant to the hypothesis.

E. No. The stonemasons' level of experience is not relevant to whether or not they referred to a scale drawing.

3. **B**   `Principle Match`

Match the answer choices to the editorialist's argument. The editorialist argues that the government should not fund essential health services with lottery revenues because those funds could decline in the future. The credited response will match this argument.

A. No. The discussion of essential versus non-essential services is not mentioned in the argument, so this does not match.

B. Yes. This matches the argument that says the government should not fund essential services with unreliable funding sources.

C. No. This does not match because the argument does not discuss all types of government services.

D. No. The argument discusses types of funding for essential services. A discussion of what is essential is not in question in the editorialist's argument.

E. No. The argument does not mention setting aside funds for shortfalls in the future.

4. **C**   **Strengthen**

The credited response for this Help question will improve the argument. The scientist hypothesizes that the heating of a squirrel's tail probably plays a role in repelling snakes. The scientist supports the hypothesis by noting that squirrel's puff and wag tails to repel snakes and that their tails heat up at the same time. The scientist also notes that snakes have infrared sensors that can detect body heat. In making the hypothesis, the scientist assumes that two things that are correlated have a causal relationship, so the credited response will support the argument by addressing this causal flaw.

A. No. A rattlesnake's ability to heat its tail is not relevant to whether a squirrel's heating of its tail plays a role in repelling snakes.

B. No. This does not address whether the heat in a squirrel's tail is designed to repel snakes.

C. Yes. This would help the argument by providing additional evidence that the heat in a squirrel's tail repel snakes.

D. No. Other predators are irrelevant to the argument about whether heat in a squirrel's tail repels snakes. It is possible, for instance, that heat in the tail repels snakes as well as other beasts.

E. No. A mammal's ability to sense heat is not relevant to the argument about whether heat in the tail will repel a reptile.

5. **C**   **Flaw**

This question asks you to describe a flaw in the argument. The critic argues that we should reject Fillmore's argument because Fillmore's conclusion is beneficial to Fillmore. The critic's argument is flawed because it assumes that a conclusion that is beneficial to its author is invalid without providing evidence for the conclusion's incorrectness. The credited response will describe this flaw.

A. No. The critic does not confuse necessary and sufficient clauses in the argument. The critic's argument is flawed because it does not provide evidence for the wrongness of Fillmore's argument.

B. No. The critic mentions that there is evidence that supports Fillmore's conclusion.

C. Yes. The only evidence the critic offers for Fillmore's wrongness is the fact that Fillmore's conclusion is self-beneficial.

D. No. The critic does not make appeals to another argument.

E. No. There are no inconsistent claims stated in the critic's argument.

6. **A** **Weaken**

The question asks you to weaken the conclusion so the credited response will hurt the argument. The argument concludes that the best approach to prescribing medicine would be to give patients a lower dose along with grapefruit juice. The author provides evidence that grapefruit juice has an effect on the absorption of medicine in which normal doses act like higher doses. This argument is flawed in that it assumes that grapefruit juice has no other effects on the drug's interaction with the body than to amplify the dose. The credited response will provide a reason that taking lower doses of some medicines with grapefruit juice is not the best medical approach.

A. Yes. This choice provides a reason not to take lower doses along with grapefruit juice. It weakens the argument by saying that the dose recommendation in the argument would be unreliable.

B. No. The cost of grapefruit juice is not relevant to the argument that the best medical approach is to take a lower dose of some medicines along with the juice.

C. No. The argument states that the chemical in grapefruit juice is the cause of the amplification of the drug absorption. The removal of the chemical from the juice is not relevant to the argument that the best medical approach is to take a lower dose of some medicines along with the juice.

D. No. The cause of the amplification of the drug absorption in grapefruit juice is not relevant to the question of the best medical approach of doses of some medicines along with the juice.

E. No. Doctor recommendations to avoid consuming grapefruit juice with some medications do not provide a medical reason that consuming grapefruit juice with a lower dose is not the best approach. To weaken the argument, an answer choice must provide a direct reason that the conclusion is wrong.

7. **E** **Principle Match**

The credited response should match the salesperson's argument as closely as possible. The salesperson advised that, given two equally priced options, the landlord should choose the option that was powerful enough rather than the option that was the most powerful option.

A. No. The advice in this choice does not match the salesperson's advice to choose the good enough option instead of the most powerful option.

B. No. This choice does not match the salesperson's advice because the two options in the argument are of equal price.

C. No. This choice does not match the salesperson's advice because the two options in the argument are of equal price.

D. No. This choice does not match the salesperson's advice because there is no mention of commission for the salesperson in the argument.

E. Yes. This choice matches the argument that suggests the good enough option over the most powerful option.

8. **A** **Necessary Assumption**

In this question, the credited response will help the argument by providing an assumption that is required by the argument. Use the Negation Test to confirm your answer choice. The argument concludes that focusing on the flaws of our leaders is a pointless distraction. The editorialist supports the conclusion by stating that the real question we should focus on is how our institutions and policies allow flawed leaders to get elected. There is a language shift between the "real question" in the evidence and "pointless distraction" in the conclusion. The credited response will connect these two things by stating directly that looking at the flaws of our leaders is not relevant to understanding how those leaders were elected.

A. Yes. This choice helps the argument by connecting the premises with the conclusion. Use the Negation Test. If examining the flaws of our leaders does reveal something about how institutions and procedures influence elections, then looking at these flaws is not a pointless distraction.

B. No. The relative rate of discussions of flawed leaders is not relevant to whether those discussions are pointless distractions.

C. No. This choice is not required by the argument. Use the Negation Test. If the procedures and institutions do not guarantee the election of flawed leaders, it may still be important to understand how they allow the election of flawed leaders.

D. No. Whether people have attempted to answer the real question is not relevant to whether looking at flawed leaders is a pointless distraction.

E. No. Satisfaction with the nation's leaders is not relevant to whether focusing on flawed leaders is a pointless distraction.

9. E **Resolve/ Explain**

In this question, the credited response will help the argument by providing an explanation for the seemingly disparate statements. The argument states that some doctors prescribe calcium supplements with lead despite the fact that lead is a dangerous substance even in small amounts.

A. No. The fact that lead is present in fruits and vegetables does not explain why doctors would prescribe calcium supplements that contain lead.

B. No. Removing lead from the body is not relevant to the fact that doctors sometimes prescribe calcium supplements with lead.

C. No. The fact that there are other potentially dangerous health concerns does not explain why doctors would prescribe calcium supplements with lead.

D. No. This choice does not explain the issue at hand. The fact that high calcium diets make small amounts of lead more dangerous makes the claim that doctors prescribe calcium supplements with lead even more contradictory.

E. Yes. This explains why some doctors would prescribe calcium supplements with lead over no supplement at all because the calcium supplements with lead may actually result in less lead in the bloodstream.

10. E **Principle Strengthen**

In this question, the credited response will help the argument by linking the principle to the conclusion in the application. The argument states that Matilde should not buy the vase for sale online because people should buy only antiques that can be authenticated and because the antique is intrinsically valuable. The credited response will show how this principle applies to Matilde specifically.

A. No. This choice does help because it does not state that Matilde finds the vase intrinsically valuable.

B. No. This choice does help because it does not state that Matilde finds the vase intrinsically valuable.

C. No. This choice is attractive, but it mistakes necessary and sufficient conditions. By addressing two factors that must be met in order to buy an antique, the principle does not actually address when someone should buy an antique. Instead, it points to two reasons that a buyer should not make a purchase.

D. No. This choice does not help because it does not state that Matilde has verified the authenticity of the vase.

E. Yes. Since Matilde cannot verify the authenticity of the vase, she should not buy it according to the principle.

11. **D** Inference

The credited response will be supported by information in the paragraph. The critic states that Waverly's textbook claims to be objective but that writing about art cannot be objective and that, in fact, Waverly writes better about art she likes than art she does not. The credited response will be supported by these facts.

A. No. The critic does not mention Waverly's views on art historians, so this is not supported by the text.

B. No. The critic does not mention that Waverly has strong opinions about the works in the textbook, so this is not supported by the text.

C. No. The critic states that Waverly intended to remain objective in writing her book.

D. Yes. The critic states that Waverly intended to remain objective in writing her book but that objectivity is impossible in writing about art. Therefore, Waverly failed to remain objective.

E. No. There is no evidence in the text that Waverly does not really believe she could be objective.

12. **E** Sufficient Assumption

The credited response will help the argument by proving that the conclusion is true based on the evidence. The argument concludes that the Sals did not smelt iron. This conclusion is based on evidence that there are smelting furnaces and tools for smelting copper and bronze and the Sals had words for copper and bronze but no words for iron. There is a language shift from the premises, which state that there are no words for iron, to a conclusion about not smelting iron.

A. No. This choice goes in the wrong direction. It states that having a word for something guarantees that it happened, but it does not help the argument that states that NOT having a word for something means it did not happen.

B. No. The familiarity of a culture with a metal is not relevant to the conclusion that the Sals did not smelt iron.

C. No. The link between words and actions for smelting copper and bronze is not directly connected to a link between not having a word for iron and the question of whether the Sals smelted iron.

D. No. The familiarity of a culture with a metal is not relevant to the conclusion that the Sals did not smelt iron.

E. Yes. This choice helps the argument by connecting the action of smelting a metal with having a word for that action.

13. **A** Main Point

This question asks for the main conclusion of the argument so the credited response will match the conclusion stated in the argument. The argument concludes that community organizations that want to enhance support for programs should convince the public that these programs are beneficial to society. This is based on premises that state that it is easier to get public support for a program that is seen to be beneficial to society than a program that is not.

A. Yes. This matches the conclusion of the argument.

B. No. This is a premise.

C. No. This is a premise.

D. No. This is a premise.

E. No. The argument does not explicitly state that higher education is beneficial to society. It states that showing people that it is would increase public support.

14. **D** Reasoning

The credited response will describe the role of the statement that the risk of satellites colliding will increase. The argument concludes that the risk of satellites colliding will increase in the future because a single collision will result in many fragments that will increase the risk of collision. The credited response will state that the claim in question is the conclusion.

A. No. The claim in question is the main conclusion of the argument. It does not support any other claims in the argument.

B. No. The claim in question is the main conclusion of the argument. It does not support any other claims in the argument.

C. No. The claim in question is the main conclusion of the argument. It does not support any other claims in the argument.

D. Yes.

E. No. The claim in question is the main conclusion of the argument. It does not support any other claims in the argument.

15. **E** Resolve/ Explain

In this question, the credited response will help the argument by providing an explanation for the seemingly disparate statements. The paragraph states that young chicks given a new treatment for *Salmonella* had a lower incidence of infection than chicks not given the new treatment. However, the chicks given the new treatment did have a higher concentration of some bacteria than those that were not.

A. No. If the treatment takes several weeks, this choice would not explain why the chicks had a lower incidence of infection.

B. No. This choice does not explain why chicks given the treatment had a lower incidence of infection but higher concentrations of bacteria.

C. No. The information about what happens in adulthood does not explain why young chicks had different concentrations of bacteria.

D. No. This choice does not explain why chicks who received the treatment had a lower incidence of infection but a higher concentration of some bacteria.

E. Yes. This choice explains why chicks who received treatment had a lower incidence of *Salmonella* and that this reduction in *Salmonella* bacteria simultaneously caused an increased concentration of other bacteria.

74

16. **D** [Flaw]

In this question, the credited response will hurt the respondent's argument by describing the problems with it. The respondent claims that the hierarchy present in lecturing is a strength based on premises that state that all teaching requires hierarchy. This argument is flawed in that it is based on a problematic comparison between hierarchy of information (arithmetic is simpler than calculus) and hierarchy of power (teacher is superior to student).

A. No. The respondent does not concede to any of the debater's assumptions.

B. No. The respondent does not mention teaching methods in any subject.

C. No. The respondent's argument is about the strength of the hierarchy, so other potential weaknesses are not relevant to the conclusion.

D. Yes. This choice points to the comparison flaw in the respondent's argument.

E. No. The problem is not that the hierarchy of information mentioned in the respondent's argument is not present outside of math. The flaw is that the hierarchy of information is not the same as the hierarchy of power.

17. **A** [Strengthen]

In this question, the credited response will help the argument by improving the evidentiary support for the conclusion. The argument concludes that Han purple was probably discovered by accident. This is based on evidence that states that the process of synthesizing Han purple uses the same ingredients as the process of producing white glass during the period. The argument is flawed because it does not provide evidence of the happenstance creation of Han purple, so the credited response will likely provide some concrete link between the glass production and the finding of Han purple.

A. Yes. This further links the creation of Han purple with the production of glass in the region.

B. No. This choice shows how Han purple and glass are different, thereby hurting the conclusion.

C. No. This choice shows how Han purple and glass are different, thereby hurting the conclusion.

D. No. While this information shows a similarity between Han purple and glass, it does not provide additional evidence that the two are related other than their similar ingredients.

E. No. The relative occurrence of Han purple and glass is not relevant to whether Han purple was discovered by accident during the creation of glass.

18. **A** `Flaw`

In this question, the credited response will hurt the argument by describing the flaw in the argument. The medical researcher concludes that mild sleep deprivation is not unhealthy, but may instead bolster the body's defense systems. This is based on evidence from a survey that showed that people who get at least 8 hours of sleep have more illness than those that sleep significantly less. This argument is flawed in that the survey does not prove a causal relationship between sleep and illness. It also fails to show that those who get significantly less sleep suffer from "mild sleep deprivation."

A. Yes. This choice describes the causal flaw in the argument.

B. No. The medical researcher does not show that sleep is one of the factors in the frequency of illness.

C. No. There is no evidence that getting at least 8 hours of sleep is sufficient to cause illness.

D. No. This choice goes in the wrong direction.

E. No. Other negative impacts of getting at least 8 hours of sleep are not relevant to whether getting that amount of sleep causes a greater frequency of illness.

19. **A** `Parallel`

In this question, the credited response will match the structure of the original argument. The argument concludes that temperatures did not drop below freezing last week based on the premises that state that if the temperatures had dropped below freezing last week, then the impatiens would have died and not continued to bloom. However, the impatiens did continue to bloom. The structure shows that A → B and B → C and given that ~C we can conclude ~A. The credited response will match this structure.

A. Yes. This argument follows the structure of the original argument.

B. No. This argument does not match because it states that A → B and B → C and given ~C we can conclude ~B.

C. No. The premises of this argument do not match the A → B and B → C structure of the premises in the original argument.

D. No. This argument concludes what should or should not be done rather than what is or is not true, so it does not match the original argument.

E. No. This argument concludes what should or should not be done rather than what is or is not true, so it does not match the original argument.

74

20. **E** **Sufficient Assumption**

In this question, the credited response will help the argument by proving its conclusion is true based on the premises. The argument concludes that building the new convention center will increase tax revenues because several large organizations will hold conferences in the new convention center. There is a shift from several national organizations holding conferences to the fact that several large conferences will take place at the convention center. The credited response will show that large organizations hold large conferences.

A. No. The argument does not discuss other ways to increase tax revenue.

B. No. The argument does not mention how increased numbers of visitors will increase tax revenue.

C. No. Other ways to increase tax revenues is not relevant to increase revenue due to the convention center.

D. No. The argument states that large conventions will cause increased numbers of visitors, so it does not need for current visitors to continue to visit in order to gain an increase in tax revenue.

E. Yes. This choice shows a link between national organizations and large conventions.

21. **B** **Evaluate**

The credited response will mention information that is missing from the argument that would help in evaluating the argument. The argument states that dogs have an aversion to being treated unfairly because the dog that did not receive a reward stopped obeying commands. The argument assumes that the dog stopped obeying due to unfair treatment, so it would be helpful to know why the dog stopped obeying commands.

A. No. The likelihood of obeying the initial command is not relevant to the discussion of dogs that stopped obeying the command after not receiving a reward.

B. Yes. This would provide additional information about why the dogs stopped obeying command by showing whether the unfair treatment has the same result as equally not giving rewards.

C. No. Differences outside of the trials are not relevant to why dogs in this trial stopped obeying commands.

D. No. Dogs that became more inclined to obey are not relevant to understanding why dogs stopped obeying commands.

E. No. The number of repetitions is not relevant to understanding why dogs stopped obeying commands.

22. **E** **Inference**

In this question, the credited response will be supported by the facts of the argument in the text. The argument states that a survey shows that people's satisfaction with income depends largely on how that income compares to their neighbors and not with the amount they make. The passage also states that people live in neighborhoods of people in the same economic class. The credited response will use this information.

74

A. No. This is not supported by the text, which states that people's satisfaction with their income is not strongly correlated with the amount they make.

B. No. This is not supported by the text since the text does not distinguish between age groups.

C. No. This is contradicted by the text, which states that people live in neighborhoods that are in their same economic class and that amount of income is not strongly correlated with satisfaction. Therefore, neighborhood should not strongly correlate to satisfaction.

D. No. The passage does not show the relative impact of satisfaction of income with satisfaction of life as a whole.

E. Yes. If satisfaction is correlated most strongly with income equality, increasing everyone's will not impact equality and will therefore not impact overall satisfaction.

23. **D**   Weaken

In this question, the credited response will hurt the conclusion by attacking the flaw in the argument. The geologist argues that people who argue against the dominant view of petroleum formation are incorrect because they are refuted by the presence of petroleum in biomarkers. The argument is flawed because it fails to link the presence of petroleum in biomarkers to proof that petroleum deposits were formed by fossilized remains instead of carbon deposits around at the formation of Earth.

A. No. The presence of biomarkers in fossils is not relevant to whether the presence of petroleum in biomarkers proves that petroleum came from living creatures and not carbon deposits.

B. No. The rise of living organisms is not relevant to whether the presence of petroleum in biomarkers proves that petroleum came from living creatures and not carbon deposits.

C. No. This fact does not address the argument against the dominant view of petroleum formation.

D. Yes. This would weaken the argument by linking the presence of petroleum in biomarkers to the presence of carbon deposits deep in the earth. This would show that the evidence does not weaken the argument put forth by people who go against the dominant view of petroleum formation.

E. No. This does not link the presence of petroleum in biomarkers to the view that petroleum was formed by carbon deposits deep in the earth.

24. **B**   Inference

In this question, the credited response will be an inference that is supported by the text in the argument. The passage states that drivers in accidents that cause personal injury or more than $500 in property damage must report the accident to the DMV unless they are incapable of doing so and that Ted was a driver in an accident who does not need to report the accident.

A. No. There is no evidence that Ted was injured or that his injury would be linked to a small amount of property damage.

B. Yes. If Ted's property was damaged more than $500, he would be required to report the accident unless he's incapable of doing so. Since the text says he does not need to report the accident, it must be true that any accident he is in that causes more than $500 in property damage also causes him to be incapable of reporting said accident.

C.   No. There is no evidence that Ted's accident caused personal injury or more than $500 in property damage.

D.   No. There is no evidence that a person must be incapable of reporting an accident due to injury.

E.   No. There is no evidence that Ted is not incapable of reporting his accident to the DMV.

25.   **D**   Parallel Flaw

In this question, the credited response will match the flaw of the original argument. The student states that people who have an immunity to a microorganism will not have harmful symptoms from that microorganism and concludes based on this that a person who does not develop harmful symptoms must have an immunity. This argument confuses a sufficient condition (having an immunity leads to a certain situation) with a necessary condition (that a certain situation must be due to immunity). The credited response will also confuse a sufficient condition with a necessary condition.

A.   No. This does not confuse necessary and sufficient conditions. The flaw in this choice is that the conclusion contradicts the original premise.

B.   No. This argument has a comparison flaw. It assumes that two groups that are dissimilar in one way are dissimilar in another way.

C.   No. This choice does not contain a flaw.

D.   Yes. This choice confuses a sufficient condition (excessive taxation leads to decline in expansion) with a necessary condition (a decline in expansion must be caused by excessive taxation).

E.   No. This does not confuse necessary and sufficient conditions. The flaw in this choice is that it assumes that because doctors are less likely to perform an activity that the activity does not impact health.

Section 2: Games

Questions 1–5

This is a 1D ordering game with range clues, so it a ranking game. The inventory consists of six musicians—G, K, P, S, T, and V—with 1-to-1 correspondence and no wildcards.

Clue 1. G ≠ 4

Clue 2. P—K

Clue 3. V—K—G

Clue 4. P—S—T or T—S—P

Combine clues 2, 3, and 4 to get two possible arrangements.

In one scenario, you know that P cannot be third, fourth, fifth, or sixth. G cannot be first, second, third, or fourth (rule 1), so it must be either fifth or sixth. You also know that S cannot be first or last, and since G must be fifth or sixth and T must be after S, that S cannot be fifth either. T cannot be first or second and K cannot be first, second, or fifth. V cannot be fourth or fifth. This means that P must be first or second, G must be fifth or sixth, and the sixth spot must be either T or G.

In the other scenario, K and G must be fifth and sixth, respectively, and V can be first, second, third, or fourth, so that means that T must be first or second, S must be second or third, and P must be third or fourth.

Your diagram should look like this:

G, K, P, S, T, V

Clue 1: G ≠ 4
Clue 2: P—K
Clue 3: V—K—G
Clue 4: P—S—T
        or
        T—S—P

1. **C** Grab-a-Rule

   A. No. This violates rule 1 because G is fourth.

   B. No. This violates rule 4 because both T and P are before S.

   C. Yes. This choice does not violate any rules.

   D. No. This violates rule 2 because K is before P.

   E. No. This violates rule 2 because K is before P.

2. **D** Specific

   Make a new line in your diagram and add the new information. If P is before S, then you need the first setup noted above.

   A. No. This is possible according to the first setup, but it doesn't have to be true. P could be first or second.

   B. No. This is possible according to the first setup, but it doesn't have to be true. P could be first or second.

   C. No. This is possible according to the first setup, but it doesn't have to be true. V could be before or after S.

   D. Yes. According to rule 4, P and T cannot both be before S, so since P is before S, T must be after S.

   E. No. This is possible according to the first setup, but it doesn't have to be true. S could be before or after K.

3. **E** **General**

Use the deductions, prior work, and trying the answers to determine which answer choice could be true.

A. No. K cannot be first (rule 2).

B. No. According to the deductions, G must be fifth or sixth.

C. No. According to the deductions, G must be fifth or sixth and S cannot be fifth or sixth, so S must be before G.

D. No. By combining the second and third rules, you can deduce that since P is before K and K is before G, then P must be before G.

E. Yes. In the first setup, K can be before S.

4. **A** **General**

This question asks for who cannot be third. Looking at the deductions, G can never be third, and that happens to be (A), the credited response.

5. **E** **Specific**

Make a new line in your diagram and add the new information. If the violinist is fourth, then both setups could apply. Fill in what you know. For the first setup, K and G would have to be fifth and sixth (rule 3) and P, S, and T would have to be first, second, and third, respectively. For the second setup, K and G would still have to be fifth and sixth, and T, S, and P would have to be first, second, and third, respectively. In either case, S must be second, V must be fourth, K must be fifth, and G must be fifth. The only things that could be false are that T and P are first or third. This makes (E) the credited response.

Questions 6–10

This is a 2D order game. There are four historians—F, G, H, and J—each giving a different one of four lectures—L, O, S, and W. Since order matters, put 1 through 4 on top of the diagram and make one row for the historians and one for the lectures. The clues are all range clues and there is one wildcard, S.

Clue 1. O—L

W—L

Clue 2. F—O

Clue 3. H—G & H—J

From the first rule, note that L cannot be first or second and that both O and W cannot be fourth. From the second rule, note that F cannot be fourth, O cannot be first, and F cannot be with O. From the third rule, note that H cannot be third or fourth and that neither G nor J can be first. Combine the first and second rules to see that F—O—L so L cannot be second and F cannot be third. Since there are only four times, if H and F cannot be third or fourth, then they must both be either first or second, which means that G and J must be either third or fourth. Since L cannot be first or second, it must be third or fourth, and since the first lecture cannot be L or O, it must be S or W. Since the fourth lecture cannot be O or W, it must be L or S. This is actually a very restricted setup, and a little patience making deductions has a big payoff in being able to find the answers quickly.

Your diagram should look like this:

historian: F, G, H, J
lectures: L, O, S, W

	1	2	3	4
historian	~G ~J		~H ~F	~F ~H
lecture	~L ~O	~L		~O ~W

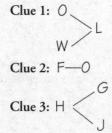

Clue 1: O
W L

Clue 2: F—O

Clue 3: H G
J

6. **E** Grab-a-Rule

A. No. This violates rule 1 since both O and W are after L.

B. No. This violates rule 3 since J is before H.

C. No. This violates rule 3 since H is after G.

D. No. This violates rule 2 since O is before F.

E. Yes. This arrangement does not violate any of the rules.

7. **B** General

Use the deductions, prior work, and trying the answers to determine what must be true.

A. No. Since S can be first, F does not have to be earlier than S.

B. Yes. From the deductions above, you know that H must be either first or second and that L must be either third or fourth. Thus, H must always be earlier than L.

C. No. Since S can be fourth, it does not have to be earlier than G.

D. No. Since S can be fourth, it does not have to be earlier than J.

E. No. Since W can be third, it can be with G and does not have to be earlier than G.

8. E   **Specific**

Make a new line in your diagram and fill in the information given. If W is third, then L must be fourth since L cannot be first or second (rule 1). Since O cannot be first (rule 2), that means it must be second, putting S first. Since F and H must be first and second, since O is second, that forces F into the first place (rule 2). That means H is second. J and G are interchangeable in the third and fourth spots. Cross off any answers that must be false since you are looking for what could be true. Choice (E) is the credited response.

9. A   **General**

Use the deductions, prior work, and trying the answers to determine what must be false.

A. Yes. From the deductions above, you know that F must be either first or second and that L must be third or fourth, so they can never be at the same time. This must be false.

B. No. From the deductions above, you know that S can be fourth and so can G, so it could be true that S and G are at the same time. Question 10 also pairs G with S.

C. No. It was possible for G to be with W in question 8.

D. No. H was at the same time as O in question 8.

E. No. It was possible for J to be with W in question 8.

10. A   **Specific**

Make a new line in your diagram and fill in the information given. If G and S are at the same time, then that must be either third or fourth. Since L must also be third or fourth (rule 1) and so must J (deduction), that means that G/S and L/W must fill the third and fourth times interchangeably. This leaves F, H, O, and W for the first and second times. Since F must be before O (rule 2), F and W are first and H and S are second. Eliminate answers that must be false.

A. Yes. If L is third, then S is fourth. This could be true.

B. No. O must be second so it cannot be third.

C. No. S is third or fourth with G. W must be first.

D. No. S is third or fourth with G. O must be second.

E. No. W must be first with F and O must be second with H.

Questions 11–16

This is a group game with fixed assignment. The diagram consists of three groups plus an out column. The inventory is six different colors, five of which are used in the three groups and one of which will be out. The clues are mainly spatial, conditional, and antiblock, and there are no wildcards.

Clue 1. W → W _ _ ; _ / _ _ → ~W

Clue 2. O → OP ; ~P → ~O

Clue 3. ~FT

Clue 4. ~PT

Clue 5. ~PY

The key to most grouping games is determining, if possible, how many spaces are in each group. Given that there are only five colors used over the three rugs, the number of colors per rug is limited to either: _ _|_ _|_ or _ _ _|_|_ . Don't forget, if W is used, it must go in group 3 (rule 1). In addition, any rug with O must have at least two colors due to rule 2. Combine rule 2 with rules 4 and 5 to deduce that T and O can never be together, and Y and O can never be together.

Make some deductions about each possible arrangement. For the _ _|_ _|_ arrangement, W is left out as per rule 1 and O and P make up one of the rugs with two colors. That leaves F, T, and Y to place. Since F and T can never be together (rule 3), one of them must be with Y in the other rug with two colors and the other must be alone. For the _ _ _|_|_ arrangement, either W is in the rug with three colors or W is out. If W is in, either O and P are with W, or O is out since it can't be alone (rule 2). This also means that with F, P, T, and Y left, then Y has to be with W as does one of F or T, and P must be a single-color rug. If W is out, then O and P have to be in the rug with three colors. Since O and P cannot be with T or Y, they must be with F, making T and Y the single-color rugs.

Your diagram should look like this:

	1	2	3	unused
Choose Five				
F, O, P, T, W, Y				
(1)	O P	F/T Y	T/F	W
(2)	_ _ _	_	_	_

Clue 1: W → W _ _

Clue 2: O → O P
         ~P → ~ O

Clue 3: F̶T

Clue 4: P̶T

Clue 5: P̶Y

11.   **A**   General

This is almost a Grab-A-Rule question, but it is missing the color that is left out. That's not too hard to keep track of, though, so this question operates like a true Grab-A-Rule.

A. Yes. This does not violate any rules.

B. No. This violates rule 5 by putting P and Y in the same rug.

C. No. This violates rule 2 because O is in a rug without P.

D. No. This violates rule 3 because F and T are in the same rug.

E. No. This violates rule 1 by having W in a two-color rug.

12. **C** General

Use the deductions, prior work, and trying the answers to determine which answer choice must be true.

A. No. This combination was used successfully in question 13. You also know from the deductions that F can be in a rug with W or with O and P, so it is possible.

B. No. This combination was used successfully in question 16, (B). You also know from deductions that F and T are somewhat interchangeable in the multicolored rugs with three colors.

C. Yes. If P is out, then O must be in, but O cannot be in without P (rule 2). This means that P must always be used.

D. No. Question 16, (C), worked with T not being used. If T is out, then W can be with O and P and the other two rugs can be F and Y.

E. No. It is possible for Y to be out. If Y is out, then W can be with O and P and the other two rugs can be F and T.

13. **E** Specific

Make a new line in your diagram and fill in the information given. If P is a single-color rug, then O is out. That means that W must be in a three-color rug. According to the deductions, this is the WY F/T | T/F | O combination. This makes (E) the credited response.

14. **D** Specific

Make a new line in your diagram and fill in the information given. With two solid rugs, then the third rug must have three colors. You are asked to determine which two colors cannot be the solid rugs. Prior work can cut down on your Process of Elimination time rather than trying out every answer.

A. No. F and P were used successfully as the two solid rugs in question 13.

B. No. If F and Y are the two solid rugs, then one possible combination is to have W with O and P in the multicolored rug and T out. This does not violate any rules.

C. No. P and T were used successfully as the two solid rugs in question 13.

D. Yes. If P and Y are the two solid rugs, F and T will be forced together in the same rug since O will have to be out (rule 2 and rule 3).

E. No. If T and Y are the two solid rugs, then one possible combination is to have W with O and P in the multicolored rug and F out.

15. **B** Specific

Make a new line in your diagram and fill in the information given. If F and P are in the same rug, then the OPF | T | Y | W (out) arrangement is in play. This makes (B) the credited response.

16. **A** Specific

Make a new line in your diagram and fill in the information given. If Y is a solid rug, then one of the _ _ _ | _ | _ arrangements must be used. This makes (A) the credited response since there cannot be exactly one solid rug.

Questions 17–23

This is a group game with fixed assignment since the inventory cannot be repeated. At least two of the six photographers available—F, G, H, K, L, and M—are assigned to one of two graduation ceremonies. Since not all the inventory has to be used, you also need an out column. The clues consist of a fixed choice clue and three conditional statements. There are no wildcards.

Clue 1. FH = in

Clue 2. L & M → ~LM

Clue 3. G = S → L = T; ~L = T → ~G = S

Clue 4. ~K = T → HM = T ; ~H = T or ~M = T → K = T

The key to most grouping games is determining, if possible, how many spaces are in each group. Since there must be at least two people assigned to each ceremony, the minimum number of the inventory used is four, leaving two to be either in or out. Since none of the clues force someone to be out, it is possible that all six people are used and that no one is out.

In addition, you can link together some of the clues. Clues 3 and 4 are both connected to clue 2. From clue 3, if G is in S, then L is in T. Now, take that to clue 2 to see that if L is in T, then M is either in S or out. Either way, K must then be in T (clue 4). The reverse of this is if K is not in T, then H, F, and M must all be in T (clues 4 and 1). Since M is in T, then L is either in S or out (clue 2), which means that G is either in T or out (clue 3).

Your diagram should look like this:

F, G, H, K, L, M

Clue 1: [FH] = S/T

Clue 2: [LM]

Clue 3: G = S → L = T

L ≠ T → G ≠ S

Clue 4: K ≠ T → [HM] = T

H ≠ T or M ≠ T → K = T

S	T	out
_ _	K/HM _	_

17. **E** `Grab-a-Rule`

    A.   No. This violates the third rule by having G and L assigned to the same group.

    B.   No. This violates rule 1 because F and H are not included.

    C.   No. This violates rule 2 since L and M are in the same group.

    D.   No. This violates rule 4 because K is not in T, which means M and H must be.

    E.   Yes. This does not violate any of the rules.

18. **D** `Specific`

Make a new line in your diagram and fill in the information given. If H is in the same group as L, then according to rule 1, F must also be in that group. From the deductions, the only way for H and L to be in the same group is in the first scenario. Be careful here—just because G in S guarantees that L is in T does not mean that L in T guarantees that G is in S. If L is in T, we know nothing about G—all we know is that M could be in S or be out and that K is in T. This makes (D) the credited response.

19. **B** `General`

Use the deductions, prior work, and trying the answers to determine which answer choice could be everyone assigned at the same time to group S.

    A.   No. According to the deductions, if G is in S then K is in T, and if K is in S, then G is either in T or out.

    B.   Yes. With G in S, F and H must be together, but they can be in either S or T, so this works.

    C.   No. According to the deductions, if G is in S then K is in T, and if K is in S, then G is either in T or out.

    D.   No. This would violate the rule that H and F must be in the same group.

    E.   No. This would violate the rule that if K is not in T, then both M and H must be in T.

20. **B** `General`

Use the deductions, prior work, and trying the answers to determine which answer choice includes everyone that can never be in the out column. From the initial deductions you know that G, L, and M can be out, so eliminate (C), (D), and (E). The difference between (A) and (B) is K. What happens if you try to put K in the out column? Well, according to rule 4, then H and M must be in T, and F has to be in T as well (rule 1). M in T means L could be in S or be out, and if L is not in T, then G must be in T or be out. This means that at most L is in T, and the setup says that there must be at least two people in each group. That means (B) is the credited response.

21. **A** `Specific`

Make a new line in your diagram and fill in the information given. If exactly four people are in, then two must be out. Since F and H must always be together in one of the groups, they must be there alone for this scenario. According to the deductions, if K is in S, then M, F, and H must all be in T. This won't work in this scenario, so K is in T, which means H and F are in S. Since the question asks for who must be in S, your work here is done; the credited response is (A).

22. **B** General

Use the deductions, prior work, and trying the answers to determine which answer choice contains a group of people who cannot be together in T.

A. No. This combination could work if K is in S based on the second scenario of the deductions.

B. Yes. This combination could never work. Since each group must have at least two people assigned, then with these four in T, G and L would be forced together in S, violating rule 3.

C. No. This combination worked in question 17.

D. No. This combination worked in questions 17 and 19.

E. No. This combination worked in question 19.

23. **C** Complex

This question asks you to replace a rule with another rule that will yield the same deductions. Since the initial rule is a conditional, look to see if any of the answers describes the contrapositive. The initial rule is ~KT → HT & MT so look for something that aligns with ~HT or ~MT → KT or even with the initial condition.

A. No. This symbolizes to KS → ~MS & ~HS. This does not match the original condition or its contrapositive.

B. No. This works out to KS → LS, which does not match the original condition or its contrapositive.

C. Yes. This becomes ~KT → HT & MT, which matches the original condition.

D. No. This becomes ~KT → ~ HL same, which does not match the original or its contrapositive.

E. No. This becomes ~HT & ~MT → KT. Be careful here! The initial "or" gets negated to "and" when you change "unless" to "if not." This does not match the original condition or its contrapositive.

Section 3: Reading Comprehension

Questions 1–8

The main point of the first paragraph is to question why great perfume isn't taken as seriously as other works of art. The second paragraph claims a parallel between perfume and other arts and details some of the characteristics of oil paintings. The main point of the third paragraph is to detail the characteristics of fine perfume that parallel the characteristics of fine oil paintings. The main point of the third paragraph is to discuss one possible reason that perfumes are not respected as art: that modern companies tamper with old formulas in a way that degrades quality. The Bottom Line of the passage as a whole is that fine perfume should be viewed as art and treated with similar respect.

1. **D** [Big Picture]

Use your Bottom Line of the passage to help you to evaluate the choices. The correct answer will describe the main idea of the passage.

   A.   No. In the fourth paragraph, the author criticizes modern perfume companies for tampering with formulas.

   B.   No. While this answer choice is supported by the passage, it is a premise that the author sets out in support of the main point.

   C.   No. The author's discussion of the declining quality of perfume is limited to the last paragraph of the passage.

   D.   Yes. This accurately matches the Bottom Line that fine perfume should be viewed as art and treated with similar respect.

   E.   No. While this answer choice is supported by the passage, it is a premise that the author sets out in support of the main point.

2. **E** [RC Reasoning]

The question is asking for a situation that would be compatible with the author's views about changing perfume formulations. In the last paragraph, the author criticizes modern companies for altering classic formulas by substituting cheap chemical compounds, so the correct answer will respect the original formulas.

   A.   No. While the author thinks that *Joy Parfum* is a masterpiece, he does not indicate that other perfumes should smells just like it.

   B.   No. This is what the author criticizes in the fourth paragraph.

   C.   No. While tempting, the author does not argue that natural chemical compounds are better than synthetic ones, he merely criticizes substitutions of chemical compounds (which could be natural or synthetic) for rarer, better ingredients.

   D.   No. The author does not discuss popularity.

   E.   Yes. The author criticizes changing perfumes from their original formulas so he or she would support undoing those changes.

3. **A** [Extract Infer]

The correct answer will be the statement that is best supported by evidence within the passage text. The passage says that the "noses" experiment with olfactory elements and produce sensations, so the correct answer should reflect that they are involved in the design and production of perfume.

   A.   Yes. Perfumers are involved in the design and production of perfume.

   B.   No. Collectors would not be producing sensations.

   C.   No. Perfumes would not be experimenting.

   D.   No. Marketing people would not be involved in experimenting with smells.

   E.   No. Pricing people would not be involved in experimenting with smells.

4. **A** **Extract Infer**

The correct answer will be the statement about art that is best supported by evidence within the passage text.

A. Yes. At the end of the second paragraph, the author argues that a brilliant perfumer, like other artists, can call upon memories.

B. No. This answer choice is extreme. It is not supported that this combination can be detected in *any* work of art.

C. No. This answer choice is extreme. The author does not argue that aiming for commercial success *inevitably* results in failure.

D. No. This answer choice is extreme. The author discusses that the Old Masters used oil paints that causes changes in appearance over time, but there is no argument that they are the best.

E. No. The author does not argue the relative superiority of forms of art, only that perfume should be considered an art.

5. **B** **Extract Infer**

The correct answer will be the statement about *Joy Parfum* that is best supported by the evidence within the passage text.

A. No. There is no mention of increased appreciation of *Joy Parfum*, only a comment that colleagues do not eagerly seek it out.

B. Yes. The author describes it as a masterpiece in the first paragraph and spends the next two paragraphs detailing how perfume parallels other art.

C. No. This answer choice is extreme. While the author calls *Joy Parfum* a masterpiece, there is no support for the idea that it was the foremost accomplishment of its time.

D. No. There is no discussion of who appreciates it.

E. No. There is no discussion of how it compares to other perfumes of its era.

6. **B** **RC Reasoning**

The question is asking for analogous behavior to that of the "cynical bean counters." In the fourth paragraph, the author argues that the bean counters tamper with old formulas in order to reduce costs and presume customers won't notice the difference, so the correct answer should involve a reduction of costs without regard for quality.

A. No. This does not involve saving money.

B. Yes. This involves saving money without regard for how it will affect quality.

C. No. While this answer choice may be tempting due to the budget reduction, the second half of it does not match with the situation in the passage as there is no anticipation of declining revenue as a motivation for cost-cutting measures.

D. No. This does not involve curtailing costs.

E. No. While this answer choice may be tempting because it mentions slashing a budget, there is no favoritism of one project over another in the passage.

7. **B**   Extract
            Infer

The correct answer will be the statement that is best supported by the evidence within the passage text.

A. No. There is no discussion of consumer knowledge of perfume names.

B. Yes. The last paragraph discusses that corporations are substituting cheap chemical compounds that only approximate rarer, better ingredients in order to increase profits.

C. No. There is no discussion of what consumers want.

D. No. This answer is extreme. There is no support for the claim that perfume makers of the past would *never* tamper with a formula.

E. No. There is no discussion of which perfumes result in the highest profits.

8. **D**   Structure

The correct answer will correctly follow the organization of the passage. Use your notes on the main point of each paragraph to evaluate the answer choices.

A. No. While the first paragraph makes an observation that perfumes are not respected as art, the middle paragraphs do not elaborate on that idea; rather, they argue that perfume should be art. The explanation in the final paragraph is not an alternative.

B. No. The first paragraph does not offer a thesis, and the final paragraph does not reject a challenge.

C. No. While this answer choice may be tempting, the final paragraph describes a possible reason for the conventional wisdom rather than support for the idea that perfume should be treated as art.

D. Yes. The first paragraph asks why perfume isn't respected as art, the middle paragraphs discuss why perfume should be respected as art, and the final paragraph discusses one reason that perhaps perfume is not respected as art.

E. No. The first paragraph does not describe a problem, there are no consequences in the middle paragraph, and the final paragraph is focused on a possible explanation even though it makes mention of who's likely to blame.

Questions 9–16

The main point of the first paragraph is to introduce the idea of "stealing thunder"—revealing negative information in court before the other side uses it. The main point of the second paragraph is that lawyers' commonly held belief in the effectiveness of stealing thunder is supported by both simulated trials and by psychological experiments. The third paragraph provides another reason that stealing thunder may be effective and notes a limitation on its effectiveness. The Bottom Line of the passage as a whole is that stealing thunder is likely an effective trial strategy based on psychological research and experiments in simulated trials.

9. **C** Big Picture

Use your Bottom Line of the passage to help you to evaluate the choices. The correct answer will describe the main point of the passage.

A. No. The author notes that the effectiveness of stealing thunder has not been tested in actual trials.

B. No. While the author discusses a limitation of the strategy, the passage is not focused on unintended consequences of its use.

C. Yes. This accurately paraphrases the Bottom Line.

D. No. The focus of the passage is on the effectiveness of the technique rather than its risks.

E. No. The passage does not address the idea that the simulated trial experiments revealed limitations on the stealing thunder strategy.

10. **B** Extract Infer

The correct answer will be an example of stealing thunder that is best supported by the evidence within the passage text. The author describes stealing thunder as the defense attorney revealing negative information about his client before the opposing side has a chance to do so.

A. No. This describes information revealed about the wrong side.

B. Yes. This involved revealing negative information about the defendant before the other side brings it up.

C. No. The goal of stealing thunder is to bring the negative information up before the other side mentions it, not to respond to it.

D. No. The answer choice does not involve revealing negative information.

E. No. Mitigating circumstances are not negative information.

11. **D** Extract Fact

The question is asking for a factor that probably contributes to the success of the stealing thunder strategy. The correct answer will be explicitly supported by the passage.

A. No. The passage does not discuss the length of time between when the two sides discuss the negative information.

B. No. The passage does not discuss lawyers' skill.

C. No. The passage does not discuss how the negative information is revealed.

D. Yes. This is explicitly stated in lines 51–54.

E. No. The passage does not discuss juror screening.

12. **A** Structure

The question is asking why the author mentions the "cognitive framework" that jurors create. The passage states that a negative impression formed early in a trial can create a filter that jurors process additional information through as part of the discussion about why it's important that the negative information be framed positively.

A. Yes. This reflects the author's discussion of a filter that jurors may view additional information through.

B. No. The author does not discuss any preconceived notions that jurors may have.

C. No. The relative impact that a piece of information may have at various points in a trial is not discussed in the final paragraph.

D. No. The last paragraph focuses on the risk of a negative impression formed early on and not on the timing of the information relative to the other side.

E. No. The author does not contrast the benefits of positively framing negative information with gaining credibility; rather, both are components of successful stealing thunder.

13. **D** Extract Infer

The question is asking how the author feels about stealing thunder. The author argues that stealing thunder is likely a successful strategy based on the evidence, so the correct answer will reflect a positive view.

A. No. This answer choice is too negative, and the passage does not discuss how commonly used the technique is.

B. No. The author does not discuss precisely when the negative information should be revealed.

C. No. This answer choice is too negative, and there's no mention in the passage of crucial omitted evidence.

D. Yes. This answer agrees with the Bottom Line of the passage and is supported by the author's discussion of why stealing thunder works.

E. No. This answer choice is too negative, and there's no discussion of the experience of attorneys using the stealing thunder strategy.

14. **E** Extract Fact

The question is asking what support the author gives for his characterization of stealing thunder as a likely successful strategy. The correct answer will be explicitly supported by the passage.

A. No. The passage does not discuss client reactions.

B. No. The passage explicitly states that no studies have been done on actual trials.

C. No. The passage explicitly states that no studies have been done on actual trials.

D. No. The passage does not discuss analogous techniques.

E. Yes. The author discusses both simulated trials and psychological research in the second paragraph.

15. **A** Extract Infer

This question is asking what the author means by suggesting that the stealing thunder technique is effective. The passage discusses that stealing thunder, when used appropriately, lessens the weight of negative information and can help jurors view subsequent information in a more favorable light.

A. Yes. Effective use of the technique would make jurors view the side using it more favorably than they otherwise would.

B. No. While there is some discussion of early positive framing in the passage, counterarguments are discussed as things that would potentially be formed by jurors, not introduced by attorneys.

C. No. This answer choice is extreme. While effective use of stealing thunder would aid the side using it, the passage does not support this idea of invariably favorable results.

D. No. The passage discusses the potential of the technique to make jurors think that negative evidence is less important.

E. No. While the negative information must be revealed prior to the opposition revealing it, it is intended to lessen the weight of the information and is not intended to be dramatic.

16. **D** Extract Infer

The correct answer will be the statement that is best supported by the evidence within the passage text.

A. No. The author discusses the potential importance of framing the information positively for effectiveness, but does not mention it in the context of deciding whether to steal thunder.

B. No. The passage does not discuss jurors' outside knowledge.

C. No. The passage does not discuss reactions of opposing counsel.

D. Yes. The first paragraph of the passage discusses that there is no point in revealing negative information unknown to or unlikely to be used by the other side and that most lawyers believe in stealing thunder when the opposition would try to derive an advantage.

E. No. The passage discusses psychological research as a reason that stealing thunder might be effective, but it is not discussed in the context of a lawyer's decision to use the strategy.

Questions 17–21

Passage A

The first chunk introduces the idea that recent neuroscience findings change the way we think about the law, specifically that someone may be totally rational but not in control of his or her action. The second chunk argues that the criminal-justice system ought not to be justified based on retribution. The Bottom Line of passage A is that neuroscience findings mean that punishment should not be based on retribution because there is no preventative value. Passage A is persuasive in tone.

Passage B

The first paragraph argues that neuroscience fuels determinism, but determinism can coexist with free will. The second paragraph outlines the theory of "soft determinism" by distinguishing free actions and constrained actions. The third paragraph continues the discussion of free versus constrained. The Bottom Line of passage B is that actions from a disease-free brain are free actions unless they are constrained. Passage B is academic in tone.

17.   **B**   Big Picture

The correct answer will reflect the Bottom Line of each passage.

   A.   No. Passage B does not discuss punishment.

   B.   Yes. Both passages discuss how neuroscience findings impact views about free will.

   C.   No. Passage B does not discuss punishment.

   D.   No. Passage B does not discuss punishment.

   E.   No. Passage A does not discuss physical coercion.

18.   **A**   Extract Fact

The passage is asking for a concept that is mentioned in passage B but not mentioned in passage A.

   A.   Yes. Passage B mentions mental disorders in line 43 as an example of an external source that constrains actions.

   B.   No. Both passages discuss free choice or free will. Passage A discusses it in line 10, and passage B discusses it starting in lines 35–36.

   C.   No. Both passages discuss actions that are caused by forces beyond someone's control. Passage A discusses them starting in line 8, and passage B discusses them starting in line 39.

   D.   No. This is discussed in passage A, but it is not mentioned in passage B.

   E.   No. This is discussed in passage A, but it is not mentioned in passage B.

19.   **B**   Structure

The question is asking why the author of passage B mentioned David Hume. After claiming that it has long been argued that free will can coexist with determinism, the passage discusses that David Hume was a philosopher two centuries prior who argued that free actions can exist in a deterministic world, just as Ayer argued in the 1950s.

   A.   No. The author is bolstering Ayer's argument, not criticizing him.

   B.   Yes. The author is bolstering Ayer's theory of soft determinism by showing that it has been argued for a long time.

   C.   No. The author is arguing the theory's continued relevance.

   D.   No. There is no discussion of how long mechanistic descriptions of the brain have existed.

   E.   No. The author is supporting the claim that soft determinism has been argued for a long time.

20.   C   **Big Picture**

The question is asking about the relative tones of the passages. Use your Bottom Line of each passage.

A.   No. This answer choice is reversed. Passage A is advocating a point of view, while passage B is presenting a theory.

B.   No. Neither passage is negative in tone.

C.   Yes. Passage A is advocating a point of view, while passage B is presenting a theory without passing judgment.

D.   No. Neither passage uses irony.

E.   No. Neither passage is negative in tone.

21.   C   **RC Reasoning**

The question is asking for an argument analogous to that in passage A. Passage A argues against the current punishment system because of new neuroscience findings. (Note: You can approach this question similarly to the way you would approach a Parallel the Reasoning Arguments question.)

A.   No. Passage A does not discuss reducing features.

B.   No. While this answer may be tempting because it mentions rationality, passage A does not discuss irrational actions.

C.   Yes. As in passage A, this answer argues against a current system because of updated information about the brain.

D.   No. Passage A rejects a justification based on new findings about the brain.

E.   No. This answer choice does not discuss rejecting a current system.

Questions 22–27

The main point of the first paragraph is that while Mario Garcia's study of Mexican American activism succeeds on one level, it also suffers from two big flaws. The main point of the second paragraph is to discuss the first flaw: that Garcia inconsistently argues political diversity while also claiming underlying consensus among opposing groups. The main point of the third paragraph is to discuss the second flaw: that Garcia may be overstating the degree to which activists' views represent the people. The Bottom Line of the passage as a whole is that Garcia's study of Mexican American activism is undermined by two big flaws.

22.   E   **Extract Fact**

The question is asking for something that is true of the League of United Latin American Citizens that is not true of the Congress of Spanish-Speaking People. The author discusses that the League encouraged a strategy of assimilation, while the Congress advocated bilingualism and equal rights. The correct answer will be directly supported by the text of the passage.

A.   No. The passage does not discuss what was popular with other citizens.

B.   No. The passage states that the Congress was the organization that fought for equal rights.

C.   No. The passage does not discuss these groups' positions on immigration.

D.   No. The passage states that the League advocated assimilation.

E.   Yes. In lines 21–22, the passage states that the League encouraged a strategy of assimilation into the United States political and cultural mainstream.

23.   **A**   **Extract Infer**

The question is asking for a statement about Garcia regarding the Mexican American political activists of the 1930s and 1940s that is best supported by the evidence within the passage text.

A.   Yes. In the first paragraph, the passage states that Garcia gives persuasive evidence that activists of the 1930s and 1940s anticipated the reforms of the 1960s and 1970s.

B.   No. The passage states that Garcia argues that earlier activists were more diverse than *historians* thought and does not compare the diversity of later activists.

C.   No. The passage states that Garcia argues that the activists of the 1960s and 1970s were more militant.

D.   No. This answer choice is extreme and unsupported. The passage does not discuss the proportion of activists who advocated bilingual education and equal rights.

E.   No. This answer choice is extreme and unsupported. The second paragraph discusses that activist groups were centered on liberal reform, not revolution.

24.   **B**   **Extract Infer**

The question is asking for a statement about Garcia's view of Mexican Americans between 1930 and 1960 that is best supported by the evidence within the passage text.

A.   No. In the third paragraph, the passage explicitly states that Garcia argued that the generation between 1930 and 1960 was more acculturated (assimilated to the dominant culture).

B.   Yes. In the third paragraph, the passage explicitly states that Garcia argued that the generation between 1930 and 1960 was more acculturated (assimilated to the dominant culture) and hence more politically active.

C.   No. In the third paragraph, the passage explicitly states that Garcia argued that the assimilation was a cause of increased political activity.

D.   No. In the second paragraph, the passage discusses that politically active groups were focused on reform, not revolution.

E.   No. This answer choice is extreme and unsupported. In the third paragraph, the passage explicitly states that the rhetoric of World War II was inclusive.

25. **B** `Extract Infer`

The question is asking for a statement about the author's view of Mexican American activists between 1930 and 1960 that is best supported by the evidence within the passage text.

A.   No. While the passage mentions that the activists of the 1930s and 1940s were less militant than the Chicanos of the 1960s and 1970s, there is no support for the idea that this is because of a common goal.

B.   Yes. In the second paragraph, the author argues that the groups were often diametrically opposed, yet their goals centered on liberal reform.

C.   No. There is no support for the claim that the groups reached a consensus.

D.   No. The passage does not discuss any relative numbers of those favoring assimilation versus cultural maintenance.

E.   No. The passage does not discuss whether the activists' goals were achieved.

26. **D** `Extract Infer`

The correct answer will be the statement that is best supported by evidence within the passage text. Look for language that explicitly indicated uncertainty.

A.   No. In the third paragraph, the author asserts that we cannot make such an assumption.

B.   No. The author does not discuss any assumptions of earlier historians.

C.   No. In the second paragraph, the author states that Mexican American activism in that period was characterized by intense and lively debate rather than consensus.

D.   Yes. In the third paragraph, the author states that it is "not clear" how far the politically active outlook extended beyond activists.

E.   No. In the second paragraph, the author states that these two organizations were often diametrically opposed to one another.

27. **E** `Extract Fact`

The correct answer will be the statement that is best supported by evidence within the passage text. Ethnic consciousness is mentioned at the end of the third paragraph.

A.   No. At the end of the third paragraph, the passage discusses that rates of Mexican immigration and naturalization help to create variations in ethnic consciousness, but there is no claim of direct proportion.

B.   No. The passage states that one cannot assume that an increase in Mexican Americans born in the United States necessarily increases activism and no correlation is made with ethnic consciousness.

C.   No. The passage states that patterns of bilingualism are one factor that helps create variations in ethnic consciousness, but there is no discussion of assimilation in this portion of the paragraph.

D.   No. The passage does not discuss the influence of Mexican American leaders.

E.   Yes. This is explicitly stated in lines 55–57.

Section 4: Arguments 2

1. **B**

The question task could be rephrased as "What does Carol incorrectly believe Ming is saying?" or "How has Carol misinterpreted Ming?" The question asks you to determine what Ming's false belief about Carol is, which is an extract task. Ming concludes that it is "fortunate" that trans fats have been eliminated from many manufacturers' cookies, based on the premise that trans fat is particularly unhealthy. Carol responds by challenging Ming's conclusion, and she adds the premise that desserts are not healthy foods. From Carol's response, it needs to be true that she has assumed that Ming is endorsing desserts free of trans fat, or suggesting that they are healthy. Ming does no such thing.

A. No. Nothing in Carol's comments suggests that she is responding to this kind of a claim.

B. Yes. The evidence suggests that Carol believes that Ming is attributing health benefits to food without trans fat. This is supported by Carol's premise that "even without trans fats" desserts are not healthy.

C. No. Nothing in Carol's comments suggests that she is responding to this kind of a claim.

D. No. Nothing in Carol's comments suggests that she is responding to this kind of a claim, but Carol's response indicates that Carol would endorse this view.

E. No. Nothing in Carol's comments suggests that she is responding to this kind of a claim.

2. **C**

This questions asks you to find the main point of the argument. This is a Disagree argument, and not all Disagree arguments have the same conclusion. The author may argue that the theory with which he or she disagrees is false, that it may be false, or simply that it is not well supported. This author picks the third option, and states "no one should accept this explanation until historical evidence demonstrates that a change in values occurred prior to the Industrial Revolution." Like many Disagree arguments, this has four parts. The first sentence is a fact both the historian and the economist agree upon. The second sentence is a statement of the economist's theory. The third sentence states the author's conclusion as well as his or her primary premise, that facts are required to support explanations. Since this follows a pattern common to Disagree arguments, knowing the pattern helps you find the conclusion. The word "should" also helps tip you off that the third sentence contains the conclusion.

A. No. This is a fact that both the historian and the economist agree upon. Since it is taken as true from the start, it is a premise.

B. No. This is a fact that both the historian and the economist appear to agree upon. Since it is taken as true from the start, it is a premise, or a very safe inference based on one premise.

C. Yes. This correctly states the conclusion of this Disagree argument.

D. No. This states that the economist's argument is false, which is a distortion of that author's actual conclusion, that the economist's argument should not be accepted without facts. This answer choice goes too far outside the scope of the argument and does not match.

E. No. The author states that in order to accept the economist's argument, we must have evidence that a change in values occurred before the Industrial Revolution. This answer choice, like some LSAT arguments, mistakes an absence of evidence for evidence of absence. The author never indicates that values did not spread, only that we need evidence that they did.

3. **E**   Strengthen

First, find the conclusion for this Strengthen argument. The argument concludes that "the donated trees are probably consistent with the master plan." This is supported by one fact, that "most" of the plants sold by the nursery are native plants. "Probably" means something is more likely than not. Thus if "most," or more than half, of the plants sold by the nursery are consistent with the plan, then the plants from the nursery are "probably" consistent with the plan. But it is not proven by the premises that most of the plants sold by the nursery are consistent with the plan, only that they are native plants. Native plant are consistent with the plan only if they do not grow to be very large. The large-growing trees present an obstacle to the argument that needs to be ruled out. If the argument can prove that most of the nursery's plants are both native and not subject to growing large, then the author can prove the claim that the plants are "probably" in accord with the plan.

A. No. This answer choice is has no relevance to the whether the donated trees are consistent with the plan.

B. No. This answer choice does not help the argument. Since cottonwood trees are not consistent with the plan, the answer provides another a reason that the plants from Three Rivers Nursery might not be consistent. While this does not meaningfully weaken the argument, it goes in the wrong direction.

C. No. Since the conclusion is only about trees, this answer about shrubs is not relevant to the conclusion.

D. No. This answer choice is about tree species not native to the area, which is largely out of scope. The nursery sells mostly native plants, and the rarity of non-native plants does not give us any information about whether the plants from the nursery are consistent with the master plan.

E. Yes. If the nursery sells mostly native plants, and no trees that grow to be very large, then the majority of the trees sold by the nursery necessarily conform to the master plan. So it is probable that the donated trees conform to the master plan. This answer choice rules out the possibility that the trees from the nursery, while probably native, are not consistent with the plan.

4. **D**   Necessary Assumption

Find the argument's conclusion first: "*Diplodocus* must have fed on plants on or near the ground, or underwater." If you use the Why Test on this, it becomes clear that the author argues that this is the case because *Diplodocus*'s neck bones prevented it from raising its long neck to reach high growing vegetation. Just because one theorized means of reaching high vegetation does not automatically mean that *Diplodocus* never fed on high-growing vegetation. One way to look at this argument is that the author assumes that neck-raising is the only way to feed on high-growing vegetation. There is also language shift here between reaching high vegetation by raising its neck and reaching high vegetation at all. Necessary Assumption answers that are phrased in the negative lend themselves particularly well to the Negation Test. If you negate (D), you get "*Diplodocus* had some other way of accessing high-growing vegetation, such as by rising up on its hind legs." This utterly destroys the conclusion and confirms that it is the right answer.

A. No. What is true of modern animals is irrelevant to what *Diplodocus* fed on.

B. No. What *Diplodocus* could see is not necessarily relevant to what it ate. It may have used other senses to find food.

C. No. This answer gives another reason why *Diplodocus* could not lift its head, a fact already established in the premise. It does not directly relate to the conclusion.

D. Yes. This answer rules out the possibility that there might have been another way to reach high-growing foliage. The Negation Test makes this clear, as explained above.

E. No. This answer rules out other ways that *Diplodocus* could have eaten underwater vegetation, and it suggests that if *Diplodocus* ate underwater vegetation, it did so by lowering its head. However, it does not help at all to rule out high vegetation as a food source. If you negate it, you get "*Diplodocus* was able..." to get to underwater food sources, which is quite consistent with the conclusion.

5. **D**   **Principle**
             Strengthen

The question task asks you to find a principle that strengthens the conclusion. For most of these Principle-Strengthen questions, the right answer will be strong and prove the conclusion. Start by finding the conclusion: "The government should not assist them in rebuilding." This statement is a recommendation, and the word "should" tips you off that this is the conclusion. The most important premise is the last sentence, which indicates that the reason for following the conclusion is that landslides in the future could cause injury. Many Principle-Strengthen questions follow a pattern of giving you a specific fact (a premise) and a specific recommendation (the conclusion). The answer choices in these arguments are general recommendations; when you add the general recommendation in the answer to the specific fact in the premise, you guarantee the specific recommendation in the conclusion. Here, you need to look for an answer choice that connects the fact about landslides and future injury with the recommendation that the government not help, and remember that the right answer needs to take you from the premise to the conclusion.

A. No. This answer choice does not connect to the main premise about landslides. You can also diagram the unless statement this way: ~Government help → ~allowed to build. This statement leads away from the conclusion instead of toward it.

B. No. This answer ignores the main premise, which states that the reason the government should not help is the risk of landslides, so it is not relevant. Even if you ignore that, it would work against the conclusion and point toward recommending that the government help.

C. No. This answer ignores the main premise, which states that the reason the government should not help is the risk of landslides, so it is not relevant. Even if you ignore that, the answer would not be relevant here for another reason: These people are committed to their community.

D. Yes. This answer choice connects the government not helping with the risk of injury. Moreover, it goes the right direction. It guarantees that if there is the chance of serious injury, then there should be no government help.

E. No. This answer is irrelevant for at least two reasons: Discouraging residents is not clearly connected to withholding help, and second, there is no evidence in the argument that this area has an extensive history of landslides.

6. **B** Necessary Assumption

Look for the conclusion. The prediction about what's possible in the future is the conclusion here: "we can control future climate change…." Use the Why Test to confirm that this is the conclusion and find the key premise. Here the author would say that we can control future climate change *because* "human behavior is responsible for climate change." Since the question task asks you to find a necessary assumption, look for something that will connect the premise to the conclusion. Check your answer using the Negation Test. The right answer, when negated, will damage the conclusion.

A. No. A "purely natural cause" for climate change is not relevant to either the premise or the conclusion.

B. Yes. This connects the premise to the conclusion. Test it with the Negation Test: Human beings *cannot* control the aspects of their behavior that have an impact on climate change. When negated, the answer choice makes it impossible to control future climate change, which demolishes the conclusion.

C. No. This answer choice deals with the past, not the future, and is not relevant to the conclusion.

D. No. The danger to other species and the comparison between the danger to humans and to other species are not relevant to the conclusion.

E. No. The relative difficulty between recognizing behaviors and changing them is not relevant to the conclusion. Additionally, this answer choice goes in the wrong direction, giving more reason why it might be difficult to change behaviors, which works against the conclusion.

7. **A** Inference

This task, along with the phrase "reasonable to conclude," tells you that you need to find an inference. Consider whether any of the statements can be combined to get a conclusion. In this case, we know two things about the patients waiting for news: They are experiencing more stress than the other group, and they are feeling less pain. At least in this instance, there seems to be a demonstrated link between uncertainty, stress, and a lack of pain.

A. Yes. This is carefully worded ("sometimes") and is supported by the passage: Stress in these patients is clearly associated with less pain.

B. No. This is quite possible, but the argument gives you no evidence of whether the pain is beneficial, harmful, or neutral. This answer is unsupported.

C. No. This answer is fairly strongly worded ("usually") and while you know the lack of the information is associated with less pain, you have no information about the effect of the lack of information on the severity of the condition.

D. No. The passage gives no information about the cause and effect relationship between stress and reduced blood flow, so this answer is unsupported.

E. No. The passage gives no reason to think this; the proportion needing surgery could just as well be the same for both groups.

8. **B** Flaw

This argument concludes that walking on hind legs is instinctive and not a learned behavior for these bears. Even though this argument does not use the words "cause" or "effect," this is an excellent example of a causal argument. One less-common causal assumption is that there can be only one cause for a particular result. This argument incorrectly rejects the possibility that the behavior is learned, simply because the shape of the bones shows that the behavior is natural. Since the question task asks for a description of the argument's flaw, the credited response will describe the problem with the argument, that one possible cause is rejected only because another possible cause exists. Look out for attractors that describe other common flaws on the test. These answer choices are both common and appealing.

A. No. This answer choice perfectly describes a sampling error. There is no evidence of a sampling in the argument, and you must accept the premise that standing and walking upright is natural for the bears.

B. Yes. This identifies the flaw in the argument. There is no evidence that the two causes for the behavior are mutually exclusive.

C. No. This is a perfect description of a shifting meanings argument, but there is no evidence in the argument that the meaning shifts.

D. No. The argument does presume that there are only two ways to explain the behavior, but it is a perfectly logical presumption. There is no other conceivable explanation for behaviors other than that they are learned or innate. The argument also fails to consider that both explanations could account for the behavior.

E. No. This is a perfect description of an appeal to authority, but there is no evidence of this. The scientists' determination is provided as a premise, and it relies on their research, not a general sense of respect for the scientists.

9. **B** Resolve/Explain

This argument establishes the premise that people are interested in and moved by "generally misleading" anecdotes. It also sets up an apparent paradox by establishing that people have fairly accurate beliefs about society. All of the facts presented are true, so you need to look for new information in the answer choice that allows the statements to be true at the same time. The only way to do this logically will be to establish that people do not base their whole belief system on these interesting and moving, but misleading anecdotes.

A. No. This answer may be appealing because it helps to explain why people are not interested in statistics. However, it does nothing to explain why people have accurate beliefs about society.

B. Yes. If people recognize the anecdotes to be unrepresentative, this shows how they can be interested and moved without the anecdotes shaping their views about society.

C. No. This may actually make the problem worse, since emotionally compelling anecdotes are misleading. This does nothing to explain why people's beliefs are surprisingly accurate.

D. No. This might explain why people like anecdotes, but since we know that most anecdotes are misleading, it does nothing to explain why people have fairly accurate beliefs.

E.   No. This answer gives no explanation of why people hold fairly accurate beliefs. This answer makes the paradox worse, since we know the anecdotes cause an emotional response and are also misleading. This would give a reason why people would have inaccurate beliefs about society.

10.   **C**   Evaluate

This argument concludes that Schweitzer's discovery helps to prove that dinosaurs are closely related to birds. Schweitzer's discovery is that *T. rex* and chickens have similar collagen proteins. Since the question task asks for an answer that is useful in evaluating the argument, look for a question whose answer would help to prove or disprove a key assumption. In this argument, the key assumption is that the similar collagen proteins shared by chickens and *T. rex* somehow mean they are related. The argument shows a language shift between "similar...proteins" and "closely related." So look for an answer that tells us whether similar proteins indicate that the animals are related.

A.   No. This does not relate to the central assumption of the argument. The rarity of the find does nothing to prove or disprove the assumption that similar proteins indicate a close relationship.

B.   No. This does not relate to the central assumption of the argument, and it does nothing to prove or disprove the assumption that similar proteins indicate a close relationship. Whether this evidence adds to the link between birds and dinosaurs is independent of whether there is any evidence against the link.

C.   Yes. The answer to this question will prove or disprove the central assumption of the argument. If it is very unlikely for unrelated animals to have similar collagen protein, that indicates the argument is very strong, since similar collagen protein would then strongly indicate a relationship between birds and dinosaurs. If it is very likely for unrelated animals to have similar proteins, then Schweitzer's finding means very little, since the animals could have similar proteins but be unrelated.

D.   No. This does not relate to the central assumption of the argument. Knowing whether this is possible or not does little to prove whether the similarity in collagen indicates a close relationship.

E.   No. This does not relate to the central assumption of the argument. Whether the discovery was surprising has no bearing on whether similar collagen indicates a close relationship between the animals.

11.   **A**   Inference

The passage establishes that the professor experienced serious subjective effects when she is sleep deprived, but that most students apparently noticed no objective changes in her when she is sleep deprived. Since the question task asks you to make an inference about the argument, the credited response will be provable using the information in the passage.

Avoid answer choices that rely on unsupported assumptions or make conclusions outside the scope of the argument.

A.   Yes. While the professor experienced serious subjective effects when she is sleep deprived, most students apparently noticed no objective changes in her when she is sleep deprived. This comparison is provable using the information in the passage, since most students noticed nothing and the professor noticed several effects.

B. No. This answer choice is not true unless it is assumed that the subjective effects are the same as the overall effects. There is no evidence in the passage that the professor's assessment was more accurate than the students' assessment of her performance, only that it was different. This answer requires unsupported assumptions.

C. No. This answer is out of scope, since it compares professors' job performance to that of others. Since we have no information about the effect of sleep deprivation on others, this answer is unsupported.

D. No. This answer is out of scope, since it compares occasional sleep deprivation to extended sleep deprivation. Since we have no information about extended sleep deprivation, this answer is unsupported.

E. No. This answer is unsupported, since we cannot assume that the university students' assessment was accurate. Even if we had that information, the passage does not prove that there is a single other instance in which university students observed something astutely.

12. **D** Resolve/ Explain

Even though the answer choices are framed as principles here, the task is to "reconcile" the apparent conflict. The answer should do what every Resolve/Explain credited response does: add a new premise that shows how the other premises can be true at the same time. As with other Resolve/Explain questions, every statement is a premise, so take every statement as true and do not look for a conclusion. The "despite the fact" shows the contrast and helps you find the conflict. Look for an answer choice that tells us why our government should give priority to satisfying the needs of our people, even though it is not objectively more important to do so, and the people are equal in worth.

A. No. This answer choice makes the conflict worse. Since we know the satisfaction of our people's needs is no more objectively important than satisfying the needs of other people, this principle would suggest that the government not attempt to satisfy its people's needs. This answer choice gives a good reason why the two premises could not be true at the same time.

B. No. This answer choice makes the conflict worse. We know that other people are equally worthy, so if this principle is true, it gives us no reason why our government should give priority to our people. This answer choice gives a good reason why the two premises could not be true at the same time.

C. No. This answer does not solve the conflict, but makes the conflict worse. This answer choice identifies the second premise, about people's objective worth, as the primary premise in determining the first premise. Rather than presenting a new reason to prioritize our people's needs, it suggests that any new reason is relatively less important than the premise already given.

D. Yes. This answer agrees with the premises in the argument and shows how they can be true at the same time. This answer gives us a new principle that provides a reason why our government should satisfy the needs of its people despite the equal worth of all people. Everyone is equally worthy, but under this principle each government looks out for its own people.

E. No. This answer choice does not solve the conflict. There is no information in the argument or answer that allows us to determine whether there is some "other way" for the group's needs to be satisfied. So the principle about another way to satisfy needs is not clearly related to the conflict, and it is unclear what effect, if any, this principle has on the passage.

13.　D　[Inference]

This passage establishes that all neighborhoods will be swept once a month. Some neighborhoods will receive an extra sweeping in addition to the monthly sweeping. Consider whether any of the statements can be combined to get a conclusion. Two factors, taken together, are sufficient to guarantee at least one extra sweeping: The neighborhood is "qualified," and the neighborhood requests it. Try to predict what wrong answers might do. Beware of extreme quantity statements such as "all" or "no." Wrong answers in any inference question dealing with necessary or sufficient conditions may confuse necessary and sufficient or may play tricks by ignoring one of the conditions.

A.　No. While excessive dirt from major construction is one circumstance that could result in a neighborhood becoming qualified, construction alone is not a factor that guarantees qualification. This is too strongly worded to be supported.

B.　No. Two factors taken together are sufficient to guarantee that a neighborhood's streets will be swept more than once a month: The neighborhood is qualified, and the neighborhood requests a sweeping. Qualification alone does not guarantee an extra sweeping. This is too strongly worded to be supported.

C.　No. This answer choice mistakes one part of a situation sufficient to guarantee more than one sweeping per month for a condition necessary to allow more than one sweeping. While any qualified neighborhood that requests a sweeping will be swept more than once a month, other neighborhoods might be swept more frequently for other reasons.

D.　Yes. Since the city will satisfy all requests for interim sweepings immediately, and since every street will already be swept once a month, this must be true. Only the first and third sentences are needed to make this inference.

E.　No. Qualified and requesting neighborhoods get an extra sweeping in addition to their regular monthly sweeping, but other neighborhoods might as well. "Qualified and Requesting → Extra Sweeping" does not mean "~Qualified → ~Extra Sweeping." This mistakes part of sufficient condition for a necessary condition.

14.　A　[Reasoning]

The question task asks for an answer that describes what the journalist is doing. These question tasks are match tasks, so you need to find an answer choice that matches what is going on in the passage. Start by identifying the argument's purpose. This argument is a Disagree argument, and the author disagrees with the view that journalists' withholding of information is "like lying...intentional deception and therefore unethical." The conclusion that the author disagrees with relies on a comparison between lying and withholding information. Understanding the common reasoning pattern helps here. The argument's author attempts to weaken this comparison in the most effective way of weakening a comparison, by pointing out a relevant difference between the two things being compared.

A.　Yes. This answer choice matches perfectly. This describes most of what the author does and does not include anything that the author does not do.

B.　No. This answer choice does not match. There is no evidence that the journalist considers the distinction between lying and withholding information to be controversial. Even more important, the author never provides a "clear instance."

C. No. This answer does not match. The author does define a concept: "to lie." But then the author's most important point is that it does not apply to all the cases under discussion. The equation of lying and withholding information is rejected.

D. No. This answer does not match. This argument is general in its approach, and it does not use examples or counterexamples.

E. No. This answer choice does not match. This argument is general in its approach, and it does not look at individual cases. The author never is quite consistent in the argument that lying is always wrong for journalists and that withholding information should not be considered lying.

15. **C** Flaw

This argument concludes that "there is no reason to lower interest rates further." This is based on the premise that one reason to lower interest rates is invalid. One reason to lower interest rates is to stimulate the economy, and this stimulation is not needed. Focus on this gap: Just because one stated reason for a course of action is not valid, it is an error of logic to conclude that the course of action is unneeded. There might be many good reasons to lower interest rates that have nothing to do with stimulating economic growth.

A. No. This answer may be appealing because the argument involves experts, but this argument actually rejects the testimony of many economists. The economist making the argument rejects the colleagues' authority in favor of a different conclusion, based on a premise that no stimulation is needed.

B. No. It is clear that stimulation is the cause, and growth is the effect. The author correctly argues that since the particular effect of growth is already occurring, no stimulation is needed to achieve that result.

C. Yes. The argument jumps from proving that there is no need to stimulate economic growth to the overbroad conclusion that there is no need to lower interest rates, as explained above.

D. No. The author effectively rules out any need to stimulate economic growth, by showing that it is already happening. It does not matter whether there are other ways of stimulating growth, since none of them are needed, at least for the purpose of stimulating growth.

E. No. While the second part of this answer repeats a premise, the first part, involving further reductions and unsustainable growth, has no basis in the argument.

16. **E** Sufficient Assumption

The argument concludes that Caravaggio's works do not fit the definition of Baroque painting, and it establishes one important fact in the premise: The definition of Baroque painting requires that it be opulent, heroic, and extravagant. We know from the premise that Caravaggio's works were realistic and showed a novel use of the interplay of light and shadow. The argument gives us no information about what those qualities mean with regards to the definition of Baroque, and no information about whether Caravaggio has the qualities necessary to be Baroque: "opulence, heroic sweep, and extravagance." We can represent this as "B → OHE" and "~OHE → ~B." Since the question tasks asks for a sufficient assumption, the credited response will clearly link Caravaggio with a lack of opulence, heroism, and extravagance, which will prove that his work does not fit the stated definition of Baroque.

A. No. This answer choice does not connect any parts of the argument or bridge any gaps. This answer choice is irrelevant.

B. No. This answer choice deals with only one premise, and it makes a statement that is already proven by that premise. Since Caravaggio had these two qualities, they can clearly exist together. This answer choice is irrelevant to the conclusion.

C. No. This answer choice deals with a prior time period and is therefore irrelevant.

D. No. This *appears* to bridge a gap in the argument, by linking realism with a lack of opulence, heroism, and extravagance. However, the language is weak, and even if a realist painting does not "usually" demonstrate these qualities, this answer does not prove that Caravaggio's paintings lacked heroism, opulence, and extravagance. So even if this were true, Caravaggio could still be considered Baroque.

E. Yes. If Caravaggio's work lacks *all* of the traits that are *required* by the definition of Baroque, this strongly worded answer proves that his work cannot fit this definition.

17. **E** ⬛ **Reasoning**

The author argues against the proponents of jury nullification by making the point that when juries are allowed to put jury nullification into practice, they often make mistakes. The author's only premise against jury nullification is the general statement that bad results often follow from this practice.

The question task here is a matching task. Watch out for appealing trap answers that describe a common pattern that does not match this argument, or other wrong answers that fail to describe the main thing this argument does.

A. No. This is a perfect description of an ad hominem or attack on the person making the argument. However, there is nothing in the argument above to indicate that the author is attacking the proponents of jury nullification rather than their arguments.

B. No. An argument with an inconsistency would have two premises that conflict with each other, and the proponents' arguments do not conflict with each other. This answer may be appealing because the word "but" appears and there is conflict in the paragraph. The conflict, however, is between the proponents' argument and the author's.

C. No. The author does not argue against any premise proposed by the proponents of jury nullification. Rather, the author brings in a new premise that shows a negative consequence of jury nullification.

D. No. This argument is very general, and the author never brings in an example. Rather, the author counters a general claim by bringing in a new general statement.

E. Yes. This is exactly what the author does, as explained above.

18. **E** ⬛ **Flaw**

This argument uses a premise about people 65–81 who suffer from insomnia, and it jumps to a conclusion that posits that people produce melatonin as they get older. In order to prove this, the argument would need a representative sample of younger people, a representative sample of older people, and evidence that the older people were deficient in melatonin. The evidence presented by the pharmacist does not provide any of these things. The sampling does not include younger people, and importantly includes only older people with insomnia. So perhaps it is the insomnia that is correlated with low melatonin, not advanced age. Perhaps insomnia occurs at the same rate in older and younger people, and any group with insomnia would respond well to melatonin supplements. No matter how large the sample the author has chosen, it could never be representative of the point the author is trying to make, since it samples only people with insomnia and does not allow us to make any comparison between younger and older people. As you read the answer choices, watch out for attractive wrong answers that describe common flaws that do not appear in this argument.

A. No. This argument does infer a cause from a proven effect, but there is no discussion of intent. The author never states the intent behind giving people melatonin.

B. No. This is an appealing answer, because the argument mentions manufacturers, who might be biased. But the argument never relies on these claims. Instead, it tries to use a factual premise to prove these claims.

C. No. This perfectly describes an equivocation or shifting meanings flaw. But there is no term in the argument that is used in two different meanings.

D. No. This answer is appealing, because the conclusion is a claim about cause, while the premise is about an effect. But the argument fails to prove that this purported cause and the purported effect are even related to each other, as explained above. So this answer fails to describe the main flaw.

E. Yes. This answer describes the flaw: The argument uses a premise about people 65–81 who suffer from insomnia, and it jumps to a conclusion that compares younger people to older people. As explained above, this particular sample could never prove the author's conclusion, no matter how large it is.

19.　**C**　Parallel

Remember that "unless" is consistently the same thing as "if not." So that means that we can properly diagram the statement "it would sell out unless it was poorly promoted" this way: "~Poorly Promoted → Sell out." The contrapositive of this statement is "~Sell out → Poorly promoted." The author then points out that the concert did not sell out. So the contrapositive statement leads right from not selling out to the logically correct conclusion, the concert was "probably not properly promoted." The premise is not presented as absolute truth, but rather as the assessment of a knowledgeable individual, so this matches the carefully worded "probably" in the conclusion. The question task is to find an answer choice that follows the same logical pattern as the argument. The statements do not need to be in the same order as the argument, but you should look for an answer that has the same kind of conclusion as the original argument and follows the same logical steps to get there.

A. No. One premise can be diagrammed as "Performed by highly skilled surgeon → patient probably survives," and the contrapositive would be "~patient probably survives → ~performed by a highly skilled surgeon." The argument establishes that the patient did not survive and then concludes that it was probably "not properly performed," a conclusion that has no basis in the premises. The "probably" in the premise also makes this argument unlike the original argument.

B. No. This argument is superficially similar to the argument above. You can diagram the conditional statement as "Is labeled properly → contains organic compounds," and the contrapositive is "~contains organic compounds → is not labeled correctly." Then the argument establishes that the sample probably did not contain organic compounds, and it concludes that the sample is not labeled correctly. The crucial point of difference between this and the original article is the "probably" in the premise. The "probably" in the conclusion of the original argument makes the argument better, since the conclusion is easier to support. But the "probably" in the premise makes the argument weaker. Furthermore, the conditional statement appears to be based on the other premise in this answer choice, and not given directly by the expert, as it is in the original argument.

74

C. Yes. This can be diagrammed thus: "Properly repaired → ~noticeable," and the contrapositive is "noticeable → ~properly repaired." The argument establishes that the damage is noticeable, and it logically follows the arrow of the contrapositive to the correct conclusion, that the repair was probably not properly done. Just as in the argument above, the conclusion is hedged with the safe "probably," and the premise is presented as the assessment of a knowledgeable person.

D. No. The conditional statement can be diagrammed as "~damaged in a storm → ~roof requires repairs," and the contrapositive is "roof requires repairs → damaged in a storm." The argument establishes that the roof requires repairs, and if it were like the original argument, it would conclude that the roof was damaged in the storm. This answer choice, however, makes a conclusion totally unlike the original argument, that the builder was probably wrong.

E. No. The conditional statement can be diagrammed as "tests properly conducted → tests find lead in soil," and the contrapositive is "~tests find lead in soil → ~tests properly conducted." The argument then establishes that the tests did find lead in the soil, and it concludes that they were properly conducted. Unlike the original argument, this answer choice does not rely on the correct contrapositive. Instead, it assumes the unsupported conditional "Tests find lead in soil → tests properly conducted." Here the author has apparently flipped the conditions without negating them. So the conclusion is unsupported, and the argument is not parallel to the original argument.

20. **D** **Flaw**

This Interpret argument puts forward the broad and fairly extreme conclusion that "global recessions can never be prevented." Statements about the future, especially statements using absolute quantity statements such as "never," are very difficult to support, no matter how strong the premises. The key premise here is that recessions can be prevented *only if* they are predictable, which can be diagrammed as "Prevented → predictable." This strong premise is followed by the weaker premise that economists, using the best techniques they have, in the past and present, consistently fail to predict recessions. So this argument would be quite strong if it were about the present. But since the conclusion leaps into the future and concludes that recessions *never* can be prevented, it is not supported. We would need a premise that economists could *never* predict a recession in order to support this extreme conclusion. So the flaw is the author's assumption that what is true of economists' ability to predict recessions will *always* be true.

A. No. This is a perfect description of a circular reasoning flaw, but there is no trace of circular reasoning in the argument.

B. No. The argument does not establish this, but whether economists claim to be able to predict or not is not relevant to the argument's validity.

C. No. This is a good description of a necessary and sufficient flaw. The argument does establish that predictability is necessary for prevention, which can be diagrammed as "Prevented → predictable." But the author never claims or assumes that predictability is sufficient for prevention, which would be diagrammed as "Predictable → prevented."

D. Yes. This perfectly matches the flaw as described above.

E. No. The argument does infer that something (prevention of recessions) will not occur. But this is not based just on the information that it is not predictable. It is based on two different things: information that economists do not seem to be able to predict it currently and a strong conditional statement that shows that prevention requires the ability to predict. This answer choice fails to describe the main components of the argument.

21. A Principle Match

This argument concludes that the "newspaper exhibits an unjustified bias." The author of the letter offers the premise that Hanlon's statements were viewed skeptically by the newspaper, and that the newspaper's skepticism is unsupported by evidence. This question task is just a variant of a typical Principle-Match question, and you need to find the principle that is most in conflict with the argument. This is a Disagree argument in which the letter to the editor attacks the newspaper's behavior. Thus, any principle that matches the newspaper's approach is likely to conflict with the argument, so look for a principle that matches the newspaper's actions.

A. Yes. This principle matches the approach apparently taken by the newspaper, since the newspaper was skeptical about an extraordinary claim that was not supported by the evidence. The author of the letter appears to think the opposite, that such an extraordinary claim, unbacked by evidence, should be accepted without criticism. So this answer is in sharp contrast to the author's reasoning.

B. No. The issue of an "intermediary source" neither matches nor conflicts with the argument. It is irrelevant.

C. No. This principle fits with the author's conclusion, since the letter argues that Hanlon should not have been viewed skeptically by the newspaper.

D. No. This principle appears to relate to Hanlon's actions, not the newspaper's, so it is not in clear contrast or agreement with the author.

E. No. The author disagrees with the newspaper about the level of skepticism directed at Hanlon, not about whether the newspaper should publish an unconfirmed report. So this answer does not clearly match or conflict with anything in the argument.

22. C Flaw

This argument establishes a premise that can be diagrammed thus:

Closely related → evolved only once;
~Evolved only once → ~closely related.

The argument then establishes that the species are not closely related and concludes that they evolved more than once. In order to reach this conclusion, the author needs to assume the following:

~Closely related → ~evolved only once.

This conditional statement is derived by negating both sides of the conditional in the premise, without flipping the conditions. So this is not a correctly derived contrapositive. The argument establishes that being closely related is sufficient to prove that this specialization evolved only once, but it incorrectly assumes that if a trait evolved only once, then all animals with that trait will necessarily be closely related.

A. No. This is a good description of a causal flaw, but it does not match the argument. There is a real causal relationship between evolving only once and being closely related, but the argument misunderstands this relationship.

B. No. This is a good description of an absence of evidence flaw, but it does not match the argument. The argument never points to unconfirmed evidence to claim that something is false.

C. Yes. This describes the flaw, as explained above.

D. No. The answer describes a confusion between probability and certainty, and it does not match the argument. The argument never establishes that the trait was even likely to have evolved more than once.

E. No. This answer simultaneously describes an appeal to authority flaw and a sampling error, but it does not match the argument. The argument is not based on the biologists' credentials, but rather on their argument, and there is nothing to indicate that they are unrepresentative.

23. **E** Principle Match

This passage, like many Principle-Match questions, has no conclusion, but states two principles. Both deal with what the government of Country F must do whenever it sells a state-owned entity: First, it must seek out the highest price it can get on the market, and second, it must ensure that citizens of the country maintain a majority ownership of the company for no less than a year after the sale. This question task is just a variant of a typical Principle-Match question, and you need to find the answer that is most in conflict with the principles stated in the passage. The answer will need to match and be relevant to the principle in order to clearly conflict with it. So any answer choices that are not related to the principles stated above should be eliminated. The right answer will violate at least one principle, but the wrong answers need not match the principles at all. Note also that since the principles concern only what the government does, the right answer must present a situation in which the government actually plans the sale of a state-owned entity.

A. No. There is no part of this situation that violates a principle. The answer never shows non-citizens owning a majority share at any point in the first year.

B. No. There is no part of this situation that violates a principle. The location of sales and operations is not relevant to the principles.

C. No. There is no part of this situation that violates a principle. It is unclear whether anything about World Oil Company is relevant. If World Oil Company were majority owned by citizens of Country F, and it put in the highest bid, then the government would have violated its principles. But the answer proves neither of these things. It is unclear whether citizens own a majority share, unclear whether World Oil Company put in the highest bid, and unclear who the government is planning to sell to.

D. No. There is no part of this situation that violates a principle. The company with the highest bid is, from the information given, a company that could buy the utility in complete accord with the principles. The consortium with the second highest bid is not relevant, since there is no evidence that the government plans to sell the company to them in violation of the first principle.

E. Yes. This answer choice partially follows the second principle. It is unclear how long majority ownership will last, so it is not clear if the second principle is followed. But critically, this situation clearly violates the first principle, since the restrictions "reduce the price the government receives" and the first principle requires the government to sell the entity for the most it can get on the open market.

24. **D** Weaken

The argument concludes that Activite must be effective, since the makers of the supplement offer a month's supply free as a promotion. The argument assumes that the only benefit the company could get out of this is the continued business from happy customers, and it assumes that the company does not benefit from the customers who take advantage of the offer and then choose not to buy Activite.

Although "since" usually marks a premise, it is important in this argument not to take the "since" statement as fact. On the extremely rare occasions when the test has presented something as support for the conclusion that is not meant to be taken as a factual premise, the word "would" has been used to show that the statement is meant to be part of the author's reasoning rather than a fact. If the since statement is taken as fact then you get the conditional "~effective → ~in company's best interest," and the contrapositive "In company's best interest → effective." But because this statement is meant to be taken as the author's reasoning rather than fact, there's a way it can be false. Look for an answer that shows how the offer can be in the company's best interest without the supplement being effective.

A. No. This shows that Activite is not a necessary source of these nutrients, but it does not show that Activite is not sufficient to provide the nutrients or that Activite is not effective. Activite can be effective without being the only way to increase energy and mental effectiveness.

B. No. This indicates that there are alternatives to Activite that are a better value, but it in no way diminishes the conclusion that Activite is effective. Activite can be overpriced and still have all the efficacy its makers advertise.

C. No. This does not give any reason why Activite might not be effective. If this promotion works even partially within a month, this gives only more reason to think that Activite is even more effective than people realize within that first month.

D. Yes. This adds an additional consideration to the argument. The author ignores the possibility that the makers of Activite might benefit from the promotion even when people are unhappy with the product. If the company makes a profit on the "free" supply by charging a premium for shipping and handling, the company can make a lot of money even if every customer hates their product.

E. No. While this proves that Activite is not guaranteed to be free of side effects, it does not prove that the supplement is not effective. Even if this answer were stronger and demonstrated a likelihood of side-effects, it would not weaken the conclusion, since even the most effective treatments can have serious side-effects.

25. **A**   Parallel Flaw

This argument concludes that Theresa probably approves of the prime minister. "Probably" is a quantity statement meaning "more likely than not" and is often a proxy for the concept of "most": If more than half of people in a group have brown hair, a random member of that group "probably" has brown hair. More than half of the people who disapprove of the prime minister overall disapprove of the prime minister's support for a tax increase. However, this is not the same thing as saying that more than half of the people who are in favor of the tax increase approve of the prime minister overall. It is possible that most or all of the people who approve of the tax increase disapprove of the prime minister overall because of an unrelated issue, such as ethics violations or social policy. Most A are B is a totally different statement from saying that most non-B are non-A, and the argument confuses these statements. Since the question task directs you to find a flaw similar to this flaw, look for this same pattern in the answer choices: The right answer will assume that "Most A are B" means that most non-B are non-A.

A. Yes. This argument matches the original argument piece by piece. The error is the same. Most of the people who support logging think it will reduce risk of fire, but there is no reason to think that because Andy does not think it will reduce the risk of fire means that he is likely to oppose logging. Like the original argument, the this answer assumes that the statement "most A are B" implies "most non-B are non-A."

B. No. This answer choice switches the conditions in the second sentence, relative to the original argument. In order for it to be similar, it would have to start by establishing that Bonita does not favor a new school. This makes a different error, assuming that since most A are B, most non-A are non-B.

C. No. This answer choice switches the conditions in the second sentence, relative to the original argument. In order for it to be similar, it would have to start by establishing that Chung does believe his situation has improved. This makes a different error, assuming that since most A are B, most non-A are non-B.

D. No. This answer choice is not in error; it assumes that since most A are B, a member of A is probably a member of B. This is not what the original argument does.

E. No. This answer choice is not in error; it assumes that since most A are B, a member of A is probably a member of B. This is not what the original argument does.

26. **B**   Strengthen

The argument concludes that a loss of nesting habitat probably caused a decrease in the mourning dove population in the area. A premise establishes that mourning doves nested in the nearby orchards, but a sprinkler system made the orchards inhospitable for the doves. This is a causal argument, and the purported effect is a premise: There was a decrease in the mourning dove population. The cause of this decrease is disputable. If the orchards make up a tiny percentage of the nesting habitat, this argument is weak. If the orchards make up most or all of the nesting habitat, then the argument is stronger. The argument requires, among other things, that the orchards make up a significant portion of the area's nesting habitat.

A. No. This answer choice provides another reason the mourning doves may be declining: People may be hunting them. This slightly weakens the argument.

B. Yes. This rules out any alternative places for the mourning doves to nest, indicating that the birds lost 100 percent of their habitat in the area. So even if the argument has not proven a causal relationship perfectly, it is clear that the doves lost all their local habitat and suffered a decrease in their population.

C. No. This answer is not clearly relevant to the conclusion. This shows that the mourning doves' aversion to sprinklers also applies to blue jays. But it does nothing to show that the cause for the decrease in mourning doves in the area is the loss of habitat. What happens to blue jays is not relevant to the mourning doves.

D. No. This answer choice is not relevant to the conclusion, which links a decline in mourning doves to a loss of habitat.

E. No. The argument already shows that the mourning doves in this area had nested in orchards. What mourning doves "often" do has no direct relevance to whether a loss of habitat caused a decline in local mourning doves.

Chapter 5
PrepTest 75:
Answers and
Explanations

ANSWER KEY: PREPTEST 75

Section 1: Arguments 1		Section 2: Reading Comprehension		Section 3: Arguments 2		Section 4: Games	
1.	B	1.	C	1.	C	1.	C
2.	C	2.	A	2.	B	2.	B
3.	A	3.	B	3.	C	3.	A
4.	E	4.	C	4.	D	4.	E
5.	C	5.	A	5.	A	5.	D
6.	D	6.	D	6.	B	6.	B
7.	E	7.	E	7.	B	7.	D
8.	C	8.	B	8.	C	8.	B
9.	A	9.	A	9.	E	9.	C
10.	E	10.	A	10.	C	10.	A
11.	D	11.	C	11.	E	11.	A
12.	D	12.	B	12.	B	12.	A
13.	C	13.	C	13.	C	13.	E
14.	A	14.	E	14.	D	14.	B
15.	C	15.	C	15.	E	15.	A
16.	C	16.	A	16.	A	16.	C
17.	D	17.	D	17.	B	17.	D
18.	B	18.	C	18.	E	18.	C
19.	B	19.	E	19.	C	19.	D
20.	E	20.	B	20.	D	20.	A
21.	B	21.	E	21.	E	21.	E
22.	C	22.	B	22.	A	22.	D
23.	C	23.	A	23.	A	23.	D
24.	E	24.	D	24.	B		
25.	A	25.	B	25.	A		
		26.	B				
		27.	C				

EXPLANATIONS

Section 1: Arguments 1

1. **B** [Necessary Assumption]

The pundit's argument makes the claim that the city made a mistake when it sold the rights to collect parking fees. This is supported by the fact that the parking company raised fees and reaped profits far greater than what the city gained in the sale of the property. The pundit then speculates that if the city had not sold the rights, then the city would have made that money. This argument makes a comparison between what the private company did and what the city could have done without first establishing that the city could in fact raise rates. The credited response will establish that the city's actions could be comparable to those of the private company.

A. No. This answer discusses other private companies, which are irrelevant to the conclusion that the city's actions were a mistake.

B. Yes. This answer establishes that the actions taken by the city could be the same as those taken by the private firm.

C. No. This answer choice claims that municipalities should always handle fees. This is too strong to be the assumption behind the argument about this specific incident.

D. No. This contradicts the argument. In the argument it was the private company, not the city, which raised the parking rates.

E. No. The efficiency at which rates are collected is irrelevant to the conclusion that the city made a mistake.

2. **C** [Principle Strengthen]

This argument claims that publications should give up trying to explain new developments in science to a wide audience. The proof offered for this solution is that metaphorical writing is necessary in order to reach a wide audience. However, metaphorical writings fail to convey the science accurately. The argument also states that if the writing is more rigorous, then the science is accurate but the wider audience is not reached. The argument assumes that since scientific rigor is lost, then the attempt to reach wide audiences should be given up. The credited response will state a general rule or principle that establishes that it is better not to reach a wide audience than to be inaccurate scientifically.

A. No. The argument claims that metaphorical writing should be given up, not balanced. This is irrelevant.

B. No. The issue in this argument is not how difficult it is to explain science, but that new developments should not be explained.

C. Yes. This answer choice clearly establishes a rationale for giving up attempting to explain science in a method that may be inaccurate.

D. No. This directly contradicts the conclusion.

E. No. The conclusion is about whether explanations should be given to a wide audience, not whether scientific writing can be free from metaphors.

3. A [Necessary Assumption]

This argument claims that rock music has almost nothing going for it. This is based upon the premises that it is musically bankrupt and socially destructive. The premises allow that the LPs from the 1960s and 1970s often had innovative art. Finally, the premises state that digital music production has almost ended the run of LPs. The argument assumes that since digital music is not the same as LPs, then it can have no features in common with LPs. The credited response will establish that there are not many similarities between LPs and digital music.

A. Yes. This answer choice eliminates the possibility of digital music including the same feature that made rock LPs worthwhile.

B. No. The conclusion allows for the possibility that some rock LPs might still exist because it states that rock music has almost nothing going for it.

C. No. The conclusion is focused on rock music today, not that of the 1960s and 1970s.

D. No. The premises and conclusions allow for some LPs to still have innovative cover art. This is not the assumption in the argument.

E. No. The argument establishes a contrast between the art of LPs and digital music. Whether rock music has become more destructive is not the assumption in the argument.

4. E [Reasoning]

This argument claims that babbling is a linguistic task. This is established by explaining the method used by researchers. Babies open their mouths wider on the right. In nonlinguistic studies, people open their mouths wider on the left. The argument proceeds by establishing two alternatives: nonlinguistic and linguistic. It then provides evidence for what nonlinguistic vocalization looks like to establish that babies' communication is different. The credited response will outline this.

A. No. There is no counterargument.

B. No. This argument does not weaken a general principle. Instead, it establishes a contrast.

C. No. The test outlined is not described as a potential test, but something that was actually performed. Also, the argument never claims that this is the only method by which a hypothesis is tested.

D. No. The argument never refutes the possibility that the interpretation about babies' vocalization might be incorrect.

E. Yes. It outlines the two alternative explanations provided and that one is preferred to the other.

5. C [Weaken]

This argument claims that planting a large number of trees will help fulfill a commitment to reducing carbon dioxide emissions. This is based upon the claim that trees absorb carbon dioxide. The argument assumes that there are no other factors to consider when enacting this plan. The credited response will introduce another consideration that will cast doubt upon the success of the plan to plant large numbers of trees.

A. No. The argument is focused on what the country will do to reduce carbon dioxide emissions. Whether or not private land owners must be paid to participate is irrelevant to the conclusion that planting trees will help the country fulfill its commitment.

B. No. The amount of deforestation is irrelevant to the conclusion about planting more trees.

C. Yes. This answer choice provides a reason to doubt that planting trees will reduce carbon dioxide emissions since more will be produced than consumed.

D. No. What climate researchers believe is irrelevant to whether the proposal will be successful.

E. No. Gases other than carbon dioxide are not relevant to this argument.

6. **D** **Resolve/Explain**

This argument establishes that SUVs are safer for their occupants when involved in crashes than are smaller vehicles. The argument then establishes a paradox by stating that despite this fact, many safety analysts are alarmed at the trend of the increasing number of SUVs. The credited response will provide a reason for the analysts to be concerned about the safety of SUVs in collisions despite the fact that their occupants are less likely to be injured.

A. No. This answer choice makes the problem worse.

B. No. Be careful not to make assumptions: SUVs having a larger fuel capacity does not provide sufficient reason for safety analysts to be concerned about their use.

C. No. Be careful not to make assumptions. Regardless of whether they have more passengers, the argument still states that those passengers are safer.

D. Yes. This answer choice shows that passengers in smaller vehicles may be less safe even though the passengers in SUVs are safer.

E. No. This does not explain why analysts are concerned about the growing number of SUVs.

7. **E** **Flaw**

This argument claims that in order to break the cycle of higher taxes, then Sherwood should not be reelected to the city council. This is based upon the fact that despite Sherwood's claims to be an opponent of high taxes, during his tenure on the city council during the last 10 years taxes consistently increased year after year. This argument assumes that what is true of the council's votes as a whole must also be true of this particular individual. The credited response will identify this flaw.

A. No. While there is a generalization made about Sherwood, we are not presented with any sample of his voting record.

B. No. This is irrelevant to the argument.

C. No. There are no sufficient or necessary conditions about Sherwood's bid for reelection.

D. No. Sherwood is not attacked personally.

E. Yes. This describes the flaw that what is true of the city council as a whole is not necessarily true of Sherwood the individual.

8. C | Main Point

This argument claims that the owners of the catering company should reconsider their decision to raise their rates. The argument opens by establishing the position that the catering company is raising their rates to cover hiring and training costs. The argument then states a contrasting stance as the conclusion. This is followed by the premise that the mission of the company is low-cost gourmet catering, which will be jeopardized by this action. The credited response will correctly identify the conclusion.

A. No. This is a premise of the argument establishing the company's position.

B. No. This is a premise of the argument establishing the company's position.

C. Yes. This is the claim that the client is making.

D. No. This is a premise in support of the claim that the company should not raise its rates.

E. No. This is a premise in support of the claim that the company should not raise its rates.

9. A | Strengthen

This argument claims that the red admiral's flight style evolved as a means of avoiding predators. This is supported by the premise that they fly in an inefficient manner. The argument also notes that predators avoid poisonous butterflies, but the red admiral has to have other means of predator evasion. The argument assumes that there are no other causes for the erratic flight pattern of these butterflies. The credited response will provide additional evidence for predator evasion or will eliminate alternative reasons for the butterflies to have this flight pattern.

A. Yes. This answer choice precludes the possibility that the erratic flight style of red admirals is shared by poisonous butterflies that already have means of evading predators.

B. No. Whether or not predation is the most common cause of death is irrelevant to the claim that red admirals develop their flight pattern to evade attack.

C. No. This answer choice does not limit the erratic flight pattern to nonpoisonous butterflies.

D. No. The inefficiency of other insects is irrelevant to the claim about why red admiral butterflies have this flight pattern.

E. No. What other butterflies' predators may eat is irrelevant to the claim that red admirals evolved this flight pattern.

10. E | Principle Strengthen

This argument establishes the position that copyright statuses benefit society through their protection of original works. The argument then contrasts this protection with the cost to society through the creation of monopolies since the protection in many countries extends decades past the life of the author. The argument concludes this time frame is too long since the benefits of protection are offset by societal costs. The argument assumes that the costs of protection must not outweigh the benefits. The credited response will establish a general rule under which the benefits of a rule are not overshadowed by the costs of that same rule.

A. No. The consistency of a statute is not relevant to the claims that copyright protection is too long.

B. No. Repealing statutes is not at issue in this argument. This is irrelevant to the conclusion.

C. No. This contradicts the conclusion that copyright protection is already too long in many countries.

D. No. This argument is about the benefits and costs of copyright law to society. Limiting rights is irrelevant to this argument.

E. Yes. This answer choice stipulates that benefits of a law should exceed that law's costs.

11. **D** **Weaken**

This argument claims that the policing strategy is the cause of the crime rate falling by 20 percent. The argument assumes that the only relevant cause to the crime rate falling is the policing strategies. The credited response will introduce another consideration that may have also contributed to a lower crime rate.

A. No. The fact that the chief's city still has a higher crime rate does not weaken his claim that his strategy was the cause of the decrease.

B. No. The crime rate several decades before this time is irrelevant to the claim that the strategies were the cause of the decrease in crime during the police chief's tenure.

C. No. Just because the crime rate leveled off does not weaken the claim that the police chief's strategies were the cause of the decrease.

D. Yes. This answer choice suggests that the decrease in crime rate in the chief's city may have been part of a larger pattern in that country that would not have been affected by city-specific policies.

E. No. The variation of rates within the city is not relevant to the claim that it was the chief's policing strategy that caused the decrease.

12. **D** **Flaw**

This argument concludes that concern for the well-being of the people is a necessary condition for the successful government of Acredia. This argument opens with the conditional statement by the Duke of Acredia that concern for the welfare of the people is a necessary condition for the successful ruling of that country. The argument then establishes that if a government of Acredia has fallen, then that ruler disregarded the welfare of the people. The argument assumes that since rulers who did not focus on the people's welfare were not successful, then focusing on their welfare is a necessary condition to their rule. This confuses something that is sufficient to maintain a successful rule as necessary for that rule. The credited response will identify this flaw.

A. No. The changes in people's needs over time is irrelevant to the conclusion that concern for well-being is a necessary feature of a ruler in that country.

B. No. This reverses the premise. The absence of concern has been a feature of rulers who fell, but it is not established as always being present.

C. No. There is no appeal to a biased source.

D. Yes. This answer choice describes how the argument assumes that since a lack of concern was a feature of deposed governments that all governments in that country must be concerned for the people in order to be successful.

E. No. The argument does not assess the character of past rulers.

13. **C** Inference

This argument establishes that Professor Burns notes that the recent observations fail to confirm a previous finding of a comet reservoir. Burns is cited as using this as definitive proof that the earlier hypothesis is incorrect. The argument then states that the data Burns used were obtained under poor conditions. The credited response will be a statement that is supported by these three facts.

A. No. This answer choice makes a speculation beyond the facts mentioned. This is an unsupported prediction.

B. No. This answer choice goes beyond the fact mentioned. All that is known of the recent observations is that they were obtained in poor conditions.

C. Yes. Professor Burns's interpretation of the data is likely flawed since the data were less than optimal.

D. No. This answer choice makes a speculation beyond the facts mentioned. This is an unsupported prediction.

E. No. The data were obtained in poor conditions, but this does not necessarily mean that the data are totally worthless. This answer choice is too strong.

14. **A** Reasoning

This argument concludes that society would not be better off if the government passed laws forcing people to be polite. This is based upon the premise that such laws would create more problems than politeness does. This is in spite of the fact that if people refrained from being impolite then society would be improved. The credited response will correctly identify the role played by the statement that society would not be better off with laws enforcing politeness. In this case, this statement is the conclusion.

A. Yes. The statement in question is conclusion of the argument.

B. No. The statement in question is not used as evidence for something else in the argument.

C. No. The statement in question is not used as evidence for something else in the argument.

D. No. The statement in question is not an illustration of a premise. It is the conclusion.

E. No. The statement in question does not describe a phenomenon. It is the conclusion of the argument.

15. **C** Strengthen

This argument concludes that some of the planets in oval orbits obtained those orbits by interacting with other planets in orbit around the same star. This is supported by the premise that many of the planets in our solar system have circular orbits, while comets in our solar system have ovate orbits. The

75

argument assumes that nothing else could cause a planet around a distant star to have an oval orbit. Additionally, the argument assumes that the comparison between our solar system and a distant plant is valid. The credited response will provide additional evidence in support of the claim that another planet caused the ovate orbit or it will remove obstacles to the conclusion being true.

A.　No. The size of the affected planet is not relevant to the conclusion that the oval orbits were caused by other planets around that star.

B.　No. What failed to happen in our solar system is not necessarily relevant to what happened in another system. If anything, this choice would weaken the conclusion by demonstrating at least one example of when planets were not affected by other planets.

C.　Yes. This removes an obstacle to the conclusion since the argument never established that stars whose planets had ovate orbits also had more than one planet in orbit.

D.　No. How comets in our system obtained their oval orbits is not relevant to the claim that planets in another system got their oval orbits.

E.　No. If each of these known planets had no other known planets, then the conclusion is implausible. This would weaken the conclusion.

16.　**C**　**Reasoning**

This argument concludes that saltwater irrigation would be cheaper than other irrigation if undertaken near the ocean. This is based upon the premises that the water would not have to be pumped far and that pumping water is the single greatest cost of irrigation. The credited response will correctly identify the claim that pumping is the greatest cost of irrigation as a premise in support of the conclusion that saltwater irrigation is cheaper than other types of irrigation.

A.　No. This claim is not disproved in the argument.

B.　No. This is a stated fact in the argument, not a hypothesis.

C.　Yes. The claim is a premise in support of the conclusion.

D.　No. This is a premise and not the conclusion.

E.　No. This is a premise in support of the conclusion, but no evidence is provided for this statement.

17.　**D**　**Inference**

This argument establish that critics worry that pessimistic news reports will harm the economy by causing people to lose faith. The argument establishes that everyone has direct experience with the economy every day. Journalists contend that they cannot worry about the effects of their work. Finally, the argument establishes that people defer to journalists only when they have no direct experience in something. The credited response will be a statement that is supported by a statement or combination of these statements.

A.　No. The statements above do not support the claim that the critics are in fact wrong. This is too strong.

B.　No. Foreign policy is not mentioned by the argument. This is unsupported information.

C. No. This is the opposite of what the argument suggests. Since people have direct experience with the economy, they are not likely to defer to journalists. Thus, the journalists' pessimistic reports will not likely have an effect.

D. Yes. Since people have direct experience with the economy, they do not defer to journalists. Thus, the opinions of the journalists are not likely to affect people's opinion of the economy.

E. No. Just because journalists cannot worry about the effects of their reports in order to do their jobs well does not mean that they should not worry. This is unsupported.

18. **B**   Flaw

This argument claims that the recent accusations of graft in the precinct are unfounded. This is based upon the definition of graft as gifts of cash or objects valued at greater than $100. The police captain then states that no officer in that precinct has accepted such gifts. The argument assumes that the definition of graft is all encompassing and that no other forms of graft or bribery exist. The credited response will identify this flaw.

A. No. The captain makes a claim about the officers in his precinct based upon knowledge of those officers. This is not a limited sample.

B. Yes. This correctly describes the assumption that since no officer has accepted a specific form of graft that no graft has occurred.

C. No. The statement is about the actions of the police officers and not an appeal to their characters.

D. No. This answer choice describes other forms of corruption that are irrelevant to the conclusion, which is focused specifically on graft.

E. No. The premise does not contradict the conclusion.

19. **B**   Resolve/ Explain

This argument establishes that hourly wages vary greatly in different regions, but average hourly wages for full-time jobs in each region increased. The paradox is that despite the average in each region increasing, the country's overall hourly wage decreased. The paradox is predicated upon how averages function. The credited response will indicate a way that overall wages could go down despite the regional increases.

A. No. A decrease nationally for the past three years does not explain why the average in each region was higher.

B. Yes. If employees moved to regions with lower average wages, they may have seen their personal wages decrease while the average wage within that region might still have increased.

C. No. People who are unemployed would not have wages that are part of the full-time job wage average.

D. No. This is an established fact in the argument and does not resolve the paradox.

E. No. This does not resolve the paradox since the ratio of full-time manufacturing and service jobs is unknown.

75

20. **E** Inference

This argument establishes the fact the 35 percent of people with schizophrenia had damage to the subplate in their brains. People without schizophrenia lacked this damage. The argument then establishes that damage to the subplate must have occurred prior to the second fetal trimester. The credited response will be an answer choice that is supported by one or a combination of these statements.

A. No. Just because 35 percent of people with schizophrenia also had this type of damage does not mean that the damage in fact caused schizophrenia. This is too strongly worded.

B. No. The treatment of schizophrenia is not mentioned in this argument. This is unsupported.

C. No. Schizophrenia and damage were found together. This does not prove that the damage caused the schizophrenia. This is too strongly worded.

D. No. The facts do not establish a genetic cause for the damage to the subplate. This is unsupported.

E. Yes. This answer choice takes the correlation between the damage and the schizophrenia as a potential cause.

21. **B** Strengthen

This argument concludes that ranchers will purchase a global positioning device for their cattle at the current cost. This claim is made despite the fact that outfitting a herd of cattle with this device is far more expensive than other means of keeping cattle in their pastures. The argument assumes that there is some reason that the device will be purchased. The credited response will introduce a consideration that makes the purchase of the device a reasonable alternative to fencing.

A. No. This contradicts the conclusion, which states that ranchers will purchase the device at its current price.

B. Yes. If cattle follow the same few animals, then ranchers would not need to purchase a device for each member of their herd. They would need to purchase only a few for these cattle who lead.

C. No. The stress caused to the cattle is irrelevant to the claim that ranchers will purchase the device at its current price.

D. No. Since the device is only as effective as fences cannot explain why ranchers will purchase this device rather than just installing fences, which are established as cheaper.

E. Yes. This contradicts the conclusion, which states that ranchers will purchase the device at its current price.

22. **C** Parallel Flaw

This argument claims that it is more economical to shop at a food co-op than at a supermarket. The premise is that a food co-op is a type of consumer cooperative and that consumer cooperatives offer the same products as stores at a cheaper price. The structure of this argument is that a specific thing (food co-ops) is part of a larger group (consumer cooperatives) that has a feature that can be compared with another thing (stores). The flaw in this argument is a part to whole comparison. The argument assumes that what is true of consumer cooperatives in general is also true of food co-ops specifically. The credited response will contain a response that has this same pattern and flaw, but it will not necessarily be in the same order as the original argument.

A. No. This answer claims that sports cars use more gasoline since they burn more gas per mile than other cars. This is a comparison between two categories, not between parts and wholes.

B. No. This answer claims that it is better to purchase frozen vegetables and provides two reasons to do so. This argument is flawed, but it does not focus on part to whole relationships.

C. Yes. This answer claims that bikes belong to a larger category of private means of transportation. Since private means of transport produce more pollution than public transportation, this answer claims that bikes produce more pollution than buses. This is the same pattern and flaw as the original argument.

D. No. This answer is based on a claim about where people shop based upon the types of food they prefer. While this argument is flawed, it does not make a comparison between parts and wholes.

E. No. This answer claims that the best way to lose weight is to increase consumption of artificial sweetener. While this argument is flawed, this does not focus on the part to whole relationship between sweeteners.

23.   C   **Sufficient Assumption**

This argument concludes that it is a mistake to claim that accidents are partly the fault of railway companies when adults ignore warning signs. This is supported via an analogy about how adults are responsible for protecting small children from injury, but licensed drivers should know better. The argument assumes that knowing how to avoid danger is sufficient to prevent a railway company from being liable for any injury caused to that adult. The credited response will explicitly link the premise to the conclusion and will force the conclusion to be true.

A. No. Stating that some drivers may ignore larger gates does not force the claim that railway companies are not responsible for those injuries.

B. No. This answer choice is a necessary assumption to the claim that railways are not responsible, but it is not in and of itself sufficient for forcing the conclusion.

C. Yes. This answer choice places the responsibility fully upon capable adults who ignore warnings.

D. No. Whether or not small children are harmed when drivers go around railway gates would not force railway companies to not be at fault.

E. No. The issue in the conclusion is whether railway companies are partially at fault when adults ignore warning signs. The limits of a company's responsibility are irrelevant to this conclusion.

24.   E   **Flaw**

This argument claims that if a survey is well-constructed, then survey respondents' desire to fulfill the surveyor's expectations of them will not affect the results of that survey. This is based upon the premise that people provide answers that they perceive are desired, but that well-constructed questions preclude the possibility of indicating a desired answer. This argument assumes that the only cause for respondent bias is to be found in the questions themselves. The credited response will identify an alternative cause for respondents to provide answers that they perceive the interviewer desires.

A. No. The conclusion is focused solely on how crafting questions will prevent people from responding the way they perceive the surveyors wants them to. Other types of survey flaws are irrelevant to this argument.

B. No. This answer cites an exception to the first premise and is not a flaw in the argument.

C. No. The issue is not whether surveyors have expectations of an answer, but whether the respondents perceive that this is so. This is irrelevant to the conclusion.

D. No. This answer choice cites an exception to the first premise and is not a flaw in the argument.

E. Yes. This answer choice provides an alternative cause for respondents to provide answers they think the surveyor wants despite having well-crafted questions.

25. **A**   Parallel

This argument claims that the availability of television reduces the amount of reading that children do. This is supported by two premises, which establish that when TV is unavailable, children read more and that when TV becomes available again, they read less. The structure of this argument is that two items are correlated. The correlation holds in two different patterns. The conclusion assumes a causal relationship between the two items. The credited response will have this same pattern.

A. Yes. The two items are interest rates and money supply. When the availability of money fluctuates, so does the interest rate. When the money supply is stable, so are interest rates. This matches the premises of the original argument. The conclusion in this answer also assumes that because the availability of one thing leads to changes in the occurrence of another, then that thing must cause those changes.

B. No. This argument claims that candy consumption disrupts appetite. This claim is based on the unrelated premise that a lack of candy consumption causes hunger. This does not match the pattern in the original argument.

C. No. This is a causal argument; however, this argument has three linked causes. This does not match the correlation as causation pattern above.

D. No. This argument claims that voting behavior is influenced by things other than the candidates' records. The argument provides some proof for that claim. This does not follow the correlation as causation pattern in the original argument.

E. No. The argument must match the structure of the original argument as closely as possible. The original argument discusses the availability of an alternative, but it never claims that the children or adults were watching TV. This answer choice goes beyond the structure of the original argument by claiming that adults are performing other activities, which in turn leads to a decrease in reading.

75

Section 2: Reading Comprehension

Questions 1–7

The main point of the first paragraph is to present the question of whether the use of video by indigenous peoples has impacted indigenous culture. The second paragraph introduces the Weiner view, that the use of video technology negatively impacts indigenous cultures. The third paragraph explains the contrasting view, held by Ginsburg that video technology not only doesn't harm indigenous culture, but also can help preserve it. The final paragraph discusses evidence from Turner consistent with the Ginsburg position. The Bottom Line of the passage as a whole is that there is debate over how video technology impacts indigenous cultures and that there is some evidence to indicate that it can help preserve culture.

1. **C** **Big Picture**

   Use your Bottom Line of the passage to help you to evaluate the choices. The correct answer will describe the main idea of the passage.

   A. No. While this answer choice is supported by the passage, it captures the point of view in the second paragraph only and is too narrow.

   B. No. This answer choice is too extreme. The passage discusses that video technology can help preserve culture, but it does not go so far as to say the "colonial gaze" has been eliminated.

   C. Yes. This accurately matches the Bottom Line that there is a debate over the impact of video technology and some evidence to support the idea that it can help preserve culture.

   D. No. The passage doesn't mention long-term impact.

   E. No. While this answer choice is supported by the passage, it captures only the fourth paragraph and is too narrow.

2. **A** **Extract Infer**

   The question is asking for Ginsburg's attitude towards Weiner's point of view. The correct answer will reflect that she disagrees with his position.

   A. Yes. Ginsburg argues that video technology can strengthen indigenous culture, in direct opposition to Weiner's view.

   B. No. While Ginsburg disagrees with Weiner, she does not scold him and "censure" is too extreme.

   C. No. Ginsburg's point of view is in direct opposition to Weiner's, so "mild" does not accurately reflect her position.

   D. No. Ginsburg disagrees with Weiner.

   E. No. Ginsburg disagrees with Weiner.

3. **B** **RC Reasoning**

   The question is asking for a situation analogous to the Kayapo's use of video. As discussed in the fourth paragraph, the Kayapo's use of video aesthetically mirrors their cultural practices. The correct answer should describe the incorporation of something new while preserving the characteristics of the original.

A.   No. This answer choice involves altering the characteristics of the original.

B.   Yes. New ideas are incorporated in, but the tradition remains.

C.   No. This answer choice involves altering the characteristics of the original.

D.   No. This choice does not involve the incorporation of something new.

E.   No. This choice does not involve the incorporation of something new.

4.   **C**   **Extract Fact**

The correct response will be directly supported by the discussion of Weiner in the passage.

A.   No. This is not discussed in the passage.

B.   No. This is not discussed in the passage.

C.   Yes. This is supported by line 22.

D.   No. While this term is mentioned in the passage, it is not part of Weiner's point of view.

E.   No. This is not discussed in the passage.

5.   **A**   **Extract Infer**

The correct answer will be the question that is most directly related to evidence within the passage text.

A.   Yes. The passage discusses that the Kayapo are primarily an oral society and use video to document transactions.

B.   No. While the term "noble savage" is mentioned, the passage does not discuss its origin.

C.   No. The passage gives an example of only one culture that has adopted video technology.

D.   No. The passage does not discuss specific technologies in the fifteenth century.

E.   No. The passage mentions that video equipment is inexpensive, but it does not discuss why.

6.   **D**   **Extract Infer**

The question is asking about the relationship between Turner and Weiner's points of view. The correct answer will be consistent with the discussion of Turner and will reflect that Turner's research undermines Weiner's point of view.

A.   No. Turner does not discuss diverse practices; he discusses only what he has found with the Kayapo.

B.   No. Turner does not discuss the availability of video technology.

C.   No. Weiner is concerned with the preservation of traditional practices, he just doesn't think that video is the best way to do it.

D.   Yes. This is consistent with Turner's findings and addresses Weiner's claim that video changes cultural values.

E.   No. Turner does not discuss other technologies.

7. E Structure

The question is asking what the author means by "technological determinism." The correct answer will be directly supported by the author's discussion in the third paragraph.

A.   No. There is no discussion of an exchange of technology.

B.   No. The passage discusses use of technology by indigenous peoples rather than by anthropologists.

C.   No. The passage does not argue that there is a dependence on technology.

D.   No. The passage does not discuss ethical values.

E.   Yes. Ginsburg argues that technology does not shape culture, which is unlike Weiner's view.

Questions 8–14

The first paragraph discusses the current approach for dealing with disqualification and recusal of judges. The second paragraph sets out issues with the current approach. The third paragraph proposes a course of action to solve the problem of biased judges. The final paragraph rebuts potential objections to the author's proposal. The Bottom Line of the passage is that the current system for the disqualification and recusal of judges is inadequate and could be improved by requiring judges to explain the reasoning for their judgments.

8. B Extract Fact

The question is asking for a direct statement from the passage critiquing the current rules.

A.   No. The passage mentions that bias might interfere with judges' reasoning, but it does not argue that the rules do.

B.   Yes. This is explicitly supported by line 15.

C.   No. This answer contradicts the author's argument that transparency in judicial reasoning is important.

D.   No. This is untrue. The passage states that some jurisdictions allow parties to court proceedings to request disqualification.

E.   No. This is untrue. The passage states that the current rules focus on both impropriety and the appearance of impropriety.

9. A Structure

The question is asking for the point of the second paragraph. The correct answer should capture the author's critique of the current approach.

A.   Yes. This accurately describes that the second paragraph is critiquing the current approach.

B.   No. This answer choice confuses the order of the passage. The solution is presented in the third paragraph.

C.   No. There are no concrete examples in the second paragraph.

D. No. The second paragraph does not discuss history.

E. No. The rest of the passage focuses on a solution, not a defense of the author's critique.

10. **A** Extract
Infer

The correct answer will be supported by the author's discussion of the principle in the fourth paragraph.

A. Yes. The author introduces the principle with "under the law."

B. No. The author is not providing a definition.

C. No. The author cites the principle as rationale for his or her proposal and as a response to potential critiques of the proposal.

D. No. The author concurs with the principle and thinks it should be applied.

E. No. The principle relates to the author's proposal to change the means of addressing judicial bias.

11. **C** Extract
Infer

The correct answer will be consistent with the author's critique of the current system.

A. No. In the second paragraph, the author argues that the current rules are vague.

B. No. The current statutes are not incompatible. Additional requirements for the disclosure of legal reasoning could be added to the current rules.

C. Yes. This answer is supported by lines 22–24.

D. No. These statutes work in tandem with rules that require judges to recuse themselves.

E. No. The author does not discuss a need for a guarantee.

12. **B** Extract
Infer

The answer will be consistent with the author's proposal to require judicial reasoning in the third and fourth paragraphs.

A. No. The author concedes that this new plan may not eliminate all bias, but it will eliminate the harm caused by bias.

B. Yes. The author argues that such a proposal would eliminate harm.

C. No. This answer choice is extreme. While the author concedes that such explanations may not always reveal the judge's actual reasoning, that is not enough to support the word "usually."

D. No. The author does not discuss changes in public perception.

E. No. The author does not discuss any impact on judges recusing themselves as a result of having to reveal their reasoning.

75

13. **C**   RC Reasoning

The question is asking for an answer that is consistent with the author's description of "real reasoning," which is contrasted with the judge's stated reasoning.

A.   No. The author is discussing the reasoning behind a judge's disposition in a case, not the reasoning about recusal.

B.   No. This is outside the scope of what is discussed in the passage.

C.   Yes. This would be reasoning that a judge would not likely articulate.

D.   No. This would be the judge's stated reasoning.

E.   No. This would be the judge's stated reasoning.

14. **E**   Extract Infer

The correct answer will be supported by the author's critique of the current approach that the current rules are vague and focus on the appearance of bias.

A.   No. The author does not discuss assurances to the general public.

B.   No. The author does not discuss how judges feel about the current rules.

C.   No. The author does not discuss the frequency of removal for bias.

D.   No. The author does not discuss the frequency of removal for bias.

E.   Yes. The author discusses that the current rules focus on appearance of bias and therefore may cause actual instances of bias to be overlooked.

Questions 15–20

Passage A

The first chunk discusses that there may be some justification for lying to liars because liars forfeit their right to honesty. The second chunk discusses the moral questions that arise and concludes that while a liar has no right to the truth, that is not sufficient justification for someone to lie to a liar. The Bottom Line of passage A is that someone's dishonesty is not sufficient justification to lie to that person.

Passage B

The first paragraph introduces Kantian morality. The second paragraph applies Kant's principles to the question of whether liars have a right to honesty and concludes that they don't because by making the rational decision to lie, they are authorizing people to lie to them. The Bottom Line of passage B is that lying authorizes other people to lie to you, but it does not compel them to lie to you.

15. **C** **Big Picture**

The correct answer will reflect the Bottom Line of each passage. The Bottom Line of passage A is that someone's dishonesty is not sufficient justification to lie to that person. The Bottom Line of passage B is that lying authorizes other people to lie to you, but it does not compel them to lie to you.

A. No. Passage B does not discuss harm.

B. No. Neither passage discusses criminal wrongs.

C. Yes. The Bottom Line of each passage answers this question.

D. No. Passage A does not discuss duties.

E. No. Passage A does not discuss rational beings.

16. **A** **Extract Fact**

The correct answer will be explicitly supported by passage A, but it will not appear in passage B.

A. Yes, Passage A discusses harm as a reason not to lie to liars, whereas passage B does not mention harm.

B. No. This is not mentioned in passage A.

C. No. This is not mentioned in passage A.

D. No. This is mentioned in passage B.

E. No. No specific instances are mentioned in passage A.

17. **D** **Structure**

The correct answer will describe the logic of each passage. Both passages discuss the implications of the view that it's acceptable for liars to be lied to.

A. No. Passage A does not refute any objections.

B. No. Passage B does not use an analogy.

C. No. Neither passage uses a specific example.

D. Yes. Passage A points out the harm to society that results from lying, and passage B argues that an assertion of a duty to punish would be excessive.

E. No. Neither passage defines a term.

18. **C** **Extract Infer**

The correct answer will be best supported by the text of passage A.

A. No. Passage A does not discuss rationality; it is discussed by passage B.

B. No. Passage A does not discuss moral duties; they are discussed in passage B.

C. Yes. This answer is explicitly supported in lines 24–27 of passage A.

D. No. This answer choice is extreme. The passage states merely that a person's characteristic as a liar is not sufficient to justify lying.

E. No. Passage A does not discuss innocent persons.

19. **E** [Extract Infer]

The correct answer will reflect passage A's discussion of rights that are forfeited, based on behavior and passage B's discussion of someone obtaining the right to lie because someone else has lied.

A. No. There is no discussion of legal rights in passage A.

B. No. There is no discussion of an individual in a position of authority in passage B.

C. No. There is no discussion of groups in passage A.

D. No. Passage A discusses rights that can be forfeited.

E. Yes. This accurately captures the discussion of rights in each passage.

20. **B** [RC Reasoning]

The question is asking for something that would reconcile passage A giving an instance in which lying would not create a right to lie even though passage B says that lying is a rational act that creates a right to lie. The correct answer will be consistent with both positions.

A. No. Lying in response to a pathological lie would not be pathological.

B. Yes. If the pathological lie is not rational behavior, then according to passage B it does not create the right to lie.

C. No. Passage B would still find sufficient reason to lie in this case.

D. No. This is inconsistent with the argument in passage A that a right to lie is not created in this case.

E. No. The lowering of standards is not relevant to passage B.

Questions 21–27

The first paragraph introduces the persistent, faulty belief that glass flows and offers a potential explanation for this mistaken belief. The second paragraph introduces evidence that debunks the belief. The third paragraph goes into further detail about the evidence. The fourth paragraph gives the actual reason that glass in old windows is thicker at the bottom. The Bottom Line of the passage is that despite the beliefs of many, glass in windows does not actually flow and this is supported by evidence.

21. **E** [Big Picture]

Use your Bottom Line of the passage to help you to evaluate the choices. The correct answer will describe the main point of the passage that despite the beliefs of many, glass in windows does not actually flow and this is supported by evidence.

A. No. While this is true based on the passage, it is a detail and too narrow in scope for a main point question.

B. No. While this is true based on the passage, it is a detail and too narrow in scope for a main point question.

C. No. There is no discussion of how Zanotto calculated the time needed for glass to flow by a noticeable amount.

D. No. This is not supported by the passage. The author argues that the movement of glass did not contribute to noticeable differences in thickness.

E. Yes. This accurately paraphrases the Bottom Line.

22. **B** [Extract Infer]

The correct answer will be best supported by the passage text.

A. No. The passage discusses the differences in pre- and post-nineteenth-century techniques, but it does not address differences between the seventeenth century and medieval times.

B. Yes. This is explicitly addressed in the fourth paragraph.

C. No. This is outside the scope of the passage. There is no mention of the existence or lack of windows before medieval times.

D. No. This answer choice pulls language from multiple parts of the passage, but there is no discussion of the type of glass used in uneven windowpanes.

E. No. The passage mentions that there were impurities in older glass, but it does not discuss how they got there.

23. **A** [Extract Infer]

The question is asking the author's attitude toward Zanotto's study results. The author uses the study to support his point, so the correct answer should reflect a favorable attitude.

A. Yes. This is an accurate description of the study results and reflects the author's positive view.

B. No. The passage does not indicate that there has been any additional research.

C. No. The passage does not indicate that there has been any additional research.

D. No. The results debunk only one view.

E. No. The results debunk only one view.

24. **D** [Extract Infer]

The correct answer will be supported by something the passage says about the atomic structure of glass. The passage notes that glass does not have a fixed atomic structure.

A. No. This is contradicted by the passage. At the end of the first paragraph, the author asserts that glass will behave as a solid.

B. No. This is contradicted by the passage. In the second paragraph, the author discusses Zanotto's study results showing that it would take far more than a few millennia for glass to move in a noticeable way.

C. No. The passage states that glass behaves as a solid when it's cooled below the transition temperature.

D. Yes. In the third paragraph, the passage states that glass could have the ability to flow when raised to over 350 degrees Celsius.

E. No. This is contradicted by the passage. In the first paragraph, the author discusses that glass does not have a fixed crystalline structure, but still behaves as a solid.

25. **B** Extract Infer

The question is asking about the reason that the author gives for people believing that glass flows noticeably downward. In the first paragraph, the author states that the mistaken belief is likely due to a misunderstanding about glass's lack of crystalline structure.

A. No. While the confusion is related to the lack of crystalline structure, it arises out of a knowledge that there is no crystalline structure and misunderstanding about the consequences of that fact.

B. Yes. The author states that the cause is likely a misunderstanding of the consequences of a lack of crystalline structure.

C. No. The author does not discuss glassmaking methods in the first paragraph.

D. No. The author's discussion of transition temperatures is in a different part of the passage and is unrelated to the mistaken belief people held.

E. No. The language in this answer choice is tempting, but the author argues that the misunderstanding stems from an assumption that liquid and solid glasses are similar rather than dissimilar.

26. **B** RC Reasoning

The question is asking for a situation similar to the mistaken belief about glass. The persistent mistaken belief was based on a misunderstanding of the structure of glass, while the real cause of thicker glass at the base of windows was the manufacturing process. The correct answer will match this logic.

A. No. This does not match the passage. The passage does not discuss correction as an issue in the misunderstanding.

B. Yes. This matches the mistaken attribution of an effect to the glass itself rather than the manufacturing process.

C. No. This does not match the passage. The passage makes no mention of a shortened life span.

D. No. This does not match the passage. The passage does not discuss quality in relation to the mistaken belief.

E. No. This does not match the passage. The passage does not discuss durability.

27. **C** Extract Infer

The correct answer will be the statement best supported by the passage's discussion of the transition temperature of glass. The passage states that this is a range of a few hundred degrees Celsius, below which glass behaves as a solid.

A. No. The passage does not provide relative transition temperatures.

B. No. The passage does not indicate that Zanotto calculated the temperature precisely, merely that he has calculated the time needed for a noticeable flow.

C. Yes. The passage states that glass would need to be heated to at least 350 degrees for any sort of noticeable flow, and given that the range is a few hundred degrees, the top end of the range would need to be a few hundred degrees above 350.

D. No. This is unsupported by the passage. Glass within the transition temperature range would be able to flow downward.

E. No. This is contradicted by the passage. The passage states that it is a range of a few hundred degrees, not a specific temperature.

Section 3: Arguments 2

1. **C** **Main Point**

In this question, the credited response will fill in the blank an answer choice that is supported by the premises stated in the argument. The argument states that individuals who have skills and knowledge to apply new technology will prosper and those that do not may lose jobs. Similarly, firms that do not resist technology will overcome those firms that do resist innovation. The credited response will match these premises and make a point that combines the facts presented.

A. No. There is no information presented in the argument about dislocating workers, so this does not match the argument.

B. No. The argument presents information pointing out that companies who resist technological innovation will lose jobs to those firms that do not resist such innovation.

C. Yes. The argument presents information pointing out that companies who resist technological innovation will lose jobs to those firms that do not resist such innovation.

D. No. The argument presents information pointing out that companies who resist technological innovation will lose jobs to those firms that do not resist such innovation.

E. No. There is no information presented in the argument about prioritizing new technology over new industries.

2. **B** **Necessary Assumption**

This question asks you to help the argument. Identify the conclusion and premises; then look for a language shift or gap between them. The argument concludes that the Hydro can likely attribute its success to customers who want to appear environmentally conscious. The argument bases this conclusion on premises that state that sales of the Hydro are rising and that the Hydro is comparable in price and fuel efficiency to its competitors. In order to attribute the success of the Hydro to the appearance of being environmentally conscious, the author must assume that the Hydro appears to be uniquely environmentally conscious among its competition.

A. No. The argument seeks to explain the reason for the Hydro's increased sales based on it appearing to be environmentally conscious. The author makes no argument about its popularity.

B.   Yes. In order to attribute the success of the Hydro to the appearance of being environmentally conscious, the author must assume that the Hydro appears to be uniquely environmentally conscious among its competition.

C.   No. The safety record of the Hydro is irrelevant to the argument about it appearing to be environmentally conscious.

D.   No. The author states that buyers of the Hydro want to appear environmentally conscious to their neighbors but makes no assumption that the neighbors are also buyers of the Hydro.

E.   No. The actual interest of Hydro buyers in environmental causes is not relevant to the argument about whether they want to appear environmentally conscious.

3.   C   **Principle Strengthen**

The argument concludes that it would be unfair for McBride's complaint to be dismissed simply because she was given an incorrect form to file the complaint. The credited response will be a principle that proves this conclusion based on the facts presented in the argument.

A.   No. A rule requiring information for those wishing to file complaints would not address the conclusion that dismissing the complaint would be unfair.

B.   No. There is no information presented in the argument that Form 283 or Form 5 are unduly burdensome, so this does not address the conclusion that dismissing the complaint would be unfair.

C.   Yes. This would prove the conclusion is true based on the premises stated in the passage.

D.   No. There is no evidence that the agency gave McBride the incorrect form because the process is too complex, so this choice does not address the conclusion that dismissing the complaint would be unfair.

E.   No. There is no evidence presented to indicate whether the business in this situation could defend itself, so this choice does not address the conclusion that dismissing the complaint would be unfair.

4.   D   **Inference**

In this question, the credited response will be supported by the text. The passage states that the size of a bird's spleen is an indicator of that bird's health. The passage also states that birds killed accidentally have larger spleens than those killed by predators.

A.   No. The passage does indicate that predators tend to kill sickly birds, but there is no information to suggest that predators are unable to kill healthy birds.

B.   No. This choice is the reverse of what is stated in the passage. It is possible that most sickly birds are not killed by predators.

C.   No. The passage does indicate that predators tend to kill sickly birds, but it does not state why or how they do so.

D.   Yes. The passage does indicate that predators tend to kill sickly birds since sickly birds have smaller spleens and the birds killed by predators have smaller spleens.

E.   No. The passage indicates that spleen size is an indicator of health but provides no evidence that spleen size causes poor health.

5. A **Resolve/ Explain**

The credited response to this question will make sense of the seeming contradiction in the passage. The conflict as described is that on one hand, home ownership is an indicator of financial prosperity. On the other hand, home ownership correlates with high levels of unemployment.

A.   Yes. This explains one reason that homeowners may have a high level of unemployment since relocating to a place with a job is more challenging if one is a homeowner.

B.   No. This would make the conflict worse by showing that jobs are more readily available near homeowners.

C.   No. This choice shows that the correlation between home ownership and unemployment is ubiquitous but does not explain why such a correlation exists.

D.   No. This would make the conflict worse by showing that homeowners have a greater support network helping them find jobs.

E.   No. This cannot explain the correlation between home ownership and unemployment because there is no link between economic security and unemployment.

6. B **Strengthen**

The credited response to this question will help the hypothesis that when hornworms' first meal is from a nightshade, they enjoy the chemical in nightshade and nothing else tastes as good. The scientists base this hypothesis on the fact that hornworms that feed first on nightshade will not eat other plants later in life, but those that feed first on other plants will eat other plants later in life.

A.   No. The preference for specific varieties of nightshade plant is irrelevant to whether the hornworm becomes habituated to indioside D.

B.   Yes. If removing the taste receptors makes hornworms feed on other plants, then the taste receptors must be responsible for the preference to nightshade. This would support the hypothesis that the taste receptors are habituated to indioside D present in nightshade plants.

C.   No. The location of eggs is not explicitly relevant to the appetites of hornworms.

D.   No. This would weaken the hypothesis by pointing out an alternative reason for the food preferences of hornworms.

E.   No. This choice is not strong enough to help the argument. There is no evidence that the taste receptors have reactions to chemicals in plants.

7. B **Flaw**

This question asks for a description of the flaw in the employee's argument. The employee argues that her boss is incorrect in stating that her presentation should have included detailed profit projections. The employees bases this conclusion on the premise that people's attention wanders when they get too much detail. The argument is flawed in that it assumes more detailed profit projections would provide too much detail to the audience.

A.   No. The argument makes no assumptions about the boss's previous assertions about the employee's presentations.

B.   Yes. The argument assumes more detailed profit projections would provide too much detail to the audience.

C.   No. Other reasons an audience's attention may wander during a presentation are not relevant to whether providing more detailed profit projections would cause the audience's attention to wander.

D.   No. The conclusion is about a single case and bases it on information about that case that may fit a generalization.

E.   No. The employee is consistent in her use of the term "detail."

8.   **C**   **Main Point**

The conclusion states that the local media shows too much deference toward public officials. This is based on premises that the local media believe Clemens is an honest politician, that Clemens was caught up in a scandal, and that the reporters failed to expose the scandal sooner. The credited response will match the conclusion of the argument.

A.   No. This is a premise.

B.   No. The author states that the media were wrong about Clemens being an honest politician and this is offered as a premise.

C.   Yes. This matches the conclusion and the other statements in the argument support it as the main point.

D.   No. This is a premise.

E.   No. This is an assumption made by the author in making the point that the local media show too much deference toward public officials.

9.   **E**   **Parallel**

The original argument concludes that there has never been life on the Moon. This is based on premises that state that if life existed on the Moon, there would be signs of life there and numerous trips to the Moon have occurred without noticing any of these signs. The credited response will offer a similar argument that bases a conclusion on an absence of evidence to the contrary despite numerous attempts to collect the evidence.

A.   No. This argument does not base its conclusion on an absence of evidence despite an opportunity to collect the evidence.

B.   No. The original argument concludes something that is certain, "there has never been life on the Moon," while this argument concludes the likelihood of something being true.

C.   No. This argument concludes that voters will go with Hendricks because Hendricks is tough on crime, but it does so by pointing to one factor (out of many possibilities) that would lead to Hendricks's winning of the election. It assumes that since there is one pathway to winning the election that the pathway must be true.

D. No. This argument assumes that evidence of rodents in the warehouse is an indication of causation. There is no premise about the lack of evidence.

E. Yes. This argument concludes that the army is not planning an attack because if it were planning an attack there would be evidence and reports do not show the evidence.

10. **C** Flaw

This question asks for a description of the flaw in the television host's argument. The host claims that there must be evidence the defendant is not completely innocent despite the fact that there was a strong alibi and exculpatory evidence and a jury found the defendant not guilty. The host bases the conclusion on the premise that the prosecutor wouldn't have brought charges unless the defendant was at least partially guilty. This argument assumes that the prosecutor has such expertise or authority that all other evidence to the contrary must be wrong. The credited response will describe this flaw.

A. No. The host provides ample evidence for the view that the defendant is not guilty but nonetheless believes the contrary because an individual believes it to be so.

B. No. This argument is not circular. The host's conclusion is based on the premise that a prosecutor must have thought the defendant was guilty and that therefore the defendant must be guilty.

C. Yes. This argument assumes that the prosecutor has such expertise or authority that all other evidence to the contrary must be wrong.

D. No. The host does not confuse two definitions of the term "guilt."

E. No. The host does not believe the jury was wrong because of the quick verdict. The host's conclusion is based on the premise that a prosecutor must have thought the defendant was guilty and that therefore the defendant must be guilty.

11. **E** Reasoning

Describe the professor's reasoning to answer this question. The professor states that the evidence against Sauk is that Sauk is more imitator than innovator and had opposing viewpoints to Providence and concludes that this evidence is insufficient to attack the writings of Sauk because it is not relevant to Sauk's writing. The critics' conclusion should therefore be rejected. The credited response will match this argument.

A. No. The professor does not take issue with the validity of the critics' premises.

B. No. The professor does not put forth any new evidence that Sauk's writing has aesthetic merit.

C. No. The professor does not mention the viewpoints of the critics.

D. No. The professor does not take issue with the validity of the critics' premises.

E. Yes. The professor states this evidence is insufficient to attack the writings of Sauk because it is not relevant to Sauk's writing.

12. **B** Principle Strengthen

This question asks for a principle that will validate the application in the passage. The policy states that the safety inspector shouldn't approve a process that has not been used safely for more than a year or if it does not increase factory safety. The author states that the safety inspector shouldn't approve a welding process because it does not increase factory safety. The credited response should fill in the missing component of the principle about a process being used safely in another factory.

A. No. This choice does not specify whether a factory has used the new process safely for the last year.

B. Yes. This choice speaks to the missing component of the principle about a process being used safely in another factory.

C. No. The principle does not require a comparison of the safety of various processes.

D. No. This choice does not specify a time frame, so it does not apply to the principle in question.

E. No. This choice does not specify whether a factory has used the new process safely for the last year.

13. **C** Weaken

This question asks for an answer choice that will weaken the administrator's claim. The administrator argues that graduate students are incorrect in their holding that teaching assistants are employees. The administrator bases this conclusion on the premises that even though assistants get paid for teaching classes, they are getting paid in order to fund their own education and would not be teaching if they could fund their own education using other funding. The administrator assumes that because they are funding their education, they should not be counted as employees and the credited response will attack this assumption.

A. No. The additional costs of granting employee benefits is not relevant to the logic of the administrator's argument.

B. No. This choice does not address the nature of the argument because there is no mention of whether adjuncts are funding an education.

C. Yes. This would weaken the argument by showing that the teaching posts have another reason for existing other than helping teaching assistants fund their education.

D. No. The fact that teaching assistants can make more money than necessary to fund their education does not address the fact that they are funding their education with money from their teaching post.

E. No. The amount or vigor of work completed by teaching assistants is not relevant to the argument about whether their funding an education prevents them from being employees.

14. **D** Parallel Flaw

The credited response will have a similar flaw to the main argument. Branson states that if people were to move from major cities to rural areas that the country's pollution would be reduced. This is based on the premise that the largest pollution comes from large cities and that these cities would pollute less with a smaller population. Branson's argument is flawed in that it assumes that pollution caused by population wouldn't disperse at the same level into rural areas at the same time it decreases in cities.

A. No. This argument assumes that Monique pays a larger housing cost because she lives in a city with high average housing costs. This is a type of comparison flaw and does not match the original argument's flaw.

B. No. This argument assumes that Karen's family would have more space in a single-family home than in an apartment because single-family homes are typically larger. This is a type of comparison flaw and does not match the original argument's flaw.

C. No. This argument assumes that because other fields are now planted with corn, that Ward's fields are planted with corn. This is a type of comparison flaw and does not match the original argument's flaw.

D. Yes. This argument concludes that Javier should eat smaller portions at meals with the largest calories and eat the remaining portions as snacks. This assumes that the calorie savings from the three meals wouldn't disperse into the snacks at the same time, as it reduces the calories of the three meals.

E. No. This argument does not contain a flaw and does not match the original argument's flaw.

15. **E** Sufficient Assumption

Identify the conclusion and premises, and then find an answer choice that validates the claim. The conclusion states that buyers were wrong in stating that safety was an important concern. This conclusion is based on premises that state that ninety percent of buyers stated that safety was an important concern, but only half of them referred to objective sources of safety, while the others referred to ads and promotional materials. The author assumes that ads and promotional materials are not valid sources and that people who think they are learning about safety do not care about safety.

A. No. The relative priorities of safety and other purchasing factors are not relevant to whether people who said safety was important were correct.

B. No. This does not prove the conclusion because it does not link incomplete safety information with whether buyers truly value safety as an important concern.

C. No. This is a necessary but not sufficient assumption since it does not speak to whether buyers who do not consult objective sources truly value safety as an important concern.

D. No. This does not prove the conclusion because it does not link knowledge of objective sources of safety information with whether buyers truly value safety as an important concern.

E. Yes. If this is true, it validates the argument by showing that half of the people who say safety is important were wrong by not consulting objective sources.

16. **A** Flaw

This question asks for a choice that hurts the conclusion by describing its flaw. The theorist argues that an organism incapable of planned movement does not have a central nervous system. This conclusion is based on premises that state that for an organism to have planned movement, it must be able to represent its environment and send messages to its muscles via a central nervous system. The argument is flawed in that it assumes one of two necessary components of planned locomotion is sufficient for planned locomotion.

A. Yes. The theorist states that a central nervous system is a necessary component in the premises, and the conclusion assumes it is a sufficient component.

B. No. The theorist states that an organism must be able to represent its environment in order to have planned locomotion.

C. No. The theorist states that the ability to represent its environment is necessary for planned locomotion but does not assume that the ability serves no other purpose.

D. No. Adaptations are not relevant to the theorist's argument.

E. No. The theorist does not make or assume a connection between the ability to represent an environment and a nervous system.

17. **B** **Necessary Assumption**

Help this argument by finding a necessary assumption. The author concludes that rocket engines must have both short and long nozzles to work most effectively throughout their ascents. This is based on premises that state that rocket engines are most effective when the pressures of exhaust gasses and the atmosphere are equal and that a short nozzle achieves this equalization at lower altitudes and a longer nozzle achieves this equalization at higher altitudes. The author assumes that having both nozzles is a way to be most effective and that it is the only way to be most effective.

A. No. The difficulty of equipping nozzles onto a rocket is not relevant to the argument about the way to make a rocket engine the most effective.

B. Yes. The author assumes that all rockets pass through both low and high altitudes. If this is not true, that rockets do not pass through the upper atmosphere, then rockets do not need long nozzles to be most effective.

C. No. The argument does not state that a rocket engine must be most effective in order to accomplish its goal of reaching higher altitudes.

D. No. The argument indicates the author believes that the pressure should change from one stage of ascent to the next.

E. No. The author argues that rockets must have both long and short nozzles, but it does not indicate that at least one engine must have both. It might be possible, for instance, that a rocket have two engines one with a short nozzle and one with a long nozzle.

18. **E** **Flaw**

Hurt the argument by describing a flaw. The consumer advocate argues that manufacturers of children's toys shouldn't overstate the dangers of their products. The advocate bases this conclusion on premises that state that a company should overstate the dangers posed by their products only if it reduces injuries but that toy companies overstate the dangers for the purpose of protecting themselves from lawsuits. The argument assumes that because companies overstate the dangers for that purpose that it doesn't also have the benefit of reducing injuries.

A. No. The author does not state necessary or sufficient reasons for actually reducing injuries caused by a product.

B. No. The argument is not about the results of overstating dangers but what reasons would justify their use.

75

C. No. There is no sample mentioned in the argument.

D. No. The argument does not assume that overstating a danger always fails to prevent injuries. The author states that preventing injuries is the only reason a manufacturer should overstate a danger.

E. Yes. The argument assumes that because companies overstate the dangers for that purpose that it doesn't also have the benefit of reducing injuries.

19. **C** **Necessary Assumption**

Help the argument by finding a necessary assumption. The argument concludes that drinking tea boosted immune systems of people in the study. This is based on premises that state that participants who drank tea and no coffee responded to germs faster than those who drank coffee but no tea. The author assumes that there is no other factor responsible for the expedited response than the consumption of tea.

A. No. The author does not assume that there are not other participants who drank both tea and coffee.

B. No. Other health benefits of coffee are not relevant to the conclusion about whether drinking tea boosted immune systems.

C. Yes. If this were true, then tea doesn't benefit immune systems because the reason tea drinkers' response was faster than that of coffee drinkers is because coffee had a detrimental effect on the immune systems. In that case, tea does not have a benefit.

D. No. This answer choice does not explicitly address the participants in the study.

E. No. Other health benefits of coffee and tea are not relevant to the conclusion about whether drinking tea boosted immune systems.

20. **D** **Reasoning**

Match the description of the reasoning to the argument. The engineer concludes that semiplaning monohulls will probably be profitable. This is based on premises that state that the semiplaning monohull, such as the airplane, offers greater speed and reliability over traditional ships. The sentence in question is premise that the author seeks to overcome by showing the similar advantages of semiplaning monohulls and jet airplanes.

A. No. This part of the analogy does not support the conclusion that semiplaning monohulls will be profitable.

B. No. The comparison between semiplaning monohulls and conventional ships is not rejected by the analogy between jet airplanes and other planes.

C. No. This part of the analogy does not support the conclusion that semiplaning monohulls will be profitable.

D. Yes. The sentence in question is a premise that the author seeks to overcome by showing the similar advantages of semiplaning monohulls and jet airplanes.

E. No. The argument's main conclusion is does not contain an analogy between types of airplanes.

21. **E** **Strengthen**

Help the argument by providing additional evidence to support the conclusion. The argument claims that Paraguay is the place where maté originated. This is based on premises that state that maté is used more widely and found in more varieties in Paraguay than anywhere else. The argument assumes that because of the variety and wide use, that it must have originated in Paraguay.

A. No. This choice supports the notion only that maté has been in Paraguay for a long time, not that it originated there.

B. No. This would weaken the argument by showing a reason that maté may have come to Paraguay with migrants from another location.

C. No. The location of the best maté in the world is not relevant to the argument about where maté originated.

D. No. That maté is not found many places outside of South America does not address the exact country of its origin.

E. Yes. This draws a link between wide use and length of time in a certain area. Therefore, if it is more widely used in Paraguay than anywhere else, it has been there longest and is likely to have originated there.

22. **A** **Resolve/ Explain**

The credited response will be the one choice that does not hurt the argument that mismanagement of the economy caused that average family income to decrease over an eight-year period.

A. Yes. The fact that there was a rise in family income in 1996 does not change the fact that over the eight years following 1996, the average family income dropped 10 percent. Since this does not hurt the argument, it is the answer.

B. No. This weakens the argument by showing a noneconomic reason for the drop in family income over the eight-year period in question.

C. No. This weakens the argument by showing a noneconomic reason for the drop in family income over the eight-year period in question.

D. No. This weakens the argument by showing that family incomes dropped due to a generational shift in the workforce, not due to economic mismanagement.

E. No. This weakens the argument by showing that policies enacted by the previous ruling party are responsible for the decline in family income.

23. **A** **Necessary Assumption**

Help this argument by finding a necessary assumption. The author concludes that gardeners who plant using the phases of the Moon are less likely to lose those plants to frost. This is based on premises that state that gardeners who plant using the phases of the Moon tend to get better results than those that do not, and those that do not, typically plant during the first warm spell of the spring, which leaves them vulnerable to late frosts.

75

A. Yes. This choice links planting with the phases of the Moon and the likelihood of frost destroying plants. If this were not true, then gardeners who plant using the phases of the Moon would not be less likely to lose plants to frost.

B. No. If the phases of the Moon affect this part of weather, then gardeners who plant during the first warm spell would not always be less successful than those that plant using the phases of the Moon.

C. No. The types of plants used by each type of gardener are not relevant to the timing of a late frost.

D. No. The reason that using phases of the Moon works is not relevant to whether it works.

E. No. Professional gardeners are not relevant to the argument about amateur gardeners.

24. **B**   Inference

The columnist states that, on average, a significant amount of money from tourism in developing countries goes to foreign owners of businesses and that this goes up as tourism becomes more established. The columnist goes on to show that tourists can spend money at local business to counteract money going to foreign businesses. The credited response will be a true statement based on the facts presented by the columnist.

A. No. The columnist does not make a recommendation about where tourists should spend their money.

B. Yes. This must be true if on average 70 percent or more of tourism dollars go to foreign business owners.

C. No. There is no evidence that this is true of any country.

D. No. There is no evidence tying money that goes to foreign business owners to an increase in poverty of local citizens.

E. No. There is no evidence that obtaining accommodations and other services from local people has no effect on foreign business owners. It is possible that these people still increase profits for those businesses indirectly.

25. **A**   Necessary Assumption

Help this argument by finding a necessary assumption. The argument concludes that it is impossible to know whether industrial pollution caused the recent decline in populations of amphibians. This is based on premises that state that populations of amphibians vary from year to year based on weather. The credited response will explain why variations based on weather make it impossible to understand the cause of a decline in these populations.

A. Yes. If this is not true, then the argument fails logically. If the species that are affected by industrial pollution are not the same ones that vary greatly due to weather, then that cannot be used as a premise.

B. No. The author does not assume that the population declines are different in making the claim that weather-related declines make knowing about pollution-related declines impossible.

C. No. The author does not assume any cause for the decline in the population in making the argument that the possibility of weather-related declines make knowing about pollution-related declines impossible.

D. No. The author does not make an assumption about a future state in which pollution either increases or declines.

E. No. The author makes no connection between pollution and weather.

Section 4: Games

Questions 1–6

This is a grouping game with fixed assignment (each item in the inventory is used once). The inventory consists of seven employees who each get either a $1,000 bonus, a $3,000 bonus, or a $5,000 bonus. The bonuses go on top of your diagram. Four of the employees—K, L, M, and P—work in Finance and the other three employees—V, X, and Z—work in Graphics. Since you know what department each employee works for you should represent this information with subscripts. There are no wildcards.

Clue 1. VG, XG, and ZG ≠ $1,000

Clue 2. E → ~E – E

Clue 3. E = LF, MF, and XG

Deductions: There are some major deductions here. First, note that LF, MF, and XG cannot be in the $1,000 group. So, the only employees who can get $1,000 bonuses are KF and PF. Next, since neither VG nor ZG can be in the $1,000 group, and XG must get a higher bonus than both of them, you know that VG and ZG both go in the $3,000 group and XG must be in the $5,000 group. Since LF and MF must get higher bonuses than KF and PF, they cannot be in the $1,000 group and must be in either the $3,000 or $5,000 groups. This means that KF and PF cannot be in the $5,000 group and must be in either the $1,000 or $3,000 groups.

Your diagram should look like this:

K L M P V X Z
F F F F g g g

Clue 1: $\begin{matrix} V & X & Z \\ g, & g, & g \end{matrix}$ ≠ 1K

Clue 2: ~ HE—HE

Clue 3: L, M, X, = HE

Combine 2 & 3: K, P—L, M
          V, Z—X

1. **C**   **Grab-a-Rule**

Use POE to eliminate answer choices that cannot be true.

A. No. This violates rules 2 and 3 because XG is in the $3,000 group.

B.   No. This violates rule 1 because ZG is in the $1,000 group.

C.   Yes. This choice does not violate any rules.

D.   No. This violates rules 2 and 3 because KF is in the same bonus group as MF.

E.   No. This violates rule 1 because VG is in the $1,000 group.

2.   **B**   Specific

Make a new line in your diagram and add the new information. If LF and MF do not get the same bonus, then one of them is in the $3,000 group and one is in the $5,000 group (rules 2 and 3). This means that both KF and PF must be in the $1,000 group (rule 2). Since LF could get either the $3,000 or the $5,000 bonus, (B) is the credited response.

3.   **A**   Specific

Make a new line in your diagram and add the new information. If only one employee can be in the $1,000 group, then it must be either KF or PF (rule 2). The other will have to be in the $3,000 group, forcing LF and MF into the $5,000 group (rules 2 and 3), making (A) the credited response.

4.   **E**   General

Use prior work and your deductions to determine which answer must be true.

A.   No. While it could be true that only one employee receives a $1,000 bonus, both KF and PF could be in the $3,000 group, forcing LF and MF into the $5,000 group (rules 2 and 3).

B.   No. If both KF and PF are in the $1,000 group and LF and MF are in the $5,000 group, then only VG and ZG are in the $3,000 group.

C.   No. Since KF and PF or LF and MF can be in the $3,000 group and VG and ZG are already there (rules 1, 2, and 3), that means there can be up to four employees in the $3,000 group.

D.   No. If LF and MF are in the $3,000 group, then XG is the only employee in the $5,000 group (see deductions).

E.   Yes. From the deductions, only LF, MF, and XG can be in the $5,000 group since they are the Highly Effective employees and must get larger bonuses than the other employees.

5.   **D**   Specific

Make a new line in your diagram and add the new information. If only two employees can be in the $5,000 group, then one of LF or MF must be in the $3,000 group since XG is already in the $5,000 group. This will force both KF and PF into the $1,000 group (rule 2), making (D) the credited response.

6.   **B**   General

Use prior work and your deductions to determine which answer must be false.

A.   No. As seen in question 4 (B), if both KF and PF are in the $1,000 group and LF and MF are in the $5,000 group, then only VG and ZG are in the $3,000 group. This could be true.

B. Yes. The maximum number of employees who could receive $1,000 bonuses is two—KF and PF. Since VG and ZG are already in the $3,000 group, and it is possible to add even more employees to this group, there is no way for there to be more employees in the $1,000 group than in the $3,000 group.

C. No. If KF and PF are both in the $1,000 group and only one of LF or MF is in the $3,000 group, then the other must be in the $5,000 group with XG, meaning that there could be the same number of employees receiving $1,000 bonuses as there are receiving $5,000 bonuses.

D. No. If LF and MF are in the $3,000 group, then both KF and PF are in the $1,000 group and XG is the only employee in the $5,000 group (see deductions). So it is possible to have more employees receive $1,000 bonuses than $5,000 bonuses.

E. No. It is possible for more employees to receive $3,000 bonuses than receive $5,000 bonuses. See question 2 (B).

Questions 7–11

This is a grouping game with fixed assignment. There are three groups—1, 2, and 3—and seven trees—H, L, M, O, P, S, and W—in the inventory. There are two wildcards.

Clue 1: HO_

Clue 2: ~MW

Clue 3: L/W = 1

Clue 4: M/O = 2

Clue 5: 3 > 1

Notice how every clue has an element that is in another clue. That means you can make deductions. Since the key to working with games with grouping is to try to narrow down the number of items that can be in each group, you should start with the HO_ block to see how it will fit in the diagram. If you try to put that block into group 1, then according to clue 5, group 3 has to have at least 4 trees. This would use all seven trees and leave none for group 2, but since you know that M/O must be in group 2 (clue 4), then HO_ cannot be in group 1. Try to put this block into group 2. Since O is in group 2, that will force M to be in a different group (clue 4). Since there are now three items in group 2, and only four items left, then only one can be in group 1 and the other three must be in group 3 (clue 5). So M must be in group 3 (clue 3). If L is in group 1, then W is in group 2 and P and S are in group 3. If W is in group 1, then L, P, and S are interchangeable in the remaining spaces.

Next, put HO_ in group 3. Since O is not in group 2, then M is (clue 4). With the block there, group 3 has exactly three items in it (clue 1), so group 1 can have one or two items. If it has one, then the remaining two items must be in group 2. If group 1 has two items, then the single remaining item must be in group 2. If L is in group 1, then W must be in group 3 because M is in group 2 (clue 2) and S and P are in group 2 with M or one is with L in group 1 and the other is with M in group 2. If W is in group 1, then L, S, and P are interchangeable in the remaining spaces, noting that L cannot be in group 1 with W.

Your diagram should look like this:

H, L, M, O, P, S, W

Clue 1: HO __ (boxed)

Clue 2: M̶W̶ (boxed, crossed out)

Clue 3: L/W = 1

Clue 4: M/O = 2

Clue 5: 3 > 1

	1	2	3
(1)	__	__ __ __	__ __
(2)	__ __	M __	H O __

7. D — Grab-a-Rule

A. No. This violates the first rule.

B. No. This violates the fifth rule.

C. No. This violates the third rule.

D. Yes. This doesn't violate any rules.

E. No. This violates the fourth rule.

8. B — Specific

Make a new line in your diagram and add the new information. If H is in group 2, then you are using the first scenario. In either case in the first scenario, M must be in group 3, making (B) the credited response.

9. C — General

Use prior work and your deductions to determine which answer is a list of any tree that can be in group 1 at any time.

A. No. H cannot be in group 1 (deductions).

B. No. H cannot be in group 1 (deductions).

C. Yes. One of L or W must be in group 1 (rule 3) and S and P are wildcards with no restrictions. See question 10 (A).

D. No. S needs to be on this list. See question 10 (A).

E. No. This violates rule 3, which says that L or W must be in group 1, so L and W need to be on this list.

10. **A**   `Specific`

Make a new line in your diagram and add the new information. If W is in group 3, then according to the deductions, you are using the second scenario. So, W is in group 3 with H and O, L is in group 1, and M is in group 2. One of S or P can be in group 1 with L and the other in group 2 with M, or both S and P can be in group 2 with M. This makes (A) the credited response.

11. **A**   `General`

This question is asking which tree, if in group 2, completely determines where all the other trees are.

A. Yes. If W is in group 2, then it is with H and O (deductions), which forces M into group 3 with P and S so that group 3 has more trees than group 1, and that leaves L for group 1.

B. No. If S is in group 2, you cannot determine where any of the other trees must be.

C. No. If P is in group 2, you cannot determine where any of the other trees must be.

D. No. If M is in group 2, then O and H are in group 3, but you cannot determine where L, W, S, or P must go.

E. No. If L is in group 2, then W must be in group 1, but you cannot determine where O, H, M, S, or P must go.

Questions 12–18

This is a 1D order game with ranking. The inventory consists of seven librarians—F, G, H, K, L, M, and Z—which are being scheduled Monday through Saturday. There is one librarian assigned each day Monday through Friday and two librarians assigned on Saturday. The days go across the top of the diagram. There are no wildcards.

Clue 1: H—L

Clue 2: H—G & M—G

Clue 3: F—K & M

Clue 4: K—Z

Clue 5: ~ L on Sat → L—F ; F – L → L on Sat

Combine the clues to get two possible arrangements.

There are lots of deductions here. From one scenario, you know that H, L, and F must be on Monday, Tuesday, and Wednesday, respectively. M and K can be on Wednesday or Thursday, and G and Z must be on Saturday together.

For the second scenario, L is on Saturday according to clue 5, so F must be on Monday or Tuesday, and H could be any day Monday through Friday, but not Saturday. M and K could be any day Monday through Friday, and one of G or Z can be on Saturday with L, but the other could be earlier in the week. G cannot be Monday, Tuesday, or Wednesday, and Z cannot be Monday or Tuesday.

Your diagram should look like this:

F, G, H, K, L, M, Z

Clue 1: H—L

Clue 2: H ⟩G
             M ⟋

Clue 3: F ⟨ K
              ⟍ M

Clue 4: K—Z

Clue 5: L ≠ Sat → L—F
            F—L → L = Sat

	M	T	W	Th	F	S
	$\frac{G}{Z}$	$\frac{G}{Z}$	_G		_F | F	$\frac{H}{M}$
(1)	H	L	F	M/K	K/M	G Z
(2)	—	—	—	—	—	L G/Z

---

12. **A**   Grab-a-Rule

   A.   Yes. This does not violate any rules.

   B.   No. This violates rule 5 because L is after F and is not on Saturday.

   C.   No. This violates rule 3 because K and M are before F.

   D.   No. This violates rule 4 because K is after Z.

   E.   No. This violates rule 1 because L is before H.

13. **E**   General

   Use your deductions to determine who cannot be on Tuesday.

   A.   No. In the second setup, F could be on Tuesday.

   B.   No. In the second setup, H could be on Tuesday.

   C.   No. In the second setup, K could be on Tuesday.

   D.   No. In the second setup, M could be on Tuesday.

   E.   Yes. In the first setup, Z must be on Saturday; in the second setup, Z must be on either Friday or Saturday, so Z cannot be on Tuesday.

14. **B**   Specific

   If K is earlier than M, then you end up with two scenarios in which M is before G. That means that K must also be before G, making (B) the credited response.

15. **A** `Specific`

Make a new line in your diagram and add the new information. If Z is on Thursday, then you are working with the second setup. This will force G into Saturday with L, since only Z or G can be on Saturday with L. So F must be earlier in the week than L, making (A) the credited response.

16. **C** `Specific`

Make a new line in your diagram and add the new information. If M is on Tuesday, then F must be on Monday (rule 3), so L must be on Saturday (rule 5), making (C) the credited response.

17. **D** `Specific`

If F is before H, L must be on Saturday (rule 5) with either G or Z. F is on Monday, and K, M, and H round out the rest of the week. This makes (D) the credited response, since M must be on a day earlier than Saturday.

18. **C** `Complex`

This question wants you to substitute a new rule for rule 3 that gets you the same deductions. Rule 3 has F before both K and M, so you need an answer that is going to make F come before both K and M.

A. No. If F can't be on Monday, Tuesday, or Wednesday, then you do not have the same deductions.

B. No. Limiting F or H to Monday may seem helpful, but if H is on Monday, then both K and M can be after F.

C. Yes. If only H and L can be earlier than F, then K and M must come after F, giving you the same deductions you had originally.

D. No. This puts F earlier than K, but M could still be before.

E. No. This puts F earlier than M, but K could still be before.

Questions 19–23

This is a variation on an ordering game in which not all the elements are used necessitating an out column. The inventory consists of four types of features—F, M, I, and T—which can not only be left out but also repeated. At least three features (note that they do not have to be different features) have to take up three or more of the five slots available in a newsletter. If there is no feature in a slot, then there is a graphic in that slot. There is one wildcard.

Clue 1. _ _+ for 1 → consecutive

Clue 2. F or T → F1 or T1 ; ~F1 & ~T1 → ~F & ~T

Clue 3. one I or ~I

There's really not much to work with here. It's worth noting that if there isn't F or T in slot 1, then both F and T are out, which means the features are made up of I and M. You might think it would be worth trying to figure out all

75

the possible combinations of features, but there are many since you can have three or more features, and graphics besides. So, you are starting off with a blank diagram.

Your diagram should look like this:

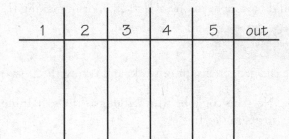

F, M, I, T, g

Clue 1: feat > 1 →
              consecutive

Clue 2: F or T → FI or TI

              ~FI & ~ TI → ~F & ~ T

Clue 3: exactly one I
              or ~ I

19. **D** Grab-a-Rule

    A.   No. This violates rule 3 since I is used twice.

    B.   No. This violates rule 2 since F or T is not in the first slot and there is another T.

    C.   No. This violates rule 2 since I is in the first slot and F is in a later slot.

    D.   Yes. This doesn't violate any rules.

    E.   No. This violates rule 1 since there is one T split up in non-consecutive slots.

20. **A** Specific

Make a new line in your diagram and fill in the information given. If T is out, and F is in slots 4 and 5, then there must be another F in slot 1 (rule 2). This makes (A) the credited response.

21. **E** General

Use the deductions, prior work, and trying the answers to determine what must be false.

    A.   No. This could be true. If I is in slot 1, then T and F are out, but there can be two or more M's.

    B.   No. This could be true. If there is one F in slot 2, then there must be T in slot 1 (rule 2). There are no other restrictions on the number or type of features.

    C.   No. This could be true. If there is one T in slot 3, then there is at least an F in slot 1. There are no other restrictions on the number or type of features.

    D.   No. This could be true. If all the features are M or T except slot 1, then as long as T is in slot 1 then this could work.

    E.   Yes. This must be false. If the features in the first four slots are either I or M, and there is a feature in slot 5, it cannot be T or F since that would violate rule 2.

22. **D** **Specific**

Make a new line in your diagram and fill in the information given. If I is in slot 1, then T and F must be out (rule 2) and there must be at least two M features. Even if one of the M's is in slot 5, the other would have to be in one of slots 2, 3, or 4, making (D) the credited response.

23. **D** **General**

Use the deductions, prior work, and trying the answers to determine what must be false.

A. No. This could be true. As long as the remaining features were all T and either the F or one of the T's is in slot 1.

B. No. This could be true. As long as there is a T in slot 1, then both F and M can be out.

C. No. This could be true. This is just exchanging an F for the T in (B). As long as there is an F in slot 1, this works.

D. Yes. This must be false. If both F and T are out and there is only 1 M, then there will not be enough features to meet the minimum requirement of three. According to rule 3, there can be only one I.

E. No. This could be true. As long as there is an F in slot 1, then both I and T can be out.

Chapter 6
PrepTest 76:
Answers and
Explanations

ANSWER KEY: PREPTEST 76

Section 1:
Reading
Comprehension

1. C
2. B
3. D
4. A
5. D
6. A
7. D
8. B
9. B
10. C
11. B
12. D
13. D
14. B
15. E
16. C
17. C
18. B
19. E
20. C
21. C
22. C
23. D
24. B
25. A
26. B
27. E

Section 2:
Arguments 1

1. B
2. B
3. C
4. C
5. C
6. D
7. C
8. E
9. B
10. B
11. A
12. B
13. D
14. E
15. A
16. C
17. D
18. B
19. C
20. E
21. B
22. A
23. E
24. D
25. D
26. E

Section 3:
Games

1. D
2. C
3. D
4. B
5. A
6. B
7. B
8. C
9. D
10. A
11. C
12. E
13. C
14. A
15. C
16. B
17. E
18. B
19. E
20. C
21. B
22. A
23. B

Section 4:
Arguments 2

1. C
2. B
3. D
4. B
5. C
6. D
7. C
8. E
9. C
10. E
11. B
12. B
13. D
14. B
15. D
16. B
17. A
18. E
19. A
20. C
21. C
22. A
23. D
24. D
25. C

EXPLANATIONS

Section 1: Reading Comprehension

Questions 1–6

The first paragraph offers a negative opinion about a piece of music. The main point of the second paragraph is that the quote refers to a Beethoven piece, but it could also characterize Schoenberg's work. The main point of the third paragraph is to show that the music of both Beethoven and Schoenberg caused controversy and that it took time for Beethoven's music to be accepted, alluding to the idea that it may take time for Schoenberg's music to be accepted. The point of the fourth paragraph is to describe the first of Schoenberg's three evolving styles. The point of the fifth paragraph is to describe the second style, which lacked tonal basis. The point of the six paragraph is to discuss the third style, which incorporated the 12-tone technique and was difficult to follow, though technically masterful. The main point of the seventh paragraph is that Schoenberg's music is most important because it captures emotions not captured before. The Bottom Line of the passage as a whole is that Schoenberg's music, while sometimes difficult to listen to, shares commonalities with other composers and moved through three phases, culminating in a style that is important because of how it captures emotions.

1. **C** **Big Picture**

    Use your Bottom Line of the passage to help you to evaluate the choices. The correct answer will describe the main idea of the passage.

    A. No. While this is a true statement based on the passage, it is too narrow and does not capture how important Schoenberg's music is.

    B. No. Though the author notes some similarities with Beethoven, the author does not claim that Schoenberg should be as highly regarded.

    C. Yes. This is a paraphrase of the predicted Bottom Line and fully captures the main idea of the passage.

    D. No. The passage states that it is Schoenberg's delineation of emotional states that makes his music essential.

    E. No. The passage does not focus on Schoenberg's acceptance.

2. **B** **RC Reasoning**

    The question is asking for a situation that parallels the way that Schoenberg's work is disturbing. The passage states that Schoenberg's work is disturbing because it unflinchingly faces difficult truths.

    A. No. This would be more similar to the incoherent, shrill, and ear-splitting characteristics that the author claims are not what make it disturbing.

    B. Yes. This is unflinchingly facing difficult truths.

    C. No. The author states that Schoenberg was the first to capture these emotional states.

D. No. This would be more similar to the incoherent, shrill, and ear-splitting characteristics that the author claims are not what make it disturbing.

E. No. The author does not discuss unfamiliarity in this portion of the passage.

3. **D** `Structure`

The question is asking why the author employs the quote from Kotzebue. The author's discussion of the quote draws a connection between Schoenberg and Beethoven.

A. No. This answer does not connect to Schoenberg.

B. No. The quote referred to Beethoven.

C. No. The author is not trying to impugn Beethoven.

D. Yes. The discussion of the quote in the next two paragraphs indicates that Beethoven's popularity grew in time.

E. No. The author does not discuss general critical consensus.

4. **A** `Extract Infer`

The correct answer will be the statement that is not supported by evidence within the passage text. The four incorrect answers will be supported by evidence in the passage.

A. Yes. Only Schoenberg began in the late-Romantic manner.

B. No. The quote in the first paragraph was written about Beethoven's work, but the author says that it is also an accurate description of Schoenberg's work.

C. No. In the second paragraph, the author states that both Beethoven and Schoenberg stirred controversy.

D. No. In the third paragraph, the author states that both Beethoven and Schoenberg worked in constantly changing and evolving musical styles.

E. No. In the third paragraph, the author states that both Beethoven and Schoenberg altered the language and extended the expressive range of music.

5. **D** `Extract Infer`

The correct answer will be the statement that is best supported by evidence within the passage text. In the seventh paragraph, the author argues that Schoenberg's work is essential because he captured emotions that had not previously been captured.

A. No. While the author acknowledges that Schoenberg had an awe-inspiring level of technical mastery, that's not what the author says makes Schoenberg's music essential.

B. No. The author does not state an opinion about this aspect of Schoenberg's work.

C. No. While this is an accomplishment that the author acknowledges, it is not what the author says makes Schoenberg's work essential.

D. Yes. In lines 50–53, the author states that this is what makes Schoenberg's work essential.

E. No. The author does not state an opinion about this aspect of Schoenberg's work.

6. **A** [Extract Infer]

The correct answer will be the statement that is best supported by evidence within the passage text. In the fourth paragraph, the author discusses that each style acknowledged tradition and lit the way for progress.

A. Yes. This is supported by the author's claim that each style lit the way for progress.

B. No. This answer is extreme. The author never claims that any of the styles are an inexplicable departure from the previous style.

C. No. This answer is extreme. The author never claims that any of the styles are an inexplicable departure from the previous style.

D. No. This answer is extreme. The author never claims that any of the styles are an inexplicable departure from the previous style.

E. No. This answer is extreme. The author never claims that any of the styles are an inexplicable departure from the previous style.

Questions 7–13

The main point of the first paragraph is to introduce the issue: that biotechnology patents may hurt basic research. The main point of the second paragraph is to discuss why researchers think that patents might hinder their research. The point of the third paragraph is to address the concerns raised about patents and argue that patents are not likely to be enforced when it comes to noncommercial research and that they create an incentive to innovate. The Bottom Line of the passage as a whole is that biotechnology patenting is not likely hindering basic research.

7. **D** [Big Picture]

Use your Bottom Line of the passage to help you to evaluate the choices. The correct answer will describe the main idea of the passage.

A. No. This is the threat that the author explores, but he or she ultimately concludes that patents don't threaten progress.

B. No. The author acknowledges the shift but does not indicate that it is controversial.

C. No. This answer choice is too negative and does not capture the main idea. At the end of the passage, the author discusses that patents have a positive impact.

D. Yes. This accurately paraphrases the Bottom Line that concerns about biotechnology patterns are not valid.

E. No. While this is mentioned in the passage, this answer is too narrow and it is not the main idea of the passage.

PrepTest 76: Answers and Explanations | **203**

8. **B** **Extract / Infer**

The correct answer will be the statement that is best supported by evidence within the passage text. The researchers in lines 30–31 are those who oppose biotechnology patents and fear that there will be prohibitively high fees to use patented materials.

A. No. Market conditions would allow the prohibitively high fees that these researchers fear.

B. Yes. Since they fear prohibitively high fees, they would favor a system without fees.

C. No. The fees that they oppose would be a measure to prevent access.

D. No. This portion of the passage discusses only corporate patent holders.

E. No. This portion of the passage does not discuss funding for research projects.

9. **B** **Extract / Fact**

The correct answer will be directly supported by the passage text. The first paragraph discusses that university researchers rely on research funding that is conditional on the patentability of results.

A. No. The passage does not discuss academic advancement.

B. Yes. This is directly supported by lines 4–7.

C. No. The first paragraph does not discuss access to basic research.

D. No. The passage does not discuss exploitation of researchers.

E. No. The passage does not discuss whether researchers would prefer a competitive or communal model.

10. **C** **Extract / Infer**

The correct answer will be the statement that is best supported by evidence within the passage text.

A. No. The passage mentioned that inventors took steps to protect their discoveries before patents were available.

B. No. This is a fear of researchers, but the passage does not argue that it actually happens.

C. Yes. This is discussed in the third paragraph. Litigation is usually undertaken only to protect market position.

D. No. The author mentioned that researchers rely on such funding but does not pass judgment on that reliance.

E. No. The passage does not discuss the innovativeness of the researchers who oppose patenting.

11. **B** **Structure**

The question is asking why the author brings up the early days of biotechnology. The passage discusses that even in the days before patents, researchers took measures to protect their work.

A. No. The passage does not provide such an account.

B. Yes. The context of this reference is that even in the days before patents, researchers took measures to protect their work.

C. No. The passage does not argue that biotechnology was untainted by commercial motives even at its inception.

D. No. There is no discussion of sophistication in this portion of the passage.

E. No. This reference is used to counter the idea that patenting biotechnological discoveries will not necessarily hinder progress.

12. **D** **Extract Infer**

The correct answer will be the statement that is best supported by evidence within the passage text.

A. No. The passage does not discuss policy makers, so we cannot infer what they are likely or unlikely to do.

B. No. This answer choice is extreme and unsupported. There is no discussion of what patent holders believe about the pursuit of basic research, only that they would be likely to sue only when market position is threatened.

C. No. This answer choice is extreme and unsupported. There is no support for a claim about whether researchers are generally unable to obtain funding.

D. Yes. The second paragraph discusses that patent holders might charge fees to use their materials for research.

E. No. This answer choice is extreme and unsupported. There is no discussion of the quantity of biologists willing to teach in academia.

13. **D** **Extract Infer**

The question is asking what the author thinks will happen with basic, noncommercial research involving patented materials. Lines 45–48 state that the author thinks that whether the patent could or would be enforced in this situation is questionable.

A. No. This is presented as a fear of some researchers, not as the author's opinion.

B. No. The author states that patent litigation is usually initiated only to protect a market position, which would not be threatened by basic noncommercial research.

C. No. The passage does not discuss whether universities restrict research due to patent concerns.

D. Yes. In the third paragraph, the author states that there has been a judicial tradition to respect a completely noncommercial research exception to patent infringement.

E. No. The passage does not discuss such offers.

Questions 14–19

The main point of the first paragraph is that wampum was used for political purposes, though it became a medium of exchange due to misinterpretations by Europeans. The second paragraph describes the two types of wampum and what they represented. The third paragraph describes wampum belts and how they were used within the Haudenosaune Confederacy to frame and enforce its laws. The Bottom Line of the passage as a whole is that the wampum symbol system evolved from religious significance into a powerful and effective political tool for the Haudenosaune group of nations.

14.   B   **Big Picture**

Use your Bottom Line of the passage to help you to evaluate the choices. The correct answer will describe the main idea of the passage.

   A.   No. This answer is untrue. The passage states that loose beads were the simplest and oldest form of wampum.

   B.   Yes. This accurately paraphrases the Bottom Line.

   C.   No. This answer is extreme and untrue. While the Europeans used wampum solely for commercial exchange, its use within the Haudenosaune was spiritual and political.

   D.   No. Wampum was used to communicate prior to the Haudenosaune Confederacy.

   E.   No. While this is suggested by the first paragraph of the passage, it is not the main idea.

15.   E   **Structure**

The question is asking why the author mentions the fishing practice in the second paragraph. The passage describes the use of wampum to communicate with the spirits thought to have created fish as an example of how the beads were used.

   A.   No. The beads were thrown into the water in this example, which would not pass on knowledge.

   B.   No. There is no discussion of whether this practice changed after contact with the Europeans.

   C.   No. The fishing practice is an example of an early religious use of wampum that came before the more formal use in the Haudenosaune Confederacy.

   D.   No. The author does not argue that this practice was learned of by studying wampum.

   E.   Yes. The author is discussing the simplest use of wampum to represent basic ideas such as the sky-yearning or earth-loving spirits who created fish.

16.   C   **Structure**

The correct answer will paraphrase the main point of the last paragraph, which describes wampum belts and how they were used within the Haudenosaune Confederacy to frame and enforce its laws.

   A.   No. While the passage mentions that wampum belts combined string wampum, the focus of the paragraph is on the symbolism and usage of the belts.

   B.   No. The focus of the paragraph is on wampum belts and their symbolism and usage.

C.   Yes. This accurately describes the contents of the final paragraph.

D.   No. The passage does not detail the contents of the Haudenosaune Confederacy's constitution.

E.   No. While the passage claims that the wampum symbol system was effective, there was no evidence given.

17.   **C**   Extract / Infer

The correct answer will be the statement that is best supported by evidence within the passage text.

A.   No. This answer is unsupported. The passage does not discuss an alternate reality.

B.   No. The author discusses the use of color prior to the Haudenosaune Confederacy.

C.   Yes. In the third paragraph, the passage discusses combining string wampum to form stylized symbols.

D.   No. The passage does not argue that the color associations shifted over time, only that the arrangements of the colors directed interpretation of symbols.

E.   No. This answer is unsupported. The passage does not discuss what would have happened if the Europeans had had different information.

18.   **B**   Extract / Infer

The correct answer will be the statement that is best supported by evidence within the passage text.

A.   No. The passage does not discuss the use of wampum for commercial purposes prior to contact with the Europeans.

B.   Yes. The third paragraph states that the formation of the Haudenosaune Confederacy was the major impetus for a more deliberate system of use of wampum.

C.   No. The passage does not discuss recodification of the laws of the Haudenosaune Confederacy.

D.   No. The passage does not provide a timeline of whether contact with Europeans came before or after the use of wampum to codify the laws of the Haudenosaune Confederacy.

E.   No. The passage does not discuss any changing of the wampum bead colors.

19.   **E**   Extract / Infer

The correct answer will be the statement that is best supported by evidence within the passage text.

A.   No. The passage does not discuss other peoples.

B.   No. This answer choice is extreme and unsupported. The passage does not mention whether Europeans were aware of wampum's true significance.

C.   No. The first paragraph states that Europeans used wampum solely to purchase goods.

D.   No. The passage states that the peoples who made up the Haudenosaune Confederacy had been warring tribes.

E.   Yes. The passage uses language such as "possibly indicating" in the third paragraph.

Questions 20–27

Passage A

The main point of the first paragraph is that Karl Popper is hyper focused on negative evidence and that theories are scientific only if they can be tested with a search for negative evidence. The main point of the second paragraph is that theories can fail for various reasons and the negative evidence is not necessarily conclusive. The Bottom Line of passage A is that Popper's obsession with negative evidence goes too far.

Passage B

The main point of the first paragraph is that an incorrect auxiliary assumption about the orbit of Uranus led to an incorrect prediction, but Newton's laws were not thought to be incorrect. The main point of the second paragraph is that Newton's theory was rejected when Einstein's new theory provided accurate results. The Bottom Line of passage B is that a prediction can be wrong either because of an incorrect auxiliary assumption or because of an incorrect theory.

20. **C**   **Big Picture**

The correct answer will be supported by the Bottom Lines of both passages.

A. No. While this is mentioned in passage A, it is not mentioned in passage B.

B. No. Passage A does not mention planetary orbits.

C. Yes. Passage A discusses the extent to which negative evidence is conclusive and passage B uses negative evidence (the actual orbits of Uranus and Mercury) to help determine the validity of auxiliary assumptions and predictive theories.

D. No. Neither passage argues for a specific technique for confirming a theory.

E. No. This answer choice is extreme. Neither passage claims that experimentation is irrelevant.

21. **C**   **Extract Fact**

The correct answer will be mentioned in passage A and there will be an example of it in passage B.

A. No. Passage B uses results to repudiate theories or assumptions, not the other way around.

B. No. Passage A does not mention revising a theory.

C. Yes. Passage A discusses using negative evidence to disprove a theory, and passage B gives the example of Mercury's orbit that was used to disprove Newton's theory.

D. No. Passage A does not mention planetary orbits.

E. No. Passage A does not mention non-testable theories.

22. **C**   **Extract Infer**

Passage A mentions a disturbing force as something that would need to be lacking for a theory's prediction to come true. The correct answer will be something in passage B that reflects this description.

A. No. Uranus was the subject of the prediction, not an outside force.

B. No. The Sun was the subject of an auxiliary assumption, not an outside force.

C. Yes. Neptune was an outside factor that was not included in the prediction's original assumptions.

D. No. Mercury was the subject of a prediction, not an outside force.

E. No. Passage B never mentions the Moon.

23. **D** Extract Infer

The question is asking what the author thinks about Popper. The author accuses Popper of believing that positive evidence has no value as evidence and that negative evidence is disproof. The correct answer will be the statement that is best supported by evidence within the passage text.

A. No. The author is arguing that Popper's idea is too extreme because the reality is more complicated than Popper treats it.

B. No. The author is arguing that Popper overestimates the value of negative evidence.

C. No. The author is not arguing that the idea fails in all cases, just that Popper takes it to the extreme.

D. Yes. The author is accusing Popper of being too extreme.

E. No. The author's criticism is that the idea is too extreme, not that it doesn't fit one particular theory.

24. **B** Structure

The question is asking for a result from passage B that would serve as evidence for the claim that negative evidence is rarely conclusive.

A. No. Passage B does not discuss the discovery of Uranus, only the difficulty predicting its orbit.

B. Yes. Newton's laws accurately predicted the orbit of Neptune and it was the assumption that Neptune didn't exist that made the prediction about Uranus inaccurate.

C. No. This would be an effective use of negative evidence.

D. No. Failure to find something is not negative evidence. Negative evidence is finding something that goes against a theory.

E. No. The successful use of a theory is positive evidence, not negative evidence.

25. **A** RC Reasoning

The question is asking for an astronomical body that serves as negative evidence like the black swan did in passage A.

A. Yes. The observed orbit of Mercury did not match Newton's prediction, serving as evidence that Newton's theory was incorrect.

B. No. The assumption that there were no other nearby planets caused the prediction to fail, not Newton's theory.

C. No. The existence of Neptune negated an auxiliary assumption, not Newton's theory. Newton's theory accurately predicted the orbit of Neptune.

D. No. Passage B does not mention Venus.

E. No. The Sun was the subject of an auxiliary assumption and did not negatively impact the validity of Newton's theory.

26. **B**   Extract
              Infer

The question is asking for a point of disagreement between passage A and passage B. The correct answer will be best supported by the text of passage B.

A. No. Passage B does not express an opinion about Popper.

B. Yes. Passage B discusses that Newton's theory was ultimately rejected even though it had accurately predicted the orbit of Neptune and other planets.

C. No. Passage B discusses the importance of auxiliary assumptions and the role they played in evaluating Newton's theory.

D. No. Passage B does not express an opinion about the logical asymmetry between positive and negative experience.

E. No. Passage B discusses one bold theory, but it does not opine on what scientific research involves.

27. **E**   RC Reasoning

The question is asking for a scenario analogous to the discovery of Neptune. The author of passage B discusses that Neptune was discovered when scientists reconsidered their assumptions that there was no other planet near Uranus after incorrectly predicting the orbit of Uranus rather than rejecting Newton's law. The orbit of Neptune was consistent with the predictions of Newton's theory. The correct answer will involve the discovery of something that was previously assumed not to exist, but its discovery is consistent with the theory at hand.

A. No. The discovery of the second high tide is not consistent with the theory.

B. No. The discovery of Neptune did not settle a debate.

C. No. This answer does not involve the discovery of something that was previously assumed not to exist.

D. No. This answer does not involve the discovery of something that was previously assumed not to exist.

E. Yes. The third undetected particle is similar to Neptune in that it was not previously assumed to exist, but then the discovery of it was consistent with the law of conservation of energy.

Section 2: Arguments 1

1. B `Flaw`

The argument concludes that industrial by-products have entered the swamp's ecosystem. This conclusion is based on the facts that industrial by-products cause elevated hormone activity, that abnormal development of certain body parts in reptiles occurs only with elevated hormone activity, and that several alligators with developmental abnormalities were discovered in the swamp. The argument mistakes a sufficient condition for a necessary condition: It assumes that nothing but industrial by-products could have caused the elevated hormone activity. The credited response will identify this flaw.

A. No. The argument is concerned only with developmental abnormalities that do result from elevated hormone activity, so other abnormalities are irrelevant.

B. Yes. This answer choice describes the flaw of mistaking a sufficient condition for a necessary condition.

C. No. Even if we knew that the industrial by-products were in food instead of or in addition to being in the swamp, the argument would still contain the flaw of assuming that the by-products are the only cause of elevated hormone activity.

D. No. The argument does not require more reptiles to have developmental abnormalities.

E. No. The argument is limited to a particular swamp, so the sample does not have to be representative of alligators in general.

2. B `Main Point`

The fill-in-the-blank space is preceded by the logical indicator "So," signaling that the credited response will be the main point of the argument. The government official states that residents who are foreign citizens cannot serve as cabinet secretaries because they cannot perform all of the duties of the position. He also states that cabinet undersecretaries are expected to serve as cabinet secretaries when the actual secretary is unavailable. The implication is that foreign citizens should not serve as cabinet undersecretaries either for the same reason: They would not be able to perform all of the duties of the cabinet secretary if they had to step in to serve when the actual secretary was unavailable. The credited response will indicate that foreign citizens should not serve as cabinet undersecretaries.

A. No. The argument is not structured to lead to a prescriptive remedy for the problem of foreign citizens' being unable to perform all of the duties of a cabinet secretary.

B. Yes. This answer choice correctly describes the conclusion that the argument is structured to lead to.

C. No. The argument does not imply that prior experience as a cabinet undersecretary is required to be a cabinet secretary.

D. No. This answer choice contradicts the argument: The argument states that the rule against appointing foreign citizens as cabinet secretaries is wise.

E. No. This answer choice contradicts the argument: We know that cabinet undersecretaries are expected to stand in for cabinet secretaries, and nothing in the argument suggests that this practice should change.

3. C **Point at Issue**

Doris concludes that we should encourage students to become involved in student government if the goal is to make students more outspoken. Her conclusion is based on her observation that all members of the student government are outspoken. She assumes that joining the student government caused the students to become outspoken. Zack concludes that encouraging students to join the student government will not make them more outspoken. His conclusion is based on his assertion that students who join the student government are outspoken before they join. Doris and Zack disagree about whether joining the student government makes students more outspoken. The credited response will identify this point of disagreement.

A. No. Neither Doris nor Zack states what should be the case regarding outspokenness.

B. No. While Doris would agree with this statement, Zack does not take a position on whether students should be encouraged to become more involved in student government.

C. Yes. Doris would agree with this statement, while Zack would disagree with it.

D. No. Doris and Zack both agree with this statement.

E. No. Neither Doris nor Zack states or implies that becoming involved in student government is a necessary condition for outspokenness.

4. C **Flaw**

The biologist concludes that critics of a behavioral study on chameleons should not doubt its results despite its small sample size. His conclusion is based on an appeal to the study author's professional standing and past record of strong research. He assumes that the study author's credentials are sufficient to prove the value of this particular study; he fails to consider that this study may be flawed despite the study author's credentials. The credited response will identify this flaw.

A. No. This answer choice describes a flaw of the study itself but not of the biologist's argument.

B. No. The mechanism of vitamin D production regulation is irrelevant.

C. Yes. This answer choice describes the flaw that the biologist focuses on the study author's reputation rather than on the study itself.

D. No. The biologist focuses on the study author while ignoring the critics' valid doubts.

E. No. The biologist defers to the study author's past record of strong research; if anything, he holds the critics to a higher standard than the study author.

5. C **Necessary Assumption**

The political scientist concludes that the government does not support freedom of popular expression, disagreeing with those who claim that the government's acceptance of the recent protest indicates that the government does support freedom of expression. He supports his conclusion by indicating that supporting freedom of expression requires accepting ideas that the government both opposes and approves of. He states that the government supported the message of the recent protest. The argument assumes that the government would not have accepted the recent protest if it had not supported the message of the protest. The credited response will establish this fact.

A. No. The government's involvement in organizing the protest rally is irrelevant.

B. No. The message of the protest rally is irrelevant.

C. Yes. This answer choice provides the sufficient side of the contrapositive of the conditional stated in the argument: If the government would not have accepted the protest rally whose message it opposed, then the government cannot be said to support freedom of popular expression.

D. No. That some groups fear a government response does not prove that the government would actually oppose the group's ideas.

E. No. Whether the government fears a backlash has no bearing on whether the government accepts or opposes an idea.

6. **D** **Principle Strengthen**

The lawyer concludes that the victim surcharge used to fund services for victims of violent crimes is unfair to nonviolent criminals. His conclusion is based on the fact that the surcharge applies to all crimes rather than just to violent crimes. He assumes that services for victims of violent crimes should be funded by surcharges collected only from violent criminals. The credited response will state a general rule or principle that establishes that services for victims of violent crimes should be funded by surcharges collected only from violent criminals.

A. No. The argument is not about deterrence.

B. No. The argument is not about the relative size of the penalties but rather about how those penalties are used.

C. No. This answer choice is a premise booster, but it does not comment on the fairness of using surcharges collected from nonviolent criminals to fund services for victims of violent criminal.

D. Yes. This answer choice establishes that surcharges collected from nonviolent criminals cannot be used to fund services for victims of more serious crimes.

E. No. The argument is not about the amount of the fine but rather about how the amount collected should be used.

7. **C** **Resolve/ Explain**

The economist concludes that, as his country has increasingly become a service economy, in which manufacturing makes up a smaller proportion of the workforce, the country has engaged in less international trade. The credited response will explain the connection between an increasing service economy and a decrease in international trade.

A. No. This answer choice makes the situation more puzzling.

B. No. This answer choice does not explain why an increasing service economy has led to a decrease in international trade.

C. Yes. This answer choice explains that most services cannot be traded internationally because they are delivered locally only.

D. No. This answer choice has no connection to international trade.

E. No. This answer choice makes the situation more puzzling.

8. **E** **Reasoning**

Merton concludes that elevated rates of heart disease are caused by air pollution from automobile exhaust. His conclusion is based on a study that showed that people who live on very busy streets have higher than average rates of heart disease. He assumes that living on such streets causes an increase in the rates of heart disease; he fails to consider other causes or relevant considerations. Ortiz suggests that Merton has failed to consider other causes, indicating that other lifestyle factors could contribute to heart disease. The credited response will describe how Ortiz responds.

A. No. Ortiz does not dispute the accuracy of the study Merton cites but rather implies that Merton has not considered all of the relevant evidence.

B. No. Ortiz does not mention other effects of air pollution.

C. No. Ortiz does not dispute the accuracy of the study Merton cites.

D. No. Ortiz does not bring up a counterexample because Merton does not state a general rule or principle.

E. Yes. Ortiz brings up other lifestyle factors as potential causes of heart disease and indicates that Merton needs to rule them out.

9. **B** **Weaken**

The argument concludes that the fishing ban at Quapaw Lake is likely responsible for the recovery of its fish population. The conclusion is based on a comparison between Quapaw Lake and Highwater Lake. Both lakes were experiencing declines in fish populations ten years ago. A moratorium on fishing was imposed at Quapaw Lake, and the fish population subsequently recovered. No such moratorium was imposed at Highwater Lake, and the fish population has continued to decline. The argument assumes that the ban caused the recovery of the fish population; it fails to consider alternate causes or relevant considerations. One such consideration is whether any fishing actually took place prior to the official ban: The argument assumes that the ban led to a change in the amount of fishing at Quapaw Lake. The credited response will introduce new evidence that undermines the conclusion or point out a relevant consideration that the argument missed.

A. No. This answer choice might explain why the fish population has continued to decline at Highwater Lake, but it is unclear how it affects the fish population at Quapaw Lake.

B. Yes. This answer choice establishes that the fishing ban did not actually change the amount of fishing at Quapaw Lake, thus suggesting that something else must have been responsible for the recovery of the fish population.

C. No. The relative size of the lakes is irrelevant.

D. No. This answer choice is too vague to weaken because we do not know whether such lakes are similar to Quapaw Lake and Highwater Lake in regards to fish population decline and fishing bans.

E. No. The argument is about the fish population only, so the variety of fish is irrelevant.

10. **B** **Sufficient Assumption**

The argument concludes that Asian elephants do not run. The conclusion is supported by the fact that Asian elephants always have at least two feet on the ground. The argument assumes that the Asian elephant cannot run with two or more feet on the ground. The credited response will explicitly link the premise to the conclusion and force the conclusion to be true.

A.   No. A premise states that the Asian elephant can accelerate, so this answer choice does not help us determine whether it can run.

B.   Yes. A premise states that the Asian elephant does not have all of its feet off the ground at once, so added to the conditional statement of this answer choice, the conclusion that the Asian elephant cannot run is proved.

C.   No. That the Asian elephant can walk as fast as some animals run does not confirm whether the elephant itself can run.

D.   No. This answer choice does not discuss running.

E.   No. This answer choice does not discuss running.

11. **A** **Resolve/ Explain**

The passage explains that, last week, Styron hammers slightly outsold Maxlast hammers. This surprising result happened despite the fact that the Maxlast hammers were on sale and displayed in a prominent position in the store while the Styron hammers were at their usual price and in their usual place in the store. The passage indicates that both brands usually have roughly equal sales figures. The credited response will explain why the Maxlast hammers were outsold despite the supposed advantages of being on sale and being in a more visible display.

A.   Yes. This answer choice explains that customers did not actually notice the Maxlast hammers (or, presumably, that they were on sale) even though they were placed in an ostensibly prominent position in the store.

B.   No. This answer choice does not explain why the sales figures changed.

C.   No. The reason customers bought the Maxlast hammers is irrelevant to why the sales figures changed.

D.   No. This answer choice makes the result more surprising.

E.   No. This answer choice does not explain why the sales figures changed.

12. **B** **Weaken**

The argument concludes that ginkgo may not have directly enhanced the memory of mice that consumed ginkgo in a study of maze navigation. The conclusion is based on the results of a comparative study that showed that mice whose diet included ginkgo were more likely to remember how to navigate a maze than mice that had a normal diet. The premises also indicate that other studies have found that ginkgo reduces stress in mice and that lowering very high stress levels is known to improve recall. The argument assumes that the mice that consumed ginkgo were actually highly stressed and that the consumption therefore reduced their high stress levels. The credited response will provide new evidence that undermines the conclusion or point out a relevant consideration that the argument missed.

A. No. Higher doses of ginkgo might still reduce stress in mice, but this answer choice does not confirm whether the mice were stressed.

B. Yes. This answer choice points out that the mice were not actually highly stressed, so the ginkgo could not have lowered very high stress levels.

C. No. This answer choice does not confirm whether the mice were stressed.

D. No. The mechanism by which ginkgo reduces stress is irrelevant to whether it actually does so. Furthermore, this answer choice does not confirm whether the mice were stressed.

E. No. The argument concerns recall, not the initial learning.

13. **D** Inference

The passage presents a single statement: Some politicians who strongly supported free trade among Canada, the United States, and Mexico now refuse to publicly support extending free trade to other Latin American countries. The credited response will be an answer choice that is supported by this statement.

A. No. The passage does not tell us anything about politicians who do support extending free trade to other Latin American countries.

B. No. The passage does not tell us anything about politicians who do support extending free trade to other Latin American countries.

C. No. The passage concerns two different instances of establishing free trade. Changing their position would mean that the politicians who supported free trade among Canada, the United States, and Mexico later decided that they are against free trade among those countries. Extending free trade to other Latin American countries is a separate issue.

D. Yes. That some politicians supported the initial free trade agreement but do not support the extension of that agreement implies that not all politicians who supported the initial free trade agreement now support the extension of that agreement.

E. No. The phrase "[refuse] to support publicly" in the passage is not synonymous with the phrase "publicly oppose" in this answer choice. Some politicians could simply remain silent on the issue, neither supporting nor opposing the idea of extending free trade.

14. **E** Principle Match

The passage presents a principle and its application, and the question stems suggests that the application is unsupported. The principle can be diagrammed as a conditional: If a person or business knowingly aids someone in infringing on a copyright, then that person or business is also guilty of copyright infringement. The contrapositive is that if a person or business is not guilty of copyright infringement, then that person or business did not knowingly aid someone in infringing on a copyright. The application of the principle indicates that the Grandview Department Store is guilty of copyright infringement. To properly make this conclusion, we need to know that the Grandview Department Store knowingly aided someone in infringing on a copyright, but the application tells us only that the store contains a self-service kiosk that a customer used to print copyrighted wedding photos. The credited response will link the idea of providing the kiosk to knowingly aiding in copyright infringement.

A. No. This answer choice does not explain how providing a kiosk constitutes knowingly aiding someone in infringing on a copyright. A comparison between self-service and full-service facilities is irrelevant.

B. No. This answer choice does not explain how providing a kiosk constitutes knowingly aiding someone in infringing on a copyright. The obligation to report illegal activity is irrelevant to the store's guilt.

C. No. This answer choice does not explain how providing a kiosk constitutes knowingly aiding someone in infringing on a copyright. Such a notice would not necessarily exonerate the store, nor do we know whether this store even posted such a notice.

D. No. This answer choice does not explain how providing a kiosk constitutes knowingly aiding someone in infringing on a copyright. Monitoring the facilities would not necessarily exonerate the store, nor do we know whether this store did in fact monitor its facilities.

E. Yes. This answer choice explains how providing a kiosk constitutes knowingly aiding someone in infringing on a copyright.

15. A **Main Point**

The fill-in-the-blank space is preceded by the logical indicator "then," signaling that the credited response will be the main point of the argument. The argument states that, although journalism's purpose is to inform people about matters relevant to the choices they must make, newspapers and television news programs often contain sensationalistic gossip that is of little relevance to people's lives. The implication is that such gossip is included for reasons unrelated to the purpose of journalism. The credited response will indicate that gossip is included in newspapers and television news programs for nonjournalistic reasons.

A. Yes. This answer choice completes the conclusion that gossip is included in newspapers and television news programs for nonjournalistic reasons.

B. No. News media might still achieve their purpose even if they contain elements that do not contribute to that purpose.

C. No. A premise states that gossip is of little relevance to people's lives, and no statements imply that such relevance has changed over the years.

D. No. The idea of keeping an audience entertained is not discussed.

E. No. People who are interested in journalism can nevertheless be interested in sensationalistic gossip as well.

16. C **Flaw**

The argument concludes that most citizens would prefer a legislature that is 40 percent Conservative, 20 percent Moderate, and 40 percent Liberal. This conclusion is based on the results of a survey that demonstrated that 40 percent of respondents would prefer a Conservative legislature, 20 percent a Moderate legislature, and 40 percent a Liberal legislature. The argument confuses the whole and the part: It assumes that the preferences of the surveyed group are also the preferences of most of the individual persons surveyed. The credited response will identify this flaw.

A. No. The conclusion does not prescribe a certain course of action but rather interprets the survey's results.

B. No. The argument does not use circular reasoning.

C. Yes. This answer choice describes the flaw of assuming that the preferences of a group represent the preferences of most individual members of that group.

D. No. The potential bias of the researchers does not affect the misinterpretation of the survey's results.

E. No. Both the premises and the conclusion refer to percentages.

17. **D** **Inference**

The city leader presents facts about the city's spending options. Adopting the new tourism plan would increase tourist revenues by at least $2 billion and create as many jobs as a new automobile manufacturing plant while costing less than building a new automobile manufacturing plant. Spending the money necessary to convince an automobile manufacturer to build a plant in the city would be a reasonable expenditure. The credited response will be an answer choice that is supported by a single statement or by a combination of statements from the passage.

A. No. The term "should" is unsupported, and the term "least expensive" is too strong: The passage does not imply which option should be pursued, nor do we know what the least expensive option would be because there may be other job-creation measures that are not discussed in the passage.

B. No. The term "in general" is too strong: The passage discusses a particular instance, but we cannot extend the reasoning to most instances.

C. No. The term "cannot" is too strong: The passage does not imply that the city can afford only one of the options.

D. Yes. If it would be reasonable to spend the money to convince an automobile manufacturer to build a plant in the city, and adopting the new tourism plan would cost less, then it is likely that spending the money to adopt the new tourism plan would also be a reasonable expenditure.

E. No. The term "only" is too strong: The passage states that building a new automobile manufacturing plant would also create jobs.

18. **B** **Necessary Assumption**

The argument concludes that one should not trust the anecdotal evidence that purportedly shows that many medical patients can predict sudden changes in their medical status. The premises rely on an appeal to an apparently analogous case that has been disproved: the claim that a disproportionately high number of babies are born during full moons. This claim has been disproved by pointing out that maternity room staff are simply more likely to remember full-moon births. The argument assumes that medical staff are likewise more likely to remember when their patients correctly predict changes to their medical status than when such predictions are incorrect. The credited response will confirm that the analogy can be extended in this way.

A. No. The argument does not require the article to be empirically disproved soon.

B. Yes. This answer choice confirms that the analogy with full-moon births can be extended to patients' predictions.

C. No. The sincerity of the patients' predictions is irrelevant to whether those predictions prove an instinctual ability to predict changes to their medical status.

D. No. The argument does not require full-moon births to be uncommon but rather requires them to be less common than they are believed to be.

E. No. The argument can be made regardless of how widely held the belief is.

19. **C**   Flaw

The politician concludes that legislators should reject the argument that increases in multinational control of manufacturing have shifted labor to nations without strong worker protections and thus decreased workers' average wages. He bases his conclusion on the fact that the argument comes from union leaders, who have an interest in seeing wages remain high. He assumes that the union leaders' self-interest cannot coincide with a valid justification for opposing multinational control; he attacks the union leaders' motives rather than the reasoning. The credited response will identify this flaw.

A. No. The term "all" is too strong: The conclusion explicitly states that legislators should reject "this argument," but this fact does not imply that one should reject all arguments made by union members.

B. No. The term "anyone" is too strong: The argument requires only that union leaders be unreliable sources.

C. Yes. This answer choice describes the flaw of attacking the union leaders' motives rather than their argument.

D. No. The term "only" is too strong: The argument does not imply that the union leaders have no other reasons for opposing multinational control.

E. No. The term "all" is too strong: The argument does not require that union leaders in non-manufacturing sectors argue against increases in multinational control of manufacturing.

20. **E**   Resolve/ Explain

The professor explains that, in the last ten years, significantly fewer people are earning chemistry degrees despite the facts that the number of university students who enter as chemistry majors has not changed in that time and that job prospects for chemistry graduates are better than ever. The credited response will explain why graduates are declining despite the apparently contradictory facts, likely by pointing out some other difference that has emerged in the last ten years.

A. No. This answer choice does not point out a difference that would explain the recent decline in the number of people earning chemistry degrees. Students may always have entered a university without the strong academic background required to major in chemistry.

B. No. The number of students earning chemistry degrees could remain constant or increase even if the number of degrees earned in the natural sciences as a whole declines, so this answer choice does not explain the decline in the number of people earning chemistry degrees.

C. No. This answer choice does not point out a difference that would explain the recent decline in the number of people earning chemistry degrees. Students may always have been unsure of their major upon entering universities.

D. No. This answer choice does not point out a difference that would explain the recent decline in the number of people earning chemistry degrees.

E. Yes. This answer choice points out a change over the years that accounts for the decline in the number of people earning chemistry degrees.

21. **B** Parallel Flaw

The argument concludes that human-borne diseases probably did not cause the mass extinction of large land animals and birds. This conclusion is supported by the facts that more than 55 different species disappeared at about the same time and that a single disease could not have wiped out so many different species. The argument fails to consider the possibility that several diseases rather than a single disease wiped out all 55 species. The credited response will match this flaw of assuming that, because a single entity cannot account for a phenomenon, a combination of such entities cannot together account for that phenomenon.

A. No. This answer choice presents a valid argument. High interest rates are neither necessary nor sufficient to cause an economic downturn, so one cannot claim that an economic downturn was caused by high interest rates.

B. Yes. Just because a single person cannot fix both the window and the door does not mean that two people could not work together to fix both.

C. No. This argument presents a flawed argument, but the flaw does not match the argument in the stimulus. The argument in this answer choice assumes that Lena, Jen, and Mark would probably not go to a restaurant outside the immediate vicinity of the theater, that they would probably not go to a restaurant that they did not all like, and that they would go home straight after the movie if they do not go out to dinner.

D. No. This answer choice presents a flawed argument, but the flaw does not match the argument in the stimulus. The painting may be great even if it was painted in a time that produced little great art.

E. No. This answer choice presents a valid argument. It is reasonable to conclude that some people benefit from the influenza vaccine if the vaccine reduces the severity of symptoms.

22. **A** Sufficient Assumption

The argument concludes that the disclaimer a tax preparation company adds to every e-mail it sends out serves no purpose. The premises indicate that the disclaimer's only purpose is to provide legal protection for the company and that the disclaimer provides no legal protection if it is contradicted elsewhere in the e-mail. The argument assumes that if the disclaimer is not contradicted elsewhere in the e-mail, then the company has no need for legal protection. The credited response will prove the conclusion.

A. Yes. This answer choice confirms that the company does not need legal protection if the disclaimer is not contradicted elsewhere in the e-mail.

B. No. Penalties are irrelevant to the argument.

C. No. Whether the disclaimer is ignored has no bearing on whether it serves a legal purpose.

D. No. Whether clients follow advice in the e-mail has no bearing on whether the disclaimer serves a legal purpose.

E. No. Penalties are irrelevant to the argument.

23. **E** `Principle Strengthen`

The argument concludes that attempts to resolve friends' marital problems are usually unjustified. This conclusion is based on the fact that such attempts usually don't work and therefore cause resentment. The argument assumes that actions that are not effective are not justified. The credited response will state a general rule or principle that establishes that only effective actions are justified.

A. No. This answer choice does not discuss whether getting involved is justified.

B. No. This answer choice would support getting involved when it is the right thing to do even if getting involved leads to resentment, so this answer choice would undermine the conclusion.

C. No. This answer choice does not discuss whether getting involved is justified.

D. No. This answer choice denies a connection between the premise and the conclusion.

E. Yes. This answer choice establishes that actions based on good intentions are justified only if they result in success.

24. **D** `Necessary Assumption`

The argument concludes that authors who write to give pleasure can impart truth. The premises claim that if the conclusion were not true, one could simply look at sales figures to determine a book's truthfulness: If a book were popular, one could claim that it gave readers pleasure and therefore that some of the book is untrue. The argument assumes that popularity is sometimes sufficient to prove that a book gives readers pleasure and that if readers derive pleasure from a book, then the author wrote the book in order to give readers pleasure. The credited response will link the ideas of deriving pleasure and writing in order to give pleasure.

A. No. Whether people are aware of a book's like effect on them has no bearing on whether the author wrote the book with a particular effect in mind.

B. No. The argument does not require authors to successfully give readers pleasure whenever they intend to do so.

C. No. Whether readers are concerned with the truth of a book has no bearing on whether the book is in fact truthful.

D. Yes. This answer choice confirms that readers can derive pleasure from a book only if the author intended the book to give pleasure.

E. No. A book that does not give readers pleasure is irrelevant to this argument.

25. **D** `Strengthen`

The argument concludes that most of the new television programs Wilke & Wilke produce for this season will be cancelled. This conclusion is based on the facts that most of the new shows they produced for the previous season were cancelled due to low viewership and that all of their new shows are police dramas, few of which have been popular in recent years. The argument assumes many things, including that Wilke & Wilke's police dramas are representative examples, that viewership from the previous season has some bearing on the current season's viewership, and that the new shows are not, for whatever reason, among those less likely to be cancelled. The credited response will provide new evidence that supports the conclusion or confirms the validity of an assumption.

A. No. The argument concludes that a certain proportion of Wilke & Wilke's shows will be cancelled, so the number of shows is irrelevant.

B. No. A premise states that most of the new shows that Wilke & Wilke produced last year were cancelled, but we do not know if the police dramas referenced in the answer choice were new shows. Furthermore, we do not know if the police dramas in the answer choice were cancelled or not.

C. No. This answer choice leaves open the possibility that Wilke & Wilke did not even produce any police dramas in the previous season—compare with (D).

D. Yes. This answer choice confirms that Wilke & Wilke have produced unsuccessful new police dramas recently, supporting the idea that their next crop of new police dramas will also fail.

E. No. A premise already states that few police dramas have been popular in recent years, so this answer choice is a premise booster.

26. **E** 　[Principle Match]

The passage describes a situation: If a corporation obtains funds fraudulently, then the corporation should be penalized for the use of those funds, and this penalty should completely cancel out any profit the corporation made in using the funds. The general rule or principle is that if one benefits from an illicit activity, then the punishment for that illicit activity should completely offset the benefit. The credited response will describe another situation that invokes this general rule or principle.

A. No. The situation does not describe a benefit arising from an illicit activity.

B. No. The situation does not describe a punishment that completely offsets the benefit: "to the satisfaction of the regulators" is a vague statement that could allow the factory's compliance expenditures to be lower than its profit.

C. No. The situation does not describe a benefit arising from an illicit activity.

D. No. The situation does not describe a penalty that completely offsets the benefit: Even if an athlete is banned from future competition, he could still retain the winnings, endorsements, etc. from previous competition. The credited response should describe reparations for past actions rather than a prohibition on future actions.

E. Yes. The criminal would profit from his crime, so all proceeds from the book sales should be donated rather than given to the criminal.

Section 3: Games

Questions 1–6

This is a 1D ordering game with 7 players and 7 spaces. Draw a diagram with the numbers 1 to 7 and the players in this game are P, Q, R, S, T, V, and W.

Clue 1: ~ST & ~TS

Clue 2: Q—R

Clue 3: VW

Clue 4: P = 4

There are several ordering deductions that can be found in this game. Draw clue 4 in the diagram. Then due to clue 2, R cannot be in 1 and Q cannot be in 7. Combine clues 3 and 4 to find that V cannot be in 3 and W cannot be in 5 since V and W must be consecutive and P is in slot 4.

Your diagram should look like this:

P, Q, R, S, T, V, W

1	2	3	4	5	6	7
-R		-V	P	-W		-Q

Clue 1: ~~ST~~ ~~TS~~
Clue 2: Q—R
Clue 3: V W
Clue 4: P = 4

1. **D** Grab-a-Rule

Use the clues and POE to eliminate answer choices that are not possible.

A. No. This violates clue 1.

B. No. This violates clue 3.

C. No. This violates clue 4.

D. Yes. This works with the clues.

E. No. This violates clue 2.

2. **C** [General]

Use previous work and try the remaining answer choices to find the possible list.

A. No. This scenario would cause a violation of either clue 2 or clue 3.

B. No. This scenario violates clue 2.

C. Yes. This scenario is possible in the work done for question 4.

D. No. This would violate clue 1.

E. No. This scenario violates clue 4.

3. **D** [Specific]

If T is second, then the players must be recruited in one of two scenarios. Either the list is Q, T, R, P, V, W, S or the list is Q, T, R, P, S, V, W. The only answer choice that is possible in either scenario is (D).

4. **B** [Specific]

If Q is immediately before R, then there are two blocks to place, one on either side of the P and each block will have S or T next to it on that side of P. For example, the list could be QRT, P, VWS or the list could be TVW, P, QRS. Because the blocks must take up two spaces, S cannot be in an even-numbered slot so the credited response is (B).

5. **A** [Specific]

If W is before R and R is before T then Q, V, and W, must all be before R in slots 1, 2, and 3. Since Q could be in slots 1 or 3, the credited response is (A).

6. **B** [Specific]

If W is immediately before Q, then the list must be V, W, Q, P, T/S, R, S/T, so R must be sixth and the credited response is (B).

Questions 7–13

This is a variable grouping game with three players, F, G, and H. The diagram should be three groups L, M, and S each with two slots.

Clue 1: Each photographer used at least once and no more than 3 times.

Clue 2: LM

Clue 3: HL = FS

Clue 4: S = ~G

Deductions: The clues in this game do not provide a great deal of deductions, so you'll start the game with a mostly blank canvas. You should write ~G above the S column.

Your diagram should look like this:

F, G, H

L | M ‖ ~G S

__ __ | __ __ ‖ __ __

Clue 1: F, G, H = 1–3 uses
Clue 2: LM
Clue 3: HL = FS
Clue 4: G ≠ S

7. B   **Grab-a-Rule**

A. No. This violates clue 4.

B. Yes.

C. No. This violates clue 2.

D. No. This violates clue 3.

E. No. This violates clue 1.

8. C   **Specific**

If both Lifestyle photos are Hue, then both Sports photos must be F (clue 4). Since at least one photo must be by Gagnon, there must be a Gagnon photo in Metro. Clue 2 states that the other Metro photo must be Hue. Therefore, (C) is the credited response.

9. D   **Specific**

If one photo in Lifestyle is Gagnon and the other is Hue, then according to clue 4, there must be exactly one F in Sports. The other sports photo cannot be G, so it must be H. The first photo in Metro must be either G or H to abide by clue 2, and the other photo would be F or G since there is a maximum of three H photos in the paper. This makes (D) the credited response.

10. A   **General**

Use previous work and clues to eliminate answer choices.

A. Yes. This can be seen in the work for question 11.

B. No. This would violate clue 3.

C. No. This would violate clue 3.

D. No. This would violate clue 2.

E. No. This would violate clue 2.

76

11.   C   [Specific]

If one Lifestyle photo is F and the other is by H, then according to clue 3, exactly one sports photo must be F. Since G cannot be in the Sports section, the other sports photo must be H. G must have at least one photo in the paper, so there must be one G photo in Metro. Clue 2 states that there must be an overlap between Lifestyle and Metro, so the other Metro photo must be either F or H. The only option that could be true in this scenario is (C).

12.   E   [Specific]

If both photos in one section belong to G, then those two photos must be in either Lifestyle or Metro since G cannot be featured in the Sports section. In the first scenario, where G takes up both spaces in Lifestyle, G must also take up one slot in Metro (clue 2). Using clue 3, the Sports section must have zero F photos so H must be in both slots in Sports. F will fill the remaining space in Metro. This scenario aligns with (E).

13.   C   [Specific]

If the photos in the Metro section are one each of F and H, then there must be a G in the Lifestyle section (clue 4). The other lifestyle photo would then have to be either F or H (clue 2). The sports section must have one H and the other could be F or H, depending what happens in the Lifestyle section (clue 3). The only one that could be true is (C).

Questions 14–18

This is a 2D ordering game with a setup that is M, T, W, R (Thursday), F each with two slots. The players are G, H, J, K, and L and each player is used twice.

Clue 1: ~XX same day.

Clue 2: LL = second

Clue 3: G = 1st; ~GG

Clue 4: K = T & F

Clue 5: HJ or JH same day

Clue 6: ~GL same day

Deductions: The repeat players and lack of specific clues defining any slots or sequences limit the deductions that can be found in this game. You will start the game with a blank diagram but should note the interactions involved in clues 2, 3, and 6 as this interaction will drive the game.

Your diagram should look like this:

G, H, J, K, L

M	T	W	Th	F
_ _	_ _	_ _	_ _	_ _

Clue 1: ~XX Same day

Clue 2: LL = Second

Clue 3: G = 1st; G̶G̶ (boxed)

Clue 4: K = T and F

Clue 5: HJ or JH (boxed)

Clue 6: G̶L̶ (boxed)

14. **A** Grab-a-Rule

A. Yes.

B. No. This violates clue 3.

C. No. This violates clue 2.

D. No. This violates clue 2.

E. No. This violates clue 3.

15. **C** General

Use prior work to eliminate answer choices that do not have to be true.

A. No. This scenario can be found in the work for question 18.

B. No. This scenario can be found in the work for question 16.

C. Yes. This is the only scenario that is not found in the work for other questions. If J is on Tuesday, then K must also be on Tuesday. This prevents J and H from appearing together because either G or L will work in the gallery on the other four days.

D. No. This scenario can be found in the work for question 16.

E. No. This scenario can be found in the work for question 16.

16. **B** Specific

Try H in the second slot on Wednesday. In this case, L must work in the second slot of Monday and Tuesday. Then clue 4 requires K to work Tuesday in the first slot. Per clues 3 and 6, G must be in the first slot on Wednesday and Friday, so K must work the second slot on Friday. Since J cannot work both slots on Thursday, it must work the first slot on Monday and either the first or second slot on Thursday along with H. J must work on Monday and Thursday, so (B) is the credited response.

17. **E** **Specific**

Try G and J on Monday. In this scenario, G is in the first slot and J is in the second. L can then be in the second slots on Tuesday and Wednesday. Clue 4 requires that K be in the first slot Tuesday. Since J and H must be together on one day, put them in both slots on Thursday. That leaves G in the first slot and K in the second slot on Friday and H to fill the first slot on Wednesday. In this scenario, it is possible that J works on Thursday, so (E) is the credited response.

18. **B** **Specific**

If K works second shift Tuesday, then L must work the second shift on Wednesday and Thursday. Since H and J must work together on one day, place them in the shifts for Monday. G cannot work with L, so G must be the morning shift on Tuesday and Friday. Then clue 4 requires K on Friday in the second shift. H and J will fill the remaining first shifts on Wednesday and Thursday. The only answer choice that could be true in this scenario is (B).

Questions 19–23

This is an In/Out game with a setup that creates two groups: fall and spring. The players are K, L, M, N, O, and P. L is a wildcard.

Clue 1: ~MP

Clue 2: KN

Clue 3: Kf → Of; Os → Ks

Clue 4: Mf → Ns; Nf → Ms

Deductions: Since this is an In/Out game, look for placeholder deductions. Clue 1 indicates that there is a space in fall with M/P and the other is in spring. Clue 4 could also provide a placeholder with M or N in spring but since you already have a placeholder with M, writing this into your diagram can create problems since M in spring would take only one space. Keep in mind that L is completely wild and can always go in either spring or fall.

Your diagram should look like this:

K, L, M, N, O, P

Fall	Spring
M/P	P/M

Clue 1: M̸P̸

Clue 2: KN

Clue 3: K_F → O_F
         O_s → K_S

Clue 4: M_F → N_S
         N_F → M_S

19. **E**   **Grab-a-Rule**

A. No. This violates clue 2.

B. No. This violates clue 1.

C. No. This violates clue 3.

D. No. This violates clue 4.

E. Yes.

20. **C**   **Specific**

If M is in fall, then clue 1 requires P in spring. Clue 4 requires N in spring and clue 2 would place K in spring as well. The only players not accounted for are L and O and the rules allow them to go in either fall or spring in this scenario. The only pair that could go in the fall with M then is L and O, so the answer is (C).

21. **B**   **Specific**

If N is published in the fall, then clue 4 places M in the spring. Clue 1 would place P in fall away from M, and clue 2 places K in fall with N. Clue 3 requires O join K in the fall. L is wild so L could be in either fall or spring. Therefore, (B) is the credited response.

22. **A**   **General**

The question task asks which additional piece of information would complete the game, so try each answer choice until you find one that proves the entire game. Since L is wild, the new piece of information must restrict L in some way. If K is in fall and L is in spring, then KNOP must be in fall and LM must be in spring. Choice (A) fully determines this scenario, so it is the credited response.

23. **B**   **Complex**

In this question, you are asked to parallel the deductions from clue 4 that create a placeholder for M/N in spring. Diagram each clue and choose the one that makes the same deduction.

A. No. This clue would restrict L instead of N.

B. Yes. Since M and P must be in different groups (clue 1), Nf → Pf is the same thing as saying Nf → Ms.

C. No. This is similar to clue 1 not clue 4.

D. No. This clue would allow both M and N to be in the fall, which is not allowed in the original clue 4.

E. No. This is the same as clue 3 not clue 4.

Section 4: Arguments 2

1. **C** **Sufficient Assumption**

The argument concludes that Vadim will be laid off. This conclusion is based on the fact that the firm has decided to lay off a programmer and on the firm's policy of laying off the most recently hired programmer when one must be laid off. The argument contains a language shift that assumes that Vadim is the most recently hired programmer. The credited response will explicitly link the premise to the conclusion and force the conclusion to be true.

A. No. The experience level of a programmer is irrelevant to the enforcement of the policy.

B. No. Vadim's understanding of the policy is irrelevant to its enforcement.

C. Yes. This answer choice confirms that Vadim is the most recently hired programmer.

D. No. Quality of work is irrelevant to the enforcement of the policy.

E. No. Whether the policy itself is justified is irrelevant to its enforcement.

2. **B** **Principle Match**

Wanda concludes that having many things in her studio is justified. She bases this conclusion on the idea that an artist requires visual stimuli to create art. She bases this idea on a comparison with writers, who require written stimuli to write. She also supports her conclusion by stating that an empty work area would hinder her creativity. Vernon suggests a potential weakness in Wanda's argument: He implies that the visual stimuli must be of a certain level of quality to inspire creativity, just as writers must be surrounded by good writing instead of poor writing such as is found in tabloids. The credited response will describe the principle underlying Vernon's reasoning.

A. No. Vernon suggests that clutter is fine as long as it is inspiring.

B. Yes. Vernon indicates that Wanda has to consider the quality of the stimuli in her studio.

C. No. Neither speaker expresses an opinion on how one should view tabloids.

D. No. Vernon suggests that messiness can inspire creativeness as long as it is the right kind of messiness.

E. No. Vernon suggests that clutter is acceptable as long as it is inspiring.

3. **D** **Resolve/ Explain**

The passage explains that listing an animal species as endangered causes the enforcement of legal safeguards designed to protect the species. The passage then introduces a paradox: Despite these legal safeguards, in some cases, a species declines more rapidly after being listed as endangered than before. The credited response will provide a reason some species declined more rapidly after being listed as endangered.

A. No. This answer choice does not explain why the decline intensifies after the listing.

B. No. This answer choice does not explain why the decline intensifies after the listing.

C.   No. The number of species on the list has no impact on the rate at which their populations are declining.

D.   Yes. After the animals are listed as endangered, their value to collectors goes up, so they are poached more aggressively.

E.   No. This answer choice makes the paradox worse.

4. **B**   `Point at Issue`

Annette concludes that Sefu should take the town council to visit other towns that have implemented development plans similar to Sefu's to convince them to implement his plan. Sefu concludes that the council's accepting the trip would give the appearance of undue influence. Sefu bases his conclusion on the fact that he has a vested interest in the council's votes. Annette and Sefu disagree about whether Sefu should take the town council on a trip. The credited response will identify this point of disagreement.

A.   No. Presumably Sefu believes that the council should adopt his plan, but Annette, although she offers advice on how to persuade the council, does not actually state whether she believes that the council should adopt the plan.

B.   Yes. Annette states that Sefu should take the council on a trip, but Sefu worries that doing so would be misguided.

C.   No. Both Annette and Sefu agree that he has an interest in the council's votes.

D.   No. Annette states that other towns have successfully implemented such plans, and Sefu tacitly agrees with this statement.

E.   No. Sefu implies that the appearance of undue influence should be avoided, but Annette does not address the issue.

5. **C**   `Flaw`

The argument concludes that any modernization will cause an increase in worshippers. The conclusion is based on the fact that some recent modernizations of language and ritual have been correlated with increases in attendance at places of worship. The argument assumes that the modernization caused the increased attendance and that there are no other causes or relevant considerations. Note that the question stem contains the phrase "presumes without giving sufficient justification": This phrase indicates that the credited response will state a necessary assumption of the argument.

A.   No. The argument does not restrict the possibility of modernization to some religions.

B.   No. The argument does not indicate whether modernization alters messages.

C.   Yes. The answer choice describes the argument's equating correlation with causation.

D.   No. The term "only" is too strong: The argument concludes that modernization is sufficient to increase worshippers but not necessary.

E.   No. The argument does not indicate that the increase in worshippers would be irreversible.

6.   **D**   **Parallel Flaw**

The argument concludes that Lily does not practice hard. The premises indicate that one must practice hard or be very talented to be in the regional band and that Lily is in the regional band and practices hard. The argument does not, however, state or imply that one cannot both practice hard and be very talented, so the conclusion is not supported. Structurally, the argument presents a conditional relationship with an "or" statement on the right side. It confirms the left-side idea and one of the right-side ideas and therefore concludes that the other right-side idea must not be true. The credited response will match this structure.

A.   No. The premises do not contain a conditional relationship with an "or" statement on the right side.

B.   No. The premises do not confirm the left-side idea and one of the right-side ideas.

C.   No. The premises do not contain a conditional relationship with an "or" statement on the right side.

D.   Yes. Staying informed requires reading a major newspaper or watching TV news every day. Julie is informed and reads a major newspaper every day, so she does not watch TV news. This answer choice matches the flaw because it fails to consider that Julie can both read a major newspaper and watch TV news every day.

E.   No. The premises do not confirm the left-side idea and one of the right-side ideas.

7.   **C**   **Reasoning**

The argument concludes that eating fish can lower one's cholesterol level. This conclusion is based on a comparative study that showed lower cholesterol levels in the group that ate a balanced diet with two servings of fish per week compared with the group that ate a similar diet without any fish. The argument further supports the conclusion by stating that the groups had similar cholesterol levels prior to entering the study. This statement rules out the possible alternate cause of the first group simply having lower cholesterol levels regardless of their level of fish consumption. The credited response will describe the function of this statement.

A.   No. The statement supports the conclusion by ruling out a possible alternate cause.

B.   No. The main conclusion of the argument is that eating fish can lower one's cholesterol level.

C.   Yes. This answer choice describes the role of the statement as ruling out a possible alternate explanation for the first group's lower cholesterol.

D.   No. The statement does not clarify why the study was undertaken.

E.   No. The statement rules out a possible alternate explanation for the conclusion.

8.   **E**   **Strengthen**

The argument concludes that satnavs save fuel and promote safety. This conclusion is supported by studies that show that drivers using satnavs make shorter journeys and thus save fuel and that drivers using satnavs drive more carefully because they do not have to take their eyes off the road to look at maps. The argument assumes that there are no other relevant considerations that would indicate that using satnavs is inefficient or dangerous. The credited response will provide new evidence that supports the conclusion or confirms the validity of the assumption.

A. No. The likelihood of a group's using satnavs reveals little about whether doing so saves fuel or promotes safety.

B. No. This fact would give drivers an incentive to use a device that would save fuel, but it does not imply that the satnav is such a device.

C. No. This answer choice suggests that a certain group of drivers would have no need for a satnav, but this fact does not imply that the use of a satnav would not save fuel or promote safety.

D. No. This answer choice suggests that some people who own a satnav would not use it, but this fact does not imply that use of the satnav would not save fuel or promote safety.

E. Yes. The satnavs give directions as they are needed, so using a satnav promotes safety because it allows drivers to drive in a less risky way.

9. **C**   **Principle Match**

The passage indicates that managers can extract the best performance from their employees by delegating responsibility to them, especially responsibility that had previously been held by the manager. It also indicates that threats of termination and promises of financial rewards are ineffective motivational strategies because employees must want to do a good job for its own sake. The credited response will describe the principle underlying the idea of delegating one's own responsibility to increase the productiveness of one's employees.

A. No. The situation does not concern one's sense of how power should be used.

B. No. The situation does not compare the desires for prestige and job security.

C. Yes. A manager can enhance his effectiveness by delegating some of his responsibilities to them.

D. No. This answer choice would support a manager's not delegating his responsibilities to his employees.

E. No. The situation does not concern the company as a whole but the performance of individual employees.

10. **E**   **Point at Issue**

Richard concludes that abstract art will eventually be seen as an aberration. His conclusion is based on the fact that abstract art is not representational and thus does not meet the fundamental representational requirement of art. Jung-Su concludes that abstract art is part of the artistic mainstream. His conclusion is based on the fact that abstract art is representational, even if it is not literally so, insofar as abstract art represents the purely formal features of everyday objects. Richard and Jung-Su disagree about whether abstract art is representational. The credited response will identify this point of disagreement.

A. No. Jung-Su states that abstract artists reject literal representation, and Richard states that abstract art is not representational, so they agree about this point.

B. No. Richard states that art must represent, but Jung-Su does not state whether representation is a requirement of art.

C. No. Jung-Su states that musicians may reject literal representation, but Richard does not discuss musicians.

D. No. Richard claims that abstract art will eventually be seen as an aberration, but Jung-Su does not speculate about how abstract art may one day be judged.

E. Yes. Richard states that abstract art fails to represent, but Jung-Su states that abstract art represents the purely formal features of everyday objects.

11. **B** **Principle Match**

The passage presents two principles that can be diagrammed as conditionals. First, if one knowingly brings about misfortune, then one should be blamed for that misfortune. The contrapositive is that if one should not be blamed for a misfortune, then one did not knowingly bring about that misfortune. Second, if one unknowingly brings about misfortune and one could not reasonably have foreseen that misfortune, then one should not be blamed for that misfortune. The contrapositive is that if one should be blamed for a misfortune, then one either knowingly brought about that misfortune or could reasonably have foreseen the misfortune. The credited response will correctly move from the left side to the right side of one of these conditionals or their contrapositives.

A. No. Riley could reasonably have foreseen the misfortune. This right-side idea does not lead to a conclusion about blameworthiness.

B. Yes. Oblicek could not have reasonably foreseen the misfortune of the business going bankrupt, so, if such a misfortune does occur, Oblicek should not be blamed.

C. No. Gougon does not know that serving the hollandaise would bring about misfortune. This right-side idea does not lead to a conclusion about blameworthiness.

D. No. Dr. Fitzpatrick does not know that the medicine would bring about misfortune. This right-side idea does not lead to a conclusion about blameworthiness.

E. No. This answer choice does not confirm whether Kapp knowingly dropped the lit cigarette to cause the fire. Without this piece, we cannot conclude that Kapp is to blame.

12. **B** **Necessary Assumption**

The researcher concludes that it is likely that the incidence of illness among people who regularly inhale the scent of lavender is reduced by their practice of inhaling the scent of lavender. This conclusion is based on research that shows that inhaling the scent of lavender tends to reduce stress and on the fact that intense stress can impair the immune system and thereby make one more susceptible to illness. The argument contains a language shift that assumes that people who regularly inhale the scent of lavender are stressed enough to have impaired immune systems. The credited response will link the ideas of inhaling the scent of lavender and being stressed enough to have an impaired immune system.

A. No. The effects of other scents are irrelevant to this argument about lavender.

B. Yes. This answer choice confirms that some people who inhale the scent lavender are stressed enough to have impaired immune systems.

C. No. The argument does not require people who inhale the scent of lavender to be representative of people in general.

D. No. The terms "anyone" and "primarily" are too strong: The argument does not require the inhalation of lavender to be the main mechanism of stress reduction.

E.   No. The term "only" is too strong: The argument does not require that diminished susceptibility to illness be restricted to those with impaired immune systems.

13.   **D**   Flaw

The argument concludes that the Andersen family's real income must have increased over the last five years. This conclusion is based on government statistics showing that the real average income for families has risen over the last five years and on the fact that the Andersen family's current income is average. The argument assumes that the Andersen family's income was not the same or higher in previous years; it assumes that what applies on average must apply to a particular case. The credited response will identify this flaw.

A.   No. The term "average" is used consistently throughout the argument.

B.   No. The argument corrects the Andersen family's income to account for inflation.

C.   No. The argument concerns a single family only, so it does not require assumptions about the distribution of most families on the income scale.

D.   Yes. This answer choice describes the flaw of failing to consider that the Andersen family's real income did not decrease over the last five years.

E.   No. The term "no" is too strong: The argument does not require the estimates to be accurate.

14.   **B**   Sufficient Assumption

The argument concludes that preventing the production of high-quality counterfeit banknotes requires making it difficult or impossible to accurately measure images on the banknotes. The premise states that some methods of making high-quality counterfeit banknotes involve making accurate measurements of such images. The argument assumes that no other prevention strategies are required to thwart would-be counterfeiters. The credited response will explicitly link the premise to the conclusion and force the conclusion to be true.

A.   No. This answer choice does not explain the relevance of accurately measuring images to the prevention of counterfeiting.

B.   Yes. This answer choice indicates that the accurate measuring of images is the only hurdle to producing high-quality counterfeit banknotes.

C.   No. This answer choice does not explain the relevance of accurately measuring images to the prevention of counterfeiting.

D.   No. This answer choice indicates that accurately measuring images is generally easy, but it does not explain the relevance of accurately measuring images to the prevention of counterfeiting.

E.   No. This answer choice does not explain the relevance of accurately measuring images to the prevention of counterfeiting.

15.   **D**   Flaw

Armstrong concludes that we should not use nutritional supplements to treat a particular disease. He supports his conclusion by pointing out that although Dr. Sullivan claims that one should use the supplements, Dr. Sullivan has an ulterior motive to promote them because he is paid to endorse a line of supplements. Armstrong assumes that Dr. Sullivan's self-interest cannot coincide with a valid justification for using the supplements; Armstrong attack's Dr. Sullivan's motives rather than the reasoning. The credited response will identify this flaw.

A. No. The term "supplement" is used consistently throughout the argument.

B. No. The argument attacks Dr. Sullivan's motives.

C. No. The argument attacks Dr. Sullivan's motives.

D. Yes. This answer choice describes the flaw of criticizing Dr. Sullivan's motives rather than his reasoning.

E. No. The argument neither states nor suggests that supplements cannot be used with other treatments. Dr. Sullivan claims that nutritional supplements should be used instead of pharmaceuticals, but these treatment options may not be the only ones available.

16. **B** **Necessary Assumption**

The economist concludes that a stronger economy is likely to make it harder to find day care. He supports this conclusion by presenting a chain of events: If the economy grows stronger, employment will increase, more parents will need to find day care, and many day-care workers will quit for better-paying jobs in other fields. The argument assumes that the day-care workers who quit will not be replaced by new workers entering the field. The credited response will confirm that those who quit will not be sufficiently replaced.

A. No. The term "most" is too strong: The argument does not require that the majority of new jobs created in a stronger economy pay well.

B. Yes. This answer choice confirms that the day-care workers who quit will not be replaced by new day-care workers.

C. No. The number of day-care workers does not necessarily need to decrease because demand for day care will definitely increase. If the number of day-care workers remained the same, it would still be more difficult to find day care due to increased demand without a corresponding increase in supply.

D. No. The term "unless" is too strong: The argument does not require the situation described in the stimulus to be the only or the most likely cause of day-care shortages.

E. No. If anything, this answer choice might weaken the conclusion by pointing out that a stronger economy will result in less competition for day care services.

17. **A** **Inference**

The passage presents facts comparing ostrich farming and cattle ranching. Ostrich farms require less acreage than cattle ranching, and ostriches reproduce faster than cattle. Starting an ostrich farm requires four ostriches and one acre of land. Starting a cattle ranch requires a large herd of cows, one bull, and at least two acres of land per cow.

Starting an ostrich farm is more costly than starting a cattle ranch. Ostrich farming can eventually bring in as much as five times as cattle ranching. The credited response will be an answer choice that is supported by a single statement or by a combination of statements from the passage.

A. Yes. Starting up an ostrich farm requires fewer animals and fewer acres of land than does starting up a cattle ranch, yet the start-up costs for an ostrich farm are still higher than those for a cattle ranch, so the ostriches probably cost more than a bull and a herd of cows.

B. No. The passage indicates that ostrich farming is a better source of income than cattle ranching, but this fact does not mean that cattle ranching is not a good source of income: Both ventures could be good sources of income with ostrich farming simply being a better one.

C. No. The passage does not discuss feed consumption.

D. No. The passage indicates that ostrich farming can eventually bring in as much as five times what cattle ranching does, but you cannot use this fact to make a specific comparison between average farms and ranches.

E. No. The passage indicates that the start-up costs for ostrich farming are high, but this fact does not imply that ostrich farmers cannot nevertheless make a profit during their first year.

18. **E** Necessary Assumption

The argument concludes that hairless dogs must have been transported between western Mexico and coastal Peru by boat, probably during trading expeditions. The argument establishes that such dogs exist in both regions and that hairlessness was very unlikely to have emerged on two separate occasions. The conclusion is supported by the fact that such dogs have never existed in the wild and that overland travel between the regions would have been difficult. The argument assumes that travel by boat was easier or at least more likely than overland travel; it also assumes that there is no other way the dogs could have come to exist in both regions. The credited response will confirm that travel by boat was easier or rule out an alternate explanation for the dogs' existence in both regions.

A. No. The term "never" is too strong: The argument does not require Mexico and Peru to be the only places where hairless dogs have been found.

B. No. Even if most trade goods were transported by boat, hairless dogs could be an exception that was transported overland.

C. No. The terms "no one" and "except" are too strong: The argument does not require trade to be the only reason for travel by boat, and even if it did, this fact would not confirm that hairless dogs were transported by boat.

D. No. This hypothetical answer choice does nothing to confirm that such transportation by boat actually occurred.

E. Yes. This answer choice confirms that travel by boat was easier than overland travel.

19. **A** Inference

The passage presents facts about the Earth's early crust. Microdiamonds are the oldest fragments of the Earth's crust yet identified. They measure 50 microns across and were formed 4.2 billion years ago. The Earth itself was formed just 300 million years before the formation of the microdiamonds. The passage indicates that the relative dates of these formations are significant. The credited response will be an answer choice that is supported by a single statement or by a combination of statements from the passage.

A. Yes. The microdiamonds, as part of the crust, were formed 300 million years after the formation of the Earth, so even if the microdiamonds were the first part of the crust to form, the crust must have begun its formation no more than 300 million years after the Earth's formation.

B. No. The researchers happen to be working in Western Australia, but nothing in the passage suggests that the Earth's crust began its formation in that region.

C. No. We can ballpark when the crust began its formation, but the passage does not provide any information about how long this formation ultimately took.

D. No. Although the statements indicate that the microdiamonds are the oldest fragments yet discovered, other undiscovered components may have formed earlier.

E. No. The term "all" is too strong.

20.   C   **Necessary Assumption**

The argument concludes that we must ensure that Internet users have at least as much freedom of expression as did people speaking in the public square in days past. The premises compare the function of the public square and the Internet: Both are important tools of democracy because they are public forums where citizens can discuss important issues. The argument contains a language shift that assumes that we should protect freedom of expression in important tools of democracy. The credited response will link the ideas of freedom of expression and maintaining effectiveness as a tool of democracy.

A. No. The term "complete" is too strong: The argument concludes that Internet users should have at least as much freedom of expression as did citizens in days past, even if that level of freedom of expression was not complete.

B. No. The terms "all" and "same level" are too strong: The argument concludes that Internet users should have at least as much freedom of expression as did citizens in days past, but this conclusion does not imply that all Internet users must have equal access.

C. Yes. This answer choice provides a reason for protecting freedom of expression.

D. No. The topic of Internet discussions is irrelevant to whether we should protect freedom of expression on the Internet.

E. No. The term "no other" is too strong: The argument does not require the Internet to be the only important tool of democracy.

21.   C   **Weaken**

The argument concludes that the reasoning power and spatial intuition required by chess-playing contributes to achievement in other intellectual areas. The conclusion is based on a study of children who completed a program where they learned to play chess. Many of the children soon showed an increase in achievement levels in all of their schoolwork. The argument assumes that completion of the program was the cause of the increased achievement; it fails to consider other causes or relevant considerations. The credited response will point out another cause for the increased achievement or identify a relevant consideration that would undermine the conclusion.

A. No. Students who did not participate in the program are irrelevant.

B. No. The baseline achievement level is irrelevant because the argument concerns an increase, which would be possible were a student starting at either a low or high level of achievement.

C. Yes. This answer choice points out an alternate cause for the students' increase in intellectual achievement: They were motivated to meet a requirement to play on the chess team.

D. No. The argument does not claim that playing chess is the only way to increase a student's intellectual achievement, so this answer choice can be true without weakening the conclusion.

E. No. Students who did not complete the program are irrelevant.

22. **A** Parallel

The argument concludes that Kate sometimes shops at the local health food store on Wednesdays. The premises indicate that Kate usually buys guava juice on Wednesdays and that the local health food store is the only place she can buy guava juice. Structurally, the argument contains a conditional statement and a "most" statement in the premises and a "some" statement in the conclusion. The credited response will match this structure.

A. Yes. The premises confirm that only teachers may use the kitchen and that most dinners are prepared in the kitchen, so the argument correctly concludes that some dinners are prepared by the teachers.

B. No. This answer choice does not contain a "most" statement in the premises or a "some" statement in the conclusion.

C. No. This argument is flawed: The premises do not indicate that teachers are the only people allowed to use the kitchen, so we cannot conclude that teachers sometimes prepare the dinners that are mostly made in the kitchen.

D. No. This argument is flawed: The premises do not indicate that teachers are the only people allowed to use the kitchen, so we cannot conclude that teachers sometimes prepare the dinners that are produced only in the kitchen.

E. No. This argument is flawed: The premises do not confirm that the kitchen is the only place teachers can prepare dinners, so we cannot conclude that dinners are sometimes prepared in the kitchen.

23. **D** Weaken

The editor concludes that the city will not see an increase in revenue from its new recycling program, disagreeing with the city's claim that they will see an increase. The new program replaces every-other-week pickup with weekly pickup. The city's claim is based on the fact that the more recyclables collected, the more revenue the city gains from selling the recyclables. The editor's conclusion is based on his assertion that there will be no increase in the volume of recyclables; instead, the same volume will be spread out over a greater number of pickups. The editor assumes that there will be no changes once the new program is implemented, including the possibility of an increased volume of recyclables being put out for pickup. The credited response will introduce new evidence that undermines the editor's conclusion or point out a relevant consideration that he missed.

A. No. Trash collection and disposal are irrelevant to the cost-effectiveness of the new recycling program.

B. No. The editor believes that the program will not be more cost-effective because it will not increase the volume of recyclables collected. This answer choice is hypothetical ("even if") and weak ("might")—compare it to the credited response, which confirms that the volume of recyclables collected will actually increase.

C. No. This answer choice is consistent with the editor's premise that the amount of recyclables collected will remain the same.

D. Yes. If the schedule is easier to follow and adhere to, then people will put out more recyclables for collection, undermining the editor's claim that the volume of recyclables collected under the new program will not increase.

E. No. This answer choice would strengthen the conclusion that the program would not be more cost-effective because the city would pay significantly more for the collection.

24. **D** **Necessary Assumption**

The professor concludes that designing introductory science courses as proving grounds has not served the purpose of allowing only those students who are the most committed to being science majors to pass. His conclusion is based on studies that show that some students who are the least enthusiastic about science have passed the courses. The argument contains a language shift that assumes that those who are the least enthusiastic about science are not also the most committed to being science majors. The credited response will link the ideas of being the least enthusiastic and not being the most committed.

A. No. The argument concludes that the courses have not served their intended purpose, not that the intended design is flawed.

B. No. The professor would agree with this statement, but it has no bearing on the argument.

C. No. The argument does not discuss students who are most enthusiastic about science.

D. Yes. This answer choice confirms that there is no overlap between those least enthusiastic about science and those most committed to being science majors.

E. No. The argument does not look forward to whether courses should continue to be designed as proving grounds.

25. **C** **Resolve/ Explain**

The passage explains that many birds and reptiles hiss to threaten potential predators. This hissing likely arose in a common ancestor. The passage then introduces a paradox: None of the potential predators of the common ancestor would have been able to hear the hissing. The credited response will provide a reason why the common ancestor would have used a threat gesture that was ostensibly ineffective.

A. No. This answer choice makes the paradox worse.

B. No. This answer choice does not explain why the common ancestor would retain among its arsenal of threat devices one that seemed to serve to purpose.

C. Yes. The hissing itself is not the threat but the fact that hissing made the common ancestor seem larger and presumably more threatening.

D. No. Even if hissing is energy-efficient, it still needs to be effective as a threat device.

E. No. Even if the common ancestor had few predators, it would still need an effective threat device to use against these predators.

Chapter 7
PrepTest 77:
Answers and
Explanations

ANSWER KEY: PREPTEST 77

Section 1: Reading Comprehension		Section 2: Arguments 1		Section 3: Games		Section 4: Arguments 2	
1.	C	1.	C	1.	A	1.	A
2.	A	2.	D	2.	B	2.	C
3.	C	3.	E	3.	D	3.	E
4.	D	4.	A	4.	C	4.	B
5.	B	5.	A	5.	C	5.	A
6.	E	6.	D	6.	E	6.	C
7.	C	7.	E	7.	D	7.	D
8.	E	8.	A	8.	C	8.	A
9.	D	9.	B	9.	A	9.	D
10.	C	10.	C	10.	B	10.	D
11.	E	11.	B	11.	B	11.	D
12.	A	12.	B	12.	A	12.	A
13.	A	13.	B	13.	B	13.	D
14.	B	14.	A	14.	C	14.	E
15.	C	15.	C	15.	A	15.	C
16.	A	16.	B	16.	E	16.	B
17.	D	17.	B	17.	E	17.	B
18.	B	18.	D	18.	E	18.	D
19.	E	19.	B	19.	C	19.	A
20.	B	20.	B	20.	B	20.	B
21.	C	21.	A	21.	B	21.	B
22.	D	22.	A	22.	C	22.	C
23.	B	23.	D	23.	C	23.	B
24.	E	24.	A			24.	D
25.	B	25.	D			25.	B
26.	A					26.	E
27.	E						

EXPLANATIONS

Section 1: Reading Comprehension

Questions 1–7

The main point of the first paragraph is that the African American artists of the Federal Theater Project (FTP) had come the closest to creating the first national black theater in the United States. The main point of the second paragraph is that the diverse and rich history of art within the African American community led to a wide range of production styles and portrayed a variety of distinct viewpoints. The main point of the third paragraph reiterates the role of the FTP in providing a way to portray the diversity of African American theater artists. The Bottom Line as a whole is that the FTP, though short-lived, provided a venue for diverse African American art and expression and was possibly the first national black theater.

1. **C**   **Big Picture**

Use the Bottom Line to choose the answer. Watch out for answer choices that contradict the Bottom Line, that are too narrow (one paragraph only), or that are too broad.

A. No. This answer choice goes beyond the information in the passage. The passage does not suggest that the artists have been rediscovered and it does not suggest that the artists are among the most talented performers of their day as compared to all other performers.

B. No. This answer choice goes beyond the scope of the passage. While the passage suggests that the FTP was important, it does not imply that its affects were the most lasting, nor does the passage compare the FTP to other government programs.

C. Yes. This answer matches the Bottom Line. This answer choice mentions that the FTP was possibly the first black national theater from the first paragraph and that it represented the wide variety of viewpoints outlined in the second paragraph.

D. No. This answer choice is too broad. The first half of the answer matches the passage; however, the passage does not discuss what the FTP is best known for today.

E. No. This answer choice shifts focus away from the Negro Units to the U.S. government. While the government is mentioned, this answer choice does not match the main idea of the passage.

2. **A**   **Extract Fact**

This question asks about specifics things that the FTP did. Since the history of the FTP is discussed in the first paragraph, this is the logical place to begin looking for textual support. Since it is an EXCEPT question, any answer choice that is found in the passage should be eliminated. The credited response will be the single answer choice NOT supported by the passage.

A. Yes. This answer choice directly contradicts line 3, which states that the FTP existed for only four years.

B. No. This is supported by the passage, which states that there were eighteen units in cities throughout the United States in lines 13–14.

C. No. This is explicitly stated by the passage in line 10.

D. No. Designers and technicians are mentioned as being among those employed in line 12.

E. No. Weekly productions are mentioned in line 6.

3. C   **Extract Infer**

This question asks which answer choice is most similar to the content and tone of the passage. Eliminate any answer choices that contradict the Bottom Line. Be wary of answer choices that match tone or content but not both. The credited response will be a statement that could likely have been excerpted from the same article as the passage was.

A. No. The issue of funding is not discussed within the passage at all. This is outside the scope of the passage and thus cannot be inferred.

B. No. The author discusses the differing viewpoints within the FTP of which the Negro Units were a part; however, these views are neither compared nor contrasted with those of the people in the FTP. The Harlem Renaissance is mentioned only as the source of the diversity of views.

C. Yes. In the second paragraph in lines 42–44, the author states that the disagreements among the members of the FTP led to a wide range of production styles and viewpoints presented.

D. No. As seen in the Bottom Line, the focus of this passage is on the FTP. There is no discussion or comparison with today's theater artists.

E. No. While both urban realistic dramas and folk dramas are discussed in paragraph two, their relative popularities are not mentioned.

4. D   **Structure**

This question asks why the author mentions the Harlem Renaissance. The Harlem Renaissance is discussed at the beginning of paragraph two. The passage states that it was a time of creativity and innovation. The next sentence begins with the word "thus" and states that there was already a diverse set of beliefs about the function of art in the African American community at the time of the founding of the FTP. The word "thus" indicates that the Harlem Renaissance was mentioned as evidence for the claim made about the diverse beliefs in the FTP. The credited response will explain why the word was included. Be wary of answers that simply define the phrase in question.

A. No. This may be what the Harlem Renaissance was; however, this is not why the author is mentioning it.

B. No. There is no discussion in that paragraph of the political advancement of the African American community.

C. No. The Harlem Renaissance occurred before the Negro Units.

D. Yes. The word "thus" in line 24 indicates that the different modes of artistic thought in the FTP were grounded in the earlier tradition of the Harlem Renaissance.

E. No. There is no discussion or comparison with mainstream U.S. culture in the paragraph.

5. **B**

This question is asking for the answer choice that provides the best paraphrase of the quoted excerpt. The credited response will be fully supported by that part of the passage. Be careful of answer choices that go beyond what can be supported by the passage.

A. No. In lines 13–14, the passage states that these units were in at least eighteen different cities, which doesn't align with the single performing arts center mentioned in this answer choice.

B. Yes. This answer choice aligns with information in both the first and second paragraphs.

C. No. This answer choice confuses the FTP, which was the federally funded project, with the Negro Units, which were a subset of the FTP. The national black theater is only referring to these units.

D. No. The body of works produced by African American playwrights is not discussed in the passage.

E. No. While there were African American units in many cities, the passage does not support the idea that these were necessarily successful. This answer goes too far beyond the information stated in the passage.

6. **E**

This question asks for an idea or opinion that the producers of *The Swing Mikado* may have had. *The Swing Mikado* was discussed in the latter half of paragraph two. The correct answer will be something that must be true based upon information in the passage. Be wary of answer choices that go beyond the scope or tone of the passage.

A. No. While the passage discusses debates about the purpose of art, there is no indication of how these playwrights felt about controversy.

B. No. While lines 41–42 indicate that some playwrights wanted solely to entertain and others to instruct, there is no indication of how *The Swing Mikado* playwrights felt.

C. No. The passage indicates that *The Swing Mikado* was a white classic in line 48, but it does not indicate whether this play was also a folk drama.

D. No. The passage indicates that *The Swing Mikado* was a white classic in line 48, but it does not indicate whether this play was an urban realistic drama.

E. Yes. The play is called a white classic in line 48, and in lines 32–35 the passage states that some playwrights advocated adapting plays written by white people.

7. **C**

Treat this question like a Strengthen Arguments question. The credited response will either introduce information in direct support of the claim or will rule out alternative claims. Trap answers will include anything that weakens the claim or that is not relevant to the claim.

A. No. The claim is that the Negro Units came closest to creating the first national black theater. If anything, this answer choice would possibly undermine that conclusion.

B. No. The presence or absence of government funding is not relevant to the claim that the Negro Units were possibly the first national black theater.

77

C. Yes. This answer choice limits early incarnations of African American theatrical arts to a small geographic region within the United States. Thus, by definition, there could be no earlier national theaters.

D. No. The size of the audience is not relevant to the claim that the Negro Units were the first national black theater.

E. No. The difficulties historians have had is not relevant to the claim being made.

Questions 8–13

The main point of the first paragraph is to introduce the idea that some economists claim that cost and benefit should be the only criteria used to determine penalties for corporate crime. The main point of the second paragraph is that the law, rather than pursuing subjective judgments of morality, should focus on affecting profit. The main point of the third paragraph is to argue that in order for cost and benefit penalties to be meaningful, detection ratios should also be taken into account. The main idea of the final paragraph is to critique the claims made by the economists and to state that something else must be added to cost and benefit analysis in order to assess fair penalties for corporate crimes. The Bottom Line is to argue that the economic viewpoint of cost and benefit, even when combined with detection ratios, is not sufficient to determine punishments for corporate crimes. The tone of the passage is critical.

8. **E**   **Big Picture**

Use the Bottom Line to choose the answer. Watch out for answer choices that contradict the Bottom Line, that are too narrow (one paragraph only), or that are too broad.

A. No. This is the main point of only the third paragraph.

B. No. This is a good summary of the economists' viewpoint, but it ignores the author's claims from the final paragraph.

C. No. This is outside the scope of the passage. The passage does not discuss the implications of the economists' arguments on communities.

D. No. The focus of the passage is to critique the sole use of cost and benefit, not to claim that the penalties assessed are too low.

E. Yes. This matches both the discussion of the need to look at detection ratios, the associated critiques, and the final claim that some other criteria must also be considered.

9. **D**   **Structure**

This question asks why the author is writing the passage. Focus on the Bottom Line and the tone of the passage. Be wary of answer choices that contradict the Bottom Line or that indicate a tone different from that found in the passage. The credited response will identify the critiques of the outlined methods that the author makes.

A. No. There is no discussion of courts in the passage.

B. No. The passage focuses on how to assess penalties of corporate crimes but does not explore why those crimes are committed.

C. No. The focus of the passage is on the punishments, not on the corporations.

D.   Yes. The passage provides an overview of the economists, provides a critique of their viewpoint, and then calls for an alternative.

E.   No. The author suggests that there must be some other criterion; however, the author does not suggest any specific ideas.

10.   **C**   [RC Reasoning]

This question provides a scenario and then asks what the author would endorse. The credited response will be in line with the author's beliefs. Trap answers will include penalties based upon other viewpoints discussed in the passage.

A.   No. This does not match any of the penalties discussed in the passage.

B.   No. This matches the example given in the first paragraph; however, that is identified as an example for the economists' cost and benefit viewpoint.

C.   Yes. This matches the author's discussion of both the advantages and dangers of using detection ratios to determine fines. Specifically, this answer choice matches the author's discussion in lines 43–47.

D.   No. This answer choice aligns with a pure view of detection ratios, which that author critiques.

E.   No. The author is against this approach as suggested in lines 43–47.

11.   **E**   [Extract Fact]

The credited response will correctly assess a point of view attributed to the economists. Be wary of answer choices that present the author's point of view.

A.   No. Paragraph two briefly mentions the use of morality in assessing fines. However, the economists are specifically against any use of morality as seen in lines 17–19.

B.   No. Paragraph two briefly mentions the use of morality in assessing fines. However, the economists are specifically against any use of morality as seen in lines 17–19.

C.   No. Paragraph two briefly mentions the use of morality in assessing fines. However, the economists are specifically against any use of morality as seen in lines 17–19.

D.   No. Paragraph two briefly mentions the use of morality in assessing fines. However, the economists are specifically against any use of morality as seen in lines 17–19. Therefore, the economists feel more strongly about the use of morality than simply claiming it is irrelevant.

E.   Yes. Paragraph two briefly mentions the use of morality in assessing fines. The economists are specifically against any use of morality as seen in lines 17–19.

12.   **A**   [Structure]

This question asks for the overall organization of the passage. Conceptually, this question asks for an answer choice that correctly outlines the passage. Rely on the Bottom Line and any notes on the overall structure. Be wary of answer choices that are only partly correct, that include the wrong tone, or that go beyond the passage.

A. Yes. A question is raised (lines 1–4), an answer is summarized (lines 4–19), an important aspect is presented (lines 19–39), a flaw in the answer is identified (lines 40–47), and the need for an alternative is affirmed (lines 47–51).

B. No. This answer is mostly correct. However, the author supports the criticism of the approach's flaw rather than rejecting it.

C. No. There is no discussion of the ethics of the economists.

D. No. Only the economists' viewpoints are discussed. There is not a second answer proposed to the question in the opening lines of the passage.

E. No. There is no discussion of the consequences of failing to resolve the question posed at the beginning of the passage.

13. **A** **Extract Infer**

This question focuses on the economists and their point of view. The credited response will align in both content and tone of the economists. The credited response should seem like it was edited out of the same summary of the economists' viewpoints from which this passage was taken.

A. Yes. The economists' point of view focuses solely on a cost and benefit analysis. In lines 34–39, the passage discusses that the economists' viewpoint implies that a just punishment for a $6 million crime would be $60 million. It is the author who raises the objection that this may put corporations out of business.

B. No. In paragraph two, the economists claim that the morality of the crime should not be a factor in determining fines. They do not state anything about assigning moral weight to a crime.

C. No. This answer choice is half right. In paragraph two, economists state that morality is not a factor. However, they make no exceptions to this statement, so this answer choice goes too far.

D. No. There is no discussion in the passage about the likelihood of repeat offences.

E. No. There is no discussion in the passage about the penalty being affected by repeat offenses.

Questions 14–19

The main idea of the first paragraph of passage A is that historical studies of women saw a shift from the focus of histories of individuals to a more abstract study of gender relations and how they shaped political and cultural interactions. The main idea of paragraph two is that the study of gender is broader than the study of women as it has more explanatory power. The main idea of paragraph three is the author speculating about what may be lost due to this shift in analytical approach. The Bottom Line of passage A is that the author evaluates how the shift from studying the history of women to gender studies has led to more explanatory power, though the author maintains doubts about what may be lost.

The main idea of the first paragraph of passage B is that Augustus responded to disorder by passing laws that put women into a particular cultural context. The main idea of the second paragraph is that due to these changes, female gender roles led to significant changes in the political sphere. The main idea of the final paragraph is that these gender roles were used artistically to portray political aspects of the Roman Empire. The Bottom Line of passage B is that Augustus responded to domestic strife by delineating specific roles for women, which led to political shifts in the Empire. The relationship between passage A and B is one of theory in passage A and application in passage B.

14. **B** `Big Picture`

This question asks for a key topic or main idea that both passages have in common. Rely on the Bottom Line for each passage. Trap answers will be choices that focus exclusively on one passage or that are too broad or narrow.

A. No. This answer choice describes passage A only.

B. Yes. Passage A discusses the role of gender in the abstract, while passage B focuses on how female gender roles were used to shape politics in Imperial Rome.

C. No. This answer choice describes passage B only.

D. No. While this phrase is used in one of the passages, it is not central to either passage.

E. No. Passage B explores gender roles rather than women's history as it is defined in passage A.

15. **C** `Extract Infer`

This questions asks which answer choice is supported by the ideas discussed in passage A. Conceptually, the credited response should sound like it was edited out of the same text that passage A was taken from. Be wary of answer choices discussing new topics or focusing on the wrong direction of the relationship between the passages.

A. No. The author of passage A does not discuss historical changes in modern versus ancient gender roles.

B. No. The author of passage A is focused on the changes in the historical study of women. There is no textual support for how the feels about the study of masculinity. This answer is outside the scope of passage A.

C. Yes. The author of passage A discusses the trend away from the study of particular women in line 5 and also worries about what may be lost due to this transition in lines 27–28.

D. No. The author of passage A does not discuss any contrasts of ancient and modern history.

E. No. This answer choices goes too far. While the study of gender roles may have more explanatory power, there is no support that historians were unaware of anything.

16. **A** `Extract Fact`

This question focuses solely on what the key shift is that is discussed in passage A. Trap answers will mention trivial ideas discussed in passage A, ideas discussed solely in passage B, and things not discussed in either passage.

A. Yes. This is a direct paraphrase of lines 7–9.

B. No. This answer choice goes too far. The shift has greater explanatory power according to the author, but there is no support that earlier research ignored women's contributions.

C. No. The focus of passage A is on historical studies of gender roles, not looking at gender biases among the researchers themselves.

D. No. The author does not critique anyone in passage A.

E. No. Shifts in domestic roles are discussed in passage B.

17. **D** ⬤ Big Picture

This question asks for the relationship between the two passages. Even though the answer choices may be abstract, refer to the Bottom Line of each passage. Wrong answer choices will confuse the relationship or introduces tones that do not match those of the Bottom Lines.

A. No. This answer is too strongly worded. Passage A discusses the historical research trends but does not endorse any particular one.

B. No. There is not an explicit relationship between the passages. Passage A does not directly refer to passage B and thus cannot criticize it.

C. No. Passage A discusses the shift in analytical trends, but it does not engage directly in analysis.

D. Yes. Passage A evaluates the shift to studying gender roles in society, and passage B is a case study that focuses on gender roles in Imperial Rome.

E. No. This answer choice is only half correct. While each passage is clearly a different frame of reference, passage A does not put forth an argument so much as evaluate a trend.

18. **B** ⬤ Extract Infer

This question refers to a specific part of passage B and asks how that matches to the ideas expressed in passage A. The cited text in passage B explains how Augustus redefined the role of all women by placing them into a more domestic context. This question can be treated similar to Principle-Match argument questions. The text in passage B is the specific case study. The information from passage A is the "principle" to which the case study conforms. As a result, trap answers will be partial matches or will be things that cannot be applied to the information from passage B.

A. No. Passage A defines the history of women in lines 23–24 as focusing on the study of specific women, but the text in passage B focuses on how the roles of women as a group were redefined by Augustus.

B. Yes. The author of passage A discusses how the focus on gender has the power to explain how male and female roles shape cultural and political contexts (lines 12–16). This matches the discussion of how roles of women were redefined to quell political strife in Rome.

C. No. This is a paraphrase of how the author of passage A defines the history of women. Passage B does not focus on particular individuals.

D. No. The lines from passage B refer to the changing role of women, not of men.

E. No. While the author of passage A briefly discusses this idea, there is nothing implied to be obscured in the cited lines from passage B.

19. **E** ⬤ Extract Infer

This question asks which answer choice is supported by the ideas discussed in passage A. Conceptually, the credited response should sound like it was edited out of the same text that passage A was taken from. Be wary of answer choices discussing new topics or focusing on the wrong direction of the relationship between the passages.

A. No. While this answer choice uses many of the key words from each passage, the author of passage A does not discuss how well integrated the new historical study of gender is with the old version.

B. No. This answer choice is too extreme. While the author of passage A discusses a shift away from the historical study of women, there is no indication that that particular field of study has been completely abandoned.

C. No. The author of passage A discusses how exploring the specific gender roles of women can explain political and cultural interactions. However, this study is not the same as studying the political influence of women.

D. No. This is contrary to the Bottom Line of passage B, which is focused specifically on the significance of gender roles in Ancient Rome.

E. Yes. Passage B specifically focused on how gender roles in Rome were crafted to lead to a political end.

Questions 20–27

The main idea of the first paragraph is that Steele is attempting to revive a defunct theory of evolution called Lamarckism and has claimed to have evidential support for it in the immune system. The main idea of the second paragraph is to show that the immune system is mysterious in evolutionary terms, such as why immune cells mutate so rapidly. The main idea of the third paragraph outlines Steele's hypothesis that DNA mutations via RNA typos can be transferred to reproductive cells via a virus. The main idea of paragraph four is to show that Steele's evidence for his hypothesis lies in the circumstantial presence of signature events of past mutations. The tone of this essay is primarily informative; however, the author clearly has doubts as evidenced by the use of the numerous rhetorical questions. The Bottom Line of this passage is that Steele claims to have found evidence of Lamarckian evolutionary change by suggesting a method for the transference of mutations in the human immune system to reproductive cells.

20. **B**   Big Picture

Use the Bottom Line to choose the answer. Watch out for answer choices that contradict the Bottom Line, that are too narrow (one paragraph only), or that are too broad.

A. No. This answer choice is too strongly worded and goes beyond the scope of the passage. The Lamarckian theory has not yet been proven correct.

B. Yes. This answer choice matches the Bottom Line of the passage.

C. No. This answer choice is too broad and too strongly worded. The passage does not state that Steele and his colleagues have succeeded in proving their claims.

D. No. While it can be inferred from the passage that the author has doubts about Steele's theory, this answer choice has the wrong focus. The Bottom Line of the passage focuses on outlining rather than critiquing Steele's theories.

E. No. This answer choice reuses many of the key words and phrases from the passage. However, Steele's research is still considered doubtful (lines 55–56). As such, there is no discussion that Steele has removed obstacles to the acceptance of Lamarckian theory.

21. **C**   Structure

This question is asking for the reason the author used the term "typo." The correct answer will provide information on why that word was used. Trap answers will be ones that explain the definition of the word instead of its purpose.

A. No. There is no discussion of adaptive characteristics in that paragraph.

B. No. The paragraph implies that the typos are important by saying that they help protect us from disease (lines 21–24).

C. Yes. The typos are a form of mutation that go through many variations in order to test different defenses.

D. No. There is no mention of the typo being overlooked.

E. No. Just because typos may also occur in written texts does not mean that the word was mentioned here specifically as an analog.

22. **D** ⬛ Extract
Infer

This question asks for how the author feels about Steele's theory. Eliminate answers that contradict the Bottom Line. The credited response will have support from the passage that proves it true. Trap answers will go beyond the scope of the passage: they will either be too strong or will be the opposite of how the author feels.

A. No. This is opposite from the passage. The author remains in doubt about the theory.

B. No. This is too strongly worded. The author is not angry about the theory.

C. No. While the author does not have much faith in Steele's hypothesis, the author doubts the theory's validity rather than its newness.

D. Yes. The author indicates doubt through the use of several rhetorical questions such as lines 44–45.

E. No. This answer choice is too strong. The author is not dismayed at Steele's hypothesis.

23. **B** ⬛ Big Picture

Use the Bottom Line to choose the answer. Watch out for answer choices that contradict the Bottom Line, that are too narrow (one paragraph only), or that are too broad.

A. No. The author is focusing exclusively on a modern revival of a historical theory rather than outlining how that theory was developed.

B. Yes. This matches the Bottom Line.

C. No. This answer choice is too narrow. Questions about the immune system are raised in paragraph two, but no answers were provided.

D. No. The author is not focusing on the merits of Lamarckian theory per se. Instead, the author is discussing the merits and plausibility of Steele's attempt to revive the theory.

E. No. The author never discusses the concept of the philosophy of science. This is too broad.

24. **E** ⬛ Structure

This question asks how to relate the topic of paragraph four to the passage as a whole. Be wary of answer choices that merely summarize the final paragraph or that are too broad.

A. No. While the last sentence suggests that there may be alternative explanations, there are no major objections raised in this paragraph. This answer is too broad.

B. No. The author describes the specific evidence that Steele cites but does not dismiss it.

C. No. This paragraph does not explain any proposed revisions to the neo-Lamarckian theory.

D. No. While skeptical scientists mention simpler explanations, the paragraph does not propose any specific lines of research.

E. Yes. This paragraph focuses on explaining the validity and nature of the hypothesis that Steele raises. In line 47, the evidence is described as circumstantial.

25. **B** Extract
            Infer

This Inference question is asking for something with which the author would agree. Use the Bottom Line to eliminate contradictory answer choices. Conceptually, the credited response should sound like it was edited out of the same text from which this passage was excerpted. Trap answers may introduce new concepts not supported by the passage or they may go beyond the scope of the passage.

A. No. This is Steele's claim rather than the author's. The author doubts the validity of Steele's theories and thus would not agree with this answer choice.

B. Yes. In lines 30–33 the passage states that Steele hypothesizes that immune RNA can undergo reverse transcription and then follows by noting that reverse transcription has been viewed in other contexts. This supports the notion that reverse transcription has not yet been observed in immune cells.

C. No. Steele proposes this as the method for transmission of mutations to reproductive cells; however, the author notes in line 39 that this is speculative.

D. No. The answer choice uses many of the key words from the passage. However, there is no discussion in the passage about the plausibility of the transmission of any inherited characteristics. This answer choice goes beyond the scope of the passage.

E. No. The author does not make any claims as to what differentiates speculation from science.

26. **A** RC Reasoning

This question should be approached in the same manner as a Strengthen question in the arguments section. Focus on the claim being made by Steele. The credited response will either introduce new information in support of Steele's claim or will rule out possible alternative explanations. Be wary of answer choices that weaken Steele's claim or that are outside the scope of his argument.

A. Yes. The author states in lines 39–43 that a virus could cause reproductive DNA to be altered but that this notion is speculative. Choice (A) provides experimental support for Steele's notion.

B. No. This answer choice would suggest that the signatures that Steele attributes to DNA mutations in lines 48–51 were not confined to immune cell DNA. If anything, this would weaken Steele's claim that those signatures support his point of view.

C. No. This has already been stated as true in lines 27–29.

D. No. Evidence of gradual change in giraffe fossils is not relevant to Steele's claim that a virus can transmit the reverse transcription mutations found in immune cells to reproductive cells.

E.   No. If the chicks receive the mutation while gestating, this would by definition be through a method other than through the parent bird's reproductive cells. As a result, this answer choice has no bearing on Steele's claim.

27.   **E**   RC Reasoning

Treat this question similar to the way you would treat a Parallel question. The question asks for the answer that is most similar to the style of evidence discussed in the final paragraph. According to the final paragraph, the evidence is circumstantial (line 47), bears a recognizable signature (line 49), and is concentrated within the particular areas under study (line 52). Thus, the evidence for copyist errors introduced at a later time should have these same features.

A.   No. This would be direct, rather than circumstantial, evidence.

B.   No. This would be direct, rather than circumstantial, evidence.

C.   No. While this is indirect hearsay evidence, this is not concentrated within the text itself. Instead, it is external.

D.   No. This evidence is external and not concentrated in the text itself.

E.   Yes. The altered vocabulary is concentrated in the text itself, has a recognizable historical pattern, and is circumstantial.

Section 2: Arguments 1

1.   **C**   Strengthen

The environmentalists take the position that the electric utility should build a waste-to-energy plant (which would double as a trash incinerator) instead of a natural gas-fired plant even though the waste-to-energy plant would produce three times as much air pollution as the natural gas-fired plant. The passage states that this position is surprising because we can reasonably assume that those who describe themselves as environmentalists would want to reduce air pollution. The credited response will provide support for the waste-to-energy plant, likely by pointing out some advantage that it has over the natural gas-fired plant.

A.   No. This comparison is irrelevant to the decision to be made between a modern natural gas-fired plant and a waste-to-energy plant.

B.   No. The energy requirements and trash production of the area are irrelevant to the levels of air pollution caused by the plants, so this answer choice provides no support for the environmentalists' position.

C.   Yes. Building the waste-to-energy plant would mean that the existing trash incinerator no longer be used, whereas building the natural gas-fired plant would mean that the existing trash incinerator remain in use. This answer choice indicates that the waste-to-energy plant alone could produce less air pollution than the combination of the natural gas-fired plant and the trash incinerator.

D.   No. This answer choice makes the environmentalists' position even more surprising if air pollution is their greatest concern, but it does not explain why they support the waste-to-energy plant.

E.   No. The source of other air pollution is irrelevant.

2. **D** Strengthen

The anthropologist concludes that the advent of cooking likely made possible getting more calories from less food (a requirement for the small human gut to support the large human brain). His conclusion is based on a correlation between brain development and fire use and on the observation that modern humans who eat only raw food have difficulty meeting their caloric needs. He assumes that cooking food allowed more calories to be stored, which in turn caused the brain to develop; he fails to consider other causes or relevant considerations. The credited response will provide new evidence that supports the conclusion or will confirm the validity of an assumption.

A. No. This answer choice does not explain how cooking allows humans to store more calories.

B. No. That different foods have different calorie counts is irrelevant.

C. No. This answer choice would weaken the argument.

D. Yes. This answer choice points out a difference between cooked and raw food that explains how cooking allows humans to store more calories.

E. No. This comparison is irrelevant.

3. **E** Necessary Assumption

The argument concludes that inbreeding is the underlying condition that has led to the adverse condition (viral or bacterial infections, pesticide poisonings, or mite infestations) that has led to the sharp decline in commercial honeybee populations. This conclusion is based on the fact that decades of breeding practices meant to maximize honeybees' pollinating efficiency have limited their genetic diversity. The argument assumes that limited genetic diversity makes honeybees more susceptible to the adverse conditions listed above. The credited response will link the ideas of limited genetic diversity and adverse conditions.

A. No. This comparison with wild honeybees is irrelevant.

B. No. The argument does not require that the results of inbreeding be reversible.

C. No. The argument is not forward-looking, so it does not require that genetic diversity continue to decline.

D. No. This answer choice indicates a correlation between certain adverse events and genetically diverse honeybees, but it does not link them causally, nor does it indicate that the diversity is limited.

E. Yes. This answer choice confirms that a lack of genetic diversity can make honeybees more susceptible to adverse conditions.

4. **A** Weaken

The argument concludes that warmer winters probably caused the increase in the northern cardinal's population in Nova Scotia. This conclusion is based on a correlation between warmer winters and an increase in the bird's population. The argument assumes that correlation proves causation; it fails to consider other causes or relevant considerations. The credited response will introduce new evidence that undermines the conclusion or will point out a relevant consideration that the argument missed.

A. Yes. The rise in bird feeders is another plausible cause of the rise in the northern cardinal's population.

B.   No. Presumably the birds have always been red and were as easy to spot in 1980 as they were in 2000.

C.   No. This answer choice confirms that the correlation holds for other songbirds, but it does not explain why they became more common.

D.   No. This comparison with migratory birds is irrelevant.

E.   No. This answer choice does not explain why the northern cardinal became more common.

5.   **A**   **Parallel**

The argument concludes that one's personality does not change over time. This conclusion is based on the facts that one's personality is linked to one's genes and that one's genes do not generally change over time. Structurally, the argument indicates that two factors are linked and that because one cannot change, the other cannot change either. The credited response will match this structure.

A.   Yes. Two factors are linked (what happened in the First World War and how historians understand that war), and because one cannot change (what happened in the war), neither can the other (historians' understanding).

B.   No. The conclusion does not state that something will not change.

C.   No. The conclusion does not state that something will not change.

D.   No. The conclusion does not state that something will not change.

E.   No. The conclusion does not state that something will not change.

6.   **D**   **Necessary Assumption**

The political analyst concludes that most people in this country will not support Brooks. He provides background information: years ago, McFarlane had Brooks arrested on charges of corruption, but McFarlane later pardoned Brooks, who then agreed to join McFarlane's government. The political analyst's conclusion is based on the facts that almost all of McFarlane's supporters believe that Brooks is guilty of corruption and that almost all of McFarlane's opponents will oppose anyone who agrees to join McFarlane's government. The argument assumes that people who believe Brooks is guilty will tend not to support him and that most people in the country are either supporters or opponents of McFarlane. The credited response will establish one of these assumptions.

A.   No. The argument does not introduce the idea of legitimacy.

B.   No. The argument does not require a relatively lower rate of corruption.

C.   No. The political positions of Brooks and McFarlane are irrelevant.

D.   Yes. If a large number of people were neutral on McFarlane, it would be possible for Brooks to have majority support in the country even if none of McFarlane's supporters or opponents supported Brooks, so the argument requires that most people in the country take a firm stance on McFarlane.

E.   No. Whether the charges were founded is irrelevant.

7. E   Strengthen

The argument concludes that pieces sold as amber are more likely to be fake if they contain normal-appearing insects than if they do not. This conclusion is based on the facts that amber is more valuable when it contains fossilized life forms and that forgers making fake amber often embed small, normal-appearing insects in it to increase its value. The argument assumes that normal-appearing insects are less likely to show up in real amber than in fake amber. The credited response will establish this likelihood.

A. No. This answer choice does not explain the connection between fake amber and normal-appearing insects.

B. No. This answer choice does not explain the connection between fake amber and normal-appearing insects.

C. No. This answer choice explains why forgers would prefer to embed insects into fake amber, but it does not explain the connection between fake amber and normal-appearing insects.

D. No. This answer choice does not explain the connection between fake amber and normal-appearing insects.

E. Yes. This answer choice explains why normal-appearing insects are more likely to indicate fake amber: genuinely fossilized insects tend to be fossilized in awkward or grotesque positions.

8. A   Principle Strengthen

The argument concludes that we should educate people about the ethical use of the Internet. This conclusion is based on the fact that widespread use of the Internet has led to an increase in certain crimes such as information theft and hacking. This fact is explained as a result of the impersonal nature of the Internet: people feel less morally constrained and thus freer to harm others when online. The argument assumes that education about the ethical use of the Internet will increase one's moral conscientiousness in using the Internet. The credited response will state a general rule or principle that establishes that ethical education will increase moral responsibility.

A. Yes. This answer choice establishes that ethical education about the use of a tool increases one's sense of moral responsibility in its use.

B. No. The conclusion is not about formulating new ethical guidelines but about providing ethical education.

C. No. This answer choice would provide a reason we should not educate people about the ethical use of the Internet.

D. No. This answer choice does not indicate whether we should educate people on the ethical use of the Internet.

E. No. This answer choice does not indicate whether we should educate people on the ethical use of the Internet.

9. B   Sufficient Assumption

The columnist concludes that video games are not works of art. He defines works of art as works that must produce an aesthetic experience that is controlled by the artist(s) who created the work. He states that video games are interactive. The argument contains a language shift that assumes that interactive works cannot also produce an aesthetic experience that is controlled by the artist(s) who created the work. The credited response will explicitly link these ideas and force the conclusion to be true.

A. No. The intention of video game creators is irrelevant.

B. Yes. Added to the premise that video games are interactive, this statement proves that video games cannot produce an aesthetic experience controlled by the artist(s) who created the work and therefore proves the conclusion that video games are not works of art.

C. No. The passage concedes that some video games could produce a rich aesthetic experience, so this answer choice does not help the conclusion.

D. No. The identity of the creators is irrelevant.

E. No. This answer choice does not confirm that video games are not works of art.

10. **C** **Evaluate**

The argument concludes that some residents must have switched to phosphate-free detergents. This conclusion is based on the correlation between the municipal ban on phosphate-containing detergents and the decrease in the level of phosphate pollution from the municipal wastewater treatment plant. The argument assumes that the ban caused the decrease in pollution; it fails to consider other causes or relevant considerations. The credited response will present a question related to this assumption.

A. No. Why some residents continued using phosphate-containing detergents is irrelevant.

B. No. The potential pollutants in phosphate-free detergents are irrelevant.

C. Yes. This answer choice asks a question that will help establish whether any other causes could account for the decline in phosphate pollution.

D. No. Whether the majority of phosphate pollution comes from the municipal treatment plant is irrelevant; it is enough that some such pollution comes from the plant.

E. No. The officials' actions are irrelevant.

11. **B** **Main Point**

The argument concludes that it would be unwise for farmers to grow genetically engineered crops. This conclusion is based on the fact that consumer confidence in such plants could be easily undermined and thus put farmers at great financial risk. The argument concedes that such crops fetch a high price, but it claims that this high price is not enough of a benefit to outweigh the risks. The credited response will indicate that farmers should be wary of growing genetically engineered crops.

A. No. This answer choice indicates an intermediate conclusion.

B. Yes.

C. No. This answer choice indicates a premise.

D. No. This answer choice indicates a premise.

E. No. This answer choice indicates a background fact.

12. **B**   **Principle Match**

The passage describes a situation: by vaccinating, doctors expose patients to a weakened form of a disease-causing pathogen so that patients can better resist that weakened form of the pathogen and become less likely to later develop a severe form of the disease. The general rule or principle is that one should experience a less-intense harm early in life so that one can develop resistance to a more-intense form of that harm later in life. The credited response will describe another situation that invokes this general rule or principle.

A. No. This answer choice indicates that actors should avoid something completely, not that they should be exposed to a less-intense form of the activity.

B. Yes. Reading fairy tales exposes children to imagined scenarios of treachery and cruelty, preparing them to face the real thing later in life.

C. No. This answer choice indicates that one should match weapons with a threat, not that one should be exposed to a less-intense harm.

D. No. This answer choice is close, but in closing down some operations, the company is preparing for a different activity (future profitability), instead of preparing for a more intense form of company closures.

E. No. This answer choice does not indicate that one should be exposed to a less-intense harm.

13. **B**   **Main Point**

The fill-in-the-blank space is preceded by the logical indicator "it follows that," signaling that the credited response will be the main point of the argument. So far, the argument states that sympathy and justice depend largely on understanding the needs and problems of others and that nations that have little interaction with one another have little knowledge of one another's needs and problems. The implication is that unless such nations interact more, they will tend to find it difficult to extend sympathy and justice to one another because they lack mutual understanding. The credited response will indicate nations that do not interact will tend to find it difficult to extend sympathy and justice to one another.

A. No. Having knowledge of one another's needs and problems is necessary but not sufficient to treating one another with sympathy and justice.

B. Yes. This answer choice completes the conclusion that nations will struggle to treat one another with sympathy and justice if they do not interact.

C. No. The argument does not try to indicate the source of most problems between nations.

D. No. The argument provides a way to at least lessen conflict between nations: interaction.

E. No. The argument states that nations that do not interact have little (but not no) knowledge of one another's needs and problems, so interaction is not required for mutual knowledge.

14. **A**   **Flaw**

The activist concludes that the only effective way to reduce the incidence of cancers and birth defects is to shut down industries known to produce pollutants that are linked to cancers and birth defects. His conclusion is based on the fact that cancer and birth defects have been linked to pollutants in water:

such pollutants are ingested by fish and move up the food chain to humans, where they accumulate in tissue. The activist assumes that only industrial pollutants cause cancers and birth defects; he fails to consider other causes. The credited response will identify this flaw.

A. Yes. This answer choice describes the flaw of assuming that only industrial pollutants cause cancers and birth defects.

B. No. The argument does not exclude this possibility.

C. No. The argument considers only one cause.

D. No. The flaw is failing to consider other possible causes of cancers and birth defects.

E. No. Having beneficial effects would not negate the negative effects, so the activist does not exclude this possibility.

15. **C** Sufficient Assumption

The political leader concludes that his side will benefit from showing a desire to compromise with the opposition. As support, he outlines the consequences of the opposition's reactions to this desire to compromise: if the opposition responds positively, a compromise will be reached. If the opposition does not respond positively, the opposition will be held responsible for the failure to reach a compromise, and the political leader's side will benefit. The argument assumes that the political leader's side will benefit if a compromise is reached. The credited response will explicitly link the premise to the conclusion and force the conclusion to be true.

A. No. The argument already functions in a world where the political leader's side is willing to compromise, so this answer choice reinforces a premise.

B. No. The argument allows for the opposition to not respond positively, so this answer choice does not fix the hole in the argument.

C. Yes. This answer choice confirms that the political leader's side will benefit if a compromise is reached.

D. No. Whether the opposition would benefit is irrelevant.

E. No. The argument allows for the opposition to not respond positively, so this answer choice does not fix the hole in the argument.

16. **B** Principle Strengthen

The argument concludes that there is harm in promoting the use of a folk remedy that has no effect. This conclusion is based on the fact that some people who are convinced to use an ineffective remedy continue to use it instead of trying conventional treatments that would almost certainly be effective. The argument assumes that promoting the use of an ineffective remedy is harmful if it interferes with one's ability to pursue a beneficial treatment. The credited response will state a general rule or principle that establishes that doing something is harmful if it interferes with one's pursuing a more beneficial option.

A. No. This answer choice does not indicate whether promoting the remedy is itself harmful.

B. Yes. This answer choice establishes that doing something is harmful if it interferes with one's pursuing a more beneficial option.

C. No. This answer choice discusses dishonesty, which is not the same as saying that something is harmful.

D. No. This answer choice discusses responsibility for harm, which is not the same thing as saying that something is harmful.

E. No. This answer choice does not discuss whether the action is harmful.

17. **B**   Reasoning

The argument concludes that the radio station's claim that its new format is popular (a claim based on the opinions of certain call-in listeners) is not persuasive. This conclusion is supported by an analogy: relying on the opinions of call-in listeners in assessing the station's popularity would be like relying on the opinions of those who already know they will vote for a particular candidate in assessing that candidate's popularity. The credited response will describe how the argument proceeds.

A. No. The people being surveyed are biased, not the party conducting the survey.

B. Yes. This answer choice correctly describes the function of the analogy in the argument.

C. No. The argument does not offer an alternative interpretation of the call-in listeners' responses.

D. No. The argument offers an analogy, not a counterexample.

E. No. The argument does not indicate any contradictions or inconsistencies.

18. **D**   Flaw

The historian concludes that those who claim that Shakespeare did not write the plays attributed to him are motivated by snobbery only. His conclusion is based on the facts that Shakespeare was the son of a glove maker, that all other writers proposed as the true author were aristocrats, and that many who make the claim are themselves descendants of aristocrats. The historian assumes that someone can have only one motivation for making a claim; he fails to consider that those making the claim might be motivated by compelling evidence even if they are also motivated by snobbery. The credited response will identify this flaw.

A. No. The conclusion is not about whether the claim is in fact true but about the motivations of those who make the claim.

B. No. The term "anyone" is too strong: the argument requires only that those making this particular claim about Shakespeare's authorship cannot have more than one motivation.

C. No. The motives of this group are irrelevant.

D. Yes. This answer choice describes the flaw that the historian fails to consider that someone might have more than one motivation for making a claim.

E. No. The argument is not circular.

19. **B**   Resolve/ Explain

The passage describes a study that compares lemurs that live in a rain forest, where the tree cover is consistent year-round, with lemurs that live in a deciduous forest, where the tree cover is thinner in winter. Both groups of lemurs are more nocturnal during the winter. The passage then introduces a puzzling difference: the deciduous forest lemurs are markedly more nocturnal during the winter than the rain forest lemurs are. The credited response will explain why the deciduous forest lemurs were significantly more nocturnal during the winter than the rain forest lemurs were, likely by pointing out some difference related to the amount of tree cover in the winter.

A. No. This answer choice does not provide a relevant nocturnal difference.

B. Yes. Both lemur populations are vulnerable during daylight hours, when their predators are on the hunt, but the deciduous forest lemurs are particularly vulnerable during winter because their habitat lacks tree cover during the day. This increased vulnerability explains why the deciduous forest lemurs are more active at night during the winter.

C. No. This answer choice does not provide a relevant nocturnal difference.

D. No. The relative population size is irrelevant.

E. No. It is unclear how this answer choice relates to daytime versus nocturnal activity.

20. **B** Reasoning

The critic concludes that the common distinction between "literary" and "genre" fiction—that the former should be interpreted while the latter should be merely enjoyed—is flawed. His main conclusion is based on an intermediate conclusion that no work should be interpreted. This intermediate conclusion is based on the idea that when we interpret a work, we cut ourselves off from the work's emotional impact. The final statement in the passage functions as support for the intermediate conclusion, which then functions as support for the main conclusion. The credited response will describe the function of this statement.

A. No. The statement functions as support for the conclusion, not as the conclusion itself.

B. Yes. This answer choice accurately describes the function of the statement as support for the conclusion.

C. No. The statement functions as support for the conclusion, not as an implication of the conclusion.

D. No. The statement functions as support for the conclusion, not as an explanation of the distinction between "literary" and "genre" fiction.

E. No. The statement functions as support for the conclusion, not as part of a potential counterargument against that conclusion.

21. **A** Principle Match

The passage presents a principle and its application, and the question stem suggests that the application is unsupported. The principle can be diagrammed as a conditional: if one does not criticize a form of behavior in oneself and one does not vow to stop the behavior, then one should not criticize that form of behavior in another. The application of the principle indicates that if Shimada does not vow to stop being tardy, then he should not criticize McFeney for tardiness. To properly make this conclusion, we need to know that Shimada does not criticize his own tardiness. The credited response will establish that Shimada does not criticize his own behavior.

A. Yes. This answer choice establishes that Shimada does not criticize his own tardiness.

B. No. This answer choice does not establish whether Shimada criticizes his own tardiness.

C. No. This answer choice does not establish whether Shimada criticizes his own tardiness.

D. No. This answer choice establishes that Shimada does in fact criticize his own tardiness, but we do not have a principle covering what is then acceptable in that situation.

E. No. This answer choice does not establish whether Shimada criticizes his own tardiness.

22. **A**   Flaw

The argument concludes that everyone should have access to more than one newspaper. This conclusion is based on an intermediate conclusion that a single newspaper would not adequately cover some important stories. This intermediate conclusion is based on the facts that there are at least two sides to each story, that all sides of an important study should be covered, and that no single newspaper covers all sides of every story. The argument assumes that if a newspaper cannot adequately cover every story, then it cannot adequately cover a particular subset of stories: important stories. The credited response will identify this flaw.

A. Yes. This answer choice describes the flaw of assuming that a newspaper cannot cover all important stories if it cannot cover all stories in general.

B. No. The argument does not imply that choosing any two newspapers will solve the problem; presumably, one would have to ensure that the combination of newspapers chosen provides one with all sides to the story.

C. No. The conclusion is about what readers should have access to, not about what newspapers should do.

D. No. The terms "everyone" and "all" are too strong: the argument indicates what "should" be the case rather than the current reality.

E. No. The argument is concerned primarily (not "only") with important stories, but defining a particular scope for an argument is not a flaw.

23. **D**   Inference

The passage presents two facts about Moradco mines: most Moradco mines in Velyena have never violated environmental regulations, and all Moradco gold mines have violated environmental regulations at least once. The credited response will be an answer choice that is supported by a single statement or by a combination of statements from the passage.

A. No. The passage does not discuss any other companies, so we cannot make a definitive statement about the relative number of mines operated by other companies.

B. No. This answer choice could be true, but we cannot prove it based on the passage because raw numbers of mines are not discussed.

C. No. This answer choice could be true as long as non-gold mines in Velyena outnumber gold mines in Velyena, but we cannot prove it based on the passage.

D. Yes. All Moradco gold mines have violated environmental regulations, so if most Moradco mines in Velyena were gold mines, it would not be possible for most such mines to have never violated environmental regulations. Therefore, most Moradco mines in Velyena must not be gold mines.

E. No. This answer choice could be true, but we cannot prove it because we do not have enough information about the worldwide prevalence of gold mines.

24. **A**

The argument concludes that politicians would be more likely to be re-elected if they voted against certain tariffs. These tariffs tend to protect the small number of people who work in industries that make the products while hurting those who do not through higher costs. The conclusion is based on polls that show that most people oppose the tariffs. The argument assumes that the polls are accurate, that people who oppose the tariffs are less likely to vote for politicians who support those tariffs, that such people actually vote in sufficient numbers to affect a politician's chances of re-election, and that people who support the tariffs are not more likely to vote or to base their vote on a politician's stance on tariffs. The credited response will establish one of these assumptions.

A. Yes. This answer choice establishes that tariff supporters are not more likely than tariff opponents are to base their vote on a politician's stance on tariffs.

B. No. The term "always" is too strong: the argument does not require politicians to act a certain way in every situation, just in this particular situation. Moreover, the conclusion is about what politicians should do, not about what is in fact the case.

C. No. The term "only" is too strong, and this answer choice does not confirm the connection between supporting such tariffs and a politician's chances of re-election.

D. No. The term "never" is too strong, and this answer choice does not discuss re-election.

E. No. This answer choice does not connect a stance on tariffs to a politician's chances of re-election.

25. **D**

The passage presents a general rule about small- to medium-sized marine mammals, such as seals and dolphins, and two comparative cases. The general rule is that the longer an animal can stay submerged during a dive, the deeper the animal can dive. Dolphins can dive deeper than northern fur seals can (which means that dolphins can stay submerged longer than northern fur seals can), and elephant seals can stay submerged longer than Weddell seals can (which means that elephant seals can dive deeper than Weddell seals can). These two cases do not overlap, so we cannot, for example, definitively state whether dolphins can dive deeper or stay submerged longer than elephant seals. The credited response will be an answer choice that violates the general rule or its specific examples.

A. No. Dolphins could fit in between elephant seals and Weddell seals in terms of diving and submerging ability.

B. No. Weddell seals could fit in between dolphins and northern fur seals in terms of diving and submerging ability.

C. No. If Weddell seals dive deeper than dolphins dive, then it must also be true that they stay submerged longer than northern fur seals because the passage indicates that dolphins dive deeper and stay submerged longer than northern fur seals do.

D. Yes. If northern fur seals stay submerged longer than elephant seals, then they must also stay submerged longer than Weddell seals. Since dolphins stay submerged longer than northern fur seals, it would not be possible for dolphins to be worse than Weddell seals in terms of diving and submerging ability.

E. No. Northern fur seals could fit in between elephant seals and Weddell seals in terms of diving and submerging ability.

Section 3: Games

Questions 1–5

This is a 1D ordering game: exactly six players will be appear in one of six time slots. The inventory consists of six players—R, S, T, W, Y, Z—with S as an unrestricted player.

Rule 1 is an ordering clue with R appearing before Z, which will provide an ordering deduction. R cannot be last, and Z cannot be first.

Rule 2 is a block clue and provides another ordering deduction. W cannot be last, and Y cannot be first.

Rule 3 shows that T can only appear in slots 2, 3, or 4.

Rule 4 shows that Z can only appear in slots 9, 10, or 11.

By combining Rules 1 and 4, you know that Z cannot be first and must appear in the morning so you can deduce that R must be in slot 9 or 10 and Z must be in slot 10 or 11.

Your diagram should look like this:

R, S, T, W, Y, Z

Clue 1: R – Z
Clue 2: [WY]
Clue 3: T = 2/3/4
Clue 4: Z = 9/10/11

1. **A** Grab-a-Rule

   A. Yes. This choice does not violate any rules.

   B. No. This violates rule 4 because Z is not in the morning.

   C. No. This violates rule 3 because T is not in the afternoon.

   D. No. This violates rule 2 because Y is not immediately after W.

   E. No. This violates rule 1 because R is not earlier than Z.

2. **B** Specific

   Make a new line in your diagram and add the new information. If W is in the morning, then according to your deductions, W must be at 11, which means that Y must be at 12.

   The question asks for what could be true. The only choice that could be true is (B).

3. **D** General

Use prior work and your deductions to determine which time slot S CANNOT be in.

A. No. From the deductions you determined that either S or R must be in the 9:00 A.M. timeslot. This could be true.

B. No. If S is at 10, then R will be at 9 and Z will be at 11. T, W, and Y will be in the afternoon timeslots. This could be true.

C. No. If S is at 11, then R will be at 9 and Z will be at 10. T, W, and Y will be in the afternoon timeslots. This could be true.

D. Yes. If S is at 2, then R and Z take up two of the morning slots, leaving one morning slot open, and T and S take up two afternoon slots, one of which is the first afternoon slot (2:00 P.M.). So, there is one morning time slot and one afternoon timeslot available, but they aren't consecutive so there is no place to put WY.

E. No. If S is at 3, then R, S, W, and Y can take up the first four slots and T can be at 4. This could be true.

4. **C** General

Use prior work and your deductions to determine the earliest time that W could be scheduled. According to the deductions, the earliest W could be scheduled is 11:00 A.M., making (C) the credited response.

5. **C** General

Use prior work and your deductions to determine which performers MUST be scheduled in the afternoon.

A. No. While T must be scheduled in the afternoon, based on the deductions Y must also be scheduled in the afternoon.

B. No. While T must be scheduled in the afternoon, according to the deductions W can be scheduled for 11:00 A.M.

C. Yes. According to clue 3, T must be scheduled in the afternoon. Based on the deductions, since the earliest W can be scheduled is 11:00 A.M., then since Y must be immediately after W that forces Y into the afternoon no matter what.

D. No. While T must be scheduled in the afternoon, according to the deductions, W can be scheduled for 11:00 A.M.

E. No. While T and Y must be scheduled in the afternoon, S can be scheduled in the morning.

Questions 6–12

This is a 1 D ordering game with an out column. The inventory consists of 8 players—L, M, N, O, P, R, S, V—6 of which will be organized into a sequence with two other players in the out column.

Rule 1 is a conditional statement that provides a M/L placeholder deduction in the out column since at least one of the two players must be out.

Since most of the rules are conditional or provide information about what cannot happen, there aren't many useful deductions you can make before moving to the questions.

Your diagram should look like this:

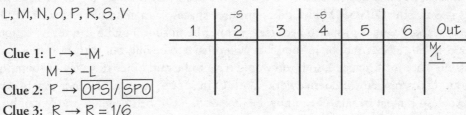

L, M, N, O, P, R, S, V

Clue 1: L → –M
         M → –L
Clue 2: P → OPS / SPO
Clue 3: R → R = 1/6
Clue 4: S ≠ 2/4
Clue 5: N → N = 5

6. **E** Grab-a-Rule

A. No. This violates the first rule because both L and M are selected.

B. No. This violates the fifth rule because N is not in spot 5.

C. No. This violates the third rule because R is not in spot 1 or spot 6.

D. No. This violates the second rule because P is not between O and S.

E. Yes. This does not violate any rules.

7. **D** Specific

Make a new line in your diagram and add the new information. Put N in spot 5. You also need to add P. According to clue 2, P must be between O and S, so look for a place you can fit those three in a row. With N in 5, they must fit in the first four spaces. Since P cannot be third (deduction), that means that P must be in spot 2. That means that either O or S must be in spot 1, making (D) the credited response.

8. **C** Specific

Make a new line in your diagram and add the new information. Put L in spot 6 and O in spot 2. Since you are looking for what must be true, fill in everything you know for sure before you go to the answers. If L is in, then M is out (clue 1). Since O is in spot 2, the only way to have P is to put P in spot 3 and S in spot 4. Neither of those can happen (deductions and clue 4), so P must be out. Now that M and P are out, everything else is in. So, R must be in spot 1 (clue 3), N must be in spot 5 (clue 5), S must be in spot 3 since it cannot be in spot 4 (clue 4), and V must be in spot 4 since it's the only one left. This makes (C) the credited response.

9. **A** Specific

Make a new line in your diagram and add the new information. Put P in spot 4. This means that O/S must be in spot 3 and S/O must be in spot 5 (clue 2). Since N cannot be in spot 5 (clue 5), then it must be out. So, R, V, and one of either L or M must be selected since the other of L or M must be out with N. R is restricted to either spot 1 or spot 6 (clue 3), so that leaves L, M, or V that could go in spot 2. This makes (A) the credited response.

10. B **Specific**

Make a new line in your diagram and add the new information. Put L in spot 1 and O in spot 4. Since L is in, M must be out (clue 1). Look for the bowl that must be out other than M (it isn't in the answers). Since the OPS/SPO block takes up three spaces, it's a good place to start. If O is in 4, then P must be in spot 5 and S in spot 6 because P cannot be in spot 3 and S cannot be in spot 2 (deduction and clue 4). Since N cannot be in spot 5, it would have to be out, but with L in spot 1 and S in spot 6, there is no place for R (clue 3), so it too would have to be out. Since there is not room for M, N, and R to be out, this arrangement doesn't work. With O in spot 4, there is no other way to arrange the OPS/SPO block so P must be out. N can now be in spot 5, S can be in spot 3, and V can be in spot 2. This means (B) is the credited response.

11. B **General**

Use prior work and your deductions to determine which answer is a bowl that must be selected. According to the deductions, if either O or S is out, then P must also be out. Since this would mean three pots were out, this cannot happen. So, both O and S must be in. Only O is in the answers, making (B) the credited response.

12. A **Specific**

Make a new line in your diagram and add the new information. If N is selected, it must be in spot 5 (clue 5). If P is in, then S and O are as well. As in question 7, with N in 5, the OPS/SPO block must fit in the first four spaces. Since P cannot be third (deduction), that means that P must be in spot 2, leading to either O or S in spot 1 and in spot 3. Since spot 1 is taken by either O or S, that means R must be in spot 6 (clue 3). Since N is in spot 5 and R is in spot 6, that makes (A) the credited response.

Questions 13–17

This is a 1D twisted game that has elements of grouping and ordering. The inventory consists of 4 employees—J, L, P, T—that must be assigned to four offices—W, X, Y, Z—based on preferences. The rules in this game state that there can be only one employee per office and that the assignment will be based on an employee receiving their most preferred choice that remains when it is that employee's turn.

Your diagram should look like this:

J, L, P, T

W | X | Y | Z

Clue 1: no doubles
Clue 2: only one office
per employee
Clue 3: highest remaining

13. B **General**

Use your deductions and prior work to determine which answer could be the right match of employees to offices. This is NOT a Grab-a-Rule question. The trick is that the answers are not in the order the employees selected the offices. You have to figure that part out yourself. Thank goodness for deductions! For each answer, you know that X or Y must be selected first, and W must be selected last.

A.   No. Note that Y is L's fourth choice and X is P's third choice. Since X or Y must be selected as a first choice, this does not work.

B.   Yes. Z is J's third choice, X is L's first choice, P is last with W, and Y is T's second choice. Since there is only one first choice, then L selects X first, T selects Y second, J selects Z third, and P is last with W.

C.   No. Note that every selection is each person's second or third choice. Since X or Y must be selected as a first choice, this does not work.

D.   No. Y is J's first choice, but all the other selections are each person's third choice. The second selection must be someone's first or second choice, so this does not work.

E.   No. This may be deceiving since there is a first, second, third, and fourth choice. Follow the possible order. J would have to select Y first, but in order for L to select Z (third choice) someone else must select X first and X is P's third choice.

14.   **C**   General

Use your deductions and prior work to determine which answer must be true.

A.   No. Since both X and Y are ranked first, it is possible that one person selects X (or Y) as a first choice. The next person then selects Y (or X), which means that there can be more than one first choice selected.

B.   No. In the deductions, you determined that both the second and third choices could be ranked second.

C.   Yes. Seems almost too easy, but yes, the first person to choose must select their first-ranked office.

D.   No. In the deductions, you determined that both the first and second selections could be ranked first, and the third selection could be ranked third. For example, P selects Y(1) first, T selects X(1) second, J selects Z(3) third, and L ends up with W(3) last. No one gets the office he ranked second.

E.   No. In the deductions, you determined that both the first and second selections could be ranked first, and the third selection could be ranked second. For example, T selects X(1) first, J selects Y(1) second, L selects Z(2) third, and P is last with W(4).

15.   **A**   General

Use your deductions and prior work to determine which answer could be true.

A.   Yes. This happens in question 14, (D). In the deductions, you determined that both the first and second selections could be ranked first, and the third and fourth selections could be ranked third. For example, P selects Y(1) first, T selects X(1) second, J selects Z(3) third, and L ends up with W(3) last.

B.   No. Since the same office cannot be chosen by more than one person, then that would mean that L must choose Y last since everyone else ranks W fourth. But you determined in the deductions that Y cannot be chosen last, so this does not work.

C. No. From the deductions, you know that the first person must choose his first-ranked choice, and that W, which is ranked third or fourth, must be chosen last. This leaves room for only two people to select the offices they ranked second.

D. No. From the deductions, you know that the first person must choose his first-ranked choice, and that the second person must choose either his first- or second-ranked office. This leaves room for only the last two people to choose the offices they ranked third.

E. No. This could never happen since each person must choose the highest-ranked office from the offices that are left.

16. **E** **Specific**

IF P selects W, then P selects fourth. That means that X, Y, and Z are all selected before P gets a turn. You can therefore disregard P and W when determining if each answer could be true.

J: Y, X, Z, (W)
L: X, Z, (W), Y
T: X, Y, Z, (W)

A. No. If the person who goes first selects X(1), then either J selects Y(1), which means two people selected their first choice, or one of Y(2) or Z(2) is selected and J selects Z(3). In either case, there can't be two people who select their second choices.

B. No. From the deductions, you know that the first selection must be ranked first, and the second selection must be ranked first or second. The only way two people could select the office each ranks third is if L selects W. Since P selects W in this question, this does not work.

C. No. Since X and Y are the only offices ranked first, there could never be more than two people who select their first-ranked office.

D. No. The only way J could select X(2) is if P selects Y(1) first.

E. Yes. If both J and T select offices before L, then L will select Z. This works.

17. **E** **General**

Use your deductions and prior work to determine which answer must be true.

A. No. In question 16, (D) describes a scenario in which J could select X. If P goes first and selects Y(1), then if J goes second, he will have to select X(2).

B. No. From the deductions, you know that anyone who chooses last selects W.

C. No. If T goes first and selects X(1), then if L goes second, he will have to select Z(2).

D. No. As described in (C), T can select X if he goes first.

E. Yes. P ranks X third. The only way P could select X is if both Y and Z are selected by others first. J would have to select Y(1) first, but both L and T rank X second. If P goes second, he will have to select Z(2). P cannot select X.

Questions 18–23

This is a grouping game. The inventory consists of five players—H, J, K, M, N—that must be assigned to three groups—X, Y, Z. Each group will have a leader, treasurer, and secretary, so mark those assignments in your diagram. The game has nine spaces to fill so some players will repeat.

Rule 1 states that whenever N is assigned, it must be the leader.

Rule 2 indicates that M can never repeat.

Rule 3 states that K must be in group Y, but not Z.

Rule 4 states that J must be the secretary in group Y and not be assigned to either of the other groups.

Combining rules 3 and 4, you know that J and K cannot be in group Z so the other three players, H, M, and N must be in group Z, with N as the leader.

Rule 2 states that M cannot repeat, and J cannot be in group X so group X must be N, H, and K with N as the leader. M cannot appear in group Y so that group must have both K and J along with either H as the treasurer or N as the leader.

Your diagram should look like this:

H, J, K, M, N

Clue 1: N → N = L

Clue 2: M used 1 time

Clue 3: K = Y
        K ≠ Z

Clue 4: J = Ysec

	$^{-M\ -J}$ X	$^{-M}$ Y	$^{-K\ -J}$ Z
L	N	K/N	N
S	H/K	J	M/H
T	K/H	H/K	H/M

18. **E** [General]

Use prior work and deductions to determine which answer could be the makeup of committee Z. According to the deductions, Z must consist of N, M, and H. Eliminate (A), (B), and (C). N must always be the leader (clue 1), making (E) the credited response.

19. **C** [Specific]

Make a new line in your diagram and add the new information. According to the deductions, K is already assigned to X and Y. If K is the treasurer in X, then H must be the secretary. If K is the treasurer in Y, then N or H could be the leader. You are looking for what must be false. Since H cannot be the treasurer for X, (C) is the credited response.

20. **B** [General]

Use prior work and deductions to determine which answer choice could be false.

A. No. From the deductions, you know that H must be on committee X.

B. Yes. From the deductions, you know that N, J, and K could be the members of committee Y, so H does not have to be assigned to Y.

C. No. From the deductions, you know that K must be on committee X.

D. No. From the deductions, you know that M must be assigned to committee Z.

E. No. From the deductions, you know that N must be assigned to committee X

21. **B** [Specific]

Make a new line in your diagram and add the new information. If K is to be the leader of a committee, it must be Y. From the deductions, you know that if K is the leader of Y, then H is the treasurer since J is already the secretary (clue 4). This has no impact on the assignments of the volunteers on the other committees, making (B) the credited response.

22. **C** [General]

Use prior work and deductions to determine which answer choice allows you to determine the exact position of each person on all three committees.

A. No. If H is the leader of a committee, it must be Y (deductions). This only allows you to determine the makeup of Y.

B. No. If H is the secretary for two committees, then according to the deductions, they must be X and Z. This will allow you to determine the exact makeup of these two committees, but this has no impact on the makeup of committee Y.

C. Yes. If H is the treasurer for all three committees, you can determine the exact makeup of each committee. From the deductions, you know that N must be the leader in X and Z, H and K must be on X and H and M must be on Z. So, if H is the treasurer, you know that K is the secretary in X and M is the secretary in Z. For committee Y, J is the secretary (clue 4) and K must also be included (clue 3). If H is the treasurer, then K must be the leader.

D. No. If K is the treasurer for two committees, they must be X and Y (clue 3 and deductions). This only allows you to determine the makeup of those two committees. You don't know the makeup of Z.

E. No. From the deductions, you already know that N must be the leader of committees X and Z and that does not determine who must be the secretary or treasurer for those groups.

23. **C** [Complex]

This question is asking you to find a substitute for clue 2 (only 1 M) that yields the same deductions. This means you are looking for information that would limit M to one position on committee Z.

A. No. Since there are no restrictions on which committee H can be on, you can't limit M to committee Z.

B. No. According to clue 4, J is on only one committee. This would require that M is not on any committee.

C. Yes. Since K is limited to two committees and cannot be on Z (clue 3) and J must be limited to only committee Y (clue 4), that means that neither J nor K can be on Z, so H, M, and N must be on Z and there can be only one Z.

D. No. If M is assigned to more than one committee, then there is not only one M.

E. No. According to the deductions, N must be on two committees but could be on all three. This means that M could be on one committee (if N is on two) or two committees (if N is on three). This also doesn't restrict which committees M could be on.

Section 4: Arguments 2

1. **A** Principle Strengthen

The pundit's argument follows a disagree pattern: the pundit concludes that Grenier will almost certainly not be elected as mayor. The pundit notes that Grenier's current position in support of raising city employees' wages is different from her earlier position against doing so. The pundit argues that most voters will see Grenier as insincere even though Grenier sincerely claims that she has learned more about the issue since then. The pundit's argument is flawed because it assumes that if most voters see a politician as insincere, then the voters will not elect that politician. In other words, the argument overlooks the possibility that a politician could still be elected even if most voters see that politician as insincere. The credited response to this Principle-Strengthen question will help the argument by providing a general rule that supports the idea that seeing a politician as insincere affects a voter's decision on whether to vote for the politician.

A. Yes. This answer directly connects the premise (voters would find Grenier insincere) to the conclusion (voters will not elect Grenier): if voters are unlikely to vote for a politician whom they perceive to be insincere, then Grenier almost certainly will not be elected.

B. No. This answer is irrelevant; the argument addresses whether voters find Grenier to be insincere when she describes why her position has changed, but not whether voters would notice that her stance has changed.

C. No. This answer is irrelevant; the argument addresses whether voters find Grenier to be insincere when she describes why her position has changed, but not whether voters agree with the politician's current positions.

D. No. This answer is irrelevant; the argument addresses whether voters find Grenier to be insincere when she describes why her position has changed, but not whether voters believe she understands their financial concerns.

E. No. This answer is irrelevant; the argument addresses whether voters find Grenier to be insincere when she describes why she changed her beliefs, but not whether she holds the same beliefs as the voters.

2. **C** Point at Issue

Albert argues that Swenson's book is valuable because it has stimulated new research on sun exposure, even though it is a model of poor scholarship. Yvonne disagrees and says that calling Swenson's book valuable because it stimulated research is like calling a virus valuable because it stimulates epidemiologists. In effect, Yvonne is saying that the poor scholarship of Swenson's book makes it dangerous, like a virus, and therefore that Albert is incorrect to call Swenson's book valuable. The credited response to this Point at Issue question will be an answer that Albert and Yvonne would disagree about the truth of. Use information extracted from each person's argument to prove whether they would agree or disagree with each answer, and find the answer for which Albert and Yvonne would give opposite responses: Albert argues that Swenson's book is valuable, while Yvonne disagrees and argues that Swenson's book is not valuable.

A. No. Neither Albert nor Yvonne specifically states whether he or she agrees that sun exposure harms skin cells, but they both seem to disagree with the scholarship of Swenson's book, which claims that sun exposure does not. So, either no opinion is stated on this matter, or else they both agree on this matter.

B. No. Albert specifically states that Swenson's book is a model of poor scholarship, while Yvonne does not specifically state an opinion. However, Yvonne has a negative opinion on Swenson's book, so if she has any opinion, it would likely agree with Albert's on this question.

C. Yes. Albert specifically states that Swenson's book is valuable, while Yvonne contradicts him and states that his opinion that the book is valuable is similar to claiming that a virus is valuable. In effect, Yvonne is saying that Albert is wrong to call the book valuable.

D. No. Albert specifically states that Swenson's book has stimulated research on sun exposure; Yvonne does not express any opinion on whether the book has stimulated research.

E. No. Neither argument addresses the value of books that do not stimulate new research.

3. **E**   Resolve/
             Explain

The argument presents a surprising finding by researchers: the percentage of people starting new businesses is higher in countries with higher average incomes than in countries with moderate average incomes; however, the percentage is highest in lower-income countries. The credited response to this Resolve/Explain question will help the passage by explaining why it makes sense that the percentage of people starting new businesses would be higher in high-income countries than in moderate-income countries, and yet be highest in low-income countries.

A. No. This answer makes the problem worse by describing a way in which low-income and high-income countries are similar, which does not help to explain why the percentage is different.

B. No. This answer makes the problem worse: if governments in higher-income countries provide more assistance in starting new businesses, then the percentage should be higher in high-income countries than in low-income countries, but the passage states that low-income countries have the highest percentage.

C. No. This answer does not resolve the two facts; it merely says that the failure rate is not higher in low-income countries than in high-income countries, which does not help explain why the percentage of people starting new businesses is highest in low-income countries.

D. No. This answer does not resolve the two facts. Even if people in high-income countries who start new businesses find out later that the perceived advantages were illusory, this does not help explain why low-income countries would have an even higher percentage of people starting new businesses.

E. Yes. This answer shows a logical difference between high-income countries and low-income countries that would explain the discrepancy: in low-income countries, the lack of employment options makes starting a new business one of the only options available for many people, leading to the highest percentage of people starting new businesses.

4. B   Strengthen

The film director's argument follows a disagree pattern. It concludes that it is inaccurate to say that low attendance of the director's film was caused by one or two negative reviews. The director supports this conclusion by suggesting that the cause of the small opening weekend audience was due to competition with several other films that appeal to the same small niche of filmgoers. The argument is flawed because it assumes that filmgoers wouldn't go see more than one film in a weekend if the filmgoers find multiple films appealing. The credited response to this Strengthen question will help the film director's conclusion by supporting the idea that the presence of competing similar films caused the small audiences for the film director's film.

A. No. This answer weakens the film director's argument; if the film had only one or two negative reviews, but no positive reviews, then the lack of positive reviews, rather than the competing films, could have been the cause of the small audience.

B. Yes. If filmgoers seldom see more than one film in a weekend, then the presence of competing films that appeal to the same audience could have reduced the audience for the film director's film.

C. No. This answer weakens the film director's argument: if audiences were larger than average that weekend, then this eliminates smaller-than-average audiences as a possible cause of the low attendance.

D. No. This answer weakens the film director's argument: if the other competing films received some positive reviews, while the film director's film received some negative reviews, the reviews could be the cause of the low attendance, rather than simply the fact that they appeal to the same niche audience.

E. No. This answer is irrelevant. The argument states that the film appeals to a small niche audience, so the movie tastes of most filmgoers is irrelevant to the argument.

5. A   Strengthen

The argument concludes that some scientific studies that would be most interesting to readers are usually not covered in popular magazines. The argument's conclusion is based on the premises that some scientific issues are too complex to be well understood by such readers, even though they would be the most fascinating issues to those readers. The argument is flawed because it assumes that popular magazines do not cover issues that their readers would not understand well. The credited response to this Strengthen question will provide additional evidence that supports the idea that magazines do not cover stories about issues that their readers cannot understand well.

A. Yes. If editors of popular magazines do not approve stories that cannot be well understood by their readers, and those are the types of stories that the readers would find most interesting, then the magazines would not cover some of the stories that would be most interesting to their readers.

B. No. This answer either weakens the argument (because popular magazines would go out of business if they did not publish stories that are interesting), or it is irrelevant to the argument (because the magazine might publish articles that the readers find interesting, even if the magazine doesn't cover some stories that the readers would find "most interesting").

C. No. This answer is irrelevant, because it does not address whether issues that cannot be understood will be covered by popular magazines, but instead discusses how common it is for highly complex issues to arise in various branches of science.

D. No. This answer is irrelevant; whether readers can assess their own understanding of complex issues has no bearing on whether the stories will be covered by popular magazines.

E. No. This answer is irrelevant; whether readers are willing to seek out other sources to read about complex issues does not help explain whether such stories will be covered by popular magazines.

6. **C**   Flaw

The letter to the editor concludes that the newspaper's advertisement has made a false claim when it says that it provides coverage of the high school's most popular sports. The letter's conclusion is based on the premise that more of the high school students compete on the track team than the basketball team, and therefore that track is more popular than basketball, even though basketball gets more coverage. The letter to the editor presents an argument that includes a shifting meanings flaw: it confuses the traditional meaning of "popular" (having the most popularity, such as fans or interest) with the idea that "popular" simply means "having the most people playing." The credited response to this Flaw question will correctly identify the shifting meanings flaw.

A. No. The argument does not include a causal flaw, in which one thing is assumed to have caused another thing.

B. No. The argument does not include a surveys and samples flaw.

C. Yes. This answer matches the flaw of the argument: the argument misinterprets a key word ("popular") in the newspaper's advertisement.

D. No. The argument does not include a circular flaw (a flaw in which the conclusion is a mere rephrase of one of the argument's premises).

E. No. This argument does not include an attacks flaw, in which the argument attacks the person or source making the claim rather than addressing the logic of the claim.

7. **D**   Reasoning

This argument follows a disagree pattern, which is a common pattern in Reasoning questions: it claims that the idea that food should always be purchased locally can sometimes be wrong, because some foods will have less of an environmental impact if they are not produced locally. The credited response to this Reasoning question will match this pattern by identifying the role played in the argument by the first sentence: it is a claim with which the argument disagrees.

A. No. The first sentence of the passage is not a principle on which the argument's reasoning is based; rather, it is a statement with which the argument disagrees.

B. No. The first sentence is not used to support a particular activity; rather, the remainder of the argument passage provides evidence against the idea stated in the first sentence.

C. No. This answer reverses the roles of the statements in the argument. The first sentence is not a general principle that is used to reject another activity; rather, the first sentence is the idea that the rest of the argument finds to be untrue (at least in part.)

D. Yes. This answer matches the role of the first sentence: it is a view (opinion) that the rest of the argument argues is incorrect.

E. No. The first sentence is not the conclusion of the argument; rather, it is a statement that is contradicted by the remainder of the argument.

8. **A**   [Main Point]

The argument concludes that technology is radically improving the quality of life in some communities, and doing so not just through direct application of innovations. The conclusion is based on the premises that the development of technology is in itself an industry that helps grow communities. The credited response to this Main Point question will match the argument's conclusion: technology is rapidly improving life in some communities in ways that go beyond simply using new innovations.

A.   Yes. This answer matches the conclusion of the argument. Use the Why Test: does each of the other statements in the argument support the idea that direct application of innovations is not the only way technology improves life in some communities? Yes. So, this answer matches the conclusion of the argument.

B.   No. This answer is a premise. Use the Why Test: does each of the other statements in the argument support the idea that the development of new technology has itself become a growing industry that helps some communities? The first sentence of the argument does not. Therefore, this answer does not match the argument's conclusion.

C.   No. This answer is a premise. Use the Why Test: does each of the other statements in the argument support the idea that companies involved in development of new technology create jobs, add to the tax base, and improve spirit? The first sentence of the argument does not. Therefore, this answer does not match the argument's conclusion.

D.   No. This answer is too strong and goes beyond the argument by saying that the quality of life in most communities is being radically improved. Therefore, this answer does not match the argument's conclusion.

E.   No. This answer is too strong and goes beyond the argument by saying that the only ways that technology helps is through creating jobs, adding to the tax base, and so on, while these are simply examples of the benefits. Therefore, this answer does not match the argument's conclusion.

9. **D**   [Flaw]

The argument concludes that Joshi is letting campaign contributions influence his vote. The conclusion is based on the premises that he has received more monetary support from property developers and that his voting record is more favorable than those of other councilors toward property developers. This argument includes a causal flaw: it assumes that Joshi's favorable voting record toward property developers was caused by the campaign contributions. Since it is also possible that the causation is reversed—property developers contribute more financial support to Joshi because of his past favorable voting toward them—the argument is flawed. The credited response to this Flaw question will correctly identify this causal flaw.

A.   No. Although this answer identifies a causal flaw, the argument does not state which events occurred earlier or later in time, so this answer does not describe the flaw of the argument.

B.   No. The argument does not include a conditional statement flaw, in which necessary factors are confused with sufficient factors.

C.   No. This answer is too strong, because it states that only a factual judgment can be justified regarding the premises of the argument; also, this answer does not identify the causal flaw.

D. Yes. This answer matches the flaw of the argument: the argument assumes that the financial support received from developers was the cause of Joshi's voting record, when it could just as well be an effect of his past voting record.

E. No. This argument does not include a circular flaw, in which the argument's conclusion is merely a paraphrase of one of its premises.

10. **D** **Inference**

The columnist states that some people argue that the government should not take over failing private banks because the government would not know how to manage a bank. The passage further notes that the government could simply select new management for the bank, and that doing so would be similar to appointing top military officials, who have at least as great a responsibility as managing a bank. Combining these facts leads to the inference that the government could successfully take over a bank if the government appoints good management for the bank. The question asks which answer could be rejected on the basis of the columnist's statements. The credited response to this Inference question will be a statement that is contradicted by information extracted from the passage.

A. No. This answer does not contradict the statements in the passage, since the passage does not discuss the amount of knowledge required by either military command or bank management.

B. No. This answer does not contradict the statements in the passage, since the passage does not address whether politicians do an adequate job of appointing military officials.

C. No. This answer does not contradict the passage; rather, it is consistent with the statement made in the first sentence of the passage.

D. Yes. This answer contradicts the passage: if the government can select the bank's senior management, and the government appoints top military officials with at least as much responsibility as the senior management of a bank, then it follows that the government could take over a bank and appoint people who would manage the bank effectively.

E. No. This answer does not contradict the passage, since the passage discusses only the possibility of taking over failing banks and does not address government takeover of banks that are financially sound.

11. **D** **Weaken**

The argument concludes that people with a university education are more likely than members of the overall population to favor keeping or increasing the level of social services (or, in other words, oppose reducing the level of social services). The argument's conclusion is based on a poll showing that graduating students are more likely than entering students to oppose reducing social services. The argument includes a surveys and samples flaw: it makes a conclusion about the opinions of people with a university education based only on data about graduating university students. The views of graduating university students may not be the same as the views of university graduates as a whole. The credited response to this Weaken question hurt the argument by providing evidence that people with a university education might actually favor reducing the level of social services.

A. No. This answer strengthens the argument, because it provides evidence that the poll was designed to avoid taking an unrepresentative sample of graduating students from any single academic discipline.

B. No. This answer strengthens the argument, because it provides additional evidence that graduating students might tend to oppose reducing the level of social students as a result of influence from professors.

C. No. This answer strengthens the argument by showing that among retired people, those with university degrees are less likely than those without university degrees to favor reducing the level of social services.

D. Yes. If polls show that five years after graduation, university graduates are more likely than the general population to favor reducing social services, then the opinion held by graduating students may not be representative of the population of university graduates as a whole.

E. No. This answer is irrelevant. Whether the graduating students were more likely than the entering students to express strong opinions does not affect how the opinions of university graduates compare to the opinions of the overall population.

12. **A**   Flaw

The argument follows a disagree pattern. It concludes that the critics have made an untrue claim that is potentially harmful to the moviemakers' reputations. The argument's conclusion is based on the premise that the critics' claim (that the movie would inspire people to act in socially irresponsible ways) relies entirely on deeply flawed survey data. The argument includes an absence of evidence flaw: it concludes that the critics' claim is false and damaging simply because it is based on flawed data, when an appropriate conclusion would be that the critics' claim may be false because of the flawed data. The credited response to this Flaw question will correctly identify the absence of evidence flaw.

A. Yes. This answer matches the flaw of the argument: the argument concludes that the critics' claim is false on the basis that the survey evidence used to support the claim is deeply flawed, when in fact an appropriate conclusion would be that the critics' claim may be false.

B. No. This answer suggests that a true, but pejorative claim could be more damaging than a false claim, but the fact that other claims could be more harmful does not hurt the conclusion, which simply says that the claim is potentially harmful.

C. No. This answer is irrelevant, because the argument does not rely on any survey or sample. The argument made by the critics does, in fact, rely on survey data, but the question does not ask for the flaw in the argument made by the critics. In any case, the argument states only that the survey data are deeply flawed, and it does not address whether an unrepresentative sample was involved.

D. No. The argument does not include an attacks flaw (a flaw in which the argument attacks the person or source making the claim rather than addressing the logic of the claim).

E. No. While this answer does identify a type of absence of evidence flaw, it is the reverse of the credited response. This answer suggests that even if the critics' claim is false, the supporting data for the claim could be true, while the issue of this argument is that even if the supporting data for the critics' claim is false, the critics' claim still might be true.

13. **D**   Inference

The passage involves quantity statements. The first statement provides that a majority of skilled banjo players are also skilled guitar players. The second statement provides that a majority of skilled guitar players are not skilled banjo players. The only way both of these statements can be true is if more skilled guitar players exist than skilled banjo players. If necessary, try using some numbers as an illustration: what would happen if there were 100 skilled guitar players and 100 skilled banjo players? Then 51 or more of the skilled banjo players would also be skilled guitar players, while at the same time 51 or more of the 100 skilled guitar players would NOT be skilled banjo players, which would be impossible. If,

77

however, there were 200 skilled guitar players and 100 skilled banjo players, then the statements would work together. The credited response to this Inference question will be proved by information extracted from the passage.

A. No. The statements in the passage do not provide enough information to calculate the number of people who are skilled at both guitar and banjo.

B. No. The statements in the passage do not address whether one is more likely to succeed.

C. No. The statements in the passage do not address the level of skill needed for the guitar or the banjo.

D. Yes. As mentioned above, this statement is proved by the statements in the passage.

E. No. This answer is a reversal of (D).

14. **E**   Reasoning

The argument concludes that lack of managerial skills and lack of entrepreneurial ability each can inhibit the development of successful companies. The argument's conclusion is based on two premises: first, entrepreneurial ability is needed to start a successful company, and second, lack of managerial skills can cause a company to fail (as supported by the example of failure to analyze market trends, leading to the failure to manage company growth). The credited response to this Reasoning question will match the role played by the proposition that certain entrepreneurs fail in managing company growth: it is an example used to support the premise that lack of managerial skills can cause a company to fail, which is in turn used to support the overall conclusion that both lack of managerial skills and lack of entrepreneurial ability can inhibit the development of successful companies.

A. No. The proposition that certain entrepreneurs fail in managing company growth is not the main conclusion; rather, it is an example used to support a premise that is in turn used to support the conclusion.

B. No. The proposition that certain entrepreneurs fail in managing company growth is not used to support the phenomenon the argument seeks to explain; rather, it is used to support the idea that entrepreneurs may fail later due to lack of managerial skills. The argument does not seek to explain why entrepreneurs fail due to lack of managerial skills—it seeks to explain that two separate factors (lack of entrepreneurial ability and lack of managerial skills) each can inhibit the development of successful companies.

C. No. The proposition that certain entrepreneurs fail in managing company growth is not meant as an aside; rather, it is an example used to support a premise that is in turn used to support the conclusion.

D. No. The proposition that certain entrepreneurs fail in managing company growth does not support the main conclusion directly; instead, it is an example used to support the idea that entrepreneurs may fail later due to lack of managerial skills, which in turn is used to support the conclusion.

E. Yes. This answer matches the role of the proposition that certain entrepreneurs fail in managing company growth: it is an example used to support a premise that is in turn used to support the conclusion.

15. **C**   Inference

The passage includes conditional statements. The second sentence can be expressed as a conditional statement: if attempts at creativity are not grounded in relevant experience, then such attempts are futile. The contrapositive of this statement is as follows: if attempts at creativity are successful (i.e., not futile), then the attempts were grounded in relevant experience. In other words, successful attempts at creativity require relevant experience. The third sentence can also be expressed as a set of conditional statements: if a problem can be solved, then it will be solved by people who really understand the problem, and if people really understand a problem, then those people have experience. In other words, solutions require people who really understand a problem and therefore have experience. The credited response to this Inference question will be proved by information extracted from the passage.

A. No. This answer includes an unsupported comparison. The statements in the passage do not provide any comparisons between the level of experience a person has and the level of creativity that person has; rather, the passage simply says that successful attempts at creativity require relevant experience.

B. No. The word "rarely" makes this answer is too strong. The argument does not address how often experienced people overlook creative solutions.

C. Yes. This answer can be expressed as a conditional statement: if a solution is creative, then the solution will come from people with experience. In other words, creative solutions require experienced people. This answer is proved by the combination of the second sentence of the passage (which states that attempts at creativity require experience) and the third sentence of the passage (which states that solutions require people with experience).

D. No. This answer goes beyond the statements in the passage. The passage does not address the amount of experience that is required based on a field's complexity.

E. No. This answer goes beyond the statements in the passage. The passage does not address the amount of training required before being given responsibility in a field.

16. **B**   Reasoning

This argument follows a disagree pattern, which is typical for Reasoning questions: it concludes that paleobiologists who think all dinosaurs were cold-blooded are mistaken. The conclusion is based on the premises that fossil records show that some dinosaurs lived in areas where temperatures drop below freezing and that only warm-blooded animals can survive such temperatures. The credited response to this Reasoning question will match the role played by the last sentence of the passage: it is a premise offered in support of the conclusion that some paleobiologists are mistaken.

A. No. The last sentence of the passage is not a counterexample to the main conclusion; rather, it supports the main conclusion (that the paleobiologists are mistaken).

B. Yes. This answer matches the role of the last sentence: it is a premise offered in support of the main conclusion (that the paleobiologists are mistaken).

C. No. The last sentence of the passage is not presented as counterevidence to the idea that dinosaurs lack turbinates; rather, it is presented as counterevidence to the idea that all dinosaurs were cold-blooded, in support of the main conclusion (that the paleobiologists are mistaken in saying that all dinosaurs are cold-blooded).

D. No. The last sentence of the passage is not the main conclusion; rather, it is evidence that supports the main conclusion (that the paleobiologists are mistaken).

E. No. The claim that some dinosaurs lived in Australia and Alaska does not support the claim that only warm-blooded creatures can survive temperatures below freezing.

17. **B** `Strengthen`

The argument presents an application of a principle. The principle is presented as a conditional statement: if expressing a true belief would be harmful to people generally, then the government should not prevent someone from expressing that belief. The application of the principle concludes that the government was wrong to prevent Calista from publicly expressing her beliefs about cancer and cell phones. The application of the principle is flawed because it does not provide evidence that Calista truly believes what she said and or evidence that expressing this belief would not be harmful to people generally. The credited response to this Strengthen question will help the application of the principle by providing evidence that Calista truly believes what she said or that expressing this belief would not be harmful and that, therefore, the government should not have prevented Calista from expressing it.

A. No. This answer is irrelevant, because the amount of research conducted by the government regarding cell phones and cancer does not affect whether Calista's expression of her belief would be harmful to people generally.

B. Yes. If several studies have found evidence of a connection, this supports the idea that Calista truly believes what she says; furthermore, if it would benefit people to know this. Then expressing the belief would not be harmful to people generally, and therefore, according to the principle, the government should not have prevented Calista from expressing the belief.

C. No. This answer is irrelevant, because the principle does not require that Calista believe that knowing this information would benefit people; rather, it requires that expressing the belief would not be harmful to people generally. Whether Calista believes it would benefit people does not affect whether it would actually benefit or harm people.

D. No. This answer is irrelevant, because the principle does not address whether expressing this sort of belief would usually be harmful; rather, it addresses whether expressing this specific belief would actually be harmful.

E. No. This answer is irrelevant. Whether most people would reduce their use of cell phones is not relevant to the application of the principle, which only addresses whether expressing the belief would harm people generally. If Calista's beliefs are taken as true, reducing use of cell phones might turn out to be a benefit, but without additional evidence, such as the evidence provided by (B), there is no way to know whether Calista's beliefs have any actual credence and therefore, whether there would be any benefit or harm as a result.

18. **D** `Inference`

The passage involves quantity statements and conditional statements. The first two sentences present conditional statements: if one learns to read an alphabetic language, then one must have both phonemic awareness and an understanding of how sounds are symbolically represented by letters. The last sentence states that many (an ambiguous amount that is effectively the same as saying "some") children taught by the whole-language method learn to read alphabetic languages. These statements can be combined: the children taught by the whole-language method who learn to read alphabetic languages must have somewhere gained both phonemic awareness and an understanding of how sounds are symbolically represented by letters. The credited response to this inference will be proved by information extracted from the passage.

A. No. This answer is too strong. The statements in the passage do not support the idea that the whole-language method invariably succeeds at any goals.

77

B. No. This answer is the converse of one of the conditional statements at the beginning of the passage (in other words, it reverses the conditional statement). The fact that learning to read an alphabetic language requires an understanding of how sounds are symbolically represented by letters does not mean that every time you gain such an understanding, you learn to read an alphabetic language.

C. No. This answer misinterprets the conditional statements at the beginning of the passage: The contrapositive of those statements would be that if one either lacks phonemic awareness or lacks an understanding of how sounds are symbolically represented by letters, then one cannot learn to read an alphabetic language. This answer, on the other hand, simply tries to negate the conditional and says that if one cannot read the alphabetic language, then one lacks both phonemic awareness and an understanding of how sounds are symbolically represented by letters, which is not supported by the passage.

D. Yes. This answer is proved by combining the statements in the passage. If a child being taught by the whole-language method successfully learns to read alphabetic languages (as stated in the last sentence), then the child must have both phonemic awareness and an understanding of how sounds are symbolically represented by letters (as stated in the first two sentences), and so the child must not have been prevented from learning those things.

E. No. This answer goes beyond the argument. It is very tempting, however, because it is very close to the correct answer. The passage states that many students taught by the whole-language method learn to read alphabetic languages, which means that those students must also have learned how sounds are symbolically represented by letters. However, the passage does not state that the whole-language method actually taught that concept to the students; the students could have gained that knowledge in another method besides the whole-language method.

19. **A**   Weaken

The argument notes that more pedestrians are struck by cars when they use crosswalks than when they do not use crosswalks. The argument concludes that the reason they are struck by cars more often in crosswalks is that strong sense of security provided by crosswalks causes pedestrians to be less likely to look both ways before crossing. The argument includes a causal flaw: the argument assumes that the cause of the higher number of pedestrians struck by cars in crosswalks is the strong sense of security provided by crosswalks, and it overlooks other possible factors that could explain why a greater number of pedestrians are struck in crosswalks than outside crosswalks. The credited response to this Weaken question will hurt the argument's conclusion by pointing out another potential cause of the higher number of pedestrians being struck in crosswalks.

A. Yes. If the overwhelming majority of pedestrians in high-traffic areas (areas with the most opportunity for car accidents) cross in crosswalks, then the higher number of accidents is simply due to the higher number of people crossing in crosswalks; in this case, the cause of the accidents need not be carelessness on the part of the pedestrians as a result of the strong sense of safety provided by crosswalks.

B. No. This answer is irrelevant. The fact that the number of pedestrians hit by cars overall has increased in recent years does not help explain the reason why more accidents happen to pedestrians in crosswalks.

C. No. This answer strengthens the argument by providing another example that supports the idea that crosswalks give pedestrians a strong sense of safety that could increase their chances of being struck.

D.   No. This answer is irrelevant; even if drivers are alert to pedestrians in crosswalks, careless pedestrians could still be struck in crosswalks.

E.   No. This answer strengthens the argument using the principle that measures intended to promote safety tend to make people less cautious, supporting the idea that crosswalks could cause people to look the other way less often when crossing.

20.   **B**   Sufficient Assumption

The argument notes that Selena claims to have psychic powers, and it concludes that if we find out whether Selena's claim to be psychic is true, then we will determine whether it is possible to have psychic powers. The argument is flawed because it would be valid in one circumstance but would not be valid in another: if we find Selena's claim to be true (and, therefore, that she has psychic powers), then this would confirm that it is possible to have psychic powers. However, if we find Selena's claim to be false (and, therefore, that she does not have psychic powers), then the argument does not explain why this would confirm whether psychic powers are possible. The correct answer to this Sufficient Assumption question will help the argument by providing an assumption that makes the conclusion valid.

A.   No. This answer is not sufficient to make the conclusion valid. If no one else has yet been found to have psychic powers, then the problem still remains in the argument: if we find that Selena has no psychic powers, why would that help us confirm whether psychic powers are possible?

B.   Yes. This answer connects the premises of the argument in a way that is sufficient to make the conclusion valid, by providing a conditional statement that ties the premises to the conclusion: if it is possible to have psychic powers, then Selena has them. The contrapositive of this conditional statement is as follows: if Selena does not have psychic powers, then it is not possible to have psychic powers. So, if this assumption is added to the argument, then the conclusion will be valid in any circumstance: If Selena's claim is true, then she has psychic powers, and we have confirmed that psychic powers are possible. If, on the other hand, Selena's claim is false, then she does not have psychic powers, which means psychic powers are not possible.

C.   No. This answer is not sufficient to make the conclusion valid. Even if we assume that it is possible to determine whether Selena has psychic powers, the problem still remains in the argument: if we find that Selena has no psychic powers, why would that help us confirm whether psychic powers are possible?

D.   No. This answer is not sufficient to make the conclusion valid. This answer simply states the flaw of the argument, but it does not help the argument by resolving that flaw.

E.   No. This answer is not sufficient to make the conclusion valid. It provides a conditional statement: if we do not find out whether Selena's claim is true, then we will not be able to determine whether psychic powers are possible. This does not help the argument, because the credited response needs to explain why finding Selena's claim to be false would help successfully determine whether psychic powers are possible.

21.   **B**   Resolve/ Explain

The passage presents an apparent contradiction: the current prices for common pharmaceutical drugs from bulk wholesalers were 60 to 80 percent below the suggested wholesale prices in an annual price guidebook. The credited response to this Resolve/Explain EXCEPT question will be the answer remaining after eliminating four answers that help explain the current prices would be 60 to 80 percent below the suggested prices published in the annual guidebook; the remaining answer will either not help explain the apparent contradiction, or will make the problem worse.

A. No. This answer helps explain the apparent contradiction; since this is an EXCEPT question, it should be eliminated. If a price war began just before the study was conducted, this would explain why the current prices are lower than the prices previously published in an annual guidebook.

B. Yes. This answer does not help explain the apparent contradiction; since this is an EXCEPT question, it is the credited response. It helps explain why prices for the most common drugs would be lower than the prices of less common drugs, but it does not help explain why the current prices for the most common drugs are lower than the prices for the same drugs published in an annual guidebook.

C. No. This answer helps explain the apparent contradiction; since this is an EXCEPT question, it should be eliminated. If the wholesale prices of drugs fluctuate dramatically from month to month, this would explain why the current prices could be significantly lower than the prices previously published in an annual guidebook.

D. No. This answer helps explain the apparent contradiction; since this is an EXCEPT question, it should be eliminated. If the prices published in the annual guidebook are calculated to allow wholesalers to make substantial profits, then this would explain why the current prices could be lower than the prices previously published in an annual guidebook—wholesalers might be currently accepting lower prices and lower profits than the substantial profits provided by the prices in the guidebook.

E. No. This answer helps explain the apparent contradiction; since this is an EXCEPT question, it should be eliminated. If the prices in the guidebook are for sales of relatively small quantities of drugs, then this would explain why the current prices are lower than the prices previously published in an annual guidebook, since the passage specifies that the study was of wholesalers who specialize in bulk sales and, therefore, might charge substantially less for the same drug when selling in large quantities.

22. **C**   `Reasoning`

The argument concludes that if the meaning of a piece of music is found in the emotion it elicits, then this means only that the music produces the core of that emotion. The conclusion is based on several premises: certain pairs of emotions have the same core feeling; those pairs are distinguishable only in terms of surrounding social conditions and the resulting behavior caused by the emotions; and music, being merely sound, is unable by itself to create social conditions or human behavior. The credited response to this Reasoning question will match the role played in the argument by the first claim that music is merely sound: it is one of three premises used to support the conclusion of the argument.

A. No. The claim that music is merely sound is not used to undermine another viewpoint; rather, it is used in combination with the other premises to support the conclusion of the argument.

B. No. The claim that music is merely sound is not part of the conclusion of the argument. Although the claim is in the same sentence as the conclusion, the word "for" marks the end of the conclusion and the beginning of a premise supporting the conclusion. Sometimes on the LSAT, a conclusion will make up only part of a sentence, and words such as "for," "because," and "since" will indicate that part of the same sentence is a premise that supports the conclusion.

C. Yes. This answer matches the role of the claim that music is merely sound: it is one of three claims that, together, support the conclusion.

D.   No. This answer is too strong. The argument does not state that the truth of the idea "music is merely sound" is necessary to establish the conclusion of the argument. Note that the word "necessary" would mean that the idea "music is merely sound" is part of a conditional statement, but it is not.

E.   No. The argument does not reject the idea that "music is merely sound"; rather, it uses that claim to support the conclusion of the argument.

23.   **B**   Parallel

The argument presents a conditional statement: if a computer is intelligent, then it must have creativity or self-awareness or the ability to learn from its mistakes (or some combination of those traits). The argument further notes that the AR3000 is not creative and not self-aware. The argument concludes that if the AR3000 is intelligent, it must have the ability to learn from its mistakes. This argument is valid; its premises logically match to the conclusion and, therefore, the argument is not flawed. The credited response to this Parallel the Reasoning question will match the logic, structure, and strength of language of the argument, which follows this sort of pattern: "To be Z, a thing needs to have A or B or C. Thing X does not have A or B. So, if Thing X is Z, then Thing X must have C."

A.   No. This answer does not match the passage, because it adds a new element (living viral cells) that does not fit into the original argument's structure and is missing an element to match the "being intelligent" element of the original argument. In order to match the conclusion of the argument, the conclusion of this answer choice would need to include something like "If vaccine X is _____, then it must be an attenuated-virus vaccine."

B.   Yes. This answer matches the structure of the argument: A virus that is commonly used is either dead-virus or attenuated-virus or pure DNA; Vaccine X is not two of those three things; so, if Vaccine X is commonly used, it must be the third of those three things.

C.   No. This answer does not match the passage, because it is missing an element to match the "being intelligent" element of the original passage. In order to match the conclusion of the original argument, the conclusion of this answer choice would need to include something like "If vaccine X is _____, then it must be an attenuated-virus vaccine."

D.   No. This answer does not match the passage, because it adds a new element (it stimulates the production of killer T cells, unlike any pure DNA vaccine) that does not fit into the original argument's structure, and because its conclusion does not match the structure of the original argument. In order to match the conclusion of the original argument, the conclusion of this answer choice would need to include something like "If vaccine X is commonly used, then..." instead of "if it is not a dead-virus vaccine...."

E.   No. This answer does not match the passage, because its conclusion concerns the three options (dead-virus, attenuated-virus, and pure DNA, which match the elements of creativity, self-awareness, and ability to learn from mistakes in the original argument), when the conclusion should concern whether the vaccine is commonly used (which matches the element of intelligence in the original argument).

24.   **D**   Sufficient Assumption

The argument notes that Mallotech portrays itself as socially responsible and that critics charge that Mallotech factory employees work in unsanitary conditions. The argument concludes that unless the critics are mistaken, Mallotech is not accurately portraying itself (in other words, Mallotech is not socially responsible). The argument is flawed because it does not explain why the unsanitary factory conditions necessarily prove Mallotech is not socially responsible. The credited response to this Sufficient Assumption question will help the argument by providing an assumption that makes the conclusion valid: the argument assumes that if employees work in unsanitary factory conditions, then the employer is not socially responsible.

A. No. This answer is not sufficient to make the conclusion valid. The argument does not state that Mallotech lied about the working conditions of its employees, so this answer does not help prove Mallotech is not socially responsible.

B. No. This answer is not sufficient to make the conclusion valid. The argument does not state that Mallotech concealed information from the public, so this answer does not help prove Mallotech is not socially responsible.

C. No. This answer is not sufficient to make the conclusion valid. The number of employees working in unsanitary conditions does not add anything to the argument, which already provides that critics charge that employees in many Mallotech factories work in unsanitary conditions. The question at issue is whether the existence of unsanitary conditions proves that Mallotech is not socially responsible, and this answer does not help to connect those ideas.

D. Yes. This answer connects the premises to the conclusion in a way that is sufficient to make the conclusion valid: if a socially responsible company would not have employees working in unsanitary conditions, then if Mallotech has employees working in unsanitary conditions, Mallotech is not socially responsible, and is therefore portraying itself inaccurately.

E. No. This answer is not sufficient to make the conclusion valid. The argument does not address whether Mallotech is well managed, so this answer does not help prove Mallotech is not socially responsible.

25. **B** Parallel Flaw

The argument concludes that mutually exclusive dichotomous classifications (in simpler terms, "seeing things as only black or white") should be abandoned. The conclusion is based on the premises that, although many concepts are dichotomous pairs (good/bad, right/wrong), science has shown some long-used dichotomies to be untenable (such as matter/energy or animals/plants). The argument includes a part-to-whole comparison flaw: it concludes that all dichotomous classifications should be abandoned simply because some of them have been proved untenable. The argument overlooks the possibility that even though some are untenable, many others may work just fine. The credited response to this Parallel Flaw question will match the pattern and strength of language of the argument's flaw: because some things in a category turned out to be invalid, the entire category of things should be abandoned.

A. No. This answer reverses the pattern, concluding that some computers aren't powerful enough because a consultant recommended that all computers be replaced with more powerful models.

B. Yes. This answer matches the part-to-whole comparison flaw in the original argument: some antianxiety drugs turn out to be untenable, so all antianxiety drugs should be abandoned.

C. No. This answer does not include a part-to-whole comparison flaw; instead, it concludes that, since all intoxicated drivers are dangerous, they should all be kept off the roads.

D. No. This answer does not include a part-to-whole comparison flaw; here, the peaches seem to be fine but are simply thrown out before they begin to rot.

E.   No. This answer does not include a part-to-whole comparison flaw; instead, it includes a past-to-future comparison that appears to be valid, since the argument states that the past revenue figures show the assumption to be untenable.

26.   **E**   **Necessary Assumption**

The argument follows a solve pattern. It notes a problem: when ballast tanks are adjusted to maintain stability during loading and unloading, sea creatures are sucked in and then deposited in other habitats, where they cause environmental damage. The argument proposes a solution to this problem: empty and refill the ballast tanks midocean, so that coastal creatures are not transported to other coastal habitats. Since the argument follows a Solve pattern, one potential flaw in the argument is that the solution could backfire, or simply fail to solve the problem. The credited response to this Necessary Assumption question will help the argument by providing a statement that is necessary in order for the solution to work or to prevent the solution from backfiring. The answer will also satisfy the Negation Test.

A.   No. This answer is too strong. The argument does not assume that the midocean refilling would ensure that no sea creatures pumped in would be able to disturb the ecology in a new habitat; rather, the argument states that the creatures pumped in midocean usually cannot survive in coastal habitats.

B.   No. This answer is too strong. It is not necessary to the argument that the procedure has to be done in calm, flat seas. Note that the Negation Test does not work on this answer: if the tanks could be refilled midocean in other weather, that would actually help the argument.

C.   No. This answer is too strong. It is not necessary to the argument's proposed solution that environmental damage has rarely, if ever, resulted from depositing creatures in a new habitat except when the creatures are able to survive there. Note that the Negation Test does not work on this answer: if environmental damage has sometimes resulted from depositing creatures in a new habitat even when they are able to survive there, that still doesn't destroy the idea that the proposed solution could help reduce the problem.

D.   No. This answer is too strong. It is not necessary to the argument's proposed solution that the current procedure involve pumping water in and out only during loading and unloading. Note that the Negation Test does not work on this answer: if the pumping of water in and out happens at other times as well, that has no effect on the argument, or perhaps makes the solution even more necessary.

E.   Yes. In order for this midocean clearing and refilling solution to work, it would be necessary that at least some ships could maintain their stability long enough to empty and refill the tanks. Try negating this choice: if no ships could remain stable long enough to empty and refill the tanks, then the solution would be impossible. Therefore, this choice is necessary for the conclusion (the solution) to be valid.

Chapter 8
PrepTest 78:
Answers and
Explanations

ANSWER KEY: PREPTEST 78

Section 1:
Arguments 1

1. A
2. E
3. A
4. E
5. B
6. B
7. B
8. C
9. A
10. C
11. A
12. C
13. D
14. D
15. E
16. A
17. E
18. E
19. E
20. D
21. E
22. A
23. B
24. E
25. C

Section 2:
Games

1. C
2. D
3. A
4. E
5. B
6. C
7. E
8. A
9. D
10. E
11. A
12. C
13. B
14. D
15. A
16. E
17. B
18. D
19. C
20. C
21. E
22. B
23. A

Section 3:
Arguments 2

1. A
2. D
3. B
4. C
5. E
6. B
7. E
8. A
9. E
10. D
11. E
12. B
13. A
14. C
15. C
16. B
17. A
18. C
19. B
20. C
21. A
22. E
23. C
24. E
25. D
26. D

Section 4:
Reading
Comprehension

1. E
2. D
3. C
4. D
5. E
6. A
7. B
8. C
9. E
10. D
11. C
12. B
13. A
14. E
15. A
16. D
17. B
18. B
19. C
20. C
21. A
22. B
23. E
24. A
25. D
26. D
27. B

EXPLANATIONS

Section 1: Arguments 1

1. **A** 〔Principle Strengthen〕

Grecia makes the point that the survey respondents' employment status must be tracked by age and suggests that respondents be asked to provide their ages. Hidalgo notes that results need not be provided for every single age and thereby concludes that asking respondents for an age range is sufficient while more specific data is not necessary. The credited response will provide a principle that allows for representative data collection with limited specificity.

A. Yes. This answer choice states that data gathered for a specific purpose should not be more detailed than necessary to meet its goal.

B. No. There is no indication that respondents would be unlikely to answer a question about age inaccurately.

C. No. There is no indication that the data being collected is not stored securely, nor that a respondent's age or age range is sensitive personal information.

D. No. There is no indication that the survey is not gathering the data necessary to meet its goal.

E. No. There is no indication that respondents are not aware of the type of data they'll share prior to their participation.

2. **E** 〔Necessary Assumption〕

The argument's author concludes that the excavation site believed to be that of Troy, the location of the ten-year-long Trojan War described in Homer's epic the *Iliad,* could not possibly be Troy because of the small size of the excavation site. The argument's author goes on to say that a city of such size could not possibly withhold a ten-year siege. The passage assumes that descriptions in the *Iliad* of the Trojan War and the city laid siege are accurate descriptions. The credited response will show that the descriptions provided in the *Iliad* are legitimate, thereby showing that the excavation site could not be the modern-day location of ancient Troy.

A. No. Whether scholars knew of other possible locations for Troy is irrelevant.

B. No. Knowing that the *Iliad* does not offer additional clues to the whereabouts of Troy's location does nothing to show the excavation site is not the actual location of Troy.

C. No. While lack of evidence of a siege might help one to infer that the excavation site is not ancient Troy, it does nothing to address the evidence the author offers as to why the site cannot be Troy, and is therefore not an assumption made by the argument.

D. No. This answer choice would work to show that the excavation site is Troy, while the argument's conclusion is that the site could not be Troy.

E. Yes. By recognizing that the *Iliad* accurately represented the duration of the war, and accepting the fact that a city of the size of the excavation site could not withstand a ten-year siege, it can be concluded that Dörpfeld's excavation site was not the location of the Trojan War.

3. **A**   Reasoning

Flynn makes the argument that letting people collect large sums if they successfully sue corporations benefits consumers, since it incentivizes corporations to reduce safety risks associated with product in order to avoid penalty. Garcia responds by pointing out that corporations could be destroyed if limits are not placed on damage awards, leading to loss of productivity and jobs. Garcia concludes that the impact of this loss on the economy harms consumers, countering Flynn's argument. The credited response will show that the impact of Flynn's policies could actually have negative outcomes, rather than the benefit Flynn suggests.

A.   Yes. This answer choice indicates that Garcia points out the possible negative consequences of Flynn's suggested policy.

B.   No. Garcia offers no evidence that undermines one of the premises of Flynn's argument.

C.   No. Garcia's argument offers no such comparison as the answer choice describes.

D.   No. Garcia does not attempt to show that Flynn's argument could be used to support an inconsistent policy.

E.   No. Garcia offers an alternative outcome, or conclusion, but does not question the premise of Flynn's argument.

4. **E**   Point at Issue

Monroe concludes that the project has been a failure based on the fact that the goal was to reduce the number of homes in the county that do not have electricity by as much as possible, and 2,000 homes still have no electricity. Wilkerson responds by pointing out that over 5,000 homes were without electricity before the project began, and concludes that bringing electricity to the 3,000 homes they did should be considered a success. Monroe and Wilkerson disagree over what should be considered a success, and the credited response will help to define what would be necessary to consider the project a success or to deem it a failure.

A.   No. The number of homes that remain without electricity is not in question.

B.   No. The number of homes that were without electricity at the beginning of the project is not in question.

C.   No. While we know that Wilkerson does not agree with this statement, we do not definitively know that Monroe would agree with this statement.

D.   No. The stated goal of the project is not in question.

E.   Yes. While Monroe would agree that leaving 2,000 homes without electricity counts as a failure, Wilkerson would not agree.

5. **B**   Weaken

The argument describes a study conducted among a group evenly split between fifty-year-olds and twenty-year-olds who are asked whether they give blood. Based on their answers, the researchers determined that fifty-year-olds are generally more altruistic than twenty-year-olds because a much larger percentage of fifty-year-olds claim to sometimes give blood. The author concludes, however, that there is reason to be skeptical, and then presents the evidence that some do not admit their true behavior if that behavior does not conform to societal norms.

A. No. Whether the sample is representative is not in question; the question is the validity of the data provided by the sample set.

B. Yes. The author offers the alternative possibility that those surveyed may not have been entirely honest.

C. No. The argument does not mention direct observation of altruism.

D. No. The author's argument addresses the actions of those surveyed, not the surveyors.

E. No. The author does not offer a counterexample, only an alternative reading of the data.

6. **B** Point at Issue

Mario argues that there must be little demand for rugs in Glendale since the only rug store there went out of business. He goes on to suggest that if one is planning to open a business in the area, one should consider a product other than rugs. Renate concedes that the only rug store is now closed, but insists its closing was not entirely about the product sold there, and concludes that the Glendale rug market is now open for entrepreneurs. Mario and Renate disagree over whether Glendale's rug market is no longer viable, and the credited response will suggest that it is or is not viable.

A. No. Neither Mario nor Renate mention anything about the quality of the rugs sold.

B. Yes. Mario does not agree that it would be a good idea to open a rug store in Glendale, while Maria believes there is opportunity in the Glendale rug market.

C. No. Both Mario and Renate have offered theories on the Glendale rug market, so, if anything, they agree that the market can be determined; they just disagree over whether the market is good for rugs or not.

D. No. Neither Mario nor Renate mentions any other stores or markets other than those for rugs in Glendale.

E. No. While we know Mario agrees that rug stores can close because of a lack of demand for rugs, Renate does not mention demand.

7. **B** Flaw

In the argument, a city council considers whether to increase the amount of air traffic allowed at an airport, reaching beyond the airport's original design capacity. Some council members argue that the increase would not decrease safety since the increase would come along with the purchase of the latest in safety technology. The author concludes that the increase would decrease safety, and cites evidence of studies from 30 years ago that found that, even in cases in which the latest safety technology had been implemented, the safety declined at every airport where traffic was increased above original design levels. A major flaw in the argument is making a comparison between a present-day situation and a similar situation 30 years past. The credited response will point out the dissimilarity between the current situation and the evidence cited by the author in order to formulate the conclusion that an increase in air traffic beyond original design specifications would lead to a decrease in safety.

A. No. The number of instances from which the inferences has been drawn is not at issue.

B. Yes. The answer notes that the argument's author has failed to consider that the latest technology might allow for more air traffic without decreasing safety, thereby identifying the flaw in comparing the latest technology from 30 years ago with current-day technology.

C. No. Whether council members are aware of the studies is not at issue.

D. No. The argument cites evidence from the past, so there is no absence of evidence.

E. No. The amount of decrease in safety is not at issue.

8. **C**   Reasoning

While it has been argued that morality must be completely a product of culture and is not grounded in a universal human nature, the philosopher concludes that this argument is wrong. The philosopher goes on to cite research that suggests that certain moral attitudes are shared across cultures. He then begins an analogy likening universal tastes, such as sweetness or saltiness, as the basis for many cuisines to our answer choices. The credited response will show that morality is not entirely the product of culture, but rather can be based on universally shared attitudes.

A. No. This answer states that moral codes come from specific instances, rather than universal attitudes.

B. No. While this answer might be tempting, it goes too far to say that most cultures resemble each other; as well, the phrase "in many respects" is vague.

C. Yes. This answer confirms that morality may come from universal attitudes.

D. No. The understanding of the basis of moral codes is in question, but it does not logically complete the statement.

E. No. Whether moral codes can be adapted is not at issue.

9. **A**   Flaw

The author concludes that having more plant species improves a prairie's ability to support plant life based on the evidence found in a recent field study in which the more plant species a plot had, the more vigorously the plants grew. The author fallaciously infers a causal relationship of a large number of plant species as the reason for the success of a prairie plot. The credited response will point out that the author has inferred a causal relationship where there is only a correlation.

A. Yes. The author credits the large number of plant species as the cause for a prairie plot's success without considering that it might be the prairie plot that allows for the wide variety of plant species.

B. No. The mechanism by which the productivity is increased is not at issue, while the causation is.

C. No. We do not know that only one prairie plot was used in the study.

D. No. There is no indication that the data is unlikely to be representative.

E. No. The argument does not confuse an increase in number with an increase in proportion.

10. C `Weaken`

The anthropologist describes an experiment in which two groups are taught to make prehistoric stone tools; one group is guided through verbal explanation paired with demonstration, while the second group received visual instruction only. Given that there was not a significant difference between members of the two teams in proficiency or speed, the anthropologist concludes that Neanderthals also could have created stone tools without language. The question asks to weaken the anthropologist's argument, so the credited response will show that the comparison between the subjects in the experiments and the Neanderthal tool-makers is not a valid comparison.

A. No. Additional evidence suggesting Neanderthal language is irrelevant to weakening the anthropologist's argument.

B. No. Regardless of whether one group was allowed to discuss the techniques while the other was not, both groups ended with approximately the same proficiency.

C. Yes. If the tools made by the subjects of the experiment were significantly easier to make, it brings into question the validity of the comparison.

D. No. Regardless of whether one group's teacher was more proficient than the other, both groups ended with approximately the same proficiency.

E. No. A comparison to Neanderthal-aged humans is not relevant to weakening the anthropologist's argument.

11. A `Inference`

The passage indicates that modest amounts of exercise can cause a dramatic improvement in cardiovascular health, and that, while more vigorous exercise is more effective, it is not necessary for improvement. The passage also states that one should exercise most (more than half) of the days of the week, and suggests the equivalent of a half hour of brisk walking on those days to fulfill the exercise requirement.

A. Yes. The argument states that one should work out most days of the week, and that a vigorous workout is more effective than less strenuous, so strenuous exercise most days of the week would fulfill the exercise requirements for improved cardiovascular health.

B. No. The passage states that exercising most days of the week produces dramatic improvement of cardiovascular health; it is unknown if exercising fewer days out of the week for a longer period of time would provide the same benefits.

C. No. No such comparison is made in the passage.

D. No. While the passage indicates that exercise can provide dramatic improvement in cardiovascular health, it does not imply that exercise is the only way to improve cardiovascular health.

E. No. The passage states that a dramatic improvement in cardiovascular health can be recognized through modest amounts of exercise most days of the week, but no requirement for strenuous exercise.

12. C `Strengthen`

The argument lays out the premise that a movie review should help readers determine whether they are apt to enjoy a film. It then states that a person who is likely to enjoy a certain movie will be more likely to realize that by reading a movie review by Sartore rather than Kelly, even though Sartore is the more likely of the two to give an unfavorable review. The argument thus concludes that Sartore is the superior movie critic. The credited response will strengthen the claim that Sartore is the better reviewer by showing that he better helps readers identify films that they are more likely to enjoy.

A. No. Technical knowledge of film is irrelevant to strengthening the conclusion.

B. No. This answer choice does nothing to strengthen claim that Sartore is the better reviewer.

C. Yes. By showing that readers are more likely to recognize a movie they will not enjoy by reading a review by Kelly, the answer shows that readers are better able to determine whether or not they are apt to enjoy a movie, in line with the premise.

D. No. The amount of enjoyment is not at issue, as the ability to determine whether one will enjoy a film or not is.

E. No. The overlap of reviews between Sartore and Kelly is irrelevant to strengthening the argument.

13. **D** Inference

The argument claims that specially bred aquarium fish with brilliant colors and unique body shapes are inferior to ordinary fish. As evidence, the author points to the fact that these fish are hampered by their elaborate tails and strangely shaped fins, which keep them from reaching food as quickly as the ordinary fish that compete with them for food, leaving specialty fish underfed. The credited response will support the claim that ordinary fish are at an advantage over specially bred aquarium fish.

A. No. There is no indication that special care must be given for specially bred fish to survive, only that they are at a disadvantage to ordinary fish.

B. No. There is no indication that connoisseurs are not interested in fish that are not brightly colored or uniquely shaped.

C. No. There is no evidence that a majority of specially bred fish are purchased by connoisseurs.

D. Yes. As ordinary fish are at an advantage over specially bred fish, and a couple of the disadvantages attributed to these fish are elaborate tails and strangely shaped fins, it can be presumed that ordinary fish do not have this disadvantage.

E. No. There is no information about the fish's reproductive abilities.

14. **D** Necessary Assumption

The ethicist concludes that it is not always true that if one ought to do something, then one can do that thing. As an example, the ethicist supposes that someone promises to meet a friend at a specific time, but is then unable to meet at the promised time due to traffic. The premise brings up a promise, while the conclusion shifts the conversation to what one ought to do. The credited response will close the gap between the idea of what one ought to do and what it means to promise something.

A. No. This answer presumes that what a person ought to do and what a person promises are interchangeable, which goes beyond the scope of the argument and is not an assumption necessary to the argument.

B. No. This answer focuses on the traffic jam that serves as an arbitrary example to help make the argument's point.

C.   No. This answer is simply a negation of the stated principle.

D.   Yes. If the obligation created by a promise were relieved by the fact that the promise could not be kept, then the conclusion that the principle "if one ought to do something, then one can" does not always hold true would no longer be possible (i.e., it is true that if one ought to do something, then one can). The assumption is necessary to the argument.

E.   No. Whether someone should have made the promise to begin with is outside the scope of the question.

15.   **E**   Principle Match

The passage states that producing leather and fur for clothing is labor-intensive, and as a result they are generally more expensive than other fashion materials. As well, fashion has trended away from leather and fur, causing a price drop while other more fashionable materials that are less expensive to produce have seen an increase in price. The argument outlines how demand drives prices. The credited response will offer a generalization that states that demand dictates price rather than the labor involved in creating materials alone.

A.   No. This answer choice presumes that what is most fashionable is what is most in demand.

B.   No. There is no mention of a material's need to be practical.

C.   No. There is no indication that less labor intensive fabrics are generally more fashionable.

D.   No. There is no mention of the impact of a manufactured good's appearance.

E.   Yes. This answer points out that demand (cultural trends) determines the price of materials.

16.   **A**   Strengthen

The argument's author concludes that the expected outbreak of tussock moths should not be countered because the moth is beneficial in areas of the forest where forest fire suppression has left the forest unnaturally crowded with immature trees. To logically complete the argument, the credited response will provide a reason that, even though the tussock moth is known to eat trees, steps should not be taken to prevent an expected outbreak.

A.   Yes. The argument states that the moths are helpful in areas where fire suppression measures have left the forest overgrown with immature trees. If a majority of the forest is overgrown with immature trees, then allowing the moth outbreak is beneficial in the majority of the forest and should not be countered.

B.   No. The maturity of the trees eaten by the moths is irrelevant.

C.   No. The proportion of mature to immature trees destroyed by forest fire is irrelevant.

D.   No. This answer choice implies only that steps must be taken if the outbreak is to be prevented, not provide a reason for why those steps should not be taken.

E.   No. The ability, or lack thereof, to counter the moths is irrelevant.

78

17.   E   **Resolve/ Explain**

The passage describes a city, Gastner, which has built a new highway that links some of its suburbs to its downtown area in order to relieve traffic congestion. Since then, though, the average commute for workers in downtown Gastner has increased. The credited response will help to explain how, even with the new highway, average commute time of downtown workers has increased.

A.   No. If most people working in Gastner's downtown commute from the suburbs, it should follow that the new highway would positively impact the drive time of workers.

B.   No. The size of the suburb is not at issue.

C.   No. The stoplight upgrades for other roads is irrelevant in explaining how the commute time for downtown workers has increased.

D.   No. If the road repair work began after the completion of the highway, one might conclude that it is the cause of additional delays, but since the repair is done in tandem with the building of the new highway, the answer does not work.

E.   Yes. If, since the new highway was opened, traffic on the surrounding roads in the downtown area has become more congested, then drivers may still save time on their commute via highway, only to be slowed down on another street that used not to have delays, thereby increasing the commute time.

18.   E   **Principle Strengthen**

The passage presents the point of view of an office worker who has two equally important projects, both incomplete. The worker decides that, since the first project is late already, all focus should be put into the second project in the hopes of finishing it prior to its deadline, even though it may not be possible to complete the second assignment in time. If the worker was to instead focus on the first project, there is no way the second would be completed in time to meet its deadline, meaning the worker believes that it is better to turn in one of the projects on time than neither of the projects. The credited response will provide a principle that establishes that completing one of the assignments on time is preferable to completing an assignment that is already late as long as both projects are equally important.

A.   No. This response does not address deadlines.

B.   No. This response does not address deadlines.

C.   No. The introduction of optional projects is irrelevant.

D.   No. Whether one worries about the failure to complete a project is irrelevant.

E.   Yes. The answer indicates that it is better to finish one project on time rather than try to finish a first, already late project that's not more important than the second project.

19.   E   **Necessary Assumption**

The science teacher begins with the premise that an abstract knowledge of science is not regularly useful for decision making in adult's daily lives. It follows that with the fact that the skills taught in secondary school should be useful for decision making in adult daily lives. The teacher then concludes that secondary school science courses should teach students to evaluate science-based arguments about practical issues instead of or in addition to abstract science. The conclusion introduces the topic of science-based arguments, whereas the premises state only that abstract science knowledge is not useful in decision making, and secondary school classes should teach classes that help with decision-making skills. Therefore, the science teacher assumes that evaluating science-based arguments will be useful in teaching decision-making skills to students.

A. No. While this answer choice boosts the premise that secondary schools should teach skills useful for decision making in adult lives, it does not address evaluating science-based arguments.

B. No. The science teacher states that abstract knowledge is not as useful for decision making, and secondary school should teach skills useful to decision making instead of or in addition to abstract science, implying that teaching abstract science is not as important as teaching students to evaluate science-based arguments.

C. No. No such comparison is made in the argument nor can be inferred from the premises.

D. No. Whether courses teaching the evaluation of science-based courses already exist is irrelevant to the argument.

E. Yes. This answer choice states that the ability to evaluate science-based arguments does help in decision making, thereby closing the gap between the premises and conclusion.

20. **D** Point at Issue

Lyle concludes that modernizing the language of premodern plays is valuable for teaching history because it makes plays accessible to students that otherwise would not be able to enjoy them, but concedes that some aesthetic value is lost in the process. Carl, on the other hand, claims that modernizing the language of certain plays is of no use for teaching because it keeps students from gaining deep knowledge of the past because modernizing the language prevents students from fully understanding what was said to premodern audiences. The credited response will show that Lyle and Carl disagree over whether modernizing the language of premodern plays has value in teaching history.

A. No. While Lyle might agree that changing the language changes the pedagogical value (lessening it aesthetically, but increasing its accessibility), Carl states that the new translations would have no pedagogical value rather than a difference in value.

B. No. While Lyle addresses a loss in aesthetic quality, Carl does not, so there is no way of knowing his opinion on such loss (be careful not to confuse aesthetic quality with teaching value).

C. No. Neither Lyle nor Carl addresses seeing the plays as originally performed.

D. Yes. Lyle and Carl disagree over the value that modernized plays have in teaching.

E. No. While Lyle addresses a loss in aesthetic quality, Carl does not.

21. **E** Parallel Flaw

The argument states that most types of soil contain clay, and almost all types of soil contain either sand or organic material. Based on this, the argument concludes that there must be at least one type of soil that contains both clay and sand and at least one type of soil that contains both clay and organic material. The argument overlooks that, even though there is a majority of types of soil that contain clay, there could still be no overlap between soil that contains clay and soil that contains sand or organic material. The credited response will offer an example of another argument that also presumes that, because a majority of X (soil) contains A (clay) and some X contains B (sand) or C (organic material) or both B and C, some X contains A and B and some X contains A and C. Each answer choice uses the example of pharmacies selling cosmetics, shampoo, and toothpaste. For these examples, X would be pharmacies, A would be cosmetics, B would be shampoo, and C would be toothpaste.

A. No. This answer says that a majority of X sells A, some X sells B or C or B and C, and if some X sells A and C, then some X sells A and B. This does not match the pattern of flawed reasoning described in the passage.

B. No. This answer says that a majority of X sells A because some X sells B or C or B and C, and some X sell A and B and some X sell A and C, which shifts the conclusion to most X sells A from some X sells A and B and some X sells A and C. This does not match the pattern of flawed reasoning described in the passage.

C. No. This answer says a majority of X sells A, and some X sells B or C or B and C, and therefore if there are not some X that sells A and C, then some X sells A and B. This does not match the pattern of flawed reasoning described in the passage.

D. No. This answer says some X that sells B also sells C and a majority of X sells A, so some X sells A and C and some X sells A and B. This does not match the pattern of flawed reasoning described in the passage.

E. Yes. This answer says that some X sells B or C or B and C, and a majority of X sells A, so some X sells A and B and some X sells A and C.

22. **A**   Flaw

The argument states that an environmental group studied the levels of toxic chemicals in the bodies of eleven volunteers and found that scientifically valid inferences could not be made, even though the results were interesting. The argument then goes to draw its conclusion, that the research proves that a regulation put in place in the 1970s was effective, based on inferences that it admits are not scientifically valid. The credited response will point out that the effectiveness of a regulation cannot be proven by scientifically invalid research findings.

A. Yes. This answer points out that it is inconsistent to state that valid inferences cannot be drawn from the findings, but then continues to draw a conclusion from invalid inferences.

B. No. Whether multiple chemicals produce the same result is irrelevant.

C. No. The conclusion does not state that the generalization is not true because it has not been proven false, but rather uses invalid inferences to draw its conclusion.

D. No. The argument does not include a causal flaw.

E. No. The rate at which effects become apparent is irrelevant.

23. **B**   Parallel

The argument states that a spy fails when he or she is caught, and generally spies reveal their methods only after being caught. Furthermore, a successful spy is never caught. The argument therefore concludes that the data about spy methods is skewed as it is made available only by unsuccessful spies who've been caught, meaning little is known about what makes a spy successful. In essence, the methods of successful spies are unknown because successful spies are never caught and therefore do not reveal their methods. The credited response will match the pattern of reasoning used, concluding that some information is skewed by the data available.

A. No. This does not match the reasoning that some data are skewed due to the information available.

B. Yes. Since people are unable to acknowledge unconscious motives, people are less likely to speak of them, thereby sharing only conscious motives. Thus, the information about motives is skewed by that fact that certain motives are never addressed.

C. No. This answer suggests that data is unclear due to unclear definitions, which is not a part of the passage's reasoning.

D. No. This answer indicates that a term should apply to a larger group than it generally does, which does not match the reasoning of the passage.

E. No. This answer indicates that data cannot be drawn from a situation that does not happen, while in the passage the spies that are not caught do exist.

24. **E** **Necessary Assumption**

The argument concludes that parents in families with underage children should be given additional votes to cast on behalf of these children because these families make up a significant portion of the population. Since only adults can vote, the premise continues, democratic lawmakers do not pay enough attention to families with underage children. This presumes that the additional votes given to parents of underage children will fairly represent the interests of these families, and the credited response will establish a principle that states that this method will allow for fair representation.

A. No. While this answer may be tempting, the conclusion that a group's interest should be directly proportional to the voters in that group still leaves out the underage (nonvoter) population.

B. No. The suggestion of a child being mature enough to decide wisely is irrelevant.

C. No. The suggestion of a child's best interests is irrelevant to the conclusion.

D. No. The argument is not about the fairness of lawmakers.

E. Yes. The answer states that the group of families with underage children can be fairly represented by only parents, a principle that is necessarily assumed for the conclusion to be considered valid.

25. **C** **Weaken**

The critic states that the *Gazette-Standard* has increased its editorial staff in order to combat factual errors. Compared to its competitor, however, the *Gazette-Standard* runs significantly more corrections acknowledging factual errors. The critic uses these facts to draw the conclusion that the increase in editorial staff did not work to combat factual errors. The credited response will offer something that indicates that the increase in editorial staff might actually be working or something that explains the apparent discrepancy in the increase in staff and higher number of corrections in comparison to the competitor.

A. No. The staff salaries are irrelevant to the critic's conclusion.

B. No. The length of time the newspapers have been in business is irrelevant to the critic's conclusion.

78

C. Yes. If the *Gazette-Standard* more actively follows up on reader complaints about errors than does its competitor, that would explain why there are more acknowledged errors in the *Gazette-Standard,* thereby weakening the critic's conclusion that hiring the additional editorial staff is not working.

D. No. If this was true, it would strengthen the author's conclusion that additional editorial staff has not combated factual errors.

E. No. A decrease in another department's staff is irrelevant to the critic's conclusion about the increase in the editorial staff.

Section 2: Games

Questions 1–5

This is a 1D in-out game: exactly three of seven workers will be chosen for a project, one of whom will be the leader. The inventory consists of seven workers—Q, R, S, T, V, W, and X— with X as an unrestricted element.

Rule 1 gives you a Q/R placeholder in the out column because they cannot both be the leader. Rule 3 gives you a W/R&V placeholder in the out column.

Your diagram should look like this:

Q, R, S, T, V, W, X

In	Out
_ _ _ _	$^Q/_R$ $^W/_{R+V}$ _ _
leader	

Clue 1: Q → Q = lead
Q ≠ lead → –Q
R → R = lead
R ≠ lead → –R

Clue 2: S → T
–T → –S

Clue 3: W → –R and –V
R or V → –W

1. **C**   Grab-a-Rule

A. No. This answer choice violates rule 3 because W is in but R is also in.

B. No. This answer choice violates rule 1 because Q is in but is not the leader.

C. Yes. This answer choice does not violate any rules.

D. No. This answer choice violates rule 2 because S is in but T is out.

E. No. This answer choice violates rule 3 because W is in but V is also in.

2. **D**   Specific

Make a new line in your diagram, and add the new information. If T is the leader, R and Q are out. If W is in, V is out. So, one of S or X must be in.

A.   No. Q must be out because T is the leader.

B.   No. Q must be out because T is the leader.

C.   No. R and V must be out because W is in.

D.   Yes. This must be true.

E.   No. V must be out because W is in.

3. **A**   General

Use deductions, prior work, and testing the answer choices to determine which answer choice allows V to be the leader. For V to be the leader, Q, R, and W must be out. Two options remain for the in column: VST or VTX.

A.   Yes. If Q and S are out, V could be project leader.

B.   No. This selection leaves S in, which would require T to be in.

C.   No. Only one of S or T can be out because Q, R, and W must be out.

D.   No. Only one of S or X can be out because Q, R, and W must be out.

E.   No. This selection leaves S in, which would require T to be in.

4. **E**   Specific

Make a new line in your diagram, and add the new information. If T is out, S is out. The placeholders therefore permit three options for the out column: TSRV, TSRW, or TSQW. In all three cases, X must be in.

A.   No. Q could be out.

B.   No. R could be out.

C.   No. V could be out.

D.   No. W could be out.

E.   Yes. If T is out, then X must be in.

5. **B**   General

Use deductions, prior work, and testing the answer choices to determine which answer choice completely determines the selection.

A.   No. The work for questions 2, 3, and 4 shows different arrangements with both Q and S out.

B. Yes. If T is out, S is out. W must also be out because if it were in, both R and V would be out, but then you would have too many elements out. So, QTSW is out, and therefore RVX is in, with R as the leader.

C. No. The work for questions 2 and 3 shows different arrangements with both Q and X out.

D. No. The work for questions 3 and 4 shows different arrangements with both R and W out.

E. No. The work for questions 2 and 4 shows different arrangements with both R and V out.

Questions 6–11

This is a 1D ordering game with an out column: exactly four of six students will be assigned a history project from four consecutive years. The inventory consists of six students—L, M, O R, T, and Y—with Y as an unrestricted element.

Combine rules 3 and 4. It is also worth looking at the OR block in rule 4 more closely: because of rule 1, the OR block, if assigned, must be assigned to 1921 and 1922. This implies that if the OR block is assigned, M must be out. So, you can make a new deduction: if M is assigned, T and R are out, and its contrapositive, if T or R is assigned, M is out. You can therefore add a placeholder to the out column: M/T&R. Also because of the OR block, R cannot be assigned to 1921 or to 1924 and T cannot be assigned to 1921 or to 1922. You can also deduce that O cannot be out: if it were, at least one of T or R would be assigned, which would require O to be assigned. L cannot be assigned to 1921 or to 1922 because if it were, T would be assigned to 1923, which would require the OR block to be assigned to 1921 and 1922.

Your diagram should look like this:

L, M, O, R, T, Y

1921	1922	1923	1924	Out
		L/T		— —

Clue 1: 1923 = L or T

Clue 2: M → M = 1921 or 1922
M ≠ 1921 and M ≠ 1922 → –M

Clue 3: T → R
–R → –T

Clue 4: R → [OR]
–[OR] → –R

6. **C** Grab-a-Rule

A. No. This answer choice violates rule 1 because R is assigned to 1923.

B. No. This answer choice violates rule 3 because T is assigned but R is out.

C. Yes. This answer choice does not violate any rules.

D. No. This answer choice violates rule 4 because O is not assigned to the year immediately prior to R's year.

E. No. This answer choice violates rule 2 because M is assigned to 1924.

7. **E** **General**

Use deductions, prior work, and testing the answer choices to determine which answer choice forces M to be assigned to 1922.

A. No. The work for question 10 shows that M could be out when L is assigned to 1924.

B. No. The work for questions 8 and 10 shows that M could be out when O is assigned to 1921.

C. No. If O is assigned to 1924, L could be assigned to 1923, Y could be assigned to 1922, and M could be assigned to 1921, with both R and T out.

D. No. The work for questions 8 and 10 shows that M could be out when T is assigned to 1923.

E. Yes. If Y is assigned to 1921, both R and T must be out because there is no room for the OR block at 1921 and 1922. Therefore, the only remaining spot for M is 1922.

8. **A** **Specific**

Make a new line in your diagram, and add the new information. If R is assigned, the OR block is assigned to 1921 and 1922. T or L must be 1923, so Y must be 1924. M must be out with one of T or L.

A. Yes. This could be true.

B. No. M must be out because the OR block is assigned to 1921 and 1922.

C. No. O must be assigned to 1921 because it must be assigned to the year immediately before R.

D. No. Y must be assigned to 1924 because T or L is 1923 and the OR block must be assigned to 1921 and 1922.

E. No. R must be assigned to 1922 because it must be assigned to the year immediately after O.

9. **D** **General**

This question asks how many students could be assigned to 1921. Looking at the deductions, L, R, and T cannot be assigned to 1921, and previous work confirms that M, O, and Y can be, so the credited response is (D).

10. **E** **Specific**

Make a new line in your diagram, and add the new information. If Y is out, M must also be out because both T and R cannot be out. Therefore, the OR block is assigned to 1921 and 1922, and T and L can be assigned to 1923 and 1924 in either order.

A. No. If L is out, M, O, and R are assigned, but you cannot both assign M and place the OR block.

B. No. If R is out, T is assigned, and if T is assigned, R must be assigned.

C. No. If T is out, M, O, and R are assigned, but you cannot both assign M and place the OR block.

D. No. If O is assigned to 1922, R is out (because you cannot place the OR block at 1922 and 1923), but if R is out, T is in, which would require R to be in.

E. Yes. This could be true.

11. **A**

This question asks who cannot be assigned to 1922. Looking at the deductions, L and T cannot be assigned to 1922, so the credited response is (A).

Questions 12–17

This is a 1D ordering game: six antiques will be ordered on six consecutive days. The inventory consists of six antiques—H, L, M, S, T, and V—with a 1:1 correspondence and no unrestricted elements.

Rule 4 gives you two options, each of which you can combine with rule 3 to create two distinct scenarios. In the first scenario, H or L must be first because S cannot be. You will also have to track the conditional in rule 2 because it may or may not apply.

In the second scenario, L must be first because S cannot be, so the only variation is that M and V can switch between third and fourth: all other elements are forced into place: S is second, T is fifth, and V is sixth. Because L is first, the conditional in rule 2 does not apply.

In both scenarios, S cannot be first, fifth, or sixth because of rules 1 and 3; M and V cannot be second or third because of rules 1 and 3; and T cannot be first or sixth because of rule 4. In the first scenario, H or L must be first, and in the second scenario, L must be first, so add an H/L placeholder to slot 1 in the diagram.

Your diagram should look like this:

H, L, M, S, T, V

Clue 1: S ≠ L
Clue 2: H – L → L – M
　　　　 M – L → L – H
Clue 3: S < M
　　　　　　 V
Clue 4: H – T – V
　　　　 or
　　　　 V – T – H

$\begin{array}{c}-V\\-M\\-S-T\end{array}$	$\begin{array}{c}-M\\-V\end{array}$			–S	–S
1	2	3	4	5	6
H/L					

12. **C**

A. No. This answer choice violates rule 2 because L is before M.

B. No. This answer choice violates rule 4 because T is after both H and V.

C. Yes. This answer choice does not violate any rules.

D. No. This answer choice violates rule 1 because S is first.

E. No. This answer choice violates rule 3 because V is before S.

13. **B**   General

Use deductions, prior work, and testing the answer choices to determine which answer choice could be true.

A. No. If T is second and L is third, H must be first and before L, but then M cannot fit before L.

B. Yes. The work for question 14 shows that this could be true.

C. No. From rule 3, S must be before M.

D. No. From rule 3, S must be before V.

E. No. From rule 3, S must be before M and V, but there is not enough room to put both M and V after S.

14. **D**   Specific

Make a new line in your diagram, and add the new information. T after both M and V is possible in the second scenario only.

A. No. In the second scenario, H is after T.

B. No. In the second scenario, T is after L.

C. No. In the second scenario, T is after S.

D. Yes. In the second scenario, M and V can be third and fourth in either order.

E. No. In the second scenario, S is after L.

15. **A**   General

This question asks which element cannot immediately precede V. From rule 4, T must be between H and V, so the credited response is (A).

16. **E**   General

Use deductions, prior work, and testing the answer choices to determine which answer choice could be true.

A. No. From the deductions, M cannot be second.

B. No. L could be second in the first scenario only, which would make H first. If H is first, it is before L, but then M must also be before L. You could add the deduction that L cannot be second to your diagram.

C. No. From the deductions, V cannot be second.

D. No. L could be third in the first scenario only, which would make H first. If H is first, it is before L, but then M must also be before L. If M is second, however, it is not after S. You could add the deduction that L cannot be third to your diagram.

E. Yes. The order could be LSVTMH.

78

17. **B** General

Use deductions, prior work, and testing the answer choices to determine which answer choice could be true.

A. No. From the deductions, S cannot be fifth.

B. Yes. The order could be LHTSMV or LHTSVM.

C. No. If L is fifth and M is sixth, H must be before L, but then M is not before L.

D. No. If T is third and L is fourth, H must be first and S must be second, but then M cannot fit before L.

E. No. From rule 4, T must be between H and V.

Questions 18–23

This is a 2D ordering game: six singers will audition one after the other, with the audition either recorded or not recorded. The inventory consists of six singers—K, L, T, W, Y, and Z—with no unrestricted elements. K's and L's auditions will be recorded, and the other four auditions will not be.

Combine rules 3 and 4. Several of the rules overlap, and a glance at the questions reveals that most of them are general, so chances are you can make several deductions.

From rule 1, K cannot be fourth; from rule 3, K cannot be first; and from rule 4, K cannot be sixth.

From rule 1, L cannot be fourth, and from rule 3, L cannot be first, but it also cannot be sixth: if it were, K would be fifth, and you would not be able to satisfy rule 4.

From rule 2, T cannot be fifth, and from combining rules 3 and 4, T cannot be first or second.

From combining rules 3 and 4, W cannot be fourth, fifth, or sixth, but is also cannot be third: if it were, you would not be able to satisfy all three of rules 1, 2, and 4.

From rule 2, Y cannot be fifth, and from rule 5, Y cannot be first, but it also cannot be second: if it were, you would not be able to satisfy all three of rules 1, 2, and 4.

From rule 2, Z cannot be fifth, and from rule 5, Z cannot be sixth.

Your diagram should look like this:

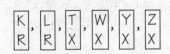

−T −K −Y −T −L	−Y −T	−W	−K −W −L		−K −L −Z −W
1	2	3	4	5	6

singer   W/Z .... K/L

recorded ⟨X⟩ .... ⟨X⟩ ...... R

Clue 1: 4 ≠ recorded

Clue 2: 5 ≠ recorded

Clue 3: W ⟨ K / L

Clue 4: K – T

Clue 5: Z – Y

18. D Grab-a-Rule

    A.   No. This answer choice violates rule 3 because W is after K.

    B.   No. This answer choice violates rule 5 because Z is after Y.

    C.   No. This answer choice violates rule 2 because the fifth audition is not recorded.

    D.   Yes. This answer choice does not violate any rules.

    E.   No. This answer choice violates rule 1 because the fourth audition is recorded.

19. C General

This question asks whose audition cannot be second. Looking at the deductions, T and Y cannot be second, so the credited response is (C).

20. C General

This question asks whose audition could be sixth. Looking at the deductions, either T or Y must be sixth, so the credited response is (C).

21. E Specific

Make a new line in your diagram, and add the new information. K cannot be fifth because T would not fit after it, so L must be fifth. The KY block cannot be second and third because both W and Z must come before it. The KY block must therefore be third and fourth, forcing T sixth. W and Z must be first and second in either order.

    A.   No. K must be third.

    B.   No. T must be sixth.

    C.   No. W must be first or second.

    D.   No. Y must be fourth.

    E.   Yes. Z could be first or second.

78

22. **B** `General`

Use deductions, prior work, and testing the answer choices to determine which answer choice could be true.

A. No. From the deductions, Y cannot be fifth.

B. Yes. The work for question 21 shows that Y could be fourth.

C. No. If Y were third, T would be fourth (because the fourth audition must be recorded, W cannot be fourth, and Z must come before Y), but then T would not be after K. You could add the deduction that Y cannot be third to your diagram.

D. No. From the deductions, Y cannot be second.

E. No. From the deductions, Y cannot be first.

23. **A** `Complex`

This question asks for a parallel rule, so consider the deductions of the rule you need to replace. Eliminate answer choices that are more or less restrictive than the rule you need to replace.

A. Yes. The original rule states that W is before K and L. By combining that rule with rule 4, you also know that W is before T. So, under the original set of rules, the only element that could come before W is Z. This answer choice paraphrases that deduction.

B. No. This rule is less restrictive because it allows K or L to come before W.

C. No. This rule is less restrictive because it allows K to come before W.

D. No. This rule is less restrictive because it allows K or L to come before W.

E. No. This rule is less restrictive because it allows K or L to come before W.

Section 3: Arguments 2

1. **A** `Flaw`

The argument concludes that most of the 5,000 people surveyed by the nonprofit organization agreed with the organization's position on a social issue. This conclusion is based on the results of the survey, which had only 300 respondents, 283 of whom agreed with the organization's position. The argument includes a surveys and samples flaw: it presumes that the opinions of the 300 respondents to the survey are representative of the opinions of the full group of 5,000, when in fact the 4,700 people who didn't respond might have had opposing opinions. The credited response to this Flaw question will correctly identify the surveys and samples flaw.

A. Yes. This answer matches the flaw of the argument: the argument bases its conclusion on data about a sample that is likely not representative of the population as a whole.

B. No. Whether the opinions of the respondents might vary if they were surveyed on different occasions is irrelevant.

C. No. The issue is not whether the responses to the survey correctly reflect the opinions of the respondents. The issue is whether the survey data correctly reflects the opinions of those who did not respond.

D. No. This answer is a reversal of the predicted answer. The argument uses data about a small portion of the population to support a conclusion about the broader population, while this answer suggests the argument used data about a large portion of the population to make a conclusion about a small portion of the population.

E. No. Whether the letter had an influence on the opinions of most of the recipients is irrelevant. Rather, the issue is whether the opinions of the respondents are representative of the opinions of the recipients as a whole.

2. **D**   Strengthen

The argument concludes that the fall of the Roman empire was probably caused by an unstable climate. The conclusion is based on tree-ring analysis that shows extreme climate fluctuations during the time of Rome's decline and fall, which must have led to reduced food production and therefore to difficulties ruling and defending the empire. The argument includes a causal flaw: it assumes that the decline and fall of the Roman empire was caused by climate fluctuations and not by some other cause. The credited response to this Strengthen question will provide evidence to support the idea that climate can affect the stability of an empire, or eliminate another possible factor that could have caused the decline.

A. No. This answer weakens the argument by providing evidence of reversed causation: the political decline caused the reduced food production, rather than the reduced food production causing the political decline, as suggested by the argument.

B. No. This answer weakens the argument by providing a counterexample: if the areas of greatest climatic instability did not have high levels of political unrest, then climate fluctuations are unlikely to be a major cause of political decline.

C. No. This answer weakens the film director's argument by providing an alternate possible cause of the political decline: poor farming practices that led to depleted soil.

D. Yes. This answer strengthens the argument by providing additional evidence that climate fluctuations affect political stability. If the Roman empire thrived during consistent favorable weather and also declined during climate fluctuations, this provides additional evidence of a causal relationship between climate and political stability.

E. No. This answer is irrelevant. The relative level of food production between the years 550 and 250 does not help determine whether climate fluctuation causes political decline.

3. **B**   Main Point

The argument follows a Solve pattern, which is a common pattern in Main Point questions: it notes that natural superstar salespeople are rare, but that many salespeople can perform like superstars if they have a good manager. The credited response to this Main Point question will provide the conclusion to this Solve pattern argument: companies should hire good managers so that many of their salespeople can perform like superstars.

A. No. This answer does not logically complete the argument. The argument does not discuss training or evaluation of salespeople.

78

B.   Yes. This answer matches the conclusion of the argument. Use the Why Test: does each of the other statements in the argument support the idea that companies should devote more effort to finding good managers than to finding natural superstars? Yes, because natural superstars are rare, but good managers help many salespeople perform like superstars. So, this answer matches the conclusion of the argument.

C.   No. This answer does not logically complete the conclusion of the argument. The argument does not discuss the number of salespeople for whom a manager should be responsible.

D.   No. This answer does not logically complete the conclusion of the argument. The argument does not suggest that promoting superstar salespeople to management positions would be helpful.

E.   No. This answer does not logically complete the conclusion of the argument. The argument does not discuss how much employees should be rewarded.

4.   **C**   Reasoning

This argument follows a disagree pattern, which is a common pattern in Reasoning questions: it claims that there are exceptions to the economists' general rule that demand for a commodity is inversely proportional to its price, because lace showed a drop in demand once its price dropped significantly. The credited response to this Reasoning question will match this pattern by identifying the role played in the argument by the second sentence: it is an example of a situation in which the general rule does apply (steel demand increased when steel became cheaper), as contrasted with the example of lace, which shows an exception to the general rule.

A.   No. This answer does not match the purpose of the example about steel, because the argument does not suggest that the example about steel is inadequate, but rather that it contrasts with the example about lace.

B.   No. This answer does not match the purpose of the example about steel, because the example about steel is not an exception to the generalization in the first sentence. Rather, the example about lace is an exception to the generalization in the first sentence.

C.   Yes. This answer matches the role of the example about steel: it an example of the generalization (about the rule of supply and demand) that the argument says does not hold in all cases (because the example about lace shows an exception to the rule).

D.   No. This answer is too extreme. The argument does not suggest that the economists' hypothesis is false; rather, it merely suggests that there are exceptions to the general rule.

E.   No. The argument does not suggest modifying the economists' general assumption; rather, it simply suggests that there are exceptions to the general rule.

5.   **E**   Flaw

The resident concludes that at least 60 percent of the town's houses have a problem that threatens their integrity. The conclusion is based on the premise that 30 percent of the town's houses have inadequate drainage and 30 percent also have structural defects. The residents' argument includes a percentages and numbers flaw: it presumes that the houses with inadequate drainage are different houses from the houses with structural defects, when in fact some or all of the town's houses could have both inadequate drainage and structural defects, making the portion of houses with integrity problems less than

60 percent. The credited response to this Flaw question will correctly identify the percentages and numbers flaw.

A. No. The total number of houses in the town does not affect the percentage of houses that have a structural defect.

B. No. The argument does not overlook the possibility that inadequate drainage can make a house unsafe; rather, the argument specifically assumes that inadequate drainage can threaten the houses' integrity.

C. No. Whether problems with houses are easy to fix is irrelevant. The issue is what portion of the houses have a problem that threatens their integrity.

D. No. The argument does not overlook the possibility that many houses do not have such problems. The argument concludes that at least 60 percent of the houses have a problem, which allows for the possibility that as many as 40 percent do not.

E. Yes. This answer matches the flaw of the argument: some houses may have both inadequate drainage and structural defects, making the total portion of houses with a problem less than 60 percent.

6. **B** `Principle Strengthen`

The argument follows a disagree pattern: it concludes that one should not regret the missed opportunities of youth, because if one had seized such an opportunity, one would miss out on some close personal relationships, which everyone deeply cherishes. The argument is flawed because it does not explain why gaining relationships you cherish outweighs the regret over missing opportunities. In other words, it assumes that if you gain something you cherish by missing an opportunity, then you should not regret missing the opportunity. The credited response to this Principle-Strengthen question will help the argument by providing a general rule that supports the idea that gaining something you cherish outweighs potential regret over missing an opportunity.

A. No. This answer is irrelevant; the argument is not concerned with having a greater number of close personal relationships. Rather, it is concerned with having fewer close personal relationships because of missed opportunities.

B. Yes. This answer directly connects the premise (bringing about close relationships that are cherished) to the conclusion (do not regret missing opportunities): if a decision helps bring about something that one cherishes, then one should not regret making the decision to miss the opportunities.

C. No. This answer contradicts the argument; the argument claims that one should not regret decisions that bring about close personal relationships, not decisions that had little effect on one's life.

D. No. This answer is irrelevant; the argument is not concerned with how deeply people cherish relationships. Rather, the argument is concerned with whether one should regret decisions if they helped bring about cherished close relationships.

E. No. This answer is irrelevant; the argument is not concerned with people who have few close personal relationships. Rather, the argument is concerned with whether one should regret decisions if they helped bring about cherished close relationships.

7. **E**

The passage states that the Kuna who live on their native islands generally have low blood pressure, while those who move to the mainland do not. The passage further states that Kuna who live on the islands drink cocoa high in flavonoids, while those on the mainland do not. Combining these facts supports the idea that cocoa high in flavonoids may help prevent high blood pressure. The credited response to this Inference question will be a statement that is supported by information extracted from the passage.

A. No. This answer is not supported by the statements in the passage. The passage does not provide any information about the availability of foods high in flavonoids on the mainland.

B. No. This answer is not supported by the statements in the passage. The passage does not provide any information about the beliefs of the Kuna with respect to the effect of cocoa on their health.

C. No. This answer contradicts the statements in the passage. If the Kuna have a genetic predisposition to low blood pressure, then those living on the mainland should generally have low blood pressure as well.

D. No. This answer is an unsupported comparison. The passage does not provide any information about the blood pressure of people living on the mainland other than the Kuna.

E. Yes. This answer is supported by the statements in the passage: if the Kuna living on their native islands drink cocoa high in flavonoids and have low blood pressure, while the Kuna living on the mainland do not drink cocoa high in flavonoids and do not have low blood pressure, then it follows that drinking cocoa high in flavonoids may help prevent high blood pressure.

8. **A**

Legal theorists hypothesize that jurors find scientific evidence more credible in a courtroom context because judges prescreen scientific evidence for credibility. The legal theorists' hypothesis contains a causal flaw: it assumes that the jurors' opinion is caused by prescreening by the judges and not by some other factor. The question stem asks for information that would be useful to evaluate the argument. The credited response will provide a question that, depending on how it were answered, would either help or hurt the hypothesis.

A. Yes. If jurors did not know that judges prescreen evidence, then the hypothesis that the prescreening causes the jurors to find the evidence more credible as a result would be incorrect. However, if the jurors were aware of the prescreening, this would be consistent with the legal theorists' hypothesis.

B. No. Whether some jurors are influenced by other jurors is irrelevant to the question of what caused the jurors to find the evidence more credible when presented at trial.

C. No. The manner in which the jurors determine the credibility of an expert witness is irrelevant to the question of what caused the jurors to find the evidence more credible when presented at trial.

D. No. Whether jurors draw on their own scientific knowledge does not help determine what caused the jurors to find the evidence more credible when presented at trial.

E. No. The manner in which the jurors respond to conflicting assessments is irrelevant to the question of what caused the jurors to find the evidence more credible when presented at trial.

9. E Resolve/Explain

The passage presents two apparently contradictory facts: word-of-mouth marketing works better when the booster admits to being part of a marketing campaign. Unexpectedly, this actually results in consumers being less skeptical toward word-of-mouth campaigns than they would be toward advertisements. The credited response to this Resolve/Explain question will help the passage by explaining why it makes sense that people would be less skeptical toward word-of-mouth campaigns even when the booster admits to being part of a marketing campaign.

A. No. This answer does not resolve the two facts. If word-of-mouth marketing campaigns are used for specialty products, this still does not explain why people are less skeptical of word-of-mouth marketing even when the booster admits to being part of a marketing campaign.

B. No. This answer does not resolve the two facts. Even if those who are most receptive to mass-media marketing are the least likely to be receptive to word-of-mouth marketing, this still does not explain why people are generally less skeptical of word-of-mouth marketing even when the booster admits to being part of a marketing campaign.

C. No. This answer does not resolve the two facts. The fact that most boosters are themselves recruited by word-of-mouth marketing does not help explain why people are less skeptical of word-of-mouth marketing even when the booster admits to being part of a marketing campaign.

D. No. This answer does not resolve the two facts. The cost of word-of-mouth campaigns does not help explain why people are less skeptical of word-of-mouth marketing even when the booster admits to being part of a marketing campaign.

E. Yes. If the fact that the booster admits being part of a marketing campaign helps foster a relaxed and in-depth discussion of the product, this would help explain why people are less skeptical toward word-of-mouth marketing.

10. D Sufficient Assumption

The argument concludes that if Whalley sticks with her current platform, she will win the election. The conclusion is based on the premise that if she sticks with her current platform, she will get a small percentage (less than half) of the under-50 vote, but a larger percentage (more than half) of the 50-and-over vote. The argument includes a percentages and statistics flaw, because it assumes there are an equal number of voters above and below 50, or that there are more 50-and-over voters than there are under-50 voters. The credited response to this Sufficient Assumption question will help the argument by providing an assumption that makes the conclusion valid: the argument assumes that the number of 50-and-over voters will be greater than or equal to the number of under-50 voters.

A. No. This answer is not sufficient to make the conclusion valid. The argument does not consider any potential changes Whalley could make to her platform.

B. No. This answer is not sufficient to make the conclusion valid. The argument does not consider which issues are of most concern to either voting group.

C. No. This answer is not sufficient to make the conclusion valid. The argument does not consider any actions that Whalley's opponent might take.

D. Yes. This answer connects the premises to the conclusion in a way that is sufficient to make the conclusion valid: the number of 50-and-over voters will be greater than or equal to the number of under-50 voters.

E. No. This answer is not sufficient to make the conclusion valid. The argument does not consider whether Whalley thinks any particular action will help her have a better chance to win.

11. **E** Principle Match

The passage describes two facts: Britain's economy grew fivefold from 1800 to 2000, but its per capita carbon dioxide emissions were the same in 1880 and in 2000. The credited response to this Principle-Match EXCEPT question will be a statement that contradicts the situation described in the passage, while the four incorrect responses will consist of principles that match the situation described in the passage.

A. No. This answer is compatible with the statements in the passage. If the economy grew but per capita emissions remained the same, then it would be possible that decreases of emissions never happen during periods of economic growth.

B. No. This answer is compatible with the statements in the passage. If countries without economic growth are unable to enact regulations restricting emissions, then it would be possible that countries with economic growth are able to do so, which would be consistent with Britain's stable emissions during a period of economic expansion.

C. No. This answer is compatible with the statements in the passage. If economic growth leads both to increased emissions and to new technologies that decrease emissions, then this would be consistent with Britain's stable emissions during a period of economic expansion.

D. No. This answer is compatible with the statements in the passage. If the emissions always increase proportionally to population, then per capital emissions would always remain constant, which would be consistent with the statements in the passage.

E. Yes. This answer directly contradicts the statements made in the passage. If economic growth always inevitably leads to increases in per capita emissions, then Britain's situation as described in the passage, in which its per capita emissions remained stable during a period of high economic growth, would be impossible.

12. **B** Necessary Assumption

The argument concludes that a lawyer's expert advice is always worth paying for when needing a will. The conclusion is based on the premises that, while consulting a lawyer is much more expensive than using software, a lawyer will tailor your will to your particular circumstances, just as you would pay your doctor for expert advice about an illness. The argument assumes that the lawyer's ability to tailor your will to your particular circumstances is worth paying for because it is superior to the ability of do-it-yourself software. In other words, the argument fails to consider that computer software might also be able to tailor your will to your particular circumstances. The credited response will help the argument by providing information that is necessary for the conclusion to be valid and will satisfy the Negation Test.

A. No. This response is not necessary in order for the conclusion to be valid. The level of expertise of a lawyer compared to that of a doctor is irrelevant to whether a lawyer's personal tailoring of a will is worth the fees.

B. Yes. In order for the lawyer's advice to be worth paying for, it is necessary that the lawyer's services be superior to the cheaper do-it-yourself software. If the do-it-yourself software cannot personally tailor a will as well as a lawyer, then this supports the idea that the lawyer's advice is worth the fees. Try negating this choice: if do-it-yourself software can tailor a will to personal circumstances as well as a lawyer, then there would be no reason to pay extra fees for a lawyer to do it.

C. No. It is not necessary that people be unsatisfied with the results of do-it-yourself software in order for it to be true that lawyers' fees are worth extra money.

D. No. Whether a majority of valid wills do not meet the needs of the persons for whom they were prepared is irrelevant to the question of whether a lawyer's advice is worth extra fees.

E. No. Whether an ill person can obtain a prescription without consulting a doctor is irrelevant to the question of whether a lawyer's advice is worth extra fees.

13. **A** | Parallel

The passage concludes that wherever there are people who are indifferent to their environment, nature's balance is harmed. The conclusion is based on the premises that wherever there are people who are indifferent to their environment, pollution is a problem, and that wherever there is pollution, nature's balance is harmed. The answer to this Parallel the Reasoning question will match the structure of the argument: if people are indifferent to their environment, then pollution is a problem, and then nature's balance is harmed; so, if people are indifferent to their environment, then nature's balance is harmed; in more simple terms, if X, then Y, then Z; so, if X, then Z.

A. Yes. This choice matches the structure of the argument: if a dessert has chocolate (X), then it is high in calories (Y), and then it is fattening (Z). So, if a dessert has chocolate (X), then it is fattening (Z).

B. No. This choice does not match the passage, because one of the conditional statements is reversed: if a dessert has chocolate (X), then it is high in calories (Y), and if a dessert is fattening (Z), then it is high in calories (Y). This does not match the pattern of the argument.

C. No. This choice does not match the passage: if a dessert is high in calories (X), then it has chocolate (Y), and if a dessert is high in calories (X), then it is fattening (Z). This does not match the pattern of the argument.

D. No. This choice does not match the passage, because the conclusion is reversed: if a dessert has chocolate (X), then it is high in calories (Y), and if a dessert is high in calories (Y), then it is fattening (Z); so, if a dessert is fattening (Z), then it has chocolate in it (X).

E. No. This choice does not match the passage, because it replaces one of the conditional statements with a quantity statement about "many desserts."

14. **C** | Reasoning

This argument follows a disagree pattern, which is a common pattern in Reasoning questions: it notes that there are many arguments that use principles of mechanism to prove the superiority of monarchy as a form of government, and that some believe that this means that mechanism must be in tension with democracy. The argument concludes that this belief is wrong, and that it is more likely that the many arguments in favor of monarchy were all wrong, and that mechanism is more compatible with democracy. The credited response to this Reasoning question will match this pattern by identifying the role played in the argument by the second sentence of the passage: it is the belief that the argument questions.

A. No. The second sentence of the passage is not a principle the argument seeks to establish; rather, it is a belief with which the argument disagrees.

B. No. The second sentence of the passage is not a phenomenon the argument seeks to explain; rather, it is a belief with which the argument disagrees.

C. Yes. This answer matches the role of the second sentence: it is a hypothesis that the rest of the argument challenges.

D. No. The second sentence of the passage is not evidence in support of the conclusion; rather, it is a belief with which the argument disagrees.

E. No. The second sentence of the passage is not the conclusion of the argument; rather, it is a belief with which the argument disagrees.

15. **C** Flaw

The argument concludes that Ishiko must be a good manager. The conclusion is based on the premises that being a good manager requires being able to defuse tense situations, which in turn requires understanding people, and that Ishiko is able to defuse tense situations. The argument contains a necessary versus sufficient factors flaw (or, in other words, a conditional statements flaw): it mistakes the idea that the ability to defuse tense situations is necessary to be a good manager with the idea that defusing sense situations is sufficient to make you a good manager. The credited response to this Flaw question will correctly identify the necessary versus sufficient factors flaw.

A. No. This answer describes a necessary versus sufficient factors flaw, but it does not match the problem in the argument. Understanding people is a required factor in the argument, but the argument does not confuse this point; rather, it confuses whether defusing tense situations is necessary or sufficient.

B. No. The argument does not involve correlation and causation.

C. Yes. This answer matches the flaw of the argument: the argument confuses a necessary factor for being a good manager (being able to defuse tense situations) with a factor that is sufficient to guarantee being a good manager.

D. No. Whether different managers defuse tense situations in different ways is irrelevant to whether being able to defuse tense situations is sufficient to guarantee being a good manager.

E. No. This answer choice is a reversal of the pattern of the argument: the answer says the argument concludes that because all good managers have a certain quality (defusing tense situations), then Ishiko must have that quality (defusing tense situations). The argument, on the other hand, concludes that because Ishiko has the required quality (defusing tense situations), that she must be a good manager.

16. **B** Resolve/ Explain

The passage presents two apparently contradictory facts: babblers defend their group with loud barks, but the loud barks make the predators aware of their location, which would otherwise be well camouflaged. The credited response to this Resolve/Explain question will help the passage by explaining why it makes sense that the birds would use loud barks to defend their group, even though it reveals their location.

A. No. This answer does not resolve the two facts. While the fact that the babblers can fly faster than their predators would help explain why they are safe, it doesn't explain why they would bark loudly for defense when they are sitting still and hidden.

B. Yes. If the predators are intimidated by large numbers of babblers, then this would explain why they would all make loud barking noises in order to show that a large group is present.

C. No. This answer does not resolve the two facts. Whether more than one type of predator exists that preys on babblers does not help explain why they bark loudly for defense.

D. No. This answer does not resolve the two facts. If the predators have weak hearing, this still would not explain why they would make barking noises that would reveal their location.

E. No. This answer does not resolve the two facts. Whether other animals near the babblers are also preyed on by the predators does not help explain why the babblers bark loudly for defense.

17. **A** **Reasoning**

This argument concludes that there is reason to believe that life may exist on Europa. The conclusion is based on the premises that a photograph shows that the icy surface of Europa appears to have buckled because of turbulent water beneath the ice, that the buckled ice indicates the existence of a warm sea beneath the ice, and that scientists consider such a warm sea to be a primary factor in the early development of life. The credited response to this Reasoning question will match this pattern by identifying the role played in the argument by the second sentence: it is a claim supported by the premise that the ice buckled because of turbulent water, but it is also a premise that supports the conclusion that there is reason to believe there may be life on Europa.

A. Yes. This answer matches the role of the second sentence: it is a subsidiary conclusion (because it is supported by the premise that the ice buckled because of turbulent water beneath it), and it is also used to support the primary conclusion (that there is reason to believe there may be life on Europa).

B. No. The second sentence is not the overall conclusion of the argument. The last sentence is the conclusion. Use the Why Test: why is there reason to believe there may be life on Europa? Because there is a warm sea beneath the icy surface. Therefore, the last sentence is the primary conclusion.

C. No. This answer reverses the roles of the statement: it is used to support a theory, not discredit a theory.

D. No. The second sentence of the passage is not the only consideration: the conclusion is supported by multiple premises.

E. No. The second sentence is not presented as support for a subsidiary conclusion; it is itself a subsidiary conclusion, because it is supported by the premise that the ice buckled because of a turbulent sea beneath, and it is also used to support the primary conclusion (that there is reason to believe there may be life on Europa).

18. **C** **Main Point**

The argument follows a disagree pattern, which is a common reasoning pattern for Main Point questions. The argument notes that the most enjoyable consumer experience is feeling lucky, and that retailers use this fact to their advantage. The argument concludes that retailers are wrong to use advertised price cuts too often, because they cut into margins and hurt customer loyalty. The credited response to this Main Point question will match the argument's conclusion: retailers too often resort to using advertised price cuts to promote their wares.

A. No. This answer is a premise. Use the Why Test: does each of the other statements in the argument support the idea that the most emotional experience is feeling lucky? The second sentence of the argument (that retailers too often resort to advertised price cuts) does not. Therefore, this answer does not match the argument's conclusion.

B. No. This answer is a premise. Use the Why Test: does each of the other statements in the argument support the idea that retailers use the fact that customers enjoy feeling lucky to their advantage? The rest of the second sentence of the argument (that retailers too often resort to advertised price cuts) does not. Therefore, this answer does not match the argument's conclusion.

C. Yes. This answer matches the conclusion of the argument. Use the Why Test: does each of the other statements in the argument support the idea that retailers too often resort to using advertised price cuts? Yes. So, this answer matches the conclusion of the argument.

D. No. This answer is a premise. Use the Why Test: does each of the other statements in the argument support the idea that using advertised price cuts reduces profit margins and undermines customer loyalty? The rest of second sentence of the argument (that retailers too often resort to advertised price cuts) does not. Therefore, this answer does not match the argument's conclusion.

E. No. This answer is too strong; it goes beyond the conclusion of the argument. While the argument does conclude that one way of making customers feel lucky (using advertised price cuts to promote their wares) is overused, this does not mean that making customers feel lucky is usually not a good formula for success.

19. **B** Reasoning

This argument follows a solve pattern, which is a common pattern in Reasoning questions: it notes that in order to keep the legal system just, it is important to guarantee that lawbreaking does not give lawbreakers an unfair advantage. The argument concludes that this problem can be solved by ensuring that the criminal justice system attempt to make criminal wrongdoing remain profitless. The credited response to this Reasoning question will match this pattern by identifying the role played in the argument by the first sentence: it is a general rule, or principle, on which the conclusion (that the justice system should attempt to make wrongdoing profitless) is based.

A. No. This answer is too strong: the first sentence provides a condition (guaranteeing that lawbreakers do not get an unfair advantage) that is described as a necessary factor in order for the legal system to remain just, but it is not described as a factor that is by itself enough to ensure that the legal system remains just.

B. Yes. This answer matches the role of the first sentence: it is a principle (general rule) that is offered as support for the conclusion.

C. No. This answer does not match the role played in the argument by the first sentence: the first sentence is not a conclusion; rather, it provides a general rule that supports the solution provided in the conclusion (the second sentence).

D. No. This answer is too strong: the argument does not state that the goal of making wrongdoing profitless is the most important goal of criminal punishment.

E. No. This answer does not match the argument: the argument does not mention any claim that criminal punishment has other goals, or try to refute any claim.

20. **C** `Sufficient Assumption`

The argument notes that the company president says that procedural changes happened before she or Yeung was told about them. However, Grimes says that the contract requires that either the company president or a lawyer in the company's legal department must be informed about changes before they happen. The argument concludes that unless Grimes or the company president was incorrect, the contract was violated. The argument is flawed because it does not state whether any lawyer in the company's legal department was notified. The credited response to this Sufficient Assumption question will help the argument by providing an assumption that makes the conclusion valid: the argument assumes that none of the lawyers in the company's legal department was notified before the procedural changes happened.

A. No. This answer is not sufficient to make the conclusion valid. Even if Yeung is a lawyer in the company's legal department, there still could be another lawyer in the company's legal department that was notified, in which case the contract was not violated.

B. No. This answer is not sufficient to make the conclusion valid. Even if Grimes and Yeung were not told about the procedural changes before they happened, there still could be a lawyer in the company's legal department that was notified, in which case the contract was not violated.

C. Yes. This answer connects the premises to the conclusion in a way that is sufficient to make the conclusion valid: if no lawyer in the company's legal department was told about the procedural changes before they happened, then the contract was definitely violated.

D. No. This answer is not sufficient to make the conclusion valid. The correct response needs to be sufficient prove that the contract was violated; this assumption describes a condition in which the contract would not be violated.

E. No. This answer is not sufficient to make the conclusion valid. This answer is similar in its wording to the credited response, but it does not actually state whether any lawyer was actually notified. The credited response must prove that the conclusion is valid—that the contract was violated.

21. **A** `Strengthen`

The journalist concludes that limiting one's intake of foods rich in iron should reduce the chance of contracting Parkinson's disease. The journalist's conclusion is based on the premise that people whose diets contain a large amount of iron are more likely to develop Parkinson's disease than those whose diets contain a lower amount. The argument's conclusion is based on a causal flaw: it assumes that there is not another factor other than a diet high in iron that might be the actual cause of Parkinson's disease. The credited response to this Strengthen question will help the journalist's conclusion by supporting the idea that a diet high in iron, and not some other factor, is a cause of Parkinson's disease.

A. Yes. If those who have a predisposition to Parkinson's disease do not have more iron in their diets than those without such a predisposition, this eliminates a possible other factor (genetic predisposition) that could have instead been the cause of the higher incidence of Parkinson's disease.

B. No. This answer weakens the journalist's argument: if a diet with iron-rich vegetables does not increase the incidence of Parkinson's disease, then this means that diets high in iron are unlikely to be a cause of Parkinson's disease.

C. No. This answer is irrelevant. The amount of iron required by the diets of adults or children does not affect the likelihood that diets high in iron cause Parkinson's disease.

D. No. This answer is irrelevant. The fact that the iron in some foods is more easily absorbed than the iron in other foods does not affect the likelihood that diets high in iron cause Parkinson's disease.

E. No. This answer is irrelevant. The fact that the amount of iron consumed by people declines as they age does not affect the likelihood that diets high in iron cause Parkinson's disease.

22. **E** [Inference]

The Chairperson states that Maples (the Modern Party Candidate) would be a better mayor than Tannett (a member of the Traditionalist Party) and that every member of the Modern Party is better qualified to be mayor than any member of the Traditionalist Party. The question asks which answer must be false on the basis of the Chairperson's statements. The credited response to this inference EXCEPT question will be a statement that is contradicted by information extracted from the passage.

A. No. This answer does not contradict the statements in the passage: the passage does not discuss seniority of members or past party memberships, so it could be true, based on the statements in the passage, that Maples is a member of the Modern Party and previously a member of the Traditionalist Party.

B. No. This answer does not contradict the statements in the passage: the passage does not discuss the relative strengths of Traditionalist Party members against one another, so it could be true, based on the statements in the passage, that Tannett would be better than any other member of the Traditionalist Party.

C. No. This answer does not contradict the statements in the passage: the passage does not discuss the beliefs of local residents, so it could be true, based on the statements in the passage, that few residents of Riverdale believe Maples would be a better mayor than Tannett.

D. No. This answer does not contradict the statements in the passage: the passage does not discuss the relative strengths of Modern Party members against one another, so it could be true, based on the statements in the passage, that Maples would be the worst mayor of all the Modern Party members.

E. Yes. This answer contradicts the passage: if any Modern Party member is better qualified to be mayor than any Traditionalist Party Member, then Tannett (a Traditionalist Party member) cannot possibly be better qualified than the Modern Party Chairperson (a Modern Party member).

23. **C** [Evaluate]

The businessperson concludes that his or her tardiness to the meeting was caused by the closure of the parking area in front of the building. The conclusion is based on the premises that if the maintenance had been done a different day, he or she would have arrived on time, because it took 15 minutes to find a parking space once he or she discovered that the parking lot was not available. The argument contains a causal flaw: it assumes that the businessperson's tardiness would not have been delayed for some other reason even if the parking area were open. The question stem asks for information that would be useful to evaluate the argument. The credited response will provide information that would either help or hurt the argument's conclusion.

A. No. The reason for the maintenance on the parking area is irrelevant to the question of whether the maintenance was the only factor that caused the businessperson's tardiness.

B. No. Whether other members were late on the same day does not affect the chances that the maintenance was the only factor that caused the businessperson's tardiness on that day.

C. Yes. If the parking patterns on days when the parking area is open would also lead to 15-minute delays, then this would weaken the businessperson's conclusion. However, if the parking patterns generally do not lead to delays, then this would strengthen the businessperson's conclusion.

D. No. Whether the businessperson has a tendency to be late to meetings does not affect the chances that the maintenance was the only factor that caused the businessperson's tardiness on that day.

E. No. Whether it was particularly important to arrive on time does not affect the chances that the maintenance was the only factor that caused the businessperson's tardiness on that day.

24. E   Inference

The passage presents a series of conditional statements. First, if a work is to be rightly thought of as world literature, then it must be received and interpreted within the writer's national tradition and within external national traditions; and second, if a work is to count as being interpreted within a national tradition, then authors from a particular national tradition must use a work in at least one of three specific ways, then the work counts as being interpreted within a national tradition. The question asks which answer is most strongly supported by the statements in the passage. The credited response to this inference question will be a statement that is supported by information extracted from the passage.

A. No. This answer is not supported by the statements in the passage. The passage does not mention any relationship between being well received by a writer's national tradition and by an external national tradition.

B. No. This answer is not supported by the statements in the passage. The passage does not compare how much a work offers to readers within different national traditions.

C. No. This answer is not supported by the statements in the passage. The passage does not discuss how meaningful a work would be to readers within different national traditions.

D. No. This answer is not supported by the statements in the passage. The passage does not discuss what a work of world literature might be influenced by; rather, it discusses what works the work of modern literature might itself influence.

E. Yes. This answer matches the contrapositive of the first statement in the passage: if a work affects the development of only one national tradition, then it cannot be received and interpreted both within the writer's own national tradition and within external national traditions; and therefore, the work cannot be rightly thought of as world literature.

25. **D** **Parallel Flaw**

The argument concludes that there must be more sociology majors than psychology majors enrolled in Intro to Social Psychology. The conclusion is based on the premise that most of the sociology majors are taking Intro to Social Psychology, but most of the psychology majors are not. This argument is based on a statistics flaw: it assumes that the number of psychology and sociology majors is equal, when in fact there could be many more psychology majors at the school than sociology majors, in which case there might be more sociology majors enrolled in the class than psychology majors. The credited response to this Parallel Flaw question will match the pattern and strength of language of the argument's flaw, because a majority of one group but a minority of another group are members of another group, there must be more members from the former group than the latter.

A. No. The conclusion of this answer choice (the museum owns "few if any" of the displayed paintings) does not match the pattern of the argument's conclusion (there must be more sociology majors than psychology majors).

B. No. This answer choice does not match the pattern of the original argument. The original argument involves portions of two groups that make up a third group, while this answer choice discusses two different subsets of one group.

C. No. This answer choice does not match the pattern of the original argument: it assumes that one subset of a group (the trees in the city arboretum) is representative of the group as a whole (all the trees in the area), while the original argument assumes that two separate groups are similar in size.

D. Yes. This answer matches the statistics flaw in the original argument: most of one group (veggies at Valley Food) is part of a group (organic food), but less than half of another group (veggies at Jumbo Supermarket) is part of that group (organic food), so there must actually be more of the first group.

E. No. This answer choice reverses the pattern of the argument. This answer states that most of the houses for sale, but less than half of the condos for sale, are displayed in photos on the website, so there must be more houses than condos for sale. However, in order to match the pattern of the argument, this answer would need to conclude that more than half of the photos on the website are photos of houses for sale.

26. **D** **Weaken**

The film director concludes that there is little risk that the studio will not recover the very high production costs of the latest film. The film director's conclusion is based on the premise that even if the film is unpopular, much of its costs are being used to develop innovative special-effects technology that could be used in future films. The argument is flawed because it assumes that the innovative special-effects technology will be used in future films and will save enough money to recover the high production costs. In other words, the argument overlooks the possibility that the innovative special-effects technology might not be used in the future or might not make enough money to recover the costs. The credited response to this Weaken question will hurt the argument by providing evidence that there is a risk that the film studio will not recover the production costs of the film.

A. No. This answer strengthens the argument. The fact that the studio owns and could control the use of the technology in future films increases the likelihood that the film studio could generate revenue from the technology sufficient to recover the production costs.

78

B. No. This answer strengthens the argument. The fact that the films that introduce innovative special-effects technologies generally draw large audiences of people increases the likelihood that the film studio would be able to recover its production costs through ticket sales.

C. No. This answer does not weaken the argument. The fact that ticket sales are unlikely to completely offset the costs does not change the fact that the costs might still be recovered in the future through the use of the new innovative special-effects technology.

D. Yes. This choice hurts the argument by pointing out that if the film is unpopular, then it is likely that the innovative special-effects technologies would be abandoned, thereby making the film studio unlikely to recover the film's production costs.

E. No. This answer strengthens the argument. The fact that the new special-effects technology would lower the production costs of other future films increases the likelihood that the film studio could generate savings from the technology sufficient to recover the production costs.

Section 4: Reading Comprehension

Questions 1–6

Passage A

The first paragraph describes what jury nullification is and some reasons that juries might employ it. The author then outlines three big problems with jury nullification: that we don't know how often it's used, that juries often do not have enough information to make a good nullification decision, and that, unlike the legislature, jurors are unelected and unaccountable. The Bottom Line of passage A is that jury nullification is problematic because the place for disagreement about laws is in public.

Passage B

The first paragraph characterizes jury nullification as a check on overzealous police and prosecutors. The second paragraph points out that jury nullification assists the legislature by helping tailor the broad language of laws to a particular defendant, and the third paragraph argues that jury nullification further helps legislatures by shedding light on problematic laws. The final paragraph notes that improper instances of nullification are likely to be extremely uncommon. The Bottom Line of passage B is that jury nullification is useful because it provides a check on law enforcement and aids the legislature.

1. **E**   Extract
Infer

The question is asking for a justification of jury nullification. The correct answer will be the statement that is best supported by evidence within passage B.

A. No. The passage never mentions complicated laws.

B. No. The passage never mentions outdated laws.

C. No. The passage never mentions laws that are too permissive.

78

D.   No. The passage never mentions laws that are too intrusive.

E.   Yes. The second paragraph of passage B discusses that jury nullification helps the legislature because legislatures have to create general laws because they cannot foresee every variation in circumstance that may occur.

2.   **D**   [Big Picture]

The question is asking how passage B's attitude towards juries differs from the attitude of passage A. Passage A expresses concern about jury nullification, while passage B praises it.

A.   No. Passage B is more trusting of juries.

B.   No. Neither passage discusses the capacity of juries to understand laws.

C.   No. While passage A expresses concern about the fact that juries are not required to provide their reasoning, passage B does not an express an opinion about this fact.

D.   Yes. Passage A expresses concern about the use of jury nullification, and passage B discusses that jury nullification happens only in compelling situations and can serve as a check on law enforcement and an aid to the legislature.

E.   No. Neither passage expresses disappointment in juries.

3.   **C**   [RC Reasoning]

The question is asking for a relationship that is analogous to that between passage A and passage B. Passage A expresses concerns about jury nullification, and passage B highlights positive aspects of jury nullification, so the correct answer should reflect that contrasting relationship.

A.   No. While passage A expresses concern, "Perversion of Justice" is excessively strong language. Passage B is solidly in favor of jury nullification, rather than discussing pros and cons.

B.   No. While passage A does point out three issues, there is nothing unexpected in the benefits discussed in passage B.

C.   Yes. Passage A discusses problems with jury nullification, and passage B discusses how juries assist the legislature through jury nullification.

D.   No. Passage A does not discuss history, and passage B does not focus on motives.

E.   No. Passage A does not go so far as to say that jury nullification should be banned, and passage B does not argue that its use is inevitable.

4.   **D**   [Extract Infer]

The question is asking what the authors of the two passages disagree about. The correct answer will be the statement best supported by evidence in both passages.

A.   No. While passage A mentions that juries are not to required to explain their verdicts, neither passage advocates that they should or shouldn't be more forthcoming.

B.   No. Both authors would agree with this statement. Passage A argues that revisions of laws should be scrutinized and debated in public, and passage B argues that jury nullification can serve to indicate to the legislature that a law may be flawed.

C.   No. Neither passage argues that elected officials are biased in their decision making.

D.   Yes. Passage A argues that it is up to the legislature to pass laws and judges to interpret them, not juries. Passage B argues that juries assist the legislature by deciding whether a law should be applied to a particular defendant.

E.   No. Passage A does not mention the discretion of police and prosecutors.

5.   **E**   RC Reasoning

The question is asking for something that the author of passage A would say to weaken passage B's assertion that it's okay for juries to nullify when they view cases as too trivial. The correct answer will be the statement that is best supported by evidence in passage A.

A.   No. Passage A does not mention prosecutors, so no inference can be made about what the author of passage A would say about them.

B.   No. Passage A does not mention prosecutors, so no inference can be made about what the author of passage A would say about them.

C.   No. Passage A does not discuss the likelihood of juries agreeing.

D.   No. Passage A does not discuss juror expertise.

E.   Yes. The third paragraph of passage A discusses that juries often have insufficient evidence to make a reasoned nullification decision.

6.   **A**   Big Picture

The correct answer will reflect the Bottom Line of each passage.

A.   Yes. This answer choice reflects passage A's criticism of jury nullification and passage B's discussion of the benefits of jury nullification.

B.   No. Passage B does not discuss any improvements to jury nullification.

C.   No. Passage A does not include any evidence; it merely makes claims. Passage B does not offer a hypothesis.

D.   No. While passage A does point out potential problems with jury nullification, passage B does not think there are problems and offers no solutions.

E.   No. Passage A does not raise a question; rather, it points out potential problems with a practice.

Questions 7–14

The main point of the first paragraph is that while most sociohistorical interpretations of art view a body of work as a dominant class imposing its ideals, these interpretations do not clarify the different ways this may happen. The main point of the second paragraph is to enumerate the two ways elites commission art: for display and to express ideals. The main point of the third paragraph is to point out issues with sociohistorical critics' focus on art as an expression of elites' ideals, namely that elites do not necessarily have recognizable identities and that there is a possibility that artists subvert the ideals of their patrons. The main point of the fourth paragraph is that elites do not necessarily have tastes that tend to produce enduring art and therefore talented artists sometimes had to find patronage from more eccentric individuals. The main point of the final paragraph is to discuss the psychological contortions that some sociohistorical critics have to do in order to account for art that went against the grain of elite values. The Bottom Line of the passage is that sociohistorical interpretations of art do not always account for all factors.

7. **B**   **Big Picture**

Use your Bottom Line of the passage to help you to evaluate the choices. The correct answer will describe the main idea of the passage.

A.   No. While this is mentioned in the passage, it is too narrow and is not the overall main idea.

B.   Yes. This answer accurately paraphrases the Bottom Line.

C.   No. The passage makes no such comparison.

D.   No. While this is mentioned in the passage, it is too narrow and is not the overall main idea.

E.   No. While this is mentioned in the passage, it is too narrow and is not the overall main idea.

8. **C**   **Extract Infer**

The question is asking what the phrase "something for display" suggests about a piece of art. The passage gives an example of someone commissioning a famous architect to design his house in order to reflect great credit on his taste, even if the house isn't functional. The correct answer will be the statement best supported by evidence in the passage.

A.   No. The passage mentions political elites, but not political statements.

B.   No. The passage doesn't mention attracting customers.

C.   Yes. This is directly supported by the example of hiring a famous architect to design a house to reflect good taste.

D.   No. The passage doesn't mention reflecting the artist's broader body of work.

E.   No. The passage doesn't mention personal satisfaction.

9. **E**   **Extract Infer**

The question is asking how Matthew Arnold feels about the aristocratic and middle classes. In the fourth paragraph, the author states that Arnold identified them as Barbarians and Philistines, respectively. The correct answer will be on the negative end of the attitude spectrum and will encompass these two adjectives.

A.   No. This answer is too positive. Arnold expresses a negative opinion.

B.   No. This answer is too positive. Arnold expresses a negative opinion.

C.   No. This answer is too neutral. Arnold expresses a negative opinion.

D.   No. There is no indication that the nineteenth-century English elites failed to live up to some expectation that Arnold had for them.

E.   Yes. This captures Arnold's description of the elites as Barbarians and Philistines.

10. D `Extract Fact`

Four of these answer choices will be explicitly mentioned in the passage as complications for the socio-historical interpretation and the correct answer will not be mentioned.

A. No. This is explicitly mentioned in lines 29–30.

B. No. This is explicitly mentioned in lines 43–44.

C. No. This is explicitly mentioned in lines 34–36.

D. Yes. Reselling is never mentioned in the passage.

E. No. This is explicitly mentioned in lines 46–47.

11. C `Extract Infer`

The question is asking for a statement that follows from Taruskin's position as it is described by the passage. The correct answer will be supported by evidence from the passage.

A. No. Matthew Arnold makes an argument about more talented artists, but Taruskin does not.

B. No. Taruskin does not mention contemporary artists.

C. Yes. In the first paragraph, Taruskin states that a defining attribute of high art is that it's produced by and for elites, and in the fifth paragraph, the author argues that Taruskin must claim that art that overtly goes against the grain of elite values actually embodies those ideals in hidden ways.

D. No. The passage does not compare artists who are members of the elites to those who are commissioned by elites.

E. No. Matthew Arnold makes an argument about more talented artists, but Taruskin does not.

12. B `Structure`

The question is asking how the third paragraph functions in the passage. The third paragraph points out issues with sociohistorical critics' focus on art as an expression of elites' ideals, namely that elites do not necessarily have recognizable identities and that there is a possibility that artists subvert the ideals of their patrons.

A. No. This paragraph is consistent with the author's argument in the first paragraph that sociohistorical interpretations fail to clarify the different ways that art was produced by and for the elites.

B. Yes. The third paragraph points out that in order for the analysis of critics like Taruskin, first outlined in the first paragraph, to work, the elites have to have a recognizable identity and one must be able to eliminate the possibility that artists subverted the will of their patrons.

C. No. The discussion in the third paragraph expands upon the second paragraph.

D. No. There is no conclusion reached in the second paragraph.

E. No. The third paragraph raises issues, but it does not draw a definitive conclusion.

13. **A**   Structure

The question is asking why the author mentions "Raphael's frescoes in the Vatican apartments." In the second paragraph, the frescoes are introduced as an example of a work that expressed and mirrored one's ideals and way of life.

A. Yes. This accurately paraphrases the discussion in the second paragraph.

B. No. While the frescoes are in the Vatican, the passage does not discuss the influence of religion.

C. No. This answer choice is extreme and is unsupported. While the passage says that sociohistorical interpreters prefer to analyze this type of relationship, the passage does not argue that it is the most common type of relationship.

D. No. An artist subverting the ideals of a patron is not mentioned until the third paragraph.

E. No. The frescoes are mentioned as an example of the relationship that is preferred by sociohistorical critics.

14. **E**   Extract
             Infer

The question is asking for Matthew Arnold's perspective on the primary reason people in the middle class became patrons of the arts. In the fourth paragraph, Arnold described the middle class as "Philistines, obsessed with respectability." The correct answer will be supported by evidence from the text.

A. No. The importance of the arts to society does not relate to respectability.

B. No. The passage does not indicate that the middle class would go against the interests of the aristocracy.

C. No. The passage does not tie patronage to profits.

D. No. The passage does not discuss the quality of the art sponsored by the middle class.

E. Yes. The passage says that Arnold believes that members of the middle class were obsessed with respectability.

Questions 15–22

The first paragraph introduces the discovery of abstract symbols on clay tablets from around 3000 B.C. as well as clay tokens from around 4000 B.C. that had largely been ignored by archeologists before Denise Schmandt-Besserat. The second paragraph describes the clay tokens in further detail and presents Schmandt-Besserat's theory that inscribed clay envelopes containing tokens served as official records of contributions to grain and livestock pools. The third paragraph describes the evolution of the token system into mature writing. The Bottom Line of the passage is to describe Denise Schmandt-Besserat's theory about the use of tokens and their evolution into mature writing.

15. **A**   Big Picture

Use your Bottom Line of the passage to help you to evaluate the choices. The correct answer will describe the main idea of the passage.

A. Yes. This accurately paraphrases the Bottom Line of the passage.

B. No. While the discovery of clay tablets is mentioned in the passage, this answer choice is too narrow and does not fully capture the overall point.

C. No. The passage does not mention puzzlement over sudden appearance of sophisticated crafts.

D. No. The passage does not go into detail about the evolution of the tokens into modern languages.

E. No. The passage does not present a Schmandt-Besserat hypothesis that the abstraction of language is tied to the abstraction of arts and crafts.

16. **D** **Extract Infer**

The question is asking for a statement about the clay tokens that is best supported by the passage's description of Schmandt-Besserat's point of view.

A. No. The passage does not discuss a strong centralized government.

B. No. The passage does not compare religious rituals to agriculture and trade.

C. No. This answer choice is extreme and unsupported. While there is mention of temple-based grain and livestock pools, the passage does not argue that whatever is produced by any individual is common property.

D. Yes. In the third paragraph, the author describes an example of markings on a clay tablet that represent the tokens according to Schmandt-Besserat's hypothesis.

E. No. The passage does not speculate about what could or could not have happened without a supply of raw clay.

17. **B** **Extract Fact**

The question is asking for something that is true about the writing on the clay tablets found in Uruk. The correct answer will be directly supported by evidence in the passage.

A. No. The passage does not state when the writing was deciphered.

B. Yes. This is explicitly stated in line 5 of the passage.

C. No. The passage argues that the clay tokens were part of an evolution to an abstract and flexible linguistic system, not necessarily the writing on the clay tablets.

D. No. The passage does not mention the language spoken along the Jordan and nearby rivers.

E. No. The passage does not argue that this writing was a transcription of an older language.

18. **B** **Extract Fact**

The question is asking for something that is true about the token system. The correct answer will be directly supported by evidence in the passage.

A. No. The passage does not state why the token system was abandoned, only hints that it may have been redundant once abstract writing began to develop.

B. Yes. This is explicitly stated in lines 36–37.

C. No. This answer choice is extreme and unsupported. The passage states that inscriptions are clearly traceable to later, known inscriptions of farm products, but it does not argue that that is the only reason they could be understood.

D. No. The passage describes only the theory of Schmandt-Besserat. It is unknown what most archaeologists thought.

E. No. The passage never states that the tokens were unwieldy or cumbersome.

19. **C** **Extract Infer**

The question is asking what the author suggests by characterizing the cuneiform inscriptions in Uruk as abstract. The author sets up a contrast by stating that the writing uses relatively few pictographs. The correct answer will be the one best supported by evidence in the passage.

A. No. The passage doesn't argue that the meaning of the inscriptions was hard to decipher.

B. No. The examples given are symbols for sheep and metal, which are tangible concepts.

C. Yes. The passage states that the symbols were not pictographs and gives the example of a circled cross to represent a sheep.

D. No. The examples given are symbols for sheet and metal, which are specific things.

E. No. There is no mention of ceremonial use.

20. **C** **Extract Infer**

The question is asking for something that is true based on the discussion of clay tokens in the second paragraph. The correct answer will be the one best supported by evidence in the passage.

A. No. This is not mentioned in the passage.

B. No. The passage does not discuss what was preferred for temple-based pools.

C. Yes. At the end of the second paragraph, the author states that after 4000 B.C., hundreds of new token forms developed including figurative forms.

D. No. The passage did not discuss the relative importance of tasks performed by token system users.

E. No. Abstraction and flexibility of later written languages is not discussed until the third paragraph.

21. **A** **Extract Infer**

The question is asking for something that is true based on the information given about the sign for "sheep" in the passage. The correct answer will be the one best supported by evidence in the passage.

A. Yes. The symbol for sheep is described an the abstract symbol of a circled cross, which does not directly relate to any characteristics of a sheep.

B. No. The symbols for sheet and metal are presented as two examples of the same practice.

C. No. The passage does not make this distinction when discussing the symbol for sheep.

D.   No. The passage notes that clay tokens were often ignored by archeologists prior to Schmandt-Besserat, but it makes no such claim about the cuneiform markings.

E.   No. The passage does not discuss the political life of those who use the cuneiform writing.

22.   **B**   RC Reasoning

The question is asking for a piece of information that would weaken Schmandt-Besserat's theory in the second paragraph. Schmandt-Besserat's theory is that the marked clay envelopes contained official records of villagers' contributions of temple-based grain and livestock pools. The correct answer will make it less likely that the clay envelopes indicate such contributions.

A.   No. This would not weaken the theory. Variety in styles of envelopes could indicate variety in contributions.

B.   Yes. This answer suggests that the envelopes could serve a purpose other than recording grain and livestock contributions to pools.

C.   No. Schmandt-Besserat's theory is about the clay envelopes with tokens inside, so information about the significance of the clay tablets would not be relevant.

D.   No. A lack of evidence regarding the intended use of the envelopes is not evidence against the theorized use of the envelopes.

E.   No. If labor was accounted for, that would strengthen the idea that something would be used to track contributions of grain and livestock as well.

Questions 23–27

The first paragraph introduces the ozone layer and its role in filtering out the ultraviolet light that contributes to skin cancer. The main point of the second paragraph is that scientists Molina and Rowland have shown that CFCs break down under ultraviolet radiation into chlorine and other component elements and that chlorine is harmful to the ozone layer. The mail point of the third paragraph is that the scientists claimed that the quantity of CFCs in the atmosphere would continue to deplete the ozone layer for years, even if production and use of CFCs ceased. The main point of the fourth paragraph is that, though Molina and Rowland's work was attacked by critics, their views have been corroborated and CFCs have been banned both domestically and internationally.

23.   **E**   Extract Infer

The correct answer will be the question most readily answered by evidence in the passage.

A.   No. The passage did not specify what laboratory experiments were conducted.

B.   No. The passage only states that in 1974 there was an estimated 5 years' worth of CFC production.

C.   No. While the passage notes that Molina was invited to testify before Congress, the year is not given.

D.   No. The passage does not discuss the impact of other chemicals.

E.   Yes. The passage states that chlorine is devastating to the ozone layer.

24. **A** RC Reasoning

The question is asking for a new piece of information that would make Molina and Rowland's claims about the long-term effects of CFCs more likely to be true. Molina and Rowland argue in the third paragraph that the depletion of the ozone layer would "continue for years, if not decades," even if the production and use of CFCs stopped immediately.

A.   Yes. This makes it more likely to be true that CFCs continued to harm the ozone layer even after the production and use of CFCs stopped.

B.   No. Other chemicals are not relevant to the conclusions about CFCs.

C.   No. Other chemicals are not relevant to the conclusions about CFCs.

D.   No. The fact that other scientists used to have unfounded criticisms does not make Molina and Rowland's conclusions more likely to be true.

E.   No. The question is asking about long-term effects of CFCs in the stratosphere, not the troposphere.

25. **D** Extract Infer

The correct answer will be the statement best supported by evidence in the passage.

A.   No. This answer choice is extreme and unsupported. The passage states that in the absence of pollutants, ozone remains stable due to an equilibrium of natural production and destruction.

B.   No. This answer choice is extreme and unsupported. While the passage states that ultraviolet light contributes to skin cancer, it does not go so far as to say that UV light is the primary cause.

C.   No. This answer choice is extreme and unsupported. The passage does not discuss whether other chemicals can release chlorine into the upper atmosphere.

D.   Yes. Since regulating the use of CFCs helps preserve the ozone layer and the ozone layer screens out ultraviolet light, it can help protect against skin cancer.

E.   No. While there is a hole in the ozone layer over Antarctica, the passage does not indicate that that's the only place that CFCs flow into the stratosphere.

26. **D** RC Reasoning

The question is asking for a test that would determine whether a chemical could avoid the harmful effects of CFCs. The passage states that the chlorine from CFCs has a devastating effect on the ozone layer.

A.   No. Reactions with other forms of oxygen wouldn't help determine effects on the ozone layer.

B.   No. Reactions with other chemicals wouldn't help determine effects on the ozone layer.

C.   No. A reaction with chlorine would not be relevant because there isn't chlorine in the ozone layer.

D. Yes. Since chlorine has a devastating effect on the ozone layer, determining similarities with chlorine would be useful to determine whether a chemical might damage the ozone layer.

E. No. It is not the fact that CFCs break down into components that is the problem, but rather that one of the components is chlorine, which damages the ozone layer.

27. **B** **Extract Infer**

The correct answer will be the statement best supported by evidence in the passage.

A. No. This answer choice is extreme and unsupported. The passage does not discuss whether alternative chemicals were available.

B. Yes. The passage states at the end of the fourth paragraph that the banning of CFCs has led to the development of more environmentally friendly refrigerant chemicals.

C. No. This answer choice is extreme and unsupported. The passage does not discuss the energy efficiency of CFCs.

D. No. The passage states that CFCs were banned in North America approximately a decade prior to the Montreal Protocol.

E. No. The passage only states that the banning of CFCs has led to the development of more environmentally friendly refrigerant chemicals.

78

Chapter 9
PrepTest 79:
Answers and
Explanations

ANSWER KEY: PREPTEST 79

Section 1: Arguments 1		**Section 2:** Reading Comprehension		**Section 3:** Games		**Section 4:** Arguments 2	
1.	C	1.	C	1.	B	1.	D
2.	E	2.	B	2.	C	2.	A
3.	D	3.	A	3.	A	3.	D
4.	D	4.	C	4.	B	4.	A
5.	B	5.	D	5.	D	5.	D
6.	B	6.	D	6.	E	6.	B
7.	A	7.	E	7.	C	7.	D
8.	E	8.	B	8.	D	8.	B
9.	B	9.	E	9.	D	9.	A
10.	C	10.	E	10.	E	10.	A
11.	C	11.	C	11.	B	11.	E
12.	A	12.	A	12.	A	12.	E
13.	E	13.	B	13.	A	13.	C
14.	E	14.	C	14.	B	14.	D
15.	A	15.	B	15.	A	15.	A
16.	B	16.	B	16.	C	16.	D
17.	C	17.	E	17.	D	17.	A
18.	A	18.	D	18.	D	18.	B
19.	D	19.	D	19.	E	19.	B
20.	D	20.	A	20.	A	20.	B
21.	E	21.	A	21.	C	21.	C
22.	E	22.	E	22.	C	22.	C
23.	D	23.	B	23.	C	23.	B
24.	B	24.	C			24.	B
25.	A	25.	E			25.	C
26.	E	26.	A				
		27.	C				

EXPLANATIONS

Section 1: Arguments 1

1. **C** **Resolve/Explain**

This argument establishes that the new system of electronic tolls resulted in a decline in delays at interchanges, travel time per car trip, and tailpipe pollution for each car trip. It also establishes that total air pollution from vehicles did not decline. The paradox is that some causes of pollution have decreased, but not overall pollution. The credited response will address both sides of the paradox and explain why total pollution did not decrease despite the decreases in travel time and tailpipe pollution.

A. No. This might explain a decrease in traffic, but it does not explain why total air pollution did not decrease.

B. No. Even with occasional long delays, the argument established that average travel time decreased, and this answer does not explain why total air pollution did not decrease.

C. Yes. Additional cars using the highway would explain why overall pollution didn't decrease even though travel time and pollution per car trip did.

D. No. Even if travel time for shorter trips did not decrease, the argument established that average travel time and per trip pollution decreased by 10%.

E. No. The argument established that average travel time and per trip pollution decreased, so this does not explain why total pollution did not decrease.

2. **E** **Flaw**

The argument claims that a lack of trust in one's neighbors causes a lack of respect for the law. This is supported by a study that shows a correlation between burglary rates and door locking. The conclusion contains the common flawed assumption that correlation equals causation in a particular direction and fails to account for the possibility that people routinely lock their doors because of the burglaries. The credited response will describe this error.

A. No. The argument contains a Causal flaw, but this answer describes a Necessary/Sufficient flaw.

B. No. This answer choice is outside the scope of the argument. The argument does not mention morality.

C. No. The data in the argument is not contradictory.

D. No. The argument contains a Causal flaw, but this answer choice describes a Circular argument.

E. Yes. This accurately describes the Causal flaw.

79

3. **D**   **Resolve/Explain**

This argument establishes that the government's efforts to fight counterfeiting and remove counterfeit bills from circulation have been successful. It also establishes that counterfeiters are still able to pass counterfeit bills to merchants and banks without difficulty. The paradox is that one would think that counterfeit bills would be more difficult to pass given the government's efforts to fight counterfeiting. The credited response will address both sides of the conflict and explain why counterfeiters are not having difficulty passing counterfeit bills despite successful efforts to fight counterfeiting.

A. No. This answer explains how the government is fighting counterfeiting, but it would make it more difficult to pass counterfeit bills and would not explain why counterfeiters are not having difficulty.

B. No. This answer explains how the government is fighting counterfeiting, but it would make it more difficult to pass counterfeit bills and would not explain why counterfeiters are not having difficulty.

C. No. The awareness or lack of awareness of counterfeiters regarding the percentage of fake bills in circulation is not relevant to how difficult counterfeit bills are to pass.

D. Yes. This addresses both sides of the paradox by explaining why it would be easy to pass counterfeit bills in spite of government crackdowns on counterfeiting.

E. No. This answer explains how the government is fighting counterfeiting, but it would make it more difficult to pass counterfeit bills and would not explain why counterfeiters are not having difficulty.

4. **D**   **Necessary Assumption**

This argument claims that scientists can rule out the possibility of finding a nearby civilization as technologically advanced as our own. This is supported by the facts that if such a civilization exists, it would have found evidence of intelligent life on Earth and that the civilization would have the ability to easily contact Earth. The argument assumes that a civilization with the ability to contact Earth would have chosen to do so. The argument also assumes that those on Earth would be able to recognize that they had been contacted by another civilization. The credited response will either establish that a civilization with the ability to contact Earth would choose to do so or that we would be able to recognize any such communication.

A. No. The argument is focused on other civilizations contacting Earth, rather than the search for evidence of extraterrestrial life forms.

B. No. This answer is outside the scope of the argument. The argument makes no claims about civilizations more than 50 light years from Earth.

C. No. While this answer choice relates to the assumption that scientists would be able to recognize communication from another planet, it is too extreme. The argument does not require that we be able to fully decipher any message.

D. Yes. This answer choice eliminates the possibility of a civilization that is able to communicate with Earth, but chooses not to.

E. No. The premises establish that technologically advanced civilizations on other planets would have found evidence of intelligent life on Earth. This answer choice is not the assumption.

5. **B** Resolve/Explain

This argument establishes that traffic lights and street markings were temporarily removed from a busy street in a city. It also establishes that the street experienced no reduction in traffic. The paradox is that even with the same amount of traffic and an expected increase in accidents, the number of accidents was greatly reduced. The credited response will explain the unexpected reduction in traffic accidents given the factors that suggest an alternate result.

A. No. Had the number of accidents remained the same as it was before the removal of the lights and street markings, this answer would be helpful, but it does not explain why the number of accidents was greatly reduced.

B. Yes. An increase in caution would explain how traffic accidents could go down in spite of the removal of traffic lights and street markings.

C. No. If drivers were not aware of the changes to the street, they might be more likely to get in accidents. This does not explain why the number of accidents went down.

D. No. This answer is outside the scope of the argument. Considerations other than safety are not related to an explanation of why traffic accidents were greatly reduced when the traffic lights and street markings were removed.

E. No. Had there been a reduction in traffic, this answer choice would have helped to explain it, but there was not, in fact, a reduction in traffic and advance notice of the conditions does not explain why there was a reduction in traffic accidents.

6. **B** Flaw

The argument presents the claim that body size influences mating decisions throughout all societies. This is based on evidence self-reported by university-age students and culled from personal ads in newspapers. The argument assumes that these two sources are representative of the entire populations of all societies. This is an example of a sampling flaw. Specifically, that university-age students and those who place personal ads are representative of society as a whole.

A. No. This answer choice describes a different type of flaw pattern. The gap between the conclusion and premises does not involve causation.

B. Yes. This answer addresses the sampling error by pointing out that university-age students and those who place personal ads may not be representative of the population of all societies.

C. No. This answer choice describes a different type of flaw pattern. The gap between the conclusion and premises does not involve causation.

D. No. This answer choice describes a different type of flaw pattern. The argument uses information about segments of the population to draw a conclusion about entire societies, not the other way around.

E. No. The argument does not specify how many reports from university-age students or how many personal ads were used as evidence and therefore leaves open the possibility that it was a large number.

7. **A**   `Necessary Assumption`

The journalist claims that the new mayor is not an introspective person. The journalist bases this claim on the fact that the mayor is bold and makes assertions with utter certainty and confidence. The journalist also notes that these assertions make the mayor popular with the public. There is a language shift from a premise about being bold and making assertions with utter certainty and confidence to the conclusion about being an introspective person. The credited response will close this gap.

A.   Yes. This answer closes the language gap and explicitly connects the mayor making assertions with utter certainty and confidence to not being introspective.

B.   No. The author states that assertions made with utter certainty and confidence may make the mayor popular with the public, so this is not an assumption.

C.   No. While the journalist states that the mayor is both bold and makes assertions with utter certainty and confidence, the conclusion is about introspection. This answer choice does not address the gap between the conclusion and premises.

D.   No. The argument makes an assumption about someone whose assertions are made with certainty and confidence, not people whose assertions are uncertain and lack confidence.

E.   No. The conclusion is about being introspective. This answer choice does not address the gap between the conclusion and premises and the journalist makes no claims about those who are not bold.

8. **E**   `Inference`

The passage states that baby macaque monkeys readily imitate scientists when the scientists smack their lips and stick out their tongues and that adult macaque monkeys smack their lips and stick out their tongues when interacting with baby monkeys. The passage also establishes that the babies stare impassively when scientists open and close their mouths and make hand gestures. The passage also establishes that adult macaques do not open and close their mouths or make hand gestures when interacting with babies. The credited response will be supported by either one or a combination of these statements.

A.   No. This answer choice is contradicted by the facts in the passage. The passage states that baby macaques do not imitate all of the scientists' actions.

B.   No. This is an example of a "crystal ball" answer choice. The passage does not discuss why baby macaques do not imitate hand gestures, so we cannot speculate about the reason.

C.   No. This is an example of a "crystal ball" answer choice. The passage does not discuss the motivations of the adult macaques, so we cannot speculate about why they might use lip smacking and stick out their tongues.

D.   No. This is an example of a "crystal ball" answer choice. We cannot know what the baby macaques are thinking when they see the scientists.

E.   Yes. The passage states that of the four gestures used by the scientists, the baby macaques imitate only the two gestures used by adult macaques when interacting with babies.

9. **B**   Main Point

This argument disputes the belief that small humanoid skeletons found on an Indonesian island are the remains of human beings with a growth disorder. The argument concludes that it is more likely that these small skeletons represent a distinct human species that became smaller over time due to environmental pressure. This conclusion is supported by the premises that these skeletons do not fit the pattern of known growth disorders and that there is evidence suggesting other species on the island evolved into smaller versions of their common counterparts.

A. No. This is the claim that the argument refutes.

B. Yes. This answer choice accurately paraphrases the argument's conclusion.

C. No. This is a premise in support of the argument's rejection of the belief that the smaller skeletons are not the result of a growth disorder.

D. No. This is a premise in support of the conclusion that it is more likely that the smaller skeletons are from a distinct species rather than from a growth disorder.

E. No. While this answer choice is supported by one of the premises, it is not the author's overall claim.

10. **C**   Strengthen

The argument claims that the greater of the area of Earth's surface that is covered with snow and ice, the cooler, on average, the global atmosphere is likely to become. This is supported by the premises that the more sunlight the Earth reflects back into space, the cooler the atmosphere tends to become and that snow and ice reflect much more sunlight back into space than do ocean water or land not covered in snow. The argument assumes that there are no other relevant factors to be considered when drawing a conclusion about the temperature of the global atmosphere. The credited response will supply an additional premise, bolster the given premises, or rule out an obstacle to the conclusion.

A. No. While scope is broader for Strengthen questions, this answer choice does not add any information that makes the conclusion more likely to be true.

B. No. While this answer choice does not mention how other factors affect the cooling of the Earth's atmosphere, if anything it weakens the conclusion because it attacks an assumption that is required by the conclusion.

C. Yes. This answer choice strengthens the conclusion by adding a premise. If more of the Earth's surface is covered by snow and ice, less of the Earth's surface will consist of ocean water and land heated by sunlight and therefore there will be less warming of the atmosphere, contributing to a cooler atmosphere.

D. No. The conclusion is about what cools the atmosphere, so information about how it is warmed does not help strengthen that conclusion.

E. No. While this answer choice might help explain why snow and ice reflect more sunlight back into space than the ocean or land, that fact is already established by the argument, and this does not make the conclusion more likely to be true.

11.   C   **Point at Issue**

Nick concludes that the university should not give the contract for building its new library to the Pincus family's main competitor. He supports this conclusion by stating that the Pincus family and its construction company has supported the university financially for decades and that awarding the contract to someone else would be disloyal to the Pincus family. Pedro concludes that the construction contract should be awarded to whichever company makes the most competitive bid. He supports this conclusion by declaring that accepting a donation does not oblige the university to give any special treatment to a donor. He also believes that granting special privileges would render a donation not a charitable contribution. The credited response will be an answer that Nick and Pedro would disagree about the truth of. One speaker should explicitly agree with the answer and the other speaker should explicitly agree with the negative of the answer.

A.   No. While Nick cites disloyalty as a reason to not give the contract to the Pincus family's main competitor, Pedro does not express any opinion about loyalty.

B.   No. Neither Nick nor Pedro expresses any opinion about why the Pincus family donated to the university.

C.   Yes. Nick explicitly agrees with this statement because he argues against being disloyal to a donor of the university; Pedro explicitly disagrees with this statement because he says that accepting a donation does not oblige the university to give a donor any special privileges.

D.   No. While Nick comments that the Pincus family has financially supported the university for decades, he does not express an opinion about how relative length of donation history should impact the university's gratefulness to a donor. Pedro does not express an opinion about gratefulness, though he would disagree with this statement if gratefulness equated to special privileges since he does not believe donors should receive any special privileges.

E.   No. Nick does not express an opinion about which construction company had the most competitive bid, and while Pedro argues that the contract should be given to the company with the most competitive bid, he also does not express an opinion about whether or not that bid was from the Pincus family.

12.   A   **Strengthen**

The argument concludes that ampicillin and other modern antibiotics are likely to result in an outbreak of diseases caused by drug-resistant bacteria. This is supported by the premises that these antibiotics kill a much wider variety of bacteria than penicillin does and that profit incentives could cause a penicillin shortage, leading to use of the more powerful antibiotics in cases in which they are otherwise unnecessary. The argument assumes that using antibiotics that kill a much wider variety of bacteria will make people susceptible to drug-resistant bacteria. The credited response will close this gap by confirming that this assumption is true.

A.   Yes. This answer closes the gap between the conclusion and premises. If doctors are using antibiotics that kill a wide variety of bacteria, and drug-resistant bacteria flourishes in the absence of competition from a wide variety of other bacteria, there is likely to be an outbreak of diseases stemming from drug-resistant bacteria.

B.   No. The conclusion is about the result of increased use of modern antibiotics, so historical information about older antibiotics does not have an impact on the conclusion.

C. No. This answer choice is not strongly connected to the argument. The conclusion is about the impact of a proliferation of the newer antibiotics, so an additional consequence of a penicillin shortage would not have an impact.

D. No. This answer choice is not strongly connected to the argument. The conclusion is about the diseases that will result from the proliferation of these new antibiotics, so information about the cost of treatment would not have an impact.

E. No. This is merely a restatement of a premise. The argument already establishes that the new antibiotics kill a wide variety of bacteria that are not killed by penicillin; thus this answer does not have any additional impact on the conclusion.

13. **E**   Flaw

The author concludes that Weingarten's claim that keeping animals in zoos is unethical should be rejected. The author bases his argument on the fact that Weingarten's reason for his claim is seemingly inconsistent with another of Weingarten's views. Specifically, Weingarten objects to keeping animals in zoos because it involves placing animals in unnatural environments merely for the sake of human amusement, yet Weingarten does not object to owning pets, which the author argues also involves placing animals in unnatural environments merely for the sake of human amusement. The author does not address the merits of Weingarten's claim and instead assumes that the claim should be rejected because Weingarten holds inconsistent views. The credited response will point out this faulty assumption.

A. No. The argument discusses Weingarten's views about owning pets, which does not hinge on whether he actually owns or does not own pets.

B. No. The conclusion is specific to Weingarten's views and does not generalize.

C. No. There is no indication that Weingarten's claim is anything other than what the author says that it is.

D. No. There is no assertion that placing animals in unnatural environments merely for the sake of human amusement is necessary to make a practice unethical.

E. Yes. This answer choice accurately describes the faulty assumption made by the author that a proponent holding inconsistent views is sufficient to justify rejecting one of those views.

14. **E**   Principle Strengthen

The activist argues that President Zagel should resign. This argument is supported by the premise that she is unable to govern effectively due to widespread belief that she rigged the election. The activist assumes that inability to govern effectively is sufficient reason to resign. President Zagel argues that she should not resign. Her argument is supported by the premises that her resignation would result in the rest of the world seeing her country's political system as hopelessly unstable due to two other recent presidential resignations. The credited response will provide a general rule or principle that establishes that President Zagel should resign even if it will result in the rest of the world seeing her country's political system as hopelessly unstable.

A. No. This principle does not apply to the dispute in this argument because the election procedures are alleged to not be resistant to illegal manipulation.

B. No. President Zagel argues that her resignation would not improve her country's international reputation for political stability, so this answer choice would weaken the activist's argument, not justify it.

C. No. There are no details given about the scandals that forced the two prior presidents to resign, so no determination can be made about whether the widespread belief that President Zagel rigged the election is a more serious scandal and this does not justify the activist's argument.

D. No. The activist only states that there is widespread belief that President Zagel rigged the election, not that it can be conclusively proven, so this does not justify the activist's argument.

E. Yes. Since we have to accept the premise that President Zagel cannot govern effectively as true, under this principle, the ineffectiveness outweighs President Zagel's concerns about being viewed as unstable and the activist's argument that she should resign is justified.

15.   **A**   **Flaw**

The author of the argument disagrees with a book's claim that people who are successful in business have, without exception, benefitted from a lot of luck on their way to success, calling this claim ridiculous. The author supports this position with the premise that success requires a lot of hard work. This argument contains a necessary/sufficient flaw. It takes the book's claim that those successful in business have always benefitted from luck and treats it as if the book argues that luck is a sufficient factor to ensure success, rather than as one of potentially several necessary factors (including hard work). The credited response will point out this flaw.

A. Yes. This answer choice accurately describes the flaw. The author mistakes the claim that luck is required for success for the claim that those successful in business only need luck.

B. No. This is inconsistent with what happens in the argument. The author disputes a view rather than taking it as authoritative.

C. No. This answer choice describes another flaw pattern, circular arguments, which rarely occur in LSAT arguments. In circular arguments, the conclusion and premises are paraphrases of one another and that is not the case here.

D. No. This answer choice describes another flaw pattern, causal assumptions, which do not occur here. The author does not make a causal claim in this argument.

E. No. This answer choice describes another flaw pattern, appeals and attacks (specifically ad hominem attacks), which does not occur here. The author does not attack the source of the argument.

16.   **B**   **Parallel Principle**

This argument proceeds by asserting that a faculty member's falsification of research was not evidence of the university's low standards as proclaimed by the media; rather, it was merely a case of dishonestly. The author further claimed that there is a benefit to the academic standards having become a topic of discussion because vigilance with respect to the standards is always necessary. The principle illustrated by the argument is that some good came out of some people misattributing the blame for a scandal because it prompted discussion, and the issue they misattributed it to is always important. The structure of the argument is that a particular scandal was not caused by characteristic A, as claimed by some; rather it resulted from characteristic B. It is good that discussion of characteristic A has been prompted, however, because attention to characteristic A is always important. The credited response will parallel this same general principle.

A. No. This answer choice does not match the original argument. Unlike the original argument, this answer choice argues that a particular issue not be the only topic of discussion.

B. Yes. This answer choice matches the structure and general principle of the original argument. The government scandal is misattributed to lack of oversight (characteristic A) rather than simple corruption (characteristic B). The author states that the discussion of oversight (characteristic A) is welcome because oversight (characteristic A) is important.

C. No. This answer choice does not match the original argument. Unlike the original argument, this answer choice attributes a scandal to two causes.

D. No. This answer choice does not match the original argument. It lacks the portion of the argument claiming that the misattribution actually had a positive consequence and instead introduces harm.

E. No. This answer choice does not match the original argument. It lacks the claim that the mis-attributed characteristic is important.

17. **C** Evaluate

The politician claims that the plan to, over the next decade, replace all of the street signs in a city with ones designed for improved readability is a colossal waste of time and money. As evidence, the politician offers the premise that no one is complaining about the current signs. The argument assumes that the plan to replace all of the signs would cost more time and money than if the plan were not enacted. The question stem asks for information that will help evaluate the truth of the conclusion. The credited response will provide a question that, depending on how it is answered, would either help or hurt the conclusion.

A. No. The features that are supposed to improve the readability of the signs are not relevant to the question of whether replacing the signs would be a waste of time and money since no one is complaining about the current signs.

B. No. If the answer to this question were yes, it would strengthen the idea that the new signs are a waste of money, though it would not necessarily support the idea of wasted time. If the answer to this question were no, however, it would not weaken the conclusion, so it is not particularly useful in evaluating the conclusion.

C. Yes. If it were known that the city replaces at least 10% of its signs annually, all of the signs would be replaced over the course of a decade anyway and the new more readable signs would not add time or expense, thus weakening the conclusion. If far fewer than 10% of the signs are replaced annually, however, replacing all of the signs over the decade would take more time and money than following the usual replacement plan, thus strengthening the conclusion that the replacement is a waste of time and money. This answer choice therefore helps evaluate the conclusion.

D. No. The conclusion is about a plan for one particular city, so information about other cities is not relevant to an evaluation of the conclusion.

E. No. The answer to this question would not have an impact on the conclusion. If experts were consulted during the design of the new street signs, that fact would not necessarily make the signs cost more.

18. **A** **Necessary Assumption**

The argument concludes that most of the scientists surveyed reject the Minsk Hypothesis. This is based on the premises that almost all of the surveyed scientists accept Wang's Law and almost all know the results of the Brown-Eisler Experiment. The argument further establishes that the results of the Brown-Eisler Experiment together with Wang's Law contradict the Minsk Hypothesis. The argument shifts from discussing a law and experimental results that scientists were surveyed about to a hypothesis, assuming that the surveyed scientists know of the Minsk Hypothesis and know that the experimental results and Wang's Law combine to contradict the hypothesis.

A. Yes. This answer choice closes the gap between the experimental results and law that the surveyed scientists know about and the hypothesis that is the focus of the conclusion.

B. No. This answer choice is too extreme. The "almost all" who accept Wang's Law and the "almost all" who know the results of the Brown-Eisler Experiment have to overlap by at least some scientists, but two "almost all" groups do not have to be exactly the same.

C. No. The way in which the Brown-Eisler experimental results were obtained is not relevant to rejection of the Minsk Hypothesis since the argument already establishes that almost all scientists accept the experimental results.

D. The argument does not generalize to scientists in the field; rather, the conclusion is specific to those scientists surveyed.

E. No. The truth of Wang's Law is not relevant to rejection of the Minsk Hypothesis since the argument already establishes that almost all scientists accept Wang's Law.

19. **D** **Principle Strengthen**

The argument claims that even the most skillful literary translation will be at best a flawed approximation of the original work. This is based on the premises that any literary translation is a compromise between faithfulness to the meaning of the text and faithfulness to the original author's style and that the two goals cannot be entirely reconciled. The argument contains a language shift and introduces the idea of a flawed approximation in the conclusion. The argument assumes that a translation that is not completely faithful to the meaning of the text and to the original author's style is a flawed approximation of the original work. The credited response will provide a general rule that closes this gap and links the premises to the conclusion.

A. No. This answer choice does not mention the concept of a flawed approximation and therefore does not close the gap in the argument.

B. No. This answer choice is contradicted by the argument. The argument already establishes that even a skillful compromise between faithfulness to the meaning of the text and faithfulness to the original author's style will result in a flawed approximation of the original work.

C. No. This answer choice does not mention the concept of a flawed approximation and therefore does not close the gap in the argument.

D. Yes. Since the argument establishes that any translation will be a compromise between faithfulness to the meaning of the text and faithfulness to the original author's style and that the two goals cannot be entirely reconciled, such a translation will not be entirely faithful to both and therefore will be at best a flawed approximation of the work.

E. No. This answer choice does not mention the concept of a flawed approximation and therefore does not close the gap in the argument.

20. **D** **Inference**

The passage indicates that electronic media encourages imprecise, uncritical thinking. It also establishes that critical thinking is the only adequate protection against political demagogues, those who seek to exploit people by using emotionally loaded language as an objective description of reality. This is an EXCEPT question, so four of the answer choices will be statements that are within the realm of possibility given the statements in the passage. The credited response will be the statement that must be false because it is contradicted by the passage.

A. No. This answer choice could be true. While electronic media encourages uncritical thinking, it does not completely prevent critical thinking and it is possible for some highly technological societies to lack political demagogues.

B. No. This answer choice could be true. The passage does not limit the use of emotionally loaded language as an objective description of reality to demagogues.

C. No. This answer choice could be true. The passage does not mention highly emotional people or less emotional people, so this statement is within the realm of possibility.

D. Yes. This answer choice is contradicted by the passage. The passage states that critical thinking is the "only" adequate protection against political demagogues, so it is not possible that the mere presence of an orderly system of government provides adequate protection.

E. No. This answer choice could be true. The passage does not mention media freedoms, so it is possible that the presence of electronic communications technology offers adequate protection against the erosion of those freedoms.

21. **E** **Weaken**

The argument presents the problem that people with higher-than-average blood levels of homocysteine are much more likely to be diagnosed with Alzheimer's disease. The argument then presents a solution, claiming that the risk of developing Alzheimer's disease could be reduced by including large amounts of B vitamins and folic acid in one's diet. The author thinks this solution will work because B vitamins and folic acid are substances known to convert homocysteine into substances unrelated to Alzheimer's disease. This argument illustrates the common causal flaw pattern. The argument assumes that the higher levels of homocysteine are causing the Alzheimer's diagnoses when in fact it could be that the Alzheimer's disease is causing an increase in homocysteine or that some third factor is causing both the Alzheimer's disease and the higher level of homocysteine. The credited response will weaken the argument by attacking this assumption.

A. No. This answer choice is not strong enough. "Many" is an indeterminate term that could refer to only a few people. Regardless of the number, the argument only states that higher levels of homocysteine are correlated with an increased likelihood of diagnosis, which leaves open the possibility that some individuals with normal levels are diagnosed.

B. No. While this would be an unfortunate consequence of this plan and is therefore a tempting answer choice, the conclusion is focused only on whether the risk of developing Alzheimer's disease could be reduced and unrelated harmful effects are therefore irrelevant.

C. No. The argument recommends including high levels of B vitamins and folic acid in one's diet, which could come in the form of various foods and not vitamin-mineral supplements, so the efficiency of such supplements does not have an impact on the conclusion.

D. No. This answer choice does not mention or connect to levels of homocysteine and therefore would not have an impact on the argument that increasing substances that convert homocysteine would decrease the incidence of Alzheimer's disease.

E. Yes. This answer choice negates the assumption that the homocysteine is causing the Alzheimer's disease and in doing so weaken the conclusion.

22. **E**   Reasoning

The consumer advocate refutes the claim that price gouging is efficient by disputing that claim's premise that price gouging allocates goods to people whose willingness to pay more shows that they really need those goods. The consumer advocate asserts that willingness to pay is not, in fact, proportional to need and therefore concludes that a price increase will allocate goods to the people with the most money and not to those with the most need. The question is asking for the role played by the claim that willingness to pay is not proportional to need.

A. No. This is not an accurate description of the structure of the argument. The statement disputes a claim, not an explanation.

B. No. The overall conclusion of the argument is that a price increase will allocate goods to the people with the most money and not to those with the most need.

C. No. This statement is part of the author's reasoning. The author disputes the claim that willingness to pay shows that goods are needed.

D. No. The statement is a premise of the author's argument, not something that the author questions.

E. Yes. This answer choice accurately describes the statement's role in refuting the premise of the argument that the author objects to.

23. **D**   Strengthen

The argument claims that prehistoric European cave bears were not exclusively herbivores. In support of this claim, the author presents the facts that animals that eat meat exhibit high concentration of heavy nitrogen in their bodily tissues because heavy nitrogen becomes more heavily concentrated as it moves up the food chain from plants to herbivores to meat eaters. The author further states that bone samples from Europeans cave bears of the Ice Age and blood samples from present-day bears fed meat-enriched diets had identical levels of heavy nitrogen. The argument exhibits the comparison flaw pattern, specifically the argument assumes that the heavy nitrogen levels in Ice Age bone samples are indicative of the levels that would have been in the bears' blood. The credited response will make the conclusion more likely to be true by validating this assumption.

A. No. This answer choice has no impact on the conclusion. The source of the heavy nitrogen in plants has no bearing on whether levels in bone samples are indicative of levels in blood.

B. No. While this answer choice lends some support to the idea that bone samples can offer information about blood levels, it is about herbivores rather than carnivores.

C. No. While this answer choice gives some support regarding the overall soundness of the study, it does not directly address the potential flaw in the argument regarding the difference between bone samples and blood samples.

D. Yes. This answer choice strengthens the conclusion by affirming the assumption that heavy nitrogen levels in bone samples are exactly indicative of levels in blood samples and therefore a conclusion can be validly drawn from their comparison.

E. No. This answer choice weakens the conclusion by suggesting that the amount of meat a bear eats does not affect the level of heavy nitrogen in its bones.

24. **B** **Necessary Assumption**

The biologist claims that computer scientists are mistaken when they imagine that all that is required for making an artificial intelligence is to create a computer program that encapsulates the information contained in the human genome. This conclusion is supported by the premise that the operation of the human brain is governed by the interactions of proteins whose structures are encoded in the human genome. The argument assumes that a computer program that encapsulates the information contained in the human genome would not include the information required to make the interaction of proteins that govern the operation of the human brain to occur.

A. No. The biologist does not claim that a computer could not simulate the functions of the human brain; rather, he or she merely claims that the data from the human genome would not be enough for such a simulation to occur.

B. Yes. Use the Negation Test. If the interactions of the proteins that govern the operation of the human brain ARE determined by the information contained in the human genome, then a computer program that encapsulates the information contained in the human genome would be sufficient for artificial intelligence and the author's conclusion would be refuted. This answer choice is therefore necessary for the conclusion to be true.

C. No. This answer choice is too extreme. The biologist claims that the computer scientists' conception of how to make an artificial intelligence is incorrect but leaves open the possibility of many other ways of creating artificial intelligence.

D. No. The biologist's conclusion is about whether a computer program that does contain all of the information in the genome would be sufficient for artificial intelligence, so the ease of creating such a program is not relevant to that claim.

E. No. The biologist's conclusion is about whether a computer program that contains all of the information in the genome would be sufficient for artificial intelligence; the difficulty of writing such a program is outside the scope of the argument.

25.   A   **Inference**

The passage describes home computers that are offered to certain consumers free of charge. These computers are offered by advertisers who play advertisements continuously on the screens of these computers when they are in use. The advertisers also receive information about the browsing patterns of users, which allows them to transmit tailored advertising to consumers. The passage asserts that the advertisers can afford to offer the free computers because they receive increased revenue from this precisely targeted advertising. The credited response will be supported by either one of or a combination of these statements.

A.   Yes. The passage states that the advertisers have increased sales resulting from this targeted advertising, so it must be true that at least some consumers with these computers are spending more money on products from these advertisers than they otherwise would have.

B.   No. This answer choice is extreme and unsupported. The passage discusses only increased revenue that results from targeted advertising. It is possible that there are advertisers who offer promotions that give away free computers for other purposes.

C.   No. This is an example of a "crystal ball" answer choice. The passage does not offer information to indicate what consumers would have done had they not browsed the Internet. Furthermore, the information in the passage does not require that little if any money was spent with an advertiser prior to being exposed to the advertising, only that the advertising resulted in an increase.

D.   No. This is an example of a "crystal ball" answer choice. The passage does not offer information to indicate what would happen if the advertisements did not play continuously. It is possible that the advertisers could still have increased revenue if the advertisements played 90% of the time.

E.   No. The passage does not specify whether consumers have the opportunity to opt out of the browsing pattern reporting some of the time; the passage merely states that advertisers receive information. This information could be collected anywhere from one hour per week to all of the time.

26.   E   **Parallel Flaw**

The argument claims that no speakers who resort to obscenity impress their audiences. This conclusion is based on the premises that some eloquent speakers impress their audiences with the vividness and clarity of the messages conveyed and that speakers who resort to obscenity are not genuinely eloquent. The structure of this argument is that some members of Group A (eloquent speakers) do Thing B (impress their audiences). People who do Thing C (resort to obscenity) are not genuinely members of Group A (eloquent speakers); therefore, no people who do Thing C (resort to obscenity) do Thing B (impress their audiences). The flaw is that the argument improperly assumes that only members of Group A (eloquent speakers) can do Thing B (impress their audiences). The credited response will contain an argument that has this same pattern and flaw, but it will not necessarily be in the same order as the original argument.

A.   No. This answer choice lacks the concept of "some" and therefore doesn't match the original pattern and flaw.

B.   No. The conclusion of the argument in this answer choice is about "some" authors, but the conclusion in the original argument is about "none" of the speakers, so this answer choice does not match the pattern and flaw of the original argument.

C. No. This answer choice substitutes "always" for the concept of "some" in the premise of the original argument and therefore does not match the original pattern and flaw.

D. No. The conclusion of the argument is this answer choice includes the uncertain "probably," but the conclusion in the original argument is firm that none of the speakers impress their audiences, so this answer choice does not match the pattern and flaw of the original argument.

E. Yes. This answer choice matches the pattern and flaw of the original argument. Some members of Group A (sculptors) do Thing B (produce significant works of art). People who do Thing C (musicians) are not genuinely members of Group A (sculptors); therefore, no people who do Thing C (musicians) do Thing B (produce significant works of art).

Section 2: Reading Comprehension

Questions 1–7

The first paragraph of passage A provides context: there must be a plausible explanation for muscle memory, a phenomenon most bodybuilders have experienced. The second paragraph proposes an explanation: the body adapts to consistent training by increasing the percentage of muscle fibers that are stimulated by neurons during maximal lifts, and this increased capacity remains intact even after a period of inactivity. Therefore, when you restart training, you have greater strength and can thus make quicker progress. The final paragraph admits that there may be another plausible explanation: when you restart training, you're already aware of your strength, so you add weight more rapidly than when you first started training because you know you can handle it.

The Bottom Line of passage A is that muscle memory may be explained by a physiological adaptation to consistent training, but other explanations (including psychological) may also account for the phenomenon.

The first paragraph of passage B states the main point: muscle memory is explained by the fact that muscles retain a certain property even after you stop training. The second paragraph explains this property: with exercise, muscle cells gain nuclei by merging with stem cells. The final paragraph describes a study that refutes the previous belief that these extra nuclei are killed when muscles atrophy.

The Bottom Line of passage B is that muscle memory is explained by the fact that with exercise, muscle cells gain nuclei by merging with stem cells and therefore have greater capacity to make muscle proteins when restarting training.

1. **C** Big Picture

   This question asks for a key topic or main idea that both passages have in common. Rely on the Bottom Line for each passage to choose the answer. Be wary of answer choices that focus exclusively on one passage or that are too broad or too narrow.

   A. No. Neither passage generalizes to exercise physiology; both focus on a particular phenomenon, muscle memory.

   B. No. Neither passage speculates on the best way to restart training after a period of inactivity.

   C. Yes. Passage A offers two explanations, and passage B offers one explanation.

   D. No. Passage B does not discuss the psychological aspect of muscle memory.

   E. No. Passage B does not discuss the psychological aspect of muscle memory.

2. **B** Structure

This question asks for a technique used in passage B but not in passage A. Rely on the Bottom Line for each passage to choose the answer. Be wary of answer choices that discuss techniques from passage A only, from both passages, or from neither passage.

A. No. Neither passage questions the reality of muscle memory.

B. Yes. Passage A presents explanations without referencing studies, but passage B presents an explanation supported by the study described in the final paragraph.

C. No. Passage A appeals to the reader's personal experience, but passage B does not.

D. No. Passage A considers a psychological explanation, but passage B does not.

E. No. Both passages speculate on the explanation for muscle memory.

3. **A** Extract Fact

This question asks which answer choice is explicitly stated in passage B but not in passage A. Evaluate each answer choice against both passages to find an idea that is explicitly stated in passage B only. Be wary of answer choices that state ideas from passage A only, from both passages, or from neither passage.

A. Yes. This is stated in lines 44–47.

B. No. Both passages discuss adaptations from training.

C. No. Passage A discusses psychological factors, but passage B does not.

D. No. Passage B discusses apoptosis, but its role in muscle memory is denied, not given as an explanation.

E. No. Passage A discusses neurons that stimulate muscles, but passage B does not.

4. **C** Extract Infer

This question asks which answer choice is supported by the ideas or tone of passage A. Evaluate each answer choice against passage A to find support. Be wary of answer choices that introduce new ideas, that contradict ideas from passage A, or that are too extreme.

A. No. Both passages are certain of the existence of muscle memory.

B. No. The passages offer differing explanations for muscle memory.

C. Yes. Had the author of passage A been aware of this research, he might have been expected to bring it up as a potential explanation for muscle memory.

D. No. Passage A does not discuss muscle nuclei.

E. No. Passage A does not describe experiments or discuss different species.

5. **D**   Big Picture

This question asks for the relationship between the intended audiences of each passage. Be wary of answer choices that confuse the relationship, that are half correct, or that are a poor match for the Bottom Line.

A. No. Passage A does not seek to convince skeptics, and passage B is aimed at a general audience. Passage A is aimed at those with direct experience.

B. No. Passage A is aimed at bodybuilders, and passage B is aimed at a general audience.

C. No. Passage A does not imply the use of a personal trainer, and passage B does not imply that people are working out on their own.

D. Yes. Passage A references bodybuilders and weight lifting in lines 2, 4, 13, and 15 and addresses the second person, e.g., "The first time you trained, you didn't know how much you could lift" in lines 31–32. Passage B is written in lay terms and summarizes a new scientific explanation for a common phenomenon many people experience when training.

E. No. Passage A mentions a possible psychological explanation, but the context of the passage indicates that bodybuilders are the primary audience. Passage B is aimed at a general audience.

6. **D**   Extract Infer

This question asks which answer choice is supported by the ideas or tone of passage B. Evaluate each answer choice against both passages to find support. Be wary of answer choices that introduce new ideas, that contradict ideas from passage B, that are too extreme, or that are supported by passage A only.

A. No. Passage B does not invalidate bodybuilders' experiences; it merely offers a different explanation for their experience of muscle memory.

B. No. Passage A's explanations are consistent with athletes' experiences, even if they are ultimately incorrect.

C. No. We cannot speculate on which explanations athletes would find convincing.

D. Yes. Passage B's explanation differs from those offered in passage A, and because this explanation is supported by research while those in passage A are not, the author of passage B might think his is the better explanation.

E. No. Passage B does not discuss the psychological aspect of muscle memory.

7. **E**   Extract Fact

This question asks which answer choice is explicitly stated in passage B but not in passage A. Evaluate each answer choice against both passages to find an idea that is explicitly stated in passage B only. Be wary of answer choices that state ideas from passage A only, from both passages, or from neither passage.

A. No. Passage A discusses muscle condition before retraining in lines 23–26, and passage B discusses it in lines 38–41.

B. No. Both passages discuss muscles' adaptation to exercise.

C. No. Passage A discusses the percentage of muscle fibers in lines 13–15, but passage B does not.

D. No. Passage A discusses the prevalence of discussions in scientific publications in lines 3–4, but passage B does not.

E. Yes. This is a paraphrase of lines 43–44.

Questions 8–14

The first paragraph states the main point: Eileen Gray had a multifaceted career informed by her work in lacquer. The second paragraph describes the aesthetic qualities and structural requirements of lacquer and her evolution from small objects to interior design. The final paragraph describes a further evolution from interior design to architectural design and explains that lacquer demands attention to the entirety of an object, an aesthetic concern that applies to all of her work.

The Bottom Line is that Eileen Gray's artistic career ranged from small objects to architectural design and was informed by her use of lacquer, which demands attention to the entirety of an object, an aesthetic concern that applies to all of her work.

8. B   **Big Picture**

Rely on the Bottom Line to choose the answer. Be wary of answer choices that contradict the Bottom Line or that are too narrow or too broad.

A. No. Her career included ornaments, so "from interior to exterior design" is too narrow. Moreover, the passage does not state or imply that her work in lacquer prevented her from garnering critical acclaim.

B. Yes. This answer choice matches the Bottom Line: it mentions the full range of her work, from small objects to interior design to architectural design, and explains how lacquer informed this work.

C. No. The passage states in line 1 that she is best known for her work in lacquer, not in modern materials such as tubular steel for the design of furniture and houses.

D. No. The passage does not discuss how identifiable her work is.

E. No. The passage does not discuss dissatisfaction with Japanese traditional art.

9. E   **Extract Infer**

This question asks which answer choice describes a work that would fit with Gray's aesthetic sensibilities. Return to the passage to find characteristics of her work: she prefers straight lines and the juxtaposition of simple forms (lines 16–17), she produces work that has hidden details (28–32), she tailors furniture to fit its environment and meet its occupants' needs (lines 34–39), and she believes interior and exterior design should not be distinct (lines 41–43). Evaluate each answer choice against these characteristics. Be wary of answer choices that introduce new ideas, that contradict the passage, or that are too extreme.

A. No. She eschews flowing, leafy lines as stated in lines 14–15.

B. No. The passage does not suggest that carvings or bright colors exemplify her work.

C. No. The passage does not suggest that containers should resemble their contents, but it does suggest that she prefers simple, austere forms to ornate designs.

D. No. The passage does not suggest that unlacquered wood, glass beads, pearls, or colorful shells exemplify her work.

E. Yes. This is supported by lines 34–39.

10. **E** [Extract Infer]

This question asks which answer choice is supported by the ideas of tone of the passage. Evaluate each answer choice against the passage to find support. Be wary of answer choices that introduce new ideas, that contradict the passage, or that are too extreme.

A. No. The passage states in line 1 that she is best known for her work in lacquer, so she is not "primarily" known for her range of styles and media.

B. No. The passage does not discuss whether she was involved in furniture construction.

C. No. The passage states that applying lacquer to wood was a time-consuming process little-known in Europe, but it does not state or imply whether it was "generally" considered an "inappropriate" medium.

D. No. The passage does not discuss whether her objects were intended for viewing.

E. Yes. Her career progressed from small objects to interior design to architectural design, and the latter two were meant to be used and appreciated, as discussed in the second and final paragraphs.

11. **C** [Extract Fact]

This question asks which answer choice presents a question that is explicitly answered by the passage. Evaluate each answer choice against the passage to find a question that is explicitly answered. Be wary of answer choices that ask questions about new ideas.

A. No. Line 11 states that the tradition was little-known in Europe during her early career, but the passage does not provide a definitive answer to when it became known.

B. No. The passage does not discuss different types of wood or state which is the "best" for traditional Japanese lacquer work.

C. Yes. Lines 13–17 contrast traditional lacquer work with Art Nouveau, stating that the former prefers straight lines and the juxtaposition of simple forms, while the latter prefers flowing, leafy lines.

D. No. The final paragraph states that she believes that structural design cannot be separated from interior design, but it does not discuss the influence of the natural landscape.

E. No. The specific materials discussed in the passage are wood and tubular steel, but neither is linked to superior strength.

12. **A** **Big Picture**

This question asks for the author's attitude toward Gray's artistic accomplishments. Rely on the Bottom Line to choose the answer. Be wary of answer choices that contradict the Bottom Line or that are a poor match for the Bottom Line.

A. Yes. This answer choice matches the Bottom Line: her work ranged in materials and in scope, and she eschewed contemporary movements (lines 13–17).

B. No. The passage does not suggest that she was "on the periphery of the art world."

C. No. The passage states that she worked in the Japanese tradition of lacquer (lines 7–10), but this is not an architectural tradition.

D. No. The passage does not emphasize the speed of her evolution from small to large, nor does it describe her as avant-garde.

E. No. The passage does not suggest that she revolutionized structural design.

13. **B** **Extract Infer**

This question asks which answer choice describes a principle that was used in Gray's work. Evaluate each answer choice against the passage to find support. Be wary of answer choices that introduce new ideas, that contradict the passage, or that are too extreme.

A. No. The passage discusses lacquering wood only.

B. Yes. The final paragraph discusses the relationship between the interior and exterior: she believes that they should be designed together as an integrated whole (lines 43–45).

C. No. The passage suggests that her artistic style evolved, not that she merely applied identical techniques to increasingly larger objects.

D. No. Lines 16–17 state that she prefers straight lines and the juxtaposition of simple forms.

E. No. The passage states that the interior and exterior should be designed together as an integrated whole (lines 43–45), but this does not suggest that one can determine hidden materials by looking at the visible materials.

14. **C** **Extract Infer**

This question asks which answer choice the author would agree with regarding Gray's architectural work. Evaluate each answer choice against the passage to find support. Be wary of answer choices that introduce new ideas, that contradict the passage, or that are too extreme.

A. No. The passage does not discuss the opinions of other architects of her time.

B. No. The passage states that her work in lacquer and interior design prefigures her work as an architect (lines 40–41), so her evolution is natural, not a "radical shift."

C. Yes. Line 1 states that she was best known for her work in lacquer, so "at least some of her other work" is less well known.

D. No. The passage does not discuss how controversial any of her work was.

E. No. The influence for her architectural work is not discussed. Moreover, the passage states that her own work in lacquer, which was definitely influenced by an established tradition of Asian art (lines 7–10), prefigured her architectural work, so it is reasonable to say that her architectural work was so influenced, even if indirectly.

Questions 15–22

The first paragraph states the common view of Mesolithic woodland clearings: they had an economic use. It then disputes this view, stating that the archeological evidence for it is lacking. The second paragraph indicates that other evidence may support a different, noneconomic model of the clearings. The third paragraph lays the groundwork for this different model by summarizing the work of geographer Yi-Fu Tuan, who claims that human behavior is driven by fear of the wilderness. The fourth paragraph builds off of Tuan's claim, hypothesizing that this fear may account for the establishment of woodland paths in prehistory. The final paragraph states the alternative to the common view: Mesolithic woodland clearings can be explained by noneconomic factors, such as paths expanding into clearings.

The Bottom Line is that the common, economic-model view of woodland clearings may be incorrect because evidence suggests that they could also be explained by a noneconomic model.

15. **B** 〔Big Picture〕

Rely on the Bottom Line to choose the answer. Be wary of answer choices that contradict the Bottom Line or that are too narrow or too broad.

A. No. This answer choice is too narrow.

B. Yes. This answer choice matches the Bottom Line: although the economic (resource-procurement) model is widely accepted, other evidence may support a different, noneconomic model.

C. No. Both the economic and noneconomic models are supported by ethnographic evidence (lines 22–27).

D. No. The paleoecological record is discussed in lines 10–14, but it is not linked with the movement of Mesolithic human populations via established paths.

E. No. This answer choice is too definitive: the passage shows that both models have some evidence, but neither is "clear and unambiguous."

16. **B** 〔Extract Fact〕

This question asks which answer choice about the resource-procurement model is explicitly stated in the passage. Evaluate each answer choice against the passage to find an idea that is explicitly stated. Be wary of answer choices that introduce new ideas or that contradict the passage.

A. No. Movement along paths supports the noneconomic model.

B. Yes. This is a paraphrase of lines 4–7.

C. No. The passage does not discuss domesticated animals.

D. No. Use of clearings as resting sites supports the noneconomic model.

E. No. The passage does not discuss planting crops.

17. E RC Reasoning

Treat this question like a Strengthen question. Focus on the proposal in lines 41–45: fear of the wooded surroundings is one of the main motivators in establishing paths in premodern societies. Look for an answer choice that introduces new evidence in support of this proposal or that rules out an alternate explanation. Be wary of answer choices that weaken the proposal or that are outside the scope of the proposal.

A. No. This answer choice does not relate to fear.

B. No. This answer choice does not relate to fear.

C. No. This answer choice does not relate to fear.

D. No. This answer choice does not relate to premodern societies.

E. Yes. Performing rituals for the purpose of protection suggests that there is something to fear and protect oneself from.

18. D Extract Infer

This question asks which answer choice is supported by the ideas of tone of the passage. Evaluate each answer choice against the passage to find support. Be wary of answer choices that introduce new ideas, that contradict the passage, or that are too extreme.

A. No. Line 22 indicates that they used fire to increase grazing areas but not that they were the first to do so.

B. No. Lines 39–41 states that movement along prescribed pathways is a new idea but not that Mesolithic human populations were the first to do so.

C. No. The passage does not discuss what they may or may not have worshipped.

D. Yes. The noneconomic model offered as an alternative to the economic model relies on wilderness as a motivating concept for Mesolithic human populations (lines 51–54).

E. No. The passage does not discuss the complexity of the Mesolithic economic system.

19. D Structure

This question asks why the author mentions Yi-Fu Tuan's argument in the third paragraph. Return to the passage to determine the context of the third paragraph: the end of the second paragraph states that ethnographic evidence suggests a noneconomic model for Mesolithic woodland clearings, and Tuan's argument provides the basis for this model. Evaluate each answer choice against this function. Be wary of answer choices that incorrectly describe the function of the third paragraph or that describe the function of a different part of the passage.

A. No. Tuan's argument sets the stage for the noneconomic model.

B. No. Tuan's argument has no relation to the resource-procurement model.

C. No. Tuan's argument is not about the clearings themselves but about a driver of human behavior in general.

D. Yes. Tuan's argument is that fear of the wooded surroundings is one of the main motivators in establishing paths in premodern societies, and this argument provides the basis for the noneconomic model.

E. No. Tuan does not have a view on the clearings.

20. **A**   **Extract Infer**

This question asks which answer choice is supported by the ideas of tone of the passage. Return to the passage to determine why the author is not convinced of the resource-procurement model for clearings: in the first paragraph, the passage states that this model lacks corroborating archaeological evidence. Evaluate each answer choice against this criticism to find one that responds to it. Be wary of answer choices that introduce irrelevant ideas.

A. Yes. Lines 14–17 indicate that a lack of such evidence is a weakness of the economic model for clearings.

B. No. Such evidence already exists, as described in the first paragraph.

C. No. The passage does not criticize the model because it has not been reproduced in controlled experiments.

D. No. Evidence that some premodern societies used fire to increase grazing areas is given in support of the economic (resource-procurement) model (lines 18–22), so such evidence might undermine that model.

E. No. An increase in the number of woodland clearings would provide little evidence of the reason for the clearings.

21. **A**   **Structure**

This question asks for the meaning of the phrase "purely social phenomena." Return to the passage to determine the context of this phrase: the final passage describes an alternative hypothesis to the common view that clearings had an economic use (lines 4–8). This alternative hypothesis is that fear motivated the establishment of paths (lines 41–45), which then became permanent and attracted activity (lines 48–51). Evaluate each answer choice against this contrast (economic versus purely social). Be wary of answer choices that define "purely social" in a way not implied by the passage.

A. Yes. The passage contrasts the economic and noneconomic models for clearings.

B. No. The passage does not discuss phenomena that are unique to human societies.

C. No. The passage does not discuss phenomena that strengthen communal ties.

D. No. The passage does not discuss phenomena intentionally created for social benefit.

E. No. The passage does not discuss phenomena that reveal cultural and economic development.

22. **E**   **RC Reasoning**

Treat this question like a Parallel question. Focus on the structure of the argument in the second paragraph: one hypothesis is supported by circumstantial evidence (line 23–24, "some ethnographic evidence has been used to bolster the resource-procurement model"), while another, competing hypothesis is supported by different circumstantial evidence (line 24–26, "other ethnographic evidence may suggest a different vision, a noneconomic one"). Look for an answer choice that matches this structure. Be wary of answer choices that describe a different type of evidence or that are half correct.

A. No. The prosecution and defense use different types of evidence when they should be the same type.

B. No. The prosecution and defense use the exact same evidence when they should use different evidence that is nevertheless the same type.

C. No. The defense's evidence is not described.

D. No. Eyewitnesses generally provide direct, not circumstantial, evidence.

E. Yes. The prosecution and defense use different circumstantial evidence to arrive at different conclusions.

Questions 23–27

The first paragraph claims that specific performance, sometimes used by courts to settle breach-of-contract disputes as an alternative to monetary damages, is not a suitable remedy in all cases. The second paragraph concedes that specific performance is the only remedy in some cases. The final paragraph claims that monetary damages are nevertheless preferable in other cases, particularly those involving employment contracts.

The Bottom Line is that specific performance is suitable in some breach-of-contract cases, but monetary damages are suitable in others, particularly those involving employment contracts.

23. **B** **Extract Infer**

This question asks which answer choice is supported by the ideas of tone of the passage. Return to the passage to determine how it defines specific performance: participants are compelled to do what they have agreed to do in the contract (lines 1–4). Evaluate each answer choice against this definition. Be wary of answer choices that introduce new ideas, that contradict the passage, or that are too extreme.

A. No. Specific performance would compel the company to publish the manuscript.

B. Yes. Both parties are compelled to fulfill their contractual obligations.

C. No. Specific performance would compel the builder to complete the project.

D. No. It is unclear what the terms of the contract are.

E. No. Specific performance would compel the engineer to work and the company to compensate him.

24. **C** **Extract Infer**

This question asks which answer choice is supported by the ideas of tone of the passage. Return to the passage to determine what it states about such a case: monetary payment would be preferable to specific performance (lines 27–30 and 34–39). Evaluate each answer choice against this claim. Be wary of answer choices that introduce new ideas, that contradict the passage, or that are too extreme.

A. No. This is contradicted by the final paragraph, which states that specific performance can be problematic.

B. No. The passage does not compare the costs to the court of either remedy.

C. Yes. The final paragraph describes the negative consequences of specific performance in employment cases (lines 39–46).

D. No. The passage discusses which is preferable in theory, not what should happen if a person refuses to adopt a particular approach.

E. No. The passage does not discuss which remedy is more often considered by the courts.

25. **E** [Big Picture]

Rely on the Bottom Line to choose the answer. Be wary of answer choices that contradict the Bottom Line or that are too narrow or too broad.

A. No. The passage does not make a prediction.

B. No. The passage does not describe either remedy as a new legal measure.

C. No. The passage describes the difference between the two remedies but more specifically differentiates when each should be applied.

D. No. The passage does not discuss how evidence is evaluated.

E. Yes. The passage claims that specific performance is appropriate in some cases, such as when monetary damages cannot adequately compensate the victim, and that monetary damages are appropriate in other cases, such as those involving employment contracts.

26. **A** [Extract Infer]

This question asks which answer choice is supported by the ideas of tone of the passage. Evaluate each answer choice against the passage to find support. Be wary of answer choices that introduce new ideas, that contradict the passage, or that are too extreme.

A. Yes. This is a paraphrase of lines 9–12.

B. No. The passage states that specific performance is sometimes the only reasonable remedy (lines 15–18), but not that it is "usually the most appropriate" remedy.

C. No. The passage does not object to coercive remedies because they are unfair but because they are detrimental to those involved in the dispute (lines 30–33).

D. No. The passage states that specific performance is appropriate when monetary value cannot be assigned to personal property (lines 18–26), which not the same thing as its value is being low. Furthermore, it is not implied that this is the only case in which specific performance can be successful.

E. No. The passage does not imply that disputants should choose the resolution method.

27. **C** [RC Reasoning]

Treat this question like a Strengthen question. Focus on the author's position about remedies in employment contract cases: he believes that monetary payment is preferable to specific performance (lines 27–30 and 34–39). Look for an answer choice that introduces new evidence in support of this position or that rules out a potential obstacle. Be wary of answer choices that weaken the position or that are outside the scope of the position.

A. No. This would weaken the author's position by suggesting that monetary damages, while ideal in theory, do not work in practice.

B. No. The passage does not provide an exhaustive list of court-ordered remedies, so the term "all" is too strong.

C. Yes. This rules out a potential obstacle (that the party required to pay has no money).

D. No. The passage does not compare the legal issues in different types of contract disputes.

E. No. The passage does not discuss the rights of particular groups.

Section 3: Games

Questions 1–5

This is a 1D ordering game. The elements are the six neighborhoods: H, L, N, O, P, and S. The core of the diagram is the days of the week. Since there are six elements and five days, there will be a "not visited (NV)" column on your diagram as well.

Now symbolize the clues.

Clue 1 is a concrete clue and can be drawn above the diagram.

Clue 2 is conditional: $O \rightarrow \boxed{OH}$ and its contrapositive: $\boxed{\cancel{OH}} \rightarrow \sim O$

Clue 3 is also conditional: $L \rightarrow L_w$, where the subscript notes the day it is visited. Its contrapositive is $\sim L_w \rightarrow \sim L$.

Clue 4 has two parts. For challenging clues, remember to at least create some sort of shorthand note: N and S but $\boxed{\cancel{NS}}$ or $\boxed{\cancel{SN}}$

Once all the clues have been symbolized and double-checked, make deductions. From clue 1, H cannot be on Friday or NV. Mark this on your diagram.

From clue 3 and its contrapositive, L can be only in one of two places: W or NV. Mark this on your diagram.

Finally, from a combination of clues 1 and 2, O cannot be on Thursday. Doing so would force H onto Friday, which would violate rule 1. Mark this on your diagram.

Your diagram should look like this:

H, L, N, O, P, S

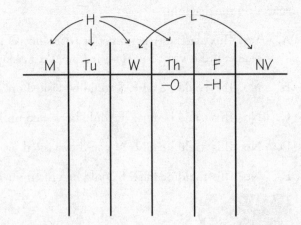

Clue 1: H = M/Tu/W/Th

Clue 2: O → [OH]

[OH] → −O

Clue 3: L → L = W

L ≠ W → −L

Clue 4: N and S [NS] [SN]

1. **B** Grab-a-Rule

   A. No. This violates rule 3 since L is visited but is not on Wednesday.

   B. Yes. This does not violate any rules.

   C. No. This violates rule 4 since N and S are on consecutive days.

   D. No. This violates rule 2 since O is visited but H is not on the following day.

   E. No. This violates rule 1 since H is visited on Friday.

2. **C** General

   Use previous work and deductions to determine which neighborhood CANNOT be visited on Thursday.

   A. No. If H is on Thursday, then O would be on Wednesday. L would be NV, and there is still room for N and S to be placed in non-consecutive places.

   B. No. If N is on Thursday, O could be NV and L could be W. There is still enough room in the diagram for S to be on Monday or Tuesday.

   C. Yes. If O is on Thursday, then H would have to be on Friday, which violates clue 1. This also matches a deduction.

   D. No. If P is on Thursday, then N or S could be Friday. There is still enough room in the diagram for S and the OH block if L is NV.

   E. No. If S is Thursday, then L could be Wednesday and O could be NV. Then H could be on Monday, N on Tuesday, and P on Friday.

3. **A** Specific

   Make a new line on your diagram and add the new information. If H is on Monday, there is no room for O, so that neighborhood is not visited (NV). This means that L must be visited Wednesday. Finally, since N and S cannot be visited consecutively, one of the two neighborhoods must be on Tuesday.

The question asks for what must be true, so the credited response should match one of the marked spaces on the diagram.

A. Yes. This matches what must be true since O must be NV, then L has to be visited. According to clue 3, if L is visited, it is visited on Wednesday.

B. No. This could be false. S could be visited on Tuesday and N later in the week.

C. No. This could be false. P could be visited on Friday as well.

D. No. This could be false. N could be visited on Tuesday and S later in the week.

E. No. This could be false. S could be visited on Thursday or Tuesday instead.

4. **B** Specific

Make a new line on the diagram and add the new information. If H is on Wednesday, the L is not visited. This means that O must be visited, so O is visited on Tuesday. Finally, either N or S must be visited on Monday since they must be non-consecutive.

This question asks for what must be true. The credited response should match one of the fixed places on the new line of the diagram. Eliminate answers that could be false.

A. No. This could be false. S could be visited on Monday and N sometime on Thursday or Friday.

B. Yes. This must be true. O must be on Tuesday since it will be visited and the position of H is fixed by the question.

C. No. This could be false. P could be visited on Thursday as well.

D. No. This could be false. N could be visited on Monday and S could be on Thursday or Friday.

E. No. This could be false. P could be visited on Thursday and S on Friday.

5. **D** Specific

Make a new line on the diagram and add the new information. If N is on Thursday, then S must be on either Monday or Tuesday. This flexibility means that the game should be played and eliminate answers based on POE. Start with S on Tuesday. There is no room for the OH block, so O is NV, which means L is on Wednesday, H is on Monday, and P is on Friday.

Since this question asks what must be true, eliminate answers that could be false:

A. No. The diagram shows this could be false.

B. This is currently true.

C. No. The diagram shows this could be false.

D. This is currently true.

E. This is currently true.

Now play the game a second time with S on Monday. This is one possible play. If S is on Monday, then O could be Tuesday and H on Wednesday. L would have to be NV, so P would have to be on Friday.

A.   No. Already eliminated.

B.   No. The second scenario shows this could be false. L could be NV.

C.   No. Already eliminated.

D.   Yes. This must be true as seen in both scenarios.

E.   No. The second scenario shows this could be false.

Questions 6–12

This is a 1D grouping game. The three groups are the numbered areas 1, 2, and 3. These form the core of the diagram. The elements are the park rangers: J, K, L, M, O, and P. The setup also stipulates a maximum and minimum for the assignments: each area must have at least one ranger and no more than three rangers.

Next, symbolize the clues.

Clue 1 is a concrete clue and should be placed on the diagram.

Clue 2 is also a concrete clue and should be placed on the diagram.

Clue 3 is a block clue with several parts. Be sure to diagram each part of the clue: $\boxed{LK}$ / $\boxed{LM}$ but $\boxed{L\cancel{K}M}$

Clue 4 is a complex conditional. Diagram this clue in two steps, beginning with the more straightforward if… then… statement.

O_2 → $\boxed{JK}$ where the subscript represents the area of the park that O is placed in.

Now, before doing the contrapositive, note the remainder of the clue. The word "otherwise" indicates all situations where O is not in area 2. Thus, this diagrams as

$\sim O_2$ → $\boxed{\cancel{JK}}$

Once the clues have been double-checked, make deductions.

The first deduction is related to the restrictions from the setup. Since every area must have at least one but no more than three rangers, the areas will have either a 2 – 2 – 2 pattern or a 1 – 2 – 3 pattern (in any order). There cannot be a distribution with four areas, nor will there be two areas that each have three rangers.

The second deduction is related to clue 3. Since L must be with either M or K, but cannot be with both, then K cannot be with M. This can be symbolized as:

$\boxed{\cancel{K}M}$ or can be placed on the diagram in conjunction with clue 1.

Finally, note how both clues two and four mention O. Since O cannot be in area 1, it must be in either two or three, each of which affects the grouping of J or K. O is the most restrictive element and will likely control the game.

Your diagram should look like this:

J, K, L, M, O, P

Clue 1: M = 3

Clue 2: O/P ≠ 1

Clue 3: LK / LM
        LMK

Clue 4: O = 2 → JK
        O ≠ 2 → J̶K̶

		−O −P			−K
	1		2		3	
	—		—		M	

6. E   Grab-a-Rule

Test each rule against the answers and eliminate false answers as they are found.

A.   No. This violates clue 3 since L is with neither K nor M.

B.   No. This violates clue 4. Since O is in area 2, then J and K must be together.

C.   No. This violates clue 2 since P is in area 1.

D.   No. This violates clue 1 since M is in area 2.

E.   Yes. This does not violate any rules.

7. C   Specific

Make a new line on the diagram and add the new information from the question. Place O in area 2 and M in area 3. Since O is the only ranger in area 2 and since P cannot be placed in area 1, P must be in area 3. According to clue 4, J and K are a block, so they must go to area 1. Finally, since L must be with either K or M, it can be in either position.

Note that the question asks for which could be a complete list. According to the diagram, the complete list could be either MP or MPL.

A.   No. If O is the only ranger in area 2, then P must also be in 3. This answer must be false.

B.   No. If O is the only ranger in area 2, then P must also be in 3. This answer must be false.

C.   Yes. This matches the diagram if L is in area 1.

D.   No. If O is the only ranger in area 2, then P must also be in 3. This answer must be false.

E.   No. If O is in area 2, then J and K must be together. This answer must be false.

8. D   Specific

Make a new line on the diagram and add the new information from the question. The new information can initially take the place of a distribution deduction.

Now, keep the pencil moving. Start placing elements beginning with the most restrictive, O.

Now eliminate answers that are false.

A. This is currently true.

B. This is currently true.

C. No. This could be false.

D. This is currently true.

E. No. This could be false.

Now repeat the process and eliminate more false answers.

A. No. This could be false.

B. No. This could be false.

C. No. This was already eliminated.

D. Yes. This must be true.

E. No. This was already eliminated.

9. **D**   General

Use prior work and deductions to determine which ranger cannot be in area 3.

A. No. If O is in area 2, JK can be in area 1 and so M, L, and P can all be in area 3.

B. No. If O is in area 2 with M, then L and K can be in area 1 and J and P can be in area 2.

C. No. If O is in area 2, JK can be in area 1 and so M, L, and P can all be in area 3.

D. Yes. If K is in area 3 with M, then L would also have to be in area 3. However, this would violate clue 3. This also matches a deduction.

E. No. If J is in area 3 with M, then O could be there also. L and K would be in area 1 and P would be in area 2.

10. **E**   Specific

Make a new line on the diagram and add the new information from the question. If K is in area 2, then O must be in area 3. Thus, J must be in area 1. L must be with either K or M, so L and P could be in either areas 2 or 3.

A. No. This must be false since J cannot be with K if O is not in area 2.

B. No. This must be false. If J was in area 3 with M and O, then either P or L would be alone in area 1, which would violate a clue.

C. No. L cannot be in area 1 if K is in 2 and M is in 3. This must be false since it would violate clue 3.

D. No. If O were in area 2 with K, then J would have to be there as well. The maximum number of elements per area is three, so L would have to be placed with M forcing P into area 1, which violates clue 2.

E. Yes. This matches one of the two possibilities on the diagram and could be true.

11. **B** Specific

Make a new line on the diagram and add the new information from the question. If L and O are together, they can be placed in either area 2 or area 3. Since L must also be with either K or M, there will be one of two blocks of three elements: KLO or MLO. Start by placing the one that is more restrictive. According to clue 1, M must be in three, so place L and O there as well. If O is in area 3, then P must be in area 2, and J and K can alternate into areas 1 or 2.

A. No. This must be false. If J is in area 3 with M, then the LO block from the question would be in area 2. K would have to be in area 3, and P would have to be in area 1, but this would violate clue 2.

B. Yes. This could be true according to the diagram.

C. No. This must be false since O must be with L and O cannot be in area 1.

D. No. This must be false. If O and L are in area 2, then K must pair with L according to clue 3. However, according to clue 4, J must also be with K, putting L O J K into area 2. This violates the setup.

E. No. This must be false. If P is in area 3 with M, then O would be forced into area 2. This would then cause L, J, and K to all be in area 2 as well.

12. **A** Specific

Make a new line on the diagram and add the new information from the question. Put J in area 2 and put M in area 3. The next element that should be placed is the restrictive element O. If O is in area 2, then K would have to be in area 2 as well. However, this would cause either L or P to be alone in area 1, both of which would violate clues. Thus, O must be in area 3. This would force K to be in area 1. L could be in either area 1 or 3, and P could be in either area 2 or 3, so they cannot be placed with certainty on the diagram.

A. Yes. This must be true according to the diagram.

B. No. This could be false since L could be in area 3.

C. No. This must be false.

D. No. This could be false since P could be in area 3.

E. No. This could be false since P could be in area 2.

Questions 13–17

This is a 1D grouping game. The three courses (groups L, M, and P) form the core of the diagram. The elements are the teaching assistants, R, S, T, V, Y, and Z. The setup stipulates a minimum of one assistant on every course.

Next, symbolize the clues.

Clue 1 states that M has exactly two assistants. This is a placeholder clue so add this directly to the diagram. If it helps, add the word only underneath the placeholders.

Clue 2 states that S and T are together. This is a block clue: $\boxed{ST}$

Clue 3 says that V and Y cannot be together. This is an antiblock: $\boxed{\diagup\!\!VY}$

Clue 4 is a conditional clue. Be sure to put the "if" clause on the left side of the conditional arrow:

Y_P or $Z_P \rightarrow \boxed{YZ}_P$, where the subscript P means placed on Pricing. Also, diagram the contrapositive:

$\sim\!\boxed{YZ}_P \rightarrow \sim\!Y_P$ and $\sim\!Z_P$

Once the clues have been double-checked, make deductions. There are two important deductions. First, combining clue 1 with the setup, there are three possible distributions to the clues. L could have one assistant, M two, and P three; each could have two assistants; or L could have three, M could have two, and P one. Add these as placeholder deductions to your diagram.

The next deduction is based upon a comparison of the block clues with the distributions above. The most restrictive elements in this game are the block ST and the potential block of YZ. However, there are no clear placements for any single elements. As a result, treat the blocks as the most restrictive elements and place them as soon as possible on the diagram.

Your diagram should look like this:

R, S, T, V, Y, Z

Clue 1: M = Z
Clue 2: $\boxed{ST}$
Clue 3: $\boxed{\diagup\!\!VY}$
Clue 4: Y = P → Z = P
         Z = P → Y = P

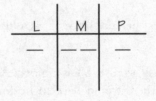

13. **A**   General

Use prior work and deductions to eliminate answers that must be false. If you still have remaining answers, diagram them one at a time. The first one that is valid is the credited response.

A.   Yes. If RYZ are in pricing, then ST would have to be in M and V would be on course L. This could be true.

B.   No. If Y is on P, then Z would also have to be on P. This violates clue 4 and must be false.

C.   No. This violates the distribution deductions. If there are four assistants on P, then there would not be enough assistants remaining to staff both places on M and the one place on L.

D.   No. This must be false since S and T are a block and have to be staffed together.

E.   No. This must be false since it violates clue 3 which says that V and Y cannot be staffed together.

79

14. B General

Use prior work and deductions to eliminate answers that ARE a complete list of assistants who can be staffed on L at the same time. Since every answer choice has exactly two elements, use distribution 2 from the deductions. Diagram as necessary.

A.   No. This could be true since ST could be on M and YZ on P.

B.   Yes. This must be false. If RZ are together, then V and Y would have to be together at some point.

C.   No. This could be true since YZ could be on M and VR on P.

D.   No. This could be true since RY could be on M and ST on P.

E.   No. This could be true since ST could be on M and RV on P.

15. A General

Use prior work and deductions to find the answer that could be true. If necessary, diagram answer choices. The first one that works is the credited response.

A.   Yes. This could be true using distribution 2. If RV are on M, then ST could be P and YZ on L.

B.   No. This must be false since ST is a block. This would put three assistants on M, which violates clue 1.

C.   No. This must be false since ST is a block. This would put three assistants on M, which violates clue 1.

D.   No. This must be false. ST is a block. Additionally, according to clue 4, if Z is on P, then Y must be as well. There would have to be four assistants on P, which would violate the distribution deductions.

E.   No. This must be false. If Z is on P, then Y must be also. This would violate clue 3.

16. C Specific

Make a new line on your diagram and add the new information. If V is with Z, then this block cannot be placed on P. This means that the VZ block will be on either L or M. Try VZ in L then try it again in M. Eliminate answer choices that can be true.

A.   No. If VZ is in M, this can be true.

B.   No. If VZ is in M, this can be true.

C.   Yes. If T was on markets, then S would also be on markets. The VZ block would have to be on L forcing Y to P. However, this would violate clue 4.

D.   No. If VZ is in L, this can be true.

E.   No. If VZ is in L, this can be true.

17. **D** `Specific`

Make a new line on your diagram and add the new information to it. Since R is the only student assigned, then the distribution will be either 1 or 2 from the deductions. Place R on the diagram followed by ST and eliminate any answer that could be false. If R is on P and ST is on P, then Y Z is on M and V is on P.

A. No. This can be false so eliminate it.

B. No. This can be false so eliminate it.

C. This is currently true.

D. This is currently true.

E. This is currently true.

Now repeat the process, placing R on P to try the other distribution. If R is the only element on P, then S T can be on L. V and Y have to be separate, so one must be on L and the other on M. Since M must have two elements, Z must be on M in this play.

A. No. Already eliminated.

B. No. Already eliminated.

C. No. This can be false so eliminate it.

D. Yes. This must be true. If Z were on P, then Y would be as well. This would force V to be with R, violating the condition from the problem. If Z were on L, then R would have to be alone on P, forcing V and Y to be together, violating clue 3.

E. No. This can be false, so eliminate it.

Questions 18–23

This is an ordering game with a twist. According to the setup, a single computer was infected and then passes the virus to the network. Since a computer can pass the virus to more than one computer, this can branch into a second dimension. The computers form the elements P, Q, R, S, T and U. The order of infection creates the core of the diagram. However, it is more efficient to use arrows to show the order of infection rather than create a grid for this game.

Next, symbolize the clues.

Clue 1 says the maximum transmission is to two other computers. This should be noted down: max to 2 computers

Clue 2 says that S transmitted to exactly one computer. Symbolize transmission using arrows.

S → ___ only

Clue 3 says that the same computer transmitted a virus to both S and R.

Clue 4 says that either R or T transmitted the virus to Q.

R → Q / T → Q

Clue 5 says that either T or U transmitted the virus to P.

T → P / U → P

Once the clues have been double checked, it is time to make deductions. First, since Q, P, R, and S are all preceded by an element, none of these computers can be the first one infected. Therefore, the first computer infected was either T or U.

1st

T/U →

The next series of deductions deal with possible orderings. Since both R and S are infected by the same computer, there can be a maximum of 5 infection events. Since S must infect something else, there is a minimum of three infection events. This helps constrain the number of possible orderings of infections.

Your diagram should look like this:

P, Q, R, S, T, U

Clue 1: max to 2 computers
Clue 2: S to 1 computer only
Clue 3: —⟨ R
                  S
Clue 4: R → Q
                 or
            T → Q
Clue 5: T → P
                 or
            P → T

18. **D**   General

Use prior work and deductions to eliminate every answer that must be false. If necessary, diagram the remaining answers: the one that works is the credited response.

A.   No. This must be false since either T or U must infect P. This violates clue 5.

B.   No. This must be false since the same computer infects both R and S. This violates clue 3.

C.   No. This must be false since either R or T must infect Q. This violates clue 4.

D.   Yes. This could be true.

E.   No. This must be false since if P infects R, it must also infect S according to clue 3. However, this would then use all the elements so S couldn't infect a computer, violating clue 2.

19.   **E**   **General**

Use prior work and deductions to determine which answer could be the first computer. Eliminate any answer that must be false.

A.   No. P cannot be first since clue 5 says that it is infected by either T or U.

B.   No. Q cannot be first since clue 4 says that it is infected by either R or T.

C.   No. R cannot be first since clue 3 says that both it and S are infected by the same computer.

D.   No. S cannot be first since clue 3 says that both it and R are infected by the same computer.

E.   Yes. This can be true and matches one of the deductions made.

20.   **A**   **Specific**

Make a new diagram beginning with the new information, and then add elements to the diagram that must be true. If T did not transmit the virus, then it must be a dead end on the diagram. Based on the deduction that either U or T must be first, this means that U must be first. According to clue 5, U must then transmit to P. According to clue 4, R must transmit to Q since T cannot. S must also transmit the virus to something, so P must transmit to R and S. In other words, the full diagram is constrained.

A.   Yes. This must be true according to the diagram.

B.   No. This must be false since R must transmit the virus to Q.

C.   No. This must be false since U can transmit the virus only to P.

D.   No. This must be false since P must transmit the virus to both R and S.

E.   No. This must be false since R must transmit the virus to Q.

21.   **C**   **General**

Use prior work and deductions to eliminate any answers that could infect two computers. The credited response will be the computer that cannot infect two others. If necessary, diagram each answer choice. If it creates a valid diagram, then eliminate it. Prior work from questions 18, 20, and 23, all show that P can infect multiple computers.

A.   No. This can be true based on prior work so eliminate it.

B.   No. This can be true.

C. Yes. This cannot be true since a computer must infect both R and S and since S must infect one computer. If R were to also infect two computers, all elements would be used but either clue 4 or clue 5 would be violated.

D. No. This can be true.

E. No. This can be true.

22. **C** `General`

Diagram each answer choice. The credited response will be the one that precludes any flexibility in the diagram. In other words, by diagramming the answer choices, every single element must be placed.

A. No. If R transmits to Q, no other elements must be placed. This does not determine the diagram.

B. No. If T transmits to Q, no other elements must be placed. This does not determine the diagram.

C. Yes. If T transmits to S, it must also transmit to R. Since T is now transmitting the virus to two computers, R must transmit to Q according to clue 4 and U must transmit to P according to clue 5. Since clue 2 stipulates that S must transmit to something, then S must transmit to U.

D. No. If U transmits to P, no other elements must be placed. This does not determine the diagram.

E. No. If U transmits to R, it must also transmit to S. This means that T must transmit to P; however, T or R can still transmit to Q, so this diagram is not fully determined.

23. **C** `Specific`

Make a new diagram beginning with the new information, and then add elements to the diagram that must be true. Since R and S are infected by the same computer, then P must be the one that is infecting them. P must be infected by either T or U, and S must infect something as well. Finally, Q must be infected by either T or R, but there is a lot of flexibility in the diagram for the position of Q. Eliminate any answer choices that could be false based on the diagram.

A. No. This could be false since S can transmit to U.

B. No. This could be false since U could transmit the virus to P.

C. Yes. This must be true since all elements are in play except for Q. Q can be infected by either T or R, but it cannot infect any other computer.

D. No. This could be false since R could infect Q.

E. No. This could be false since U could infect P.

Section 4: Arguments 2

1. D Resolve/Explain

The passage states that muscle power in cold-blooded creatures weakens as temperature drops and that indeed, the veiled chameleon suffers a decline in the ability to retract its tongue as temperature drops. Oddly, the veiled chameleon does not suffer a similar decline in its ability to extend its tongue. The credited response will explain the difference in the effect of a drop in temperature on the tongues of veiled chameleons.

A. No. General activity does not explain the difference in the effect of a drop in temperature on the tongues of veiled chameleons.

B. No. The distance a veiled chameleon can extend a tongue does not address the difference in the effect of a drop in temperature on the tongues of veiled chameleons.

C. No. The range of temperatures in the habitat of a veiled chameleon does not explain the difference in the effect of a drop in temperature on the tongues of veiled chameleons.

D. Yes. This would explain why the ability of a veiled chameleon to retract its tongue declines due to a weakening of muscle power but that its ability to extend its tongue is unaffected since it is not related to muscle power.

E. No. The relative strength of the veiled chameleon's retraction muscles compared to other cold-blooded creatures does not address the difference in the effect of a drop in temperature on the tongues of veiled chameleons.

2. A Necessary Assumption

The argument concludes that Acme will have to declare bankruptcy because it overstated its earnings for the last year. This is based on the premise that Acme must declare bankruptcy if it had to pay back a bank loan immediately and that Acme must pay back the bank loan should its earnings fall below $1 million in a year. The argument assumes that Acme overstated its earnings to be above $1 million but that it really earned less than $1 million and would need to pay back the loan immediately. The credited response will help the argument by providing this necessary assumption.

A. Yes. In order to know that Acme will declare bankruptcy, we must assume that its earnings fell below $1 million.

B. No. The argument does not require the holding of any other debts in order to be true. Acme would have to declare bankruptcy with only its bank loans if its earnings fell below $1 million.

C. No. Other years that Acme has overstated its earnings are not relevant to whether its overstating earnings in this year will cause it to declare bankruptcy.

D. No. The argument assumes that Acme's earnings fell below $1 million in the last year and that it will have to repay its loan immediately leading it to declare bankruptcy. This year's earnings are not relevant to that conclusion.

E. No. Other ways in which Acme may declare bankruptcy are not relevant to the situation in which Acme would have to declare bankruptcy by immediately repaying its bank loans.

3. **D** `Resolve/ Explain`

The passage states that hospital patients typically have lower rates of infection in private rooms as compared to semiprivate rooms, but that patients at Woodville hospital have similar rates of infection to those in other nearby hospitals despite Woodville's patients staying in semiprivate rooms as compared to mostly private rooms in other hospitals nearby. The passage states that the hospitals have similar patients and similar lengths of stay, so the credited response will need to explain the similar rates of infection (instead of expected higher rates at Woodville) by pointing to another difference between the hospitals.

A. No. The similarity in doctors would not address an important difference that explains why Woodville has lower than expected rates of infection relative to other hospitals in the area.

B. No. The age of hospitals is not directly relevant to explaining why Woodville has a lower than expected rate of infection relative to other hospitals in the area without making additional assumptions about how age would impact rates of infection.

C. No. This would explain only why people in semiprivate rooms tend to have higher rates of infection than those staying in private rooms.

D. Yes. Despite having only semiprivate rooms, if this is true, it is possible that the lower rates of infection are due to de facto private rooms at Woodville hospital.

E. No. The location of the hospitals is not directly relevant to explaining why Woodville has a lower than expected rate of infection relative to other hospitals in the area without making additional assumptions about how that location would impact rates of infection.

4. **A** `Sufficient Assumption`

The economist claims that unemployment will soon decrease. This is based on two facts. 1) Significant increases in government spending will spur the economy and cause a decrease in unemployment. 2) Significant decreases in government spending will cause business to retain earnings and hire more workers thereby causing a decrease in unemployment. The argument assumes that government spending will soon increase or decrease significantly.

A. Yes. If this is true, then one of the two scenarios will soon occur and unemployment will decrease.

B. No. Government policies intended to reduce unemployment are not relevant to the economist's argument about government spending.

C. No. The economist's argument is not based on a claim of increased demand for workers.

D. No. The argument does not make assumptions about the long-term economic impacts of increases in government spending.

E. No. The facts of the argument state that a significant decrease in spending will cause businesses to retain earnings.

5. **D** `Reasoning`

Marisa argues that zoning regulations should be relaxed because the regulations reduce the value of undeveloped property. Tyne disagrees by pointing out that the value of natural, undisturbed areas is preserved by the regulations. The argument hinges on two different definitions of value. Marisa uses value in a monetary sense, whereas Tyne uses value to mean something more general.

A.   No. The two refer to the same understanding of the word "regulations."

B.   No. The two refer to the same understanding of the word "development."

C.   No. Only Marisa refers to the word "prohibitive."

D.   Yes. The argument hinges on two different definitions of value. Marisa uses value in a monetary sense, whereas Tyne uses value to mean something more general.

E.   No. Only Marisa refers to the word "significantly."

6.   **B**   **Necessary Assumption**

The scientist argues that the conditions of laboratory animals can be responsible for skewing the results of studies that use these animals. The scientist offers the fact that animals in labs are well fed and receive very little exercise, that these conditions are only assumed to be healthy, and an example of a study in which such conditions would impact the results. The argument assumes that the conditions of laboratory animals are actually unhealthy.

A.   No. The conclusion is not about animals on a calorie-restricted diet.

B.   Yes. In order to claim that these conditions impact the study of laboratory animals, the author must assume that the conditions are unhealthy.

C.   No. The conclusion is not about animals that do not live in laboratory settings.

D.   No. The conclusion is not about studies that take into consideration the differences between animals in a lab and those outside of a lab.

E.   No. The amount of a food an animal with unlimited food would eat is not relevant to the health conditions of laboratory animals that may or may not be offered unlimited food.

7.   **D**   **Principle Strengthen**

The trade negotiator argues that it is wrong for a country to adopt a trade policy that would hinder the growth of another country because increased economic prosperity leads to political freedoms. The credited response should address the link between political freedoms and trade policies.

A.   No. The trade negotiator does not address policies that encourage political freedoms.

B.   No. This does not link the increase in political freedoms with trade policies set by a country.

C.   No. This does not link the increase in political freedoms with trade policies set by a country.

D.   Yes. If this is true, the argument's conclusion must also be true. A country that should do nothing to impede the increase in political freedoms shouldn't adopt trade policies that would hinder political freedoms.

E.   No. The argument is not about the inhabitants of a country that imposes trade policies, but instead on the inhabitants of other countries.

8. **B**

The argument concludes that great works of art are rare. This is based on the fact that a great work of art must be the result of an artist with great artistic skill and a high degree of creativity. The author assumes that having a combination of great skill and high levels of creativity is rare.

A. No. The author assumes that the combination of great skill and high creativity is rare, but does not make any assumptions about these factors individually.

B. Yes. This must be true for the argument's conclusion to hold. If the combination is not rare, then it is possible that great works of art are not rare.

C. No. This choice confuses necessary and sufficient conditions. The author does not state that the combination always results in great art.

D. No. The author assumes that the combination of great skill and high creativity is rare, but it does not make any assumptions about these factors individually.

E. No. The author makes no claims about the production of an individual who has both necessary factors to make great artworks.

9. **A**

The advertisement claims that by eating the cereal you will be on the most effective path toward fitness. This is based on the fact that those who eat cereal daily are more likely to exercise regularly, and regular exercise is the most effective way to become fit. The argument assumes that because people who eat cereal are more likely to exercise regularly, that eating cereal causes the regular exercise. The argument also assumes that this particular cereal does not contain ingredients that would hinder someone's ability to become fit.

A. Yes. The argument assumes that because people who eat cereal are more likely to exercise regularly, that eating cereal causes the regular exercise.

B. No. The author makes no claims about nutrition or its role in becoming physically fit.

C. No. The author never shows how cereal contributes to the result except how it is related to regular exercise.

D. No. The studies make a factual claim about adults. There is no evidence the sample used in the studies is unrepresentative.

E. No. The author does not make assumptions about individual adults.

10. **A**

The journalist concludes that critics who believe the quality of reporting has decreased with the increase in entertainment news are wrong. This is based on the fact that the best journalists have been the most entertaining journalists. The author fails to establish whether the best journalists are those who have quality reporting. In this Help question, the credited response will provide some link between these two concepts in order to help the conclusion follow from the facts presented.

A. Yes. This links the quality of reporting with the entertainment of the best journalists.

B. No. This fails to establish whether the best journalists are those who have quality reporting.

C. No. This fails to establish whether the best journalists are those who have quality reporting.

D. No. This fails to establish whether the best journalists are those who have quality reporting.

E. No. The qualities of the worst journalists would not help this argument.

11. **E** Main Point

The argument concludes that Austronesian-speaking peoples must have originated in Taiwan and moved to other islands. This is based on facts that state that three of the four Austronesian languages are unique to Taiwan, and the fourth is spread out over a vast number of islands in the Pacific. The author also states that these languages must all have started in the same geographic location. The credited response will match the conclusion of the argument.

A. No. This is a premise.

B. No. The author never mentions the length of time a language has been spoken.

C. No. The author never mentions the length of time a language has been spoken.

D. No. The author never mentions the length of time a language has been spoken.

E. Yes. This matches the conclusion drawn in the argument.

12. **E** Reasoning

West concludes that Haynes is the company's worst inspector because more than half of the poor quality returns were inspected by Haynes. Young points out that Haynes inspects more than half the appliances to provide another reason than quality of inspector that could explain why Haynes has more than half the returns.

A. No. Young provides additional facts to counter West's claim.

B. No. Young does not specifically address West's conclusion in her statements.

C. No. Young does not take issue with any of West's premises.

D. No. Young does not specifically address West's conclusion in her statements.

E. Yes. Young points out another factor to explain the premises that West attributes to poor performance.

13. **C** Principle Match

The situation establishes that both John and Emma ignored the potential for danger, but that John alone should be responsible for consequences since John was responsible for the errant throw. The credited response will match this situation.

A. No. This does not match because only one actor is responsible for the potential for danger.

B. No. The two actors performing the action are not responsible for the potential danger.

C. Yes. Both actors ignored the potential for danger; one of them alone caused an accident and is held responsible for the consequences.

D. No. A previous renter is responsible for the potential danger, and a fourth actor is held responsible for the consequences.

E. No. The party responsible for the consequences is not one of the two people who ignored the potential for danger.

14. **D** Strengthen

The researchers concluded that parents who sing to their infants do so with an emotion that noticeably affects the sound of their singing. This is based on a study in which parents sing with and without an infant, and researchers were able to identify whether an infant was present by listening to the recordings. The argument assumes that there are no other factors than emotion that lead to the change in the sound of the singing when an infant was present.

A. No. The conclusion is about the feeling of emotion when singing to their children specifically. Findings about singing to other children would not be relevant to the conclusion.

B. No. Knowledge of recordings is not directly relevant to whether emotion impacted singing. This choice provides a potential reason to weaken the claim by providing an alternative reason for the change in sound.

C. No. The conclusion is about the feeling of emotion when singing to their children specifically.

D. Yes. This provides an additional reason to believe the hypothesis is correct by pointing to a physiological response to emotions.

E. No. What the parents believed to be true is not relevant to whether the sound of their singing was affected by emotion.

15. **A** Principle Strengthen

The argument concludes that claims about Shakespeare's portrayal of Richard III are not relevant to appreciate the play. This is because Richard III is both fascinating and illuminating regardless of its historical accuracy. The credited response will help the conclusion by showing how a fascinating portrayal of aesthetics and morals is relevant to appreciating a play.

A. Yes. This would help the argument by showing that the historical inaccuracies are not relevant to appreciating the play.

B. No. This would hurt the argument by stating that Shakespeare's portrayal shouldn't have historical inaccuracies.

C. No. The argument does not state that Shakespeare is beyond the scope of criticism. It focuses on a specific criticism.

D. No. The argument does not mention the winning side.

E. No. The argument does not mention whether the inaccuracies in Shakespeare's play impugn Richard III in a way that should be corrected.

16. D **Parallel Flaw**

The argument concludes that the prime minister must be looking for a job with an international organization. This is based on the premise that the prime minister is travelling a lot and that travel is a necessary component of looking for a job with an international organization. The argument assumes that travel is also a sufficient factor. The credited response will contain a necessary/sufficient flaw.

A. No. This is the wrong flaw. It contains a numbers flaw.

B. No. This argument assumes that the evidence is enough to conclude that Franklin will lose the election.

C. No. This is the wrong flaw. It contains a causal flaw.

D. Yes. This argument contains a necessary/sufficient flaw.

E. No. This is the wrong flaw. It contains an absence of evidence flaw.

17. A **Main Point**

The argument concludes that debating the truth of a law is pointless, because it doesn't matter if the law can be defended based on the standard rules of debate. The credited response will paraphrase the first sentence of the argument.

A. Yes. This is the argument's conclusion.

B. No. This is a premise.

C. No. This is a premise.

D. No. The argument does not argue that the participants must hold the law in common.

E. No. This is a premise.

18. B **Flaw**

The argument concludes that many students should not go to college because many high school students already have the qualities valued in a college education. The argument fails to recognize that there may be other factors a job prospect would want to go to college.

A. No. The argument doesn't discuss whether colleges would provide the valued qualities since many students already possess these qualities.

B. Yes. If getting a college education is required for many jobs, there is a good reason many people would go to college.

C. No. The argument does not assume that only people with these qualities are hired.

D. No. The other reasons a person would go to college other than to get a job are not relevant to the conclusion.

E. No. How a student gained the valued qualities is not relevant to the conclusion.

19. **B** [Weaken]

The argument states that Neanderthals probably smoked meat because evidence of smoke producing fodder for fires has been found in Neanderthal fireplaces. The argument assumes that there is no other reason that Neanderthals chose lichens and grass over wood to make fires other than to smoke meats. The credited response will weaken the argument by providing an alternative reason.

A. No. This does not address the argument over whether Neanderthals smoked meat.

B. Yes. This states that Neanderthals had no other choice but to use lichens and grasses for their fires.

C. No. The challenge associated with using lichens and grasses is not relevant to whether they could have used other types of fodder for their fires.

D. No. Other types of Neanderthals are not relevant to the conclusion.

E. No. This choice is not relevant to the conclusion.

20. **B** [Point at Issue]

Edgar argues that it is okay to hurt an animal species in order to avoid inconveniencing people. Rafael argues that the threat to the fish indicates that there is a problem with the water supply and that therefore, the water pumps should be turned off.

A. No. Rafael never takes a stance on this issue.

B. Yes. Edgar would agree with this statement, while Rafael would disagree.

C. No. Rafael never takes a stance on this issue.

D. No. Neither speaker takes a stance on the legality of the issue.

E. No. Neither speaker takes a stance on whether the fish will be protected.

21. **C** [Necessary Assumption]

The argument provides an analogy between the relationships of scientific fields. In order for this analogy to be valid, the notion of purpose in machines, which can only be found through engineering, must be similar to the operational principles of human organs found only through physiology.

A. No. For the analogy to function there must be a link made between humans and machines.

B. No. For the analogy to function there must be a link made between humans and machines.

C. Yes. This states the link between the notion of purpose in machines and the operational principles of human organs.

D. No. For the analogy to function there must be a link made between humans and machines.

E. No. For the analogy to function there must be a link made between humans and machines.

22. **C** [Strengthen]

The argument concludes that the virus is at least 25 million years old based on premises that state that the virus is present in the same place in two different bird species that branched from each other approximately 25 million years ago. The argument assumes that a virus in the same place on the DNA must have occurred naturally before the two species split.

A. No. The argument is not concerned with the reasons a species may split.

B. No. The argument is not concerned with the existence of other viruses.

C. Yes. If this is true, then it is very unlikely that the two birds would have the virus in the exact same place.

D. No. The argument is not concerned with other bird species.

E. No. The survival of the animal species that contain the DNA of the virus is not relevant to the argument about the age of the virus.

23. **B** [Inference]

The passage states that *H. Subflexa* caterpillars eat only *Physalis* fruits, which do not contain an acid that other insects require for growth as well as the production of a chemical called volicitin. *H. Subflexa* does not have volicitin in its saliva.

A. No. There is no evidence to support the claim since the only evidence provided states that the diet of this caterpillar does not contain the acid.

B. Yes. The passage states that most caterpillars have volicitin in their saliva and that the acid is required for the production of volicitin.

C. No. The passage does not state that the acid causes the insects to produce volicitin, only that it is necessary for them to do so.

D. No. There is no evidence that discusses the impact of the acid on the caterpillar.

E. No. There is nothing in the passage to indicate that only the one species of caterpillar eats the fruits of *Physalis* plants.

24. **B** [Role]

The argument concludes that governmental monitoring of Internet conversations would be a setback for democracy because democracy requires that there be no restrictions on the ability of citizens to communicate freely. The question asks for the role of the first statement in the argument, which is a premise.

A. No. While the statement in question is a premise, it supports both of the statements that follow it.

B. Yes. The statement in question is a premise that is used to support both of the statements that follow it.

C. No. The statement in question is a premise for which no support is given.

79

D.   No. The statement in question is a premise for which no support is given.

E.   No. The statement in question is a premise for which no support is given.

25.   **C**   Inference

The passage states that one can compare two chess-playing programs by looking at performance on a given computer with fixed time limits per move. It also states that a single program will have a greater chance of winning a fixed-time game on a faster computer than the same program would on a slower computer because that program could calculate more moves in the same amount of time.

A.   No. There is no information in the passage that would allow one to compare two programs chances of winning based on speed. The passage tells us we can compare performance, but it is possible that a slower program could perform better than a faster program.

B.   No. There is no information about the requirements to run a chess-playing program.

C.   Yes. The last sentence states that a single program is more likely to win on a faster computer because it can calculate more moves in the time allotted.

D.   No. There is no information in the passage that would allow one to compare two programs' chances of winning based on speed. The passage tells us we can compare performance, but it is possible that a slower program could perform better than a faster program.

E.   No. There is no information that would allow one to compare programs based on speed in different time limits.

Chapter 10
PrepTest 80:
Answers and
Explanations

ANSWER KEY: PREPTEST 80

Section 1:
Arguments 1

1. D
2. A
3. A
4. E
5. A
6. B
7. D
8. C
9. D
10. D
11. D
12. C
13. A
14. C
15. C
16. B
17. E
18. D
19. A
20. A
21. B
22. D
23. E
24. E
25. C

Section 2:
Reading
Comprehension

1. A
2. D
3. B
4. A
5. E
6. C
7. E
8. A
9. D
10. A
11. D
12. C
13. B
14. D
15. B
16. C
17. E
18. B
19. D
20. B
21. A
22. D
23. E
24. A
25. E
26. C
27. B

Section 3:
Games

1. C
2. D
3. D
4. E
5. B
6. D
7. E
8. B
9. D
10. A
11. B
12. A
13. A
14. E
15. D
16. B
17. E
18. D
19. C
20. A
21. A
22. E
23. D

Section 4:
Arguments 2

1. A
2. C
3. D
4. D
5. C
6. A
7. B
8. A
9. E
10. C
11. A
12. E
13. A
14. E
15. E
16. B
17. B
18. E
19. B
20. E
21. B
22. B
23. A
24. E
25. D
26. B

EXPLANATIONS

Section 1: Arguments 1

1. D Resolve/ Explain

The passage presents two apparently contradictory facts: in a study, one group had a 69 percent reduction in dust-mite allergen, while the control group had no reduction. Unexpectedly, neither group had a reduction of allergy symptoms. The credited response to this Resolve/Explain question will help the passage by explaining why it would make sense that a 69 percent reduction in dust-mite allergens would still not reduce allergy symptoms.

A. No. This answer does not resolve the two facts. If dust-mite allergens in bedding are more irritating than in other locations, this would not explain why reducing allergens in bedding did not lead to a reduction in allergy symptoms.

B. No. This answer does not resolve the two facts. Even if people tend to exaggerate their allergy symptoms, they would still be expected to have fewer allergy symptoms after the dust-mite allergens were reduced.

C. No. This answer does not resolve the two facts. If the medical community does not fully understand how dust-mite allergens cause allergy, this would not explain why reducing the allergens did not reduce allergy symptoms.

D. Yes. If the only way to get relief from allergies is to reduce dust-mite allergens by 90 to 95 percent, this would help explain why both groups still experienced the same allergy symptoms even when one group had a 69 percent reduction in allergens.

E. No. This answer does not resolve the two facts. If both groups knew that only one group would be receiving mite-proof bedding, this still would not explain why the group with mite-proof bedding did not experience reduced allergy symptoms.

2. A Flaw

The argument concludes that Wilson's net income from sales of its hair dryer must be half of what it was five years ago. This conclusion is based on the fact that, over the past five years, Wilson's market share dropped from 50 percent to 25 percent of national hair dryer sales, while Wilson's net income per hair dryer has not changed over that time. The argument contains a percentages and numbers flaw: it presumes that the percentages of the national market are calculated based on the same total amount. That is, if the total national hair dryer sales market is the same size now as five years ago, the argument might work, but if the market has increased greatly, Wilson could be making more net income today with 25 percent of a much larger national market than it did when it had 50 percent of a smaller national market. The credited response to this Flaw question will correctly identify this percentages and numbers flaw.

A. Yes. This answer matches the flaw of the argument: the argument confuses a change in Wilson's percentage share of the national market with a change in the actual number of hair dryers sold by Wilson.

B.   No. Specific information about the profits generated by hair dryers is irrelevant to whether Wilson's net income from hair dryer sales has dropped over the past five years.

C.   No. Sales of products other than hair dryers are irrelevant. The conclusion is focused only on whether net income from sales of hair dryers has dropped over the past five years.

D.   No. The retail price of Wilson's hair dryers is irrelevant, because the argument states that the net income Wilson receives per hair dryer sold has remained constant. Therefore, an increase in retail price would not help, since it must have been offset by increased costs in order to generate the same net income per hair dryer.

E.   No. Whether the hair dryer is one of Wilson's least profitable products is irrelevant. The conclusion is focused only on whether net income from sales of hair dryers has dropped over the past five years.

3.   **A**   **Main Point**

The argument follows a typical Interpret pattern: it notes that virtues are always praiseworthy, and that resentment is never considered virtuous, even though it involves a type of faithfulness. The argument concludes that whether faithfulness is called virtuous depends on the object of the faithfulness. The credited response to this Main Point question will match that conclusion.

A.   Yes. This answer matches the conclusion of the argument. Use the Why Test: does each of the other statements in the argument support the idea that the object of a person's faithfulness partially determines whether or not the faithfulness is virtuous? Yes, because resentment is not praiseworthy, so it is never considered virtuous, even though it involves faithfulness. Therefore, this answer is the conclusion.

B.   No. This answer does not match the conclusion of the argument; rather, it is a premise. Use the Why Test: does each of the other statements in the argument support the idea that virtuous behavior is praiseworthy by definition? The first sentence does not support this idea, so this answer is not the conclusion.

C.   No. This answer does not match the conclusion of the argument; rather, it is a combination of two premises of the argument: the premise that virtues are by definition praiseworthy, and the premise that resentment involves faithfulness to hatreds or animosities. However, the conclusion is the first sentence of the argument: the object of a person's faithfulness partially determines whether or not the faithfulness is virtuous.

D.   No. This answer does not match the conclusion of the argument; rather, it comes from the premises of the argument. The conclusion is the first sentence of the argument: the object of a person's faithfulness partially determines whether or not the faithfulness is virtuous.

E.   No. This answer goes beyond the argument. The argument does not address whether resentment should be considered virtuous; the argument states in its premises that no one considers resentment virtuous, which is different. The conclusion is the first sentence of the argument: the object of a person's faithfulness partially determines whether or not the faithfulness is virtuous.

4.   E   Principle Strengthen

The columnist's argument follows a disagree pattern: it concludes that the legislator's proposal (to scrap the dam project that was approved, and instead use water bill revenue to construct new roads) is unacceptable. The argument is flawed because it does not explain why it is unacceptable to divert the funds in this manner. The credited response to this Principle-Strengthen question will help the argument by providing a general rule that supports the idea that it is unacceptable to scrap an approved dam project and instead spend the water bill revenues on road construction.

A.   No. This answer is irrelevant; the argument is not concerned with whether the customers have a right to know how their money is spent. Rather, it is concerned with whether spending the money on road construction is unacceptable.

B.   No. This answer is irrelevant; the argument does not state that road construction would benefit only some members of the community. If the argument had stated that the dam project would benefit the entire community but that the road construction would benefit only some members of the community, then this answer would strengthen the argument. However, the argument did not address this question.

C.   No. This answer is irrelevant; the argument does not address whether most of the utility's customers disapprove of the road construction project.

D.   No. This answer is irrelevant; the argument states that the water utility has already received legislative approval for the additional charge.

E.   Yes. This answer directly connects the premise (the new road construction project, which is not water-related) to the conclusion (that it is unacceptable to collect an additional charge for such a project): if an additional charge is not to be used for water-related expenditures, then it is unacceptable for the water utility to collect that additional charge.

5.   A   Necessary Assumption

The argument concludes that the leopard magpie moth is in danger of extinction, based on the premise that the Natal grass cycad, which provides the toxin that protects the moth from predators, is in danger of extinction. The argument is flawed because it presumes that lacing its body with toxins from the Natal grass cycad is the only way the moth can protect itself from predators. In other words, the argument overlooks the possibility that the moth could avoid extinction by protecting itself from predators in some other way. The credited response to this Necessary Assumption question will help the argument by providing a statement that is necessary in order for the moth to be in danger of extinction. The answer will also satisfy the Negation Test.

A.   Yes. In order for the moth to be in danger of extinction, it would be necessary that feeding on the Natal grass cycad is the only way for the moth to protect itself from predators. Try negating this choice: if feeding on the Natal grass cycad is not the only way for the moth to protect itself, then the moth would not be in danger of extinction. Therefore, this choice is necessary for the conclusion to be valid.

B.   No. This answer is too strong. It is not necessary that the moth be unable to escape from any of its potential predators in order for the moth to be in danger of extinction.

C. No. This answer does not help the conclusion. If a predator cannot determine from appearance alone whether a moth is laced with toxins, then this would make the conclusion less likely: the moth might not be in danger of extinction.

D. No. This answer is too strong. It is not necessary that the moth be unable to locate Natal grass cycads unless they are abundant. The moth could be in danger of extinction even if it could locate the cycads when they are rare.

E. No. This answer is too strong. The argument does not assume that none of the potential predators of the moth have developed a tolerance to the toxin; if only some predators have developed a tolerance, the moth could still survive and not be threatened by extinction.

6. **B**   Main Point

The argument follows a typical Disagree pattern, which is very common in Main Point passages: it concludes that using a budget surplus to pay down the national debt would make no sense, because national infrastructure is decaying, and to pay debt without repairing it would be similar to a homeowner paying off a mortgage early while neglecting the upkeep of the home. The credited response to this Main Point question will match the conclusion: using a budget surplus to pay down the national debt would make no sense.

A. No. This answer does not match the conclusion of the argument; rather, it is a premise. Use the Why Test: does each of the other statements in the argument support the idea that homeowners should not pay off their mortgage early while neglecting upkeep? The two sentences do not support this idea, so this answer is not the conclusion.

B. Yes. This answer matches the conclusion of the argument. Use the Why Test: does each of the other statements in the argument support the idea that using a budget surplus to pay down the national debt would make no sense? Yes, because national infrastructure is decaying, and to pay debt without repairing it would be similar to a homeowner paying off a mortgage early while neglecting the upkeep of the home. Therefore, this answer is the conclusion.

C. No. This answer does not match the conclusion of the argument; rather, it is a premise. Use the Why Test: does each of the other statements in the argument support the idea that a homeowner's personal finances are comparable to a nation's budget? The first two sentences do not support this idea, so this answer is not the conclusion.

D. No. This answer does not match the conclusion of the argument; rather, it is a premise. Use the Why Test: does each of the other statements in the argument support the idea that the nation is not maintaining adequate standards in the services it provides? The first two sentences do not support this idea, so this answer is not the conclusion.

E. No. This answer does not match the conclusion of the argument; rather, it is a premise. Use the Why Test: does each of the other statements in the argument support the idea that government leaders want to pay down the national debt? No, the argument concludes that this idea makes no sense. Therefore, this answer is not the conclusion.

7. D Point at Issue

Peraski argues that even though gas-guzzling cars pollute more than small cars, those who drive small cars when they could ride bicycles would be hypocrites to speak out against gas guzzlers. Jackson disagrees and says that even though the behavior is hypocritical, it would be worse not to speak out against gas guzzlers. The credited response to this Point at Issue question will be an answer that Peraski and Jackson would disagree about the truth of. Use information extracted from each person's argument to prove whether he or she would agree or disagree with each answer, and find the answer for which Peraski and Jackson would give opposite responses: Peraski argues that people who are hypocrites should not speak out, while Jackson argues that people should speak out even if they are hypocrites.

A. No. Peraski and Jackson agree about this statement. Peraski states that driving a gas guzzler produces greater pollution than a smaller car, while Jackson agrees and refers to them as greater sources of pollution.

B. No. Peraski and Jackson agree about this statement. Peraski states that if one speaks out against gas guzzlers when one drives a smaller car but could ride a bicycle, this would reveal hypocrisy. Jackson agrees and acknowledges that to do so would be hypocritical.

C. No. Peraski and Jackson agree about this statement. Peraski states that driving a bicycle would be better than driving a small car, and Jackson agrees that Jackson could do better in this area.

D. Yes. Peraski specifically states that one should not speak out if it reveals one's hypocrisy, while Jackson contradicts Peraski and states that it would be worse not to speak out, even if one's behavior is hypocritical.

E. No. Neither Peraski nor Jackson would agree with this statement, because neither of them addresses whether there is no moral difference between driving a gas guzzler and a smaller car.

8. C Resolve/ Explain

The passage presents two apparently contradictory facts: the only way for a small abalone species to develop into a large abalone species is by spending less energy on finding food and avoiding predators and more energy on competition in mating, and yet one species of large abalones developed only after otters that prey on abalones dominated their environment. The credited response to this Resolve/ Explain question will help the passage by explaining why it would make sense that the arrival of otters that prey on abalones would help abalones spend less energy on finding food and avoiding predators and more energy on competition in mating.

A. No. This answer does not resolve the two facts; rather, it makes the problem worse. If otters compete for the same types of food as abalones, then the arrival of otters would cause the abalones to spend more energy on finding food, and so the small abalone species would have a harder time developing into a large abalone species.

B. No. This answer does not resolve the two facts. Even if this situation involves only one of two known species of large abalones, this does not help explain why the arrival of otters helped this species to develop into large abalones.

C. Yes. If the otters prey on abalones' competitors for food, then the abalones would be able to spend less energy on finding food, which might help the species develop into large abalones even though they would have to spend energy avoiding the otters.

D.   No. This answer does not resolve the two facts. The speed at which small and large abalone species reproduce does not help explain why the arrival of otters helped this species to develop into large abalones.

E.   No. This answer does not resolve the two facts. If the otters prefer large abalones over small abalones, this would mean that the domination of otters in the environment should make it harder for the species of small abalones to develop into a species of large abalones.

9.   **D**   Sufficient Assumption

The argument concludes that stiff competition can undermine the result it was intended to achieve: maximization of employee performance. The conclusion is based on the premise that when one employee is perceived as clearly superior, this makes other competitors anxious about and doubtful of their own ability. The argument is flawed because it does not state that being anxious about and doubtful of one's own ability would affect employee performance. The credited response to this Sufficient Assumption question will help the argument by providing an assumption that makes the conclusion valid: the argument assumes that being anxious about and doubtful of one's own ability could affect one's ability to perform.

A.   No. This answer is not sufficient to make the conclusion valid. The argument is not concerned with how often employees who are considered superior win; rather, the argument is concerned with maximizing overall employee performance.

B.   No. This answer is not sufficient to make the conclusion valid. The argument is not concerned with whether employees who exert the most effort win; rather, the argument is concerned with maximizing overall employee performance.

C.   No. This answer is not sufficient to make the conclusion valid. The argument is not concerned with a situation in which competitors perceive the competition as winnable; rather, the argument is concerned with a situation in which employees consider one employee as clearly superior.

D.   Yes. This answer connects the premises to the conclusion in a way that is sufficient to make the conclusion valid: being anxious about and doubtful of one's own ability can affect one's ability to perform.

E.   No. This answer is not sufficient to make the conclusion valid. The argument is not concerned with competitors who work to undermine others; rather, the argument is concerned with competitors who are considered to be clearly superior.

10.   **D**   Inference

The passage states that creating a database of all recorded plant species was not easy, because botanists have often historically named plants that they didn't know were already named, and because DNA analysis has shown that plants that botanists thought were of the same species actually were not. The credited response to this inference EXCEPT question will be a statement that *contradicts* information extracted from the passage. Eliminate any statements that do not contradict information extracted from the passage.

A.   No. This answer does not contradict the passage. The passage states that for centuries, botanists have been naming plants that were already named. Therefore, it would be possible that most of the errors have not yet been cleared up.

B. No. This answer does not contradict the passage. The passage states that for centuries, botanists have been naming plants that were already named. Therefore, an accurate database of plant species could aid botanists by helping them prevent this extra work and the resulting confusion.

C. No. This answer does not contradict the passage. The passage does not discuss fields other than botany, so there is no reason to reject this statement based on information extracted from the passage.

D. Yes. This answer contradicts the passage: if for centuries, scientists have been naming plants that were already named, and if DNA analysis helps to identify plants that are actually of different species, then botanists must have some sort of technique for determining that this is the case.

E. No. This answer does not contradict the passage. The passage states that for centuries, botanists have been naming plants that were already named. Therefore, a person who looked up only one of a plant's names may miss other information that is included under another name for the same plant.

11. **D**   Strengthen

The argument concludes that hospital staff became much more meticulous about patient care when they knew their errors were being carefully monitored. The conclusion is based on the premise that the hospitals had attempted to reduce patient injuries due to staff errors by implementing a system to record all such errors, and that the number of injuries has decreased since that time. The argument includes a causal flaw: it assumes that because there was a correlation between the implementation of the new system and the decrease in patient injuries, that the decrease in patient injuries must have been caused by the implementation of the system. The credited response to this Strengthen question will provide evidence to support the idea that the reduction in patient injuries was caused by the implementation of the system, or eliminate another possible factor that could have caused the decline.

A. No. This answer weakens the argument by providing evidence that the hospitals had already had a policy of investigating such errors before the reduction in injuries began, which reduces the likelihood that the new system was the cause of the decrease.

B. No. This answer weakens the argument by providing evidence that another hospital that did not participate in the system also saw reductions in injuries during the same period, which reduces the likelihood that the new system was the cause of the decrease.

C. No. This answer is irrelevant. The argument is concerned only with errors that caused patient injuries, not errors that could have caused injuries but did not.

D. Yes. This answer strengthens the argument by providing evidence that in each hospital, the reduction in injuries did not begin until after staff became aware that the records were beginning to be analyzed. This increases the likelihood that awareness of the system caused the reduction in injuries.

E. No. This answer is irrelevant. The argument is concerned only whether awareness of the error-recording system caused a reduction in patient injuries, not the particular type of punishment given to staff members who made errors.

80

12. C Resolve/
Explain

The passage presents two apparently contradictory facts: wolves were introduced to an island to control the growing moose population. The wolves prospered, but unexpectedly, the moose population continued to grow. The credited response to this Resolve/Explain question will help the passage by explaining why it would make sense that the moose population continued to grow even after wolves were introduced to the island.

A. No. This answer does not resolve the two facts. Even if the wolves discouraged other predators from moving into the area, this does not explain why the wolves did not themselves reduce the moose population.

B. No. This answer does not resolve the two facts. Even if other attempts to control moose populations have failed, this still does not explain why the wolves did not themselves reduce the moose population.

C. Yes. If wolves often kill diseased moose that would have spread the disease to other moose, then this would explain why the wolves actually helped the moose population continue to grow, by reducing the number of moose that died due to disease.

D. No. This answer does not resolve the two facts. Whether healthy moose consume more vegetation than diseased or injured moose does not help explain why the wolves did not reduce the moose population.

E. No. This answer does not resolve the two facts. Even if older moose are just as likely to die of natural causes as they do from a wolf attack, that still does not explain why the wolves did not themselves reduce the moose population.

13. A Flaw

The argument begins by presenting a conditional statement: if the purpose of laws is to make people happy, then we can criticize existing laws and propose new laws. The argument then concludes that if the purpose of laws is not to make people happy, then we have no basis to evaluate existing laws, and therefore existing laws acquire legitimacy simply because they are the laws. The argument contains a necessary versus sufficient conditions flaw (in other words, a conditional statement flaw): it proposes that because a conditional statement is true (if laws make people happy, then we can criticize), the inverse of that conditional statement must also be true (if laws don't make people happy, then we can't criticize). However, a conditional statement can only prove its contrapositive (if we can't criticize, then the laws aren't to make people happy). The credited response to this Flaw question will correctly identify this necessary versus sufficient conditions flaw: the argument improperly took the sufficient portion of a conditional statement (the left side) and swapped it to become the necessary portion of the conditional statement (the right side), which is logically invalid.

A. Yes. This answer matches the flaw of the argument: the argument confuses a sufficient condition for a necessary condition. In other words, it swapped the left and right sides of a conditional statement, which is not a valid logical conclusion.

B. No. This answer describes a causal flaw. The argument does not infer a causal relationship based on a correlation. The argument simply presents a conditional statement and then concludes that the inverse of the conditional statement is true, which is logically invalid.

C. No. This answer describes a shifting meanings flaw. The argument does not change the meaning or sense of any words. Instead, the argument presents a conditional statement and then concludes that the inverse of the conditional statement is true, which is logically invalid.

D. No. This answer does not describe the flaw of the argument. The argument does not make any claims about how the world should be. Instead, the argument presents a conditional statement and then concludes that the inverse of the conditional statement is true, which is logically invalid.

E. No. This answer describes a part-to-whole comparison flaw. The argument does not compare a set of things (existing laws) to each member of the set of things (each existing law). Instead, the argument presents a conditional statement and then concludes that the inverse of the conditional statement is true, which is logically invalid.

14. **C**   Parallel

The argument begins by presenting a conditional statement: the existence of life on planet P23 requires the presence of water on the planet's surface. However, since there is no water on the planet's surface, the argument concludes that there must be no life on planet P23. The answer to this Parallel the Reasoning question will match the pattern of the argument's structure: in simple terms, "X requires Y. Y does not exist; therefore, X is impossible."

A. No. This choice does not match the passage, because it adds additional elements and because it uses weaker language than that of the argument: being successful (X) requires efficient employees (Y); knowledgeable and hardworking employees (Z) are probably efficient (Y); thus, being successful (X) requires knowledgeable and hardworking employees (Z).

B. No. This choice does not match the passage, because it adds additional elements and because it uses weaker language than that of the argument: being flustered (X) might result from surprise (Y); if so, then there is a low probability of being guilty (Z); thus, being flustered (X) does not necessarily mean a suspect is guilty (Z).

C. Yes. This choice matches the structure of the argument, even though it rearranges the order of the sentences: if companies plan to increase drilling (X), then they would be buying new drilling equipment (Y); they are not buying drilling equipment (Y), so they are not planning to increase drilling (X).

D. No. This choice does not match the passage: if the town's economy were improving (X), then real estate prices would increase (Y); the price of real estate is increasing (Y); thus, the town's economy is improving (X). In order to match the passage, this answer would need to note that the price of real estate was not increasing, and then conclude that the town's economy was not improving.

E. No. This choice does not match the passage: whenever exports decrease (X), trade deficit increases (Y); exports have recently decreased (X); thus trade deficit increased (Y). In order to match the passage, this answer would need to note that trade deficit had not increased, and then conclude that the exports had not decreased.

80

15. **C** Point at Issue

Sanchez argues that the school's sixteen new computers were not as expensive as people assumed, and concludes that the school didn't spend too much on the computers. Merriweather responds by arguing that the problem wasn't that the computers weren't worth the price, but that the computers were much more elaborate than they needed to be. The credited response to this Point at Issue question will be an answer that Sanchez and Merriweather would disagree about the truth of. Use information extracted from each person's argument to prove whether he or she would agree or disagree with each answer, and find the answer for which Sanchez and Merriweather would give opposite responses: Sanchez believes the school did not spend too much because the computers were less expensive than people assumed, while Merriweather believes that the school spent too much because it bought computers that were overly elaborate.

A. No. Sanchez and Merriweather do not disagree about this statement. Merriweather says that the computers were more elaborate than they needed to be, which implies that there was some need for new computers. However, Sanchez does not address whether the school needed new computers in any way.

B. No. Neither Sanchez nor Merriweather agree with this statement. Sanchez argues that the school didn't spend too much on computers, so Sanchez does not agree that the school purchased more computers than it should have. Merriweather says the computers were simply more elaborate than they needed to be, which implies that the computers were needed. Thus, Merriweather also does not agree that the school purchased more computers than it should have.

C. Yes. Sanchez believes the school did not spend too much because the computers were less expensive than people assumed, while Merriweather believes that the school spent too much because it bought computers that were overly elaborate.

D. No. Sanchez and Merriweather do not disagree about this statement. Merriweather disagrees with the statement, indicating that the school did not spend more on the computers than they were worth. However, Sanchez does not address whether the computers were worth the price; rather, Sanchez only addresses the price of the computers compared to people's expectations.

E. No. Sanchez and Merriweather do not disagree about this statement. Neither Sanchez nor Merriweather addresses whether the school was harshly criticized for purchasing the computers.

16. **B** Flaw

The airport administrator concludes that the chance of a plane straying off course while landing is 1 out of 2 million, low enough to allow runways to be safely built closer together. The administrator's conclusion disagrees with opponents who claim that the chance is 1 out of 20,000, based on air traffic control tapes, which the administrator believes are unreliable compared to the reports from pilots themselves that were reviewed in order to calculate the 1 out of 2 million figure. The argument contains a surveys and samples flaw: the administrator concludes that a study based on reports from individuals who commit errors is more reliable than a study based on a review of flight control tapes. The argument overlooks the possibility that there may be a problem with the study that produced the 1 out of 2 million figure. The credited response to this Flaw question will correctly identify this surveys and samples flaw: the argument overlooks the possibility that there may be a problem with the study that produced the 1 out of 2 million figure.

A. No. This answer is irrelevant. The argument does not address whether building runways closer together would make pilots more cautious; rather, the argument concludes that the risk of errors while landing is already low enough to allow runways to be built closer together.

B. Yes. This answer correctly identifies the flaw of the argument: the airport administrator's preferred study was based on flight reports from pilots, who may be unreliable sources of information about errors they have made while landing.

C. No. This answer describes an appeals and attacks flaw, but the argument did not attack the integrity of the opponents. Rather, the argument argues that the study used by the opponents is less reliable than the study used by the airport administrator.

D. No. This answer is too strong. The argument does not presume that the air traffic control tapes are inaccurate, but rather that the review of them was only partial, and therefore unreliable. Furthermore, the actual flaw in the argument is that the study preferred by the administrator may actually be less reliable.

E. No. This answer is too strong. The argument does not presume that the higher number is inaccurate, but simply relatively unreliable compared to the lower number. Furthermore, the actual flaw in the argument is that the study preferred by the administrator may actually be less reliable.

17. **E**   Necessary Assumption

The argument concludes that anglers who seek lake trout in partially iced-over lakes in late winter should fish in a shallow bay or close to the surface off a rocky point, rather than in the normal summer locations of those fish. The conclusion is based on the premise that a temperature distribution "turnover" occurs in fall and late winter, causing the lake trout to move to the new location of colder water. The argument is flawed because if an angler is visiting these lakes in late winter, it is not clear whether the late winter "turnover" would have already happened at that point, which would return the lake trout to their normal summer locations. The credited response to this Necessary Assumption question will help the argument by providing a statement that is necessary in order for the lake trout to be in different locations from their summer haunts. The answer will also satisfy the Negation Test.

A. No. This answer is irrelevant. The argument is not concerned with the ease of catching lake trout at various times of years and water temperatures; rather, the argument is concerned with the best location to look for lake trout during late winter in partially iced-over lakes.

B. No. This answer is irrelevant. The argument is not concerned with the density and weight of colder water compared to warmer water; rather, the argument is concerned with the best location to look for lake trout during late winter in partially iced-over lakes.

C. No. This answer is too extreme. It is not necessary that lake trout be found exclusively in deep temperate lakes in order for them to be found in shallow bays or near the surface off a rocky point during late winter in partially iced-over lakes.

D. No. This answer is irrelevant. The argument does not address the feeding habits of lake trout at various times of year; rather, the argument is concerned with the best location to look for lake trout during late winter in partially iced-over lakes.

E. Yes. In order for the lake trout to have moved from their summer haunts to the shallow bays, the fall "turnover" would need to have occurred and the late winter "turnover" would have to still be in the future. Try negating this choice: if the late winter "turnover" has already occurred, then the trout would already have returned to their summer haunts, and the conclusion would be incorrect. Therefore, this choice is necessary for the conclusion to be valid.

18. **D** Point at Issue

Liang argues that watching movies in which violence is portrayed as an acceptable way to resolve problems increases aggression in viewers, and so children should be restricted from watching such movies. Sarah responds by arguing that violence in dramas allows viewers to purge aggressive emotions, and so that mature audiences should not be restricted from viewing such dramas. The credited response to this Point at Issue question will be an answer that Liang and Sarah would agree about the truth of. Use information extracted from each person's argument to prove whether he or she would agree or disagree with each answer, and find the answer with which Liang and Sarah would both agree: Liang believes violent movies increase aggression in viewers, while Sarah believes violent movies help viewers purge aggressive emotions.

A. No. Liang and Sarah disagree about this statement. Liang disagrees, stating that violent movies increase aggression in viewers, while Sarah agrees, stating that violent movies help views purge emotions.

B. No. Liang and Sarah disagree about this statement. Liang disagrees, stating that violent movies increase aggression in viewers, while Sarah agrees, stating that violent movies help mature audiences purge emotions.

C. No. Liang and Sarah do not agree about this statement. Liang does not actually address whether violence is caused, only levels of aggression, and only recommends restricting the access of children. Sarah does not address a situation in which violent movies cause violence in viewers.

D. Yes. Liang and Sarah agree with this statement. Liang believes that dramatic depictions of violence on audiences increase levels of aggression in viewers, which must mean that Liang believes the effects of violent movies are at least partially understood. Sarah believes that dramatic depictions of violence on audiences allow viewers to purge aggressive emotions, which must mean that Sarah also believes the effects of violent movies are at least partially understood.

E. No. Liang and Sarah do not agree about this statement. Neither Liang nor Sarah addresses whether children or adults are more likely to be attracted to violent movies.

19. **A** Weaken

The politician concludes that Thompson is the best candidate to lead the nation. The politician's conclusion is based on the premises that Thompson opposes higher taxes, and that many people would agree that people who oppose higher taxes will make better leaders than people who support them. The argument is flawed because it does not explain why opposing higher taxes would actually result in good leadership (other than noting that many people believe it would); effectively, the argument assumes that the only relevant factor related to national leadership is opposition to higher taxes. The credited response to this Weaken question will hurt the argument by providing evidence that Thompson may not be the best person to lead the nation.

A. Yes. This choice hurts the argument by providing evidence that Thompson is not the best candidate to lead the nation. If opposing higher taxes is not a factor that contributes to good leadership, then Thompson would not necessarily be the best candidate to lead the nation.

B.   No. This answer does not affect the argument; it is too weakly stated to affect the conclusion. Even if being opposed to higher taxes is not sufficient on its own to cause good leadership, this doesn't mean that is it not a factor that contributes to good leadership.

C.   No. This answer is irrelevant. The argument does not provide any reason why having questionable opinions about important issues other than taxes would have an effect on leadership ability. The issue with the argument is its failure to connect the idea of opposing higher taxes to the quality of good leadership.

D.   No. This answer is either irrelevant or it strengthens the argument. If all past leaders who supported higher taxes performed their jobs adequately, this increases the likelihood that supporting higher taxes contributes to good leadership, or at least adequate leadership.

E.   No. This answer is either irrelevant or it strengthens the argument. If all past leaders who supported higher taxes were hardworking, this either increases the likelihood that supporting higher taxes contributes to good leadership (if being hardworking contributes to leadership), or has no effect on the argument (if being hardworking is unrelated to leadership).

20.   **A**   Reasoning

Patterson argues that music first arose during the Upper Paleolithic period, because the earliest evidence of music is bone flutes dating from that period. Garza responds by noting that bone typically survives well for centuries, unlike other materials, such as wood, that are commonly used to make musical instruments. Therefore, Garza is suggesting that music could have arisen earlier if wooden musical instruments from earlier periods simply haven't survived. The credited response to this Reasoning question will match the argumentative technique used by Garza to respond to Patterson: Garza pointed out that Patterson's evidence didn't necessarily prove Patterson's point, because some early musical instruments simply may not have lasted long enough to be discovered.

A.   Yes. This answer matches the technique used by Garza: Garza argues that the body of evidence (musical instruments made of bone) is insufficient for Patterson's purposes, because other evidence (earlier wooden musical instruments) simply might not have lasted long enough to be discovered.

B.   No. This answer does not match the passage because it is too strong. Garza does not challenge the truth of Patterson's premise (that bone flutes are the earliest evidence of music); rather, Garza suggests that other evidence might be missing that could disprove Patterson's point.

C.   No. This answer does not match the passage. Garza does not present a counterexample to Patterson's conclusion; rather, Garza suggests that other evidence might be missing that could disprove Patterson's point. To present a counterexample, Garza would need to have presented actual evidence of other musical instruments from an earlier period than the Upper Paleolithic.

D.   No. This answer does not match the passage. Garza does not present an analogous argument to Patterson's argument; rather, Garza suggests that other evidence might be missing that could disprove Patterson's point. To present an analogous argument, Garza would need to have presented an example of a similar discovery in another field that turned out to not prove its point.

E.   No. This answer does not match the passage. Garza does use Patterson's evidence to draw a different conclusion; rather, Garza suggests that the evidence used by Patterson is not sufficient to prove Patterson's point.

21. **B**

The passage presents a principle: occupations should not require licensing unless incompetence in performing regular occupational tasks poses a plausible threat to human health or safety. This principle can be rephrased as a conditional statement: if an occupation is to be subject to a licensing requirement, then incompetence in the performance of regular occupational tasks must pose a plausible threat to human health or safety. Also consider the contrapositive of the conditional statement, which applies equally: if incompetence in the performance of regular occupational tasks does not pose a plausible threat to human health or safety, then no licensing requirement should apply. The credited response to this Principle-Match EXCEPT question will be a statement that correctly applies this principle: it will follow the rules set forth in the conditional statement or its contrapositive.

A. No. This answer does not correctly apply the principle. If only some of the duties of police officers have no connection to human health or safety, the principle does not apply. The principle applies to the tasks normally carried out within the occupation, not to just some of the duties involved in the occupation.

B. Yes. This answer correctly applies the principle: if there are no dangers to humans related to interior design, then the occupation should not be subject to a licensing requirement.

C. No. This answer reverses the order of the conditional statement stated in the passage: if hospital administrator decisions do affect human health or safety, this does not trigger the conditional statement. The conditional statement is triggered only when an occupation's tasks do not pose a threat (meaning that no requirement should be imposed) or when a licensing requirement is imposed (meaning that the job must involve a threat to human health or safety).

D. No. This answer reverses the order of the conditional statement stated in the passage: if hair stylist products can pose a threat to human health or safety, this does not trigger the conditional statement. The conditional statement is triggered only when an occupation's tasks do not pose a threat (meaning that no requirement should be imposed) or when a licensing requirement is imposed (meaning that the job must involve a threat to human health or safety).

E. No. This answer reverses the order of the conditional statement stated in the passage: if unsanitary tattoo artists can pose a threat to human health or safety, this does not trigger the conditional statement. The conditional statement is triggered only when an occupation's tasks do not pose a threat (meaning that no requirement should be imposed) or when a licensing requirement is imposed (meaning that the job must involve a threat to human health or safety).

22. **D**

The passage states that most (more than half) of the new cars sold by Regis last year were purchased by local residents. The passage further states that Regis sold more new cars last year than ever before. Finally, the passage states that most (more than half) of the new cars purchased by local residents were not from Regis. The credited response to this Inference question will be a statement that is supported by information extracted from the passage.

A. No. This answer is too strong. While Regis did sell more new cars last year than ever before, and sold more than half of last year's cars to local residents, it is still possible that Regis sold more cars to local residents in a previous year than it did last year. For example, Regis might have sold 1,000 cars last year, the highest number it ever sold, and sold 501 of those cars to local residents. However, Regis could have sold 900 cars the year before, and could have sold 600 of them to local residents.

B. No. This answer is too strong. While Regis did sell more new cars last year than ever before, and sold more than half of last year's cars to local residents, it is still possible that local residents purchased more cars in a previous year than they did last year. For example, Regis might have sold 1,000 cars last year, the highest number it ever sold, and sold 501 of those cars to local residents. However, local residents might have bought 2,000 cars last year, and 3,000 cars the year before.

C. No. This answer is too strong. While local residents did purchase more vehicles from other dealers than from Regis last year, the passage does not state whether any one specific car retailer made more sales than Regis did to local residents.

D. Yes. This answer is supported by the statements in the passage: if Regis sold more new cars last year than ever before, and sold more than half of last year's cars to local residents, and if local residents bought more than half of their cars from other dealerships than Regis, then the number of cars purchased by local residents must be greater than the number of cars sold by Regis. For example, Regis might have sold 1,000 cars last year, the highest number it ever sold, and 501 of those cars were sold to local residents. If this were the case, then local residents must have purchased at least 502 cars from other car retailers, and that number must be more than half the total number of cars they purchased. Therefore, local residents would have to have purchased at least 1,003 cars last year in order to have purchased more than half from retailers other than Regis.

E. No. This answer is too strong. While Regis did sell more new cars last year than ever before, and sold more than half of last year's cars to local residents, it is still possible that Regis's share of the local new car market decreased from the year before. For example, Regis might have sold 1,000 cars last year, the highest number it ever sold, and sold 501 of those cars to local residents. If local residents bought 2,000 cars last year, then Regis's share of the market would be approximately 25%. However, Regis might have sold 600 cars in the previous year, while local residents might have bought only 1,200 cars that year, making Regis's share of the market 50% the year before last.

23. **E** **Strengthen**

The argument concludes that delaying the start time of school would cause a reduction in the number of car accidents involving teenagers driving to school. The conclusion is based on the premises that teenagers are sleepy if made to wake up before 8 A.M. and that when Granville's start was moved later, the overall number of teenage car accidents in Granville declined. The argument contains a causal flaw: because there was a correlation between the change in the start time and the reduced number of car accidents involving teenagers, the argument concludes that the change in the start time must have caused the reduction. The argument assumes that the change in the start time is the only possible cause of the reduced number of accidents. The credited response to this Strengthen question will provide evidence to support the idea that the change in the start time caused the reduction in car accidents involving teenagers, or eliminate a possible alternative cause that could have led to the reduction in car accidents involving teenagers.

A. No. This answer is irrelevant. The argument is not concerned with when young children start and stop releasing melatonin; rather, it is concerned with reducing the number of car accidents involving teenagers.

B. No. This answer is irrelevant. The argument is not concerned with tardiness to school; rather, it is concerned with reducing the number of car accidents involving teenagers.

80

C. No. This answer is irrelevant. The argument is not concerned with teenagers who work at jobs during the day; rather, it is concerned with reducing the number of car accidents involving teenagers driving to school.

D. No. This answer is irrelevant. The fact that many of the car accidents involving teenage driving occurred in the evening rather than the morning does not change the fact that accidents did occur while driving to school; the argument is concerned only with whether reducing the number of car accidents involving teenagers driving to school would be reduced.

E. Yes. This answer strengthens the argument by providing evidence that car accidents involving teenage drivers rose in the region during the time they declined in Granville. If this is the case, then this strengthens the idea that there is a casual connection between the change in the start time and the reduction in car accidents.

24. **E** ▐ Parallel Flaw

The argument states that Lucinda will soon attend National University as an engineering major, and notes that at National University, most (more than half) of the residents of Western Hall are engineering majors. The argument concludes that Lucinda will probably live in Western Hall. The argument contains a statistics flaw: it assumes that because more than half of Western Hall is engineering majors, that Lucinda will probably live there. The argument overlooks the possibility that there may be many other places where engineering majors live other than Western Hall. The credited response to this Parallel Flaw question will match the pattern and strength of language of the argument's flaw: because the residents of Western Hall (group X) are mostly made up of engineers (group Y), then a person who is an engineer (group Y) is probably in Western hall (group X).

A. No. This answer choice reverses the pattern of the original argument, because it states that most cities with shopping malls (group X) are regional economic hubs (group Y), and concludes that because our city is getting a shopping mall (group X), that it will become an economic hub (group Y).

B. No. This answer choice does not match the pattern of the original argument, because it uses conditional (if-then) statements instead of quantity statements involving "most" of a group.

C. No. This answer choice does not match the pattern of the original argument, because it uses conditional (if-then) statements instead of quantity statements involving "most" of a group.

D. No. This answer choice does not match the pattern of the original argument, because it contains a comparison flaw. It concludes that because one city experienced economic growth because of a shopping mall, most cities would also do the same. However, the original argument contained a statistics flaw.

E. Yes. This answer matches the statistics flaw in the original argument: most of the cities that are regional economic hubs (group X) contain regional shopping malls (group Y); our city is getting a shopping mall (group Y), and therefore, it will probably become a regional economic hub (group X).

25. C

The argument concludes that carbon dioxide should be pumped deep into the oceans in order to substantially reduce the amount of carbon dioxide in the Earth's atmosphere. The conclusion is based on the premise that the carbon dioxide would be trapped in the dense water in the ocean depths for centuries. The argument follows a "solve" pattern: it proposes a solution to a problem. The argument is flawed because it presumes that the solution will work, and that there are not problems that will prevent the solution from succeeding. The credited response to this Necessary Assumption question will help the argument by providing a statement that is necessary in order for the plan to pump carbon dioxide into the oceans to be successful. The answer will also satisfy the Negation Test.

A. No. This answer is irrelevant. The argument is not concerned with how thoroughly carbon dioxide dissolves when pumped into warm water compared to cool water; rather, the argument is concerned only with pumping carbon dioxide into cool water in the ocean depths.

B. No. This answer is irrelevant. The argument is not concerned with evaporation of warmer ocean water; rather, the argument is concerned only with cool water in the ocean depths.

C. Yes. In order for the plan to work, the carbon dioxide needs to not escape back into the atmosphere more quickly than planned. Try negating this choice: if the dissolved carbon dioxide escapes back into the atmosphere a long time before the cool water mixes with the warmer water, then the amount of carbon dioxide in the Earth's atmosphere would not be significantly reduced. Therefore, this answer is necessary in order for the conclusion to be valid.

D. No. This answer is too extreme. It is not necessary that density play the main role in trapping carbon dioxide in order for the plan to succeed in reducing the amount of carbon dioxide in the Earth's atmosphere.

E. No. This answer is too extreme. It is not necessary that the carbon dioxide be trapped for hundreds of years in order for the plan to succeed in substantially reducing the amount of carbon dioxide in the Earth's atmosphere.

Section 2: Reading Comprehension

Questions 1–6

The main point of the first paragraph is that Rawls was reacting to utilitarianism, a philosophy that has some problematic consequences. The second paragraph posits that the key to Rawls's theory is that fair procedure determines justice. The author calls this ingenious.

The main point of the third paragraph is that Rawls cleverly suggests the veil of ignorance (removing potential for bias) to achieve fairness and the author provides an example. In the fourth paragraph, the author describes Rawls's thought experiment called the original position, in which an individual's motivations would not be to the detriment of anyone because the individual would not know his or her station in life. The main point of the fifth paragraph is that Rawls thinks that all people want rights and liberties, powers and opportunities, and income and wealth and these are needed to accomplish goals, which results in a redistributionist point of view for those in the original position. The Bottom Line of the passage as a whole is to discuss how Rawls's theory of justice responds to the problems with utilitarianism. The author has a positive view towards Rawls, as indicated by language such as "ingenious" and "clever."

80

1. **A**

Extract Fact

The question is asking for a device that Rawls uses to explain his theory. The correct answer will be directly supported by evidence in the passage.

A. Yes. The passage explicitly describes Rawls's original position thought experiment in the fourth paragraph.

B. No. The passage does not discuss process of elimination.

C. No. The passage does not discuss an empirical study or social institutions.

D. No. The passage does not mention deduction.

E. No. The passage does not discuss the meaning of words.

2. **D**

Structure

The question is asking why the author includes the question "What else should we do but try to achieve the most satisfaction possible for the greatest number of people?" The author is indicating what makes utilitarianism seem plausible at first sight.

A. No. The question indicates what makes utilitarianism plausible, not implausible.

B. No. The author's discussion of problems with utilitarianism is later in the paragraph.

C. No. This answer choice is too extreme. The author states only that utilitarianism seems plausible.

D. Yes. The question indicates what makes utilitarianism seem plausible at first sight.

E. No. The question is posed rhetorically.

3. **B**

Big Picture

Use your Bottom Line to help you evaluate the choices. The credited response will describe the author's primary purpose.

A. No. The focus of the passage is on Rawls's theory of justice, not the abandonment of utilitarianism.

B. Yes. The author describes how Rawls's theory of justice responds to utilitarianism and calls his response ingenious.

C. No. The passage does not discuss the history of Rawls's theory.

D. No. There is only one mention of an unfortunate consequence of Rawls's ideas, and the author's attitude towards Rawls's theory is positive.

E. No. The author constructs the argument by rejecting utilitarianism.

4. **A**

Extract Infer

The question is asking for a statement that evidence in the passage indicates both the author and Rawls would agree with.

A. Yes. In the first paragraph, the passage indicates that both the author and Rawls have a problem with the concept of executing an innocent person to appease a mob.

B. No. This is a component of Rawls's theory, but the author does not indicate agreement.

C. No. This is a consequence of Rawls's theory, but the author indicates disagreement by using the word "unfortunately."

D. No. The passage does not discuss which of the primary goods is most valuable.

E. No. This statement is in line with the utilitarianism that Rawls and the author object to.

5. E **Big Picture**

The question is asking for the author's attitude toward Rawls's theory. The author expresses a positive attitude, though he or she expresses some concern about the redistributionist idea that results.

A. No. The author is positive rather than neutral, describing Rawls's theory as ingenious and clever.

B. No. There is no indication that the author's positive language toward Rawls's theory is insincere, nor is there any indication of disdain.

C. No. The author expresses concern about one of the results of the theory but does not criticize its cogency.

D. No. The author does not criticize the theory's practicality.

E. Yes. The author describes the theory as ingenious and clever, but notes that the redistributionist ideas that result are unfortunate.

6. C **RC Reasoning**

The question is asking for a piece of information that would weaken the idea that any individual in the original position would agree that everyone should get at least a minimum amount of the primary goods. The credited response will introduce a new piece of information that makes this claim less likely to be true.

A. No. This statement is consistent with the passage. The claim is about an individual in the original position, and a person who does not know his or her own preferences.

B. No. The claim assumes an individual in the original position, so it is not relevant whether that position can actually occur in practice.

C. Yes. This weakens the claim because some people would not agree that everyone should get some amount of the primary goods.

D. No. This is not relevant because the claim does not address satisfaction.

E. No. The claim discusses only that each person should get a minimum amount of primary goods, so the estimation of availability and need is not relevant.

Questions 7–13

The first paragraph begins by introducing the three catalysts of the Great Migration of African Americans from the south to the north beginning in 1915. In the second paragraph, the authors discuss that 1915 was the beginning because of the income gap, but not that the reasons for its continuation and acceleration are murkier. The main point of the third paragraph is the authors' hypothesis that migration momentum develops because current migration reduces the three sources of difficulty and cost of future migration. Paragraph four outlines how the actions of early migrants addressed all three of these causes of difficulty and cost. The Bottom Line of the passage is that though the north-south income gap triggered the Great Migration, it was sustained and grew because current migration reduces the difficulty and cost of future migration.

7. **E**   **Big Picture**

The question is asking for the main idea of the passage. Use your Bottom Line to help you evaluate the choices.

A.   No. While this is true based on the passage, it is only a detail and does not capture the larger main idea.

B.   No. While this answer choice mentions two of the three triggers of the Great Migration discussed in the passage, it does not discuss the continuation and acceleration of the migration that are necessary components of the main idea.

C.   No. While this is true based on the passage, it is only one detail and does not capture the larger main idea of the passage.

D.   No. This answer choice is too broad. The passage is about the Great Migration, which is not mentioned by this answer choice.

E.   Yes. This is an accurate paraphrase of the Bottom Line and captures the full main idea.

8. **A**   **Extract Fact**

The question is asking why the Great Migration did not start earlier than 1915. In the second paragraph, the passage states that the Great Migration began in 1915 and not earlier because it was only then that the income gap became large enough. The credited response will paraphrase this evidence from the passage.

A.   Yes. This answer choice paraphrases the reason given in the second paragraph of the passage.

B.   No. In the second paragraph, the authors explicitly state that the migration did not begin until the income gap was wide enough. Cost of living is not mentioned as a cause of the Great Migration.

C.   No. In the second paragraph, the authors explicitly state that the migration did not begin until the income gap was wide enough. The passage does not discuss specialized training for jobs.

D.   No. In the second paragraph, the authors explicitly state that the migration did not begin until the income gap was wide enough.

E.   No. In the second paragraph, the authors explicitly state that the migration did not begin until the income gap was wide enough. The passage mentions that labor demand was reduced by the boll weevil infestation, but there is nothing to support that agricultural jobs in the South paid very well.

9. **D**   **Structure**

The question is asking for the purpose of the third and fourth paragraphs. The third paragraph introduces the authors' hypothesis that migration grows over time because current migration reduces the difficulty and cost of future migration and the fourth paragraph details how the three sources of difficulty and cost were addressed by early migrants during the Great Migration.

A. No. These paragraphs discuss why the Great Migration lasted, while the first paragraph discusses why the Great Migration began.

B. No. Repercussions of the Great Migration are not discussed.

C. No. A thesis is presented in the third paragraph and evidence is presented in the fourth paragraph.

D. Yes. The second paragraph presents the question of why migration continued and accelerated as income differences were narrowing, the third paragraph presented a hypothesis to answer that question, and the fourth paragraph provided evidence for that hypothesis.

E. No. The claims made in the first paragraph were about catalysts for the Great Migration, but the third and fourth paragraphs discuss reasons that the Great Migration was sustained.

10. **A**   Extract Infer

The credited response will be the statement best supported by evidence in the passage.

A. Yes. The passage indicates in the second paragraph that migration accelerated even when income differences were narrowing. The authors of the passage explained in the fourth paragraph that difficulties and costs of migration were diminished during the Great Migration, encouraging migration even though expected financial gains were lower.

B. No. The authors do not discuss what triggered nineteenth-century migrations in their explanation of the Great Migration, so there's no support for the idea that they insist on the inclusion of those triggers.

C. No. The authors discuss migration movements in general in the third paragraph and the authors draw no distinction between the Great Migration and other migration movements.

D. No. This answer choice is too extreme. The authors discuss multiple factors that affect large-scale migrations, including information about the labor- and housing-market conditions and physical costs, so the authors would not agree that movement of people from lower- to higher-income regions would be an adequate explanation of most large-scale migrations.

E. No. The passage states that the Great Migration of African Americans occurred in the early twentieth century, but there is no support for the idea that other migrations did not before that particular migration.

11. **D**   Structure

The question is asking for the purpose of the final sentence of the second paragraph. The sentence states that the fact that migration continued and accelerated as North-South income differences narrowed is not as easily explained as the timing of the start of the Great Migration. The authors spend the rest of the passage explaining this paradox.

A. No. The authors do not criticize any previous research on the Great Migration; they merely note that the explanation of the continuation of the migration is less clear.

B. No. The authors discuss the causes of the Great Migration in the first paragraph. The end of the last paragraph is introducing the topic of the acceleration and continuation of the migration.

C. No. The sentence mentions that the income gap was narrowing, but that still means that Northern wages were higher than Southern wages, just to a lesser degree.

D. Yes. The remainder of the passage explains the fact that the Great Migration continued and accelerated despite the narrowing income gap.

E. No. The authors spend the rest of the passage explaining the Great Migration.

12. **C** Extract
Infer

The credited response will be the statement best supported by evidence in the passage.

A. No. The passage does not discuss the pay of any particular industries.

B. No. The passage does not go into enough specifics to support this statement. If anything, costs were likely lower for later migrants because of the factors discussed in the fourth paragraph.

C. Yes. The passage states that increased demand for labor in the North and decreased demand for labor in the South were catalysts for the Great Migration, which began when the income gap increased sufficiently.

D. No. The passage does not provide information about average wages over time.

E. No. This answer is too extreme. While the passage mentions that first-time migrants often traveled with earlier migrants returning from a visit, the passage does not support that most migrants made such a trip.

13. **B** RC Reasoning

The question is asking for a new piece of information that would strengthen the authors' discussion of the Great Migration. The credited response will be consistent with the Bottom Line.

A. No. If the average amount of time for new migrants to find employment grew, that would be an additional obstacle for later migrants, which is inconsistent with the authors' contention that migration accelerated because migration was less difficult for later migrants.

B. Yes. This would contribute to the ability of early migrants to pass information to new migrants, provide cultural cushion, and reduce physical costs by accompanying new migrants.

C. No. If housing prices were unpredictable, that would be an additional obstacle for later migrants, which is inconsistent with the authors' contention that migration accelerated because migration was less difficult for later migrants.

D. No. While recruitment is listed as one of three catalysts of the Great Migration, the authors do not discuss it as a factor sustaining the migration.

E. No. A reverse migration would weaken the authors' contention that migration accelerated during the Great Migration.

Questions 14–19

Passage A

Passage A begins by defining insider trading. In the second paragraph, the author contends that the actions that constitute insider trading are actually just a part of a well-functioning market. The third paragraph argues that since stock prices reflect an amalgamation of everyone's information and opinions about a company, it is helpful for those with inside information to act. The fourth paragraph continues this idea and asserts that acting on inside information ensures that prices are accurate, which is good for everyone in the market. The fifth paragraph analogizes to the non-criminality of the widespread practice of refraining from trading due to inside knowledge. The Bottom Line of passage A is that insider trading isn't problematic because it helps keep prices accurate, which is good for the stock market.

Passage B

Passage B begins by asserting that transparency is a basic principle of the stock market so that everyone has the same chance, and success is based on skill in analyzing information that is available to all. The second paragraph argues that insider trading unfairly compromises the market. The main point of the third paragraph is that insider trading causes a loss of investor confidence, which could lead to the breakdown of the market because people won't invest. The Bottom Line of passage B is that insider trading is harmful to the market.

14. **D**   **Big Picture**

The question is asking for a question that is answered by the Bottom Line of each passage. The passages are concerned with advocating for or against the harmfulness of insider trading.

  A.   No. While each passage does define insider trading, this is a detail rather than the primary concern of the passages.

  B.   No. Neither passage discusses the severity of penalties for insider trading.

  C.   No. Neither passage discusses the motivations for insider trading.

  D.   Yes. The primary purpose of passage A is to argue that insider trading is not harmful to the stock market, while the primary purpose of passage B is to argue that insider trading is harmful to the stock market.

  E.   No. Neither passage discusses ways to regulate insider trading.

15. **B**   **Big Picture**

The question is asking for the respective attitudes of passage A and passage B toward insider trading. Passage A argues that insider trading is helpful to the stock market, and passage B argues that insider trading is harmful to the stock market.

  A.   No. Passage B is negative, not neutral.

  B.   Yes. Passage A is positive, and passage B is negative.

  C.   No. Passage A is positive, not neutral.

  D.   No. Neither passage is neutral.

  E.   No. Passage A is positive, not negative.

16. **C** **Extract / Infer**

The question is asking what the authors of the two passages agree about. The credited response will be the statement best supported by evidence in both passages.

A. No. While this statement is explicitly supported by the third paragraph of passage B, passage A does not specifically address investor confidence and argues that insider trading is good for the stock market.

B. No. While this statement is consistent with passage B's contention that the stock market should be transparent, passage A argues that stock markets work best when relevant information is spread quickly and advocates that those with information act before others have the information.

C. Yes. While the passages differ on whether insider information is rightly included in that analysis, passage A praises analyzing stocks in the second paragraph and passage B advocates for skill in analyzing investments in the first paragraph.

D. No. While the author of passage A might agree with this statement because he or she thinks neither practice should be criminal, passage B does not discuss insider nontrading.

E. No. This answer choice is extreme and unsupported. While passage A argues that insider trading helps disseminate information, the author does not argue that it is the best method. Passage B argues against insider trading.

17. **E** **RC Reasoning**

The question is asking for a law that is consistent with the position of passage A that insider trading is good for the market, but inconsistent with the position of passage B that insider trading is harmful to the market. Treat this question like a Principle-Match question in Arguments.

A. No. This answer choice is reversed. This law would be consistent with the position in passage B and inconsistent with the position in passage A.

B. No. This answer choice is reversed. This law would be consistent with the position in passage B and inconsistent with the position in passage A.

C. No. Passage A does not discuss investor confidence, and this law would be consistent with the position in passage B.

D. No. Passage A does not differentiate between insider buying and selling, so this law would be inconsistent with passage A.

E. Yes. This is consistent with passage A's argument for insider trading but inconsistent with passage B's argument against insider trading.

18. **B** **Structure**

This question is asking for the way in which passage A's argument is structured. The credited response will be something that passage A does, but passage B doesn't do.

A. No. Passage A does not provide a particular example.

B. Yes. Passage A points out the uncontroversial and widespread practice of insider nontrading. Passage B does not discuss any uncontroversial activities.

C. No. Both passages discuss the consequences that they think result from insider trading.

D. No. Both passages discuss how the activity of insider trading relates to the stock market as a whole.

E. No. Passage A does not discuss any actor's motivations.

19. **D** **Structure**

The question is asking how each passage uses its reference to analysis of stocks. Passage A describes analysis as an activity that takes advantage of knowledge that others don't have. Passage B describes analysis as a skill that dictates success given equal access to information.

A. No. Passage A does not dismiss analysis; rather, it compares analysis to insider trading.

B. No. Passage A does not argue that the market needs to compensate for a lack of transparency. Passage B does not claim that the viability of analysis is conditional.

C. No. Passage A presents analysis as part of an argument that insider trading is not unfair. Passage B makes no such claim about the relationship between analysis and transparency.

D. Yes. Passage A describes analysis as an activity that takes advantage of knowledge that others don't have. Passage B describes analysis as a skill that dictates success given equal access to information.

E. No. Passage A does not limit analysis to stock market professionals.

Questions 20–27

The main point of the first paragraph is that while brain scans are valuable for medical diagnosis, there are problems when they are used in psychology, which relies on the modular theory of mind. The second paragraph critiques the modular theory of mind and argues that mental activity should not be compartmentalized. There is a shift in the third paragraph as the author concedes that there are well-defined areas of the brain that depict differential rates of oxygen use for different cognitive tasks, but this is based on a subtractive method. The fourth paragraph points out that the brain scans obscure the distributed brain functions because of this problematic subtractive method and that the modular theory is favored because it is illustrated by this flawed method. The Bottom Line of the passage as a whole is that brain scans do not necessarily prove that cognitive tasks are modular because the subtractive method is problematic.

20. **B** **Big Picture**

Use your Bottom Line to evaluate the answer choices.

A. No. The passage does not focus on the growth of brain scan technology in psychology; it merely mentions that is it widespread.

B. Yes. This is an accurate paraphrase of the Bottom Line of the passage.

C. No. This answer choice is too narrow. While the passage mentions the popular press and the separation of reason and emotion in the second paragraph, that is not the main point of the passage.

D.   No. The passage does not argue that the fMRI is not a measure of metabolic activity; rather it critiques the subtractive method that obscures the baseline distributed brain activity.

E.   No. The passage critiques the modular theory of mind.

21.   **A**   **Extract Fact**

The question is asking for something that is true about mental activity within the modular theory of mind. The credited response will be directly supported by evidence in the passage.

A.   Yes. In the first paragraph, the passage defines the modular theory of mind as the premise that the mind can be analyzed into separate and distinct modules that are in localized brain regions.

B.   No. The author discusses metabolic activity across the brain as part of his or her critique of the modular theory of mind.

C.   No. The passage does not discuss whether the physical processes that constitute mental activity are controllable.

D.   No. The amygdala and the prefrontal cortex are discussed in the second paragraph as examples of particular areas that the popular press claims are the respective seats of emotion and reason, while the author defines the modular theory of mind in the first paragraph.

E.   No. The author criticizes the modular theory of mind by arguing that reason-giving cannot be separated from other mental processes such as emotion.

22.   **D**   **Extract Infer**

The question is asking for a statement about the subtractive method that is supported by evidence in the passage. In the fourth paragraph, the author argues that the subtractive method obscures the fact that the entire brain is active in both the baseline and second fMRI scans.

A.   No. While the author does criticize the subtractive method for masking distributed brain functions, he or she states in the first paragraph that the value of brain scans for medical diagnosis is straightforward and indubitable.

B.   No. The author argues that the subtractive method supports the modular theory of mind, which Uttal disagrees with the in the second paragraph.

C.   No. The author argues that the subtractive method gives a false impression of neat functional localization and would therefore create the impression that emotion is seated in the amygdala.

D.   Yes. This is a paraphrase of the last sentence of the passage.

E.   No. The author agrees that the subtractive method depicts differential rates of oxygen use, but disagrees with the interpretation of what that differential use means.

23.   **E**   **Structure**

The question is asking what the purpose of the final paragraph is. The fourth paragraph points out that even if brain scans depict differences in oxygen use, they obscure the distributed brain functions because of the problematic subtractive method, and the modular theory is favored because it is illustrated by this flawed method.

A. No. The author states that the differential oxygen use research results in the third paragraph seem to support the basic premise in the first paragraph that the mind can be analyzed in distinct modules.

B. No. The author states that the differential oxygen use research results in the third paragraph seem to support the basic premise in the first paragraph that the mind can be analyzed in distinct modules.

C. No. The research method detailed in the third paragraph is in contrast with the distributed mental activity theory described in the second paragraph, and there is no indication that the author thinks the distributed mental activity theory is outdated. If anything, the author believes the modular theory of mind described in the first paragraph is outdated.

D. No. While the author criticizes the modular theory of mind outlined in the first paragraph, he or she does not criticize the distributed mental activity theory discussed in the second paragraph.

E. Yes. In the fourth paragraph, the author describes why the evidence detailed in the third paragraph is flawed.

24. **A** **Structure**

The question is asking for the author's purpose in analogizing brain scans and X-rays. In the first paragraph, the author says that brain scans and X-rays are similar as applied to medical diagnosis, but argues that the use of brain scans in psychology is different.

A. Yes. The author argues that brain scans, like X-rays, are valid for medical diagnosis, but not valid for psychological analysis.

B. No. The author does not indicate that either procedure is new technology.

C. No. The author does not compare the precision of brain scans and X-rays.

D. No. X-rays are mentioned only with respect to medical diagnoses and are not used in the author's critique of the modular theory of mind.

E. No. The author does not claim that brain scans are derived from X-rays.

25. **E** **Extract Fact**

The question is asking for a statement that Uttal would agree with. The credited response will be something directly supported by evidence in the passage.

A. No. In the second paragraph, Uttal argues that mental processes are distributed throughout the brain and are not independent modules.

B. No. This answer choice is too extreme. While the second paragraph does argue that reason cannot be separated from emotion, these are merely examples of two of many mental processes that Uttal believes are distributed throughout the brain.

C. No. Uttal's view is discussed in the second paragraph and oxygen use differentials do not come up until the third paragraph.

D. No. Interpretations of brain scans using the subtractive method support the modular theory of mind, which Uttal disagrees with.

E. Yes. This is an accurate paraphrase of Uttal's contention in the second paragraph.

26. **C** **Extract Infer**

The credited response will be the answer choice that is best supported by evidence in the passage.

A. No. This answer choice is extreme and unsupported. The author argues that it may be that mental activity cannot be decomposable into independent modules.

B. No. The modular theory of mind is supported by the subtractive method of interpreting brain scans, which the passage says shows a differential rate of oxygen use. There is no claim that the baseline oxygen use is close to zero.

C. Yes. As described in the passage, certain areas of the brain "light up" when the oxygen use in those areas is higher than the baseline oxygen use rate.

D. No. The passage does not give any information about the relative baseline oxygen use rates for different regions of the brain.

E. No. The passage does not specify what happens on brain scans when a subject experiences anger; it merely presents Uttal's disagreement with the popular press's belief that the amygdala is the seat of emotion and the prefrontal cortex is the seat of reason.

27. **B** **RC Reasoning**

This question is asking for a scenario that is consistent with the typical interpretation of fMRI scans as described in the passage. The author contends the fMRI scans are typically interpreted as showing metabolic activity only in specific areas, though this is a result of a subtractive method.

A. No. There is no subtractive method at work in this scenario.

B. Yes. The difference between the baseline number of shoppers and the increase in the summer is used to indicate that something happened just in the summer, much like the difference in oxygen use between the baseline and the spikes in a particular area is used to argue that there is activity just in that area.

C. No. There is no subtractive method at work in this scenario.

D. No. There is no subtractive method at work in this scenario.

E. No. There is no subtractive method at work in this scenario.

Section 3: Games

Questions 1–5

This is a 1D In/Out game (two groups are played like In/Out games). The core of the diagram will be the two research teams, green and red. The elements are the five students: J, K, L, M and O. The twist to this game is the facilitator position. The placements are relatively fixed with two students on one team and three on the other. As a result, there are only two possible distributions for this game.

Now symbolize the clues.

Clue 1 is an antiblock clue:

Clue 2 is a concrete clue and can be placed directly on the diagram.

Clue 3 is informational: K ≠ F

Clue 4 is also informational: O = F

Once all the clues have been symbolized and double-checked, make deductions. From clue 1, J and O are always on different teams. This can be symbolized as a placeholder deduction on the diagram.

This deduction establishes the placement of three of the five elements of the game. Also, since O must be a facilitator, the placement of either J or O will dictate who can or cannot be a facilitator.

Your diagram should look like this:

J, K, L, M, O

	Green	Red
(1)	_ J/O L	_ O/J
(2)	J/O L	_ _ O/J

Clue 1: J̶O̶

Clue 2: L = G

Clue 3: K ≠ facilitator

Clue 4: O = facilitator

1. **C** Grab-a-Rule

    A. No. This violates clue 1 since both J and O are on the green team.

    B. No. This violates clue 4 since O is not a facilitator.

    C. Yes. This answer agrees with all clues.

    D. No. This violates clue 2 since L is not on the green team.

    E. No. This violates clue 3 since K is a facilitator.

80

2. **D** General

Use previous work and deductions to determine which response must be true.

A. No. J can be placed on the green team with L, while O, M, and K can be on the red team. O would be the facilitator for the red team and either J or L would be the facilitator for the green.

B. No. J could be the facilitator for one team and O could be the facilitator for the other.

C. No. If J is assigned to the green team, then O would have to be assigned to the Red. There is enough flexibility in the other elements to allow this.

D. Yes. There can be only one facilitator per team. If J is the facilitator of one and M the facilitator of the other, then it would not be possible for O to be a facilitator. This violates clue 4.

E. No. K cannot be a facilitator; however, it is possible for J to be a facilitator of one team and O the facilitator of the other.

3. **D** General

Use previous work and deductions to determine which response must be false. Any answer choice that could be true should be eliminated.

A. No. This could be true. L could be the facilitator of the green team with K and J. O and M would be on the red team with O as the facilitator.

B. No. This could be true. M could be the facilitator of the red team with J and K. O and L would be on the green team with O as the facilitator.

C. No. This could be true. O and M could be on the red team with O as the facilitator. J, K, and L could be on the green team with either J or L as facilitator.

D. Yes. This must be false. If L is on a different team than J, then O must be on the same team as L. However, both L and O cannot both be facilitators. This violates the setup of the game.

E. No. This could be true. M could be the facilitator of the green team with L and J. O would be the red facilitator with K.

4. **E** Specific

Make a new line on the diagram and add the new information. If L is a facilitator, then according to clue 4, the two facilitators must be L and O. This means that J and L are on the green team, while O is on the red team.

The specific distribution does not matter here. There is a maximum of one more element that can be placed on the green team and a minimum of one element that must be on the red team. This question asks for what could be true. The credited response will be the answer choice that doesn't violate what is here. Eliminate answers that must be false.

A. No. This must be false. As seen on the diagram, J must be on the green team.

B. No. This must be false. As seen on the diagram, J must be on the green team.

C. No. This must be false. As seen on the diagram, O must be on the red team.

D. No. This must be false. As seen on the diagram, O must be on the red team.

E. Yes. This could be true. M could be on the red team with O, and K could be placed on either team.

5. **B**   Specific

Make a new line on the diagram and add the new information. If M is on the green team with L, the placeholder deduction stipulates that the distribution must be three on the green team and two on the red. Since the distribution is known, then K must be on the red team. O will be a facilitator for one of the teams, but the other facilitator is flexible.

Since this question asks what must be true, eliminate answers that could be false. The credited response will likely match something on the diagram:

A. No. The diagram shows this could be false.

B. Yes. This must be true.

C. No. The diagram shows this could be false.

D. No. If O is on the green team, then L wouldn't be a facilitator. This could be false.

E. No. If O is on the green team, then M wouldn't be a facilitator. This could be false.

Questions 6–11

This is a 1D ordering game. The seven chapters form the core of the diagram and the clues—R, S, T, U, W, X, and Z—are the elements of the game.

Next, symbolize the clues.

Clue 1 provides concrete information and should be noted on the diagram. The (~) symbol can be used to indicate "not."

Clue 2 is a block clue since the word "exactly" appears in the clue. Symbolize this in a block and use spaces for the empty placeholders: | T __ __ W |

Clue 2 is an antiblock clue. Be careful to symbolize both possible orderings: |S̶Z̶| / |Z̶S̶|

Clue 4 is a similar antiblock clue: |W̶X̶| / |X̶W̶|

Clue 5 is a block clue but the order is not specified. Symbolize both possibilities: | U X | / | X U |

Once the clues have been double-checked, make deductions.

The first deduction is based on the block from clue 2. Since there must be a minimum of three positions after T, then T cannot be in chapter 5, 6, or 7. Likewise, W must follow at least three other elements, so W cannot be in chapter 1, 2, or 3. If we combine clue 2 with clue 1, then W cannot be in chapter 4 either. These can be added to the deduction line on the diagram.

80

Elements T and W are the most restrictive of the game. Combined with the numerous other block and antiblock clues, this is the key deduction to make. However, there are two more deductions that can be made that are based upon this crucial deduction. Based upon the previous deduction, the only positions for W are chapters 5, 6, or 7. Clue 4 stipulates that X cannot be adjacent to W. Since W has only three options, if X were placed in chapter 6, there would be no place for W in the diagram. Finally, since U and X must be adjacent, U cannot be in chapter 7 since this would force X into chapter 6. Mark these on the diagram as well.

Your diagram should look like this:

R, S, T, U, W, X, Z

-W -T 1	-W 2	-W 3	-W 4	-T 5	-X -T 6	-U -T 7

Clue 1: T ≠ 1

Clue 2: T _ _ W

Clue 3: S̶Z̶ / Z̶S̶

Clue 4: W̶X̶ / X̶W̶

Clue 5: UX / XU

6. **D** Grab-a-Rule

Test each rule against the answers and eliminate false answers as they are found.

A. No. This violates clue 2 since there are three chapters between T and W.

B. No. This violates clue 1 since T is in the first chapter.

C. No. This violates clue 5 since U and X are not in adjacent chapters.

D. Yes. This answer does not violate any clues.

E. No. This violates clue 4 since W and X are adjacent.

7. **E** Specific

Make a new line on the diagram and add the new information from the question. Place X in chapter 1. This forces U into chapter 2. Next, place the large block clue. T could be in chapter 3, so W is in 6. Since S and Z are an antiblock, one of these must be in chapter 6. There is one other possible permutation for the clues. X is in chapter 1 and U is in chapter 2, but T could be in chapter 4 and W in chapter 7. In this permutation, either S or Z must be in chapter 3.

This question asks for which answer choice could be true. Eliminate any answer choice that cannot be true.

A. No. This must be false. If R is in chapter 3, then either clue 2 or clue 3 would be violated.

B. No. This must be false. If R is in chapter 7, then either clue 2 or clue 3 would be violated.

C. No. This must be false. U must be in chapter 2 according to clue 5.

D. No. This must be false. W cannot be in chapter 5 since that would place T in chapter 2.

E. Yes. This could be true according to the second permutation discussed above.

8. B Specific

Make a new line on the diagram and add the new information from the question. Place U in chapter 3. Next place X next to U in chapter 2 since X cannot be next to W. This forces T into chapter 4 and W into chapter 7. Finally, either S or Z must be in chapter 1.

The credited response will be an answer choice that could be true based upon the diagram. Eliminate any answer choice that must be false.

A. No. This must be false. If R was in chapter 1, then S and Z would have to be adjacent, violating clue 3.

B. Yes. This could be true. If R was in chapter 5, then S or Z could go in chapter 6.

C. No. This must be false. W must be in chapter 7.

D. No. This must be false. W must be in chapter 7.

E. No. This must be false. X must be in chapter 2; otherwise, X and W would be adjacent.

9. D Specific

Make a new line on the diagram and add the new information from the question. If Z is in chapter 7, then there are only two remaining places for W. If W was in chapter 6, then T would be in chapter 3. There is enough room in this diagram for the UX/XU block and for the two remaining elements. Alternatively, W could be in chapter 5 and T in chapter 2. The XU block would have to be in chapters 4 and 5 in that specific order.

The question asks for which answer choice could be true. Eliminate any answers that must be false based upon the diagram.

A. No. This must be false. Either T or X must be in chapter 3.

B. No. This must be false. Either T or X must be in chapter 3.

C. No. This must be false. T cannot be in chapter 4 since that would force W into chapter 7.

D. Yes. This is possible. U could be in 1, X in 2, T in 3, S and R in 4 or 5, W in 6, and Z in 7.

E. No. This must be false. If X were in chapter 5, it would be next to W.

10. A General

Use deductions and prior work to eliminate or identify possible answer choices. The question asks for which could be true. Eliminate any answer choice that must be false according to the deductions. Any answer choice that matches a valid play from prior work will be the credited response. Any remaining answer choices should be diagrammed.

A. Yes. This could be true.

B. No. This must be false, as seen in the deductions.

C. No. This must be false, as seen in the deductions.

80

D.   No. This must be false, as seen in the deductions.

E.   No. This must be false, as seen in the deductions.

11.   **B**   Complex

This Complex question asks for which credited response will have the same effect on the game as clue 1. Clue 1 stipulates that T cannot be placed in chapter 1. The credited response will prevent T from being placed in chapter 1 but will not have any other effect on the game. Rely heavily on Process of Elimination. If necessary, compare answer choices against prior work. If all prior valid plays remain valid, that answer choice may be the credited response.

A.   No. Preventing U from being placed in chapter two would not force T away from chapter 1. This answer choice would also invalidate the permutations from question 7.

B.   Yes. If W could not be in chapter 4, then according to the block in clue 2, T could never be placed in chapter 1. This has the same effect on the game.

C.   No. This is already true according to deductions. However, the creation of this rule would allow T to be placed in chapter 1.

D.   No. While this would prevent T from being in chapter 1, it would place a larger restriction on the game than clue 1 does. It would invalidate one of the possible diagrams from question 9.

E.   No. This would still allow T to be placed in chapter 1 since T X U W is a possible block of elements.

Questions 12–18

This is a 2D grouping game. The four walls form the core of the diagram. There are two elements for each student: oil and watercolor. Use subscripts to signify the different elements. Finally the second dimension is the upper or lower portion of the wall.

Next, symbolize the clues.

Clue 1 states that no wall has only watercolors. This is a vertical antiblock clue:

Clue 2 states no student has both paints on a single wall. There are four students, so symbolize this with four vertical antiblocks:

Clue 3 is a vertical antiblock dealing with F and I:

Clue 4 states that GW is above FO. Symbolize this as a vertical block clue.

Clue 5 is a concrete clue. It should be symbolized on the diagram.

Once the clues have been double-checked, make deductions. Begin with the more restrictive antiblock clues. Clue one states that no watercolors may be on the same wall. Since there are four watercolors, four oil paintings, and eight positions for the elements, then no wall may have two oil paintings either. In other words, all vertical blocks will contain one oil and one water:

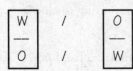

The next important deduction comes from a combinations of the previous deduction and various clues. First, the upper painting on wall four must be a W since the lower painting is an O. However, the upper painting cannot be I_W based on clue 2. Based on clue 3, the upper painting cannot be F_W. Finally, G_W must be paired with F_O, so it cannot be that one either. Therefore, the only painting remaining is H_W. Mark this on the diagram.

The final deduction helps dictate the last two vertical pairings. Since F and I cannot be on the same wall, the two remaining elements must be in separate vertical blocks. Thus, F_W will pair with one of either H_O or G_O, and I_W will pair with the other.

Your diagram should look like this:

F_O, F_W, G_O, G_W
H_O, H_W, I_O, I_W

	1	2	3	4
Upper				H_W
Lower				I_O

Clue 1: W / W

Clue 2: F/F G/G H/H I/I

Clue 3: F/I I/F

Clue 4: G_W / F_O

Clue 5: I_O = 4, lower

80

12. **A**   General

This is not a Grab-a-Rule question since it does not deal with the entire diagram or use all the elements. Use prior work, the rules, and deductions to eliminate answer choices.

A. Yes. This could be true.

B. No. This must be false. Based on a deduction, H_W must be on the upper position.

C. No. This must be false. Clue 5 states that I_O must be the in the lower position on wall 4.

D. No. This must be false. Clue 4 states that G_W must be in the upper position.

E. No. This must be false. Based on a deduction, H_W must be on the upper position.

13. **A**   Specific

Make a new line on the diagram and add the new information from the question. If F_O is on wall 3, then the $G_W F_O$ vertical block is on wall 3. Pick a position for I_W on wall 2. Finally, according to clue 3 or deductions, F_W must be on wall 1.

This question asks which painting must be on wall 1. The credited response should match a fixed position on the diagram.

A. Yes. F_W must be in either the upper or lower position on wall 1.

B. No. This could be false. G_O could be on wall 2.

C. No. This must be false. If F_O is on wall three, then G_W must be on wall 3 as well.

D. No. This could be false. H_O could be on wall 2.

E. No. This must be false. H_W must be on wall 4.

14. **E**   Specific

Make a new line on the diagram and add the new information from the question. Place H_O on wall 2. Next, place the block from clue 4 on either wall 1 or wall 3. Finally, place G_O on the remaining empty wall since no wall can have two oil paintings.

The question asks for which could be true. Eliminate any answer choice that must be false based upon the diagram.

A. No. This must be false since F_O is part of a block clue.

B. No. This must be false since G_W is part of a block clue.

C. No. This must be false since this would put two oil paintings on the wall. This violates a deduction.

D. No. This must be false. This violates the deduction that H_W must be on wall 4.

E. Yes. This could be true as seen in the example above.

15. **D** Specific

Make a new line on the diagram and add the new information from the question. Place the G_OF_W block on any of the empty walls. Next, place the block from clue 4. Finally, place the remaining two elements.

The question asks which must be true. Eliminate any answer choices that could be false.

A. No. This could be false. G_O could be in the lower position.

B. No. This must be false since it violates clue 1.

C. No. This could be false. H_O could be in the lower position.

D. Yes. This must be true since I_W was the only element remaining after the clues and deductions.

E. No. This could be false. I_W could be in the upper position.

16. **B** Specific

Make a new line on your diagram and add the new information. If F_O is on wall 1, then it is in the lower position and G_W is in the upper position. F_W and I_W must be on separate walls due to clue 3, so one is on wall 2 and one is on wall 3. Finally, G_O and H_O fill the remaining positions on wall 2 and wall 3. According to the clues, the vertical positions on wall 2 and 3 cannot be determined.

The question asks for which could be true. Eliminate any answer choice that must be false based on the diagram above.

A. No. This must be false since both paintings on wall 4 are known from deductions.

B. Yes. This could be true. G_O could be on wall 2.

C. No. This must be false since G_W must be in the position above F_O according to clue 4.

D. No. This must be false since H_W must be in the upper position of wall 4.

E. No. This must be false since this would violate clue 4.

17. **E** General

Use previous work and deductions to eliminate every answer choice that must be false. If any answer choices are remaining, begin diagramming them one by one. Since the question asks for which answer could be true, the first answer that produces a valid diagram will be the credited response.

A. No. This must be false. Placing G_W in a lower position would violate clue 4.

B. No. This must be false. Placing F_O in an upper position would violate clue 4.

C. No. This must be false. Placing F_O in an upper position would violate clue 4.

D. No. This must be false. Placing G_W in a lower position would violate clue 4.

E. Yes. This could be true.

18. **D**

Use prior work and deductions to eliminate every answer that could be true. The credited response will possibly match a deduction. If necessary, diagram remaining answers and eliminate every answer choice that produces a valid diagram.

A. No. This could be true as seen in prior work.

B. No. This could be true as seen in prior work.

C. No. This could be true as seen in prior work.

D. Yes. This must be false. Based on a deduction, H_W must be in the upper position of wall 4.

E. No. This could be true as seen in prior work.

Question 19–23

This is a complex grouping game. Three corporations—R, S, and T—own buildings that are named. Each building is classed as either 1, 2, or 3. The buildings will be traded. It is more efficient to use arrows to show the trades rather than create a grid for this game. Group the elements according to the corporations that own them and use numerals (or subscripts) to indication the class of each building:

R = G1 Y3 Z3

S = F1 L2

T = K2 M2 O2

Next, symbolize the clues.

Clue 1 says that a trade could be for any two equivalent class buildings:

1 ←→ 1 / 2 ←→ 2 / 3 ←→ 3

Clue 2 states that class 1 can be traded for two class two buildings:

1 ←→ | 2 2 |

Clue 3 states that a class 2 building can be traded for two class 3 buildings:

2 ←→ | 3 3 |

Once the clues have been double-checked, it is time to make deductions. Since R is the only corporation with class 3 buildings, then they cannot be traded one for one. Thus, the only way that R can trade the class 3 buildings is as a block for a class two building. There are only two class one buildings, so they can be swapped. However, since no corporation has either four class 2 buildings or a class 1 and two class 2 buildings, then no corporation can obtain both class 1 buildings. Note these deductions in crib note form:

Both 3 buildings stay together

No corp. gets both class 1.

Your diagram should look like this:

R = G1, Y3, Z3 — Both 3 buildings stay together
S = F1, L2 — no corp. gets both class 1
T = K2, M2, O2

Clue 1: 1 ↔ 1, 2 ↔ 2, 3 ↔ 3
Clue 2: 1 ↔ $\boxed{2\ 2}$
Clue 3: 2 ↔ $\boxed{3\ 3}$

19. **C** General

Used prior work and deductions to determine which could be the buildings owned after a single trade. Since the trades are between two corporations, one corporation's buildings must match the original setup. Eliminate any answer that must be false.

A. No. This must be false. R cannot have both class 1 buildings.

B. No. This must be false. This would mean that R and T traded two class 3 for two class 2, violating clue 1.

C. Yes. The single trade was L2 for Y3 and Z3. Corporation T made no trades.

D. No. This must be false. This would involve R and T trading a single class 3 for a single class 2, violating clue 3.

E. No. This must be false. This would involve S and T trading a class 1 for a single class 2, violating clue 2.

20. **A** General

Use prior work and deductions to determine which answer choice must be false. The credited response might match a deduction. Eliminate any answer choices that could be true. If any answer choices remain, diagram them and eliminate any that produce a valid diagram.

A. Yes. This must be false according to deductions. R would have to keep G1 but could trade only Y3 and Z3 for a single class 2. There would be no way to trade up to another class 1.

B. No. This could be true. S could trade L2 for M2 in a single trade.

C. No. This could be true. S could trade F1 for G1 in a single trade.

D. No. This could be true. T could trade both K2 and M2 for F1 in a single trade.

E. No. This could be true. T could trade both K2 and O2 for G1 in a single trade.

21. **A** **Specific**

Write out the new information in a diagram. For R to have only class two buildings, then G1 would have to be traded to T for two class 2 buildings. Then R would have to trade both class three buildings to either S or T. See one possible example below:

R = K2 M2 L2

S = F1 Y3 Z3

T = G1 O2

S could then trade the two class 3 for the remaining class 2 in T. Likewise, S and T could trade the class 1 buildings.

The question asks for which answer must be true. Eliminate any answer choice that could be false.

A. Yes. This must be true. R would have to get two class 2 buildings if it got rid of all class 1.

B. No. This could be false. T could trade any of the class 2 buildings with R.

C. No. This could be false. S could have a class 1 and two class 3 buildings.

D. No. This could be false. S could trade both class 3 buildings for one of the class 2 buildings held by T.

E. No. This could be false. S could trade its class 1 for the class 1 that T holds.

22. **E** **Specific**

Write out the new information in a diagram. In order for T to have no class two buildings, it would need to trade both up and down for class 1 and class 3. This means that T would have one class 1 and two class 3 buildings. The specific class 1 building is irrelevant since it can be traded for the other class 1. See an example below:

R = K2 M2 O2

S = F1 L2

T = G1 Y3 Z3

Based on buildings values, R could swap any or all of its buildings with S. Likewise, S and T could swap the class 1 buildings. The question asks for which answer choice must be true. The credited response will possibly match the diagram. Eliminate any answer choice that could be false.

A. No. This could be false. R could have all class 2 buildings.

B. No. This could be false. S could have a class 1 building.

C. No. This could be false. T could make all trades with R.

D. No. This could be false. T could trade G1 for F1.

E. Yes. This must be true since T would have to trade down to class 3 to get rid of its final class 2 building.

23. **D** General

Use prior work and deductions to determine which answer choice must be false. The credited response might match a deduction. Eliminate any answer choices that could be true. If any answer choices remain, diagram them and eliminate any that produce a valid diagram.

A. No. This could be true.
R = L2 M2 O2
S = F1 Y3 Z3
T = G1 K2

B. No. This could be true.
R = F1 Y3 Z3
S = G1 M2
T = K2 L2 O2

C. No. This could be true.
R = G1 Y3 Z3
S = K2 M2 O2
T = F1 L2

D. Yes. This must be false. Z cannot be traded alone, but must always be with Y.

E. No. This could be true.
R = K2 M2 Y3 Z3
S = F1 O2
T = G1 L2

Section 4: Arguments 2

1. **A** Flaw

The community organizer concludes that this year's cleanup will be a success. This conclusion is based on the fact that, last year, 77 local residents signed up to participate, but over 100 showed up (100 participants is sufficient to guarantee a successful cleanup), and that, this year, 85 local residents have signed up.

The argument assumes that a prediction can be made about this year's cleanup based on last year's cleanup; it fails to consider that fewer residents may show up even though more have signed up than last year. The credited response will identify this flaw.

A. Yes. The answer choice describes the flaw that the argument assumes that last year's cleanup can be used to make a prediction about this year's cleanup.

B. No. The argument does not require that the same people participate in both years.

C. No. The argument claims that the participation of at least 100 residents is sufficient to guarantee success, not that it is required.

80

D.   No. The argument does not imply that participants must be local, so it is not overlooking this possibility.

E.   No. Success is guaranteed if the cleanup has at least 100 participants, but this definition does not imply that success is inevitable.

2.   **C**   `Point at Issue`

Bell concludes that Klein should continue to be the leader because her policies (although unpopular) avoided an impending catastrophe. Soltan concludes that Klein should step down because she will not have the political support to make important decisions in the future. They disagree about whether Klein should remain leader. The credited response will identify this point of disagreement.

A.   No. Soltan states that Klein's policies have been effective, and Bell implies as much in saying that her policies avoided an impending catastrophe, so they agree on this point.

B.   No. Bell states that Klein's policies are unpopular, but Soltan does not discuss or imply anything about the popularity of the policies.

C.   Yes. Bell states that Klein is the person we need making decisions in the future, while Soltan states that Klein should step down.

D.   No. Both Bell and Soltan state that important decisions will need to be made in the future, so they agree on this point.

E.   No. Bell states that Klein's policies avoided an impending catastrophe, but Soltan does not discuss or imply anything about an impending catastrophe.

3.   **D**   `Resolve/ Explain`

The psychologist identifies an apparent discrepancy seen in a study: when given a chance to purchase a coffee mug, participants were not willing to pay more than $5, but when given a similar mug and asked how much they would sell it for, most participants would not sell for less than $5. The credited response will explain why participants would try to sell a mug for more than they themselves are willing to pay for it, likely by pointing out some difference related to having an object versus wanting an object.

A.   No. This answer choice does not explain why the inherent properties of an object would change depending on whether one owns it or is trying to buy it.

B.   No. The passage does not discuss objects that have been owned for a long period of time.

C.   No. The passage does not discuss objects that have been sold in the past.

D.   Yes. This answer choice provides a relevant difference related to having an object versus wanting an object.

E.   No. The passage does not compare objects that one has been given and objects that one has purchased; the distinction is between objects one has been given and objects one wants to purchase.

4.   **D**   `Strengthen`

The ecologist offers an explanation for why male starlings decorate their nests with fragments of aromatic plants: to attract female starlings. His explanation is based on the fact that such decoration stops once egg-laying begins. However, because the plants are rich in compounds known to kill parasitic insects that are potentially harmful to nestlings, other researchers explain the nest-decoration as protection for nestlings.

The ecologist assumes that his explanation is better than the competing explanation; he fails to consider that they might both be wrong. The credited response will support the ecologist's explanation, likely by bolstering the plausibility of that explanation.

A.   No. This answer choice is irrelevant because the competing explanation is about protection for nestlings, not adult starlings, and because it has no bearing on the ecologist's explanation.

B.   No. This answer choice strengthens the competing explanation by stating that when the alleged cause (parasitic insects) is absent, so too is the alleged effect (decorating nests with fragments of aromatic plants as protection against those parasitic insects).

C.   No. This answer choice weakens the explanation by pointing to another possible explanation: something in the aromatic plants helps nestlings grow faster.

D.   Yes. This answer choice bolsters the plausibility of the ecologist's explanation by reinforcing the cause-and-effect relationship.

E.   No. This fact is consistent with either explanation presented in the argument.

5.   **C**   **Sufficient Assumption**

The argument concludes that the commission's report will not be effective. The premises state that the report will be effective only if the commission speaks with a unified voice and that individual members of the commissions have repeatedly expressed their own opinions in the news media in advance of the report.

The argument contains a language shift that assumes that if members voice their opinions in the media, the commission will not be able to speak with a unified voice. The credited response will explicitly link these ideas and force the conclusion to be true.

A.   No. This answer choice does not bring up the idea of the commission speaking with a unified voice.

B.   No. This answer choice does not bring up the idea of the commission speaking with a unified voice.

C.   Yes. Added to the premises that the report will be effective only if the commission speaks with a unified voice and that the members have repeatedly expressed their own opinions in the news media, this statement proves that the report will not be effective.

D.   No. This answer choice does not bring up the idea of the commission speaking with a unified voice.

E.   No. This answer choice does not bring up the idea of the commission speaking with a unified voice.

80

6. **A** **Principle Match**

The engineer concludes that a technical fix to slow or reverse global warming by blocking out a portion of the sun's rays would encourage more carbon dioxide emissions and thereby possibly increase global warming. This conclusion is based on the fact that wider roads have been shown to encourage drivers to take more risks.

The engineer assumes that the situations are analogous and based on the same general rule or principle: taking steps to avoid a particular problem can result in behavior that exacerbates that problem. The credited response will describe the principle underlying the engineer's reasoning.

A. Yes. Widening roads and blocking out a portion of the sun's rays are the conditions, and driving riskily and emitting more carbon dioxide are the risk-taking.

B. No. The argument is not about the nature of the solution but its effects.

C. No. The argument does not discuss the endurance of technical fixes.

D. No. The conclusion is about encouraging certain behavior, not about not discouraging certain behavior.

E. No. The argument does not discuss unresolved problems.

7. **B** **Strengthen**

The argument concludes that urushiol probably did not evolve in such plants as poison oak and poison ivy as a chemical defense. This conclusion is based on the fact that it appears that only humans develop contact rashes from urushiol-containing plants and that wood rats even use such plants in building their nests.

The argument assumes that some animals not yet identified do not also suffer reactions to urushiol, that wood rats use part of the plant that contains urushiol, that wood rats are more typical than are humans in their (lack of) reaction to the oil, and that the plant did not evolve to contain urushiol at a time when many more animals did experience a reaction to it. The credited response will provide new evidence that supports the conclusion or will confirm the validity of an assumption.

A. No. This answer choice might weaken the argument if dead, brittle branches do not contain urushiol.

B. Yes. This answer choice provides new evidence that suggests that many more animals do not react to urushiol.

C. No. This answer choice is irrelevant; "common" does not imply that all plants have chemical defenses.

D. No. This answer choice is a premise booster.

E. No. Where poison oak and poison ivy grow is irrelevant.

8. **A** **Principle Strengthen**

The politician concludes that legislation to encourage renovation and revitalization of aging urban areas should not be commended. This conclusion is based on the fact that the main beneficiaries of such legislation have been well-to-do professionals who could afford to restore deteriorating buildings, while long-term residents (who were intended to benefit from the legislation) have been displaced due to increased rent and taxes.

The politician assumes that one should not commend legislation that negatively affects those it was intended to help. The credited response will state a general rule or principle that establishes that judging legislation requires considering not only its intentions but also its results.

A.   Yes. This answer choice establishes that both results and intentions are relevant to the evaluation of legislation.

B.   No. The conclusion is not about whether wealthier members of society should have undue influence on its governance.

C.   No. The conclusion is not about whom tax laws and zoning regulations should apply to.

D.   No. The argument states that the legislation was to the benefit of the well-to-do professionals in the society, so this principle does not apply to the premises.

E.   No. The conclusion is not about whether such laws can benefit society as a whole.

9.   **E**   Main Point

The argument concludes that it is good to have national leaders voted out of office after a few years. This conclusion is based on the fact that change usually happens early in a new government, so if leaders do not address a problem quickly and it becomes a problem later, they must either deny the existence of the problem or deny the availability of a solution to the problem, unless they are willing to take responsibility for the persistence of the problem. The credited response will indicate that national leaders should be voted out of office every few years.

A.   No. This answer choice states an idea that is not stated in the argument.

B.   No. This answer choice indicates a premise.

C.   No. This answer choice indicates a premise.

D.   No. This answer choice states an idea that is not stated in the argument.

E.   Yes. This is the main point of the argument.

10.   **C**   Strengthen

The farmer concludes that, for the most part, only government-sponsored research investigates agricultural techniques that do not use commercial products. This conclusion is based on the fact that no private for-profit corporation will sponsor research that is unlikely to lead to marketable products.

The farmer assumes that, for the most part, agricultural research without commercial products can be sponsored only by either governments or private for-profit corporations; he fails to consider that other entities could sponsor such research. The credited response will provide new evidence that supports the conclusion or confirm the validity of an assumption.

A.   No. Just because the government sponsors some agricultural research without commercial products does not mean that other entities could not also sponsor such research.

B.   No. This answer choice has no relevance to the funding source of the research.

80

C. Yes. This answer choice confirms the assumption that other entities rarely sponsor such research.

D. No. Agricultural research of commercial products is out of scope.

E. No. Just because most government-sponsored agricultural research does not include commercial products does not mean that most such research is government-sponsored (and even if it did, it would not mean that other entities could not also sponsor such research).

11. **A**   Flaw

The university spokesperson concludes that the university should rehire Hall Dining next year. This conclusion is based on the belief that the university should adhere to the preferences of the students. Several vendors have publicly expressed interest in working with the university, and most of the students surveyed said that they would prefer a new vendor. However, the only viable alternative is Hall Dining Services, which was university's food vendor until this past year.

The spokesperson assumes that the students know that Hall Dining is the only alternative to the current vendor. The credited response will identify this flaw.

A. Yes. This answer choice describes the flaw of assuming that the students knew about the available vendor options in responding to the survey.

B. No. The survey was of the students, and the premise states that the students' preferences should be adhered to, so the sample is representative of the proper population.

C. No. The premise states, "other things being equal," so it has accounted for other factors.

D. No. The argument states that most (not necessarily all) students favor switching, so the survey results are consistent with disagreement among students.

E. No. The survey results indicate that switching vendors would be popular but not that switching specifically to Hall Dining Services would be popular.

12. **E**   Inference

The passage presents three facts about cat food: cats fed canned cat food eat fewer ounces of food per day than do cats fed dry cat food, canned cat food contains more calories per ounce than does dry cat food, and feeding a cat canned cat food usually costs more per day than does feeding a cat dry cat food. The credited response will be an answer choice that is supported by a single statement or by a combination of statements from the passage.

A. No. Although canned cat food is more calorie-dense than dry cat food, we don't have enough information about the exact differences in calorie-density and amount eaten to make this inference.

B. No. A typical cat's diet is not discussed.

C. No. The term "only" is too strong: we don't know what factors affect the price of cat food.

D. No. This answer choice does not specify whether it is talking about canned or dry cat food, so while it could be true, it depends on the type of food the cats are eating.

E. Yes. Cats that eat canned cat food eat fewer ounces, but it still costs more to feed such cats, which suggests that canned cat food costs more per ounce.

13.   A   **Resolve/Explain**

The passage states that the Frauenkirche, a historic church destroyed by bombing in World War II, has been reconstructed to serve as a place for church services and cultural events. It then introduces a puzzling fact: although the foundation doing the reconstruction took care to return the church to its original form, it chose to build a modern organ instead of rebuilding the eighteenth-century baroque organ originally designed for the church. The passage rules out one possible explanation for this puzzling fact: a donor was willing to pay for the full cost of rebuilding the original organ, so a lack of funding is not the problem. The credited response will explain why the foundation chose not to rebuild the original organ even though doing so was seemingly in line with their goal of returning the church to its original form.

A.   Yes. The goal of reconstructing the church was to serve as a place for current church services and cultural events, and this answer choice explains that rebuilding the original organ would not align with that goal.

B.   No. If anything, having more features than modern organs might provide a reason to have rebuilt the original organ.

C.   No. This answer choice reinforces an already-known fact.

D.   No. The choice was between a modern organ and the original organ, not between a modern organ and a modified version of the original organ.

E.   No. Eighteenth-century church services are irrelevant.

14.   E   **Principle Match**

The passage presents two principles and a conclusion, and the question stem suggests that we must provide the missing piece that would allow the conclusion to be properly supported by one of the principles. The principles can be diagrammed as conditionals.

First, if reducing taxes on imports would financially benefit many consumers in its domestic economy, a government should reduce taxes on imports. The contrapositive is that if a government should not reduce taxes on imports, the import would not financially benefit many consumers in its domestic economy.

Second, if the added competition from reducing taxes on imports would significantly harm at least one domestic industry, a government should not reduce taxes on imports. The contrapositive is that if a government should reduce taxes on imports, the added competition from reducing taxes on imports would not significantly harm any domestic industries.

The conclusion indicates that the government should not reduce taxes on textile imports. To properly make this conclusion, we need to know that the added competition from reducing taxes on textile imports would significantly harm at least one domestic industry, so the credited response will establish this idea.

A.   No. This answer choice does not establish that the added competition from reducing taxes on textile imports would significantly harm at least one domestic industry.

B.   No. This answer choice does not establish that the added competition from reducing taxes on textile imports would significantly harm at least one domestic industry. Just because it would "not benefit" the textile industry does not imply that it would harm it—it could have no effect.

80

C. No. This answer choice does not establish that the added competition from reducing taxes on textile imports would significantly harm at least one domestic industry.

D. No. This answer choice does not establish that the added competition from reducing taxes on textile imports would significantly harm at least one domestic industry, so taxes should not be reduced.

E. Yes. This answer choice establishes that the added competition from reducing taxes on textile imports would significantly harm at least one domestic industry.

15. **E**   Inference

The passage presents two facts about rising global sea levels: global warming has contributed to a rise in sea levels both because it causes glaciers and ice sheets to melt and because it causes water volume to increase, and the rise in global sea levels is not as great as it could be because artificial reservoirs contain a large amount of water that would otherwise reach the sea. The credited response will be an answer choice that is supported by a single statement or by a combination of statements from the passage.

A. No. The passage does not state or imply that there is a dispute about the magnitude of the rise.

B. No. The reservoirs do not cause sea levels to rise, so presumably any rises pre-reservoir could be explained in the same or some other way.

C. No. The passage states what is known: global warming causes glaciers and ice sheets to melt and causes water volume to increase, which in turn contributes to a rise in global sea levels.

D. No. The passage does not compare the amount of water in reservoirs to the amount of water resulting from the melting of glaciers and ice sheets, so the phrase "about equal" is too specific.

E. Yes. The passage states that some melted water ends up in artificial reservoirs rather than reaching the sea, so looking only at the rise in global sea levels would miss part of the overall picture.

16. **B**   Flaw

The argument concludes that Juan entered the software company's contest. The premises provide a rule and a fact: everyone who entered the contest got a certain T-shirt, and Juan has that T-shirt.

The argument confuses necessary and sufficient conditions; it fails to consider that even those who did not enter the contest could have the T-shirt. The credited response will identify this flaw.

A. No. The conclusion is not causal.

B. Yes. This answer choice correctly identifies the flaw of confusing necessary and sufficient conditions.

C. No. The conclusion is about a single person, not about every member of a group.

D. No. The argument is not circular.

E. No. The conclusion is about a single person, not a generalization.

17. **B**   Inference

The passage presents facts about expert witness testimony: jurors often do not understand such testimony and are therefore unable to evaluate it, expert witnesses on opposing sides often make conflicting claims, and expert witnesses on both sides often seem competent, leaving jurors unable to assess the reliability of their conflicting testimonies. The credited response will be supported by a single statement or by a combination of statements from the passage.

A. No. The passage does not discuss whether legal teams should have limits on technical information in preparing a case.

B. Yes. Because jurors cannot assess the reliability of expert witness testimony, jury decisions in cases involving such testimony do not always hinge on the reliability of such testimony.

C. No. The passage is concerned primarily with jurors who do not understand the technical information, so this answer choice is out of scope. Furthermore, just because one understands technical information does not imply that one understands its legal implications.

D. No. The passage does not discuss jury selection.

E. No. The passage does not discuss whether opposing expert witnesses would agree about technical claims; if anything, being on opposing sides might suggest that they have differing evaluations of technical claims.

18. **E** **Necessary Assumption**

The tax reformer concludes that the legislation is framed correctly. This conclusion is based on the fact that a single statement cannot be both too specific and too vague, so criticism from the right (that the legislation is too specific) and from the left (that the legislation is too vague) is unjustified.

The tax reformer assumes that the right and left were not referring to different parts of the legislation in making their judgments; that conflicting interpretations of a given statement are impossible; and that the only possible evaluations of the legislation are that it is too specific, too vague, or just right. The credited response will establish one of these assumptions.

A. No. The rarity of criticism is irrelevant.

B. No. Implementation of the legislation is irrelevant.

C. No. The specific critics are less important than is the substance of their critique, so it is not essential that no other groups have criticized the legislation.

D. No. The intent of the legislation is irrelevant.

E. Yes. This answer choice rules out the obstacle that the right and left were referring to different parts of the legislation in making their judgments.

19. **B** **Parallel**

The employee implies that employees should not be banned from accessing non-work-related websites. He disagrees with his company, which claims that such websites distract employees and prevent them from doing their best work. As support, he offers an analogy: offices that have windows or nice decorations can also be distracting, but nobody claims that employees do their best work in an undecorated, windowless room.

He assumes that the analogy is relevant and justifies his implied conclusion. The credited response will match the structure of the argument by implying that something should not be banned by pointing to an analogous situation where something else was not banned despite having a common characteristic.

A. No. This argument does not contain an analogy.

B. Yes. The argument implies that an electronic device should not be banned. It disagrees with activists who claim that prolonged exposure to the device while it is in use causes cancer in lab animals. As support, it offers an analogy: most chemicals probably cause cancer in very high doses, but nobody claims that all chemicals should be banned.

C. No. This argument does not contain an analogy.

D. No. This argument does not contain an analogy.

E. No. This argument does not contain an analogy.

20. **E** Sufficient Assumption

The argument concludes that some students taking French Literature 205 are not French-literature majors. The premises state that some students taking French Literature 205 are also taking Biology 218 and that all students taking Biology 218 are biology majors.

The argument contains a language shift that assumes that biology majors cannot also be French-literature majors. The credited response will explicitly link these ideas and force the conclusion to be true.

A. No. This answer choice does not link biology and French-literature majors.

B. No. This answer choice does not link biology and French-literature majors.

C. No. The relative number of biology and French-literature majors is irrelevant; the important question is whether one can double-major in both subjects.

D. No. The relative number of biology and French-literature majors is irrelevant; the important question is whether one can double-major in both subjects.

E. Yes. Added to the premises that some students taking French Literature 205 are also taking Biology 218 and that all students taking Biology 218 are biology majors, this statement proves that some students taking French Literature are not French-literature majors.

21. **B** Inference

The critic presents two conditional statements: if a book is a literary classic, it reveals something significant about the human condition. If something reveals anything significant about the human condition, it is worthy of serious study. These conditionals have a common term and can be linked to prove that if a book is a literary classic, it is worthy of serious study. The credited response will be supported by a single statement or by a combination of statements from the passage.

A. No. This answer choice is backwards: the correct statement is that *only* books worthy of serious study are literary classics.

B. Yes. This answer choice links the two conditionals as described above.

C. No. This answer choice is contradicted by the statements in the passage, which imply that all literary classics are worthy of serious study.

D. No. Being worthy of serious study is necessary (but not sufficient) to reveal anything significant about the human condition, so this answer choice could be true.

E. No. Revealing something significant about the human condition is necessary (but not sufficient) to be a literary classic, so this answer choice could be true.

22. **B**   Evaluate

The argument concludes that we must abandon the belief that the *T. rex* developed its characteristic physical qualities (oversized head, long hind legs, and tiny forelimbs) in order to accommodate its great size and weight. This conclusion is based on the discovery of a nearly complete skeleton of an earlier dinosaur that had the characteristic *T. rex* features but was one-fifth the size and one-hundredth the weight.

The argument assumes that the skeleton is representative of its species and that its differing physical characteristics disprove the previous belief. The credited response will present a question related to one of these assumptions.

A.   No. The ratio of head size to body size is not discussed in the argument, so its relevance is unclear.

B.   Yes. If the recently discovered dinosaur died before it was fully mature, its skeleton might not be a representative example of the species.

C.   No. The argument does not require *T. rex* to have been the largest or heaviest prehistoric predator.

D.   No. The argument states that the dinosaur had similar features, but it does not require it to have been related to *T. rex*.

E.   No. Prey is not discussed in the argument, so its relevance is unclear.

23. **A**   Parallel Flaw

The argument concludes that *Bliss* is currently the highest-rated show on television. The premises state that YXK currently has the highest overall number of viewers of any television network and that *Bliss* is currently YXK's highest-rated show.

The argument assumes that the television network with the highest overall number of viewers must have the highest-rated show (whole-to-part flaw); it fails to consider that the highest-rated individual show could be on a network that is not the highest-rated overall. The credited response will have the same whole-to-part flaw.

A.   Yes. The argument assumes that the sport with the most leg injuries (soccer) must have the athlete with the most leg injuries (Linda Wilson).

B.   No. This argument assumes that awards indicate teaching ability, but it does not contain a whole-to-part flaw.

C.   No. This argument is valid.

D.   No. This argument tries to use two data points (highest and lowest earners) to support an inference about average earners, but it does not contain a whole-to-part flaw.

E.   No. This argument assumes that the film earning the most at the box office in the country is the most successful film in the country, but it does not contain a whole-to-part flaw.

80

24. **E**

The passage provides two principles that can be diagrammed as conditionals.

First, if a contract is valid, one party accepted a legitimate offer from another party. The contrapositive is that if one party did not accept a legitimate offer from another party, the contract is not valid.

Second, if someone in the position of the party to whom the offer was made would reasonably believe that offer to have been made in jest, the offer is not legitimate. The contrapositive is that if an offer is legitimate, someone in the position of the party to whom the offer was made would not reasonably believe that offer to have been made in jest.

The credited response will correctly move from the left side to the right side of one of these conditionals or their contrapositives.

A. No. This right-side idea (legitimate offer) does not lead to a conclusion about contract validity.

B. No. Just because Kenta doesn't *know* it was made in jest doesn't mean that he couldn't *believe* it to have been made in jest, so we cannot conclude that the offer was not legitimate, which in turn means we cannot conclude that the contract is not valid.

C. No. There are no principles about when one will accept an offer.

D. No. Hai made a legitimate offer, but this right-side idea does not lead to a conclusion about contract validity.

E. Yes. This answer choice confirms that Sal's only offer to Veronica was not legitimate and correctly concludes that they have no valid contract.

25. **D**

The scientist concludes that the ancestors of a certain species of iguana must have rafted on floating debris across the Pacific Ocean from the Americas to a small group of islands near Australia. This conclusion is based on the fact that this or closely related species of iguana are found in both the Americas and the islands (but nowhere else) and that the islands formed long after the fragmentation of Gondwana, the ancient supercontinent that included present-day South America and Australia.

The scientist assumes that there is no other explanation for the distribution of the iguanas; he fails to consider other possible explanations. The credited response will introduce new evidence that undermines the plausibility of his explanation or provide an alternate explanation.

A. No. Other animals are out of scope.

B. No. This answer choice is consistent with the statement that the iguanas found in the Americas are "closely related"—the argument does not state that they are genetically identical.

C. No. This answer choice is too weak and consistent with the argument: "uncommon" does not imply that it never happens.

D. Yes. This answer choice points to an alternate explanation: the iguanas originated in Australia, not in the Americas.

E. No. This answer choice is out of scope because the islands formed after the fragmentation of Gondwana.

26.   **B**   **Flaw**

The argument concludes that a recently discovered tomb must be that of Alexander the Great. The premises state that this is the largest tomb ever found in the region and that Alexander the Great, because he was the greatest Macedonian in history, would have had the largest tomb.

The argument assumes that the greatest Macedonian would have had the largest tomb, that Alexander the Great's corpse would have been interred in a tomb in the region, and that the largest tomb found so far is in fact the largest tomb that ever existed in the region. The final assumption is the most tenuous, so the credited response will identify this flaw.

A.   No. The term "only" is too strong, and this answer choice does not address the flaw of the largest tomb found being the largest tomb in existence.

B.   Yes. This is the credited response. This answer choice correctly identifies the assumption that the largest tomb found is the largest tomb in existence.

C.   No. Tombs from other regions are out of scope.

D.   No. The argument states that he is the greatest Macedonian and that his empire collapses after his death, so it implies that the collapse does not diminish his greatness.

E.   No. Even if archaeologists were incorrect in their determination of the tomb's size, the argument would stick with its assumption that the largest tomb found is the largest tomb in existence, so this answer choice does not identify the flaw.

80

Chapter 11
PrepTest 81:
Answers and
Explanations

ANSWER KEY: PREPTEST 81

Section 1:
Reading
Comprehension

1. D
2. C
3. D
4. B
5. E
6. A
7. E
8. B
9. C
10. E
11. A
12. D
13. C
14. D
15. C
16. A
17. D
18. B
19. D
20. E
21. C
22. A
23. D
24. B
25. C
26. B
27. D

Section 2:
Arguments 1

1. D
2. B
3. D
4. B
5. E
6. B
7. C
8. D
9. C
10. E
11. B
12. A
13. A
14. C
15. D
16. A
17. D
18. A
19. C
20. A
21. B
22. D
23. A
24. C
25. D
26. E

Section 3:
Arguments 2

1. E
2. C
3. A
4. E
5. D
6. E
7. B
8. B
9. B
10. B
11. A
12. A
13. B
14. A
15. A
16. C
17. D
18. D
19. C
20. E
21. C
22. D
23. B
24. B
25. E

Section 4:
Games

1. E
2. B
3. C
4. D
5. A
6. B
7. D
8. A
9. E
10. D
11. E
12. D
13. C
14. B
15. B
16. A
17. C
18. B
19. D
20. A
21. D
22. A
23. E

EXPLANATIONS

Section 1: Reading Comprehension

Questions 1–7

The main point of the first paragraph is that Wynton Marsalis once had tremendous influence in the jazz world, but his future is now uncertain. The second paragraph provides detail on the state of Marsalis's career in the early 2000s as well as the state of jazz in the record industry. The main point of the third paragraph is that many critics blame Marsalis for the lack of support for jazz. The main point of the fourth paragraph is that Marsalis's emphasis on honoring old masters while creating new music influenced record companies to focus mostly on old masters. The final paragraph notes that record companies are incentivized to focus on old masters rather than new artists because of the economic incentives. The Bottom Line of the passage as a whole is that the record industry is not investing in the development of new jazz artists perhaps because of Wynton Marsalis's promotion of traditional jazz music. The author's tone is negative toward the current state of jazz, but he or she stops short of joining the criticism of Marsalis and instead defends him.

1. **D**   Big Picture

    Use your Bottom Line to help you evaluate the choices. The credited response will describe the author's overall point.

    A.   No. The fact that Marsalis did not have a recording contract at the time the article was written is a detail in the passage. While the passage discusses a decline in support for new artists, it does not discuss why Marsalis specifically does not have a current contract.

    B.   No. While the beginning of this answer choice is true, it is too narrow, and the passage never mentions the idea that Marsalis's emphasis on past masters widened the audition for jazz, only that he sought to improve the public perception of jazz.

    C.   No. This answer choice is not supported. The passage never says that Marsalis has moved away from traditionalism.

    D.   Yes. This answer choice captures the main idea of the entire passage, including Wynton Marsalis's devotion to and promotion of traditional jazz as well as the de-emphasis of new artists by record companies.

    E.   No. While this answer choice is true based on the passage, it is the main point of the first paragraph only and not of the passage as a whole.

2. **C**   Extract Infer

    The question is asking what you can infer that the record executive means by Marsalis embodying a "retro ideology." Given that the author introduces the quote by discussing the critics' charge that Marsalis has "codified the music into a stifling orthodoxy and inhibited the innovative impulses," the credited response should reflect this rigidity.

    A.   No. The passage never claims that the musical traditions that Marsalis emphasizes have been discredited.

B. No. The passage explicitly states in the fourth paragraph that Marsalis "never advocated mere revivalism."

C. Yes. This is an accurate paraphrase of the passage's discussion of the "retro ideology."

D. No. This answer choice is too positive. The executive criticized Marsalis and called the ideology "museumlike."

E. No. The passage does not criticize the ideas of the old masters.

3. **D** RC Reasoning

The question is asking what would make the author less negative about the state of affairs of jazz. The author attributes the uncertain future of jazz to the fact that record companies have given up on developing new jazz artists. The credited response should address this concern.

A. No. The author does not attribute the problems facing the jazz genre to critics of Marsalis; the author attributes the problem to the record companies.

B. No. The author does not attribute the problems facing jazz to Marsalis; the author attributes the problems to the record companies.

C. No. The author does not attribute the problems facing jazz to Marsalis; the author attributes the problems to the record companies.

D. Yes. This answer addresses the author's criticism of record companies and their role in the decline of jazz.

E. No. While the author praises artists like Marsalis who show respect for tradition, he or she also discusses that individualistic expression is what pushes jazz forward.

4. **B** RC Reasoning

To answer this question, identify the situation that is facing Marsalis and look for an answer choice that matches the reasoning. Marsalis highlighted and advocated for traditional jazz artists and traditions in his new music, which led to record companies focusing almost exclusively on the music of the old traditional jazz artists rather than on new artists. The credited response will involve respect for tradition interwoven with new ideas, which then leads to almost exclusive attention on the tradition.

A. No. While Marsalis's situation does involve an unintended consequence, this answer choice does not involve respect for tradition.

B. Yes. The new hybrid tomatoes show respect for traditional varieties while also incorporating something new, and the result is a focus on the tradition.

C. No. This answer choice does not involve respect for tradition.

D. No. This answer choice does not involve respect for tradition.

E. No. This answer choice does not involve respect for tradition.

81

5. **E** `Extract Fact`

The question is asking for a statement made in the passage about what Marsalis encouraged young jazz musicians to do. The credited response will be something directly supported by evidence in the passage.

A. No. Critics accused Marsalis of inhibiting innovative impulses, but the author refutes that charge.

B. No. The passage does not discuss composing versus performing.

C. No. The passage says that Marsalis advocated paying attention to past masters and traditions, but it never mentions playing with them.

D. No. While Marsalis sought to improve the public perception, the passage never says that he told young musicians to ignore those perceptions.

E. Yes. In the beginning of the fourth paragraph, the passage says that Marsalis "encourage[d] young practitioners to pay attention to the music's traditions."

6. **A** `Extract Infer`

The question is asking for a statement that the author would agree with. The credited response will be the answer choice that is best supported by evidence in the passage.

A. Yes. In the third paragraph, the author states that critics accuses Marsalis of steering jazz toward classicism, though he does not advocate revivalism. By repackaging catalogs of vintage recordings rather than investing in recordings by new artists, the record companies are much more wedded to classicism.

B. No. While this could be true, the passage talks only about Marsalis's advocacy of the importance of jazz history and promotion of the genre. It does not mention his promotion of new artists.

C. No. The views of other musicians are not mentioned in the passage.

D. No. This answer choice is extreme and unsupported. The passage does not mention the views of young artists, let alone the views of most young artists.

E. No. While it is true that Marsalis released fifteen new CDs in 1999, the passage attributes the criticism of him to his emphasis on past masters and not on the quantity of music produced or the timing of its release.

7. **E** `Extract Fact`

The question is asking for something that is directly addressed by the passage. The credited response will be directly supported by evidence in the passage.

A. No. The passage mentions that Marsalis did not release a collection of new music in the two years after 1999, but he could have been composing music that was not released during that time.

B. No. The passage does not discuss the demographics of Marsalis's fans.

C. No. The passage does not discuss the specific content of Marsalis's CDs, only that he's used traditional elements to push jazz forward.

D. No. While the passage discusses that record companies have shifted their attention away from young talent, it does not state the reason that Marsalis did not have a contract after two decades as a jazz musician.

E. Yes. The last paragraph of the passage discusses that the economics of re-releasing old recordings were irresistible.

Questions 8–14

The main point of the first paragraph is that while common sense says that we know our own thoughts infallibly and infer the thoughts of others, some psychologists believe we are wrong to think that we have infallible noninferential knowledge of our thoughts. The second paragraph discusses the psychologists' attempts to explain why people hold this belief and analogizes it to our experience with expertise. The third paragraph clarifies the position of the psychologists. The Bottom Line of the passage as a whole is that people may not have noninferential and infallible knowledge of their own thoughts. The author's purpose is to correct the record and the author's tone is informative.

8. **B**   Big Picture

Use your Bottom Line to help you evaluate the choices. The credited response will describe the author's overall point.

A. No. The passage discusses that the illusion of noninferential and infallible access to thoughts is analogous to our experience with expertise, but it does not distinguish experts' access to their own thoughts from the access of others.

B. Yes. This accurately summarizes the overall point of the passage as a whole.

C. No. The passage discusses that our ability, not inability, to make quick and reliable inferences is one of the things that leads us to think we are perceiving our thoughts directly.

D. No. Psychologists use children's inability to identify their thoughts as evidence for the main thesis and do not connect it to lack of expertise.

E. No. This is explicitly contradicted in the third paragraph of the passage when the author says that the psychologists' arguments do not commit them to this claim.

9. **C**   RC Reasoning

The question is asking you to weaken the psychologists' interpretation of the experiments with children. In the first paragraph, the author discusses that the psychologists use the fact that children are less able to identify their thoughts to support the idea that thoughts are unobservable. The credited response will weaken the link between the experiments and the psychologists' thesis.

A. No. The fact that there may be a few children who can identify their thoughts as well as adults does not have a significant impact on the psychologists' claim.

B. No. The fact that older children perform similarly to adults does not weaken the psychologists' claim that people are not actually observing their thoughts.

C. Yes. The psychologists take the experimental result that children are misdescribing their thoughts to mean that they can't actually identify those thoughts, but if this statement is true, it would negate the idea that they can't identify their thoughts.

D. No. The psychologists are the ones who are distinguishing between direct and indirect access, so it does not matter whether children can.

E. No. The initial impetus of the experiments does not impact the psychologists' interpretation of the results of the experiments.

10. **E** `Extract Infer`

The question is asking what the author thinks about the quoted view. In the third paragraph, the author states that the psychologists come "perilously close" to claiming the quoted view, but that their arguments do not, in fact, commit them to it. The credited response will reflect this disagreement with the statement.

A. No. The author never attacks the study of thinking processes.

B. No. The author suggests that some might misinterpret the psychologists' claims as meaning the quoted view, but not that psychologists themselves do.

C. No. The passage does not indicate that anyone ever held this view.

D. No. The author disagrees with this view.

E. Yes. The third paragraph explains why the view is incorrect.

11. **A** `RC Reasoning`

The question is asking for a scenario that is consistent with the reason that people fail to notice that they are making inferences with their thoughts. In the second paragraph of the passage, the author explains that we fail to notice that we're making inferences because we become so good at making them incredibly quickly. The credited response will match this rationale.

A. Yes. Just like we become experts at making inferences about our thoughts, the anthropologist is an expert at studying culture.

B. No. The author's rationale does not hinge on limitations.

C. No. The passage discusses that comfort with making inferences causes us to overlook those inferences, but here the comfort leads to overlooking something other than the thing that the children are comfortable with.

D. No. The author's rationale does not involve conflict of interest.

E. No. The author's rationale does not involve the idea of being too busy or preoccupied with something else.

12. **D** `Extract Infer`

The question is asking what the passage suggests is the result of gaining greater expertise in a field. In the second paragraph, the passage discusses that greater expertise alters our perception and leads us to believe that we see and understand things directly rather than making inferences about them. The credited response will be the answer that is best supported by evidence in the passage.

A. No. The passage says that expertise affects our perception, but it does not discuss how that impacts our expression of our opinions.

B. No. The passage distinguishes direct and indirect understanding, but does not discuss level of detail.

C. No. The passage does not suggest that expertise leads people to overlook errors, only that we overlook the fact that we're making inferences.

D. Yes. This accurately paraphrases the author's statements in the middle of the second paragraph.

E. No. The passage does not make any claims about reliance on sensations and emotions.

13. **C** ▸ Extract Fact

The question is asking what causes the illusion of direct knowledge of our own thoughts. The passage states in the second paragraph that this is prompted by the fact that we become experts at making inferences. The credited response will be the answer that is directly supported by the text of the passage.

A. No. In the third paragraph, the author notes that the inferences we make are reliable.

B. No. This answer choice takes language from the passage and distorts it. The passage discusses that our expertise in making inferences is what causes us to overlook the fact that we make them.

C. Yes. This answer accurately paraphrases the author's discussion at the end of the second paragraph.

D. No. While it is true that our inferences about our own thoughts are reliable, the passage does not claim that we make extremely accurate perceptions of the world.

E. No. The passage does not discuss clouded thoughts or uncertainty.

14. **D** ▸ Extract Infer

The question is asking what the passage suggests is advantageous about using children in the discussed experiments. The credited response will be the answer that is best supported by evidence in the passage.

A. No. The passage never discusses the creativity of children or whether it would be advantageous for results to be interesting.

B. No. The inaccuracy of children's description of their thoughts is what led to the experimenters' conclusions. If children's reports were more accurate, they would be less useful.

C. No. The author calls the belief in infallible access to thoughts illusory in the second paragraph.

D. Yes. The experimenters' conclusions here were based on the cognitive errors made by the children.

E. No. The experiments were about knowledge about one's own thoughts, not the thoughts of others.

Questions 15–20

The first paragraph describes what dowsing is and how it works. The second paragraph describes the criticism of dowsing from its skeptics. The third paragraph introduces the point of view of proponents of dowsing and addresses some of the skeptics' concerns. The fourth paragraph details evidence corroborating the claims of dowsing proponents. The Bottom Line of the passage as a whole is that though there are skeptics of dowsing's efficacy, study results corroborate the claim that dowsers can have higher success rates locating groundwater than geologists and hydrologists. The author's attitude is positive towards dowsing.

15. C   **Structure**

The question is asking for the purpose of the second paragraph. The second paragraph describes the skeptics' criticisms of dowsing. The credited response will accurately reflect the organization of the passage.

A. No. The first paragraph outlines what dowsing is and the second paragraph describes criticisms, not details.

B. No. The second paragraph contains the perspective of skeptics only, and the final paragraph is support for the position of the dowsing proponents given in the third paragraph.

C. Yes. The second paragraph describes criticisms of dowsing and the third paragraph responds to those criticisms.

D. No. The second paragraph does not discuss any ramifications.

E. No. The second paragraph discusses only one perspective on dowsing.

16. A   **Extract Fact**

The question is asking for a statement about the dowsing skeptics' beliefs that is supported by evidence in the passage. The skeptics' views are discussed in the second paragraph.

A. Yes. This is admitted by the skeptics in the middle of the second paragraph.

B. No. The beliefs of scientists are not mentioned by the skeptics. The second paragraph does say that numerous studies show that the success rate for dowsers is inconsistent, but this is not strong enough to support the extreme "generally rejected" nor were these studies necessarily done by scientists.

C. No. This is claimed by the proponents in the third paragraph, but it is not acknowledged by the skeptics.

D. No. This is claimed by the proponents in the third paragraph, but it is not acknowledged by the skeptics.

E. No. This is claimed by the proponents in the third paragraph, but it is not acknowledged by the skeptics.

17. D   **RC Reasoning**

The question is asking for a scenario with reasoning that matches that of dowsing's skeptics. The skeptics argue that inert tools indicate that the dowsers themselves are making the predictions, that the success rate of dowsers is inconsistent, and that dowsers confine their predictions to areas where there is likely to be groundwater everywhere, increasing the likelihood that they will find water. The credited response will match one of these arguments.

A. No. Computer modeling is inconsistent with the skeptics' discussion of inert tools.

B. No. The skeptics do not criticize the proponents for a lack of evidence; rather they critique the quality of the evidence.

C. No. The skeptics do not argue that successful dowsers have success because of practice.

D. Yes. This matches the skeptics' claim that dowsing is done in areas where groundwater is expected to be ubiquitous and therefore water could be expected to be found in any spot.

E. No. The skeptics' claims have nothing to do with memories or the potential causes of those memories.

18.　B　**Extract Infer**

The question is asking for a statement about the results of the groundwater-locating study in the third paragraph that is supported by evidence in the passage. In the study, dowsers were more successful than geologists and hydrologists at predicting drill sites in areas they all were unfamiliar with.

A. This answer choice is extreme and unsupported. While the dowsers were more successful, that does not mean that the geologists and hydrologists did not have some success and that their success would not be useful.

B. Yes. In the final sentence of the passage, the author states that the study results suggest that dowsers can detect variations in subsurface conditions, so it is possible that they do it by detecting changes in the electromagnetic field.

C. No. This answer choice is too extreme. The author discusses only one study and that one study only compares dowsers to geologists and hydrologists. It is possible that other studies would show that other techniques are even more successful.

D. No. The passage does not indicate that the dowsers used different tools during the study.

E. No. The study results do help refute the skeptics' arguments, specifically the argument that dowsers make subconscious determinations using clues derived from surface conditions.

19.　D　**Extract Infer**

The credited response will be the answer choice that is best supported by evidence in the passage.

A. No. The passage never discusses a timeline for the practice of dowsing.

B. No. The passage does not discuss the impact of rain.

C. No. The passage mentions forked sticks, pendulums, and metal rods as possible tools used by dowsers, but it never discusses which tools are used by successful dowsers.

D. Yes. In the first paragraph, dowsing is defined as detecting resources or objects, which can include many things other than water.

E. No. The passage mentions that surface clues could be used, but it does not specify what they are.

20. **E** 〔Extract / Infer〕

The credited response will be the answer choice that is best supported by evidence in the passage.

A.   No. This answer choice takes language from the passage and distorts it. In the fourth paragraph, the passage mentions that the study was concentrated on finding groundwater in narrow, tilted fracture zones in arid countries, but there is no indication that there is a higher likelihood of finding those zones in particular regions.

B.   No. The fact that the passage doesn't mention any such studies is not enough to infer that none exist.

C.   No. The passage does not discuss whether a dowser would use a different tool depending on the resource that the dowser is attempting to locate.

D.   No. The passage states only that the dowsers were asked to locate a dry fracture zone, and it does not mention whether the geologists and hydrologists were asked as well.

E.   Yes. In the third paragraph, the dowsing proponents note that successful dowsers are not well represented in the typical study, but the study in the final paragraph utilized the most successful dowsers.

Questions 21–27

Passage A

Passage A begins by noting two objections to trial court judges conducting independent research. The second paragraph addresses the first objection, and the third paragraph addresses the second objection. The Bottom Line of passage A is that an absolute prohibition on independent research by trial judges is not justified, especially with respect to scientific research.

Passage B

Passage B begins by asserting that appellate courts should not conduct independent research, but it does not take a position on what trial court judges should do. The second paragraph discusses that appellate courts lack the live testimony and cross-examination that can help ensure an accurate determination of the facts at the trial level. The third paragraph expands on this point and notes that independent research at the appellate level usurps the trial court's fact-finding function. The final paragraph argues that independent research, regardless of the medium of the source, can cause an appellate court to ignore its function as a court of review. The Bottom Line of passage B is that appellate courts should not conduct independent scientific research.

21.   **C** 〔Big Picture〕

The question is asking for a principle underlying both passages. The credited response will be consistent with the Bottom Line of both passages.

A.   No. Passage A does not discuss whether or not it is appropriate for appellate judges to conduct independent research.

B.   No. While passage A mentions that independent research can help trial judges avoid errors in scientific admissibility decisions, passage B does not discuss the admissibility of evidence.

81

C. Yes. Passage A states that independent research "supplements rather than replaces" evidence presented at trial, and passage B argues that independent research is unreliable at the appellate level because of the lack of live testimony and cross-examination that can occur only at the trial level.

D. No. While passage B notes that judges can question live witnesses, it is discussed in a way to test the credibility and reliability of scientific literature. Passage A does not discuss judges' questioning of witnesses.

E. No. Passage B argues that appellate judges should not conduct research.

22. **A**   `Extract Infer`

The question is asking for a statement that both authors would agree with regarding research conducted independently by judges. The credited response will be the answer choice best supported by evidence in the passages.

A. Yes. Passage A argues this in its third paragraph, and passage B discusses that a trial provides critical tools for determining facts.

B. No. Both passages note that judges may wind up using questionable sources.

C. No. This is explicitly contradicted by the final paragraph of passage A.

D. No. Passage A does not mention the appellate level.

E. No. This is argued by passage B, but passage A is in favor of independent research to aid the trial court in fact-finding.

23. **D**   `Structure Function`

The question is asking you to find the phrase in passage B that parallels how the author of passage A uses the quoted phrase. In passage A, the author is expressing concern that judges will wind up using outlier or discredited materials in their research. The credited response will be a phrase from passage B that is also used in the author's expression of concern about the materials that judges might use in their independent research.

A. No. This phrase is referring to an advantage of live testimony.

B. No. This phrase is referring to the judge's interaction with a live witness at trial.

C. No. This phrase isn't critiquing the content of the outside literature. Instead it states that the literature is not subject to cross-examination.

D. Yes. This phrase is referring to the potentially unreliable outside research materials that a judge might use.

E. No. The critique is passage A is not that a source is external, but that it may be of poor quality. This phrase does not describe the quality of the material.

24. **B**   `Extract Infer`

The question is asking for a statement from passage A that the author of passage B would disagree with based on the statements about cross-examination. In lines 39–43, passage B discusses that cross-examination (the "greatest legal engine ever invented") can be used to test the credibility and reliability of scientific literature. The credited response will be a statement from passage A that passage B explicitly contradicts.

A. No. Passage B does not explicitly state whether independent research is justified or unjustified at the trial level; it merely discusses that the trial level offers some protections when it comes to fact-finding.

B. Yes. Passage B calls cross-examination the "greatest legal engine ever invented," and would therefore disagree with the statement that the adversarial system is ill-suited for handling specialized knowledge.

C. No. Passage B does not discuss admissibility decisions.

D. No. Passage B does not discuss erroneous decisions.

E. No. This is consistent with passage B's discussion of the protections that a trial court offers.

25. **C** Structure

The question is asking you to find the word in passage B that parallels how the author later uses the word "crucible." The author of passage B uses "crucible" to refer to the adversarial system and the practice of testing literature with live comment. The credited response will play this same role elsewhere in the passage.

A. No. Be wary of words that you might associate with crucible outside of the context of the passage. Here, "temptation" is referring to the design to conduct independent research.

B. No. "Credibility" is referring to the validity of the material itself rather than to the process used to vet it.

C. Yes. The author is calling cross-examination and the adversarial system the greatest legal engine ever invented, which is the same thing that is discussed in the third paragraph of passage B.

D. No. "Function" refers to the job of the trial court, not the adversarial process of cross-examination.

E. No. "Medium" refers to the material that a judge might examine in his or her research, not the cross-examination process.

26. **B** RC Reasoning

The question is asking you to identify the relationship between passage A and passage B and then apply that same relationship to answer choices on topics unrelated to the passage. Passage A discusses reasons that independent research might be acceptable at the trial level, while passage B discusses why independent research is not acceptable at the appellate level. The credited response should reflect the idea that something is acceptable under one set of circumstances, but not acceptable under a different set of circumstances.

A. No. Both of these titles view salt negatively.

B. Yes. The first title says salt is acceptable under one set of circumstances, but the second title indicates that salt is not acceptable under a different set of circumstances.

C. No. While the first title seems to match with passage A, passage B takes a definitive stance rather than failing to draw a conclusion.

D. No. Neither passage evaluates alternatives to independent research.

E. No. Both of these titles seem to view salt positively.

27. **D** Big Picture

The question is asking for each author's attitude toward independent research on the part of trial judges. Passage A gives reasons in favor of independent research by trial judges, and passage B does not state a position with respect to trial judges.

A. No. Passage A's tone is positive, not reluctant, and passage B's tone is neutral, not negative.

B. No. Passage A's tone is positive, not neutral.

C. No. Passage A's tone is positive, not negative, and passage B's tone is neutral, not negative.

D. Yes. This accurately matches the attitudes in passages A and B.

E. No. Passage A's tone is positive, but not forceful, and passage B's tone is neutral, not negative.

Section 2: Arguments 1

1. **D** Resolve/Explain

The passage presents two apparently contradictory facts: for the first few weeks of life, the dunnart has to breathe through its thin skin, which thickens as it matures inside the mother's pouch. However, all other warm-blooded mammals need thick skin their entire lives in order to maintain body temperature and reduce water loss. The credited response to this Resolve/Explain question will help the passage by explaining why it would make sense that a dunnart is able to survive for a few weeks with thin skin, even though no other warm-blooded mammal can do so.

A. No. This answer does not resolve the two facts. If respiratory muscles begin to develop after a few days, this still would not explain why the dunnart can survive with thin skin.

B. No. This answer does not resolve the two facts. If the dunnart has higher body temperatures than other warm-blooded mammals, this still does not explain how the dunnart can reduce water loss (the other necessary purpose of thick skin stated in the passage).

C. No. This answer makes the conflict worse. If adult dunnarts experience more heat and water loss than other mammals, this makes it even more difficult to understand why the dunnart can survive with thin skin.

D. Yes. If the mother's pouch keeps the newborn dunnart warm and reduces water loss, this would help explain why the newborn dunnart could survive for a few weeks in the mother's pouch until the skin thickens.

E. No. This answer does not resolve the two facts. If respiratory muscles begin to develop after a few days, this still would not explain why the dunnart can survive with thin skin.

2. **B** Main Point

The argument follows a typical Interpret pattern: it notes that stand-up comedians use humor to keep the audience's attention for hours and present information in such a way that the audience remembers it. It further notes that many comedians also use humor to make interesting points about serious topics. The argument then notes that university professors hope to achieve the same result in their lectures. Since the argument compares the goals of university professors to the goals of comedians, the credited response to this Main Point question will recommend that university professors could use comedy techniques to achieve their goals.

A. No. This answer does not match the argument; the argument does not suggest that university professors and comedians have the same skill set. Rather, it should suggest that they have similar goals, and therefore could use some of the same techniques to achieve those goals.

B. Yes. This answer matches the argument. Use the Why Test: does each of the other statements in the argument support the idea that incorporating humor into university lectures would help achieve the professors' goals for those lectures? Yes, because the argument states that university professors and comedians have similar goals, and therefore that professors could use the same techniques to achieve that similar goal. Therefore, this answer is an appropriate conclusion.

C. No. This answer is too extreme. The argument does not suggest that humor is the only possible way that university professors can achieve their goals for their lectures; rather, it simply states that university professors and comedians have similar goals, and therefore that university professors could use similar techniques to achieve that similar goal.

D. No. This answer is too extreme. The argument does not suggest that there is no reason to suppose that long lectures cannot hold an audience's attention. Rather, it simply states that comedians are able to keep the audience's attention for hours, and it implies that university professors might be able to use some of the same techniques in their lectures.

E. No. This answer is too extreme. The argument does not suggest that university professors should treat even the most serious topics in a serious way. Rather, it simply states that comedians are able to make interesting points about serious topics by using humor.

3. **D** Sufficient Assumption

The argument concludes that the advice in management books is of limited use to most managers. The conclusion is based on the premises that almost all management books are written from the perspective of the CEO, and that most managers don't have the same perspective as a CEO. The argument is flawed because it does not state that a book that is written from a different perspective than a manager's will be of limited use to the manager. The credited response to this Sufficient Assumption question will help the argument by providing an assumption that makes the conclusion valid: the argument assumes that a book that is not written from one's perspective will be of limited use.

A. No. This answer is not sufficient to make the conclusion valid. The argument is not concerned with how often advice books take the perspective of their intended audience; rather, the argument is concerned with whether books that do not take the perspective of their intended audience are of limited use to that audience.

81

B. No. This answer is not sufficient to make the conclusion valid. The argument is not concerned with whether people who read management advice books aspire to be CEOs; rather, the argument is concerned with whether books that do not take the perspective of their intended audience are of limited use to that audience.

C. No. This answer is not sufficient to make the conclusion valid. The argument is not concerned with whether CEOs have experience as lower level managers; rather, the argument is concerned with whether books that do not take the perspective of their intended audience are of limited use to that audience.

D. Yes. This answer connects the premises to the conclusion in a way that is sufficient to make the conclusion valid: if a book is written from a different perspective from the intended audience, then the book is of limited use to that audience.

E. No. This answer is not sufficient to make the conclusion valid. The argument is not concerned with what sort of books most managers prefer to read; rather, the argument is concerned with whether books are of limited use to managers.

4. **B**   Weaken

The argument states that the mayor has been accused of taking a bribe because a consultant that does business with the city paid for improvements to the mayor's vacation house. The mayor's defense is that he has paid every bill that was presented to him. The mayor's argument contains an absence of evidence flaw: the mayor does not provide any evidence that the consultant did not pay for improvements to the mayor's house. The credited response to this Weaken question will hurt the mayor's argument by pointing out that, even if the mayor's statement is true, the consultant could still have paid for improvements to the mayor's house.

A. No. This answer strengthens the argument. If the consultant is being investigated for taking bribes, then the consultant may have been willing to bribe the mayor as well.

B. Yes. This choice hurts the argument by providing evidence that the mayor was aware that bills were presented to the consultant, which might mean those bills were paid by the consultant.

C. No. This answer is irrelevant. Whether the contractor for the improvements to the mayor's house has done business with the city in the past does not help determine whether the consultant paid for the improvements to the mayor's house.

D. No. This answer is irrelevant. The fact that the improvements to the mayor's house were expensive does not help determine whether the consultant paid for those improvements.

E. No. This answer is irrelevant. The fact that the city's payout to the consultant exceeded the cost of the improvements does not help determine whether the consultant paid for the improvements to the mayor's house.

5. **E**   Necessary Assumption

The argument notes that the earliest evidence of controlled fire use in Europe dates to 400,000 years ago. The argument concludes that this evidence casts doubt on the idea that mastery of fire was a necessary prerequisite for human migration to Europe. In other words, the argument concludes that because the earliest evidence of controlled fire use dates to 400,000 years ago, mastery of fire must not have been needed in order to migrate to Europe. The argument is flawed because it does not state when

81

humans first migrated to Europe. In other words, the argument overlooks the possibility that humans may have migrated to Europe fewer than 400,000 years ago, after controlled fire use was already occurring. The credited response to this Necessary Assumption question will help the argument by providing a statement that is necessary in order to show that mastery of fire was not needed to live in Europe. The answer will also satisfy the Negation Test.

A. No. How humans used fire is not relevant to the conclusion about whether humans needed fire.

B. No. The argument states that Europe has a cold winter climate, but does not assume that the climate was colder than it is today.

C. No. The argument is primarily concerned with humans' mastery of fire. Thus, information about humans using naturally occurring, rather than mastery of fire, is not directly relevant to the conclusion.

D. No. This choice states that cold weather was a prerequisite for the mastery of fire which is the reverse of the statement in the argument.

E. Yes. In order to show that mastery of fire was not needed to live in Europe, it would be necessary for humans to have lived in Europe more than 400,000 years ago, before controlled fire use began. Try negating this choice: if no humans lived in Europe before 400,000 years ago, then the argument would not tell us whether or not mastery of fire was needed in order to live in Europe. Since the argument fails if the answer choice is negated, the choice must be necessary for the conclusion to be valid.

6. **B**   **Principle Strengthen**

The astronomer's argument follows a disagree pattern: it concludes that canceling the telescope project would be a mistake, even though it is way over budget, because if the project is canceled, the money already spent (more than the amount required to complete the project) would be wasted. The argument is flawed because it does not explain why a project shouldn't be canceled even if more than half of the money for a project has already been spent. The credited response to this Principle-Strengthen question will help the argument by providing a general rule that supports the idea that if more than half of the funds for the telescope project have already been spent, then the telescope project should not be canceled.

A. No. This answer is irrelevant; the argument is not concerned with the money spent relative to the agency's overall budget. Rather, it is concerned with the money spent relative to the total project budget.

B. Yes. This answer directly connects the premise (more than half of the telescope project costs have been spent) to the conclusion (that it would be a mistake to cancel the telescope project): if more than half of a project's cost has been spent, then it would be a mistake to cancel the project.

C. No. This answer is irrelevant; the argument does not address whether the total cost of the project will be more than double the original budget. Rather, it is concerned with the money spent relative to the total amount required to complete the project.

D. No. This answer is irrelevant; this answer addresses whether to commit additional funding to a project, while the argument is about whether a project should be canceled because it is over budget.

81

E.   No. This answer is irrelevant; the argument does not address whether the project is likely to lead to important new discoveries. Rather, it is concerned with the money spent on the project relative to the total project budget.

7.   **C**   Inference

The passage states that different nonhuman primate species exhibit different behaviors. A chimpanzee presented with a screwdriver is likely to examine it, play with it, and then lose interest. On the other hand, an orangutan is likely to pretend to ignore the tool and then later use it to dismantle its cage. The credited response to this Inference question will be a statement that is supported by information extracted from the passage.

A.   No. This answer is too strong. The passage does not state that orangutans are the most intelligent of nonhuman primates.

B.   No. This makes an unsupported comparison. The passage does not compare the memories of orangutans to those of chimpanzees.

C.   Yes. This answer is supported by a statement in the passage: if an orangutan is likely to pretend to ignore the tool and then later use it to dismantle its cage, then the orangutan is capable of deception.

D.   No. This makes an unsupported comparison. The passage does not compare how much orangutans and chimpanzees dislike being caged.

E.   No. This answer is not supported by the passage. While the passage does state that a chimpanzee is likely to lose interest in a screwdriver, this does not prove that the chimpanzee does not understand tool use generally.

8.   **D**   Flaw

The argument concludes that Liang should not receive a bonus this year. The conclusion is based on the premises that the only employees that should receive a bonus this year are those who were exceptionally productive last year, and that Liang works in a division that failed to meet its productivity goals for the year. This argument contains a comparison flaw: it assumed that if Liang's corporate division did not meet its productivity goals, that Liang must not have been exceptionally productive herself. The credited response to this Flaw question will correctly identify this comparison flaw.

A.   No. Whether the standards for judging productivity vary between corporate divisions is irrelevant to whether Liang was personally exceptionally productive last year.

B.   No. Whether the corporation as a whole is profitable is irrelevant to whether Liang was personally exceptionally productive last year.

C.   No. This answer does not match the flaw of the argument. While the argument does include a comparison flaw, it does not compare one group's performance to the performance of a wholly different group. Rather, it makes a conclusion about Liang's performance based on the performance of her group as a whole.

D.   Yes. This answer matches the flaw of the argument: the argument makes a conclusion about Liang's individual performance based only on the performance of her corporate division as a whole.

E.   No. Whether an employee who is unproductive one year will be exceptionally productive in future years is irrelevant to whether Liang was personally exceptionally productive last year.

9. **C**   **Sufficient Assumption**

The argument states that the journalist thought that the informant was untrustworthy, that the journalist promised not to reveal the informant's identity so long as the information provided did not turn out to be false, and that the journalist will publicly reveal the informant's identity if ordered to do so by a judge or her editor, since the information concerns safety violations at a power plant. The argument concludes that the journalist will reveal the informant's identity even if the information is accurate. The argument is flawed because it does not state that the journalist will be ordered to reveal the identity of the informant. The credited response to this Sufficient Assumption question will help the argument by providing an assumption that makes the conclusion valid: the argument assumes that the journalist will be ordered to reveal the identity of the informant by her editor or a judge.

A. No. This answer is not sufficient to make the conclusion valid. The argument is not concerned with what the journalist will do if the information is false. Rather, the conclusion concerns whether the journalist will reveal the identity even if the information is accurate.

B. No. This answer is not sufficient to make the conclusion valid. If the journalist's editor will not order her to reveal the identity unless the information is accurate and concerns public safety, this is not enough to prove that the journalist would surely reveal the informant's identity. It shows only that the journalist's editor might possibly order the journalist to reveal the informant's identity.

C. Yes. This answer connects the premises to the conclusion in a way that is sufficient to make the conclusion valid: since the information concerns safety at a power plant, the judge will order the journalist to reveal the informant's identity, and so the journalist will surely reveal the informant's identity.

D. No. This answer is not sufficient to make the conclusion valid. The argument is not concerned with whether the information can be verified. Rather, the argument is concerned with whether the journalist will reveal the identity even if the information is accurate.

E. No. This answer is not sufficient to make the conclusion valid. The argument is not concerned with whether the informant understood that the journalist might break the promise. Rather, the argument is concerned with whether the journalist will reveal the identity even if the information is accurate.

10. **E**   **Principle Match**

The passage presents a principle: when a person has borrowed an item and promised to return it by a certain date, then that person should return the item on time if it's not difficult to return a borrowed item on time, and if the person hasn't been given permission to return the borrowed item late. The contrapositive of this conditional statement states that if it's okay for a person to return an item late, then either it must have been difficult to return on time, or the person must have been given permission to return the item late. The credited response to this Principle-Match question will be an argument that correctly applies this principle: it will follow the rules set forth in the conditional statement or its contrapositive.

A. No. This answer does not correctly apply the principle. This answer concludes that it would be wrong to return a book early, which is a different situation from the one described in the original argument, which is about whether an item can be returned late.

81

B. No. This answer does not correctly apply the principle. This answer concludes that a bicycle should be returned even if doing so is difficult, but the principle stated in the argument provides that if the returning an item is difficult, then there's no need to return the item on time.

C. No. This answer does not correctly apply the principle. This answer concludes that a car should be returned on time even if permission was given to return it late, but the original argument provides that if permission is given to return an item late, then it may be returned late.

D. No. This answer does not correctly apply the principle. This answer concludes a computer should be returned, but since the argument did not state whether Yesenia promised to return the computer on time, the principle described in the original argument does not apply.

E. Yes. This answer correctly applies the principle: since Oliver promised to return the guitar on time, it's easy for Oliver to return it on time, and Madeline has not given Oliver permission to return it late, then Oliver should return the guitar on time.

11. **B** **Necessary Assumption**

The argument notes that human skin gives off gases, including carbon dioxide and lactic acid, both of which attract mosquitoes. But neither of those substances, alone or combined, attract mosquitoes as much as a human arm, even in darkness. The argument concludes that human skin gives off some other gaseous substance that attracts mosquitoes. The argument includes a causal flaw: it assumes that the mosquitoes must have been attracted by gaseous substances and not by some other factor. In other words, the argument overlooks the possibility that the mosquitoes were attracted to something other than a gaseous substance. The credited response to this Necessary Assumption question will help the argument by providing a statement that is necessary in order to show that the mosquitoes are attracted to some gaseous substance given off by human skin.

A. No. This answer does not help the conclusion. Whether mosquitoes communicate with one another does not help determine whether the mosquitoes are attracted to a gaseous substance given off by human skin.

B. Yes. In order to show that mosquitoes are attracted to some other gas given off by human skin, it would be necessary that the mosquitoes not be attracted by some other factor, such as body heat. Try negating this choice: if mosquitoes are attracted to body heat, then the mosquitoes are probably not attracted to some other gaseous substance emitted by human skin. Since the argument fails if the answer choice is negated, the choice must be necessary for the conclusion to be valid.

C. No. This answer does not help the conclusion. Whether human skin gives off different amounts of gaseous substances during the day compared to the night does not affect whether mosquitoes are attracted to a gaseous substance given off by human skin.

D. No. This answer does not help the conclusion. Whether mosquitoes are more successful at finding human skin in darkness versus light does not help determine whether the mosquitoes are attracted to a gaseous substance given off by human skin.

E. No. This answer is too strong. It is not necessary that the human skin never gives off a gaseous substance that repels mosquitoes. Mosquitoes could still sometimes be attracted to a gaseous substance given off by human skin even if the human skin emits a substance that repels mosquitoes at other times.

81

12. **A** Resolve/Explain

The passage presents two apparently contradictory facts: an analysis of paint samples from an Italian painting suggested that the painting used cobalt blue, a pigment not used in Europe before 1804. But a further analysis suggested that the painting might have been made before 1804. The credited response to this Resolve/Explain question will help the passage by explaining why it would make sense that a painting could have been produced before 1804 might have pigments in it that were not used until 1804.

A. Yes. If the cobalt was only in the topmost layer, then the cobalt blue could have been added to the painting after 1804.

B. No. This answer does not resolve the two facts. The fact that the 2009 analysis could detect much smaller amounts of cobalt does not help explain how the painting could have cobalt in it if it was produced before 1804.

C. No. This answer does not resolve the two facts. The fact that the 2009 analysis took more samples than the 1995 analysis does not help explain how the painting could have cobalt in it if it was produced before 1804.

D. No. This answer makes the problem worse. If many experts date the painting to the 1700s, this still does not help explain how the painting could have cobalt in it if it was produced before 1804.

E. No. This answer makes the problem worse. If cobalt blue was used only rarely in Italy in the years immediately following 1804, this still does not help explain how the painting could have cobalt in it if it was produced before 1804.

13. **A** Strengthen

The argument notes that a six-month health campaign tried to limit the flu by encouraging people to wash their hands frequently and avoid public places if they had flu symptoms, and that the incidence of flu turned out to be much lower than predicted during that period. The argument concludes that the public apparently heeded the campaign. The argument includes a causal flaw: it assumes that because there was a correlation between the health campaign and the reduced incidence of the flu, that the campaign must have caused the reduced incidence of the flu. In other words, the argument overlooks the possibility that the reduced incidence of the flu was caused by some other factor. The credited response to this Strengthen question will provide evidence to support the idea that the reduced incidence of the flu was caused by the health campaign and not by some other factor.

A. Yes. This answer strengthens the argument. If there was also a lower incidence of other illnesses that can be controlled by hand-washing, this is additional evidence that the public may have heeded the campaign recommending frequent hand-washing.

B. No. This answer either weakens the argument or is irrelevant. Whether the incidence of the common cold remained about the same as usual during this period does not help explain what caused the incidence of the flu to decrease, or perhaps suggests that people did not actually wash their hands more frequently (and thus did not actually heed the public health campaign).

C. No. This answer weakens the argument by providing evidence of another potential cause of the reduced incidence of the flu. If there were fewer public gatherings than usual during this period, then this could have caused the reduced incidence of the flu during the period.

D. No. This answer weakens the argument by providing evidence of another potential cause of the reduced incidence of the flu. If the news media also spread the message recommending frequent hand-washing, then people may have been heeding the news media rather than the public health campaign.

E. No. This answer either weakens the argument or is irrelevant. If people believed they should do more to limit the spread of the flu, then perhaps that belief itself, rather than the health campaign, led them to change their behavior. In any case, whether people believe they should do more does not help determine whether or not they heeded the public health campaign.

14. **C** **Main Point**

The argument follows a typical Solve pattern: it notes that most company meetings show diminishing returns after 30 minutes, and produce little after 60 minutes. Also, the most productive meetings were those with a clearly established time frame. The argument's conclusion is a conditional statement: if the company wants maximum productivity at a meeting, then the meeting needs a clear time frame and should last no more than 30 minutes. The credited response to this Main Point question will match the conclusion of the argument.

A. No. This answer does not match the argument's conclusion: it reverses the conditional statement. The answer suggests that if a meeting lasts no more than 30 minutes and has a clear time frame, then the meeting will achieve maximum productivity. This is a reversal of the conclusion, which states that if a meeting is to achieve maximum productivity, then it needs a clear time frame and should last no more than 30 minutes.

B. No. This answer does not match the argument's conclusion. Instead, it restates one of the premises.

C. Yes. This answer matches the argument's conclusion. Use the Why Test: does each of the other statements in the argument support the idea if a meeting is to be maximally productive, then it should have a clear time frame and last no more than 30 minutes? Yes, because each of the other premises in the argument supports this idea. Therefore, this answer matches the conclusion.

D. No. This answer does not match the argument's conclusion. Instead, it restates one of the premises.

E. No. This answer does not match the argument's conclusion. Instead, it restates one of the premises.

15. **D** **Inference**

The passage states that more than half of fad diets prescribe a single narrow range of nutrients for everyone. Also, because foods contain differing nutrients, dietary needs vary from person to person.

Finally, all people should eat plenty of fruits and vegetables. The credited response to this Inference question will be a statement that is supported by information extracted from one or more statements in the passage.

A. No. This answer contradicts the passage. The passage states that most fad diets prescribe a single range of nutrients for all people, but this answer states that most fad diets require that everyone eat plenty of fruits and vegetables.

B. No. This answer is too strong. While the passage does state that everyone should eat plenty of fruits and vegetables because they contain nutrients that protect against a wide range of health problems, the passage does not state that fruits and vegetables are the only foods that can do this.

C. No. This answer is too strong. While the passage does state that dietary needs vary from person to person, the passage does not state that any two people have different health problems and different dietary needs.

D. Yes. This answer is supported by the statements in the passage: if most fad diets prescribe a single narrow range of nutrients, but dietary needs vary widely from person to person, then most fad diets must not satisfy the dietary needs of at least some people.

E. No. This answer is too strong. While the passage does state that fruits and vegetables protect against a wide range of health problems, the passage does not state that there are few or no nutrients contained in every other food.

16. **A**   Evaluate

The argument states that caffeine in coffee stimulates the production of irritating stomach acid, but that darker roasts of coffee contain more NMP than lighter roasts, which tends to suppress production of stomach acid. The argument concludes that if you drink caffeinated coffee, a darker roast will irritate your stomach less. The argument contains a comparison flaw: it assumes that the reduction of stomach acid caused by the NMP in a darker roast will outweigh the increase in stomach acid due to the caffeine in the coffee. In other words, the argument overlooks the possibility that the increase in stomach acid caused by the caffeine in the coffee might not be completely counteracted by the reduction in stomach acid caused by the NMP. The question stem asks for information that would be useful to evaluate the argument. The credited response will provide a question that, if answered, would either help or hurt the argument's conclusion.

A. Yes. If extending the roasting time of coffee beans to create a darker roast increases the amount of caffeine present in the coffee, this fact would hurt the conclusion by suggesting that the reduction of stomach acid caused by the NMP in the darker roast might be outweighed by the increase in stomach acid caused by the increased caffeine due to the increased roasting time. If, on the other hand, the extended roasting time does not increase the caffeine level of the coffee, then a darker roast would definitely irritate the stomach less than a lighter roast.

B. No. This answer is irrelevant. Whether a reduction in acid production in the stomach has an adverse effect on stomach function does not help determine whether the darker roasts will irritate the stomach less.

C. No. This answer is irrelevant. Whether coffee drinkers would drink more coffee if they drank coffee with less caffeine does not help determine whether the darker roasts will irritate the stomach less.

D. No. This answer is irrelevant. Whether coffee drinkers increase their coffee consumption does not help determine whether the darker roasts will irritate the stomach less.

E. No. This answer is irrelevant. Whether lighter roasts of coffee have important health benefits does not help determine whether the darker roasts will irritate the stomach less.

17. **D**   Inference

The passage states that film historians find it difficult to determine the typical audience response to films from the early twentieth century, noting that box office figures indicate only financial success and not what audience members found emotionally affecting. Also, historians find newspaper and magazine reviews to be generally unhelpful. The credited response to this Inference question will be a statement that is supported by information extracted from one or more statements in the passage.

A. No. This answer is not supported by statements in the passage. The passage does not state when newspaper and magazine reviews of films are written in relation to the film's release.

B. No. This answer is too strong. While the passage does state that it's difficult to determine the audience members' responses to early twentieth-century films, the passage does not state whether it is easy to determine audience members' responses from more modern films.

C. No. This statement is not supported by statements in the passage. The passage states that box office figures do not help determine audience responses, but the passage does state whether box office figures depend on viewers' emotional reactions to the film.

D. Yes. This answer is supported by statements in the passage. The passage states that film historians have difficulty determining typical audience members' responses to particular films, and that they find that that newspaper and magazine reviews of films fail to provide much insight.

E. No. This answer is not supported by the passage. While the passage does state that film historians find that that newspaper and magazine reviews of films fail to provide much insight into typical audience members' reactions, the passage does not state whether early twentieth-century films were typically reviewed by newspapers or magazines.

18. A Reasoning

The argument follows a typical Solve pattern. It notes that based on surface observation, astronomers generally agree that pulsars are made up of neutrons. However, some pulsars behave as if they are filled with quarks. Because a quark-filled pulsar would be positively charged, the argument concludes that quark-filled pulsars attract a layer of negative particles that then support an outer crust of neutrons, which would explain why surface observation made astronomers think pulsars are all made up entirely of neutrons. The credited response to this Reasoning question will match the role played in the argument by the statement that the core of a quark-filled pulsar would be positively charged: it is a premise that supports the conclusion that quark-filled pulsars might have an outer crust of neutrons.

A. Yes. This answer matches the role played by the statement that the core of a quark-filled pulsar would be positively charged: it is a premise that supports the conclusion that quark-filled pulsars might have an outer crust of neutrons, which explains how the pulsar could appear to be made only of neutrons even if it has a core of quarks..

B. No. This answer contradicts the argument. The statement supports the idea that some pulsars may be made of quarks; it does not challenge that claim.

C. No. This answer contradicts the argument. The argument does not state that astronomers are not recognizing pulsars as pulsars.

D. No. This answer contradicts the argument. The statement that the core of a quark-filled pulsar would have a positive charge is not described as a new finding, and it doesn't in itself challenge the consensus view. It merely supports the claim that some pulsars may have an outer crust of neutrons and a core made up of quarks, which modifies the consensus view.

E. No. This answer does not match argument. Nothing in the argument suggests that pulsars would not have a mass roughly equal to the mass of our Sun.

19. C Inference

The passage states that if a new natural-gas-powered electrical generation station is constructed, then it needs to be located near a natural-gas pipeline, a large body of water, and transmission lines, and located in a region where residents will not oppose construction. Also, our country's natural gas pipelines run near only three large bodies of water, and residents would oppose construction in each of these sites. When these statements are combined, the passage states, effectively, that there are no reasonable locations for new natural-gas-powered electrical generation statements anywhere in the country, unless a new pipeline is constructed near a body of water where the residents would not oppose construction. The credited response to this Inference question will be a statement that is supported by information extracted from one or more statements in the passage.

A. No. This answer is too strong. The passage does not state that future electrical needs cannot be satisfied by natural-gas-powered generation. Rather, the passage states that no new stations can be built using the currently existing pipeline network.

B. No. This answer goes beyond the passage. The passage does not state whether residents would move away if a new station were constructed.

C. Yes. This answer is supported by the statements in the passage: if a new station needs to be located near a pipeline and a large body of water, in a region where residents will not oppose construction, and there are no such sites currently available, then no sites will be available until more pipelines are constructed.

D. No. This answer goes beyond the passage. The passage does not address the location of any currently existing stations.

E. No. This answer goes beyond the passage. The passage does not address the feelings of residents about construction of new transmission lines.

20. A Flaw

The argument notes that people over 65 have high voter turnout, while young adults have low voter turnout. The argument concludes that citizens are becoming increasingly disconnected from politics with each passing generation. The argument contains a comparison flaw. It assumes that the group of over-65 voters is comparable to the group of young adult voters. In other words, it overlooks the possibility that the difference in voter turnout could be due to something other than the passing of generations. The credited response to this Flaw question will correctly identify this comparison flaw.

A. Yes. This answer matches the flaw of the argument: the argument compares an early state of one generation to a later stage of another generation, which means the difference in voter turnout could be due to the age and maturity level of the voter, or other factors, rather than simply due to the passing of generations.

B. No. This answer is irrelevant. The relative sizes of the generations involved does not help determine the reason for the difference in voter turnout.

C. No. This answer does not match the argument. The argument does provide an explanation for the phenomenon: the argument states that increasing disconnection from the political system is the explanation for the phenomenon of decreasing voter turnout.

D.   No. This answer does not match the argument. The argument does propose that increasing disconnection from the political system caused the change in voter turnout. However, the argument does not confuse the cause (disconnection from the political system) with the effect itself (low voter turnout).

E.   No. This answer is irrelevant. The possibility of future changes in voting patterns does not help to explain the reason for the difference in voter turnout.

21.   **B**   **Parallel**

The argument notes that in order to build a new office complex, a local marsh would need to be drained. Since marshes often play crucial roles in purifying groundwater and no assessment has been done of this marsh's role, the argument concludes that the city should block the construction until an assessment is done. The principle underlying the argument is that if a proposed project could potentially have costly, damaging effects, and if a scientific assessment could determine whether the project is safe, that the project should be blocked until the assessment is made. The credited response to this Parallel the Principle question will match the underlying principle of the argument.

A.   No. This choice does not match the argument. The argument in this answer choice concludes that a proposal should be rejected because of the cost of the scientific assessment that needs to be carried out to determine safety, while the original argument concludes that a proposal should be blocked until an assessment is carried out.

B.   Yes. This choice matches the structure of the argument: defective products in a new line could be costly to a manufacturer, but they could be tested for defects to prevent such problems, so the new line should be delayed until the testing is done. This is parallel to the original argument, which states that if a proposed project could potentially have costly, damaging effects, and if a scientific assessment could determine whether the project is safe, that the project should be blocked until the assessment is made.

C.   No. This choice does not match the argument. The argument in this answer choice concludes that a report about the scientific assessment cannot be released at this time, because the assessment is not complete, while the original argument concludes that a proposal should be blocked until an assessment is carried out.

D.   No. This choice does not match the argument. The argument in this answer choice involves comparing the safety of two routes, while the original argument involves blocking a single proposal until a scientific assessment is carried out.

E.   No. This choice does not match the argument. The argument in this answer choice concludes that a route must be built to avoid future problems, while the original argument involves blocking a single proposal until a scientific assessment is carried out.

22.   **D**   **Weaken**

The argument notes that in a study, a group of participants who watched video recordings of themselves running on treadmills reported exercising, on average, one hour longer than the other group, which watched recordings of other people running on treadmills. The argument concludes that watching a recording of yourself exercising causes you to be motivated to exercise more. This argument is flawed because it makes a conclusion about people's motivation to actually exercise based on premises about the number of hours people reported exercising. The argument also includes a causal flaw: it assumes that the first group reported exercising longer because the first group was motivated to exercise more, rather than for some other reason. In other words, the argument overlooks the possibility that the first group reported exercising longer due to some other cause. The credited response to this Weaken question will hurt the argument by providing an alternative reason why the first group might have reported working out for an additional hour.

A. No. This answer strengthens the argument. If people in a similar situation (watching recordings of themselves lifting weights) actually did increase their behavior (exercising) more than other people, this supports the idea that watching a recording of yourself exercising actually can motivate you to exercise more.

B. No. This answer strengthens the argument. If people in a similar situation (hearing stories about people they identified with giving money to charity) were motivated to increase their behavior (giving to charity), this supports the idea that watching a recording of yourself exercising actually can motivate you to exercise more.

C. No. This answer is irrelevant. The behavior of people who were already highly motivated to exercise does not help determine the effect on the actual groups in the study.

D. Yes. This choice hurts the argument by providing evidence that people in a similar situation (observing their identical twin reading) were simply motivated to overreport the amount of time spent reading, rather than to actually read more. This supports the idea that the first group actually have just overreported their hours spent exercising, rather than being motivated to actually exercise more.

E. No. This answer strengthens the argument. If people in a similar situation (watching recordings of themselves sitting) actually did increase that behavior (sitting) more than other people, this supports the idea that watching a recording of yourself exercising actually can motivate you to exercise more.

23. A **Necessary Assumption**

The argument follows a typical Disagree pattern. The argument concludes that attempts to reduce carbon use (by convincing people to reduce their personal use of fossil fuels) cannot be successful. The conclusion is based on the premises that even if most people changed their behavior, their changes in personal use would not be enough to make the needed reductions, which can be achieved only through government policy changes. The argument is flawed because it overlooks the possibility that convincing people to focus on their own carbon use might help influence the government to change government policies about the use of fossil fuels. The credited response to this Necessary Assumption question will help the argument by providing a statement that is necessary in order to show that convincing people to focus on their personal carbon use cannot achieve the goal.

A. Yes. In order to show that efforts to convince people to focus on their personal carbon use cannot achieve the goal, it would be necessary that the changes in people's personal opinions would not lead to governmental changes in policy. Try negating this choice: if convincing people to focus on their personal carbon use would lead to government policy changes, then the effort could succeed in its goal. Since the argument fails if the answer choice is negated, the choice must be necessary for the conclusion to be valid.

B. No. This answer is too strong. Even if the calculations needed to determine how best to reduce fossil fuels are too complex for individuals, this does not mean that individuals wouldn't be able to reduce fossil fuels in some way other than the best way.

81

C. No. This answer is irrelevant. Whether the efforts to convince people to change their behavior are made by government policy makers does not help to determine whether the effort to convince people to change their behavior would be able to achieve its goal.

D. No. This answer is irrelevant. Whether it is easier to convince the government to change its policies than it is to convince people to change their personal behavior does not help to determine whether the effort to convince people to change their behavior would be able to achieve its goal.

E. No. This answer hurts the argument. If people who are concerned about environmental issues are more likely to support political candidates who support environmental issues, then the efforts to convince people to change their behavior would actually be more likely to succeed. Since the conclusion states that the efforts cannot achieve their goal, this answer choice would hurt the argument.

24. **C**   Parallel

The argument begins by stating that there are only two plausible views about the source of a painting's aesthetic value: either its purely formal qualities or its meaning. But since there is no compelling general account of how a painting could derive value from its purely formal characteristics, the argument concludes that the source must be the meaning. The answer to this Parallel the Reasoning question will match the pattern of the argument's structure: in simple terms, "the source of X must be either A or B; there is no convincing explanation for how A is possible, so the source must be B."

A. No. This choice does not match the passage: it concludes that surgery is not the best choice because of the difficulty of recovering from surgery, while the original argument rejects a choice because there is no compelling reason given in favor of it.

B. No. This choice does not match the passage: it concludes that the company expects to win a bid because one of the two options if it is outbid would not be an option. On the other hand, the original argument rejects a choice because there is no compelling reason given in favor of it.

C. Yes. This choice matches the structure of the argument: history (X) is driven primarily by economic forces (A) or political forces (B); there is no convincing explanation of how it could be economic forces (A), so it must come from political sources (B).

D. No. This choice does not match the passage: it states that if the economy expands, either the inflation rate will rise or the unemployment rate will fall, but then concludes that the inflation rate will not change because the unemployment rate is not expected to change. On the other hand, the original argument rejects a choice because there is no compelling reason given in favor of it.

E. No. This choice does not match the passage: it concludes that an outcome is impossible because either of two options must happen to prevent the outcome. On the other hand, the original argument rejects a choice because there is no compelling reason given in favor of it.

25. **D**   Flaw

The argument concludes that a ban on the use of fossil fuels would be followed by an economic boom rather than the economic depression predicted by critics of the ban. The conclusion is based on the premises that substantial economic growth must be preceded by technological innovations, and that a ban on the use of fossil fuels would surely produce those sorts of technological innovations. The argument contains a necessary versus sufficient factors flaw (i.e., a conditional statements flaw): the argument assumes that because the ban on fossil fuels would satisfy a necessary factor (technological innovations), that this would be sufficient to lead to the economic boom, when in fact it is only enough to make that economic boom possible. The credited response to this Flaw question will correctly identify this necessary versus sufficient factors flaw.

A. No. This answer describes a circular flaw, which does not match the argument. The argument includes a necessary versus sufficient conditions flaw.

B. No. This answer describes an appeals and attacks flaw, which does not match the argument. The argument includes a necessary versus sufficient conditions flaw.

C. No. This answer does not match the flaw of the argument. The argument does not base its conclusion on stronger evidence than the argument requires; rather, it confuses a necessary condition for a sufficient condition.

D. Yes. This answer matches the flaw of the argument: the argument confuses a necessary condition (technological innovations) for a phenomenon (an economic boom) with a sufficient condition for that phenomenon.

E. No. This answer does not match the flaw of the argument. The argument states that technological innovations are required for an economic boom and then concludes that technological innovations are sufficient to cause an economic boom. The answer choice, on the other hand, states that the argument confuses a condition that only sometimes accompanies a phenomenon with a condition that always accompanies a phenomenon, which does not match.

26. **E** **Point at Issue**

Winston notes that Nobel Prizes are limited to three people per prize. However, many important scientific results are the work of four or more scientists. Sanjay notes that Nobel Prize rules also require that prize winners must be alive, but some scientists died before their work was fully appreciated. The credited response to this Point at Issue question will be an answer that Winston and Sanjay would both agree about the truth of. Information extracted from each person's argument must prove that both Winston and Sanjay would agree with the credited response: Winston feels that Nobel Prizes sometimes overlook scientists because the prizes are limited to only three people; Sanjay feels that Nobel Prizes sometimes overlook scientists because they died before their contributions were appreciated.

A. No. Winston does not express any opinion about whether prizes should be awarded to deceased persons.

B. No. Sanjay does not express any opinion about whether prizes should be different for science compared to other disciplines.

C. No. Neither Winston nor Sanjay argues that Nobel Prizes should not be given for particular scientific results.

D. No. Neither Winston nor Sanjay argues that the evaluation of individual achievement in science is highly subjective.

E. Yes. Winston agrees that Nobel Prizes overlook scientists because they are limited to only three people; Sanjay feels that Nobel Prizes sometimes overlook scientists because they died before their contributions were appreciated.

Section 3: Arguments 2

1. **E** [Point at Issue]

Joe and Maria are discussing stories about vampires. Joe states that because every victim of a vampire becomes a vampire, the growing number of vampires would have eliminated humans and he concludes that vampire stories are thus, absurd. Maria says that in the stories she's heard, victims of vampires usually die and don't become vampires. They therefore disagree about what happens to the victims of vampires.

A.   No. Joe states that vampires are immortal; Maria says nothing about it.

B.   No. Joe mentions this; Maria does not.

C.   No. Joe says that vampire stories are absurd, not incoherent; Maria says nothing about it.

D.   No. Neither speaker discusses how stories characterize the size of the vampire population.

E.   Yes. Joe states this explicitly in the second sentence; Maria says that only a few victims of vampires become vampires themselves.

2. **C** [Resolve/ Explain]

This passage discusses a company that wanted to make things easier for their salespeople by scanning all their papers into a computer system so they wouldn't have to take their paper files when they travel. The project failed because the salespeople refused to use the computer system and didn't allow the company to scan many of their files. The credited response will explain why the salespeople refused to use the new computer system even though it would have made their work easier to do.

A.   No. This tells us that different salespeople gave different amounts of files to be scanned, but doesn't address why the salespeople refused to use the system.

B.   No. This shows that most of the employees had computers, but doesn't explain why they wouldn't use the new computer system.

C.   Yes. This explains that salespeople were concerned about putting the information in their files into the system because it contained personal information. This answer gives us a reason they didn't want to use the computer system, which led to the project's failure.

D.   No. Training the salespeople to use the system would not explain why they didn't use it.

E.   No. Although this answer discusses what the system costs, it doesn't explain why the salespeople refused to take advantage of it.

3. **A** [Main Point]

The purpose of this argument is to interpret. The author discusses the right to free speech and the restrictions upon it. This argument begins by explaining that not all speech is protected and gives several examples. The author then concludes that the government is justified in outlawing certain forms of speech because, as in those examples, some speech can have harmful consequences. The correct answer will paraphrase this conclusion.

A. Yes. This is exactly what the conclusion is saying.

B. No. This answer choices reverses the conditional relationship in the text.

C. No. The argument is not about whether speech leads to harm, but about whether harmful speech should be criminalized.

D. No. The author does not claim that any form of speech leads to harm, only some cases. Further, whether or not speech is harmful is not the author's main conclusion.

E. No. The author does not discuss any other reasons for restricting freedom of speech.

4. **E** `Necessary Assumption`

The argument talks about how people interact with art. The author says that because people don't spend much time looking at art, they are less willing to engage with works of art than they used to. This is a language shift. There is no stated relationship between the amount of time someone spends looking at a painting and how willing they are to engage with it; however, the author assumes that the less time they spend with a piece, the less willing they are to engage with it. You should look for this shift to be resolved in the correct answer.

A. No. This is neither stated nor implied in the text. It also doesn't address how willing they are to engage with pieces.

B. No. This is a good trap, but it fails to make any connection to the idea of how engaged people are with the art.

C. No. This answer discusses enjoyment, not engagement.

D. No. Whether they look at their pictures or not, we do not know how engaged they are with the artwork.

E. Yes. This connects the premise to the conclusion and resolves the language shift.

5. **D** `Inference`

We are told fun facts about heavy tapestry fabrics. We are told that they are good only if they don't need to be laundered. As a conditional, if it needs to be washed, then it shouldn't be used. This is why it is bad for making clothing and good for decoration. The correct answer will be based on this information.

A. No. We don't know anything about other fabrics.

B. No. Swags and valances are examples of good uses for the fabric, but they are not the only applications.

C. No. Again, window treatments are an example of a good use, but are not the only application.

D. Yes. Skirts and jackets need to be washed; therefore, heavy tapestry fabrics should not be used.

E. No. We are told that this fabric shouldn't be used in ANY type of clothing. This is refuted by the passage.

6. **E** **Resolve/Explain**

We are told that a new apartment complex led to an increased number of available homes in Brewster-ville. Usually this would lower rents on existing apartments, but for some reason rents went up. Our task is to explain why rent went up instead of down.

A. No. It doesn't matter how many new apartments were built; the rule states that whenever any new apartments are built, rents should go down. So this doesn't explain why rent went up instead.

B. No. The fact that the new apartments were better than the old apartments doesn't help explain why the old apartments became more expensive.

C. No. This shows that areas nearby had decreasing rents, but doesn't explain why rents in Brewster-ville went up.

D. If people moved out of the existing apartments, that would only increase the supply of available housing, which should lower rents, not raise them.

E. Yes. Supply and demand. If the number of people looking for apartments increased, then the overall supply of available houses would go down, which would raise rents.

7. **B** **Flaw**

This argument seeks to show that attempts to increase productivity in the economy as a whole would increase the number of unemployed people. The author relies on a bad comparison, which looks at how a single corporation may increase its profitability by reducing the number of its employees. However, the economy of a country may work differently than a corporation, which is the nature of the flaw.

A. No. Although the author does believe that unemployment is a drawback to productivity, the author never recommends abandoning attempts to increase productivity.

B. Yes. This describes the comparison flaw!

C. No. We don't know what the sample size of politicians is.

D. No. The author doesn't make this assertion.

E. No. The argument is about the economy as a whole, not just one company. That's the problem.

8. **B** **Main Point**

The purpose of this argument is "Solve," and the author advocates that movie reviewers should be able to give good reviews to a movie that isn't their usual cup of tea. This is true because their tastes are different from their audience and their job is to help people decide what movies they'd like. We should find the best match to that first sentence.

A. No. This is a premise.

B. Yes. Although the conclusion is not written as a conditional, the conclusion creates a rule for ALL good reviewers, which can be expressed conditionally. This is a correct interpretation of the first sentence.

C. No. This is a premise.

D.   No. This is implied by the second sentence, but is not the conclusion.

E.   No. This is the other half of the premise from (C).

9.   **B**   Flaw

The argument tries to convince you that because skilled musicians have a bigger part of their brain than people who don't play music, that playing a musical instrument causes your brain to change shape. This is a causal/correlation flaw, and it overlooks the possibility that maybe these musicians are skilled because the parts of their brain that interpret sounds were already bigger.

A.   No. This describes a comparison flaw that is not present in the text.

B.   Yes. Reversed causation, there it is.

C.   No. Technically this is true in that the premise is about highly skilled musicians and the conclusion is about people who practice and play a musical instrument. However the argument is focused on the effect of playing music on brain structure and the premise is an appropriate example of a situation where this might occur.

D.   No. Neither the conclusion nor the premise has anything to do with listening to music.

E.   No. The argument doesn't discuss the amount of time that musicians practice.

10.   **B**   Inference

This passage discusses the consequences of hearing only one side of a phone call. It states that it can distract listeners from whatever they're doing and that the listeners are constantly trying to figure out what the other person is saying. They are also distracted because people on cell phones speak very loudly.

A.   No. This passage is about listening to someone else on a phone call, not being on a phone call themselves.

B.   Yes. We are told that listening to a person's conversation is distracting, which could detract from their performance.

C.   No. This is the opposite of everything that was said in the passage.

D.   No. We are told that listening to one side of a phone call is distracting, but we don't know if it would cause someone to lose their own train of thought.

E.   No. This is never mentioned. We aren't given any information on types of conversations other than cell-phone calls.

11.   **A**   Parallel Flaw

The argument describes a treatment that was tested in three studies. The results of all three studies were positive, but because the methodology was flawed, the author believes that the treatment is probably not effective. This is a fallacy, in which the author thinks a conclusion is false just because the reasoning was flawed, which is not necessarily the case. In the credited response, look for the answer to dismiss a conclusion because the reasoning was bad.

A. Yes. "The criteria was bad, so the winning cake must be bad" follows the same pattern as the original argument discussed above.

B. No. This reasoning may not be flawed, and it is not a good match. There is no methodology discussed in the original argument.

C. No. This choice makes too broad of a conclusion based on a single piece of information. It's flawed, but not in the same way.

D. No. This choice attempts to infer that something was originally created to serve a purpose just because that's how the object is used today. It's a flaw too, but not the same one.

E. No. This choice contains an attack flaw, which does not match the original argument.

12. A **Strengthen**

The author concludes that if car manufacturers can get the same amount of reliable data about safety features from a computer simulation as it can from performing a test crash, it will use fewer test crashes. The reason given is that computer simulations are cheaper. However, it is not known whether there are any other factors besides cost that should be considered or whether information on safety features is the only reason to perform a test crash. A correct answer would give us additional reasons to believe that car makers will phase out test crashes as long as they get the same data on safety features.

A. Yes. This states outright that information on safety features is the only reason car makers perform test crashes. This eliminates a possible objection and strengthens the argument.

B. No. The argument isn't about whether computer simulations will provide more information than test crashes or not. The author only asserts that if they can get enough information from computers they'll phase out test crashes. This answer choice doesn't address that assertion and is therefore irrelevant.

C. No. The argument isn't about making safer cars.

D. No. While this is good news for car makers, it doesn't address whether test crashes will be phased out or not.

E. No. While it is useful to know computer simulations are used in other industries, it is not known whether airplane manufacturers can or do use test crashes or how this affects the author's conclusion.

13. B **Flaw**

There are a number of flaws in this argument. This legislator is advocating that they should approve a proposed act. We are told that their colleague argues against the act because it would deter investment. The author says that because their opponent has voted for legislation in the past that was bad for investment, she must not really care about investment. This is an attack on their opponent and also implies that what is true in the past, will also be true in the future. The author then says that because they don't believe this is the real reason and because their opponent hasn't revealed it, it must not be very good. And because this reason against the act isn't good, they should pass it. This is an absence of evidence flaw. It also forgets to address the official reason the opponent opposes the bill.

A. No. At first glance this may sound like it describes an attack flaw, but it actually says that a character trait is being presented as a professional viewpoint. There is no comparison between personal and professional traits here, just past and present viewpoints.

B. Yes. The author tries to distract the reader from his opponent's critique that the act would deter investment by bringing up a second, secret critique, but notice that he never addressed whether the act would deter investment or not.

C. No. There's no discussion of whether the colleague or the legislator is in the majority.

D. No. No mention of what voters favor or oppose is made.

E. No. Whatever the colleague's reasons are, is irrelevant. We don't know what value, if any, constituent's wishes have in this debate.

14. **A**   Main Point

There is an "unless" statement here, which should be turned into a conditional statement. A new computer system will not increase efficiency unless it makes employees adopt new ways of working. So if a computer system doesn't make employees adopt new ways of working, it won't increase efficiency. Then we're told that the new computer system won't make employees change the way they work so the blank should tell us that it won't increase efficiency.

A. Yes. That's it. Thank you conditional statements!

B. No. We don't know anything about whether computer systems work.

C. No. We don't know what leaders care about.

D. No. Automation isn't discussed.

E. No. We aren't told how easy to use the new system will be.

15. **A**   Flaw

This columnist has owned three cars and never got close to the fuel economy advertised by the manufacturers. Therefore, she concludes that the manufacturers probably inflate those numbers. However, three cars is a pretty small sample to draw on.

A. Yes. That's it.

B. No. The author doesn't seem to imply that driving conditions are the same everywhere on the entire planet.

C. No. This answer is making an ad hominem attack; the author is not.

D. No. The columnist never discusses minimum fuel efficiency standards.

E. No. This is a shift in meaning flaw and is not present here.

16. **C**   Weaken

The argument claims that because tenants who don't pay for their electricity don't have a financial incentive to conserve energy, making them pay their own electric bills will make them use less energy. The correct answer will give some reason why this won't be effective.

A. No. We don't know the effect of this on rent.

B. No. If people knew how conserving energy would save them money, this would only strengthen the argument.

C. Yes. This shows that the proposal of making tenants pay for electricity removes the financial incentive for landlords to save energy.

D. No. This discusses how easy it would be to implement the idea, not whether it would work.

E. No. This does weaken the argument, but not as much as C does. Remember that "some" could be just one person.

17. **D**   Reasoning

This question is asking about the role of a specific sentence in the argument. Begin by identifying the conclusion and premise. The conclusion of this argument is the first sentence, which is that repeat offenders receiving harsher punishments is unsustainable. Why does the author believe this? Because of the chain of reasoning described after it. First the author discusses an implication of this position: it implies that what an offender did in the past is relevant to how serious their current offense is. The author then shows how that implication doesn't work out. This is a Match question, so find the description that fits best.

A. No. This answer implies that it is a subsidiary conclusion, which it isn't.

B. No. The argument doesn't wish to defend this position; it wants to attack it.

C. No. The first sentence is the main conclusion.

D. Yes. An implication of a position would be its consequence, and then they give reasons that are supposed to show why this consequence cannot be sustained.

E. No. This is a tricky one, because this sentence is a premise and there is a subsidiary conclusion; however, this answer choice best represents the third sentence of the argument, not the second and (D) is a better, more precise answer.

18. **D**   Necessary Assumption

The author claims that the partisan reporting of new media outlets represents a different business strategy when compared to newspapers. He claims that the standard of being objective developed in newspapers who needed to avoid offending people, while newer media outlets seek to differentiate themselves in a crowded market. Remember to look for implied logic, rather than stated relationships. Does partisan reporting help them differentiate themselves? Does being objective help avoid offending readers? Those are the two major assumptions in this argument.

A. No. We don't care about the individual journalists, just the reporting.

B. No. If people prefer objective reporting, it doesn't totally follow that newer media would avoid it.

C. No. The argument claims that objectivity works for newspapers and partisanship works for newer media. It doesn't indicate that one is better than the other.

D. Yes. This helps further explain why newspapers have sought to be objective. Use the negation test: if newspapers didn't think objective reporting would help them avoid offending people, why did they do it? The whole chain of reasoning falls apart from there.

E. No. This answer is a little extreme. The author isn't claiming that new media has high journalistic standards, just that their standards are different because of different business needs.

19. **C** Inference

Remember that absolute statements are conditional statements, so symbolize that first sentence: IF a practice might lead to an abuse of power AND there isn't a compelling reason to do it, then it shouldn't be done. The argument then follows with a discussion about government secrets. Make sure you understand each point as you go. Often when an Inference question contains a conditional, it's important to understand it and the contrapositive as is the case here.

A. No. The third sentence gives us reason to know that "often" the government isn't justified in keeping secrets, but we don't know if it's in "most" cases.

B. No. This jumbles the information a bit. Having a compelling reason to keep a secret is a necessary condition to justifying it, but it doesn't relate to abusing power.

C. Yes. The contrapositive of the first sentence tells us that IF a government action is justified, it either won't lead to an abuse of power OR they have a compelling reason to do so. The last sentence says that when the government conceals the existence of a secret, it'll lead to an abuse of power. This means, for it to be justified, they need to have a good reason.

D. No. Again, this mixes up the parts of the conditions of this rule. Having compelling reasons does not impact whether an action will create an abuse of power.

E. No. This again does not follow that initial conditional statement.

20. **E** Sufficient Assumption

When you see "if assumed" in the question stem, you should look for a language shift in the argument. Here the author tries to point out a contradiction. She says that some musicians claim that music is a series of sounds without meaning, but she claims their own music doesn't conform to their theory because they have an explanation of their work before they perform. The author must be drawing a connection between having an explanation and having meaning. Namely, if a musician's work has no meaning, they shouldn't have to explain it before they perform. Look for exactly that in the answers.

A. No. The human ability to think symbolically comes out of nowhere. Scratch this answer off.

B. No. The author doesn't discuss when it will be possible to compose such music.

C. No. The author doesn't discuss whether this music appeals to audiences.

D. No. Again, no one cares if anyone likes the music.

E. Yes. As with most Sufficient Assumption questions, this answer draws an almost verbatim connection between the two key phrases in the argument.

21. **C** Reasoning

Here we have to describe the reasoning, which means we have to describe how the premise of the argument is supporting the conclusion. We have an argument that makes the claim that evolution doesn't always optimize survival and this is supported by the example of moose antlers doing just that. Nothing in the actual example is helpful to you. You just need to know that this information about moose antlers is why the author doesn't think evolution always helps animals survive. Match it to an answer choice.

81

A. No. Example? Yes. Competing argument? No. A good trap answer for people who rush. Match every part to the argument.

B. No. The conclusion is about organisms evolving and the premise is an example of this, not an analogy.

C. Yes. The general claim is that evolution always optimizes survival of an organism. The challenge to the general claim is that evolution does not always optimize survival of an organism. And the moose antler discussion is the counterexample.

D. No. The author uses this example; it doesn't dispute it.

E. No. No self-contradictions here. What that would look like is "If evolution helped every animal survive, then it would make lions better hunters, which would hurt the survival of other organisms."

22. D Weaken

Always keep an eye out for flaws when doing Strengthen or Weaken questions. The argument concludes that bacteria detect red light by monitoring how much energy their chlorophyll is producing. Does the author know this? Well, there's an experiment in which bacteria move into areas of a test tube lit by red light and that red light allows them to produce more energy. But do we know that they detect red light by monitoring their own energy levels? This is a causal/correlation flaw, and the author assumes that it's only the need for energy that makes bacteria seek out red light. The correct answer will weaken this claim with new information.

A. No. This strengthens the argument by showing that the chlorophyll is responsible for their move into the red zone.

B. No. Although they can produce some energy from these other colors, we are told that they produce the most energy from red light, so this has no effect on the conclusion.

C. No. This also strengthens the argument by ruling out another factor that would explain their movement—i.e., the temperature.

D. Yes. The author claims that it's the energy levels that motivate the bacteria to go to the red zone, but if another color can give them the same amount of energy and they still go to the red zone, there must be some other reason for it.

E. No. Great, but we're talking about bacteria of only this particular species, not some other kind without chlorophyll.

23. B Flaw

When you see conditional statements in a Flaw question, check for the necessary versus sufficient flaw. IF legislation is the result of negotiation and compromise between competing groups, THEN it won't satisfy any of the groups. The contrapositive is IF legislation satisfies some of the groups, THEN it wasn't the result of negotiation and compromise between them. But the author says that since the groups are unhappy, THEN they must have compromised. This mixes up the necessary and sufficient conditions. Find that in the answers.

A. No. This describes a circular flaw, which is rare on the LSAT.

B. Yes. All the buzzwords are here. Plugging in words from the text it concludes that compromise MUST have led to the groups feeling unhappy because compromise CAN lead to the groups feeling unhappy.

C. No. This is a shift in meaning flaw, also uncommon.

D. No. It never makes this claim or implies it.

E. No. This doesn't describe anything in the text.

24. **B** `Inference`

Don't get hung up on the scientific words. Researchers found three isotopes: I, T, and C and no heavy isotopes in the atmosphere. They either came from rods or from the core. Rods don't contain T. Radioactive material directly from the core would have heavy isotopes.

PAUSE. So this means that we don't have a complete explanation of where these isotopes came from.

Next we're told that steam came up from the core and might have carried I, T, and C with it. This helps us out by giving us another possible explanation for what happened.

A. No. We aren't told this.

B. Yes. This is possible. We aren't told whether steam would carry heavy isotopes with it, but this is the most likely explanation.

C. No. This is never mentioned.

D. No. This is tricky, but if material came from the core, it would have heavy isotopes and we're told there weren't any.

E. No. This also is not stated.

25. **E** `Parallel`

Look at the basic structure here. If E and P were judged the same way, E wouldn't be successful. But E is successful. Therefore, E and P are not judged the same way. Conditional and contrapositive, no mistakes. Great. Find the best match in the answer choices.

A. No. The first sentence says if S goes up, then either price will go up or the industry will disappear. This is already different.

B. No. If G could borrow Matisse's works, then it would have the largest exhibition ever. But there isn't a demand for larger exhibitions. "Demand" is a new element that isn't in the original argument. Cross it off.

C. No. If cars are lighter and stronger in the future, then fatalities would go down. Cars will be lighter and stronger in the future. Therefore, fatalities will go down. This is a correct use of the conditional. The original argument uses the contrapositive, but this doesn't.

D. No. If P tried S, then they would be successful. But P won't try S. Oops. They reversed the conditional.

E. Yes. If E was adequate, then it would be possible to make forecasts. But it's not possible to make forecasts. Therefore, E is not adequate. It starts with a conditional and then uses the contrapositive to form a valid conclusion. This is the one.

Section 4: Games

Questions 1–6

This is a 2D ordering game: five photo essays by five photographers will be featured in the first five issues of a new magazine. The inventory consists of five photographers—F, G, H, J, and K—and five photo essay themes—three rural and two urban—with a 1:1 correspondence and H as an unrestricted element.

Rule 1: 1 = R

Rule 2: KF

Rule 3: $K_{R/U}$ & $F_{U/R}$

Rule 4: G = 3

Rule 5: J_U

Add rule 1 and rule 4 to the diagram. Based on the combination of rules 2 and 4, the game has a distribution deduction: the KF block must be either first and second or fourth and fifth. In the first scenario, H and J can be fourth and fifth in either order. In the second scenario, H must be first, and J must be second (because J's essay must be urban per rule 5). Because J's essay must be urban (rule 5) and exactly one of K's or F's essays must be urban (rule 3), both G's and H's essays must be rural in both scenarios.

Order of attack: question 1 (Grab-a-Rule), question 3 (Specific), question 2 (General), question 4 (General), question 5 (General), question 6 (Complex)

Your diagram should look like this:

F, G, H, J, K
R, R, R, U, U

Clue 1: 1 = R

Clue 2: [KF]

Clue 3: $K_{R/U}$ + $F_{U/R}$

Clue 4: G = 3

Clue 5: J_U

	1	2	3	4	5
(1) photo	K	F	G	H/J	J/H
theme	R	U	R		
(2) photo	H	J	G	K	F
theme	R	U	R	R/U	U/R

1. **E** Grab-a-Rule

   A. No. This answer choice violates rule 2 because K is not immediately before F.

   B. No. This answer choice violates rule 4 because G is not third.

   C. No. This answer choice violates rule 2 because K is not immediately before F.

   D. No. This answer choice violates the combination of rules 1 and 5 because the first essay must be rural, but J's essay must be urban.

   E. Yes. This answer choice does not violate any rules.

2. **B**   General

Use deductions, prior work, and testing the answer choices to determine which answer choice could be true.

A. No. This answer choice must be false: G must be third (rule 4), and K must immediately precede F (rule 2), so there is no room for a KFJ block.

B. Yes. This could be true.

C. No. This answer choice must be false: G must be third (rule 4), and K must immediately precede F (rule 2), so there is no room for a HKF block.

D. No. This answer choice must be false: G must be third (rule 4), and K must immediately precede F (rule 2), so there is no room for a JKF block.

E. No. This answer choice must be false: K must immediately precede F (rule 2).

3. **C**   Specific

Make a new line in your diagram, and add the new information. If the fourth essay is urban, there are two options based on the placement of the KF block (rule 2).

A. No. This answer choice could be true.

B. No. This answer choice could be true.

C. Yes. J's essay must be urban (rule 5), so if H's essay were also urban, K's and F's essays would both be rural, which would violate rule 3.

D. No. This answer choice could be true.

E. No. This answer choice could be true.

4. **D**   General

Use deductions, prior work, and testing the answer choices to determine which answer choice must be true.

A. No. This answer choice must be false: G must be third (rule 4), J's essay must be urban (rule 5), and exactly one of K's or F's essays must be urban (rule 3), so G's essay must be rural.

B. No. This answer choice could be false—use previous work from question 2.

C. No. This answer choice could be false—use previous work from question 2.

D. Yes. This must be true based on deductions.

E. No. This answer choice could be false—used previous work from question 3.

5. **A**   General

Use deductions, prior work, and testing the answer choices to determine which photographer and photo essay can't be fourth.

81

A. Yes. K must immediately precede F (rule 2), and G must be third (rule 4), so F can't be fourth.

B. No. This answer choice could be true—use previous work from question 2.

C. No. This answer choice could be true.

D. No. This answer choice could be true—use previous work from question 3.

E. No. This answer choice could be true—use previous work from question 3.

6. **B** `Complex`

This question asks for a parallel rule, so consider the deductions of the rule you need to replace.

Eliminate answer choices that are more or less restrictive than the rule you need to replace.

A. No. Even if H's essay were rural and J's essay were urban (rule 5), both K's and F's essays could be rural, so this rule is less restrictive.

B. Yes. J's essay must be urban (rule 5), so if G's and H's essays must be rural, the only options left for K's and F's essays are urban and rural, so this rule effectively replaces rule 3.

C. No. J's essay must be urban (rule 5), and prior work for questions 2, 3, and 5 shows that F's essay could also be urban, so this rule is more restrictive.

D. No. Even if J's essay must immediately follow a rural essay, both K's and F's essays could be rural, so this rule is less restrictive.

E. No. Prior work for questions 2, 3, and 5 shows that K's essay could have the same theme as both G's and H's essays, so this rule is more restrictive.

Questions 7–11

This is a 1D ordering game: seven musicians will perform consecutively, one at a time. The inventory consists of seven musicians—L, M, N, O, P, S, and T—with a 1:1 correspondence and S as an unrestricted element.

Rule 1: L — N

Rule 2: M — T

Rule 3: L_O / O_L

Rule 4: M_P / P_M

Rule 5: P = 1/7

Based on the combination of rules 4 and 5, the game has a distribution deduction: either P is first with M third, or P is seventh with M fifth.

In the first scenario, you can make the following deductions:

- N can't be second because it must be after L (rule 1).

- L can't be seventh because it must be before N (rule 1).

- O can't be fifth because if it were, it would force L to be seventh.

- T can't be second because it must be after M (rule 2).

- N can't be fourth because if it were, you wouldn't be able to satisfy rule 3.

A tougher deduction (that you might not see until you play the game) is that S can't be fourth: if it were, the L_O / O_L block (rule 3) would be forced fifth and seventh, which wouldn't allow you to satisfy both rule 1 and rule 2.

In the second scenario, you can make the following deductions:

- T must be sixth because it must be after M (rule 2).

- N can't be first because it must be after L (rule 1).

- L can't be fourth because it must be before N (rule 1).

- O can't be second because if it were, it would force L to be fourth.

A tougher deduction (that you might not see until you play the game) is that S can't be third: if it were, the L_O / O_L block (rule 3) would be forced second and fourth, which wouldn't allow you to satisfy rule 1.

Order of attack: question 8 (Specific), question 10 (Specific), question 7 (Specific), question 9 (General), question 11 (General)

Your diagram should look like this:

L, M, N, O, P, S, T

	1	2	3	4	5	6	7
(1)	P	–T –N	M	–S –N	–O		–L
(2)	–N	–O	–S	–L	M	T	P

Clue 1: L – N

Clue 2: M – T

Clue 3: L – O / O – L

Clue 4: M – P / P – M

Clue 5: P = 1/7

Order of attack: question 8 (Specific), question 10 (Specific), question 7 (Specific), question 9 (General), question 11 (General)

7. **D** General

Use deductions, prior work, and testing the answer choices to determine which answer choice could be true.

A. No. This answer choice must be false: P must be first or seventh (rule 5), and there is an M_P / P_M block (rule 4), so M can be only third or fifth.

B. No. This answer choice must be false: L must be before N (rule 1), so N can't be first.

C. No. This answer choice must be false: O can't be fifth in scenario 2, and if it were fifth in scenario 1, L would be seventh, which wouldn't allow you to satisfy rule 1.

D. Yes—use prior work from question 8.

E. No. This answer choice must be false: T can't be second in scenario 1 because it would violate rule 2, and T must be sixth in scenario 2 to satisfy rule 2.

8. **A** Specific

Make a new line in your diagram, and add the new information. O can be before M in either scenario, so try both. In the first scenario, if O is 2nd, L is fourth (rule 3), and then N, S, and T can fit into the remaining slots in any order. In the second scenario, there are several options based on the placement of the L_O / O_L block (rule 3).

A. Yes. L can't be fifth in scenario 2, and if it were fifth in scenario 1, O would be seventh (rule 3), which wouldn't allow you to satisfy the new information.

B. No. This answer choice could be true.

C. No. This answer choice could be true.

D. No. This answer choice could be true.

E. No. This answer choice could be true.

9. **E** General

Use deductions, prior work, and testing the answer choices to determine which performer can't be third.

A. No. This answer choice could be true—use prior work from question 8.

B. No. This answer choice could be true—use prior work from question 8 or 10.

C. No. This answer choice could be true—use prior work from question 8.

D. No. This answer choice could be true—use prior work from question 8.

E. Yes. S can't be third in scenario 1, and if it were third in scenario 2, the L_O / O_L block (rule 3) would be second and fourth, leaving N first, which would violate rule 1.

10. **D** Specific

Make a new line in your diagram, and add the new information. The ST block can fit in scenario 1 only, and there are two options.

A. No. This answer choice could be true.

B. No. This answer choice could be true.

C. No. This answer choice could be true.

D. Yes. If T were fifth, S would be fourth, and you wouldn't have room for the L_O / O_L block (rule 3).

E. No. This answer choice could be true.

11. **E**   General

Use deductions, prior work, and testing the answer choices to determine which answer choice completely determines the order.

A. No. Prior work for questions 8 and 10 shows more than one order with L fourth.

B. No. Prior work for question 8 shows more than one order with M fifth.

C. No. Prior work for question 8 shows more than one order with N fourth.

D. No. Prior work for question 8 shows more than one order with O third.

E. Yes. If S is first, P must be seventh (rule 5), M must be fifth (rule 4), T must be sixth (rule 2), L must be second and O must be fourth (rule 3), and N must be third (rule 1).

Questions 12–16

This is a 1D ordering game: six obstacles will be placed in order from start to finish. The inventory consists of six obstacles—R, S, T, V, W, and Z—with a 1:1 correspondence and T as an unrestricted element.

Rule 1: $S = 3/4$

Rule 2: WZ

Rule 3: ~RV / ~VR

S can't be first, second, fifth, or sixth (rule 1), Z can't be first (rule 2), and W can't be sixth (rule 2). W also can't be third because then Z would be fourth (rule 2), and you wouldn't be able to satisfy rule 1. For the same reason, Z can't be fourth. A tougher deduction (that you might not see until you play the game) is that T can't be third or fourth: If it were, S would be fourth or third, respectively, and you wouldn't be able to satisfy both rule 2 and rule 3. Rule 3 doesn't give you any initial deductions, but the antiblock will be important as you play the game. Also, you might notice that R and V are twin elements, meaning they have the exact same set of restrictions, so they will always be interchangeable unless a specific question places a further restriction on one of them.

Order of attack: question 12 (Grab-a-Rule), question 13 (Specific), question 15 (Specific), question 16 (Specific), question 14 (General)

Your diagram should look like this:

R, S, T, V, W, Z

	1	2	3	4	5	6
	−Z −S	−S	−T −W	−T −Z	−S	−W −S

Clue 1: $S = 3/4$

Clue 2: WZ

Clue 3: ~RV~ / ~VR~

81

12. **D** `Grab-a-Rule`

    A.   No. This answer choice violates rule 2 because W is not just before Z.

    B.   No. This answer choice violates rule 3 because R is just before V.

    C.   No. This answer choice violates rule 1 because S is not third or fourth.

    D.   Yes. This answer choice does not violate any rules.

    E.   No. This answer choice violates rule 3 because R is just after V.

13. **C** `Specific`

Make a new line in your diagram, and add the new information. If T is first, S can't be fourth because you wouldn't be able to satisfy both rule 2 and rule 3, so S must be third (rule 1). With T and S placed, there are two options for the WZ block (rule 2).

    A.   No. This answer choice could be false.

    B.   No. This answer choice could be false.

    C.   Yes. This must be true.

    D.   No. This answer choice could be false.

    E.   No. This answer choice could be false.

14. **B** `General`

Use deductions, prior work, and testing the answer choices to determine which answer choice gives a complete and accurate list of the options for T.

    A.   No. Prior work for question 16 shows that T could be sixth.

    B.   Yes. Prior work for questions 13 and 15 shows that T could be first, prior work for question 16 shows that T could be sixth, and the diagram above shows that T could be second or fifth. Refer to the initial deductions for an explanation of why T can't be third or fourth.

    C.   No. Refer to the initial deductions for an explanation of why T can't be third or fourth.

    D.   No. Refer to the initial deductions for an explanation of why T can't be third.

    E.   No. Refer to the initial deductions for an explanation of why T can't be third or fourth.

15. **B** `Specific`

Make a new line in your diagram, and add the new information. If R is second and S must be third or fourth (rule 1), S must be third because if it were 4th, you wouldn't be able to satisfy both rule 2 and rule 3. With R and S placed, there are two options for the WZ block (rule 2). For both options, T must be 1st.

    A.   No. This answer choice must be false.

    B.   Yes. This must be true.

C. No. This answer choice could be false.

D. No. This answer choice could be false.

E. No. This answer choice could be false.

16. **A** ◖Specific◗

Make a new line in your diagram, and add the new information. If R and V must come before T, T can't be first or second; it can't third because it would violate rule 3; it can't be fourth because if it were, S would be third, and it would still violate rule 3; and it can't be fifth because if it were, no element could be sixth: S must be third or fourth (rule 1), there's a WZ block (rule 2), and the new information is that both R and V are before T. Therefore, T must be sixth. Furthermore, S must be fourth because if it were third, you wouldn't be able to satisfy both rule 1 and rule 2. With T and S placed, there are two options for the WZ block (rule 2).

A. Yes. This must be true.

B. No. This answer choice must be false.

C. No. This answer choice could be false.

D. No. This answer choice could be false.

E. No. This answer choice could be false.

Questions 17–23

This is a 1D variable grouping game: four product managers will be sent to three cities, each manager visiting at least one city, and each city visited by exactly two managers. The inventory consists of four managers—F, G, H, and I—with no unrestricted elements.

Rule 1: *exactly* II

Rule 2: ~FH

Rule 3: GM → HT

~HT → ~GM

Rule 4: G → S

Add another I to your inventory (rule 1). Add rule 4 to the diagram. Because F and H can't visit the same city (rule 2) and G can't visit S (rule 4), I must visit S with one of F or H. Rule 3 doesn't give you any initial deductions, but the conditional will be important as you play the game. Another important aspect will be determining which of F, G, or H is doubled up to provide the final element in your inventory.

Order of attack: question (Grab-a-Rule), question 21 (Specific), question 22 (Specific), question 19 (General), question 20 (General), question 18 (General), question 23 (Complex)

81

Your diagram should look like this:

F, G, H, I

Clue 1: exactly 2 I
Clue 2: F̶H̶
Clue 3: G = M → A = T
 H ≠ T → G ≠ M
Clue 4: G ≠ S

17. **C** `Grab-a-Rule`

A. No. This answer choice violates rule 1 because I doesn't visit exactly two cities.

B. No. This answer choice violates rule 4 because G visits S.

C. Yes. This answer choice does not violate any rules.

D. No. This answer choice violates rule 3 because G visits M but H doesn't visit T.

E. No. This answer choice violates rule 2 because F and H visit the same city.

18. **B** `General`

Use deductions, prior work, and testing the answer choices to determine which answer choice completely determines the assignment.

A. No. Prior work for questions 19, 21, and 22 shows more than one arrangement with two Fs.

B. Yes. If there are two Gs, G must visit M and T because G can't visit S (rule 4), H must visit T (rule 3), I must visit S and M (rule 1), and F must visit S because every manager must visit at least one city.

C. No. Prior work for questions 19, 21, and 22 shows more than one arrangement with two Hs.

D. No. Prior work for question 19 shows more than one arrangement with F and G visiting T.

E. No. Prior work for question 21 shows more than one arrangement with G and H visiting T.

19. **D** `General`

Use deductions, prior work, and testing the answer choices to determine which answer choice must be true.

A. No. This answer choice could be false—use prior work from question 21 or 22.

B. No. This answer choice could be false—use prior work from question 21 or 22.

C. No. This answer choice could be false.

D. Yes. This must be true based on the original deductions.

E. No. This answer choice could be false—use prior work from question 21.

20. **A** [General]

Use deductions, prior work, and testing the answer choices to determine which answer choice could be true.

A. Yes. This could be true. Use prior work from question 21.

B. No. This answer choice must be false: If H doesn't visit T, G can't visit M (rule 3), and if I visits T and S (refer to the initial deductions), I can't visit M (rule 1), so the only option left for M is FH, which would violate rule 2.

C. No. This answer choice must be false: I must visit S (refer to the initial deductions), and there are exactly two Is (rule 1), so I can't visit both M and T.

D. No. This answer choice must be false: Each manager must visit at least one city, and there are exactly two Is (rule 1), so if there were also three Fs, one of G or H wouldn't be able to visit a city.

E. No. This answer choice must be false: Each manager must visit at least one city, and there are exactly two Is (rule 1), so if there were also three Hs, one of F or G wouldn't be able to visit a city.

21. **D** [Specific]

Make a new line in your diagram, and add the new information. G can't visit S (rule 4), so G and H must visit M or T. If G and H visit M, H must visit T (rule 3), I must visit S and T (rule 1), and F must visit S because every manager must visit at least one city. If G and H visit T, there are several options. For all options, H must visit T.

A. No. This answer choice could be false.

B. No. This answer choice could be false.

C. No. This answer choice could be false.

D. Yes. This must be true.

E. No. This answer choice could be false.

22. **A** [Specific]

Make a new line in your diagram, and add the new information. If I visits T and S (refer to the initial deductions), G must visit M because I can't visit M (rule 1) and F and H can't visit the same city (rule 2). Because G must visit M, H must visit T (rule 3), so there are two options based for the managers that visit M.

A. Yes. This must be true.

B. No. This answer choice must be false: There are exactly two Is (rule 1), but this answer choice would result in three Is.

C. No. This answer choice must be false: There are exactly two Is (rule 1), but this answer choice would result in three Is.

D. No. This answer choice must be false: If F visits M, G must also visit M because both Is are already placed (rule 1) and F can't visit the same city as H (rule 2), but then you wouldn't be able to satisfy rule 3 (GM → HT) because I and F would already be visiting T, leaving no room for H.

81

E.   No. This answer choice must be false: If H visits M, G must also visit M because both Is are already placed (rule 1) and H can't visit the same city as F (rule 2), but then H must visit T (rule 3), leaving no cities for F to visit.

23.   **E**   **Complex**

This question asks for a parallel rule, so consider the deductions of the rule you need to replace. Eliminate answer choices that are more or less restrictive than the rule you need to replace.

A.   No. Prior work for question 21 shows that G and I can visit the same city, so this rule is more restrictive.

B.   No. Prior work for question 19 shows that F can visit S without H visiting T, so this rule is more restrictive.

C.   No. Even if F and H can't both visit T, they could both visit S, so this rule is less restrictive.

D.   No. Prior work for question 21 shows that G and I can visit the same city, so this rule is more restrictive.

E.   Yes. If every city must have at least one of G or I, there will not be room for F and H to visit the same city.

NOTES

NOTES

NOTES

NOTES

NOTES

NOTES

NOTES

NOTES

NOTES

International Offices Listing

China (Beijing)
1501 Building A,
Disanji Creative Zone,
No.66 West Section of North 4th Ring Road Beijing
Tel: +86-10-62684481/2/3
Email: tprkor01@chol.com
Website: www.tprbeijing.com

China (Shanghai)
1010 Kaixuan Road
Building B, 5/F
Changning District, Shanghai, China 200052
Sara Beattie, Owner: Email: sbeattie@sarabeattie.com
Tel: +86-21-5108-2798
Fax: +86-21-6386-1039
Website: www.princetonreviewshanghai.com

Hong Kong
5th Floor, Yardley Commercial Building
1-6 Connaught Road West, Sheung Wan, Hong Kong
(MTR Exit C)
Sara Beattie, Owner: Email: sbeattie@sarabeattie.com
Tel: +852-2507-9380
Fax: +852-2827-4630
Website: www.princetonreviewhk.com

India (Mumbai)
Score Plus Academy
Office No.15, Fifth Floor
Manek Mahal 90
Veer Nariman Road
Next to Hotel Ambassador
Churchgate, Mumbai 400020
Maharashtra, India
Ritu Kalwani: Email: director@score-plus.com
Tel: + 91 22 22846801 / 39 / 41
Website: www.score-plus.com

India (New Delhi)
South Extension
K-16, Upper Ground Floor
South Extension Part–1,
New Delhi-110049
Aradhana Mahna: aradhana@manyagroup.com
Monisha Banerjee: monisha@manyagroup.com
Ruchi Tomar: ruchi.tomar@manyagroup.com
Rishi Josan: Rishi.josan@manyagroup.com
Vishal Goswamy: vishal.goswamy@manyagroup.com
Tel: +91-11-64501603/ 4, +91-11-65028379
Website: www.manyagroup.com

Lebanon
463 Bliss Street
AlFarra Building - 2nd floor
Ras Beirut
Beirut, Lebanon
Hassan Coudsi: Email: hassan.coudsi@review.com
Tel: +961-1-367-688
Website: www.princetonreviewlebanon.com

Korea
945-25 Young Shin Building
25 Daechi-Dong, Kangnam-gu
Seoul, Korea 135-280
Yong-Hoon Lee: Email: TPRKor01@chollian.net
In-Woo Kim: Email: iwkim@tpr.co.kr
Tel: + 82-2-554-7762
Fax: +82-2-453-9466
Website: www.tpr.co.kr

Kuwait
ScorePlus Learning Center
Salmiyah Block 3, Street 2 Building 14
Post Box: 559, Zip 1306, Safat, Kuwait
Email: infokuwait@score-plus.com
Tel: +965-25-75-48-02 / 8
Fax: +965-25-75-46-02
Website: www.scorepluseducation.com

Malaysia
Sara Beattie MDC Sdn Bhd
Suites 18E & 18F
18th Floor
Gurney Tower, Persiaran Gurney
Penang, Malaysia
Email: tprkl.my@sarabeattie.com
Sara Beattie, Owner: Email: sbeattie@sarabeattie.com
Tel: +604-2104 333
Fax: +604-2104 330
Website: www.princetonreviewKL.com

Mexico
TPR México
Guanajuato No. 242 Piso 1 Interior 1
Col. Roma Norte
México D.F., C.P.06700
registro@princetonreviewmexico.com
Tel: +52-55-5255-4495
+52-55-5255-4440
+52-55-5255-4442
Website: www.princetonreviewmexico.com

Qatar
Score Plus
Office No: 1A, Al Kuwari (Damas)
Building near Merweb Hotel, Al Saad
Post Box: 2408, Doha, Qatar
Email: infoqatar@score-plus.com
Tel: +974 44 36 8580, +974 526 5032
Fax: +974 44 13 1995
Website: www.scorepluseducation.com

Taiwan
The Princeton Review Taiwan
2F, 169 Zhong Xiao East Road, Section 4
Taipei, Taiwan 10690
Lisa Bartle (Owner): lbartle@princetonreview.com.tw
Tel: +886-2-2751-1293
Fax: +886-2-2776-3201
Website: www.PrincetonReview.com.tw

Thailand
The Princeton Review Thailand
Sathorn Nakorn Tower, 28th floor
100 North Sathorn Road
Bangkok, Thailand 10500
Thavida Bijayendrayodhin (Chairman)
Email: thavida@princetonreviewthailand.com
Mitsara Bijayendrayodhin (Managing Director)
Email: mitsara@princetonreviewthailand.com
Tel: +662-636-6770
Fax: +662-636-6776
Website: www.princetonreviewthailand.com

Turkey
Yeni Sülün Sokak No. 28
Levent, Istanbul, 34330, Turkey
Nuri Ozgur: nuri@tprturkey.com
Rona Ozgur: rona@tprturkey.com
Iren Ozgur: iren@tprturkey.com
Tel: +90-212-324-4747
Fax: +90-212-324-3347
Website: www.tprturkey.com

UAE
Emirates Score Plus
Office No: 506, Fifth Floor
Sultan Business Center
Near Lamcy Plaza, 21 Oud Metha Road
Post Box: 44098, Dubai
United Arab Emirates
Hukumat Kalwani: skoreplus@gmail.com
Ritu Kalwani: director@score-plus.com
Email: info@score-plus.com
Tel: +971-4-334-0004
Fax: +971-4-334-0222
Website: www.princetonreviewuae.com

Our International Partners

The Princeton Review also runs courses with a variety of partners in Africa, Asia, Europe, and South America.

Georgia
LEAF American-Georgian Education Center
www.leaf.ge

Mongolia
English Academy of Mongolia
www.nyescm.org

Nigeria
The Know Place
www.knowplace.com.ng

Panama
Academia Interamericana de Panama
http://aip.edu.pa/

Switzerland
Institut Le Rosey
http://www.rosey.ch/

All other inquiries, please email us at
internationalsupport@review.com